Supertagging

Supertagging: Using Complex Lexical Descriptions in Natural Language Processing

Edited by Srinivas Bangalore and Aravind K. Joshi

A Bradford Book
The MIT Press
Cambridge, Massachusetts
London, England

For information about special quantity discounts, please email special_sales@mitpress.mit.edu

This book was set in LaTex by the authors.

Printed and bound in the United States of America.

Library of Congress Cataloging-in-Publication Data

Supertagging : using complex lexical descriptions in natural language processing / edited by Srinivas Bangalore and Aravind K. Joshi.
p. cm. — (A Bradford Book)
Includes bibliographical references and index.
ISBN 978-0-262-01387-1 (hardcover : alk. paper) 1. Natural language processing (Computer science) 2. Computational linguistics—Statistical methods. 3. Semantics. 4. Lexicology. I.
Bangalore, Srinivas, 1969– II. Joshi, Aravind K. (Aravind Krishna), 1929–
QA76.9.N38S86 2010
006.3'5—dc22
                    2009028194

10 9 8 7 6 5 4 3 2 1

Contents

vi

Preface

The conventional (mathematical) wisdom in specifying a grammar formalism is to start with basic primitive structures as simple as possible and then introduce various operations for constructing more complex structures. This has the consequence that information (e.g., syntactic and semantic) about a lexical item (word) is distributed over more than one primitive structure. Therefore, the information associated with a lexical item is not captured locally, that is within the domain of a primitive structure. An alternate approach is to start with complex (more complicated) primitives for a word, which capture directly some crucial linguistic properties of the word and then introduce some general operations for composing these complex structures (primitive or derived). All the pieces of information associated with a lexical item have to be represented in the local domains of the primitive structures. In this approach, non-local dependencies are pushed to become local that is, these dependencies start out in the basic primitive structure. We refer to the primitive structure that is associated with a word as a *supertag* and characterize this approach as *complicate locally, simplify globally* (CLSG).

During this past decade, the CLSG approach has been explored in different grammar formalisms and the consequences of such a localization for computational, linguistic and psycholinguistic models of natural language processing has been extensively studied. This book is a collection of some of the research that investigates this theme. We expect that this book will be of special interest to computational linguists and researchers in speech and language processing for its perspective on the representation and its implications on computation of linguistic structure. For the machine learning community interested in language applications, we expect this book to provide an opportunity for exploring novel machine learning techniques that can exploit the richer feature space provided by supertag representations. The close coupling of lexical and syntactic information afforded by the supertag representation and its impact on language processing would be of interest to researchers of psycholinguistics interested in human sentence processing.

The book is broadly organized into five parts. The first part highlights issues concerning the creation and organization of supertags in Lexicalized Tree-adjoining Grammar (LTAG) framework. Research concerning the models for supertag disambiguation and their relation to parsing in the context of LTAG supertags are included in the second part of the book. The third part presents different instantiations of the notion of supertags in a range of grammar formalisms. Research work on some of the linguistic and psycholinguistic issues related to supertags constitute the fourth part. And finally, some of the speech and language applications that exploit supertags are highlighted in the last part of the book.

We are most grateful to the members of the XTAG group at University of Pennsylvania who helped develop the idea of supertags in LTAG formalism and for the effort in building a wide-coverage grammar of English that has served as the basis for the initial experiments. We thank all the chapter authors who kindly consented to contribute their research to the theme of this book. We would like to thank AT&T Labs-Research for continued support in this research agenda and during the preparation of the book.

List of Figures

Contributors

Jens Bäcker
Recommind, Germany

Srinivas Bangalore
AT&T Labs–Research, United States

Akshar Bharati
International Institute of Information Technology, India

Pierre Boullier
INRIA-Rocquencourt, France

Tomas By
Universität Hamburg, Germany

John Chen
Janya Inc., United States

Stephen Clark
Oxford University, England

Berthold Crysmann
DFKI and Saarland University, Germany

James R. Curran
University of Sydney, Australia

Kilian Foth
Universität Hamburg, Germany

Robert Frank
Yale University, United States

Karin Harbusch
University of Koblenz-Landau, Germany

Saša Hasan
Aachen University, Germany

Aravind Joshi
University of Pennsylvania, United States

Vincenzo Lombardo
Università di Torino, Italy

Takuya Matsuzaki
University of Tokyo, Japan

Alessandro Mazzei
Università di Torino, Italy

Wolfgang Menzel
Universität Hamburg, Germany

Yusuke Miyao
University of Tokyo, Japan

Richard Moot
LaBRI-CNRS & INRIA Futurs, France

Alexis Nasr
Université de la Méditerranée, France

Günter Neumann
DFKI and Saarland University, Germany

Martha Palmer
University of Colorado, United States

Mary Harper
Purdue University, United States

Owen Rambow
Columbia University, United States

Rajeev Sangal
International Institute of Information Technology, India

Anoop Sarkar
Simon Fraser University, Canada

Giorgio Satta
University of Padua, Italy

Libin Shen
BBN Technologies, United States

Patrick Sturt
University of Edinburgh, Scotland

Jun'ichi Tsujii
University of Tokyo, Japan

K. Vijay-Shanker
University of Delaware, United States

Wen Wang
SRI International, United States

Fei Xia
University of Washington, United States

1

Introduction

SRINIVAS BANGALORE AND ARAVIND JOSHI

The conventional (mathematical) wisdom in specifying a grammar formalism is to start with basic primitive structures as simple as possible and then introduce various operations for constructing more complex structures. These operations can be simple or complex and the number of operations (although finite) need not be limited. New operations (simple or complex) can be introduced in order to describe more complex structures.

An alternate approach is to start with complex (more complicated) primitives, which capture directly some crucial linguistic properties and then introduce some general operations for composing these complex structures (primitive or derived). What is the nature of these complex primitives? In the conventional approach the primitive structures (or rules) are kept as simple as possible. This has the consequence that information (e.g., syntactic and semantic) about a lexical item (word) is distributed over more than one primitive structure. Therefore the information associated with a lexical item is not captured locally, that is, within the domain of a primitive structure. We will illustrate this in section 1.1 in terms of the well-known context-free grammar (CFG) framework.

In contrast, in the alternate approach described in this book, we allow the primitive structures to be as complex as necessary to capture all the relevant information about a lexical item in the local domain of a primitive structure. We refer to the primitive structure as a *supertag* and is associated with a lexical item. A supertag needs to localize the following information: (a) a lexical item taken as a predicate has zero or more arguments, (b) the arguments need to satisfy certain syntactic and semantic constraints, which are determined by the lexical item, and (c) the different positions that the arguments will occupy relative to the position of the lexical item. Hence, in the alternate approach, all the pieces of information associated with a lexical item have to be represented in the local domains of the primitive structures of the formal system. Although the primitives are complex and there may be more than one primitive structure associated with a lexical item, the number of primitives is finite. Further the combining operations are kept to the minimum and they are language independent (that is, *universal*). In this approach nonlocal dependencies are pushed to become local, that is, these dependencies start out in the basic primitive structure (supertag) and hence we characterize this approach as *complicate locally, simplify globally* (CLSG). The architecture resulting from the CLSG approach has important implications for linguistics, computational linguistics, and psycholinguistics, including generation and acquisition.

There is another dimension in which formal systems can be characterized. One could start with an unconstrained formal system (Turing machine equivalent, for example) and then add linguistic constraints, which become in a sense, all stipulative. Alternatively, one could start with a formal system that is constrained and just adequate for describing language. The formal constraints then become universal, in a sense. All other linguistic constraints become stipulative and language specific. Now it turns out that the CLSG approach leads to constrained formal systems. This convergence is of interest in its own right which is not discussed in this book. Our focus will be on the CLSG approach and its implications for the architecture of the grammars, their processors, and how it has been realized in different grammar formalisms.

We begin this book by illustrating these ideas in terms of the Lexicalized Tree-Adjoining grammar (LTAG), a class of grammars that illustrates the CLSG approach by adopting it in its extreme form in section 1.3. LTAG and some of its extensions have been investigated both formally and computationally for over twenty five years (See Joshi et al., 1975; Joshi, 1985; Kroch and Joshi, 1985; Vijay-Shanker, 1987; Weir, 1988; Kroch, 1989; Kroch and Santorini, 1991; Schabes, 1992; Rambow, 1994; Resnik, 1992; Chiang, 2000; Sarkar, 2002; Abeillé, 2002; Prolo, 2003). There are several formal systems that are clearly related to LTAG. Some examples are Combinatory Categorial Grammars (CCG) (Steedman, 1996), Stabler's version of minimalist grammars (Stabler, 1997), Lexical Functional Grammars (LFG) (Kaplan and Bresnan, 1983), Head Driven Phrase Structure Grammars (HPSG) (Pollard and Sag, 1994) (for a constrained version of HPSG, (see Kasper et al., 1995). Linear Indexed Grammars (LIG) by Gazdar, and Head Grammars (HG) by Pollard. CCG and LTAG have been shown to be weakly equivalent, that is, in terms of the string sets they generate but not in terms of the structural descriptions. These relationships have been discussed extensively in Joshi et al. (1991).

In this chapter, in section 1.1, we will introduce the notions of domain of locality and lexicalization in the context of the well-known context-free grammars (CFG) and then show how lexicalized tree-adjoining grammars (LTAG) arise in the process of lexicalizing CFGs and extending the domain of locality in section 1.2. We will also show how the architecture of the building blocks of LTAG directly predicts many complex dependency patterns and then summarize some important properties of LTAG in section 1.3. In section 1.4, we introduce the perspective of supertagging for LTAG and discuss its implications for language description and language processing. In section 1.5, we mention the relevance of supertagging for psycholinguistic models of sentence processing. In section 1.6, we group the chapters of this book under thematic topics and briefly summarize their contributions towards the goal of this book.

1.1 Domain of Locality of CFGs

In a context-free grammar (CFG) the domain of locality is the one level tree corresponding to a rule in a CFG (figure 1.1). It is easily seen that the arguments of a predicate (for example, the two arguments of *likes*) are not in the same local domain. The two arguments are distributed over the two rules (two domains of locality)– $S \rightarrow NP\ VP$ and $VP \rightarrow V\ NP$. They can be brought together by introducing a rule $S \rightarrow NP\ V\ NP$. However, then the structure provided by the VP node is lost. We should also note here that not every rule (domain) in the CFG in (figure 1.1) is lexicalized.

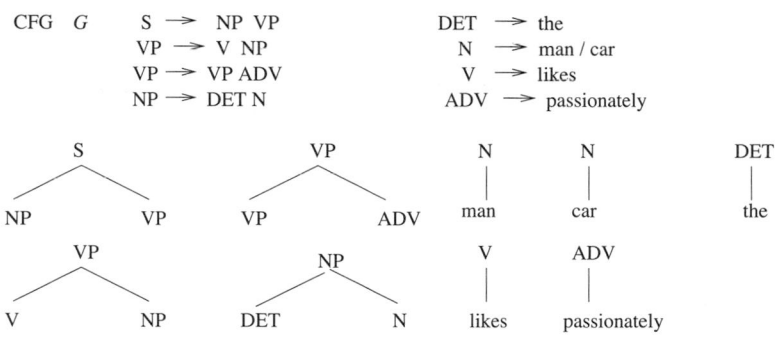

FIGURE 1.1 Domain of locality of a context-free grammar

The five rules on the right are lexicalized; that is, they have a lexical anchor. The rules on the left are not lexicalized. The second, the third, and the fourth rule on the left are almost lexicalized, in the sense that they each have at least one preterminal category (*V* in the second rule, *ADV* in the third rule, and *DET* and *N* in the fourth rule); that is, by replacing *V* by *likes*, *ADV* by *passionately*, and either *DET* by *the* or *N* by *man*, these three rules will become lexicalized. However, the first rule on the left ($S \rightarrow NP\ VP$) cannot be lexicalized, not certainly by *man*.

Can a CFG be lexicalized that is, given a CFG, G, can we construct another CFG, G', such that every rule in G' is lexicalized and $T(G)$, the set of (sentential) trees (that is, the tree language of G) is the same as the tree language $T(G')$ of G'? Of course, if we require that only the string languages of G and G' be the same (that is, they are weakly equivalent) then any CFG can be lexicalized. This follows from the fact that any CFG can be put in the Greibach normal form (see Linz, 2001) where each rule is of the form $A \rightarrow w\ B1\ B2\ ...\ Bn$ where w is a lexical item and the $B's$ are nonterminals.[1] We call this *weak* lexicalization. The lexicalization we are interested in requires the tree languages (that is, the set of structural descriptions) to be the same (that is, strong equivalence). We call this *strong* lexicalization. It is

easily seen, even from the example in figure. 1.1, that a nonlexicalized CFG cannot
be necessarily strongly lexicalized by another CFG. Basically this follows from the
fact that the domain of locality of CFG is a one level tree corresponding to a rule
in the grammar (for detail, see Joshi and Schabes, 1997). In section 1.2, we will
consider lexicalization of CFG by larger (extended) domain of locality.

Before proceeding, it would be helpful to review certain definitions. The
primitive structures of a formalism (also called elementary structures or elementary
trees, as special cases) provide a *local* domain for specifying linguistic constraints
(pieces of linguistic theory) in the sense that if the constraints are specifiable by
referring to just the structures that are associated with the elementary structures
then it is specifiable over the domain of these elementary structures. Therefore,
we refer to the domains corresponding to the elementary structures as *domains of
locality*. Formalism A is said to provide an *extended domain of locality* as compared
to a formalism B if there is a linguistic constraint that is not specifiable in the local
domains associated with B but which is specifiable in the local domains associated
with A. The goal of the CLSG approach is to look for a formalism that provides
local domains large enough so that, in principle, *all* linguistic constraints (pieces
of linguistic theory) can be specified over these local domains. In the conventional
approach (e.g., CFG-based) the specification of a constraint is often spread out
over more than one local domain, and thus the specification of a constraint is
intertwined with how the local domains are composed by the grammar; in other
words, specification of a constraint will require specification of recursion, resulting
in an effectively unbounded domain. In contrast, in the CLSG approach we seek a
system with extended (but still finite) domains of locality capable of specifying the
linguistic constraints over these extended domains. Thus, recursion does not enter
into the specification of the constraints. We call this property as *factoring recursion
away from the domains of locality.*

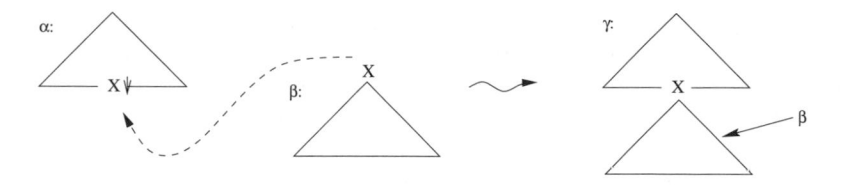

FIGURE 1.2 Substitution

1.2 Lexicalization of CFGs by Grammars with Larger Domains of Locality

Now we can ask the following question. Can we strongly lexicalize a CFG by a
grammar with a larger domain of locality? Figure 1.2 and figure 1.3 show a tree
substitution grammar where the elementary objects (building blocks) are the three
trees in figure 1.3 and the combining operation is the *tree substitution* operation

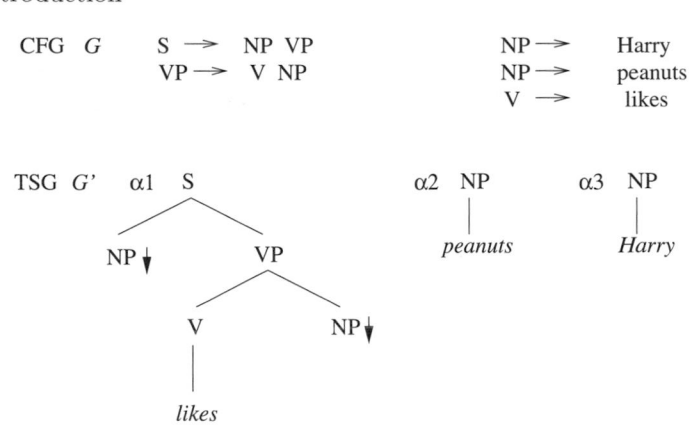

CFG *G*   S $\rightarrow$ NP VP   NP $\rightarrow$ Harry
         VP $\rightarrow$ V NP   NP $\rightarrow$ peanuts
                                          V $\rightarrow$ likes

FIGURE 1.3 Tree substitution grammar

shown in figure 1.2. Note that each tree in the tree substitution grammar (TSG), G' is lexicalized; that is, it has a *lexical anchor*. It is easily seen that G' indeed strongly lexicalizes G. However, TSGs fail to strongly lexicalize CFGs in general. We show this by an example. Consider the CFG, G, in figure 1.4 and a proposed TSG, G'. It is easily seen that although G and G' are weakly equivalent they are not strongly equivalent. In G', suppose we start with the tree α_1; then by repeated substitutions of trees in G' (a node marked with a vertical arrow denotes a substitution site), we can grow the right side of α_1 as much as we want but we cannot grow the left side. Similarly, for α_2 we can grow the left side as much as we want, but not the right side. However, trees in G can grow on both sides. In order for a tree to grow on both sides, the distance between the lexical anchor of a tree, a, and the root of the tree, S, must become arbitrarily large. Substitution makes a tree grow only at the leaves of the tree and cannot make it grow internally. Hence, the TSG, G', cannot strongly lexicalize the CFG, G (Joshi and Schabes, 1997). Thus, even with the extended domain of locality of TSGs, we cannot strongly lexicalize CFGs as long as substitution is the only operation for putting trees together.

We now introduce a new operation called *adjoining*, as shown in figure 1.5. Adjoining involves splicing (inserting) one tree into another. More specifically, a tree β is inserted (adjoined) into the tree α at the node X, resulting in the tree γ. The tree β, called an *auxiliary tree*, has a special form. The root node is labeled with a nonterminal, say X, and on the frontier there is also a node labeled X called the foot node (marked with *). There could be other nodes (terminal or nonterminal) on the frontier of β, the nonterminal nodes marked as substitution sites (with a vertical arrow). Thus, if there is another occurrence of X (other than the foot node marked with *) on the frontier of β, it will be marked with the vertical arrow, and that will be a substitution site. Given this specification, adjoining β to α at the node X in α is uniquely defined. Adjoining can also be seen as a pair of substitutions as follows: The subtree at X in α is detached, β is substituted at X, and the detached subtree is

CFG *G*   S → S S (nonlexical)
             S → a   (lexical)

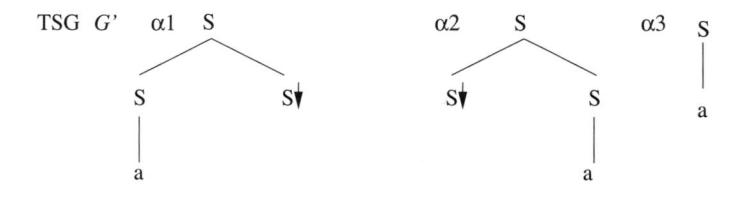

TSG *G'*   α1 S   α2   S   α3   S
                                                             |
                                                             a

FIGURE 1.4 A tree substitution grammar

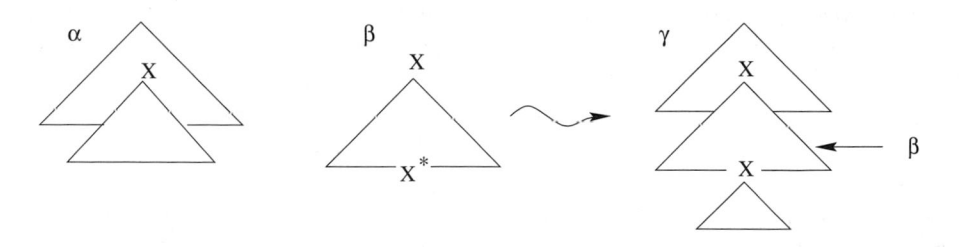

FIGURE 1.5 Adjoining

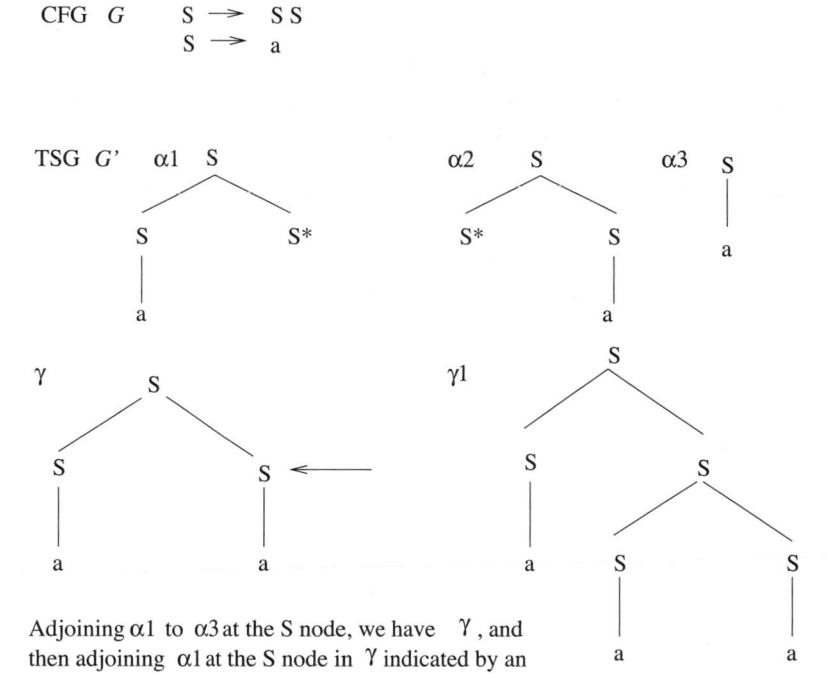

Adjoining α1 to α3 at the S node, we have γ , and then adjoining α1 at the S node in γ indicated by an arrow, we have γ1.

FIGURE 1.6 Adjoining arises out of lexicalization

then substituted at the foot node of β. A tree substitution grammar when augmented with the adjoining operation is called a tree-adjoining grammar (lexicalized tree-adjoining grammar, because each elementary tree is lexically anchored). In short, LTAG consists of a finite set of *elementary tree*, each lexicalized with at least one lexical anchor. The elementary trees are either initial or auxiliary trees. Auxiliary trees have been defined already. *Initial* trees are those for which all nonterminal nodes on the frontier are substitution nodes. It can be shown that any CFG can be strongly lexicalized by an LTAG (Joshi and Schabes, 1997).

In figure 1.6, we show a TSG, G', augmented by the operation of adjoining, which strongly lexicalizes the CFG, G. Note that the LTAG looks the same as the TSG considered in figure 1.4. However, now trees α_1 and α_2 are auxiliary trees (foot node marked with *) that can participate in adjoining. Since adjoining can insert a tree in the interior of another tree, it is possible to grow both sides of the tree α_1 and tree α_2, which was not possible earlier with substitution alone. In summary, we have shown that by increasing the domain of locality we have achieved the following: (1) lexicalized each elementary domain, (2) introduced an operation of adjoining, which would not be possible without the increased domain of locality (note that with one level trees as elementary domains, adjoining becomes the same as substitution, since there are no interior nodes to be operated upon), and (3) achieved strong lexicalization of CFGs.

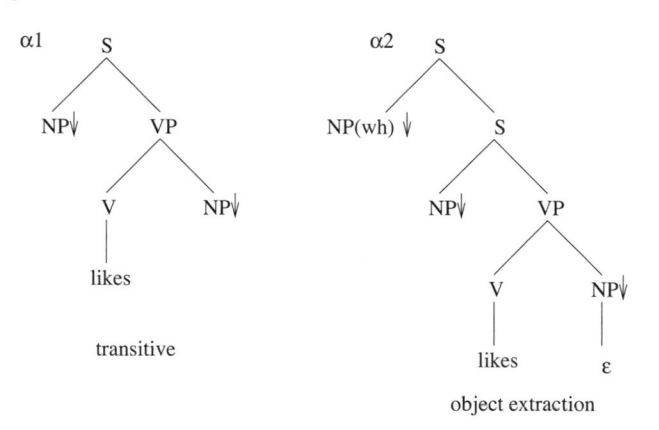

FIGURE 1.7   LTAG: Elementary trees for *likes*

1.3   Lexicalized Tree-Adjoining Grammars

Rather than give formal definitions for LTAG and derivations in LTAG, we will give a simple example to illustrate some key aspects of LTAG.[2] We show some elementary trees of a toy LTAG grammar for English. Figure 1.7 shows two elementary trees for a verb such as *likes*. The tree α_1 is anchored on *likes* and encapsulates the two arguments of the verb. The tree α_2 corresponds to the object extraction construction. Since we need to encapsulate all the arguments of the verb in each elementary tree for *likes*, for the object extraction construction, for example, we need to make the elementary tree associated with *likes* large enough so that the extracted argument is in the same elementary domain. Thus, in α_2 the node for $NP(wh)$ (the extracted argument) has to be in the tree for *likes*. Further, there is a dependency between the $NP(wh)$ node and the NP node, which is the complement of *likes* (that is, to the right of V dominating *likes*), and this dependency is local to α_2. The tree α_2 shows not only that $NP(wh)$ is an argument of *likes* but also that it is large enough to indicate a specific structural position for that argument.

Therefore, in principle, for each "minimal" construction in which *likes* can appear (for example, subject extraction, topicalization, subject relative, object relative, passive, etc.) there will be an elementary tree associated with that construction. By *minimal* we mean that all recursion has been factored away. This factoring of recursion away from the domain over which the dependencies have to be specified is a crucial aspect of LTAGs as they are used in linguistic descriptions. This factoring allows all dependencies to be localized in the elementary domains. In this sense, there will, therefore, be no long-distance dependencies as such. They will all be local and will become long-distance on account of the composition operations, especially adjoining. This will become clear as soon as we describe the derivation in figure 1.8.

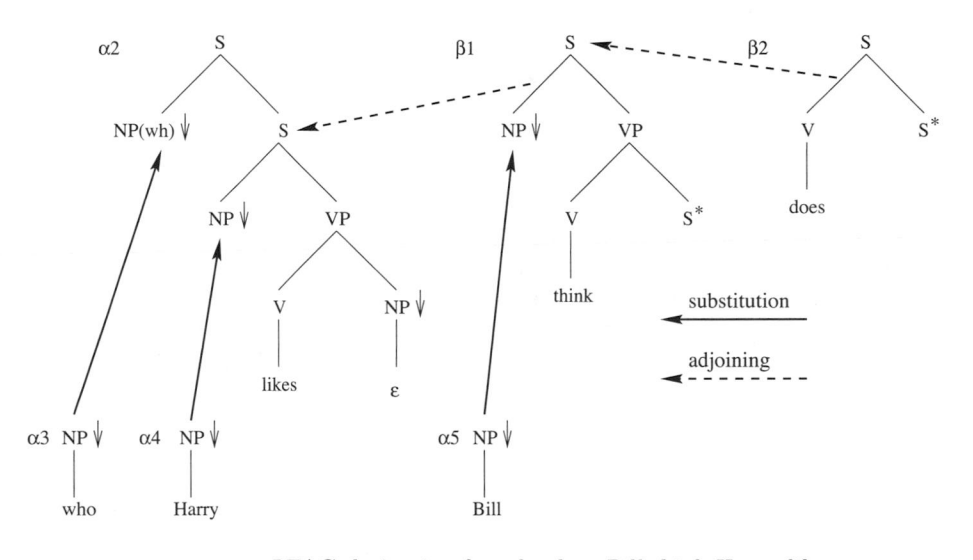

FIGURE 1.8 LTAG derivation for *who does Bill think Harry likes*

Figure 1.9 shows some additional elementary trees; trees α_3, α_4, and α_5 and trees β_1 and β_2. The β trees with foot nodes marked with * will enter a derivation by the operation of adjoining. The α trees enter a derivation by the operation of substitution.[3]

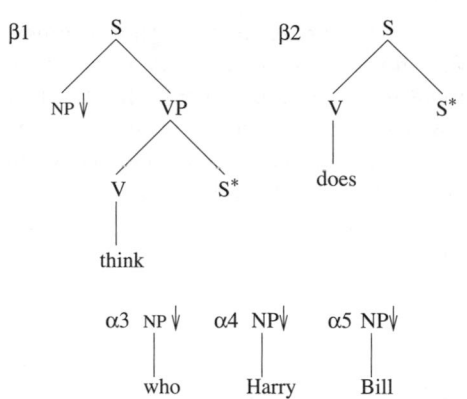

FIGURE 1.9 LTAG: Sample elementary trees

A derivation using the trees α_2, α_3, α_4, α_5, β_1, and β_2 is shown in figure 1.8. The trees for *who* and *Harry* are substituted in the tree for *likes* at the respective NP nodes, at node addresses 1 and 2.1 in α_2. The tree for *Bill* is substituted in the tree for *think* at the NP node at the node address 1 in β_1. The tree for *does* is adjoined to the root node (address 0) of the tree for *think* tree (adjoining at the root node is a special case of adjoining), and finally the derived auxiliary tree (after adjoining β_2 to β_1) is adjoined to the indicated interior S node of the tree α_2 at the address 2 in α_2. This derivation results in the *derived tree* for

Who does Bill think Harry likes

as shown in figure 1.10. Note that the dependency between *who* and the complement NP in α_2 (local to that tree) has been stretched in the derived tree in figure 1.10. It has become *long distance*. However, it started out as a local dependency. A key property of LTAGs is that all dependencies are local, that is, they are specified in the elementary trees. They can become long distance as a result of the composition operations. Figure 1.10 is the conventional tree associated with the sentence.

However, in LTAG there is also a *derivation tree*, the tree that records the history of composition of the elementary trees associated with the lexical items in the sentence. This derivation tree is shown in figure 1.11. The nodes of the tree are labeled by the tree labels such as α_2 together with its lexical anchor *likes*[4]. The number on an edge of a derivation tree refers to the node address in a tree into which either a substitution or adjoining has been made. Thus, for example, in figure 1.11 the $\alpha_3(who)$ tree is substituted at the node with address 1 in the tree $\alpha_2(likes)$, the tree $\beta_1(thinks)$ is adjoined at the address 2 in the tree $\alpha_2(likes)$, and so on. Solid edges denote substitution, and dotted edges denote adjoining.

The derivation tree is the crucial derivation structure for LTAG. It records the history of composition in terms of the elementary trees (primitive building blocks)

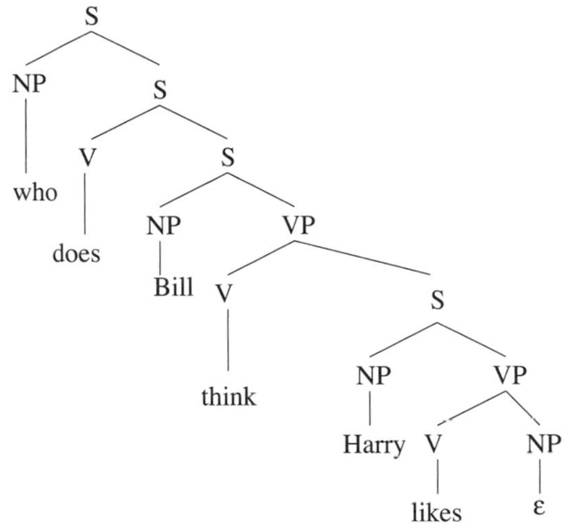

FIGURE 1.10 LTAG derived tree for *who does Bill think Harry likes*

of LTAG. The derived tree in figure 1.10 does not indicate what the component elementary trees are for the final derived tree. It should be clear that from the derivation tree we can always obtain the derived tree by performing the substitutions and adjoinings indicated in the derivation tree. So in this sense the derived tree is redundant.

Further, for semantic computation the derivation tree (and not the derived tree) is the crucial object. Compositional semantics is defined on the derivation tree. The idea is that for each elementary tree there is a semantic representation associated with it, and these representations are composed using the derivation tree. Since the semantic representation for each elementary tree is directly associated with the tree, there is no need to reproduce necessarily the internal hierarchy in the elementary tree in the semantic representation (Joshi and Vijay-Shanker, 1999; Kallmeyer and Joshi, 1999; Joshi et al., 2003). This means that the hierarchical structure internal to each elementary tree need not be reproduced in the semantic representation. This leads to the so-called *flat* semantic representation, that is, the semantic expression associated with the sentence is essentially a conjunction of semantic expressions associated with each elementary tree.[5] Of course, relevant machinery has to be provided for scope information (for details, see Kallmeyer and Joshi, 1999). The semantics need not be compositional at the level of the elementary trees. It is, however, compositional at the level of the derivation tree, i,e, at the level at which the elementary trees are assembled. This aspect of the architecture is also helpful in dealing with some of the noncompositional aspects, as in the case of rigid and flexible idioms (see Abeillé, 2002, chap. 1; Stone and Doran, 1999).

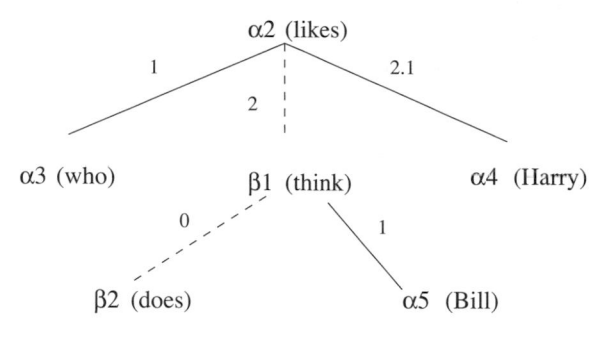

FIGURE 1.11 LTAG derivation tree

1.4   Supertagging

The elementary trees associated with a lexical item can be treated as if they are more informative parts-of-speech (super POS (parts-of-speech) or supertags) in contrast to the standard POS such as V (verb), N (noun), and so on. Now, it is well known that local statistical techniques can lead to remarkably successful disambiguation of standard POS. Can we apply these techniques for disambiguating supertags, which are very rich descriptions of the lexical items? If we can, then, indeed, this will lead to *almost* parsing. This approach is called supertagging (Joshi and Srinivas, 1994b; Srinivas and Joshi, 1998).

In figure 1.12, two elementary trees associated with the lexical item *likes* are shown. These are the same trees we have seen before. However, now we are going to regard these trees as super part-of-speech (supertags) associated with *likes*. Given a corpus parsed by LTAG grammar we can compute the statistics of supertags, statistics such as unigram, bigram, and trigram frequencies. Interestingly, these statistics combine not only lexical statistics but the statistics of constructions (as represented by the elementary trees) in which the items appear, thus combining lexical statistics with the statistics of the linguistic environments in which the lexical items appear.

Thus, for example, consider the string

The purchase price includes two ancillary companies

as shown in figure 1.13. The supertags associated with each word appear on top of that word. Some words have only only one supertag associated with them and others have more than one. In the current system there are about 15 to 20 supertags per word on the average, so there is a very high level of local ambiguity. In figure 1.14, the same supertags are shown for each word; however, for each word one supertag has been identified (in a box). This is the *correct* supertag for this word in the sense that this is the supertag associated with this word in the correct parse of this sentence. Suppose we are able to find the correct supertag for each word in this sentence by

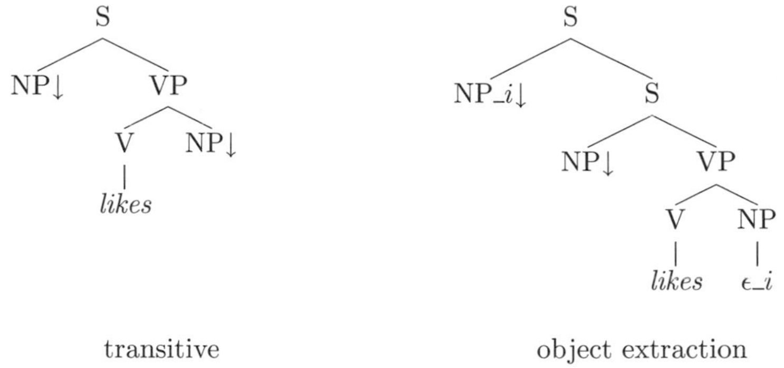

S
NP↓   VP
V   NP↓
|
likes

transitive

S
NP_*i*↓   S
NP↓   VP
V   NP
| |
likes   ε_*i*

object extraction

Some other trees for *likes*: subject extraction, topicalization, subject relative, object relative, passive, and so on.

FIGURE 1.12 Two supertags for *likes*

applying local statistical disambiguation techniques; then for all practical purposes we will have parsed the sentence. It is not a complete parse because we have not put the supertags together; hence we call it an *almost* parse.

A supertagging experiment was carried out using trigrams of supertags and techniques similar to the standard POS disambiguation techniques (Joshi and Srinivas, 1994a). The corpus used was the Wall Street Journal Corpus (WSJ). With a training corpus of 1 million words and a test corpus of 47,000 words, the baseline performance was 75% (that is, 75% of the words received the correct supertag). The baseline corresponds to the case when the supertag chosen for a word is just the most frequent supertag for this word. We know from the performance of disambiguators for the standard POS that the baseline performance is 90% or better. The lower baseline performance for supertagging is due to the fact that the local ambiguity is very high (about 15 to 20 on the average) in contrast to the local ambiguity of standard POS, which is about 1.5 for English. The performance of the trigram supertagger, on the other hand, is 92%. The improvement from 75% to 92% is indeed very remarkable. This means that 92% of the words received the correct supertag. More recent experiments based on other machine learning techniques have pushed the performance to about 93% (Chen and Vijay-Shanker, 2000; Shen and Joshi, 2003).[6]

Of course, more can be said about this supertagging approach. There are techniques to improve the performance and to make the output look more like a complete parse. We will not discuss these aspects; rather, we will talk about the abstract nature of supertagging and its relevance to the use of the CLSG approach. In supertagging we are working with complex (richer) descriptions of primitives (lexical items in our case). The descriptions of primitives (lexical items in our case) are complex because we try to associate with each primitive all

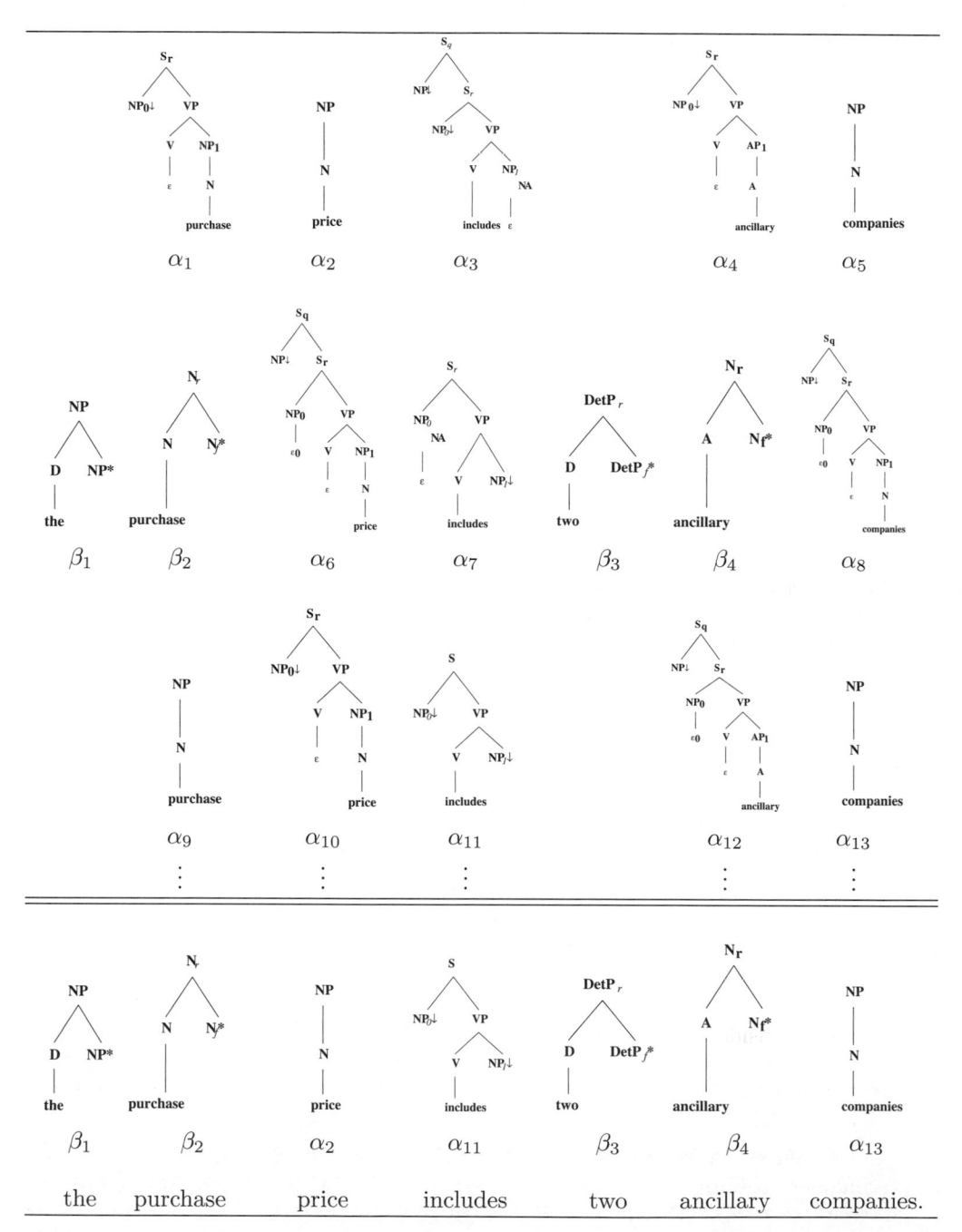

FIGURE 1.13 A selection of the supertags associated with each word of the sentence: *the purchase price includes two ancillary companies*

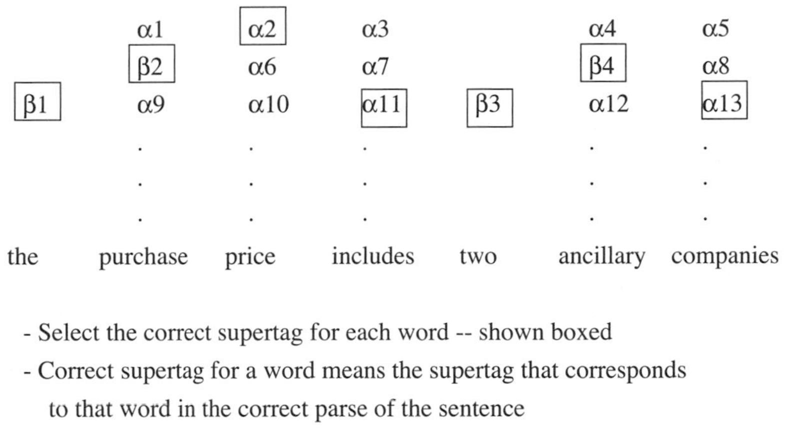

	α1	α2	α3		α4	α5
	β2	α6	α7		β4	α8
β1	α9	α10	α11	β3	α12	α13
	.	.	.		.	.
	.	.	.		.	.
	.	.	.		.	.
the	purchase	price	includes	two	ancillary	companies

- Select the correct supertag for each word -- shown boxed
- Correct supertag for a word means the supertag that corresponds
  to that word in the correct parse of the sentence

FIGURE 1.14 A sentence with the correct supertag for each word

information relevant to that primitive. Making descriptions more complex has two consequences: (1) local ambiguity is increased, that is, there are many more descriptions for each primitive, however, (2) these richer descriptions of primitives *locally* constrain each other. There is an analogy here to a jigsaw puzzle—the richer the description of each piece the better, in the sense that there are stronger constraints on what other pieces can go together with a given piece. Making the descriptions of primitives more complex allows us to compute statistics over these complex descriptions but, more importantly, these statistics are more meaningful because they capture the relevant dependencies directly (for example, word-to-word dependencies where each word is the lexical anchor of some supertag, and word-to-construction dependencies). Local statistical computations over these complex descriptions lead to robust and efficient processing. Supertagging by itself is not full parsing. However, parsing a sentence already supertagged is far more efficient (faster), on the average, as compared to parsing without supertagging. Supertagging is thus an example of a local computation on complex descriptions. Psycholinguistic relevance of supertagging is described in section 1.5.

These considerations are directly relevant to other domains, such as AI. We can illustrate this by pointing out interesting relationships to the well-known algorithm in Waltz (1975) for interpreting line drawings. What Waltz did was to make the descriptions of vertices more complex by adding information about the number and types of edges incident on a vertex. Again, there is an analogy here to a jigsaw puzzle: the richer the description of a piece the better. By making the descriptions of vertices more complex, the local ambiguity was increased, for example, an L junction (a particular kind of junction in the taxonomy of junctions of edges) has about 92 physically possible labelings. However, local computations on these complex descriptions are adequate to rapidly disambiguate these descriptions, leading to efficient computation.

Data Oriented Parsing (DOP) (Bod et al., 2003) is another framework that uses richer descriptions that extend the domain of locality of constraints. In this approach, *all* possible cuts of a parse tree are maintained and analysis of a sentence proceeds by pasting these structures together and computing the most probable derivation. The structures, however, need not be lexicalized, and the tree cuts would typically need not result in a linguistically meaningful structure. Along the lines of extending the domain of locality of CFG rules, research has been carried out on using richer (tree-local) features in machine learning techniques applied to statistical natural language parsing (Magerman and Marcus, 1991; Black et al., 1993; Magerman, 1995; Collins, 1996; Ratnaparkhi, 1997; Charniak, 2000). These features might be regarded as a bundle of constraints anchored on a lexical item just as supertags. Arbitrary feature co-constraints can be computed using tree-kernels as shown in Collins and Duffy (2002). However, in these approaches *recursion* is not factored out from the domain over which the constraints operate. As a result, feature contexts that only differ due to recursive elements are not identified leading to a large number of contexts and consequently to sparseness of data and lack of model portability issues.

1.5   Supertags in Psycholinguistic Models

In this section, we will discuss the implications of the TAG architecture for certain processing issues. These pertain to using supertags to make fine-grained distinctions between lexical and structural ambiguities and their relevance to processing.

Recently there has been increasing convergence of perspectives in the fields of linguistics, computational linguistics, and psycholinguistics, especially with respect to the representation and processing of lexical and grammatical information. More specifically, this convergence is due to a shift to lexical and statistical approaches to sentence parsing. The particular integration of lexical and statistical information proposed in Kim et al. (2002) is highly relevant from the perspective of the LTAG architecture. As we saw in section 1.3, LTAG associates with each lexical item one or more elementary structures, which encapsulate the syntactic and associated semantic dependencies. The computational results in supertagging as described earlier in section 1.4 show that much of the computational work of linguistic analysis, which is traditionally viewed as the result of structure building operations can be viewed as lexical disambiguation in the sense of supertag disambiguation. If the supertagging model is integrated in a psycholinguistics framework, then one would predict that many of the initial processing commitments of syntactic analysis are made at the lexical level in the sense of supertagging. The model proposed in Kim et al. (2002) is an integration of the Constraint-Based Lexicalist Theory (CBL) (MacDonald et al., 1994), where the lexicon is represented as supertags with their distributions estimated from corpora as in the supertagging experiments described earlier (section 1.4).

For example, in this model, there is a distinction between the prepositional phrase attachment ambiguity (PP ambiguity) as in (1) below

(1) *I saw the man with a telescope*

and the PP attachment ambiguity as in (2) below

(2) *The secretary of the general with red hair*

In the first case, the PP either modifies a noun phrase, *the man*, or a verb phrase VP, headed by *saw*. There are two supertags associated with the preposition *with*, as in figure 1.15, one with the foot and root nodes being NP (supertag $\beta 1$) or both being VP (supertag $\beta 2$). That is, the ambiguity is resolved if we pick the correct supertag for *with* anchored on the preposition *with*. Thus, this PP attachment ambiguity will be resolved at the lexical level. However, in the second case in both readings of (2) the supertag associated with *with* is the one whose root and foot nodes are both NP. Thus, in this case, the ambiguity will not be resolved at the lexical level. It can only be resolved at the level when the attachment is computed.

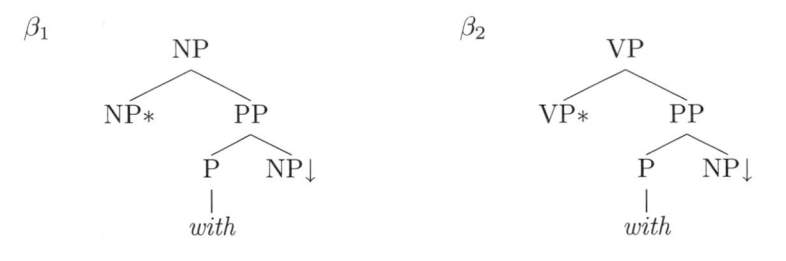

FIGURE 1.15 Two supertags for *with*

The first PP attachment ambiguity is not really an attachment ambiguity. It should be resolved at an earlier stage of processing. In the second case it will be resolved at a later stage. Similarly, the ambiguity associated with a verb such as *forgot*, because it can take either an NP complement as in (3) below

(3) *The student forgot her name*

or a VP complement as in (4) below

(4) *The student forgot that the homework was due today*

is a lexical (supertag) ambiguity and need not be viewed as a structural ambiguity. Kim et al. (2002) present a neural net based architecture using supertags and confirm these and other related results.

1.6   Outline of the Book

As discussed in the preceeding sections, the perspective of viewing the elementary trees of LTAG as supertags has provided novel and interesting insights into computational and psycholinguistic approaches to language processing. During this past decade, this theme has been explored in different grammar formalisms, and the consequences of such a localization for grammar development as well as natural language applications have been extensively studied. This book is a collection of some of the research that investigates this theme. We expect that this book will be of special interest to computational linguists and researchers in speech and language processing for its perspective on the representation and its consequences on computation of linguistic structure. For the machine learning community interested in language applications, we expect this book to provide an opportunity for exploring novel machine learning techniques that can exploit the richer feature space provided by supertag representations. The close coupling of lexical and syntactic information afforded by the supertag representation and its impact on language processing would be of interest to researchers of psycholinguistics interested in human sentence processing.

The book is broadly organized into five parts. The first part highlights issues related to supertags in LTAGs such as the creation and organization of supertags. Research concerning the models for supertag disambiguation and their relation to parsing in the context of LTAG supertags constitute the second part of the book. The third part presents different instantiations of the notion of supertags in a range of grammar formalisms. Research work on some of the linguistic and psycholinguistic issues related to supertags constitute the fourth part. And finally, some of the speech and language applications that exploit supertags are highlighted in the last part of the book.

1.6.1   Developing and organizing supertags

The construction of wide-coverage grammars had been a dominant activity in the natural language processing community during the early nineties. Broad coverage grammars and parsers were constructed in HPSG (Flickinger et al., 2000), XTAG (XTAG-Group, 2002), LFG (Butt et al., 2002). These grammar development projects involved construction of detailed analysis of linguistic phenomena and encoding them in the concerned formalisms. At the same time, parse-annotated corpora such as the Penn Treebank (Marcus et al., 1993) and NEGRA (Skut et al., 1997) were being created. Although the representations used in these treebanks were relatively shallow compared to the hand-built grammars, they provided a distributional characterization of the linguistic phenomena as evidenced in the domain from which the corpus was drawn. The two chapters in this part of the book discuss different methods for creating and organizing an inventory of supertags that rely on parsed corpora as well as hand-crafted grammars.

In chapter 2, Xia and Palmer describe methods used to transform the parse-annotated Penn Treebank corpus into a corpus of LTAG derivations and the associated set of supertags. Such an LTAG corpus has been used for training supertagging models as well as statistical LTAG parsers. This chapter also discusses the issues related to the extraction of an LTAG grammar in contrast to extracting a CFG; a key difference is the need to distinguish arguments from adjuncts in an LTAG grammar. The chapter provides coverage statistics of the extracted grammar, results of supertagging experiments, using the extracted supertag set as well as the relation of this work to similar grammar extraction methods.

An alternate method to constructing the inventory of supertags is presented in the *LexOrg* system discussed in chapter 3. The motivation for this work is to factor out the structural redundancy present in the set of supertags and instead to represent supertags as structures created by composition of tree descriptions each of which are associated with some linguistic aspect such as subcategorization, head-modifiers, syntactic variations (e.g., passivization, relativization). The tree descriptions are represented as formulae in a simplified first-order language and the model that satisfies these formulae results in the desired set of supertags. This approach not only compacts the grammar but also provides an abstract specification for the supertags based on linguistic principles. This abstract specification of supertags directly allows for rapid creation of supertag sets for new languages. This chapter discusses the creation of supertag sets for Korean and Chinese languages and compares them to the English supertag set.

1.6.2   Supertagging and parsing

The chapters in this part of the book explore different models for supertagging and explicate the relationship between supertagging and parsing.

In chapter 4, Satta reviews lexicalized formalisms such as lexicalized CFG and TAG. The focus of the chapter is a formal presentation of parsing algorithms for such lexicalizd formalisms. The crucial observation is that using algorithms designed for parsing unlexicalized grammars to parse such lexicalized formalisms leads to inefficient parsing algorithms. As a result of increase in the number of nonterminals due to lexicalization, the complexity of parsing increases by a factor of n^2 resulting in $O(n^5)$ parsing complexity for binary branching lexicalized context-free grammars(LCFG). The chapter reviews an algorithm that reduces the complexity of LCFG parsing to $O(n^4)$ and extends this same algorithm to lexicalized TAGs resulting in a reduction of complexity from $O(n^8)$ to $O(n^7)$. In all these complexity results there is an additional constant factor that is cubic in the number of grammar primitives. This constant factor typically dominates parsing performance in broad-coverage natural language grammars. The supertagging approach helps in reducing this constant factor significantly and improves the speed of the parser dramatically.

Sarkar, in chapter 5, presents two interesting research directions concerning the use of supertagging. First, the chapter provides quantitative results on how a lexicalized TAG parser's efficiency is dependent on syntactic lexical ambiguity and sentence complexity (defined in terms of the number of clauses in a sentence). The use of supertagging before parsing is shown to dramatically reduce the syntactic lexical ambiguity and radically improve parsing efficiency. A second line of research presented in the chapter concerns with using the co-training paradigm to bootstrap parse-annotated corpora. In the co-training paradigm for parsing, two statistical parsers assign probability scores to their input based on (ideally) conditionally independent features and produce the same parse output. Given unannotated sentences, the high scoring parses from one parser are used as training data for the other parser, thus the two parsers mutually benefit from a growing size of parse annotated corpus. The chapter presents improvement results in parsing accuracy using a small amount of annotated corpus in conjunction with two parsers – a supertagger-based parser and a statistical LTAG parser.

In chapter 6, Shen explains the use of discriminatively trained classification techniques for supertag disambiguation. The approach described in this chapter relies on building one classifier for each part-of-speech that predicts the supertag label given local contextual information such as lexical context, the preceeding supertag predictions, and the part-of-speech tags. This rich conditioning information is used to build a log-linear classification model. He further combines the supertags from a left-to-right disambiguation model with a right-to-left disambiguation to improve the supertagging accuracy results. In the second part of the chapter, he contrasts supertags to part-of-speech tags and shows that the richer and detailed information encoded in the supertags is indeed beneficial in improving the accuracy on the task of chunking nonrecursive noun phrases.

Models for supertagging have typically relied on estimating statistical models from annotated corpora. In chapter 7, Boullier presents an alternate approach to supertagging that exploits the structural constraints of the underlying LTAG grammar and does not rely on a statistical model for disambiguation. A drawback in statistical models of supertagging, both one-best and n-best variants, is that they might eliminate supertags that are necessary for parsing a sentence. The approaches presented in this chapter guarantee that the correct supertag will not be eliminated from the set of supertags assigned to a word. Boullier presents different supertaggers that are modeled using context-free and regular approximations of the LTAG grammar. The chapter details the construction of the supertaggers and evaluates the different approximations in terms of their precision of supertag assignment on the Wall Street Journal corpus. The speed versus precision of the supertaggers are also explored. An interesting approach of combining the nonstatistical supertagger, which has 100% recall with a statistical supertagger to improve precision is also suggested.

Nasr and Rambow in chapter 8 present a nonlexicalized chart parser (GDG) that uses the output of a supertagger and produces a dependency parse output for a sentence. In contrast to the Lightweight Dependency Analyser(LDA) (Bangalore, 2000) that uses heuristics to compute links between supertags, the GDG parser uses probabilities estimated from a parsed corpus to compute the dependency linkage structure. Also, being a full parser, unlike LDA, a globally consistent linkage structure is produced. The grammar is encoded as an Recursive Transition Network (RTN), where each finite-state automaton represents a supertag and a transition is labeled by all supertags that can substitute into that supertag at a given node. Given the supertag sequence or the n-best output from the supertagger, the chart parser uses the RTN to produce a dependency parse forest from which the first-best dependency parse is retrieved. The parser is evaluated on the Penn Treebank and different trade-offs in terms of the supertag ambiguity versus the parser efficiency and accuracies are explored. There is also a detailed discussion in the chapter on how this research is different from other recent work in dependency parsing.

1.6.3   Supertags in other related formalisms

The adoption of the notion of supertags by researchers working in different grammar formalisms is the topic of the third part of the book. Although, as one would expect, the supertags in these different formalisms result in different representations, the notion of localized structures provides a unifying theme across the different formalisms. The differences in encodings of linguistic phenomena in these formalisms could be an object of future study in its own right.

Combinatory Categorial Grammars (CCG) and Lexicalized Tree-Adjoining Grammars are perhaps the two most closely related lexicalized grammar formalisms that have been extensively compared from formal, computational and linguistic perspectives. In chapter 9, Clark and Curran extend this tradition by presenting an approach to supertagging using CCG categories and tightly integrating the supertagger with a CCG parser. Clark and Curran present a maximum entropy model for CCG supertag disambiguation which is extended to produce multiple CCG supertags per word. The tight coupling with the parser is novel in the sense that the parser requests the supertagger more supertags if the parser fails to produce a spanning analysis. Clark and Curran use a CCG grammar extracted from the Penn Treebank and train and evaluate the supertagger and parser on standard partitions of the treebank. The performance of the CCG supertagger is better than that reported for LTAG supertagger partly due to the size of the supertag sets in these two grammars. CCG supertag sets are usually smaller than the LTAG supertag sets due to the difference in granularity of localization in the two grammars. They also crucially rely on supertagging to reduce the search space during the discriminative training phase of the CCG parser.

Constraint Dependency Grammars introduced by Maruyama (1990) associates lexical items with *governor* and *need* roles that are filled in by role values that indicate the dependency relations among the words of a sentence. A parse structure in these grammars is a consistent assignment of role values to the need roles. A set of constraints operating on the lexial level (fullfillment of need roles) and at the sentence level (e.g., each word must have a single governor) are used to specify the consistency of a parse. The search for a parse proceeds as a consistraint satisfaction program. In chapter 10, Harper and Wang extend this grammar framework to accomodate for ambiguity in lexical categories (SuperARVs) and incorporate probabilistic constraints in order to model parse preferences. The SuperARVs (super abstract role values) are lexicalized representations and encode rich morpho-syntactic information. However, unlike supertags, SuperARVs do not contain constituency information. Broad-coverage statistical parsers using SuperARVs extracted from the Penn Treebank are presented in this chapter. Parsing using the two methods of (a) SuperARV disambiguation followed by dependency linking and (b) tight integration of SuperARV disambiguation as part of dependency linking are presented and compared using the Wall Street Journal parsing task. They also present comprehensive results on large vocabulary speech recognition and demonstrate the use of structural information as encoded in the SuperARV grammars improve speech recognition accuracy as compared against n-gram based language models.

The trade-off between the amount of information that is packed into supertags (granularity of supertags), the accuracy of supertagging and its relation to parsing accuracy is investigated in chapter 11. Foth and colleagues investigate the effect of incorporating ever richer information into supertags. These supertags are constructed from dependency trees for German that were extracted from the NEGRA and TIGER corpora. The obvious effect of incorporating richer information into supertags is an increase in the supertag vocabulary. However, interestingly, this increase in supertag vocabulary does not directly correlate with the supertagging error. They show that supertagging using a supertag set that includes direction of attachment information in a supertag is harder to dismabiguate than a supertag set which includes complement information in a supertag. Further, the disambiguated supertag sequence is encoded as weighted constraints and incorporated into a rule-based weighted constrained dependency grammar parser. The evaluation of parser output presented in this chapter illustrates that increasing the complexity of supertags and using the disambiguated supertags to guide the parser continues to improve the accuracy of the parser. The information encoded in the supertags counter balances the drop in accuracy of supertag disambiguation with more complex supertags.

Moot, in chapter 12, describes type-logical grammars, which trace their lineage to the Adjukiewicz-Bar-Hillel grammars. The analysis/generation of a sentence in type-logical grammars is viewed as a proof using rules of natural deduction. In order to account for linguistic phenomena that require more than context-free generative capacity, modal operators that allow for structural changes of the proof tree are introduced in this chapter. Following an introduction to type-logical grammars, Moot introduces the idea of extracting a type-logical grammar from a dependency parse treebank. He extracts a grammar from a parsed corpus of *spoken* Dutch sentences. The grammar extraction procedure is general enough that it could be directly applied to other dependency annotated treebanks. The grammar, as in LTAG, is lexicalized and by varying the information present in the type-logical supertags, Moot shows that the supertag disambiguation can be improved. Given the complexities of the spoken corpus – disfluencies and ellipses, the supertag set is quite large compared to other supertag sets and the supertagging accuracy is correspondingly lower as well.

In chapter 13, Neumann and Crysmann discuss results on statistical parsing using a richly annotated German treebank from the Verbmobil domain. The treebank is annotated using a Head-driven Phrase Structure Grammar representation. They discuss the extraction procedure that exploits the head/argument and argument/adjunct distinctions as defined by the HPSG grammar. The result of the grammar extraction is a lexicalized tree-insertion grammar (LTIG) and the lexicalized trees are used as HPSG-supertags in a probabilistic LTIG parser. They report results on parsing German sentences from the Verbmobil domain and contrast them to previous results obtained on the NEGRA corpus.

Supertags from the LTAG, CCG, and other formalisms can be viewed as localizing different kinds of linguistic information into a single elementary object. The nature and amount of information that is localized vary depending on the formalism and the linguistic analysis that is adopted in that formalism. It can be regarded as extending the domain of locality of CFG rules by operating on objects richer than single level trees. Matsuzaki, Miyao, and Tsujii present an interesting variant to the question of how to extend the localization of CFG in chapter 14. In their approach, a CFG nonterminal is enriched with latent annotations that take on specified range of values. These latent annotation variables and the values do not bear any linguistic significance, but are used to losen the independence assumptions in a context-free grammar (a motivation shared by LTAGs). A special case of this approach is the use of head-word annotation on CFG nonterminals that has been successfully exploited in statistical parsing research. The chapter discusses in detail the methods for estimating the parameters of PCFGs with latent annotations and presents parsing evaluation results as the number latent variables and the value ranges are varied.

In chapter 15, Bharathi and Sangal discuss a computational framework for Indian language processing based on Paninian Grammar. Panini had formulated a theory for Sanskrit language analysis some two thousand five hundred years ago which has been since extended and adapted for analysis of other Indian languages. This chapter discusses the adoption and suitability of Paninian theory for computational analysis of Indian languages particularly due to their relatively free word order nature. The use of *karaka* roles helps in interfacing the syntax and semantic level of representations. Post-position markers help identify word groups that satisfy the karaka roles and are central to the grammaticality of a sentence. Each verb is associated with karaka frames that specify mandatory and optional karakas. The parsing problem is framed as an integer programming problem and an efficient solution is computed using the bipartite graph-matching algorithm. The resulting parse is a dependency tree similar to a derivation tree in LTAG, but with words as nodes and karaka roles as the labels for the edges of the dependency tree. The similarities between LTAG and Computational Paninian Grammar is explicated and the use of supertagging as a means of selecting the appropriate karaka frame is suggested.

1.6.4   Linguistic and psycholinguistic issues

As discussed in the introductory sections of this chapter, the effect of localization of dependencies to be specified in a supertag has interesting linguistic and psycholinguistic implications. In the fourth part of the book, we include work from two authors who have novel proposals for syntactic analysis that are motivated by representational (syntax-prosody interface) and human sentence processing issues.

Frank (1992) first enunciated the principles that have been used as a guide in the construction of elementary trees for a linguistically motivated grammars in LTAG. The lexical head of an elementary tree is to assign a role to all the frontier nonterminal nodes in the tree. This limits the size of the elementary tree and consequently all the modifiers are factored out from this domain of role assignment. In chapter 16, Frank restates the principle to assert that *all* the syntactic relations of a lexical head are expressed in an elementary tree and questions the need for construction of a global syntactic structure. In this view, the assignment of the correct elementary structure to words would be sufficient to infer syntactic information of each word – much like the motivation underlying supertagging. In this chapter, Frank explores the consequences of not computing a global syntactic structure for deriving phonological and semantic representations. He proposes that the phonological representations are computed locally for each elementary tree and are combined using a merge operation to form a phonological representation for a sentence.

The relevance of lexicalized grammars for computational analysis of language has been explored extensively. Lexicalized grammars have also been studied as appealing representations in the human sentence processing literature (Trueswell and Tanenhaus, 1994). The domain of locality provided by supertags combined with their distributional information derived from corpora has been shown to model the relevant human sentence processing results related to processing preferences and difficulties (Kim et al., 2002). In chapter 17, Mazzei, Lombardo and Strut explore the issue of incremental sentence processing using supertag-based elementary structures. In order to address the apparent lack of delays in structure computation as evidenced from experimental literature, they propose a *strong connectivity hypothesis*. According to this hypothesis, during left to right sentence processing, each word is incorporated into the evolving syntactic structure immediately. Such a proposal requires extending the domain of locality of supertags further in order to allow for the incorporation of a word into the structure computed for the fragment of a sentence thus far. Also, they develop a dynamic version of TAG called DVTAG and introduce direction (left, right) sensitive substitution and adjunction opertation in order to combine the supertag structures. The chapter also describes the extraction of these larger supertags from annotated corpora and illustrates the size of such extracted supertag sets. The use of such supertag sets in a parser is left for further study.

1.6.5   Speech and language applications

The level of syntactic representation created by the supertagger has been exploited in a variety of speech and language applications. The enriched tagset is used for information filtering (Chandrasekhar and Bangalore, 2002), for language modeling (Srinivas, 1996), and for coreference resolution (Srinivas and Baldwin, 1996). Other interesting speech and language applications that exploit the supertag representation for semantic role labeling, spoken language understanding in dialog and mechanisms for input in devices without keyboard are presented in this final section of the book.

In chapter 18, Chen presents different methods for semantic role labeling using deep linguistic features and compares their performances against methods that use only surface linguistic features. Semantic role labeling is the task of identifying predicate-argument relations and labeling the arguments of the predicates. These labels are as defined in the Propbank (Penn Treebank with semantic role labels), annotation guide and represent deep grammatical roles, in contrast to the surface grammatical roles of subject, direct and indirect object. The chapter builds on the previous work of extracting LTAG grammars from the Penn Treebank. With the availability of Propbank, the extracted grammars would contain the role label as part of the syntactic constituent label. The extracted LTAG grammars are used to build supertaggers as well as lightweight dependency analyzers for semantic parsing. This approach is contrasted against a full statistical semantic parsing approach. The conclusions of these experiments indicate that supertags capture most of the deep linguistic information that improve the semantic role labeling task performance. Also, the use of semantic supertags (semantic roles on argument nodes) improves the performance over an approach of using a syntactic parser and then recovering the semantic role labels as a second step.

In chapter 19, Harbusch and colleagues discuss two other applications for supertagging. In the first application, the supertagger is used in the understanding component of a user-initiated dialog system in a call center. They show that the use of the supertagger enhances the robustness of the spoken language understanding component in terms of classifying the user's request as well as extracting the task parameters more accurately. The second application presented in this chapter concerns ambiguous keyboards and multitapping on small devices without a conventional keyboards. These keyboards cluster characters onto single keys and the user needs to tap multiple times to select the appropriate character. The method proposed in this chapter involves allowing the user to tap only once on the multitap keyboard and to resolve the character ambiguity generated by the single tap using sentence-based language models. The supertagger is used to provide syntactic constraints for the reordering of the sentence hypotheses and allows the user to select the appropriate sentence from the ranked suggestion list. The evaluation results support the use of supertagger in improving the interaction time compared to the word-based disambiguation methods.

1.6.6   Ongoing research related to supertags

There are several research directions related to supertags that are not covered by the topics of the chapters included in this book. We summarize these briefly in this section.

The research work on discriminative models for supertagging in conjunction with efficient statistical tree-insertion grammar parsing is available in MICA, a broad-coverage, fast English parser. The parser can be downloaded freely (Bangalore et al., 2009).

While most of the supertag disambiguation discussed in this book are for sentence analysis, there has been work on using them for *sentence generation.* Sentence generation is typically viewed as consisting of content planning, sentence planning and surface realization steps (Reiter and Dale, 2000) which are usually hand-crafted for a given application. The content planning step decides on what is to be conveyed and structures the content for the sentence planner. The sentence planner uses lexical and syntactic resources in order to convey the content. The result of sentence planning is then used by the surface realizer to create a well-formed natural language sentence. In recent work (Langkilde and Knight, 2000; Corston-Oliver et al., 2002; Bangalore and Rambow, 2000) there has been interest in creating a broad-coverage, data-driven surface realizer that could be used across different applications. The approach followed to that end is to regard the surface realizer as transforming an abstract representation (e.g., logical form or underspecified dependency trees) into a natural language sentence and to use statistical models to achieve this transformation. The supertag-based approach to a surface realizer followed in FERGUS (Bangalore and Rambow, 2000) uses underspecified (unlabeled) dependency trees as input. The nodes of the dependency tree are then annotated with supertag labels which provide the lexical ordering information. Assigning supertags to nodes of the dependency tree requires supertagging, just as in the case of sentence analysis. Generative and discriminative models for supertagging have been explored for this task (Bangalore and Rambow, 2000, 2005).

Supertags have been used in a variety of different speech and language tasks as a means of incorporating syntactic information in a inexpensive manner without incurring the cost of a full parse. Supertags have recently been used to improve the quality of phrase tables in phrase-based statistical machine translation research (Hassan et al., 2007). The authors show that assigning supertags to words of a phrase and exploiting the constraints encoded in supertags helps in improving the translation quality over a purely lexical phrase-based approach.

For speech prosody prediction, supertags have been incorporated along with acoustic information in a maximum-entropy framework (Rangarajan et al., 2007). The supertag labels are shown to provide discriminative information that improves the prosody label prediction beyond the lexical information of a sentence. Furthermore, supertags complement the acoustic information of the speech signal as well and a combination of lexical, syntactic and acoustic information is shown to perform the best in this task. A similar result is shown for dialog act labeling, where each utterance of a dialog turn is assigned a communicative intent label. Here too, exploiting the supertag label in addition to the lexical and acoustic information improves labeling accuracy significantly (Bangalore et al., 2006; Rangarajan et al., 2007).

Finally, LTAG and CCG formalisms continue to be compared on formal, linguistic, and computational grounds. While the work of viewing CCG categories as richer lexical description has been explored in chapter 9, there is also work on extending the notion of CCG categories to be closer to the notion of supertags. Supertags associated with a predicate encode not only the arguments of a predicate but also all the different structural positions the arguments may occupy in various syntactic constructions in which the predicate participates. Categorial grammars also encode argument positions, but they do not encode (in the representation of a category label associated with a predicate) the different structural positions that the arguments can occupy. These emerge during the various types of compositions and type-raisings in categorial grammars. In this sense, LTAGs are strongly lexicalized. Hence although the so-called Combinatory Categorial Grammars (CCG) (Steedman, 1996) are weakly equivalent to LTAGs (both belonging to the class of the so-called *mildly context-sensitive languages* (Joshi, 1985), they are not strongly equivalent. It is possible to construct a version of CCG that is more like LTAG. This is achieved by starting with the syntactic type assigned to a predicate by a CCG and then *unfolding* it and creating partial proof trees, analogous to the supertags in LTAG, which are then composed by appropriate rules of composition (inference), for further details see Joshi and Kulick (1997).

Notes

1. The Greibach form of the rule is related to the categories in a categorial grammar.

2. In the actual LTAG grammar, each node in an elementary tree is decorated with attribute value structures (feature structures) that encode various linguistic constraints specified over the domain of an elementary tree. There is no recursion in these feature structures. We omit these details here in as much as they are not essential for our immediate purpose.

3. This distinction between the two types of elementary trees is characterized in LTAG in terms of *initial trees* (the α trees) and the *auxiliary trees* (the β trees).

4. The derivation trees of LTAG have a close relationship to dependency trees, although there are some crucial differences. The semantic dependencies are the same, however.

5. The general notion of flat semantics is related to the notion of minimal recursion semantics (MRS) (Copestake et al., 1999). MRS has been used in the semantic computation in the HPSG framwork. In the LTAG framework, the notion of elementary trees and the derivation tree, which specifies the composition in terms of the elementary trees, directly provides a representation for computing a *flat* semantics.

6. There have been several recent experiments using different methods for extracting supertags from treebanks. Each of these extraction methods results in different sizes of supertag tagsets and hence the accuracy of the supertag disambiguation varies depending on the supertag tageset.

References

Abeillé, A. (2002). Une grammaire électronique du français. *CNRS Éditions*.

Bangalore, S. (2000). A lightweight dependency analyzer for partial parsing. *JNLE*, 6(2):113–138.

Bangalore, S., Boullier, P., Nasr, A., Rambow, O., and Sagot, B. (2009). MICA: A probabilistic dependency parser based on tree insertion grammars (application note). In *Proceedings of Human Language Technologies: The 2009 Annual Conference of the North American Chapter of the Association for Computational Linguistics, Companion Volume: Short Papers*, pages 185–188.

Bangalore, S., Fabbrizio, G. D., and Stent, A. (2006). Learning the structure of task-driven human-human dialogs. In *Proceedings of COLING/ACL*.

Bangalore, S. and Rambow, O. (2000). Exploiting a probabilistic hierarchical model for Generation. In *COLING*, Saarbucken, Germany.

Bangalore, S. and Rambow, O. (2005). Classification of structured descriptions. In *Proceedings of ICASSP*, Philadelphia.

Black, E., Jelinek, F., Lafferty, J., Magerman, D. M., Mercer, R., and Roukos, S. (1993). Towards History-based Grammars: Using Richer Models for Probabilistic Parsing. In *Proceedings of the 31st Conference of Association of Computational Linguistics*.

Bod, R., Scha, R., and Sima'an, K. (2003). *Data-Oriented Parsing*. CSLI.

Butt, M., Dyvik, H., Holloway-King, T., Masuichi, H., and Rohrer, C. (2002). The parallel grammar project. In *Proceedings of COLING-2002 Workshop on Grammar Engineering and Evaluation*.

Chandrasekhar, R. and Bangalore, S. (2002). Glean: Using syntactic information in document filtering. In *Encyclopedia of Microcomputers*, pages 111–131. Marcel Dekker.

Charniak, E. (2000). A maximum-entropy-inspired parser. In *Proceedings of NAACL*.

Chen, J. and Vijay-Shanker, K. (2000). Automated extraction of the tags from the penn treebank. In *Proceedings of the 6^{t}h International Workshop on Parsing Technology (IWPT)*, pages 65–76.

Chiang, D. (2000). Statistical parsing with an automatically extracted tree adjoining grammar. In *Proceedings of the Association for Computational Linguistics (ACL) 2000 Meeting*.

Collins, M. (1996). A New Statistical Parser Based on Bigram Lexical Dependencies. In *Proceedings of the 34th Annual Meeting of the Association for Computational Linguistics*, Santa Cruz.

Collins, M. and Duffy, N. (2002). New ranking algorithms for parsing and tagging: Kernels over discrete structures and the voted perceptron. In *ACL*.

Copestake, A., Flickinger, D., Sag, I. A., and Pollard, C. (1999). Minimal recursion semantics: An introduction. Technical report, Stanford University.

Corston-Oliver, S., Gamon, M., Ringger, E., and Moore, R. (2002). An overview of amalgam: A machine-learned generation module. In *Proceedings of INLG-02*.

Flickinger, D., Copestake, A., and Sag, I. A. (2000). HPSG analysis of English. In Wahlster, W., ed., *Verbmobil: Foundations of Speech-to-Speech Translation*, pages 254–263. Springer Verlag.

Frank, R. (1992). *Syntactic locality and Tree Adjoining Grammar: grammatical, acquisition and processing perspectives*. PhD thesis, University of Pennsylvania, IRCS-92-47.

Hassan, H., Sima'an, K., and Way, A. (2007). Integrating supertagging into phrase-based statistical machine translation. In *Proceedings of ACL 2007*, Prague.

Joshi, A. K. (1985). Tree-adjoining grammars: How much context sensitivity is required to provide reasonable structural descriptions. In D. Dowty, L. K. and Zwicky, A., eds., *Natural Language Parsing*, pages 206–250. Cambridge University Press.

Joshi, A. K., Kallmeyer, L., and Romero, M. (2003). Flexible composition in LTAG: Quantifier scope and inverse linking. In *Proceedings of the International Workshop on Computational Semantics (IWCS-5)*, Tilburg.

Joshi, A. K. and Kulick, S. (1997). Partial proof trees as building blocks for a categorial grammar. *Linguistics and Philosophy*.

Joshi, A. K., Levy, L. S., and Takahashi, M. (1975). Tree adjunct grammars. *Journal of Computer and System Sciences*, 10:1:136–163.

Joshi, A. K. and Schabes, Y. (1997). Tree-adjoining grammars. In Rosenberg, G. and Salomaa, A., eds., *Handbook of Formal Languages*, pages 69–123. Springer.

Joshi, A. K. and Srinivas, B. (1994a). Disambiguation of Super Parts of Speech (or Supertags): Almost Parsing. In *Proceedings of the 17th International Conference on Computational Linguistics (COLING '94)*, Kyoto, Japan.

Joshi, A. K. and Srinivas, B. (1994b). Disambiguation of super parts of speech (supertags): Almost parsing. In *Proceedings of the 1994 International Conference on Computational Linguistics (COLING)*, Kyoto, Japan.

Joshi, A. K. and Vijay-Shanker, K. (1999). Compositional semantics with lexicalized tree-adjoining grammar (LTAG): How much underspecification is necessary. In Bunt, H. and Thijsse, E., eds., *Proceedings of the Third International Workshop on Computational Semantics (IWCS-3)*, pages 131–145.

Joshi, A. K., Vijay-Shanker, K., and Weir, D. J. (1991). The convergence of mildly context sensitive grammatical formalisms. In Sells, P., Shieber, S., and Wasow, T., eds., *Foundational Issues in Natural Language Processing*. MIT Press.

Kallmeyer, L. and Joshi, A. K. (1999). Factoring predicate argument and scope semantics: Underspecified semantics with LTAG. In *Proceedings of the Twelfth Amsterdam Colloquium, University of Amsterdam*, pages 169–174.

Kaplan, R. and Bresnan, J. (1983). Lexical-functional grammar: A formal system of grammatical representation. In Bresnan, J., ed., *The Mental Representation of Grammatical Relations*. MIT Press.

Kasper, R., Kiefer, B., Netter, K., and Vijay-Shanker, K. (1995). Compilation of HPSG to TAG. In *Proceedings of the Association for Computational Linguistics (ACL)*, MIT Press, pages 92–99.

Kim, A., Srinivas, B., and Trueswell, J. (2002). The convergence of lexicalist perspectives in psycholinguistic and computational linguistics. In Merlo, P. and Stevenson, S., eds., *Sentence Processing and the Lexicon: Formal, Computational and Experimental Perspectives*. John Benjamin Publishing.

Kroch, A. (1989). Asymmetries in long distance extraction in a tree-adjoining grammar. In Baltin, M. and Kroch, A., eds., *Alternative conceptions of phrase structure*. University of Chicago Press.

Kroch, A. and Joshi, A. K. (1985). Linguistic relevance of tree-adjoining grammars. Technical report, Department of Computer and Information Science, University of Pennsylvania.

Kroch, A. and Santorini, B. (1991). The derived constituent structure of the west germanic verb raising constructions. In Freiden, R., ed., *Principles and parameters in comparative grammar*, pages 269–338. MIT Press.

Langkilde, I. and Knight, K. (2000). Forest-based statistical sentence generation. In *Proceedings of First North American ACL*.

Linz, P. (2001). *An Introduction to Formal Languages and Automata*. Jones and Bartlett.

MacDonald, M., Pearlmutter, N., and Seidenberg, M. (1994). Lexical nature of syntactic ambiguity resolution. *Psychological Review*, 101:676–703.

Magerman, D. M. (1995). Statistical Decision-Tree Models for Parsing. In *Proceedings of the 33rd Annual Meeting of the Association for Computational Linguistics*.

Magerman, D. M. and Marcus, M. P. (1991). Pearl: A probabilistic chart parser. In *Proceedings of the European Assoc. for Comp. Ling.*, Berlin.

Marcus, M. P., Santorini, B., and Marcinkiewicz, M. A. (1993). Building a large annotated corpus of English: The Penn Treebank. *Computational Linguistics*, 19.2:313–330.

Maruyama, H. (1990). Constraint Dependency Grammar and its weak generative capacity. *Computer Software*.

Pollard, C. and Sag, I. A. (1994). *Head-Driven Phrase Structure Grammar*. University Press of Chicago.

Prolo, C. A. (2003). *LR parsing for tree-adjoining grammars and its applications to corpus based natural language parsing*. PhD thesis, University of Pennsylvania.

Rambow, O. (1994). *Formal and computational aspects of natural language syntax*. PhD thesis, University of Pennsylvania.

Rangarajan, V., Bangalore, S., and Narayanan, S. (2007). Exploiting acoustic and syntactic features for prosody labeling in a maximum entropy framework. In *Proceedings of NAACL 2007*, Rochester.

Ratnaparkhi, A. (1997). A Linear Observed Time Statistical Parser Based on Maximum Entropy Models. In *Proceedings of the Empirical Methods in Natural Language Processing*, New Providence.

Reiter, E. and Dale, R. (2000). *Building Natural Language Generation Systems*. Cambridge University Press.

Resnik, P. (1992). Probabilistic tree-adjoining grammars as a framework for statistical natural language processing. In *Proceedings of COLING '92*, Nantes, pages 418–424.

Sarkar, A. (2002). *Combining labeled and unlabeled data in statistical natural language processing*. PhD thesis, University of Pennsylvania, Philadelphia.

Schabes, Y. (1992). Stochastic lexicalized grammars. In *Proceedings of COLING '92*, University of Chicago Press, pages 426–432.

Shen, L. and Joshi, A. K. (2003). A SNoW based supertagger the applications to NP chunking. In *Proceedings of the Association for Computational Linguistics Meeting (ACL)*, Sapporo, Japan, pages 89–96.

Skut, W., Krenn, B., Brants, T., and Uszkoreit, H. (1997). An annotation scheme for free word order languages. In *Proceedings of the Fifth Conference on Applied Natural Language Processing ANLP-97*, Washington, DC.

Srinivas, B. (1996). "Almost Parsing" Technique for Language Modeling. In *Proceedings of ICSLP96 Conference*, Philadelphia, USA.

Srinivas, B. and Baldwin, B. (1996). Exploiting supertag representation for fast coreference resolution. In *Proceedings of the International Conference on Natural Language Processing and Industrial Applications (NLP+IA '96)*, Moncton, Canada.

Srinivas, B. and Joshi, A. K. (1998). Supertagging: An approach to almost parsing. *Computational Linguistics*, 22:1–29.

Stabler, E. P. (1997). Derivational minimalism. In Retorc, C., ed., *Logical Aspects of Computational Linguistics*, pages 68–95. Springer Verlag.

Steedman, M. J. (1996). *Surface Structure and Interpretation*. MIT Press.

Stone, M. and Doran, C. (1999). Sentence planning as description using tree-adjoining grammar. In *Procceedings of the Association for Computational Linguistics (ACL) Meeting*, Madrid.

Trueswell, J. and Tanenhaus, M. (1994). Toward a lexicalist framework for constraint-based syntactic ambiguity resolution. In Clifton, C., Rayner, K., and Frazier, L., eds., *Perspectives on Sentence Processing*. Lawrence Erlbaum Associates.

Vijay-Shanker, K. (1987). *A Study of Tree-Adjoining Grammars*. PhD thesis, University of Pennsylvania.

Waltz, D. (1975). Understanding line drawings of scenes with shadows. In Winston, P., ed., *The Psychology of Computer Vision*. McGraw Hill.

Weir, D. J. (1988). *Characterizing mildly context-sensitive grammar formalisms*. PhD thesis, University of Pennsylvania.

XTAG-Group (2002). A lexicalized tree-adjoining grammar for English. Technical report, University of Pennsylvania.

Part I

Creating and Organizing Supertags

From Treebanks to Tree-Adjoining Grammars

Fei Xia and Martha Palmer

2.1 Introduction

Grammars are valuable resources for natural language processing. A large-scale grammar may incorporate a vast amount of information on morphology, syntax, and semantics. Traditionally, grammars are built manually. Hand-crafted grammars often contain rich information, but they require tremendous human effort to build and maintain. As large-scale treebanks become available in the last decade, there has been much work on extracting grammars automatically from treebanks. Such grammars are called *treebank grammars*.[1]

Many of the previous work on grammar extraction such as (Shirai et al., 1995; Charniak, 1996; Krotov et al., 1998) generate context-free grammars (CFGs). In this chapter, we present a system, LexTract, which generates both CFGs and lexicalized tree-adjoining grammars (LTAGs).

Extracting LTAGs is more complicated than extracting CFGs because of the differences between LTAGs and CFGs. First, the primitive elements of an LTAG are lexicalized tree structures (called *elementary trees*), rather than context-free rules. Therefore, an LTAG extraction algorithm needs to examine a larger portion of a phrase structure to build an elementary tree. Second, because the adjoining operation in LTAG allows an elementary tree to be inserted within another elementary tree, an elementary tree is often formed by *gluing together* several disconnected parts of a phrase structure. Third, unlike in CFGs, parse trees (also known as *derived trees* in the LTAG formalism) and derivation trees (which describe how elementary trees are combined to form parse trees) are distinct in the LTAG formalism in the sense that a parse tree can be produced by several distinct derivation trees. Therefore, to provide training data for statistical LTAG parsers, an LTAG extraction algorithm should also build derivation trees in addition to elementary trees.

There were two main considerations when we designed LexTract: First, given a parse tree, the number of distinct LTAG grammars that produce this parse tree can be exponential with respect to the number of leaf nodes in the parse tree, and most of those grammars are not linguistically plausible. In order to extract only linguistically plausible grammars, we make certain assumptions about how three major relations (predicate-argument relations, modification relations, and coordinated relations) should be handled in LTAG grammars. The assumptions are based on well-established linguistic notions such as the notion of *head*. Second, in order to make LexTract a good grammar extraction tool that can be applied to various treebanks for different languages, we put all the language-dependent or treebank-dependent information in three tables (that is, the head percolation table, argument table, and tagset table). Users can easily modify these tables to reflect their own preferences. Given the assumptions and the tables, the process of extracting grammars is totally deterministic and we extract exactly one grammar for any given treebank. We have run the system on three publicly available treebanks, and the system output has been used in various NLP tasks.

As the LTAG formalism is a general framework and its usage is not restricted to natural languages, the formalism itself does not impose any constraint that is based solely on the properties of natural languages. Because the grammars that LexTract aims to extract are for natural languages only, we impose additional constraints on the treebank grammars to reflect the properties of natural languages. In section 2.2, we introduce these constraints and describe the grammar that we intend to extract. In section 2.3, we describe the extraction algorithm and compare it with related work. In section 2.4, we report experimental results on some tasks that use extracted grammars.

2.2   The Target Grammars

Given a parse tree, the LTAG grammars that can generate the parse tree are not unique. For instance, a simple parse tree such as the one in figure 2.1a can be produced by either grammar G_1 in figure 2.1b or grammar G_2 in figure 2.1c. While both grammars are LTAGs, people with a linguistic background would prefer G_1 over G_2 because it is more plausible to have the verb (rather than the noun) anchor a clause. The question is how we can equip LexTract with such linguistic knowledge so that it will produce G_1 rather than G_2.

Recall that the LTAG formalism is a general framework. Besides natural languages, the formalism can be used to generate formal languages such as $\{a^n b^n c^n\}$. Because its usage is not restricted to natural languages, the formalism itself does not impose constraints that are based solely on the properties of natural languages. As the grammars that LexTract aims to extract are for natural languages only, we would like to impose constraints on the target grammars (i.e., the grammars built by LexTract) to reflect the properties of natural languages. These extra constraints

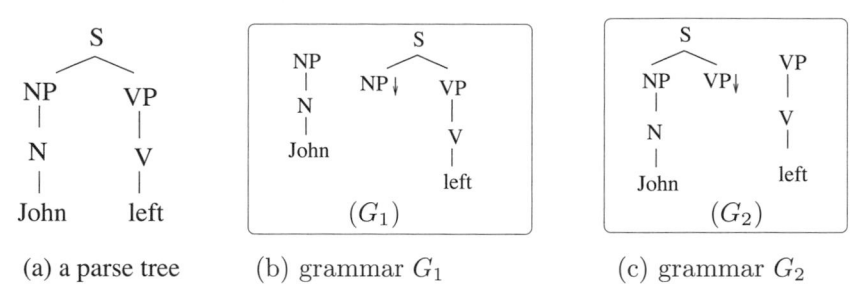

(a) a parse tree (b) grammar G_1 (c) grammar G_2

FIGURE 2.1 A parse tree and two LTAGs that can generate the parse tree

are based on well-defined linguistic notions such as the notion of *head*. As a result, the target grammars form only a subset of all possible LTAG grammars. For the example in figure 2.1, LexTract will produce only G_1, not G_2.

In this section, let us first review a few important syntactic notions and show how they are represented in linguistic theories and LTAG grammars. The notions are a head and its projections, arguments and modifiers. We shall also define three prototypes and require that each elementary tree in the target grammars fall into one of the prototypes.[2]

2.2.1 Several important syntactic notions

An important concept in many contemporary linguistic theories such as X-bar theory (Jackendoff, 1977) and GB theory (Chomsky, 1981) is the notion of *head*. A *head* determines the main properties of the phrase that it belongs to, and it may project to various levels. We call the chain formed by a head and its projections *a projection chain*. In X-bar theory (see figure 2.2a), a head X projects to $\bar{X}$, which further projects to XP. The X in this paradigm can be any part of speech such as a verb, where the XP is a phrase such as a verb phrase. GB theory divides heads into two types: lexical heads and functional heads. In figure 2.2b, V (for verb) is a lexical head, whereas C (for complementizer) and I (for inflection) are functional heads. The projections of lexical and functional heads are called *lexical* and *functional* projections, respectively. The solid arrows in the figure show the syntactic movement from a lower position to a higher position.

A head may have several arguments, and it and its projections can be modified by other components. For instance, a verb can project to a verb phrase, and it may have one or more arguments, and a verb phrase can be modified by preposition phrases, adverbial phrases, and so on.

2.2.2 Prototypes of elementary trees

Recall that LTAG is a general framework, and therefore it does not have to follow a particular linguistic theory such as X-bar theory. However, the notions of head,

(1) XP -> YP $\overline{X}$

(2) $\overline{X}$ -> $\overline{X}$ WP

(3) $\overline{X}$ -> X YP

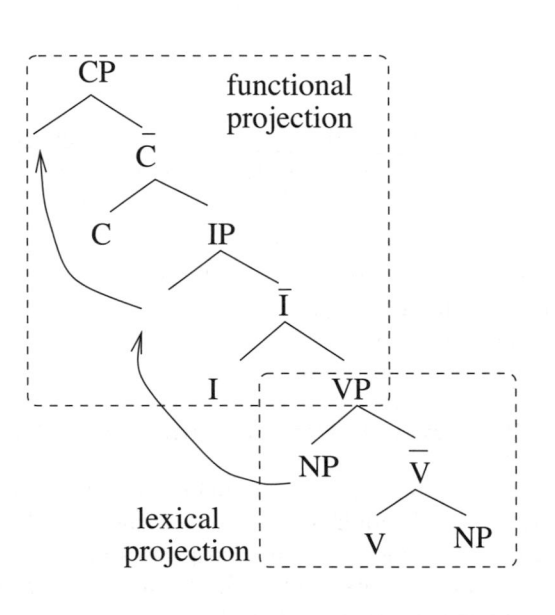

(a) rules in X-bar theory   (b) a phrase structure in GB-theory

FIGURE 2.2 The notions of *head* in X-bar theory and GB-theory

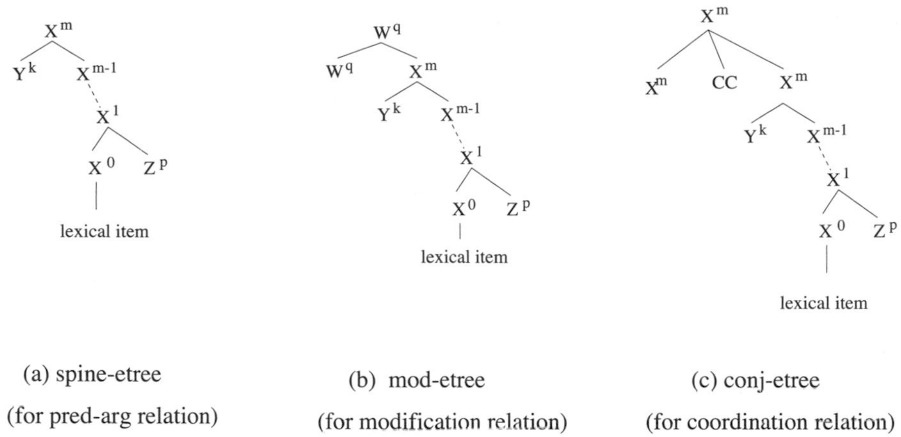

FIGURE 2.3 The three forms of elementary trees in the target grammar

projection, argument, and modifier are widely accepted in the LTAG community, and people often follow some conventions when manually crafting LTAG grammars for natural languages. For instance, they often use initial trees to express predicate-argument relations: the anchor of an initial tree is the head of the root node, and all the arguments of the head are included in the same initial tree. In contrast, auxiliary trees are used to express modification relations, where the root node and the foot node have the label of the modified element, and the modifier is a sibling of the foot node. We formalize these conventions and define three types of elementary tree (*etree* for short) according to the relations between the anchor of the elementary tree and other nodes in the tree, as shown in figure 2.3:

- *Spine-etrees* for predicate-argument relations: A spine-etree is formed by a head X^0, its projections $X^1, ..., X^m$, and its arguments. We call the path from X^0 to the root X^m a *projection chain*. The head X^0 is also the anchor of the tree, and its arguments are leaf nodes attached at various levels.

- *Mod-etrees* for modification relations: The root of a mod-etree has two children: one child has the same label (W^q) as the root, while the other child, X^m, is a modifier of W^q. The X^m child is further expanded into a spine-etree whose head X^0 is the anchor of the whole mod-etree.

- *Conj-etrees* for coordination relations: In a conj-etree, the children of the root are two conjoined constituents and one conjunction.[3] One conjoined constituent is expanded into a spine-etree whose head is the anchor of the whole tree. Structurally, a conj-etree is the same as a mod-etree except that the root has one extra conjunction child.

The similarity between the forms in figure 2.3 and rules in X-bar theory is obvious: a spine-etree is a tree that combines the first and the third types of rules in X-bar theory (see figure 2.2a); Similarly, a mod-etree incorporates all three types of rules. A spine-etree is also very similar to the basic structure in GB-theory, as in figure 2.2b.

Some explanations about the prototypes are in order. First, each node in these prototypes may have zero or more children; when it has more than one child, the order among these children is not specified in the prototypes. For instance, the prototypes allow arguments Y^k and Z^p to appear to the left or to the right of X^0. Second, in the LTAG formalism elementary trees are divided into two types: initial trees and auxiliary trees. In this section, we define three forms of elementary trees. These two classifications are based on different criteria. The former classification is based on the existence of a foot node in the tree. Our classification is based on the relation between the anchor of the tree and other nodes in the tree. In general, spine-etrees are initial trees, mod-etrees and conj-etrees are auxiliary trees; however, there are exceptions to this generalization.[4] Third, the notions of *head* and *anchor* do not always coincide: the anchor of a spine-etree is the head of the root node, whereas the anchor of a mod-etree (or conj-etree) is the head of the modifier phrase, but not the head of the root node.

Now that we have defined the prototypes, we require each elementary tree produced by LexTract to fall into one of three prototypes. For a little abuse of notation, we also use the terms *spine-etree*, *mod-etree*, and *conj-etree* to refer to the corresponding templates.

2.3   The Extraction Algorithm

The core of LexTract is an extraction algorithm that takes a phrase structure in a treebank and produces an LTAG grammar. Extracting LTAGs is more complicated than extracting CFGs because of the differences between LTAGs and CFGs. First, the primitive elements of an LTAG are elementary trees, rather than context-free rules. Therefore, an LTAG extraction algorithm needs to examine a larger portion of a phrase structure to build an elementary tree. Second, because the adjoining operation in LTAG allows an elementary tree to be inserted within another elementary tree, an elementary tree is often formed by *gluing together* several disconnected parts of a phrase structure.

Our extraction algorithm has three steps: first, we convert a treebank tree (*ttree* for short) into a derived tree in the LTAG formalism. Figure 2.4 is a *ttree* example that we shall use throughout the section. The labels come from the English Penn Treebank (Marcus et al., 1993). There is a major difference between a *ttree* and a derived tree: in a *ttree*, arguments and modifiers are not always explicitly marked and structurally distinguished, and they can be siblings of one another. In contrast, the target grammars that we just defined distinguish heads, argument, and adjuncts, and arguments and adjuncts are never siblings in an LTAG derived tree. We convert a *ttree* into a derived tree by inserting more internal nodes so that arguments and adjuncts are attached at different levels.

In the second step of the algorithm, the newly created derived tree is decomposed into a set of elementary trees (a.k.a. *etrees*). In the third step, we create derivation

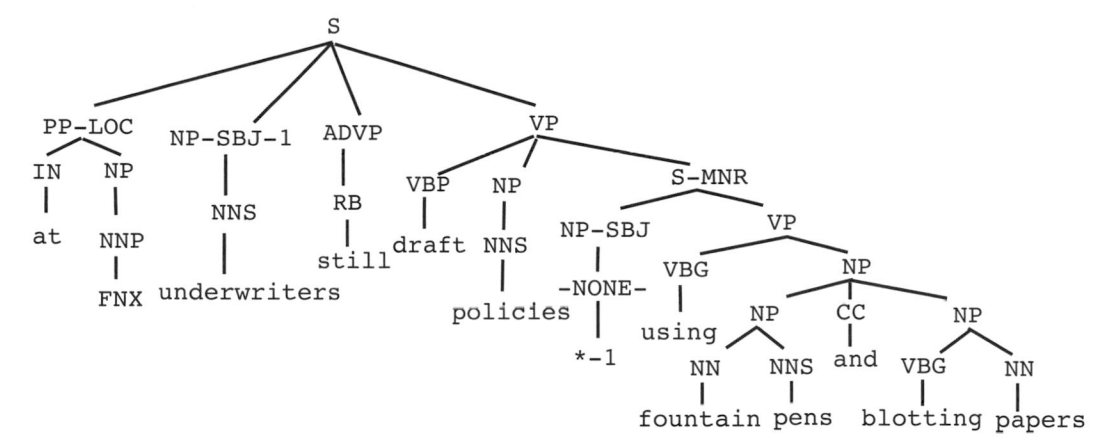

FIGURE 2.4 A treebank tree

trees, which show how *etrees* are combined to form the derived tree. The derivation trees are used to train statistical LTAG parsers.

We start the section with descriptions of three tables as part of the input to LexTract; we then describe the three steps of the extraction algorithm; finally we briefly discuss the uniqueness of the system output.

2.3.1 Distinguishing head, argument, and modifiers using three tables

In a *ttree*, the head of a phrase is not explicitly marked. Similarly, arguments and adjuncts are not structurally distinguished. In order to construct the *etrees*, which make this distinction, LexTract requires its user to provide some information about the treebank in the form of three tables: a Head Percolation Table, an Argument Table, and a Tagset Table. The Head Percolation Table is used to find the head of a phrase, whereas the Argument Table and the Tagset Table are used to make argument/modifier distinction.

In a Head Percolation Table, an entry is of the form $(x \ direct \ y_1/y_2/.../y_n)$, where x and y_i are syntactic labels, *direct* is either *LEFT* or *RIGHT*, and $\{y_i\}$ is the set of possible tags of x's head child. A *head child* of a node x in a *ttree* is the child of x which dominates the head of x. For instance, in figure 2.4, the head of the root node S is the VBP node, so the head child of S is the VP node.

A Head Percolation Table has previously been used in several statistical parsers (Magerman, 1995; Collins, 1997) to find heads of phrases. Our strategy for choosing heads is similar to theirs except that the order of the tags in the set $\{y_i\}$ does not matter in our algorithm and we do not use special rules to choose the head of noun phrases. To be more specific, to choose the head child of a node whose tag is X, we check the tags of the node's children from left to right (or vice versa according to

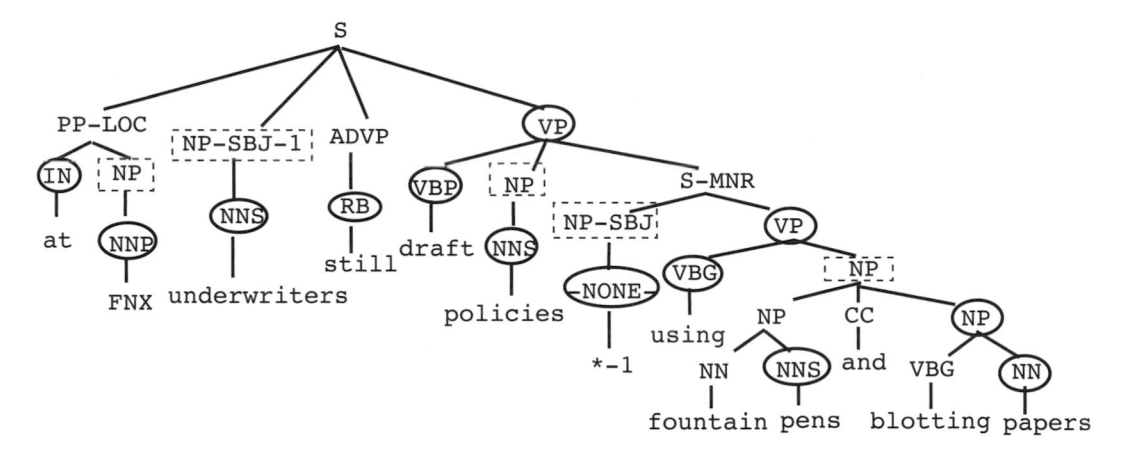

FIGURE 2.5 The *ttree* after head/argument/adjunct are distinguished,: head children are circled, and arguments are marked with dotted boxes.

direct) and find the first child whose tag is in $\{y_i\}$. Given that table, we mark the head child of every node in figure 2.4, as shown in figure 2.5.

An Argument Table specifies the number and the types of arguments that a head can take. The entry in an argument table is of the form *(head_tag, left_arg_num, right_arg_num, $y_1/y_2/.../y_n$)*: *head_tag* is the syntactic tag of a head, $\{y_i\}$ is the set of possible tags for the head's arguments, and *left_arg_num* (*right_arg_num*, respectively) is the maximal number of arguments to the left (right, respectively) of the head. For example, the entry *(IN, 0, 1, NP/S/SBAR)* says that a preposition (*IN*) does not have left arguments, and it has at most one right argument whose label is *NP*, *S*, or *SBAR*.

The Tagset Table provides types and attributes of the tags in the treebank's tagset. A few function tags (e.g., *SBJ* for subject) always mark arguments. Similarly, some function tags such as *TMP* for a temporal phrase always mark modifiers. Such information is specified in the Tagset Table. With the Argument Table and the Tagset Table, LexTract marks each sibling of a head as an argument if the sibling can be an argument of the head according to the Argument Table and none of the function tags of the sibling indicates that it is an adjunct. For example, in figure 2.4, the head of the root *S* is the verb *draft*, and the verb has two siblings: LexTract marks the noun phrase *policies* as an argument of the verb because from the Argument Table we know that verbs in general can take an NP object; it marks the clause *using fountain pens and blotting papers* as a modifier of the verb because, although verbs in general can take a sentential argument, the Tagset Table informs LexTract that the function tag -MNR (*manner*) always marks a modifier.

All three tables can be created by hand. As each table contains only dozens of entries, it should take a person no more than a couple of hours to create these tables if he understands the basic notions of heads, arguments, and adjuncts, and is familiar with the tagset of the treebank. The three sets of tables that we created for English, Chinese, and Korean Treebanks can be found in Xia (2001).

2.3.2 Step 1: Converting *ttrees* into derived trees

To extract *etrees* from a *ttree*, LexTract first converts the *ttree* into a derived tree by adding intermediate nodes to the *ttree* so that, at each level of the new *ttree*, exactly one of the following holds:

(Head-argument relation) there are one or more nodes: one is the head, the rest are its arguments;

(Modification relation) there are exactly two nodes: one node is modified by the other;

(Coordination relation) there are three nodes: two nodes are coordinated by a conjunction.

LexTract achieves this by first choosing the head-child at each level and distinguishing arguments from adjuncts as mentioned in section 2.3.1, then adding intermediate nodes so that the modifiers and arguments of a head attach to different levels. Figure 2.6 shows the new *ttree* after adding new nodes to the *ttree* in figure 2.4. The inserted nodes are in bold. It shall become clear after the next section that this new *ttree* is indeed a derived tree for the sentence if the sentence is parsed with the extracted *etrees* produced by LexTract.

2.3.3 Step 2: Building *etrees*

In this stage, each node X in the derived tree is split into two parts: the top part $X.t$ and the bottom part $X.b$. The reason for the splitting is as follows. When two *etrees* are combined during LTAG parsing, the root of one *etree* is merged with a node in the other *etree*. The resulting structure of the combined *etrees* is a derived tree. Therefore, a node in a derived tree actually has two parts (*top* and *bottom*), which could come from different *etrees*. Extracting *etrees* from a derived tree can be seen as the reverse process of parsing. Therefore, during the extraction process, each node in the derived tree is split into the top and bottom parts.

In this step, LexTract decomposes the derived tree into a set of *etrees*: LexTract removes recursive structures (which will become mod-etrees or conj-etrees) from the derived tree, and builds spine-etrees for the remaining nonrecursive structures. To be more specific, starting from the root of a derived tree, LexTract first finds the path from the root to its head. It then checks each node hc on the path. If a sibling s of hc in the *ttree* is marked as an adjunct, the algorithm factors out from the *ttree* the recursive structure that includes $hc.t$, $s.t$, and the bottom part of hc's parent p. The recursive structure becomes part of a mod-etree (or a conj-etree if hc has another sibling that is a conjunction), in which $p.b$ is the root node, $hc.t$ is the foot node, and $s.t$ is a sister of the foot node. Next, LexTract creates a spine-etree with the remaining nodes on the path and their siblings. It repeats the process for the subtrees whose roots are not on the path.

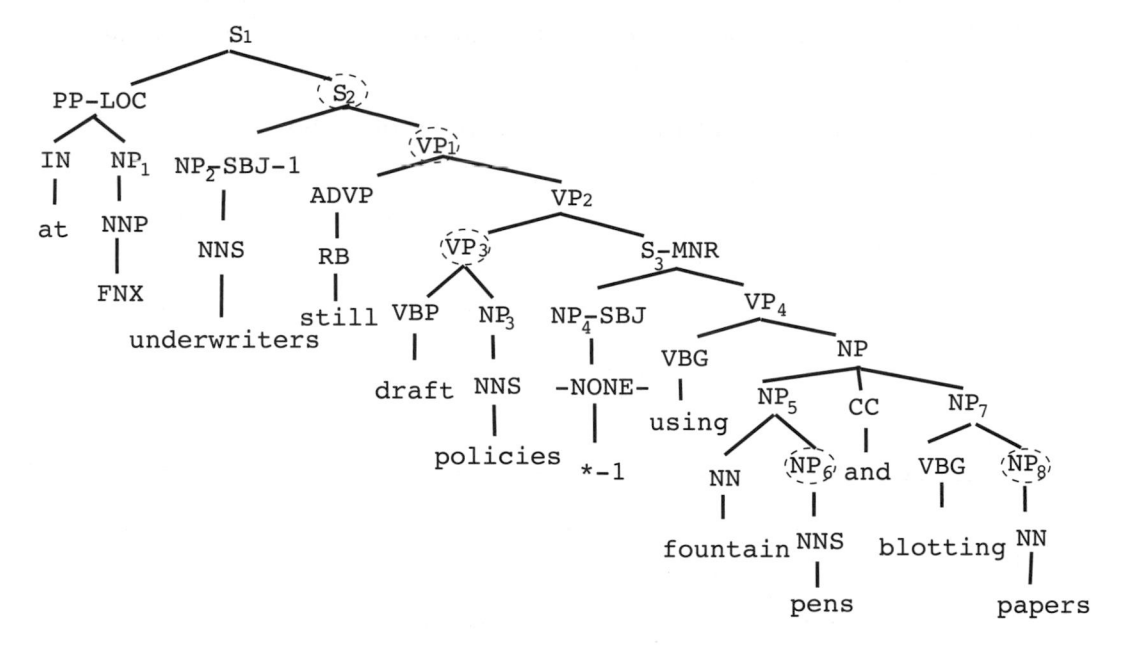

FIGURE 2.6 The new, expanded *ttree*: the five nodes in dotted circles are inserted by LexTract.

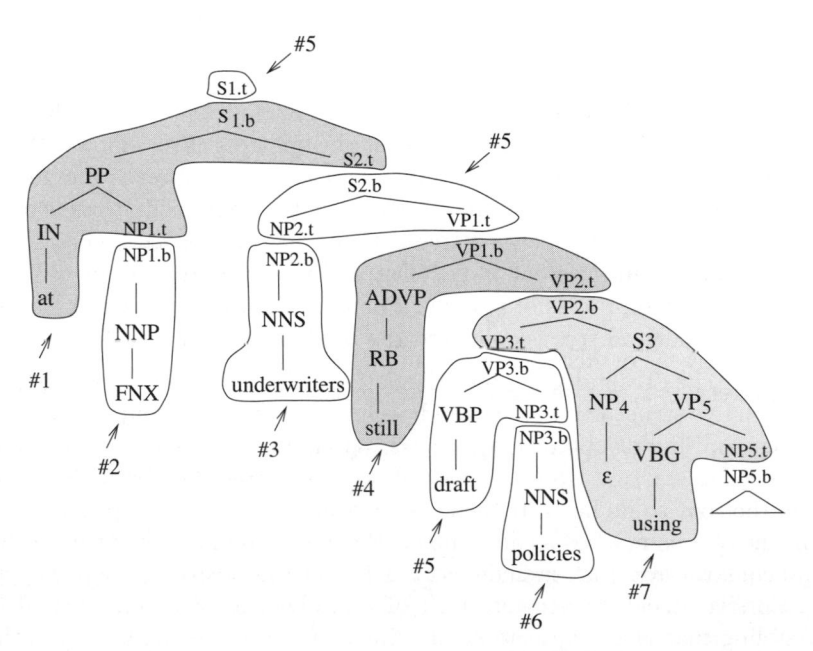

FIGURE 2.7 The extracted *etrees* can be seen as a decomposition of the new, expanded *ttree*.

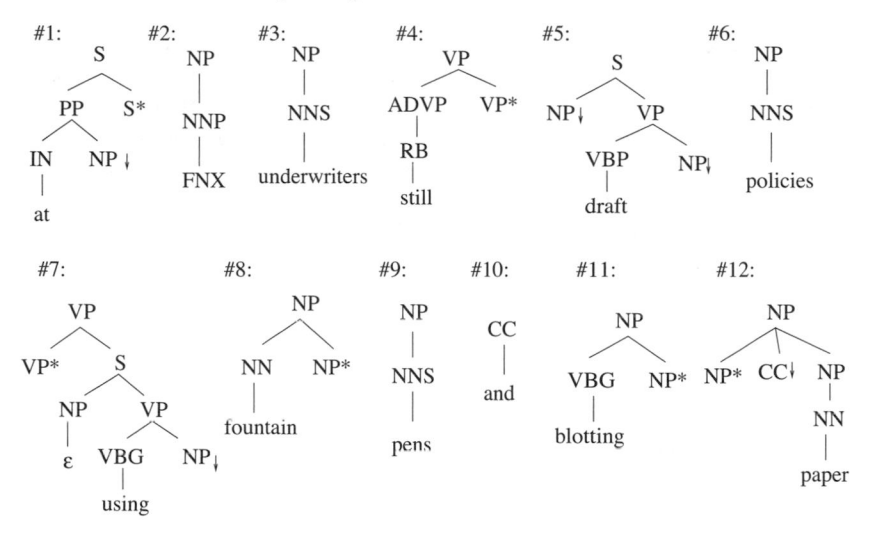

FIGURE 2.8 The extracted *etrees* from the expanded *ttree*

To see how the algorithm works, let us look at an example. Figure 2.7 shows the same derived tree as the one in figure 2.6 except that some nodes are numbered and split into the top and bottom parts. For the sake of simplicity, we show the top and the bottom parts of a node only when the two parts will end up in different *etrees*. The path from the root S_1 to the head VBP is $S_1 \rightarrow S_2 \rightarrow VP_1 \rightarrow VP_2 \rightarrow VP_3 \rightarrow VBP$. Along the path the PP "*at FNX*" has been marked as a modifier of S_2 in the previous stage; therefore, $S_1.b$, $S_2.t$, and the spine-etree rooted at PP form a mod-etree #1. Similarly, the ADVP *still* is a modifier of VP_2, and S_3 is a modifier of VP_3, and the corresponding structures form mod-etrees #4 and #7. On the path from the root to VBP, $S_1.t$ and $S_2.b$ are merged (and so are $VP_1.t$ and $VP_3.b$) to form the spine-etree #5. Repeating this process for other nodes will generate other trees such as trees #2, #3 and #6. The whole *ttree* yields twelve *etrees* as shown in figure 2.8. Notice that the tree structures that form an *etree* are often not adjacent in the derived tree. For instance, the spine-etree #5 in figure 2.7 is separated by three mod-etrees (#1, #4, and #7) in the derived tree.

2.3.4   Step 3: Creating derivation trees

For the purpose of grammar development, a set of *etrees* may be sufficient. However, to train a statistical LTAG parser, derivation trees, which store the history of how *etrees* are combined to form derived trees, are required. Recall that, unlike in CFG, the derived trees and derivation trees in the LTAG formalism are different in the sense that a derived tree can be produced by several distinct derivation trees. There are two slightly different definitions of derivation trees in the LTAG literature. The first definition adopts the no-multi-adjunction constraint, whereas the second one allows multiple adjunctions at the same nodes under certain conditions (Schabes and Shieber, 1992). The no-multi-adjunction constraint says that, when *etrees* are combined, at most one adjunction is allowed at any node in any *etree*. As a result, if a phrase XP in an *etree* E_h has several adjuncts (each adjunct belongs to a mod-etree), according to the first definition, the mod-etrees with these adjuncts form a chain in the derivation tree, with one mod-etree-adjoining to E_h and the rest adjoining to one another; whereas according to the second definition, these mod-etrees are allowed, but not required, to all adjoin to E_h. Figures 2.9 and 2.10 show two derivation trees, both combining the *etrees* in figure 2.8 to form the derived tree in figure 2.7. Note that mod-etrees #4 and #7 both modify #5 at the *VP* node, and they form a chain in figure 2.9, whereas they are siblings in figure 2.10.

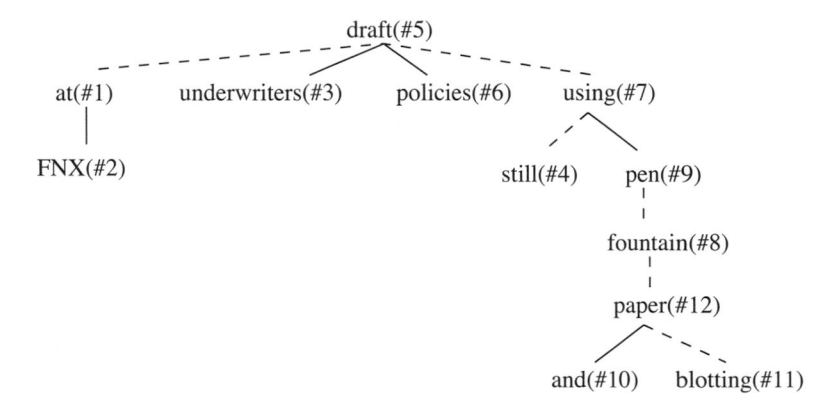

FIGURE 2.9 The derivation tree *with* the no-multi-adjunction constraint

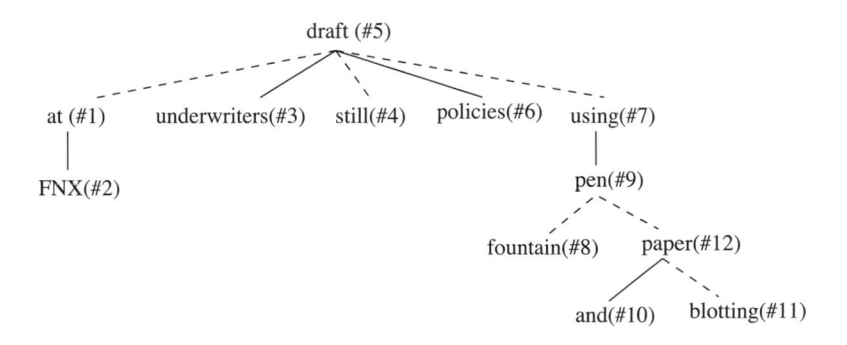

FIGURE 2.10 The derivation tree *without* the no-multi-adjunction constraint

In general, given a derived tree T and a set *ESet* of *etrees*, there may be more than one derivation tree that generates T by combining *etrees* in *ESet*. This is because, when a phrase has several adjuncts, the corresponding *etrees* could form a chain in the derivation tree and the order of these etrees on the chain is not fixed.

For instance, switching the order of trees #4 and #7 in figure 2.9 (i.e., making #4 the parent of #7 and the child of #5) will yield a different derivation tree, which generates the same derived tree. Such differences in the derivation trees arguably do not imply any ambiguity in the meaning of the sentence. Therefore, we can impose either of the following constraints to make the derivation tree unique given a derived tree T and a set *ESet* of *etrees*:

- If we adopt the first definition of derivation trees (which allows at most one adjunction at any node), we add an additional constraint which says that no adjunction operation is allowed at the foot node of any auxiliary tree. This no-adjunction-at-foot-node constraint makes the derivation tree unique by forcing the ordering of mod-etrees on the chain. This constraint has been adopted by several hand-crafted grammars such as the XTAG grammar for English (XTAG-Group, 1998) in order to eliminate this source of spurious ambiguity.
- If we use the second definition of derivation trees (which allows multiple adjunction at any node), we require all mod-etrees to adjoin to the *etree* that they modify. Because of this requirement, mod-etrees that modify the same *etree* are always siblings in the derivation tree.

The user of LexTract can choose either option and inform LexTract about one's choice by setting a parameter.[5] Once the choice is made, LexTract builds the derivation tree in two steps. First, for each *etree* in *ESet*, it finds the etree $\hat{e}$ which e substitutes/adjoins into; $\hat{e}$ will be the parent of e in the derivation tree. Second, it builds a derivation tree from those $(e, \hat{e})$ pairs. The algorithm can be found in chapter 5 of Xia (2001).

2.3.5 Uniqueness of decomposition

So far, we have discussed the extraction algorithm used by LexTract. The algorithm takes three tables with language-specific information and a *ttree T*, and creates (1) a derived tree T^*, (2) a set *ESet* of *etrees*, and (3) a derivation tree D for T^*. The derivation tree D is unique given T and *ESet* once we choose one of two options. Furthermore, in general, *ESet* is the only tree set that satisfies all the following conditions:

(C1) Decomposition: The tree set is a *decomposition* of T^*; that is, T^* can be generated by combining the trees in the set via the substitution and adjoining operations.

(C2) LTAG formalism: Each tree in the set is an elementary tree according to the LTAG formalism. For instance, each tree is lexicalized and in an auxiliary tree the foot node and the root node have the same label.

(C3) Target grammar: Each tree in the set falls into one of the three types as specified in section 2.2.2.

(C4) Language-specific information: The head/argument/adjunct distinction in the trees is made according to the language-specific information provided by the user.

This uniqueness of the tree set may be quite surprising at first sight, considering that the number of possible decompositions of T^* is $\Omega(2^n)$, where n is the number of nodes (including POS tags such as N, but excluding lexical items such as *John*) in T^*.[6] Instead of giving a proof of the uniqueness, we use an example to illustrate how the conditions $(C1)$–$(C4)$ rule out all the decompositions except the one produced by LexTract. In figure 2.11, the derived tree T^* has five nodes (i.e., S, NP, N, VP, and V). There are thirty-two distinct decompositions for T^*, six of which are shown in the same figure. Out of these thirty-two decompositions, only five (i.e., $E_2 - E_6$) are fully lexicalized – that is, each tree in these tree sets is anchored by a lexical item. The rest, including E_1, are not fully lexicalized, and are therefore ruled out by the condition $(C2)$. For the remaining five *etree* sets, $E_2 - E_4$ are ruled out by the condition $(C3)$, because each of these tree sets has one tree that violates the constraint that in a spine-etree an argument of the anchor should be a substitution node, rather than an internal node.[7] For the remaining two, E_5 is ruled out by $(C4)$ because, according to the head percolation table provided by the user, the head-child of the S node should be the VP node, rather than the NP node. Therefore, E_6, the tree set that is produced by LexTract, is the only *etree* set for T^* that satisfies $(C1)$–$(C4)$.

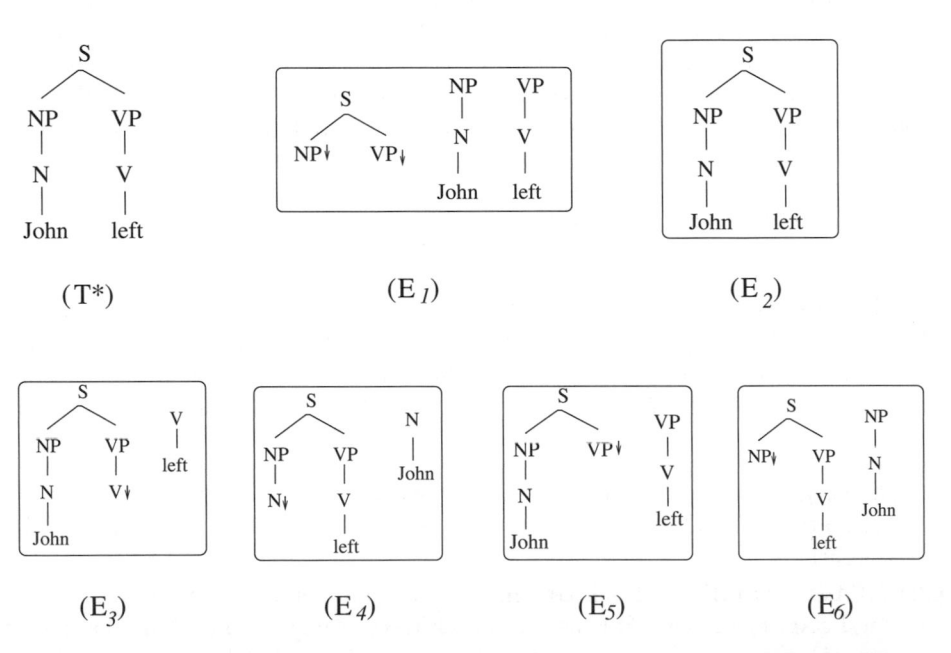

FIGURE 2.11 Six tree sets for the derived tree T^*: E_1 is ruled out by $C2$, $E_2 - E_4$ are ruled out by $C3$, and E_5 is ruled out by $C4$; E_6 satisfies all four conditions and is the one produced by LexTract.

2.3.6   Comparison with other work

LexTract is designed to extract LTAGs, but, as shown in figure 2.12, simply reading context-free rules off the templates in an extracted LTAG yields a context-free grammar. In this section, we compare LexTract with other extraction algorithms for CFGs and LTAGs proposed in the literature.

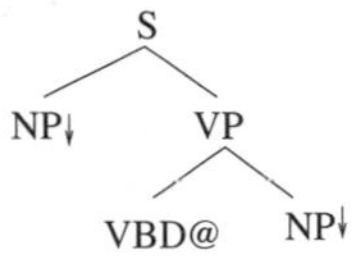

(a) a template   (b) CFG rules derived from (a)

(1) S -> NP VP
(2) VP -> VBD NP

FIGURE 2.12   The context-free rules derived from a template

CFG extraction algorithms

Many systems that use treebank context-free grammars simply read context-free rules off the phrase structures in treebanks. Because the phrase structures in the source treebanks are partially flat (i.e., arguments and adjuncts can be siblings), the resulting grammars are very large. There have been several research efforts addressing this issue. Due to space limitations, we compare LexTract with only one of these efforts, which is an algorithm that reduces the size of the derived grammar by eliminating redundant rules (Krotov et al., 1998). A rule is *redundant* if it can be "parsed" (in the familiar sense of context-free parsing) using other rules of the grammar. The algorithm checks each rule in the grammar in turn and removes the redundant rules from the grammar. For example, in a grammar that has the following three rules, the algorithm would remove Rule (1) because Rule (1) can be parsed by Rules (2) and (3):

Rule (1): $VP \rightarrow VB\ NP\ PP$
Rule (2): $VP \rightarrow VB\ NP$
Rule (3): $NP \rightarrow NP\ PP$

The rules that remain when all rules have been checked constitute the compacted grammar. The compact grammar for the PTB has 1,122 context-free rules, and the recall and precision of a CFG parser with the compact grammar are 30.93% and 19.18% respectively, in contrast to 70.78% and 77.66% of the same parser with the full grammar, which has 15,421 context-free rules.

Krotov's method differs dramatically from LexTract in several ways. First, it does not use the notion of *head* and it does not distinguish adjuncts from arguments. In the previous example, because of the existence of Rules (2) and (3), Rule (1) is considered redundant and gets removed even though the *PP* in Rule (1) can be an argument of a verb such as *put*. Second, the compacting process may result in different grammars depending on the order in which the rules in the full grammar are checked. To maintain order-independence, their algorithm removed all unary and epsilon rules by collapsing them with the sister nodes. Because of frequent occurrences of empty categories and unary rules in the treebank, we suspect that this practice will make the resulting grammars less intuitive, and it might also contribute to the low parsing accuracy when the compact grammar was used. Third, the growth of their grammar is nonmonotonic in that, as the corpus grows, the size of the grammar may actually decrease because the new rules in the grammar may cause the existing rules to become redundant and get eliminated. Although the *size* of the compact grammar might approach a limit eventually in their experiment, it is not clear how stable the grammar really is, considering the existence of annotation errors in the treebank. For example, it is possible that a few bad rules (e.g., $\{X \rightarrow X\ ZP\}$, where *ZP* can be any syntactic label) can ruin the whole grammar because they make many good rules become redundant and get eliminated. They mentioned in their paper that they developed a linguistic compaction algorithm that could retain redundant but linguistically valid rules, and they gave the sizes of two grammars built by this new algorithm. Unfortunately, the description is too sketchy for us to determine exactly how that algorithm works.

In contrast, LexTract uses the notion of *head* and it distinguishes arguments from adjuncts. For instance, LexTract determines whether the *PP* in Rule (1) is an argument or an adjunct according to the Argument Table and the Tagset Table. If it is an argument, LexTract will keep the rule; if it is an adjunct, LexTract will replace this rule with Rule (2) and another rule *VP → VP PP*. The redundant rules that Krotov's method would remove are not produced by LexTract because a context-free rule produced by LexTract never has both arguments and adjuncts as siblings. Second, the CFG produced by LexTract is order-independent, and it allows unary rules and epsilon rules. In addition, the growth of the grammar is monotonic, and the existence of bad rules would not affect the good rules. As for the number of context-free rules, the CFG built by LexTract from the PTB has 1,524 rules (see section 2.4.1), whereas in Krotov's approach, the compact grammar has 1,122 rules and the two linguistically compact grammars have 4,820 and 6,417 rules, respectively.[8]

LTAG extraction algorithms

We first published the extraction algorithm used by LexTract in Xia (1999). The algorithm was later revised and the new version and a few applications of LexTract were discussed in Xia et al. (2000a) and other papers. Besides LexTract, there are two systems that extract LTAGs from treebanks: they are (Neumann, 1998) and (Chen and Vijay-Shanker, 2000).

Neumann's lexicalized tree grammars: Neumann (1998) describes an extraction algorithm and tests it on the PTB and a German Treebank called

NEGRA (Skut et al., 1997). There are several similarities between his approach and LexTract. First, both approaches adopt notions of *head* and use a head percolation table to identify the head-child at each level. Second, both decompose the *ttrees* from the top downward such that the subtrees rooted by nonhead children are cut off and the cutting point is marked for substitution. The main difference between the two is that Neumann's system does not distinguish arguments from adjuncts, and therefore it does not factor out the majority of recursive structures with adjuncts. As a result, only 7.97% of the templates in his grammar are auxiliary trees, and the size of his grammar is much larger than ours: his system extracts 11,979 templates from three sections of the PTB (i.e., Sections 02–04), whereas LexTract extracts 6926 templates from the whole corpus (i.e., Sections 00–24). It is also not clear from his paper how he treats conjunctions, empty categories and coindexation; therefore, we cannot compare these two approaches on these issues.

Chen and Vijay-Shanker's approach: Chen and Vijay-Shanker's method (Chen and Vijay-Shanker, 2000) is similar to LexTract in that both use a head percolation table to find the head and both distinguish arguments from adjuncts. Nevertheless, there are several differences.

One major difference is the overall architecture. When we designed LexTract, we explicitly defined three prototypes of elementary trees in the target grammars. The prototypes are language independent and every *etree* built by LexTract falls into one of three prototypes. Given a treebank and three tables containing language-specific information, for each phrase structure (*ttree*) in the treebank, LexTract first explicitly inserts internal nodes to the *ttree* to form a LTAG derived tree. It then decomposes the derived tree into a set of *etrees*.

The bidirectional mapping between the nodes in this derived tree and the *etrees* makes LexTract a useful tool for treebank annotation and error detection (see section 2.4.5). LexTract also explicitly builds derivation trees. Chen and Vijay-Shanker's system does not explicitly define the prototypes of elementary trees, and it does not build derivation trees. Also it does not convert a *ttree* into an LTAG derived tree; therefore, there are no one-to-one mappings between the nodes in a *ttree* and the nodes in the extracted *etrees*. The two systems also differ in their algorithms for making argument/adjunct distinctions, their treatments for coordination, punctuation marks, and so forth.

Another way to compare these systems is to evaluate the performances of a common NLP tool that is trained by the data produced by the systems. One of such tools is Srinivas's Supertagger. In section 2.4.3, we shall report the performances of the Supertagger with the data produced by these two systems.

2.4 Applications of LexTract

In the previous section, we introduced a grammar extraction tool LexTract, which takes treebanks and three tables as input and produces grammars and derivation trees. In this section, we discuss some applications of LexTract and report experimental results. These applications roughly fall into four types:

- The treebank grammars built by LexTract are useful for grammar development and comparison (sections 2.4.1 and 2.4.2).

- The lexicon and derivation trees derived from treebanks can be used to train statistical tools such as Supertaggers and parsers (sections 2.4.3 and 2.4.4).

- The bidirectional mappings between *ttree* nodes and *etree* nodes makes LexTract a useful tool for treebank annotation (section 2.4.5).

- LexTract can retrieve the data from treebanks to test theoretical linguistic hypotheses such as the tree-locality hypothesis (Xia and Bleam, 2000).

In this section, we shall briefly discuss the first three types.[9]

All the experimental results reported in this section were conducted by us, except for the parsing results of an LTAG statistical parser in section 2.4.4, which was produced by Anoop Sarkar.[10]

2.4.1   Treebank grammars as stand-alone grammars

The treebank grammars extracted by LexTract can be used as stand-alone grammars for languages that do not have wide-coverage grammars.

We ran LexTract on the English Penn Treebank (PTB) and extracted two treebank grammars. The first one, G_1, uses PTB's tagset. The second treebank grammar, G_2, uses a reduced tagset, where some tags in the PTB tagset are merged into a single tag, as shown in Table 2.1. The reduced tagset is basically the same as the one used in the XTAG grammar (XTAG-Group, 1998), which is a large-scale hand-crafted grammar that has been under development at the University of Pennsylvania since the early 1990s. We built G_2 with this reduced tagset for two reasons. First, we use G_2 to estimate the coverage of the XTAG grammar (see section 2.4.2). Second, G_2 is much smaller than G_1 and presumably the sparse data problem is less severe when G_2 is used. For some applications such as Supertagging and testing the tree-locality hypothesis, G_2 is as good as, if not better than, G_1.

The sizes of the two grammars are in Table 2.2. The first two columns show the number of templates and elementary trees. Recall that a template is an elementary tree without the anchor word. There are 49,206 unique words in the PTB, and the third column lists the average number of elementary trees that a word anchors. The last column of the table shows the number of context-free rules when we simply read context-free rules off the templates in an extracted LTAG.

In G_1 as well as G_2, a few templates occur very often while others occur rarely in the corpus. Among 6,926 templates in G_1, 96 templates each occur more than a thousand times, and they account for 86.91% of the template tokens in the PTB. In contrast, 3,276 templates occur only once, and together they account for only 0.27% of the template tokens in the PTB. In figure 2.13, we plot the frequency of the templates as a function of the rank of the templates on doubly logarithmic axes.

TABLE 2.1 Some tags in the English Penn Treebank tagset are merged into a single tag. The reduced tagset is used in G_2 and is similar to the tagset used in the XTAG grammar.

	tags in the PTB and G_1	tags in XTAG and G_2
adjectives	JJ/JJR/JJS	A
adverbs	RB/RBR/RBS/WRB	Ad
determiners	DT/PDT/WDT/PRP$/WP$	D
nouns	CD/NN/NNS/NNP/NNPS/PRP WP/EX/$/#	N
verbs	MD/VB/VBP/VBZ/VBN V VBD/VBG/TO	V
clauses	S/SQ/SBAR/SBARQ/SINV	S
noun phrases	NAC/NP/NX/QP/WHNP	NP
adjective phrases	ADJP/WHADJP	AP
adverbial phrases	ADVP/WHADVP	AdvP
preposition phrases	PP/WHPP	PP

TABLE 2.2 Two LTAG grammars extracted from the English Penn Treebank

	template types	*etree* types	# of *etrees* per word	context-free rules
LTAG G_1	6,926	131,397	2.67	1,524
LTAG G_2	2,920	117,356	2.38	675

The curve is close to a straight line, indicating that the relationship between the rank and frequency of templates satisfies a general version of Zipf's law.[11]

Once LexTract extracts grammars from treebanks, a natural question that comes to mind is: how complete is the grammar? To answer the question, we plot the number of templates as a function of the percentage of the corpus used to generate the templates, as in figure 2.14. To reduce the effect of the original ordering of the *ttrees* in the treebank, we randomly shuffle the *ttrees* in the treebank before running LexTract. We repeat the process ten times, and calculate the minimal, maximal, and average numbers of the templates generated by a certain percentage of the corpus. The figure shows that the curves for the minimal, maximal, and average template numbers are almost identical. Furthermore, in all three curves the number of templates does not converge as the size of the treebank grows, implying that there could be many new templates in new data.

As the number of templates does not coverage as the size of the treebank grows, the next question is whether these low frequency templates are linguistically plausible. To answer this question, we randomly selected 100 templates from the 3,276 templates in G_1 that occur only once in the corpus. After manually examining

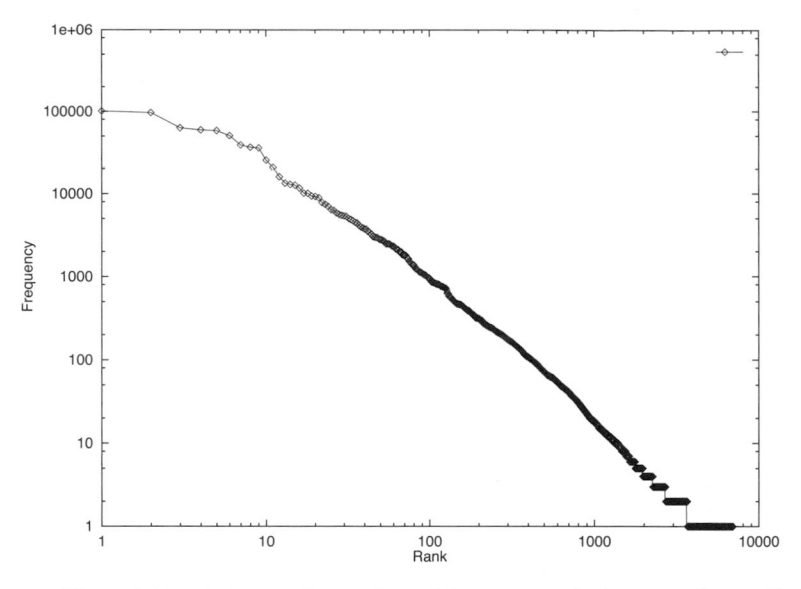

FIGURE 2.13 The relation between the rank and frequency of *etree* templates: X-axis and Y-axis show the rank and frequency of templates respectively, and both are on log scales.

them, we found that 41 templates resulted from annotation errors and two from missing entries in the language-specific tables that we made for the PTB; the remaining 57 were linguistically plausible. This experiment shows that, although the PTB is pretty large, G_1 is still missing many plausible templates for English.[12]

So far, the discussion has been based on templates, rather than on *etrees*. For parsing purposes, a more important question is: how often do the unseen *etrees* occur in new data? Recall that an *etree* is equivalent to a (word, template) pair. If an *etree* is unseen, the word can be unseen (*uw*) or seen(*sw*), and the template can be unseen (*ut*) or seen (*st*). Therefore there are four kinds of unseen pairs, where (sw, st) means both words and templates have appeared in the training data, but not the pair. Table 2.3 shows that in G_1 only 7.85% of the pairs in Section 23 of the PTB are not seen in Sections 2 to 21.[13] Of all the unseen (word, template) pairs in G_1, only 4.20% (0.31%+0.02% divided by 7.85%) are caused by unseen templates, and the remaining 95.80% are caused by unseen words or unseen combinations. This implies that the presence of unseen templates is unlikely to have a significant impact on Supertagging or parsing. In addition, most unseen (word, template) pairs are (sw, st) pairs, indicating that some type of smoothing over sets of templates (e.g., the notion of tree families in the XTAG grammar) could be helpful for improving parsing accuracy. In the table, we also list the percentages of unseen (word, POS tag) pairs in the same data for comparison. This table shows two differences between POS tags and templates. First, the number of POS tags is much smaller, and there are no unseen POS tags; consequently, the percentages for (sw, ut) and (uw, ut) are zero. Second, the percentage of unknown (word, POS tag) pairs where both words and

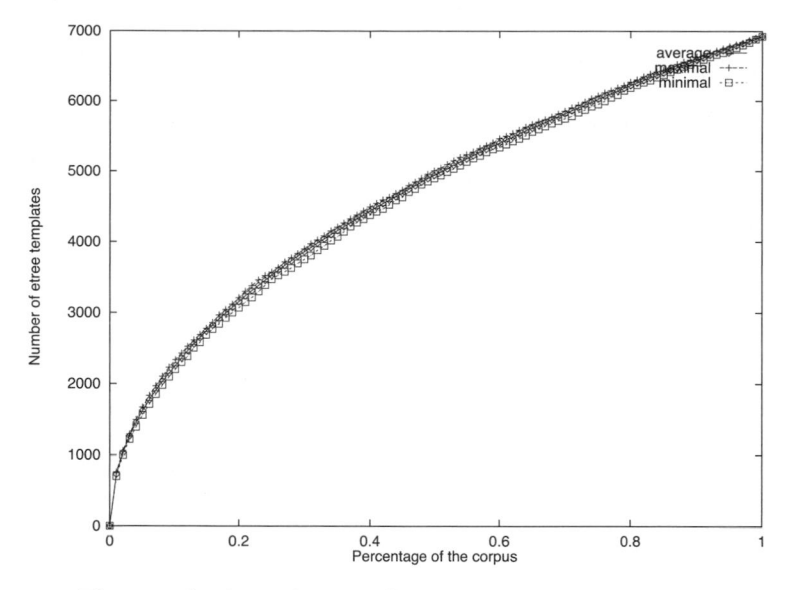

FIGURE 2.14 The growth of templates in G_1: X-axis shows the percentage of the corpus used for extraction (e.g., 0.2 means 20%), Y-axis shows the number of extracted templates.

POS tags are known is much lower than that for (word, template) pairs. Because of these differences, the baseline for POS tagging is much higher than the one for template tagging (i.e., Supertagging), as shall be discussed in section 2.4.3.

TABLE 2.3 The types of unseen (word, template) pairs in Section 23 of the English Penn Treebank

	# of tags	(sw, st)	(uw, st)	(sw, ut)	(uw, ut)	total
POS tags	48	0.44%	2.47%	0	0	2.91%
LTAG G_1	6,926	5.09%	2.43%	0.31%	0.02%	7.85%
LTAG G_2	2,920	4.20%	2.45%	0.10%	0.01%	6.76%

In addition to the English treebank, we also extracted grammars from the Chinese Penn Treebanks and the Korean Penn Treebanks.[14] The results are shown in Table 2.4. An interesting question is what kind of elementary trees and subtrees are shared among grammars for different languages. We have conducted some preliminary experiments and the results were reported in Xia et al. (2001).

An interesting question is how similar or different those treebank grammars are. In one of our previous experiments, we looked at each language pair, and counted the numbers of templates that are shared between the two corresponding treebank grammars. Then we classified the templates that appear in one grammar but not

TABLE 2.4 Grammars extracted from the English, Chinese, and Korean Penn Treebanks

	corpus size (in words)	word types	template types	*etree* types	context-free rules
English	1M	49,206	6,926	131,397	1,524
Chinese	100K	10,772	1,140	21,125	515
Korean	50K	10,035	632	13,941	152

the other. Some of the mismatches are due to spurious reasons (such as annotation errors or different annotation style), whereas the rest are due to the true differences between the two languages (for instance, some syntactic constructions appear only in one of the two languages). Our preliminary results were reported in Xia et al. (2001). The exercise helps us better understand the similarities and differences between languages with respect to their grammars. Another potential benefit of this exercise is that it produces the links between the templates in the grammars, which could be a valuable resources for transfer-based machine translation systems.

2.4.2 Treebank grammars combined with hand-crafted grammars

If a language already has a hand-crafted grammar such as the XTAG English grammar, we can use a treebank grammar to evaluate and improve the coverage of this hand-crafted grammar.

Previous evaluations (Doran et al., 2000; Srinivas et al., 1998) of hand-crafted grammars use raw data (i.e., a set of sentences without syntactic bracketing). The data are first parsed by an LTAG parser and the coverage of the grammar is measured as the percentage of sentences in the data that can be parsed.[15] For more discussion on these evaluations, see Prasad and Sarkar (2000).

Now with the treebank grammar produced by LexTract, we can estimate the coverage of a hand-crafted grammar by measuring the overlap of the hand-crafted grammar and the treebank grammar. The main idea is as follows: given a treebank T and a hand-crafted grammar G_h, let G_t be the set of templates extracted from T by LexTract. The coverage of G_h on T can be measured as the percentage of template tokens in T that are covered by the *intersection* of G_t and G_h. One complication is that the treebank and G_h may choose different analyses for certain syntactic constructions; that is, although some constructions are covered by both grammars, the corresponding templates in these grammars would look very different. To address this problem, some human effort is required. In this section, we report the main results of our experiment; the details can be found in Xia and Palmer (2000).

In our experiment, we chose G_2 as our treebank grammar (see Table 2.2 in section 2.4.1) and the XTAG grammar as the hand-crafted grammar. The former has 2,920 templates, and the latter has 1,004 templates. We first calculate how many templates in the XTAG grammar *match* some template in G_2. We define two types of matching: *t-match* and *s-match*. We say that two templates *t-match* (*t* for *template*) if they are identical barring the types of information present only in one grammar – such as feature structures in the XTAG grammars and the frequency information in G_2. The definition of *t-match* is pretty strict because it does not tolerate minor differences between two grammars such as the number of projections of a head. A more lenient measure is called *s-match*. Two templates are said to *s-match* if they are decomposed into the same set of subtemplates. A subtemplate can be a subcategorization frame, a modification pair, or a head projection chain. Note that neither type of matching is one-to-one.[16]

Table 2.5 lists the numbers of matched templates in the two grammars. The last row lists the percentage of the template tokens in the PTB that match some templates in XTAG. For instance, the first column says 173 templates in XTAG *t-match* 81 templates in G_2, and these 81 templates account for 78.6% of the template tokens in the PTB. There are 17.9% of the template tokens in the PTB that do not match any template in the XTAG grammar. There are several reasons why a template appears in G_2 but not in the XTAG grammar:

TABLE 2.5 The numbers of templates in the XTAG grammar that match some templates in G_2 and their frequencies in the English Penn Treebank

	t-match	s-match	matched subtotal	unmatched subtotal	total
# of templates in XTAG	173	324	497	507	1,004
# of templates in G_2	81	134	215	2,705	2,920
% of template tokens	78.6%	3.5%	82.1%	17.9%	100%

(T1) incorrect templates in G_2: These templates result from treebank annotation errors, and therefore they are not in XTAG.

(T2) coordination in XTAG: the templates for coordination in XTAG are generated on-the-fly during parsing (Sarkar and Joshi, 1996), and are not part of the 1,004 templates. Therefore, the conj-templates in G_2, which account for about 3.4% of the template tokens in the PTB, do not match any templates in the XTAG grammar.

(T3) alternative analyses: XTAG and G_2 sometimes choose different analyses for the same phenomena. As a result, the templates used to handle these phenomena do not *match* according to our definition.

(T4) constructions not covered by XTAG: Some constructions, such as the unlike coordination phrase (*UCP*), parenthetical (*PRN*), and ellipsis, are not currently covered by the XTAG grammar.

For the first three types, the XTAG grammar can handle the corresponding constructions although the templates used in two grammars look different and do not *match* according to our definition. To find out what constructions are not covered by XTAG, we manually classified the 289 most frequent unmatched templates in

G_2 according to (T1)–(T4) as previously defined. These 289 templates account for 16.8% of all the template tokens in the treebank. The results are shown in Table 2.6, where the percentage is with respect to all the template tokens in the treebank. From the table, it is clear that most unmatched template tokens are due to (T3); that is, alternative analyses adopted by the two grammars. Combining the results in Tables 2.5 and 2.6, we conclude that 97.2% of template tokens in the PTB can be handled by the current XTAG grammar,[17] while another 1.7% cannot. There are 2416 unmatched templates in G_2 that we have not checked manually, which account for the remaining 1.1% of template tokens in the PTB.

TABLE 2.6 Classification of 289 templates that are in G_2, but not in the XTAG grammar

	T1	T2	T3	T4	total
# of template types	51	52	93	93	289
% of template tokens	1.1%	3.4%	10.6%	1.7%	16.8%

Instead of just calculating the percentage of template tokens in the PTB that match templates in the XTAG grammar, we can also calculate the percentage of sentences in the PTB that can be parsed by the XTAG grammar. This can be done by first running LexTract to build a derivation tree for each sentence in the PTB as discussed in section 2.3.4. Each node in a derivation tree is a (word, template) pair as in figures 2.9 and 2.10. A sentence is covered by the XTAG grammar if both of the following conditions hold:

- For each (word, template) pair (w, t) in the derivation tree, there exists a template t' in the XTAG grammar such that t' t-matches or s-matches t and (w, t') is in the lexicon of the XTAG grammar.
- The new derivation tree made up of (w, t') could fit together.[18]

The average length of the sentences in the PTB is 23.8 words. For most of the sentences, their derivation trees contain at least one (word, template) pair that is not in the XTAG grammar; therefore, the percentage of sentences in the PTB that satisfies both conditions is very low. Nevertheless, this experiment provides a list of (word, template) pairs that could be added to the XTAG grammar to improve its coverage.

To summarize this section, we have presented a method for evaluating the coverage of a hand-crafted grammar – the XTAG grammar – on a treebank. First, we used LexTract to automatically extract a treebank grammar. Second, we matched the templates in the two grammars. Third, we manually classified unmatched templates in the treebank grammar to decide how many of them were due to missing constructions in the hand-crafted grammar. Some of the unmatched templates can be added to the hand-crafted grammar to improve its coverage. Our experiments showed that the XTAG grammar covers at least 97.2% of the template tokens in the English Penn Treebank. This method has several advantages. First, the whole process is semiautomatic and does not require much human effort. Second, the method provides a list of templates and (word, template) pairs that can be added to the grammar to improve its coverage. Third, there is no need to use the grammar to parse the whole corpus and manually check whether the correct parses are produced, which can be very time-consuming. Fourth, the coverage of the grammar can be estimated at either the template level or the sentence level.

2.4.3 Lexicons as training data for supertaggers

A Supertagger (Joshi and Srinivas, 1994; Srinivas, 1997) assigns an *etree* template to each word in a sentence. The templates are called *Supertags* because they include more information than part-of-speech (POS) tags. In this section, we use these two terms (i.e., template and Supertag) interchangeably, and *a word has x Supertags* means that the word can anchor x distinct *templates*. In general, a word has many more Supertags than POS tags because a word appearing in different elementary trees will have different Supertags even if the POS tag of the word remains the same. For example, a preposition has different Supertags when the PP headed by the preposition modifies a VP, an NP, or a clause. In the PTB, on average, a word *type* has 2.67 Supertags, and a word *token* has 34.68 Supertags.[19] In contrast, on average a word *type* has 1.17 POS tags, whereas a word *token* has 2.29 POS tags.[20]

Srinivas implemented an *n*-gram Supertagger and he also built a Lightweight Dependency Analyzer (LDA) that assembles a Supertag sequence to create an almost-parse for a sentence. A Supertagger can also be used as a preprocessor (just like a POS tagger) to speed up parsing, because after the Supertagging stage an LTAG parser needs to consider only one or a few templates (in case of n-best Supertagging) for each word in the sentence, instead of every template that the word can anchor. Besides parsing, Srinivas (1997) has shown in his thesis that Supertaggers are useful for other applications, such as information retrieval, information extraction, language modeling, and simplification.

One difficulty in using Supertaggers is the lack of training and testing data. To use a treebank for that purpose, the phrase structures in the treebank have to be converted into (word, Supertag) sequences first. As discussed in section 2.3.3, LexTract builds a set of elementary trees from a parse tree. As an elementary tree is a (word, Supertag) pair, LexTract can easily produce a (word, Supertag) sequence for each sentence in the treebank. Besides LexTract, there have been two other attempts at converting the English Penn Treebank to (word, Supertag) sequences in order to train a Supertagger. One is Chen and Vijay-Shanker's method (Chen and Vijay-Shanker, 2000), which has been discussed in section 2.3.6. The other was reported in Srinivas (1997), in which the author first selected a subset of templates from the XTAG grammar, then used heuristics to map structural information in the treebank into the subset of templates. Srinivas's approach differs from LexTract and Chen and Vijay-Shanker's method in that it uses a preexisting Supertag set, rather than extracting a Supertag set directly from the treebank. As a result, it is not guaranteed that the Supertag sequences in Srinivas's converted data would always fit together, due to the discrepancy between the XTAG grammar and the treebank annotation and the fact that the XTAG grammar does not cover all the template tokens in the treebank.

In our experiment, we use the data converted by these three methods to train and test the same Supertagger (i.e., Srinivas's n-gram Supertagger). Except for the conversion methods, everything else is identical, including the Supertagger, the evaluation tool, and the original PTB data. The results are given in Table 2.7. Following the convention of recent parsing work, we use Sections 02–21 for training, and Section 23 for testing. We also include the results for Section 22 because (Chen and Vijay-Shanker, 2000) is tested on that section and its results on Section 23 are not available. The results of Chen and Vijay-Shanker's method come from their paper (Chen and Vijay-Shanker, 2000). They built eight grammars. We list two of them that seem to be most relevant: C_4 uses a reduced tagset while C_3 uses the PTB tagset. As for Srinivas's results, we had to rerun his Supertagger using his data on the sections that we have chosen, because his previous results were trained and tested on different sections of the PTB.[21]

TABLE 2.7 Supertagging results based on three different conversion algorithms, everything else such as the original data and Supertagger are identical. For comparison, two sets of baselines are provided: in the first set (base1), a word is tagged with most common Supertag for that word; in the second set (base2), a word is first POS tagged using a trigram POS tagger, then tagged with the most common Supertag for that (word, POS tag) pair.

	# of templates	section	base1	base2	tagging accuracy
Srinivas's	483	23	72.59	74.24	85.78
grammar		22	72.14	73.74	85.53
our G_2	2920	23	71.45	74.14	84.41
		22	70.54	73.41	83.60
our G_1	6926	23	69.70	71.82	82.21
		22	68.79	70.90	81.88
Chen and	2366 – 8996	22	-	-	77.8 – 78.9
Vijay-Shanker's					
C_4	4911	22	-	-	78.90
C_3	8623	22	-	-	78.00

We calculated two sets of baselines. For the first set, we tagged each word in the testing data with the most common Supertag for that word in the training data. For an unknown word, the most common Supertag was used. For the second set of baselines, we used a trigram POS tagger to tag the words first, and then for each word we used the most common Supertag for that (word, POS tag) pair. The table shows that the first set of baselines for Supertagging were around 70%, which are much lower than the 91% baseline for the POS tagging task if the same method is used. This implies that Supertagging is a much harder task than POS tagging. The second set of baselines were slightly better than the first set of baselines, indicating that POS tags could help to improve the Supertagging accuracy.

A word of caution is in order. Because the sets of Supertags used by these conversion methods differ a lot with respect to the size, coverage, and so on, we cannot use Supertagging accuracy to compare the quality of grammar extraction tools that produce the training data for the Supertagger. For instance, the accuracy using G_1 is about 2% lower than the one using G_2, although both are produced by LexTract. Furthermore, higher Supertagging accuracy does not necessarily imply higher parsing accuracy when a tool (such as an LDA) is used to assemble a Supertag sequence to create a parse tree. We conducted this experiment only to show that the (word, template) sequences produced by LexTract are useful for training Supertaggers.

2.4.4 Derivation trees as training data for statistical LTAG parsers

In the previous section, we have shown that the (word, template) sequences produced by LexTract can be used to train a Supertagger. The output of a Supertagger can then be fed to an LDA or a parser to produce parse trees. A problem with this approach is that the Supertagging errors can hurt parsing performance.

Another way of using LexTract for parsing is to train an LTAG parser directly, without using a Supertagger as a preprocessor. There have been two LTAG parsers that use LexTract's output as training data. One is a head-corner LTAG statistical parser built by Anoop Sarkar. To reduce the amount of labeled data needed to train his parser, Sarkar adopts a cotraining method, which uses a small amount of labeled data, a large amount of unlabeled data, and a tag dictionary. *Labeled* data are sentences annotated with phrase structures; *unlabeled* data are sentences stripped of all annotations; and a tag dictionary is a set of (word, template) pairs. In his experiment, the labeled data are Sections 02–06 of the PTB, the unlabeled data are Sections 07–21 stripped of all annotation, and the tag dictionary includes all the (word, sequence) pairs from Sections 02–21. When tested on Section 23 of the PTB, the labeled bracketing precision and recall are 80.02% and 79.64%, respectively. Considering that the labeled data used by the parser are only about 25% of the training data used by other parsers, we believe that the results are very promising. The details of the generative model, the co-training method, and the experiment can be found in Sarkar (2001). The second parser that uses LexTract to convert the treebank data to the training data for LTAG parsers is a LR parser developed by Carlos Prolo. The details can be found in Prolo (2000).

2.4.5 LexTract as a tool for error detection in treebank annotation

Recall that given a treebank tree T, LexTract inserts additional internal nodes into it to form a new tree T^* and decomposes T^* into a set $ESet$ of elementary trees.

Because $ESet$ is a decomposition of T^*, there is a mapping between the nodes in T^* and the nodes in $ESet$.[22] If there are annotation errors in T, those errors will be passed into T^*, and then to some *etrees* in $ESet$; as a result, those corresponding *etrees* are likely to be linguistically implausible.[23] For the reversed direction, if an *etree* is linguistically implausible, it implies that the corresponding nodes in the T^* and T are not annotated correctly. Based on this relation, we use LexTract to detect annotation errors in a treebank.

The algorithm for error detection has three steps: first, we run LexTract on the whole treebank to generate a grammar G; second, we check each template in G, decide whether it is plausible and mark it accordingly; third, for each *ttree* T_i in the treebank, we run LexTract and generate a grammar G_i. Obviously, G_i is a subset of G. If G_i includes any implausible *etree* as marked in G, then we modify T_i to T'_i so that the *etrees* generated by T'_i are all plausible. It is possible that the new *ttree* T'_i yields some new *etrees* which are not in G. In that case, we mark the plausibility of such *etrees* and add them to G. In this algorithm, human effort is required with respect to two aspects: checking the plausibility of *etrees* and modifying *ttrees*.[24]

We used LexTract for the final cleanup of the Chinese Penn Treebank. The treebank contained about 100,000 words after word segmentation, and the average sentence length was 23.8 words. Before LexTract was used for the final cleanup, the treebank had been manually checked at least twice and the annotation accuracy was already above 95%. Details on the treebank can be found in Xia et al. (2000b) and at the website *http://www.ldc.upenn.edu/ctb*; the treebank is available to the public via LDC.

Before the final cleanup, the treebank grammar G_o contained 1245 *etree* templates. It took a linguistics expert about ten hours to manually examine all the templates in G_o to determine whether they were plausible. After that, it took another person (who was one of the two annotators in the Chinese Treebank project) about twenty hours to run LexTract and correct treebank annotation. After the cleanup, 169 templates in the old grammar disappeared, and 38 templates were added to the new grammar; so the new grammar has 1,114 *etree* templates. We also automatically counted the number of word tokens in the treebank that anchored distinct templates before and after the cleanup. We found 579 word tokens (which account for 0.58% of the total number of word tokens in the treebank) whose templates had changed after the cleanup. The differences may not be huge, but considering the accuracy before running LexTract was already above 95%, the results of the final cleanup were satisfactory. These errors found by LexTract can be classified as follows:

- Formatting errors in *ttrees* such as unbalanced brackets and illegal tags: when a *ttree* is not properly formatted, LexTract will give a warning and exit without further processing of the *ttree*.

- Mismatched syntactic labels (including POS tags, phrase labels and empty category tags): Except for careless typos (e.g., using the tag LC (localizer) rather than CL (classifier) for a classifier in the Chinese Treebank), mismatched syntactic labels are often due to incompatible labels at several levels. For example, in Chinese, a coordinating conjunction (CC) such as *tong* is also a preposition (IN); therefore, the sentence "*John tong/and‗with Mary zou/leave le/ASP*" means either "*John and Mary left*" or "*John left with Mary*", and both structures in figure 2.15a and 2.15b are correct.[25] However, the structure in figure 2.15c is incorrect because the POS tag *CC* and the phrase label *PP* do not match, resulting in an implausible *etree* in figure 2.15d. This type of error is relatively common because POS tagging and bracketing were done at separate annotation stages by different annotators.

```
(S (NP-SBJ (NP (NNP John))
          (CC tong)
          (NP (NNP Mary)))
   (VP (VB zou)
       (AS le)))
```

```
(S (NP-SBJ (NNP John))
   (VP (PP (IN tong)
          (NP (NNP Mary)))
       (VB zou)
       (AS le)))
```

(a) tong as a conjunction   (b) tong as a preposition

```
(S (NP-SBJ (NNP John))
   (VP (PP (CC tong)
          (NP (NNP Mary)))
       (VB zou)
       (AS le)))
```

⟹

(c) the incompatible labels   (d) the resulting *etree*

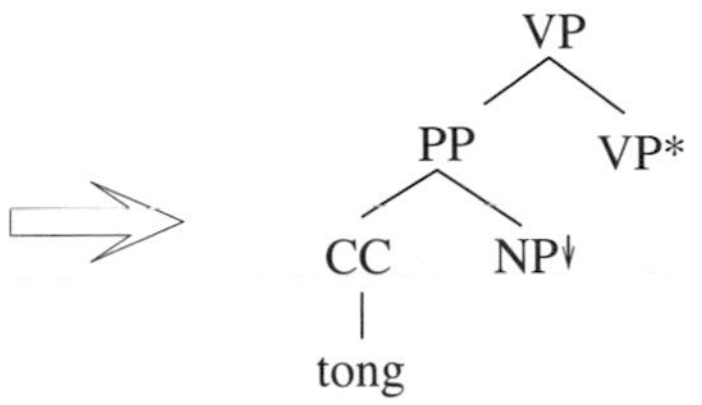

FIGURE 2.15 An error caused by incompatible labels: (a) and (b) are two correct structures; (c) has two mismatched labels (*PP* and *CC*), both marked in boldface; (d) is the elementary tree resulted from the annotation errors in (c).

• Wrong or missing function tags: LexTract uses syntactic labels and function tags to distinguish arguments from adjuncts. Wrong or missing function tags may cause an argument to be mistaken as an adjunct by LexTract or vice versa. For example, the Chinese Treebank annotation guidelines require that the subject of a verb should always have the function tag *-SBJ*, but sometimes annotators forgot to do that. In figure 2.16, the structure in (c) is identical to the one in (a) except that the subject in (c) is missing such a function tag; as a result,

LexTract treats the subject in (c) as an adjunct, and creates an implausible *etree* in (d) rather than the plausible *etree* in (b).

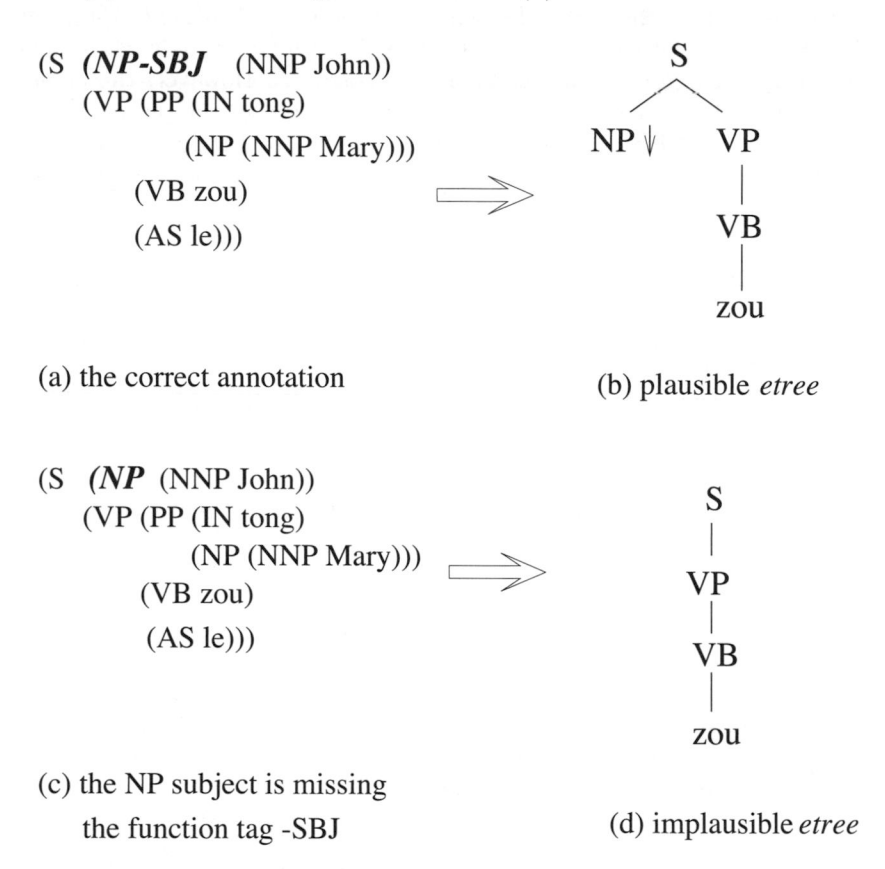

(a) the correct annotation

(b) plausible *etree*

(c) the NP subject is missing
the function tag -SBJ

(d) implausible *etree*

FIGURE 2.16 An error caused by a missing function tag: (a) is the correct structure; (b) is one of the *etrees* extracted from (a); (c) misses the function tag *SBJ*; (d) is an extracted *etree* from (c), and it is implausible because it does not contain the subject of the verb.

- Missing *ttree* nodes: One reason for this type of error in the Chinese Penn Treebank is that annotators forgot to mark dropped arguments. In figure 2.17, the dropped argument should be marked as an empty category *pro*, as in (a). Failing to do that, as in (c), would result in an implausible *etree* in (d).

- Extra *ttree* nodes: This type of error is rare and mostly caused by careless typos or misunderstanding of the annotation guidelines.

Two observations are in order. First, the main function of LexTract is extracting LTAGs and building derivation trees to train LTAG parsers and Supertaggers. Error detection is only a byproduct of the system. Consequently, there are errors that LexTract cannot detect; namely, the errors that do not result in implausible *etrees*.

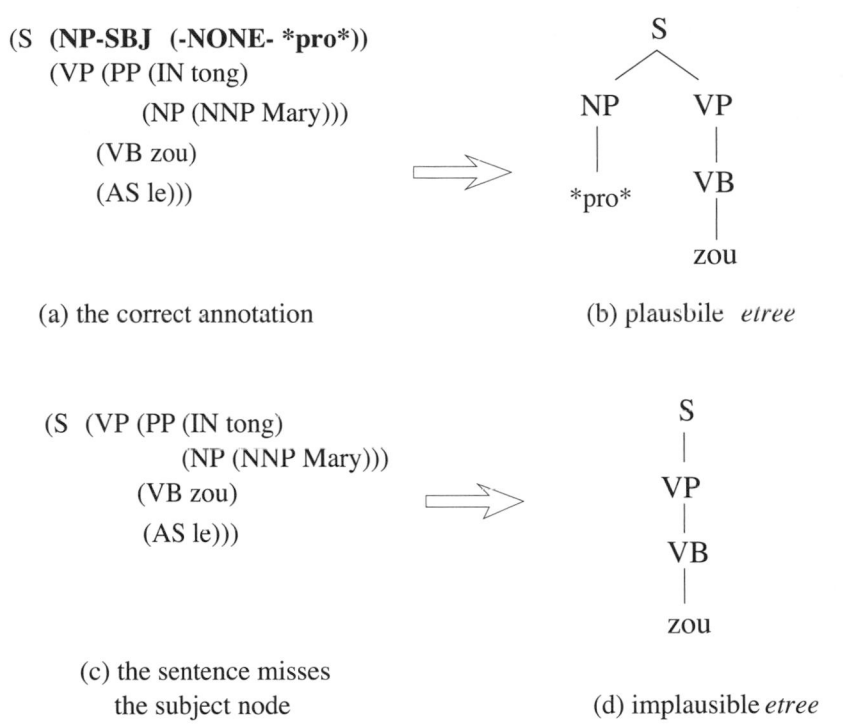

```
(S  (NP-SBJ  (-NONE- *pro*))
    (VP (PP (IN tong)
            (NP (NNP Mary)))
        (VB zou)
        (AS le)))
```

(a) the correct annotation

(b) plausbile *etree*

```
(S  (VP (PP (IN tong)
            (NP (NNP Mary)))
        (VB zou)
        (AS le)))
```

(c) the sentence misses
the subject node

(d) implausible *etree*

FIGURE 2.17 An error caused by a missing subject node: (a) is the correct structure; (b) is one of the *etrees* extracted from (a); (c) misses the *NP-SBJ* node and its child; (d) is an extracted *etree* from (c), and it is implausible because it does not contain the subject of the verb.

For example, in English, a *PP* can modify either an *NP* or a *VP*. Given a particular context, in general, only one attachment makes sense. If the treebank chooses the wrong attachment, LexTract cannot detect that error.

The second observation is that using templates can detect more annotation errors than using context-free rules. For example, in English either the subject or the object of a verb can undergo wh-movement and leave a trace in its position, as shown in figure 2.18a and 2.18b. But the subject and the object cannot be moved at the same time, as in figure 2.18c. That is, the first two templates are plausible but the third template is not. However, all three templates consist of the same set of context-free rules as in figure 2.18d, and all the context-free rules are plausible. Thus, the annotation errors that result in the implausible template in figure 2.18c can be detected only if we use templates, rather than context-free rules.

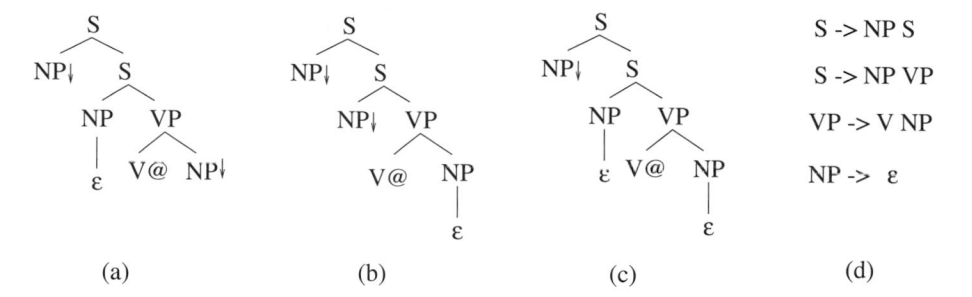

FIGURE 2.18 Three templates and corresponding context-free rules: the first two templates are plausible, while the third one is not. The context-free rules derived from these three templates are identical and each rule is plausible.

2.5   Summary

We outlined a system named LexTract, which takes a treebank and language-specific information, and produces grammars (LTAGs and CFGs) and derivation trees. LexTract has several advantageous properties. First, it takes very little human effort to build three tables (i.e., the Tagset Table, the Head Percolation Table, and the Argument Table). Once the tables are ready, LexTract can extract grammars from treebanks in a short time. Because LexTract does not include any language-dependent code, it can be applied to various treebanks for different languages. Second, LexTract builds a unique derivation tree for each sentence in the treebank, which can be used to train statistical LTAG parsers directly. Third, LexTract allows its users to have some control over the kind of treebank grammar to be extracted. For example, by changing the entries in the Head Percolation Table, the Argument Table, and the Tagset Table, users can get different treebank grammars and they can then choose the ones that best fit their goals. Fourth, the grammar produced by LexTract is guaranteed to cover the source treebank.

We have used LexTract for four types of tasks. First, treebank grammars produced by LexTract are useful for grammar development and comparison. For example, a treebank grammar can be used as a stand-alone grammar. We also used a treebank grammar extracted from the English Penn Treebank to estimate and improve the coverage of the XTAG grammar. Second, the treebank grammar and derivation trees produced by LexTract were used to train a Supertagger and a statistical LTAG parser with satisfactory results. Third, we used LexTract to detect annotation errors in the Chinese Penn Treebank. Last, we used LexTract to find all the nonlocal examples from the English Penn Treebank in order to test the tree-locality hypothesis. The details of these experiments can be found in Xia (2001). All these applications indicate that LexTract is not only an engineering tool of great value, but it is also very useful for investigating theoretical linguistics.

Notes

1. Treebank grammars may contain less information (e.g., feature structures associated with nonterminal nodes) than some hand-crafted grammars, but they are sufficient for some NLP tasks such as Supertagging and parsing as described in section 2.4.

2. Another possible name for a prototype is *template*. We do not use this name because the term *template* in the LTAG formalism is used to refer to an unlexicalized elementary tree.

3. Some users may prefer to treat the conjunction as the anchor of the tree, and treat the conjoined constituents as substitution nodes. It is also possible that two conjoined constituents are connected by two conjunctions (e.g., the conjunction pair "*both ... and ...*" in English). LexTract can accommodate both cases, but we omit the details in this chapter for the sake of simplicity.

4. One exception is the predicative auxiliary tree for verbs such as *think*. The elementary tree for the verb *think* in a declarative sentence is an auxiliary tree to handle long-distance movement, but it is also a spine-etree as it shows the predicate-argument relation of the verb.

5. This choice will not change the elementary trees extracted from a *ttree*, but they will result in different derivation trees, as in figures 2.9 and 2.10. It is possible that one option is better than the other for training a particular LTAG parser.

6. Recall that the process of building *etrees* has two steps. First, LexTract treats each node as a pair of the top and bottom parts. The derived tree is cut into pieces along the boundaries of the top and bottom parts of some nodes. In any partition, the top and the bottom parts of each node belong to either two distinct pieces or one piece; as a result, there are 2^n distinct partitions of the derived tree. In the second step, two nonadjacent pieces in a partition can be glued together to form a bigger piece under certain conditions. Therefore, each partition will result in one or more decompositions of the derived tree. In total, there are at least 2^n decompositions for any derived tree with n nodes; that is, the number of possible decompositions is $\Omega(2^n)$.

7. The prototypes actually allow the arguments of an anchor to be further expanded and lexicalized in order to handle noncompositional phrases such as *keep the bucket*; however, because the Penn Treebanks currently do not mark these noncompositional phrases, all the *etrees* extracted from the treebanks will have single anchors, and the arguments of the anchor are substitution nodes.

8. Unfortunately, we do not have access to the CFG parser they used; therefore, we cannot compare our grammar with their grammars with respect to the precision and recall rates of the parser.

9. We leave out the last type mainly because understanding our experiment for this type requires the knowledge of Multiple-Component Tree-Adjoining Grammars (MCTAG), a topic that we do not cover in this chapter.

10. Anoop Sarkar attended graduate school at the University of Pennsylvania when the experiment was conducted. He is currently a faculty member at Simon Fraser University in Vancouver, Canada.

11. Zipf's Law says that in a large corpus the rank of a word multiplied by its frequency is a constant (Zipf, 1949). The *rank* of a word is the position of the word in the word list when the list is sorted in decreasing order according to the words' frequencies in the corpus. Graphically, if the frequency of each word is plotted as a function of rank on doubly logarithmic axes, the curve is close to a straight line with slope -1. To achieve a closer fit to the empirical distribution of words, Mandelbrot (1954) derives the following more general relationship between rank and frequency:

$$freq = P(rank + \rho)^{-B}$$

where P, B, and ρ are parameters of a text, that collectively measure the richness of the text's use of words (Manning and Schütze, 1999). Interestingly, the curve in figure 2.13 shows that the relationship between the rank and frequency of templates satisfies Mandelbrot's equation.

12. Chiang (2000) did similar experiments for the tree insertion grammar that he extracted from the PTB. His grammar had 3,626 templates, of which 1,587 occur once. He found that out of 100 randomly selected once-seen templates, 34 results from annotation errors, 50 from deficiencies in the heuristics used by his extraction algorithm, and 4 from performance errors; only 12 appeared to be genuine. It is hard to compare the results of these two experiments because the treebank grammars and the extraction algorithms in his and our experiments were very different.

13. We chose those sections because most state-of-the-art parsers are trained and tested on those sections.

14. The Chinese Treebank had about 100,000 words when our experiments were conducted. Since then, the treebank has been expanded and now it contains more than 500,000 words.

15. Ideally, the coverage of a grammar should be measured as the percentage of sentences for which the *correct* parse trees can be generated by the grammar. However, because it is time consuming to manually check whether the parse trees produced by the grammar contain the correct ones, previous evaluations used a more lenient measure, which is the percentage of sentences for which the grammar will produce at least one parse tree.

16. For instance, in the XTAG grammar, the templates for intransitive verbs such as *come* and the templates for the intransitive usage of ergative verbs such as *break* in the sentence *The window broke* look the same except that the subject in the

former is named NP_0 while the subject in the latter is named NP_1. The subscript 0 implies that the NP is the agent, and the subscript 1 implies that the NP is the theme. On the other hand, the Penn Treebanks do not mark agents and themes, and therefore the templates for *come* and the intransitive usage of *break* will be identical in the treebank grammar. Because subscripts appear only in the XTAG grammar and are ignored when templates are matched, the two slightly different templates in the XTAG grammar will match the same template in G_2.

17. The number 97.2% is the sum of two numbers: the first one is the percentage of matched template tokens (82.1% from Table 2.5). The second number is the percentage of template tokens in T1–T3 (16.8% - 1.7% = 15.1% from Table 2.6).

18. It is possible that the new derivation tree cannot fit together because t and t' are not identical.

19. A *word* in this section, as usual, refers to an inflected word, rather than a lemma. The average number of Supertags per word *type* is calculated as

$$\frac{\sum_{w \in W} stag(w)}{|W|}$$

The average number of Supertags per word *token* is calculated as

$$\frac{\sum_{w \in W} stag(w) * freq(w)}{\sum_{w \in W} freq(w)}$$

where W is the set of distinct words in a treebank, stag(w) is the number of Supertags that a word w has, and *freq(w)* is the number of occurrences of w in the treebank.

20. For these four numbers, we use PTB's tagset. The numbers would decrease a little bit if we used the reduced tagset instead. A word may appear to have more Supertags (or POS tags) in the treebank than it should due to treebank annotation errors.

21. Notably, the results we report on Srinivas's data, 85.78% on Section 23 and 85.53% on Section 22, are lower than the 92.2% reported in Srinivas (1997), 91.37% in Chen et al. (1999) and 88.0% in Doran (2000). There are several reasons for the differences. First, the size of training data in our experiment is smaller than the one for his previous work, which was trained on Sections 00–24 except for Section 20 and tested on Section 20. Second, we treat punctuation marks as normal words during evaluation because, like other words, punctuation marks can anchor *etrees*, whereas he treated the Supertags for punctuation marks as always correct. Third, he predefined some equivalence classes and used them during evaluations. If the correct Supertag for a word is x, and the output of the Supertagger for that word is y, he did not consider that output to be an error if x and y appeared in the same equivalence class. We suspect that the reason that these Supertagging errors were disregarded is that they might not affect parsing results when the Supertags are combined to form parse trees. For example, both adjectives and nouns can modify other nouns.

The two templates (i.e., Supertags) representing these modification relations look the same except for the POS tags of the anchors. If a word that should be tagged with one Supertag is mistagged with the other Supertag, it is likely that the wrong Supertag can still fit with the rest of Supertags in the sentence to produce the correct parse tree. In our experiment, we did not use these equivalence classes.

22. Let R be the root of T^*. If each node t in T^* is split into a *(t.top, t.bot)* pair, and each node e in *ESet* is split into a pair *(e.top, e.bot)* except that the foot and substitution nodes have only the top part and the root nodes have only the bottom part, then there is a bidirectional function f from the set $\{t.top,\ t.bot\} - \{R.top\}$ to the set $\{e.top,\ e.bot\}$. Details can be found in section 5.4.4 in Xia (2001).

23. While the exact definition of *plausibility* could vary depending on the underlying linguistic theory, there are some requirements that most people would agree that a good elementary tree should satisfy: for example, arguments should appear in the same elementary tree as their head; if the category of a phrase is XP (e.g., *VP*), the category of the head of the phrase should be X (e.g., *V*). For the experiment described in this section, we let our linguistic expert use her own judgment to decide on the plausibility of elementary trees.

24. While the algorithm would point out the nodes in *ttrees* that need to be checked, it is up to the user of the tool to decide what kind of modification is needed to fix the errors in the *ttree*.

25. Because most of the readers are more familiar with the English Penn Treebank than the Chinese Penn Treebank, in this example we adopt the annotation convention and the tagset that are used in the English Penn Treebank (except for the tag *AS* for an aspect marker, which does not appear in the English tagset).

References

Charniak, E. (1996). Treebank Grammars. In *Proc. of the 13th National Conference on Artificial Intelligence (AAAI-1996)*.

Chen, J., Srinivas, B., and Vijay-Shanker, K. (1999). New Models for Improving Supertag Disambiguation. In *Proc. of the 10th Conference of the European Chapter of the Association for Computational Linguistics (EACL-1999)*.

Chen, J. and Vijay-Shanker, K. (2000). Automated Extraction of TAGs from the Penn Treebank. In *Proc. of the 6th International Workshop on Parsing Technologies (IWPT-2000), Italy*.

Chiang, D. (2000). Statistical Parsing with an Automatically-Extracted Tree Adjoining Grammar. In *Proc. of the 38th Annual Meeting of the Association for Computational Linguistics (ACL-2000)*.

Chomsky, N. (1981). *Lectures on Government and Binding*. Foris.

Collins, M. (1997). Three Generative, Lexicalised Models for Statistical Parsing. In *Proc. of the 35th Annual Meeting of the Association for Computational Linguistics (ACL-1997), Madrid, Spain*.

Doran, C. (2000). Punctuation in a Lexicalized Grammar. In *Proc. of 5th International Workshop on TAG and Related Frameworks (TAG+5)*.

Doran, C., Hockey, B. A., Sarkar, A., Srinivas, B., and Xia, F. (2000). Evolution of the XTAG System. In Abeillé, A. and Rambow, O., eds., *Tree Adjoining Grammar: Formalism, Computation, Applications*, CSLI Publications.

Jackendoff, R. S. (1977). *X-bar Syntax: A Study of Phrase Structure*. MIT Press.

Joshi, A. K. and Srinivas, B. (1994). Disambiguation of Super Parts of Speech (or Supertags): Almost Parsing. In *Proc. of the 15th International Conference on Computational Linguistics (COLING-1994)*.

Krotov, A., Hepple, M., Gaizauskas, R., and Wilks, Y. (1998). Compacting the Penn Treebank Grammar. In *Proc. of the 36th Annual Meeting of the Association for Computational Linguistics (ACL-1998)*, Montreal, Quebec, Canada.

Magerman, D. M. (1995). Statistical Decision-Tree Models for Parsing. In *Proc. of the 33rd Annual Meeting of the Association for Computational Linguistics (ACL-1995)*, Cambridge, Massachusetts.

Mandelbrot, B. (1954). Structure formelle des textes et communication. *Word*, 10.

Manning, C. D. and Schütze, H. (1999). *Foundations of Statistical Natural Language Processing*. The MIT Press, Cambridge, Massachusetts, USA.

Marcus, M. P., Santorini, B., and Marcinkiewicz, M. A. (1993). Building a Large Annotated Corpus of English: the Penn Treebank. *Computational Linguistics*.

Neumann, G. (1998). Automatic Extraction of Stochastic Lexicalized Tree Grammars from Treebanks. In *Proc. of the 4th International Workshop on TAG and Related Frameworks (TAG+4)*.

Prasad, R. and Sarkar, A. (2000). Comparing Test-Suite Based Evaluation and Corpus-Based Evaluation of a Wide-Coverage Grammar for English. In *Proc. of LREC Satellite Workshop Using Evaluation Within HLT Programs: Results and Trends*, Athens, Greece.

Prolo, C. A. (2000). An Efficient LR Parser Generator for TAGs. In *6th International Workshop on Parsing Technologies (IWPT 2000)*, Italy.

Sarkar, A. (2001). Applying Co-Training Methods to Statistical Parsing. In *Proc. of the Second Meeting of the North American Chapter of the Association for Computational Linguistics (NAACL-2001)*, Pittsburgh, Pennsylvania.

Sarkar, A. and Joshi, A. K. (1996). Coordination in Tree Adjoining Grammars: Formalization and Implementation. In *Proc. of the 16th International Conference on Computational Linguistics (COLING-1996)*, Copenhagen, Denmark.

Schabes, Y. and Shieber, S. M. (1992). An Alternative Conception of Tree-Adjoining Derivation. In *Proc. of the 30th Annual Meeting of the Association for Computational Linguistics (ACL-1992)*, Newark, Delaware, USA.

Shirai, K., Tokunaga, T., and Tanaka, H. (1995). Automatic Extraction of Japanese Grammar from a Bracketed Corpus. In *Proc. of Natural Language Processing Pacific Rim Symposium (NLPRS-1995)*.

Skut, W., Krenn, B., Brants, T., and Uszkoreit, H. (1997). An Annotation Scheme for Free Word Order Languages. In *Proc. of 5th International Conference of Applied Natural Language*.

Srinivas, B. (1997). *Complexity of Lexical Descriptions and Its Relevance to Partial Parsing*. PhD thesis, University of Pennsylvania.

Srinivas, B., Sarkar, A., Doran, C., and Hockey, B. A. (1998). Grammar and Parser Evaluation in the XTAG Project. In *Proc. of the Workshop on Evaluation of Parsing Systems*, Granada, Spain.

Xia, F. (1999). Extracting Tree Adjoining Grammars from Bracketed Corpora. In *Proc. of 5th Natural Language Processing Pacific Rim Symposium (NLPRS-1999)*, Beijing, China.

Xia, F. (2001). *Automatic Grammar Generation from Two Different Perspectives*. PhD thesis, University of Pennsylvania.

Xia, F. and Bleam, T. (2000). A Corpus-Based Evaluation of Syntactic Locality in TAGs. In *Proc. of 5th International Workshop on TAG and Related Frameworks (TAG+5)*.

Xia, F., Han, C., Palmer, M., and Joshi, A. K. (2001). Automatically Extracting and Comparing Lexicalized Grammars for Different Languages. In *Proc. of the Seventeenth International Joint Conference on Artificial Intelligence (IJCAI-2001)*, Seattle, Washington.

Xia, F. and Palmer, M. (2000). Evaluating the Coverage of LTAGs on Annotated Corpora. In *Proc. of LREC Satellite Workshop Using Evaluation Within HLT Programs: Results and Trends*, Athens, Greece.

Xia, F., Palmer, M., and Joshi, A. K. (2000a). A Uniform Method of Grammar Extraction and Its Applications. In *Proc. of Joint SIGDAT Conference on Empirical Methods in Natural Language Processing and Very Large Corpora (EMNLP-2000)*.

Xia, F., Palmer, M., Xue, N., Okurowski, M. E., Kovarik, J., Huang, S., Kroch, A., and Marcus, M. P. (2000b). Developing Guidelines and Ensuring Consistency for Chinese Text Annotation. In *Proc. of the 2nd International Conference on Language Resources and Evaluation (LREC-2000)*, Athens, Greece.

XTAG-Group (1998). A Lexicalized Tree Adjoining Grammar for English. Technical Report IRCS 98-18, University of Pennsylvania.

Zipf, G. K. (1949). *Human Behavior and the Principle of Least Effort*. Hafner.

3

Developing Tree-Adjoining Grammars with Lexical Descriptions

Fei Xia, Martha Palmer, and K. Vijay-Shanker

3.1 Introduction

LTAG is an appealing formalism for representing various phenomena (especially syntactic phenomena) in natural languages because of its linguistic and computational properties such as the Extended Domain of Locality, stronger generative capacity and lexicalized elementary trees. Because templates (i.e., elementary trees with the lexical items removed) in an LTAG grammar often share some common structures, as the number of templates increases building and maintaining templates by hand presents two major problems. First, the reuse of tree structures in many templates creates redundancy. To make a single change in a grammar, all the related templates have to be manually checked. The process is inefficient and cannot guarantee consistency (Vijay-Shanker and Schabes, 1992). Second, the underlying linguistic information (e.g., the analysis of wh-movement) is not expressed explicitly. As a result, from the grammar itself (i.e., hundreds of templates plus the lexicon), it is hard to grasp the characteristics of a particular language, to compare languages, and to build a grammar for a new language given existing grammars for other languages.

To address these problems, we designed a grammar development system named LexOrg, which automatically generates LTAG grammars from abstract specifications. The system is based on the ideas expressed in Vijay-Shanker and Schabes (1992), for using tree descriptions in specifying a grammar by separately defining pieces of tree structure that encode independent syntactic principles. Various individual specifications are then combined to form the elementary trees of the grammar. We have carefully designed our system to be as language-independent as possible and tested its performance by constructing both English and Chinese grammars, with significant reductions in grammar development time. The system not only enables efficient development and maintenance of a grammar, but also

Transitive verbs: (NP0 V NP1)

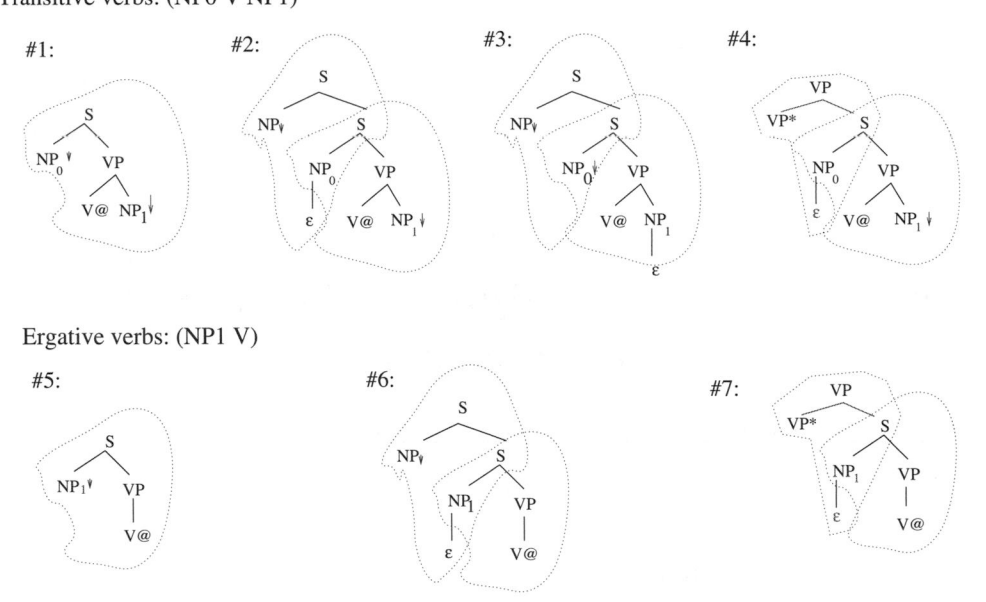

Ergative verbs: (NP1 V)

FIGURE 3.1   Templates in two tree families

allows underlying linguistic constructions (such as wh-movement) to be expressed explicitly.

The chapter is organized as follows. In section 3.2, we give an outline of the LexOrg system. In section 3.3, we define descriptions, trees, and four classes of descriptions. In sections 3.4 to 3.6, we describe the three main components of LexOrg. In section 3.7, we discuss how a user creates a set of abstract specifications for a language. section 3.8 includes a report on our experiments using LexOrg to generate grammars for English and Chinese. In section 3.9, we compare LexOrg with related work.

3.2   An Overview of LexOrg

To better understand the redundancy problem, let us look at an example. Figure 3.1 shows seven templates in two tree families:[1] the top four elementary trees are for the verbs with the subcategorization frame *(NP0 V NP1)*, and the bottom three elementary trees are for the verbs with subcategorization frame *(NP1 V)*. Of course, these are not the only trees in the tree families associated with these subcategorization frames. In the XTAG grammar for English, for example, there are nineteen templates in the transitive verb's tree family.[2]

Among these seven templates, #1, #2, #3, and #4 all share the structure in figure 3.2a; templates #2, #3, and #6 all have the structure in figure 3.2b; templates

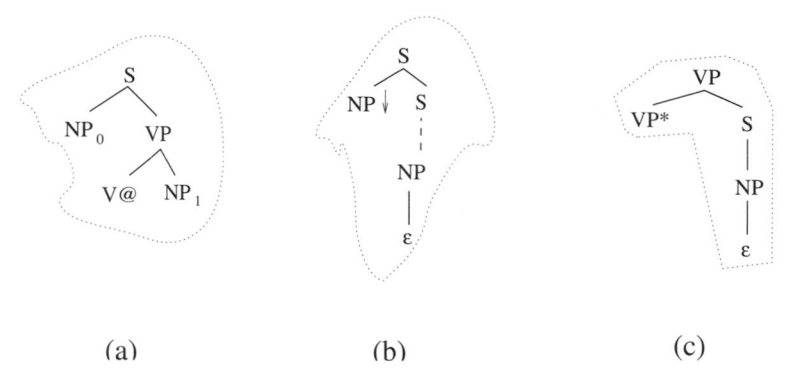

(a)   (b)   (c)

FIGURE 3.2 Structures shared by the templates in figure 3.1

#4 and #7 both have the structure in figure 3.2c. The dashed line in figure 3.2b between the lower *S* and the node *NP* indicates that the *S* node dominates the *NP* node, but it is not necessarily the parent of the *NP*.

Because of the redundancy among templates, the process of manually creating and maintaining grammars is inefficient and cannot guarantee consistency. Nevertheless, if there exists a tool that combines these common structures to generate templates automatically (as illustrated in figure 3.3), then the task of the grammar designers changes from building templates to building these common structures, providing an elegant solution. First, one can argue that the common structures form the appropriate level for stating the linguistic generalizations. Considering that these common structures are much smaller and simpler than templates and the number of the former is much less than that of the latter, the grammar development time will also be reduced significantly. Second, if grammar designers want to change the analysis of a certain phenomenon (e.g., wh-movement), they need to modify only the structure that represents the phenomenon (e.g., the structure in figure 3.3b for wh-movement). The modifications in the structure will be automatically propagated to all the templates that subsume the structure, thus guaranteeing consistency among the templates. Third, the underlying linguistic information (such as wh-movement) is expressed explicitly, making it easy to grasp the main characteristics of a language and to compare languages.

All of these advantages will be derived if the grammar designer is able to state the linguistic principles and generalizations at the appropriate level. That is, the domain of the objects being specified must be only large enough to state these principles. While the enlarged domain of locality in templates is touted as one of the fundamental strengths of LTAG, it must be noted that from the grammar development point of view each template expresses several (often independent) principles. Thus, in coming up with a template, the designer has to consider the instantiation of several principles that could interact in some cases and also instantiate the same principles multiple times (sometimes hundreds of times). We

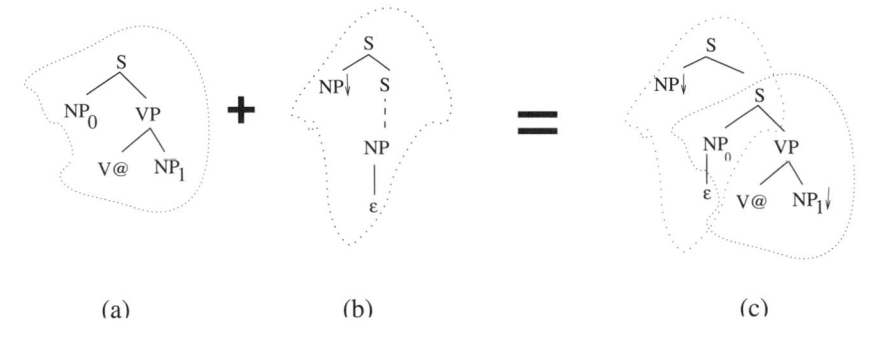

(a)   (b)   (c)

FIGURE 3.3 Combining descriptions to generate templates

believe that this aspect makes the grammar development process unnecessarily error-prone and cumbersome. Our aim in developing LexOrg is to let the grammar designer define individual grammar principles within a domain that is appropriate for that principle. (Roughly, these domains and the instantiation of principles would represent the shared structures found among templates in existing grammars as discussed earlier.) The LexOrg system then assumes the burden of considering what set of principles should fit together to make up a template and also considers the interactions and consistency of such a set of principles. Thus, the process of grammar development or prototyping can be significantly simplified, thereby made more rapid and less error-prone. Over a period of time, as the grammar is developed to further its coverage, certain principles are bound to be modified. No matter how small the modification is, ensuring that the possible effect on all the templates already designed is properly accounted for by manually checking the templates is an onerous task. However, with a tool such as LexOrg, the focus is correctly placed on the principle. The propagation of this principle and ensuring the consistency of its interactions with other principles is now mechanized.

In LexOrg, instead of manually creating templates, a grammar designer needs to provide the following specifications for a language: subcategorization frames, lexical subcategorization rules, and four different kinds of tree descriptions: head-projection, head-argument, modification, and syntactic variation descriptions. These specifications relate closely to the different aspects of LTAG elementary trees and the notion of tree families. The *subcategorization frames* associated with different lexical items specify which arguments of the lexical items the designer intends to localize within the elementary trees. Together with *the head-projection* and *head-argument descriptions* (where the grammar designer expresses how the lexical heads project and how they combine with their "subcategorized" arguments), they will cause LexOrg to produce the basic tree structure for each subcategorization frame.[3] The *lexical subcategorization rules* allow the grammar designer to specify the processes that they consider to be lexical, which define related subcategorization frames. For example, the difference between the passive and active forms can be stated using this machinery. In addition to head-projection and head-argument descriptions, there

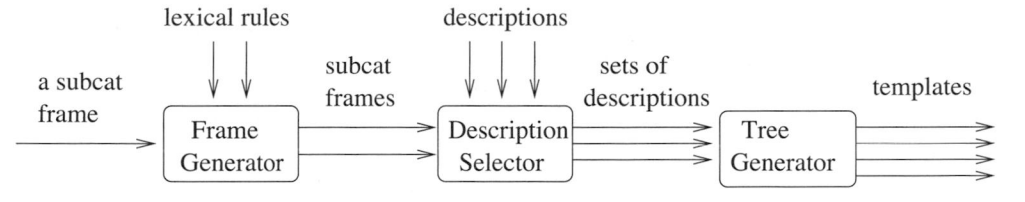

FIGURE 3.4 The architecture of LexOrg

are two additional kinds of descriptions: *modification descriptions* and *syntactic variation descriptions*. *Modification descriptions* are used to describe the other kind of elementary trees in LTAG, modifier auxiliary trees, which are used to represent the tree structures for various forms of modification. *Syntactic variation descriptions* are to be used to account for the design of the rest of the elementary trees that are not obtained from mere projections of the basic subcategorization frames or frames derived from using lexical subcategorization rules. In the next sections, we shall define each kind of specification in more detail.

We believe that most linguistic theories in some form or the other use these different types of grammatical mechanisms. We have separated them out into the different kinds of specifications as described above because of their relationship to the different aspects of elementary trees and tree families, which are now familiar to the LTAG community. Nevertheless, in spite of this connection, we make no a priori assumption about how a grammar designer should use these types of grammatical specification methods. For example, the treatment of wh-movement can be specified via syntactic variation descriptions or as a lexical process and hence by using lexical subcategorization rules; the descriptions can be structured hierarchically or could have a relatively flat organization. Because we give grammar designers such freedom in choosing appropriate grammatical specification methods, evaluation of one particular set of specifications (such as the ones given in section 3.8) is not central to LexOrg's evaluation. In the next few sections, we will describe pieces of a particular specification of an LTAG grammar. However, this should be understood as an attempt to suggest the usefulness of LexOrg and to provide examples of using the different aspects of LexOrg. Hence, by no means do we intend for this specification to suggest any particular grammatical principle to be associated with LTAG nor even how principles have to be stated in LexOrg.

Figure 3.4 shows the architecture of the LexOrg system, which has three components: a Frame Generator, a Description Selector, and a Tree Generator. The inputs to the system are subcategorization frames, lexical subcategorization rules, and tree descriptions. The Frame Generator (described in section 3.6) accepts the subcategorization frames and lexical subcategorization rules, and for each subcategorization frame it considers all the applicable lexical subcategorization rules to produce a set of subcategorization frames in a format that is appropriate for later stages. The Description Selector (described in section 3.5) automatically identifies the set of descriptions (used to construct the tree templates) appropriate for each template for each subcategorization frame. Finally, the Tree Generator (section 3.4) produces the templates corresponding to the selected descriptions and subcategorization frame. In the next section, we first describe the language used in specifying the grammatical descriptions and consider four different classes of descriptions that a grammar designer may provide.

3.3   Tree Descriptions

Tree descriptions (or *descriptions* for short) were introduced by Vijay-Shanker and Schabes (1992) in a scheme for efficiently representing an LTAG grammar. Rogers and Vijay-Shanker (1994) later gave a formal definition of (tree) *descriptions*. We extended their definition to include features and further divided *descriptions* into four classes: head-projection descriptions, head-argument descriptions, modification descriptions, and syntactic variation descriptions. This section presents the characterizations of each of these classes in detail.

3.3.1   The definition of a *description*

In Rogers and Vijay-Shanker (1994), *descriptions* are defined to be formulas in a simplified first-order language L_K, in which neither variables nor quantifiers occur. L_K is built up from a countable set of constant symbols K, three predicates (*parent*, *domination*, and *left-of* relations), the equality predicate, and the usual logical connectives ($\wedge$, $\vee$, $\neg$). We extended their definition to include features because, in the LTAG formalism, feature structures are associated with the nodes in a template to specify linguistic constraints. Feature specifications, in a PATR-II like format, are added to descriptions so that when descriptions are combined by LexOrg, the features are carried over to the resulting templates. In addition to any feature that a user of LexOrg may want to include, there are two predefined features for each constant symbol in K: one is *cat* for *category*, the value of which can be N (noun), NP (noun phrase), and so on; the other feature is *type* for node types, which has four possible values: *foot*, *anchor*, *subst*, and *internal*. The first three values are for the three types of leaf nodes in a template: foot node, anchor node, and substitution node, and the last value is for all the internal nodes in a template.

Figure 3.5a shows a description in this logical form, where $\lhd$, $\lhd^*$, and $\prec$ stand for *parent*, *domination*, and *left-of* predicates, respectively; *cat* stands for *category* and is a feature. For instance, $NP_0.cat = {}'NP'$ means that NP_0 has a feature named *cat* whose value is NP (i.e., noun phrase). Most descriptions used by LexOrg can be represented in a treelike figure. Figure 3.5b is the graphical representation for the same description. In this graph, dashed lines and solid lines stand for *domination* and *parent* predicates, respectively. The values of some features of nodes (such as the category of a node) are enclosed in parentheses. The graphical representation is more intuitive and easier to read, but not every description can be displayed as a graph because a description may use negation and disjunctive connectives. In the

$(S_0 \lhd NP_0) \wedge (S_0 \lhd S_1)$

$\wedge(NP_0 \prec S_1) \wedge (S_1 \lhd^* NP_1)$

$\wedge(NP_1 \lhd Trace) \wedge (S_0.cat = \ 'S')$

$\wedge(NP_0.cat = \ 'NP') \wedge (S_1.cat = \ 'S')$

$\wedge(NP_1.cat = \ 'NP') \wedge (Trace.cat = \ '\epsilon')$

(a) the logical representation   (b) the graphical representation

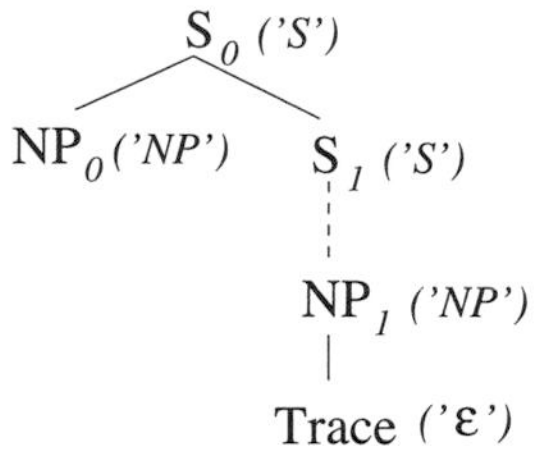

FIGURE 3.5 Two representations of a description

following sections, we shall use the graphical representation when possible and use the logical representation in other cases.

3.3.2   The definition of a *tree*

According to Rogers and Vijay-Shanker (1994), a *tree* is a structure that interprets the constants and predicates of L_K such that the interpretation of the predicates reflects the properties of the trees. A tree is said to *satisfy* a description if the tree as a structure satisfies the description as a formula in L_K. As we have extended the definition of description to include features, we also placed additional requirements on *trees* with respect to features. For instance, the category of every node in a *tree* must be specified. For more details about this revision, please see section 4.3.3. of Xia (2001).

From each satisfiable description, we can always recover a minimal tree that satisfies the description. For example, figure 3.6a is a tree that satisfies the description given in figure 3.5. In this representation, a node has the form $\{k_i\}(\{f_m = v_m\})$, where $\{k_i\}$ is a list of node names, and v_m is the value of a feature f_m. For simplicity, we often omit from this graphical representation the curly brackets and all the features except the category of a node. When $\{k_i\}$ has more than one member, it means that several nodes from different descriptions are merged in the tree. In figure 3.6a, one such case is *Obj,ExtSite('NP')*. As we will show later, *Obj* comes from a head-argument description, while *ExtSite* comes from a syntactic variation description. The two names refer to the same node in the tree. In section 3.4, we shall show that it is trivial to build a unique template from such a representation.

3.3.3   Four classes of descriptions

In section 3.4, we shall demonstrate how a component of LexOrg, namely the Tree Generator, generates templates from descriptions. Because the goal of LexOrg is to build grammars for natural languages, rather than any arbitrary LTAG grammar, descriptions used by LexOrg should contain all the syntactic information that could

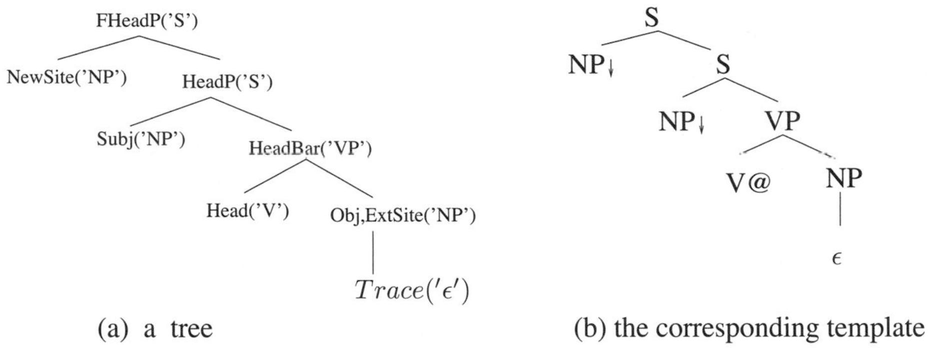

(a) a tree   (b) the corresponding template

FIGURE 3.6 A tree and the template that is built from the tree

appear in the templates for natural languages. In this section, we identify four types of syntactic information in a template and define a class of descriptions for each type of information.

Head-projection descriptions

An important notion in many contemporary linguistic theories such as X-bar theory (Jackendoff, 1977), GB theory (Chomsky, 1981), and HPSG (Pollard and Sag, 1994) is the notion of a *head*. A head determines the main properties of the phrase that it belongs to. A head may project to various levels, and the head and its projections form a projection chain.

The first class of description used by LexOrg is called a *head-projection description*. It gives the information about the head and its various projections. For instance, the description in figure 3.7a says that a verb projects to a *VP*, and the *VP* projects to an *S*. Typically this should be straightforwardly derivable from head projection principles as found in X-bar theory or similar intuitions expressed in GPSG or HPSG. But in order to give flexibility to a grammar designer to use any appropriate linguistic theory and, for example, to use any choice in the number of projection levels and categories, we do not implement the derivations from any specific linguistic principles, but rather expect the grammar designer to state the head-projection descriptions explicitly.

Head-argument descriptions

A head may have one or more arguments. For instance, a transitive verb has two arguments: a *subject* and an *object*. The second class of description, the *head-argument description*, specifies the number, the types, and the positions of arguments that a head can take, and the constraints that a head imposes on its arguments. For instance, the description in figure 3.7b says that the subject — a left argument of the head — is a sister of the *HeadBar*.[4] In this case, the feature equation in the description, given below the tree in figure 3.7b, specifies

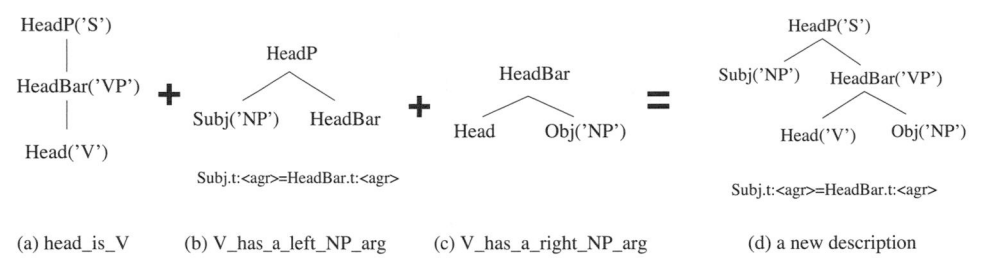

FIGURE 3.7 Subcategorization descriptions

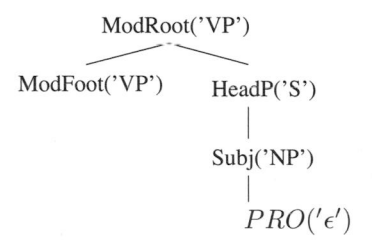

FIGURE 3.8 A description for purpose clauses

that the subject and the *HeadBar* must agree with respect to number, person, and so on. The description in figure 3.7c says that a head can take an *NP* argument, which appears as a right sister of the head. Combining head-projection and head-argument descriptions forms a description for the whole subcategorization frame, as in figure 3.7d; therefore, we use the term *subcategorization* description to refer to descriptions of either class. As we will describe in section 3.5, the Description Selector is responsible for choosing the set of descriptions appropriate for a given subcategorization frame. Again, for reasons similar to the one that we used at the end of the previous section on head-projection descriptions, for flexibility in choosing structures for head-argument realizations, we do not include in LexOrg a reliance on any specific linguistic principle governing descriptions of head-argument structures.

Modification descriptions

A syntactic phrase can be modified by other phrases. The third class of description, called a *modification description*, specifies the type and the position of a modifier with respect to the modifiee, and any constraint on the modification relation. For instance, the description in figure 3.8 says that a clause can modify a verb phrase from the right,[5] but the clause must be infinitival (as indicated by the PRO subject).

The modification descriptions are expected to describe the so-called modifier auxiliary trees in the resulting LTAG grammar, which are used to express modification in LTAG.

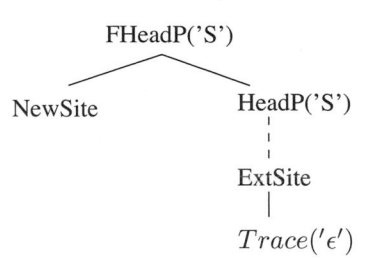

$$NewSite.t:<trace> = ExtSite.t:<trace>$$

FIGURE 3.9 A description for wh-movement

Syntactic variation descriptions

Head-projection and head-argument descriptions together define a basic tree structure for a subcategorization frame, which forms a subtree of every template in the tree family for that subcategorization frame. For instance, the structure in figure 3.7d appears in every template in the transitive tree family, as shown on the top part of figure 3.1. In addition to this basic structure, a template may contain other structures that represent syntactic variations such as wh-movement and argument drop. For example, template #2 in figure 3.1 can be decomposed into two parts: the first part, as in figure 3.2a, is the basic structure that comes from head-projection and head-argument descriptions; the second part, as in figure 3.2b, comes from the description in figure 3.9. We call this description a *syntactic variation description*, as it provides information on syntactic variations such as wh-movement. This description says that, in wh-movement, a component is moved from a position *ExtSite* under *HeadP* to the position *NewSite*, as indicated by the feature equation $NewSite.t :< trace >= ExtSite.t :< trace >$; *NewSite* is the left sister of *HeadP*; both *NewSite* and *HeadP* are children of *FHeadP*; both *FHeadP* and *HeadP* are of the category *S*.

Note that LexOrg allows descriptions to "inherit" from other descriptions; that is, a grammar designer has the flexibility of specifying a description as a further specification of other descriptions, which represent more general principles (such as X-bar theory couched in this framework). For example, a grammar designer may choose to create a description *head_has_an_arg* for the head-complement structure in X-bar theory, in which the position of the argument with respect to the head and the categories of the head and the argument are unspecified. The description is specialized further in giving the position of the argument, resulting in a new description *head_has_a_right_arg*. The latter description can be further specialized for the case where the argument has a category of *NP*, yielding a new description *head_has_a_right_NP_arg*, and for the case where the argument is an *S*, yielding another description *head_has_a_right_S_arg*. Similarly, the description in figure 3.9 can form the basis for movement specification in the grammar and can be further instantiated to cover not only wh-movement but also relative clauses, if desired. Using the inheritance among descriptions may reduce the redundancy among descriptions. For instance, if grammar designers later decide to change the representation for the head-complement structure, they need to change only the description *head_has_an_arg*, not the descriptions that inherit from this description. One final note about the inheritance relation among descriptions: while we (as the creators of LexOrg) encourage grammar designers to take advantage of this feature of LexOrg to make their descriptions more concise and hierarchical, we still allow a grammar designer to create all descriptions such that they are all "atomic" and there is no inheritance among them.

To summarize, we have discussed four classes of descriptions. In section 3.5, we will show that another component of LexOrg, namely the Description Selector, chooses descriptions according to their classes; that is, it will create sets of descriptions such that each set includes one head-projection description, zero or more head-argument descriptions, zero or one modification descriptions, and zero or more syntactic variation descriptions.

3.4 The Tree Generator

The most complex component of LexOrg is called the *Tree Generator (TreeGen)*, which takes a set of descriptions as input and generates a set of templates as output. This is done in three steps: first, TreeGen combines the input set of descriptions to get a new description; second, TreeGen builds a set of trees such that each tree in the set satisfies the new description and has minimal number of nodes; third, TreeGen builds a template from each tree in the tree set. In figure 3.10, the descriptions in (a) are the inputs to TreeGen. Combining them results in a new description in (b).[6] There are many trees that satisfy this new description, but the two trees in (c) are the only ones with minimal number of nodes. From these two trees, TreeGen builds two templates in (d). In this section, we explain each step in detail.

3.4.1 Step 1: Combining descriptions to form a new description

The Description Selector selects a set of descriptions that might potentially form one or more templates. TreeGen combines such a set of descriptions to form a new description. Recall that a description is a well-formed formula in a simplified first-order language. Given a set of descriptions $\{\phi_i\}$, the new description ϕ, which combines $\{\phi_i\}$, is simply the conjunction of ϕ_i; that is, $\phi = \phi_1 \wedge \phi_2 ... \wedge \phi_n$, where n is the size of $\{\phi_i\}$.

3.4.2 Step 2: Generating a set of trees from the new description

In the second step, TreeGen generates a set of trees, $TreeSet_{min}(\phi)$, for the new description ϕ. Let $TreeSet(\phi)$ be the set of trees that satisfies ϕ and $NumNodes(T)$

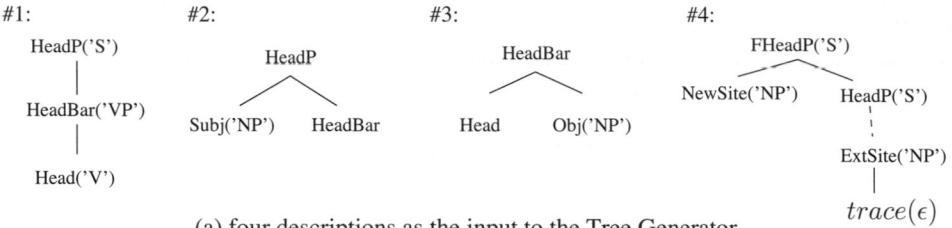

(a) four descriptions as the input to the Tree Generator

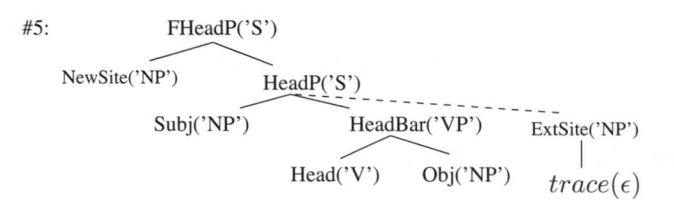

(b) the new description that combines the four descriptions in (a)

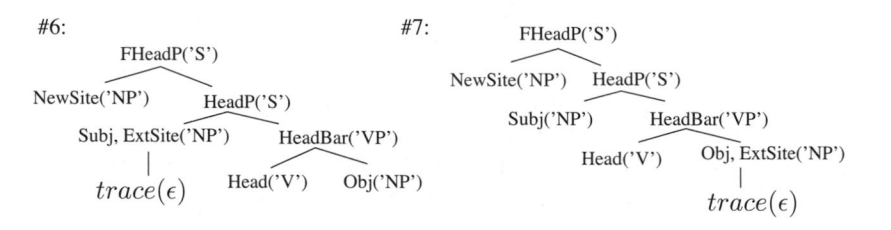

(c) trees generated from the new description

#8:

#9:

(d) the templates as the output of the Tree Generator

FIGURE 3.10 The function of the Tree Generator

be the number of nodes in a tree T, then $TreeSet_{min}(\phi)$ is defined to be the subset of $TreeSet(\phi)$ in which each tree has the minimal number of nodes; that is,

$$TreeSet_{min}(\phi) = arg\,min_{T \in TreeSet(\phi)} NumNodes(T)$$

With a little abuse of notation, we also use $NumNodes(\phi)$ to represent the number of nodes occurring in a description ϕ. According to our definition of *tree*, each node in a tree must have a category; therefore, each tree in $TreeSet(\phi)$ can have at most $NumNodes(\phi)$ nodes. Because $NumNodes(\phi)$ is finite for each ϕ, $TreeSet(\phi)$ and its subset $TreeSet_{min}(\phi)$ are finite too. As a result, $TreeSet_{min}(\phi)$ can be calculated by the following naive algorithm: first, initialize i to 1; second, generate a set $TS(i)$ that includes all the trees with i nodes; third, put into the set $TreeSet_{min}$ all the trees in $TS(i)$ that satisfy ϕ; if $TreeSet_{min}$ is empty, increase i by one and repeat the second and third steps until $TreeSet_{min}$ is not empty or i is more than $NumNodes(\phi)$. Because $NumNodes(\phi)$ is finite for any ϕ, the algorithm will always terminate; furthermore, when it terminates, $TreeSet_{min}$ is the same as $TreeSet_{min}(\phi)$ because by definition $TreeSet_{min}$ contains all the trees that satisfy ϕ with the minimal number of nodes. However, this algorithm is inefficient because it generates a large number of trees that do not satisfy ϕ and have to be thrown away in later steps.[7]

TreeGen uses a more efficient algorithm in which it first builds a new description $\hat{\phi}$ such that a tree satisfies $\hat{\phi}$ if and only it satisfies ϕ, and $\hat{\phi}$ is in the disjunctive normal form $\hat{\phi}_1 \vee ... \vee \hat{\phi}_m$, where each $\hat{\phi}_i$ uses only the conjunctive connectives. It does so by using rewrite rules that essentially capture the properties of trees to convert a negated formula into a disjunction of tree constraints, and then uses distributive rules to convert the formula into disjunctive normal form.[8] Second, for each $\hat{\phi}_i$ in $\hat{\phi}$, TreeGen builds a graph G_i. G_i is not necessarily a tree, as it might be disconnected, have loops, and so on. Third, TreeGen turns each G_i into a tree. There may be more than one possible tree for a graph; as a result, TreeGen gets a set of trees TC_i. Last, TreeGen chooses the subset of $\bigcup TC_i$ with the minimal number of nodes.

The new algorithm is in table 3.1. The major steps of the algorithm are illustrated in figure 3.11. The input description is in (a). Since the description is already in disjunctive normal form, TreeGen skips Step (A) in table 3.1. In steps (C1) and (C2), TreeGen creates a graphical representation for the description, as shown in figure 3.11b. A dashed edge (a solid edge, resp.) from the node x to y is in the graph if and only if $x \lhd^* y$ ($x \lhd y$, resp.) is one of the literals in the description. steps (C3) – (C5) convert the graph into a tree. In (C3) TreeGen removes loops in the graph. If a loop contains only dashed edges, TreeGen removes the loop by merging all the nodes on the loop.[9] If a loop contains one or more solid edges, the nodes on the loop cannot be merged; that is, the description corresponding to the graph is inconsistent, and no templates will be created from this description. In this example, the nodes C and E are on a loop in graph #2 in figure 3.11b, and after merging, they become one node in the new graph, as shown in graph #3 in figure

Input: a description ϕ
Output: $TreeSet_m$ (i.e., $TreeSet_{min}(\phi)$)
Notation: $\lhd$ and $\lhd^*$ denote *parent* and *dominance* relations, respectively.
Algorithm: void GenTreesEff(ϕ, $TreeSet_m$)

// a description $\phi \Rightarrow$ a new description $\hat{\phi}$
(A) build a $\hat{\phi}$ which satisfies the following two conditions:
   (1) $TreeSet(\phi) = TreeSet(\hat{\phi})$, and
   (2) $\hat{\phi}$ is in the disjunctive normal form and does not use
     negation connectives; that is, $\hat{\phi} = \hat{\phi}_1 \vee ... \vee \hat{\phi}_m$,
     where $\hat{\phi}_i = \psi_{i_1} \wedge \psi_{i_2}... \wedge \psi_{i_n}$ and ψ_{i_j} is a literal.

// a description $\hat{\phi} \Rightarrow$ a set of trees TC
(B) $TC = \{\}$;
(C) for (each $\hat{\phi}_i$)
   // a description $\hat{\phi}_i \Rightarrow$ a graph G_i
   (C1) draw a directed graph G_i. In G_i, there is a dashed edge
      (a solid edge, resp.) from the node x to y *iff*
      one of the literals in $\hat{\phi}_i$ is $x \lhd^* y$ ($x \lhd y$, resp.).
   (C2) store with the graph the *left-of* information that appears in $\hat{\phi}_i$.

   // a graph $G_i \Rightarrow$ a tree set TC_i
   (C3) if (G_i has cycles)
     then if (the set of nodes on each cycle are compatible)
       then merge the nodes;
       else $TC_i = \{\}$; continue;
   (C4) merge the nodes in G_i until it does not have any compatible set;
      (this step may produce more than one new graph)
   (C5) for (each new G_i)
     build a set of trees TC_i such that each tree
      includes all the edges in G_i and
      satisfies the *left-of* information;
     $TC = TC \bigcup TC_i$;

// a set of trees $TC \Rightarrow$ a set of minimal trees $TreeSet_m$
(D) $a = min_{tr \in TC} NumNodes(tr)$;
(E) $TreeSet_m = \{tr \mid tr \in TC$ and $NumNodes(tr) = a\}$;

TABLE 3.1 A more efficient algorithm for building $TreeSet_{min}(\phi)$

#1: $(A \lhd^* B) \wedge (A \lhd^* C) \wedge (C \lhd D) \wedge (C \lhd^* E)$
$\wedge (E \lhd^* C) \wedge (E \lhd F) \wedge (G \lhd H) \wedge (B \prec E)$
$\wedge (A.cat = \ 'a') \wedge (B.cat = \ 'b') \wedge (C.cat = \ 'c') \wedge (D.cat = \ 'd')$
$(F.cat = \ 'b') \wedge (G.cat = \ 'b') \wedge (H.cat = \ '\epsilon')$

(a) a description

#2:

Left-of information: $B \prec E$

(b) a graph built from the description

#3:

Left-of information: $B \prec C, E$

(c) the graph after cycles are removed

#4:

Left-of information: $B, G \prec C, E$

#5:

Left-of information: $B \prec C, E$

(d) the graphs after compatible sets are merged

#6:

#7:

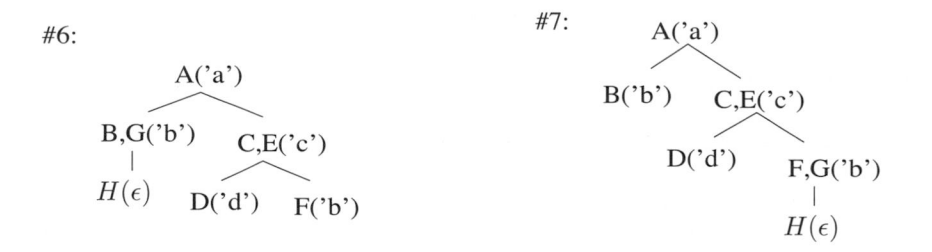

(e) the trees built from the graphs

FIGURE 3.11 An example that illustrates how the new algorithm works: (a) is the original description in logical representation; (b) shows the graph built in steps (C1) and (C2) in table 3.1; (c) shows the graph after step (C3) when cycles are removed; (d) shows two graphs produced in step (C4), in which compatible sets are merged; and (e) shows the trees produced in step (C5).

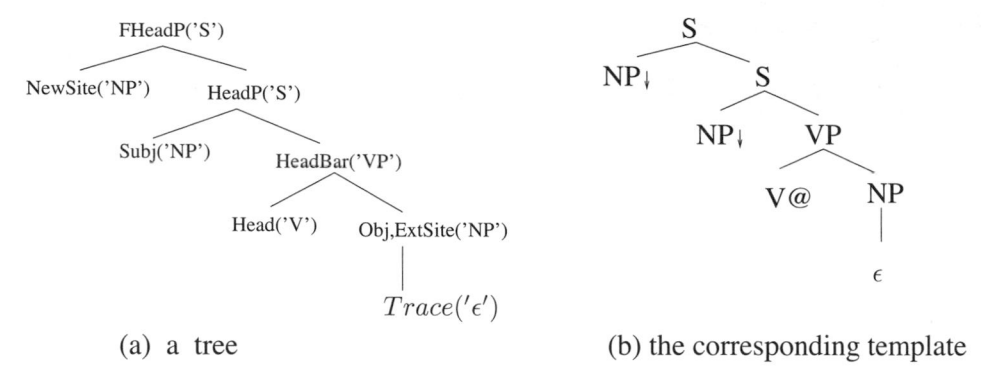

(a) a tree　　　　　　　　　　　　(b) the corresponding template

FIGURE 3.12　A tree and the template built from it

3.11c. In step (C4), TreeGen merges nodes that are compatible. A set of nodes are called *compatible* if the categories of the nodes in the set match and after merging the nodes there is at least one tree that can satisfy the new graph. In graph #3, the nodes G and B are compatible, so are G and F. Merging G and B results in graph #4 in (d), and merging G and F results in graph #5.[10] In step (C5), for each graph produced by step (C4), TreeGen builds a set of trees that satisfy that graph. In this case, step (C4) produces two graphs: #4 and #5. There is only one tree, #6, that satisfies graph #4, and one tree, #7, for graph #5. So the tree set TC after step (C5) contains two trees: #6 and #7. Notice that without the *left-of* information, the node B in graph #4 could be C's sibling, parent, or child. But with the *left-of* information, B has to be C's left sibling. In steps (D) and (E), TreeGen produces the final result $TreeSet_m$, which contains only the trees in TC that have the minimal number of nodes. In our example, the two trees in TC have the same number of nodes, so both are kept in the final result $TreeSet_m$.

3.4.3　Step 3: Building templates from the trees

In this step, TreeGen builds a unique template from each tree produced by the previous step. Recall that a node in a tree has the form $\{k_i\}(\{f_m = v_m\})$, where $\{k_i\}$ is a list of node names, and f_m is a feature and v_m is the feature value. In this step, LexOrg simply replaces $\{k_i\}(\{f_m = v_n\})$ with $l(\{f_m = v_m\})$, where l is the category of k_i (i.e., l is the value of $k_i.cat$). For a leaf node, if its type (i.e., anchor node, substitution node or foot node) is not specified by features, TreeGen determines its type by the following convention: if the leaf node is a head (an argument, a modifiee, respectively), it is marked as an anchor node (a substitution node, a foot node, respectively). Figure 3.6 (repeated as figure 3.12) shows a tree and the template built from the tree.

3.5 The Description Selector

In the previous section, we showed that the Tree Generator builds templates from a set of descriptions. The set of descriptions used by the Tree Generator is only a subset of descriptions provided by the user. The function of the second component of LexOrg, the *Description Selector*, is to choose the descriptions for the Tree Generator; to be more specific, it takes as input a subcategorization frame and the set of descriptions provided by the user, and produces sets of descriptions, which are then fed to the Tree Generator. This process, illustrated in figure 3.13, is described below.

3.5.1 The definition of a *subcategorization frame*

A subcategorization frame specifies the categories of a head and its arguments, the positions of arguments with respect to the head, and other information such as feature equations. While our definition of a *subcategorization frame* is essentially the same as the one commonly used in the literature, we can also interpret a subcategorization frame as a subcategorization description.[11] For instance, the subcategorization frame $(NP_0 \ V \ NP_1)$ can be seen as the shorthand version of the description

$$(leftarg \prec head) \wedge (head \prec rightarg) \wedge (leftarg.cat = \ 'NP') \wedge (head.cat = \ 'V')$$

$$\wedge(rightarg.cat = \ 'NP') \wedge (leftarg.subscript = 0) \wedge (rightarg.subscript = 1)$$

This interpretation allows LexOrg to treat a subcategorization frame the same way as other descriptions, as will be shown next.

3.5.2 The algorithm for the Description Selector

Recall that descriptions are divided into four classes: the ones for head-projection relations, head-argument relations, modification relations and syntactic variations. The first two classes (e.g., D_1, D_2 and D_3 in figure 3.13) are also called *subcategorization* descriptions since they specify structures for a particular subcategorization frame. Because the templates in a tree family have the same subcategorization frame, the Description Selector should put in every description set SD_i all the subcategorization descriptions for that subcategorization frame. In addition to subcategorization information, in its choice of including other descriptions, the Description Selector's guiding principle is to capture the fact that elementary trees in an LTAG grammar reflect zero or more syntactic variations, and zero or one modification relations. Therefore, each description set built by the Description Selector should include all the related subcategorization descriptions, zero or more syntactic variation descriptions, and zero or one modification descriptions.

The algorithm is quite straightforward: given a subcategorization frame Fr, a set *Subcat* of subcategorization descriptions, a set *Synvar* of syntactic variation descriptions, and a set *Mod* of modification descriptions, the Description Selector's

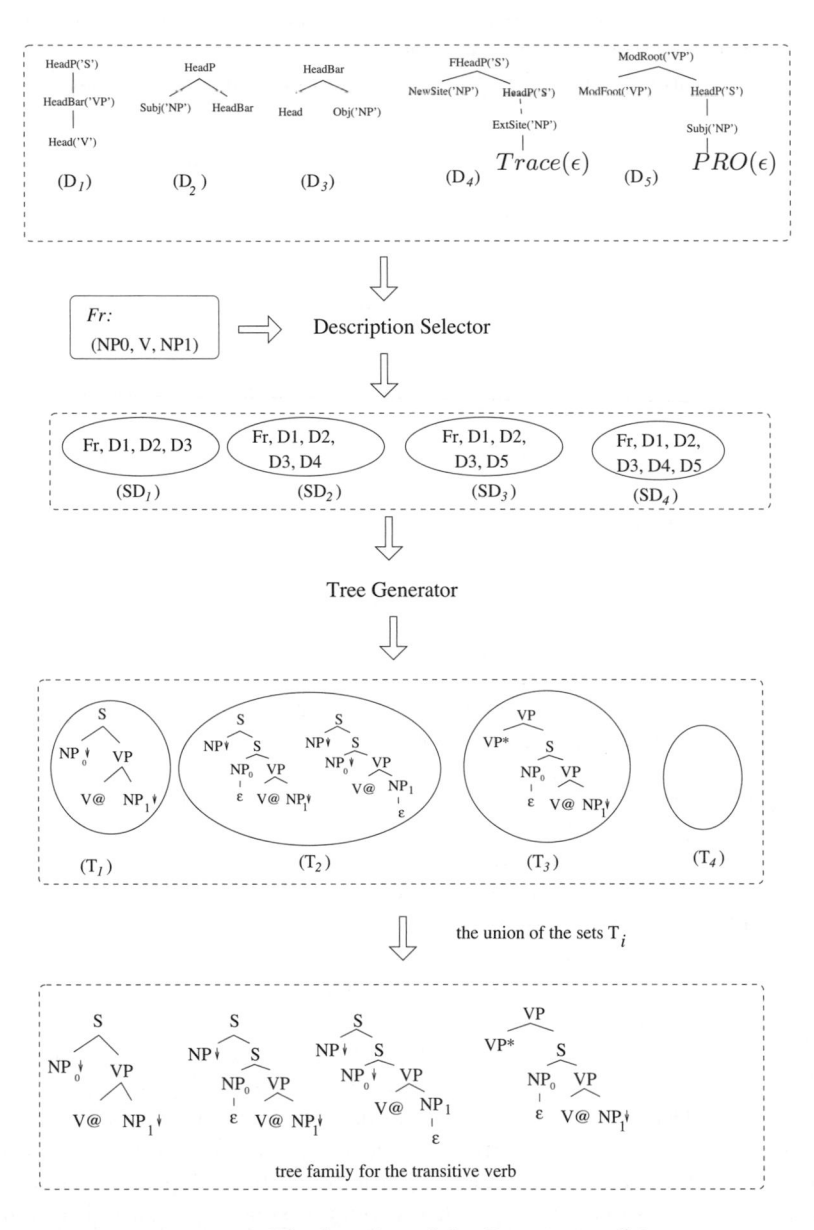

FIGURE 3.13 The function of the Description Selector

first responsibility is to select a subset $Subcat_1$ of $Subcat$ according to the arguments and category information mentioned in Fr. For instance, if Fr is $(NP_0 \ V \ NP_1)$, $Subcat_1$ will include descriptions such as $head\_is\_V$, $head\_has\_a\_left\_NP\_arg$, $head\_has\_a\_right\_NP\_arg$ and so on. As noted earlier, these descriptions need not be atomic and could be instantiations of more basic descriptions. Next, for each subset $Synvar'$ of $Synvar$ and each member m' of Mod, the Description Selector creates a set SD_i, which is $Subcat_1 \cup Synvar' \cup \{Fr\}$, and another set SD_i', which is $SD_i \cup \{m'\}$.[12] This process is illustrated in figure 3.13. In this example, $Subcat$ is $\{D_1, D_2, D_3\}$, $Synvar$ is $\{D_4\}$, and Mod is $\{D_5\}$. Given the subcategorization frame Fr, which is $(NP_0 \ V \ NP_1)$, the Description Selector first chooses a subset $Subcat_1$ of $Subcat$, which happens to be the same as $Subcat$ in this case; it then creates multiple descriptions sets, each set including $Subcat_1$ and a subset of $Synvar$. Some description sets also include a member of Mod. As a result, the Description Selector produces four description sets for Fr: SD_1, SD_2, SD_3, and SD_4. Each SD_i is sent to the Tree Generator to generate a tree set T_i. Each T_i has zero or more trees. For instance, T_2 has two trees, whereas T_4 is empty because the descriptions in SD_4 (i.e., D_4 and D_5) are incompatible. The union of the T_is forms a tree family.

Notice the Description Selector considers different combinations of the descriptions that define the principles underlying the grammar design. The TreeGen produces the trees that are defined by the combinations of these principles when the combinations lead to consistent descriptions. Thus, these two components of LexOrg together take away from the LTAG grammar designer the burden of considering which set of principles are compatible with each other and which lead to inconsistencies. Thereby, the grammar designer can now focus on stating the individual linguistic principles, while the system automatically oversees the ramifications of these principles with respect to the details of the grammar.

3.6 The Frame Generator

In an LTAG grammar, each word anchors one or more elementary trees. Figure 3.1 (repeated as figure 3.14) shows seven templates anchored by ergative verbs such as *break*. The templates belong to two tree families because the subcategorization frames for them are different, but there is a clear connection between these two subcategorization frames, and all the ergative verbs (such as *break*, *sink*, and *melt*) have both frames. Levin (1993) listed several dozen alternations and classified English verbs according to alternations that they participate in. In LexOrg, we use lexical subcategorization rules to link related subcategorization frames.[13] Figure 3.15 shows the lexical subcategorization rule that links the two subcategorization frames in the causative/inchoative alternation. The function of the third component of LexOrg, the Frame Generator, is to apply lexical subcategorization rules to a subcategorization frame and generate all the related frames.

Transitive verbs: (NP0 V NP1)

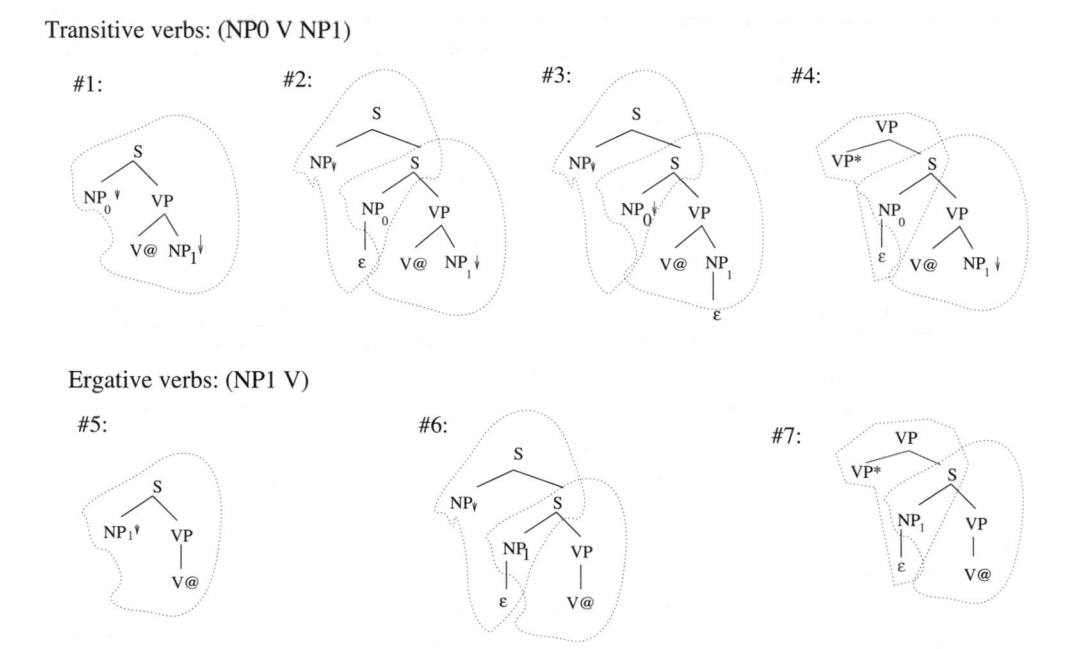

Ergative verbs: (NP1 V)

FIGURE 3.14 Templates in two tree families

$$(NP0 \; V \; NP1) => (NP1 \; V)$$

FIGURE 3.15 The lexical subcategorization rule for the causative/inchoative alternation

3.6.1 The definition of a *lexical subcategorization rule*

A lexical subcategorization rule is of the form $fr_1 \Rightarrow fr_2$, where fr_1 and fr_2 are just like subcategorization frames except that the categories of the nodes in fr_1 and fr_2 can be unspecified, in which case we will use a special label, *XP*, to represent an unspecified category. A lexical subcategorization rule $fr_1 \Rightarrow fr_2$ is said to be *applicable* to a subcategorization frame fr if fr and fr_1 are compatible; that is, fr and fr_1 have the same number of arguments and the features of the corresponding nodes can be unified.[14] Applying this rule to fr yields a new frame that combines the information in fr and fr_2. For instance, the lexical subcategorization rule $(XP\ V\ S) \Rightarrow (XP\ V\ NP)$ says that if a verb can take an S object, it can also take an *NP* object. Applying this rule to the frame $(NP_0\ V\ S_1)$ generates a new frame $(NP_0\ V\ NP)$. In this new frame, the category of the subject comes from the input frame, where the category of the object comes from the right frame of the lexical subcategorization rule. Because the category of the subject in the lexical subcategorization rule is not specified as indicated by the use of the label *XP*, the rule is also applicable to the frame $(S_0\ V\ S_1)$.

In addition to categories, the nodes in a lexical subcategorization rule may include other features. For instance, a lexical subcategorization rule for passivization is similar to the one in figure 3.15 but the feature *voice* will have the value *'active'* for the verb in the left frame, and have the value *'passive'* for the same verb in the right frame. This feature will prevent the rule from being applied to a subcategorization frame in which the verb is already in the passive voice, such as *given* in *John is given a book*.

Lexical subcategorization rules and syntactic variation descriptions are very different in several aspects. First, a lexical subcategorization rule is a function that takes a subcategorization frame as input, and produces another frame as output; a syntactic variation description is a well-formed formula in a simplified first-order logic. Second, lexical subcategorization rules are more idiosyncratic than syntactic variations. For instance, the lexical subcategorization rule in figure 3.15 is only applicable to ergative verbs, rather than to all the transitive verbs. In contrast, the description for wh-movement applies to all the verbs. Third, when lexical subcategorization rules are applied to a subcategorization frame in a series, the order of the rules matters. In contrast, if a set of descriptions includes more than one syntactic variation description (e.g., the descriptions for topicalization and argument drop in Chinese), the order between the descriptions does not matter. Last, lexical subcategorization rules can be non-additive, allowing arguments to be removed; descriptions are strictly additive, meaning that a description can only add information and it cannot remove information. Notice that LexOrg does not place any constraint on which aspect of the grammar must be specified using lexical subcategorization rules or syntactic variation descriptions, and a grammar designer might even choose to use only one of these devices. However, because we believe that they can serve different purposes and we also like to provide flexibility to the grammar designer, both of these methods of grammar specification are available in LexOrg.

3.6.2   The algorithm for the Frame Generator

The Frame Generator takes a subcategorization frame Fr and a set of lexical subcategorization rules $Rules$ as input and produces as output a set $FrSet$ of related frames. The algorithm is in table 3.2: Initially, $FrSet$ contains only one frame, Fr; the Frame Generator then applies each rule in $Rules$ to each frame in $FrSet$, and appends the resulting new frames to $FrSet$.

Input: a subcategorization frame Fr and a set of lexical subcategorization rules $Rules$
Output: a list of related frames $FrSet$
Algorithm: void GenFrames(Fr, $Rules$, $FrSet$)

(A) let $FrSet$ contain only the frame Fr
(B) for each frame f in $FrSet$
        for each lexical subcategorization rule r in $Rules$
            if r is applicable to f
                let f' be the new frame as r is applied to f
                if f' is not in $FrSet$
                    append f' to $FrSet$

TABLE 3.2 The algorithm for generating related subcategorization frames

In this process, the Frame Generator may first apply a rule r_1 to a frame f_1 and generate a new frame f_2 (which is added to $FrSet$); it may later apply another rule, r_2, to f_2 which generates f_3; and the process continucs. When that happens, we say that a sequence $[r_1, r_2, ..., r_n]$ of lexical subcategorization rules is applied to the frame f_1. The order of the rules in such a sequence is important. For example, a passivization rule is applicable after the dative shift rule is applied to the subcategorization frame for ditransitive verbs, but the dative shift rule is not applicable after a passivization rule is applied to the same frame. Rather than placing the burden of determining the order of applicability of the rules on the grammar designer, the system automatically tries all possible orders but will only succeed in producing the frames for ones with the correct ordering. Also, the set of possible sequences of lexical subcategorization rules is finite because the set of distinct lexical subcategorization rules is finite and in general each lexical subcategorization rule appears in a sequence at most once.[15] Therefore, the algorithm in table 3.2 will always terminate.

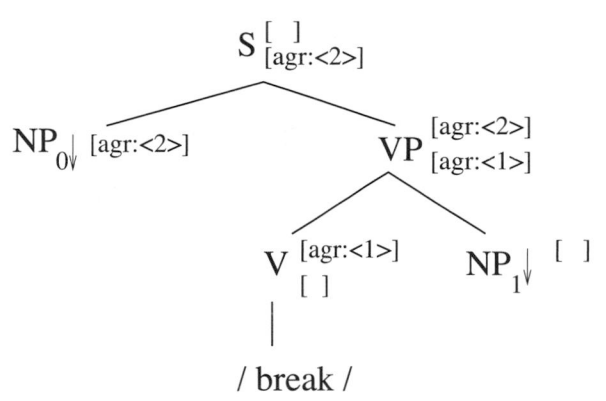

FIGURE 3.16 An elementary tree for the verb *break*

3.7   Creating abstract specifications

In previous sections, we have described the three components of LexOrg: the Tree Generator, the Description Selector, and the Frame Generator. To generate a grammar, the users of LexOrg need to provide three types of abstract specifications: subcategorization frames, lexical subcategorization rules, and tree descriptions. A natural question arises: *how does a user create such information?* In this section we briefly discuss our approach to this question.

Before we get into the details, let us first emphasize one point. Any large-scale grammar development requires a thorough study of various linguistic phenomena in the language to decide how these phenomena should be represented in the grammar, no matter whether or not tools such as LexOrg are used. The advantage of using LexOrg is that LexOrg not only *allows* but actually *requires* grammar designers to state linguistic principles and generalization at the appropriate level; that is, LexOrg forces grammar designers to state the underlying linguistic principles explicitly. For instance, figure 3.16 contains two feature equations, as indicated as the coindexes $< 1 >$ and $< 2 >$. The same equations appear in hundreds of tree templates in the XTAG grammar. If templates are created by hand, grammar designers have to consider for each template whether such equations should be included, and there is nothing to ensure that this process is done consistently. In contrast, if LexOrg is used to generate templates, grammar designers need to decide which abstract specifications such feature equations should belong to. Once the equations are added to appropriate specifications,[16] LexOrg will ensure that they are propagated to all relevant templates.

3.7.1 Subcategorization frames and lexical subcategorization rules

Only a limited number of categories (such as verbs and prepositions) take arguments and therefore have nontrivial subcategorization frames and lexical subcategorization rules. By *nontrivial*, we refer to subcategorization frames with at least one argument. Among these categories, verbs are the most complicated ones. To create subcategorization frames and lexical subcategorization rules for verbs, we studied the literature on verb classes such as Levin (1993) which discusses alternations and classifies verbs according to the alternations that the verbs can undergo.

An alternation describes a change in the realization of the argument structure of a verb, and is illustrated by a pair of sentences in which a verb can appear. For instance, the spray/load alternation is illustrated by these two sentences *"Jack sprayed paint on the wall "* and *"Jack sprayed the wall with paint."* For each alternation, if all the dependents of the verb involved in the alternation are arguments of the verb, then each sentence in the sentence pair is abstracted into a subcategorization frame, and the alternation is represented as a lexical subcategorization rule. As the goal of the current experiment was to use LexOrg to create a grammar similar to the XTAG grammar, and the XTAG grammar has a very strict definition of arguments, only a few alternations (such as the causative alternation, the dative shift alternation, and the passive alternation) fall into this category and they are represented as lexical subcategorization rules.[17]

3.7.2 Tree descriptions

To create the first three classes of descriptions (namely, head-projection descriptions, head-argument descriptions, and modification descriptions), we adopt the following approach: in a head-projection description, the head and its projections form a chain, and the categories of the head and its projection are specified; in a head-argument description, the categories of the head and its argument are specified, as well as the positions of the arguments with respect to the head; in a modification description, the categories of the modifiee, the modifier and the head of the modifier are supplied, as well as the position of the modifier with respect to the modifiee.

To build a transformation variation description, we start with the definition of the corresponding phenomenon, which is language-independent. For example, *relative clause* can be roughly defined as *an NP is modified by a clause in which one constituent is extracted (or co-indexed with an operator)*. We build a tree description (for clarity, we will call it *metablock*) according to the definition. Notice that the exact shape of the metablock often depends on the theory. For example, both metablocks in figure 3.17 are consistent with the definition of relative clause, the former follows the way that the Penn XTAG group treats the complementizer(COMP) as an adjunct, the latter follows more closely to the GB theory where COMP is the functional head of CP.

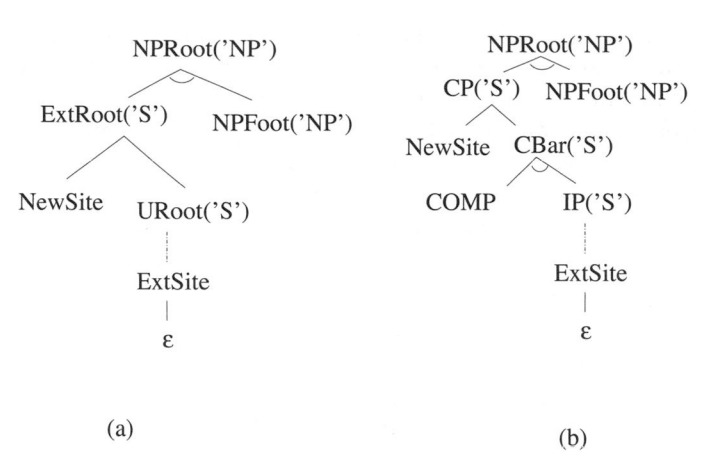

FIGURE 3.17 The possible metablocks for relative clause

	English	Portuguese	Chinese	Korean
position of NPFoot?	left	left	right	right
overt wh-movement?	yes	yes	no	no
has overt RelPron?	yes	yes	no	no
RelPron can be dropped?	yes*	yes*	-	-
position of COMP?	left	left	right	suffix
COMP can be dropped?	yes*	yes*	yes*	no
COMP and RelPron co-occurs?	no	no	-	-
COMP and RelPron both be dropped?	yes*	no	-	-

TABLE 3.3 Settings for relative clauses in four languages

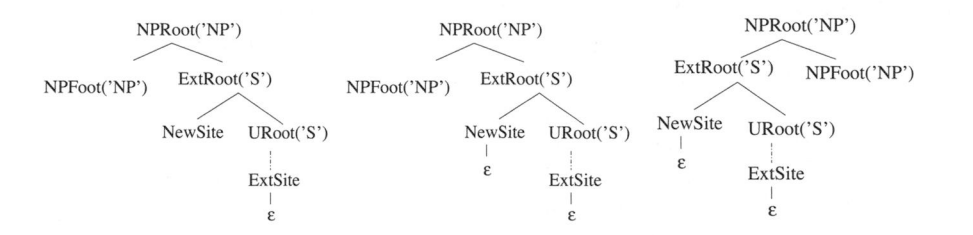

(a) English and Portuguese   (b) English and Portuguese   (c) Chinese and Korean
   with Relative Pronoun   without Relative Pronoun

FIGURE 3.18 The transformation variation descriptions for relative clauses in four
languages

The metablocks must be general enough to be language-independent; therefore, certain relations in metablocks are are not fully specified. For instance, the order between the noun phrase and the relative clause in figure 3.17 is unspecified. To generate transformation variation descriptions for a particular language, metablocks have to be combined with language-specific information. We can elicit language-specific information by asking native speakers questions that are derived from the underspecification in metablocks.

For example, figure 3.17 shows the possible metablocks for relative clauses. Table 3.3 lists the questions about those metablocks and the answers for four languages. In a relative clause, a relative pronoun(RelPron) occupies the position marked by NewSite. If we choose the metablock in 3.17a, the top four questions should be asked, and the corresponding transformation variation descriptions are shown in figure 3.18.[18] If we choose the metablock in 3.17b, all the eight questions are relevant.

Several points are worth noting. First, the setting of some parameters follows from higher-level generalizations and some pairs of parameters are related. For example, the position of NPFoot follows from the head position in that language. Korean is an SOV language, so we can infer the position of the NPFoot without asking native speakers. Second, the setting of the parameters provides a way of measuring the similarities between the languages. According to the settings, Chinese is more similar to Korean than to English.

A word of caution is also in order. Both the construction of the metablock and the correct answers to the questions require some degree of linguistic expertise. Also, certain language-specific details cannot be easily expressed as yes-no questions. For example, the asterisk-marked answers in table 3.3 mean that they are true only under certain conditions; for instance, in English, COMP and RelPron can be both dropped only when the relativized NP is not the subject.

3.8   The Experiments

To test our implementation of LexOrg, we created two sets of abstract specifications (one for English and the other for Chinese) as discussed in the previous chapter. We chose English because we wanted to compare our automatically generated grammar with the XTAG grammar, and we chose Chinese because one of the authors was very familiar with literature on Chinese linguistics which greatly facilitated the creation of the set of abstract specifications for Chinese. These languages also come from two very different language families, offering interesting points of comparison and a test of LexOrg's language independence.

At that time, the XTAG grammar contained about one thousand elementary trees. Among them, about 700 trees were anchored by verbs. Because verbs have nontrivial subcategorization frames and lexical subcategorization rules, the goal of our experiment was to use LexOrg to "*reproduce*" this subset of trees with as little effort as possible. Given a preexisting grammar where the related linguistic phenomena had been well-studied, as in the English XTAG, creating a new version with LexOrg was quite straightforward, and required no more than a few weeks

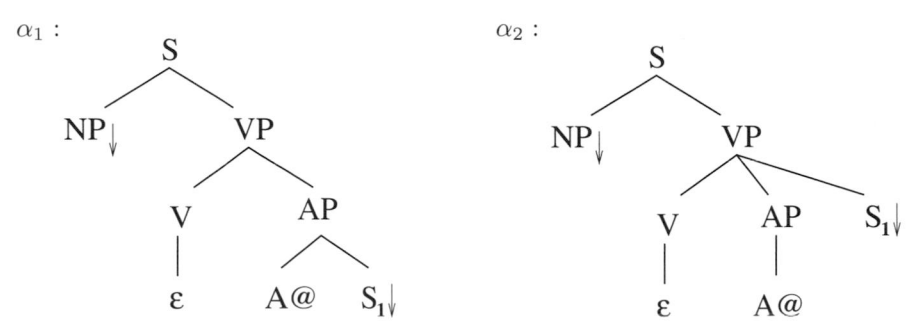

FIGURE 3.19 Two elementary trees for adjectives with sentential arguments

of effort. A tree-by-tree comparison of this new grammar and the original XTAG grammar allowed us to discover gaps in the XTAG grammar that needed to be investigated. The types of gaps included missing subcategorization frames that were created by LexOrg's Frame Generator and which would correspond to an entire tree family, a missing tree which would represent a particular type of syntactic variation for a subcategorization frame, or missing features in some elementary trees. Based on the results of this comparison, the English XTAG was extensively revised and extended.

The experiment also revealed that some elementary trees were easier to generate with LexOrg than other elementary trees. Figure 3.19 shows two elementary trees where an adjective such as *glad* takes a sentential argument. They differ in the positions of the S_1 node: in α_1 the S_1 node is a sister of the A node, but in α_2 it is a sister of the AP node. As both trees can handle a sentence such as *Mary was glad that John came to the party*, it is difficult to choose one tree over the other according to the set of sentences that each tree accepts. While it is equally easy to draw these two trees by hand, α_1 would be preferred over α_2 if LexOrg is used to generate a grammar. This is because the head-argument description in figure 3.20, which is used to generate all the elementary trees anchored by transitive verbs or prepositions, can also be used to generate α_1. In contrast, the elementary tree α_2 would require a different head-argument description. Because our grammar includes the transitive verb family and one of the trees in figure 3.19, choosing α_1 over α_2 will require a smaller set of descriptions. This example illustrates another advantage of using LexOrg besides the ease of creating and maintaining a grammar: the users of LexOrg are encouraged to create elegant, consistent, well-motivated grammars by defining structures that are shared across elementary trees and tree families.

In addition to English, we also used LexOrg to generate a medium-size grammar for Chinese. The Chinese grammar, although smaller than the English grammar, required several person-months, since many of the linguistic principles had to be defined along the way before the structures could be generated. Note that most of the time invested for the Chinese grammar was in linguistic analysis which would be applicable to any style of grammar, rather than in structure generation. In designing

Fei Xia, Martha Palmer, and K. Vijay-Shanker

HeadBar

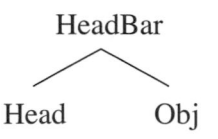

Head   Obj

FIGURE 3.20 A head-argument description

these two grammars, we have tried to specify grammars that reflect the similarities and the differences between the languages.

	English	Chinese
subcategorization frames	(NP, V, NP) (NP, V, NP, NP, S)	(NP, V, NP) (V)
lexical subcategorization rules	passive without by-phrase dative-shift	short *bei*-const *ba*-const
head-projection descriptions	S_has_V_head S_has_P_head	S_has_V_head
head-argument descriptions	V_has_NP_right_arg V_has_3_right_arg	V_has_NP_right_arg V_has_PP_left_arg
modification descriptions	NP_modify_NP_from_left S_modify_NP_from_right	NP_modify_NP_from_left S_modify_NP_from_left
syntactic variation descriptions	wh-question gerund etc	topicalization arg-drop etc.
# subcategorization frames	43	23
# lexical subcategorization rules	6	12
# descriptions	42	39
# templates	638	280

TABLE 3.4 Major features of English and Chinese grammars

To illustrate the similarities and differences between these two languages, for each language we give two examples for each type of abstract specification in table 3.4: the first example has similar content in the two languages, while the second example appears in only one language. For example, the lexical subcategorization rule for passive without the by-phrase in English is very similar to the rule for the short bei-construction in Chinese, whereas the rule for dative-shift appears only in English, and the rule for the ba-construction appears only in Chinese. Similarly, both languages have wh-movement (topicalization in Chinese), but only English has a gerund form and only Chinese allows argument drop, as indicated by the row for syntactic variation descriptions. The bottom part of the table shows that with a small set of specifications, a fairly large number of templates were produced; and in the case of the English grammar, we were able to specify a grammar with a coverage comparable to that of the then current version of XTAG: LexOrg's English grammar covered more than 90% of the templates for verbs that were found in XTAG.[19] To maintain the grammars, only these specifications need to be modified, and all the elementary trees will be updated automatically.

We are encouraged by the utility of our tool and the ease with which both English and Chinese grammars were developed. We believe that, beginning with a preexisting linguistic analysis and grammar design experience, a prototype grammar for a new language can be easily and rapidly developed in a few weeks. Furthermore, we see this approach as much more than just an engineering tool. Provably consistent abstract specifications for different languages offer unique opportunities to investigate how languages relate to themselves and to each other. For instance, the impact of a linguistic structure such as wh-movement can be traced from its specification to the descriptions that it combines with, to its actual realization in trees.

3.9   Comparison with Other Work

Systems such as Becker's HyTAG system (Becker, 1994), the one by Evans, Gazdar and Weir (1995) implemented in DATR (Evans and Gazdar, 1989), and Candito's system (Candito, 1996) have all been based on the same observation that motivated LexOrg; namely that the templates in an LTAG grammar are related to one another and could be organized in a compact way for efficient development and maintenance. This section briefly compares LexOrg to these other systems.[20]

In a lexical hierarchy, a class inherits attributes from its superclasses as illustrated by figure 3.21. (For a detailed example of a verb subcategorization frame hierarchy adhering to strict inheritance properties, see Copestake and Sanfilippo (1993) and Briscoe et al. (1994).) Although the hierarchy seems intuitive, it is difficult to build manually. Grammar designers first have to decide between a true hieararchy and a network. If a network is chosen, then conflicts between multiple superclasses must be resolved. The individual nodes also all need to be explicitly defined. For instance, could the nodes in figure 3.21 for *TRANSITIVE, SIMPLE-TRANS*, and *NP-IOBJ* be merged, or do they need to be distinct?

One major difference between LexOrg and the other three approaches is that LexOrg does not depend on a predefined hierarchy. The inheritance relations between tree families are implicit. For instance, the description set selected by LexOrg for the ditransitive verb family is a superset of the descriptions selected for the transitive verb family. Therefore, the ditransitive family implicitly "inherits" all the information from the transitive family without needing to refer directly to an explicit hierarchy or to the transitive family. [21]

3.9.1   Becker's HyTAG

A *metarule* in general consists of an input pattern and an output pattern. When the input pattern matches an elementary structure in a grammar, the application

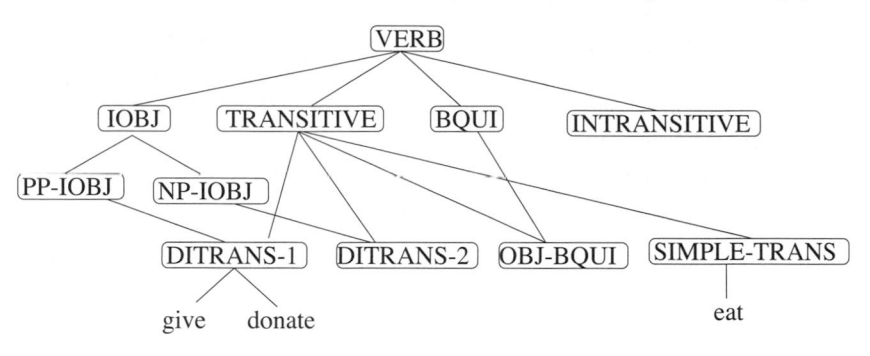

FIGURE 3.21 The lexical hierarchy given in Vijay-Shanker and Schabes (1992)

of the metarule to the structure creates a new elementary structure. Metarules were first introduced in Generalized Phrase Structure Grammar (GPSG) (Gazdar et al., 1985). Later, Becker modified the definition of metarules in order to use them for LTAG in his HyTAG system (Becker, 1994). In addition to metarules, Becker's HyTAG system also uses a handcrafted inheritance hierarchy such as the one just discussed.

In HyTAG, the input-pattern and the output-pattern of a metarule are elementary trees with the exception that any node may be a metavariable. A *metavariable* describes part of a template that is not affected if the metarule is applied. If a template matches the input-pattern, the application of the metarule creates a new template which could be added to the grammar.

A major difference between HyTAG and LexOrg is that HyTAG uses metarules to describe both lexical and syntactic rules, whereas LexOrg uses two mechanisms: lexical subcategorization rules and descriptions. Aside from the linguistic debate that argues for different treatments of lexical and syntactic rules, using different mechanisms results in LexOrg having a small number of lexical subcategorization rules which are simpler than metarules because they do not contain metavariables. This makes it easier to ensure the termination of the application process. It also allows for more modular encoding of constraints such as feature agreements.

3.9.2 The DATR system

Evans, Gazdar and Weir (1995) discuss a method for organizing the trees in a TAG hierarchically, using an existing lexical knowledge representation language called DATR (Evans and Gazdar, 1989). In the DATR system, an elementary tree is described from its lexical anchor upwards as a feature structure using three tree relations: the left, right, and parent relations. Like HyTAG, the DATR system uses an inheritance hierarchy to relate verb classes. For instance, the *VERB+NP* class inherits the structure from the *VERB* class and adds a right *NP* complement as the sister of the anchor.

The system uses lexical rules to capture the relationships between elementary trees. A lexical rule defines a derived output tree structure in terms of an input tree structure. Since the lexical rules in this system relate elementary trees rather than subcategorization frames, they are more similar to metarules in HyTAG than to lexical subcategorization rules in LexOrg. In addition to topicalization and wh-movement, lexical rules in the DATR system are also used for passive, dative-shift, subject-auxiliary inversion, and relative clauses. In the passive rules, instead of stating that the first object of the input tree is the subject of the output tree, the lexical rule simply discards the object. As a result, the relationship between the object in an active sentence and the subject in the corresponding passivized sentence is lost.

Similarly to HyTAG, the DATR system requires a hand-crafted hierarchy and does not distinguish between syntactic rules and lexical rules, in contrast with LexOrg which can generate its hierarchy automatically and which clearly separates syntactic rules and lexical subcategorization rules. There are two other major differences: (1) the descriptions used by LexOrg are constrained to be strictly monotonic, whereas the DATR system allows nonmonotonicity in its application of rules; (2) the DATR system can capture only direct relations between nodes in a tree (such as the parent-child relationship or precedence), and must use feature-equations to simulate other tree relations (such as dominance relation). This means that in their system, an abstract concept such as dominance must be specified by spelling out explicitly all of the different possible path lengths for every possible dominance relationship.

3.9.3 Candito's system

Like LexOrg, Candito's system (Candito, 1996) is built upon the basic ideas expressed in Vijay-Shanker and Schabes (1992) for the use of descriptions to encode tree structures shared by several elementary trees. Her system uses a handwritten hierarchy that has three dimensions. In the first dimension, canonical subcategorization frames are put into a hierarchy similar to the ones in HyTAG and the DATR system. The second dimension includes all possible redistributions of syntactic functions. The third dimension lists syntactic realizations of the functions. It expresses the way that the different syntactic functions are positioned at the phrase-structure level. The definitions of classes in these dimensions include descriptions and meta-equations.

A *terminal* class is formed in two steps. First, it inherits a canonical subcategorization from dimension 1 and a compatible redistribution from dimension 2. This pair of superclasses defines an actual subcategorization frame. Second, the terminal class inherits exactly one type of realization for each function of the actual subcategorization from dimension 3. A terminal class is actually a description. Elementary trees are the minimal trees that satisfy the description. For instance, a terminal class inherits the ditransitive frame (NP_0 V NP_1 NP_2) from dimension 1 and the passive redistribution from dimension 2; this yields the actual subcategorization frame (NP_1 V NP_2). It then inherits *subject-in-wh-question* and *object-in-canonical-position* realizations from dimension 3. The resulting elementary tree is anchored by a passivized ditransitive verb whose surface subject (i.e., the indirect object in the active voice) undergoes wh-movement, such as *given* in *who was given a book?*

A terminal class inherits one class from dimension 1, one from dimension 2, and one or more from dimension 3. These superclasses may be incompatible. To ensure that all the superclasses of a terminal class are compatible, the system provides several ways for its users to explicitly express compatibility constraints.

These are not needed in LexOrg, which automatically ensures that illegal combinations are ruled out.

There are many similarities between Candito's system and LexOrg as both use descriptions to encode tree structures shared by several elementary trees, and there is a separation of lexical rules and syntactic rules. There is an obvious parallel between Candito's subcategorization dimension and our subcategorization descriptions, between her redistribution dimension and our lexical subcategorization rules, and between her realization dimension and our syntactic variation/modification descriptions. However, there are also several major differences.

First, Candito's system requires a handwritten hierarchy, whereas LexOrg does not. It also requires that each terminal class should select exactly one class from dimension 2. This means that if two lexical subcategorization rules can be applied in a series (such as passive and causative) to a subcategorization frame, a node that represents that sequence must be manually created and added to dimension 2. In other words, dimension 2 should have a node for every rule sequence that is applicable to some subcategorization frame. LexOrg does not need users to build this dimension manually because the Frame Generator in LexOrg automatically tries all the rule sequences when given a subcategorization frame.

The two systems also differ in the way that syntactic variations are represented. In Candito's third dimension, each argument/function in a subcategorization frame requires an explicit representation for each possible syntactic realization. For example, the subject of a ditransitive verb has a different representation for the canonical position, for wh-extraction, and so on. So do the direct object and indirect object. To generate templates for wh-questions of ditransitive verbs, Candito's system needs to build three separate terminal classes. In contrast, LexOrg does not need descriptions for the various positions that each argument/function can be in. To generate the template for wh-questions, LexOrg only needs one wh-movement description. Combining this description with the set of subcategorization descriptions will yield all the templates for wh-questions.

3.10   Summary

In LTAG, there is a clear distinction made between a grammar and the grammatical principles that go into developing this grammar. Arguments have been made on linguistic and computational grounds that the use of a suitably enlarged domain of locality provided by the elementary trees and the operations of substitutions and adjoining provide many advantages. But it is clear that these elementary trees, especially given that they have an enlarged domain of locality, are themselves not atomic but rather encapsulate several individual independent grammatical principles. Although this fact is widely understood in the LTAG context, most of the large-scale grammar development efforts have directly produced the elementary trees, thereby in essence manually compiling out subsets of independent principles into elementary trees. Of course, as with similar hand-crafted grammars, the larger the grammar, the more prone to errors it becomes, and the harder it is to maintain.

LexOrg is a computational tool that alleviates these problems in grammar design for LTAGs. It takes three types of abstract specifications (i.e., subcategorization frames, lexical subcategorization rules, and descriptions) as input and produces LTAG grammars as output. Descriptions are further divided into four classes according to the information that they provide. In grammar development and maintenance, only the abstract specifications need to be edited, and any changes or corrections will automatically be proliferated throughout the grammar.

Given a preexisting linguistic analysis, a new grammar can be developed with LexOrg in a few weeks, and easily maintained and revised. This provides valuable time savings to grammar designers, but, perhaps even more importantly, the reuse of descriptions encourages a comprehensive and holistic perspective on the grammar development process that highlights linguistic generalizations. The users of LexOrg are encouraged to create elegant, consistent, well-motivated grammars by defining structures that are shared across elementary trees and tree families.

In addition to greatly shortening grammar development time and lightening the more tedious aspects of grammar maintenance, this approach also allows a unique perspective on the general characteristics of a language. The abstract level of representation for the grammar both necessitates and facilitates an examination of the linguistic analyses. The more clearly the grammar designer understands the underlying linguistic generalizations of the language, the simpler it will be to generate a grammar using LexOrg. In using LexOrg to create an English LTAG, we demonstrated that this process is very useful for gaining an overview of the theory that is being implemented and exposing gaps that remain unmotivated and need to be investigated. The type of gaps that can be exposed include a missing subcategorization frame that might arise from the automatic combination of subcategorization descriptions and that would correspond to an entire tree family, a missing tree which would represent a particular type of syntactic variation for a subcategorization frame, and trees with inconsistent feature equations. The comparison of the LexOrg English grammar with the preexisting XTAG grammar led to extensive revisions of XTAG, resulting in a more elegant and more comprehensive grammar. Provably consistent abstract specifications for different languages offer unique opportunities to investigate how languages relate to themselves and to each other. For instance, the impact of a linguistic structure such as wh-movement can be traced from its specification to the descriptions that it combines with, to its actual realization in trees. By focusing on syntactic properties at a higher level, our approach allowed a unique comparison of our English and Chinese grammars.

3.11   Acknowledgments

Joseph Rosenzweig is acknowledged for his original implementation of tree descriptions in Prolog which demonstrated the feasibility of this endeavor. Aravind Joshi has provided continued guidance and support and Marie Candito participated in several lengthy discussions with the authors during her visit to the University of Pennsylvania. This work has been supported by DARPA N66001-00-1-8915, DOD MDA904-97-C-0307, NSF SBR-89-20230-15 and NSF 9800658. A longer version of this chapter was published in the *Journal of Computational Intelligence*, and we would also like to thank the journal and Blackwell Publishing for granting us the permission to include this chapter in the book.

Notes

1. A tree family is a set of elementary trees that have the same subcategorization frame.

2. The XTAG grammar (XTAG-Group, 1998, 2001) is a large-scale LTAG grammar for English, which has been manually created and maintained by a group of linguists and computer scientists at the University of Pennsylvania since the early 1990s.

3. Note we use the term "subcategorization" here to mean what the designer intends to be localized with the lexical head. Lexical items with the same subcategorization frames can thus be understood to share the same tree family.

4. As a user of LexOrg, a grammar designer has the freedom to choose the linguistic theory to be incorporated in an LTAG grammar. In the examples given in this chapter (such as in figure 3.7), we do not strictly follow the X-bar theory or the GB theory. We name some nodes as *HeadBar* and *HeadP* only for the sake of convenience.

5. In the sentence "*John brought a stone to break the window*", the infinitival clause "*to break the window*" modifies the *VP* "*brought a stone.*" One may choose the analysis where the infinitival clause modifies the whole main clause "*John brought a stone*", instead of just the *VP* "*brought a stone.*" To account for this analysis, we only have to change the categories of *ModRoot* and *ModFoot* from *VPs* to *Ss*.

6. Notice that in figure 3.10b the position of *ExtSite* with respect to *Subj* and *HeadBar* is not specified.

7. Recall that the number of possible rooted, ordered trees with n nodes is the $(n-1)^{th}$ Catalan Number, where the nth Catalan Number b_n satisfies the following equation:

$$b_n = \frac{1}{n+1} \times \binom{2n}{n} = \frac{4^n}{\sqrt{\pi} \times n^{3/2}} \times (1 + O(1/n)).$$

As the notion of tree in LexOrg is more complicated than the notion of rooted, ordered trees, the number of $TS(n)$ is much larger than b_{n-1}. Furthermore, most trees in $TS(n)$ do not satisfy ϕ, and therefore are not in $TreeSet_{min}(\phi)$.

8. In first-order logic, two formulas are *equivalent* if any model that satisfies one formula also satisfies the other formula and vice versa. ϕ and $\hat{\phi}$ are not necessarily equivalent because we require only that the sets of *trees* (not *models*) that satisfy these two formulae are identical. Recall that trees are structures with special properties. For instance, given two symbols a and b in a tree, the formula $(a \prec b) \vee (b \prec a) \vee (a \lhd^* b) \vee (b \lhd a)$ is always true; therefore, a rewrite rule that replaces $\neg(a \prec b)$ with $(b \prec a) \vee (a \lhd^* b) \vee (b \lhd a)$ will not change the set of trees that satisfy a formula. The idea of using such rewrite rules originates from Rogers and Vijay-Shanker (1994). However, our goal of applying rewrite rules in this step is to get rid of negative connectives, rather than to find trees that satisfy each $\hat{\phi}_i$. Therefore, we use fewer numbers of rewrite rules and the $\hat{\phi}_i$ created by our algorithm can be inconsistent; that is, it is possible that no trees satisfy $\hat{\phi}_i$.

9. When two nodes x and y are merged, in the graphic representation they become the same node after merging; in the logic representation, let ϕ be the description before the merging, after the merging the new description is $\phi \wedge (x = y)$.

10. A node may appear in more than one compatible set. If a graph has two compatible sets, it is possible that after merging the nodes in one set, the other set is no longer compatible in the new graph. Therefore, if a graph has more than one compatible set, merging these sets in different orders may result in different graphs.

11. A subcategorization frame is different from other descriptions in that it cannot refer to any node other than the head and its arguments. For instance, it cannot refer to the *VP* which is the parent of the verb head. Another difference is that the categories of the nodes in a subcategorization frame must be specified. The reason for these differences is simply because we want to adopt the same definition of subcategorization frame as the one commonly used in the literature; namely, a subcategorization frame specifies the categories of the head and its arguments.

12. The number of description sets produced by the Description Selector is $2^{|Synvar|} \times (| Mod | + 1)$. We can actually reduce this number by not producing some description sets that are obviously unproductive. A description set is *unproductive* if there exists no templates that satisfy all the descriptions in the set; as a result, the Tree Generator will produce nothing when it takes the set as the input. For instance, if in a head-projection description the head is a verb and its highest projection is a clause, the Description Selector will select a modification description only if the modifiee in that description is a clause.

13. In our previous papers on LexOrg, we called these rules *lexical rules*. However, the term *lexical rule* is heavily overloaded. For instance, lexical rules as defined in Evans et al. (1995) can manipulate tree structures. They are used to account for wh-movement, topicalization, and so on. In contrast, the rules in LexOrg can manipulate only subcategorization frames. To avoid the confusion, in this chapter we rename the rules in LexOrg as *lexical subcategorization rules*, following a suggestion from one of the anonymous reviewers.

14. In our current implementation, a lexical subcategorization rule $fr_1 \Rightarrow fr_2$ has to specify the numbers of arguments in fr_1 and fr_2. This requirement will be relaxed in the future to allow a more general version of the passive rule $(NP_0 \ V \ NP_1 \ XP^*) \Rightarrow (NP_1 \ V \ XP^*)$, where * indicates that the argument XP is optional.

15. An arguable exception to this claim is the double causative construction in languages such as Hungarian (Shibatani, 1976). But in this construction it is not clear whether the second causativization is done in morphology or in syntax. Even if it is done at the morphological level, the two causativizations are not exactly the same and they will be represented as two distinct lexical subcategorization rules in LexOrg.

16. In the two sets of specifications that we created for English and Chinese, we added the feature equation $V.t :< agr >= VP.b :< agr >$ to the description in figure 3.7a, and the equation $VP.t :< agr >= NP_0.t :< agr >$ to the one in figure 3.7b.

17. All the other alternations contain some components that are considered to be adjuncts in the XTAG grammar. For instance, in the spray/load alternation, both the *PP* "*on the wall*" in the first sentence and the *PP* "*with paint*" in the second sentence are considered adjuncts in the XTAG grammar. As a result, no lexical subcategorization rule was created for this alternation, and the spray verbs are treated as normal transitive verbs.

18. The descriptions for relative clause in English and Portuguese look the same as in figure 3.18a and 3.18b but they differ in one aspect: when the ExtSite is not the subject, in English, both COMP and NewSite are optional, but in Portuguese, one of them must be present. The difference is captured by features which are not shown in the figure.

19. The remaining 10% of the templates are like α_2 in figure 3.19 in that they require some abstract specifications which do not quite fit with the rest of the grammar. For example, as explained before, α_2 in figure 3.19 would require a head-argument description which is very different from the one used for transitive verbs or prepositions. In order to keep our set of specifications for English elegant and well-motivated, we did not include such specification, although adding such specification will guarantee that the resulting new English grammar would cover all the templates for verbs that were found in XTAG.

20. For more details of these systems and the comparisons, see Xia et al. (2005) or Chapter 4 of Xia (2001).

21. If one wishes to make explicit this implicit inheritance hierarchy, it can be built by adding an inheritance link between every tree family pair that satisfies the following condition: the subcategorization description set selected for one family is a superset of the subcategorization description set selected for the other family.

References

Becker, T. (1994). Patterns in Metarules. In *Proc. of the 3rd International Workshop on TAG and Related Frameworks (TAG+3)*, Paris, France.

Briscoe, E. J., Copestake, A., and de Paiva, V. (1994). *Inheritance, Defaults and the Lexicon*. Cambridge University Press.

Candito, M.-H. (1996). A Principle-Based Hierarchical Representation of LTAGs. In *Proc. of the 16th International Conference on Computational Linguistics (COLING-1996)*, Copenhagen, Denmark.

Chomsky, N. (1981). *Lectures on Government and Binding*. Foris.

Copestake, A. and Sanfilippo, A. (1993). Multilingual Lexical Representation. In *Proc. of the AAAI Spring Symposium: Building Lexicons for Machine Translation*, Stanford, California.

Evans, R. and Gazdar, G. (1989). Inference in DATR. In *Proc. of the 4th Conference of the European Chapter of the Association for Computational Linguistics (EACL-1989)*, Manchester, England.

Evans, R., Gazdar, G., and Weir, D. J. (1995). Encoding Lexicalized Tree Adjoining Grammars with a Nonmonotonic Inheritance Hierarchy. In *Proc. of the 33rd Annual Meeting of the Association for Computational Linguistics (ACL-1995)*, Cambridge, Massachusetts, USA.

Gazdar, G., Klein, E., Pullum, G., and Sag, I. A. (1985). *Generalized Phrase Structure Grammar*. Basil Blackwell.

Jackendoff, R. S. (1977). *X-bar Syntax: A Study of Phrase Structure*. MIT Press.

Levin, B. (1993). *English Verb Classes and Alternations: A Preliminary Investigation*. The University of Chicago Press, Chicago, USA.

Pollard, C. and Sag, I. A. (1994). *Head-Driven Phrase Structure Grammar*. University of Chicago Press.

Rogers, J. and Vijay-Shanker, K. (1994). Obtaining Trees from Their Descriptions: An Application to Tree Adjoining Grammars. *Journal of Computational Intelligence*, 10(4):401–421.

Shibatani, M., ed. (1976). *The Grammar of Causative Constructions*. Academic Press.

Vijay-Shanker, K. and Schabes, Y. (1992). Structure Sharing in Lexicalized Tree Adjoining Grammar. In *Proc. of the 14th International Conference on Computational Linguistics (COLING-1992)*, Nantes, France.

Xia, F. (2001). *Automatic Grammar Generation from Two Different Perspectives*. PhD thesis, University of Pennsylvania.

Xia, F., Palmer, M., and Vijay-Shanker, K. (2005). Automatically Generating Tree Adjoining Grammars from Abstract Specifications. *Computational Intelligence*, 21(3):246–287.

XTAG-Group (1998). A Lexicalized Tree Adjoining Grammar for English. Technical Report IRCS 98-18, University of Pennsylvania.

XTAG-Group (2001). A Lexicalized Tree Adjoining Grammar for English. Technical Report IRCS 01-03, University of Pennsylvania.

Part II

Supertagging and Parsing

Complexity of Parsing for Some Lexicalized Formalisms

GIORGIO SATTA

4.1 Introduction

In the computational linguistic literature, and in the generative linguistic literature as well, it is widely recognized that lexical information plays a central role in determining the properties of syntactic structures. For instance, a lexical predicate usually specifies the number and the syntactic configurations of its arguments, imposing both hard and soft constraints on these elements. Not only are these constraints needed in discriminating between correct and incorrect syntactic analyses, but they also play a fundamental role in natural language processing, when preferences between alternative syntactic analyses of an input sentence must be assessed. In fact, the wide diffusion of lexicalized grammars in the natural language processing community is mainly due to the capability of these formalisms to control syntactic acceptability, when this is sensitive to individual words in the language, and to control word selection, accounting for genuinely lexical factors as well as semantic and world knowledge conditions. More discussion on the role of lexical information in syntactic processing and in generative linguistics is reported in chapters 1 and 16 of this book.

As a consequence of these considerations, much of the natural language processing literature has focused in recent years on so-called lexicalized grammars, that is, grammars in which each individual production or elementary object is specialized for one or more lexical items. Formalisms of this sort include, among others, dependency grammars (Mel'čuk, 1988), combinatorial categorial grammars (Ades and Steedman, 1982; Steedman, 2000), lexicalized tree-adjoining grammars (Schabes et al., 1988), link grammars (Sleator and Temperley, 1993), tree insertion grammars (Schabes and Waters, 1995), head automaton grammars (Alshawi, 1996) and bilexical grammars (Eisner, 1997). So-called probabilistic lexicalized grammars, where productions are associated with probabilities, have also been exploited in state-of-the-art, real-world parsers, as reported for instance in Lafferty et al. (1992), Eisner (1996), Hwa (1998), Charniak (2000), Chiang (2000), Roark (2001), Clark et al. (2002), and Collins (2003). Other parsers or language models for speech recognition that do not directly exploit a generative grammar still are heavily based on lexicalization, as, for instance, the systems presented in Manning and Carpenter (1997), Ratnaparkhi (1997), and Chelba and Jelinek (1998).

Within the parsing community, and in the speech community as well, a considerable research effort has been devoted to the important problem of selecting statistical parameters associated with lexicalized grammars and to the problem of the specification of algorithms for the statistical estimation of these parameters. In contrast, not much has been done with respect to the sentence processing problem for these formalisms. Most of the parsing systems mentioned before process the input strings using naïve adaptations of existing algorithms developed for the unlexicalized version of the adopted formalisms, possibly in combination with heuristics specially tailored to cut down the parsing search space. In this chapter[1] we show how the internal structure and the large size of formalisms derived by means of standard lexicalization mechanisms render these systems unsuitable to be processed by traditional parsing techniques. We also focus on two specific formalisms, that is, lexicalized context-free grammars and lexicalized tree-adjoining grammars, and discuss some more sophisticated parsing algorithms that overcome these computational inefficiencies.

All the algorithms we consider here are based on dynamic programming: this is by far the most widespread paradigm in parsing, and in this context it is also called tabular parsing. In tabular parsing, the input problem is decomposed in every possible way into subinstances. Solutions of these subinstances are recursively obtained and stored in a data structure called the parsing table. The solutions in the parsing table are then combined to obtain the desired solution of the original problem. Under this approach, people do not distinguish between the recognition problem, that is, the problem of deciding whether an input grammar can generate an input string, and the parsing problem, that is, the problem of providing a suitable representation of all or the desired parse trees of an input string under an input grammar. This is because the construction of the parsing table can serve as a solution of both the recognition and the parsing problems. Thus, in this chapter, we use the terms recognition algorithm and parsing algorithm interchangeably.

In order to specify our parsing algorithms, we follow Shieber et al. (1995) and express each step of the algorithm as a deduction rule. These rules abstractly specify how to induce new entries of the parsing table, starting from old entries of the same table along with some side conditions derived from the grammar. In this way, we can focus on the basic parsing strategy underlying the algorithm of interest, leaving out implementation details that only affect the control flow of the computation and that can be tuned on the basis of the specific grammar at hand.

We close this introduction with some notational conventions. Given a finite alphabet V_T, we denote as V_T^* the set of all (finite) strings over V_T, including the null string ε. Let us fix some string $w \in V_T^*$ with $w = a_1 a_2 \cdots a_n$, $n \geq 1$ and $a_i \in V_T$ for $1 \leq i \leq n$. We call **index** (for w) any integer i with $0 \leq i \leq n$. An index i is used to denote the "splitting" of w into two substrings $a_1 a_2 \cdots a_i$ and $a_{i+1} a_{i+2} \cdots a_n$. Following this convention, for indices $i < j$ we write $w_{i,j}$ to denote the substring of w represented by $a_{i+1} a_{i+2} \cdots a_j$, that is the substring obtained by splitting w at indices i and j. We also write w_i for $w_{i-1,i}$.

4.2 Parsing for Context-free Grammars

Our analysis of parsing techniques for lexicalized formalisms starts in section 4.4 with lexicalized context-free grammars. Before that, we need a brief introduction to parsing for context-free grammars.

We denote a **context-free grammar** (CFG) by a 4-tuple $G = (V_N, V_T, P, S)$, where V_N is a finite set of nonterminals, V_T is a finite set of terminals with $V_T \cap V_N = \emptyset$, $S \in V_N$ is a special symbol called the start symbol, and P is a finite set of productions having the form $A \rightarrow \gamma$, with $A \in V_N$ and $\gamma \in (V_T \cup V_N)^*$. Throughout this chapter, elements of V_T are called **lexical elements**. We assume the reader is already familiar with the derive relation that is used in CFGs to rewrite strings; see, for instance, Harrison (1978). If a nonterminal A derives a substring $w_{i,j}$ of w, for some indices i and j, we also say that A spans $w_{i,j}$. The language generated by G is denoted $L(G)$. The size of G is defined as

$$|G| = \sum_{(A \rightarrow \alpha) \in P} |A\alpha| . \tag{4.1}$$

A CFG is in **Chomsky normal form** if every production in P has one of the following two forms

- $A \rightarrow B\,C$,
- $A \rightarrow a$,

where $A, B, C \in V_N$ and $a \in V_T$. Any CFG G that does not have empty productions, that is, productions of the form $A \rightarrow \varepsilon$, can be transformed into a CFG G' in Chomsky normal form, such that $L(G') = L(G)$; see, for instance, Harrison (1978). In this chapter, we deal with CFGs in Chomsky normal form in order to simplify the presentation of some of the parsing algorithms. Note that Chomsky normal form does not allow unary productions, that is, productions of the form $A \rightarrow B$, nor empty productions. The treatment of these productions does not add any conceptual difficulty to the problem of parsing based on lexicalized context-free grammars, so we will not discuss them any further in this chapter.

We now introduce the so-called CKY recognition algorithm for context-free languages (Younger, 1967; Aho and Ullman, 1972), requiring the input CFG to be cast in Chomsky normal form. This discussion will serve in section 4.4 as the basis for the computational analysis of some inefficiencies of standard CFG parsing algorithms, when applied to lexicalized CFGs. Let $G = (V_N, V_T, P, S)$ be a CFG in Chomsky normal form, and let $w = a_1 \cdots a_n \in V_T^+$ be an input string, where $n \geq 1$

$$\frac{}{[A, i-1, i]} \quad \begin{cases} (A \to a) \in P \\ a = a_i \end{cases} \tag{4.2}$$

$$\frac{\begin{array}{c} [B, i, k] \\ [C, k, j] \end{array}}{[A, i, j]} \quad \{(A \to B\ C) \in P \tag{4.3}$$

FIGURE 4.1 Abstract specification of the CKY recognition algorithm.

and $a_i \in V_T$ for $1 \le i \le n$. Our specification of the algorithm is based on items having the form

$$[A, i, j],$$

where A is a nonterminal of G and i, j are indices for w. The deduction of such an item by the algorithm assesses that A spans substring $w_{i,j}$ of w. The algorithm accepts w if and only if it can construct the item $[S, 0, n]$. Figure 4.1 provides an abstract specification of the algorithm expressed as a deduction system, where each deduction rule corresponds to a step that the algorithm can apply in constructing new items (see section 4.1).

Rule (4.2) in figure 4.1 serves as an initialization step. It processes the productions of the form $A \to a$ to construct all items that can directly be deduced from the lexical elements in the input string. Rule (4.3) combines two items that were previously deduced by the algorithm at adjacent positions in the input string, and it produces a new item according to some specific binary production.

We now turn to the discussion of the computational complexity of the algorithm. A straightforward implementation employs a square array, or parsing table, of size $n + 1$. Each entry in the parsing table is a bit vector of size $|V_N|$. In this way the deduction of item $[A, i, j]$ by the algorithm can be recorded by selecting the entry of the parse table indexed by i, j, and by setting to 1 the entry indexed by nonterminal A in the associated bit vector. In addition, all items that are deduced by the algorithm are also added to a list of unprocessed items, usually called agenda. The algorithm implementation is then based on a main cycle, and at each iteration an item is removed from the agenda and is processed by the deduction rules in figure 4.1. If previously unseen items are produced by such iteration, they are in turn added to the parsing table and to the agenda.

Let us consider now rule (4.3). It is not difficult to see that, using the representation discussed above, this rule can be executed once in a constant amount of time, given two input items and some binary production. We should now ask how many times the algorithm needs to execute rule (4.3) for a given input grammar and string. The rule can be executed for every possible value of indices i, k and j with $0 \le i < k < j \le n$, and for every possible production in P of the form $A \to B\ C$. In the worst case, then, there may be $\mathcal{O}(n^3)$ possible choices for i, k

and j, and $\mathcal{O}(|P|)$ possible choices for binary productions in the grammar, and thus rule (4.3) is executed a number of time $\mathcal{O}(|P| \cdot n^3)$. Since a single execution of the rule can be carried out in constant time, as already observed, this is also a bound on the total amount of time charged to the rule in the execution of the algorithm. A similar analysis can be carried out for rule (4.2); we do not pursue the details here, but we point out that the dominating step in the complexity of the algorithm is represented by rule (4.3). We thus conclude that the total running time of the algorithm in figure 4.1 is $\mathcal{O}(|P| \cdot n^3)$.

4.3 2-Lexical Context-free Grammars

Context-free grammars without empty productions can be lexicalized; that is, they can be cast in a form in which every production has at least one lexical element. Several definitions have been proposed in the literature. Here we consider 2-lexical context-free grammars, which is a subclass of CFGs underlying several probabilistic formalisms that have been extensively used in natural language processing, both in statistical parsing and in language modeling; see the discussion in section 4.1. A 2-lexical CFG is a special case of CFG in Chomsky normal form. In a 2-lexical CFG, each nonterminal is associated with a lexical element, called **head**, which plays a special role in the definition of the productions of the grammar. More precisely, each binary production combines the nonterminals in its right-hand side on the basis of the associated heads. This is typically used to model the selection of complements and modifiers of a given syntactic constituent, on the basis of the involved heads.

Before presenting the formal definition of 2-lexical CFG, we discuss a simple example, taken from Eisner and Satta (1999). A 2-lexical CFG uses nonterminals of the form VP[solve], N[puzzles], and so on, where *solve* is the head associated with the nonterminal VP[solve] and *puzzles* is the head associated with the nonterminal N[puzzles]. The grammar can then encode lexically specific preferences through the productions

- VP[solve] → V[solve] NP[puzzles]
- NP[puzzles] → DET[two] N[puzzles]
- V[solve] → solve
- N[puzzles] → puzzles
- DET[two] → two

in order to allow the derivation of the string *solve two puzzles* from the nonterminal VP[solve], but meanwhile omit the similar productions

- VP[eat] → V[eat] NP[puzzles]
- VP[solve] → V[solve] NP[goat]
- VP[sleep] → V[sleep] NP[goat]
- NP[goat] → DET[two] N[goat]

since puzzles are not edible, a goat is not solvable, *sleep* is intransitive, and *goat* cannot take plural determiners. Furthermore, a stochastic version of the grammar could implement "soft preferences" by allowing the rules in the second group but assigning them various low probabilities. This was not satisfactorily captured by earlier formalisms that did not make use of lexicalization.

A **2-lexical context-free grammar** (2-LCFG) is a CFG $G = (V_N, V_T, P, S[\$])$ in Chomsky normal form, satisfying the following conditions:

1. there exists a finite, non-empty set V_D, called the set of **delexicalized nonterminals**, such that

$$V_N \subseteq \{A[a] \mid A \in V_D, \, a \in V_T\}; \qquad\qquad (4.4)$$

   set V_N is thus called the set of **lexicalized nonterminals**;

2. every production in P has one of the following forms:
   (a) $A[b] \rightarrow B[b] \, C[c]$;
   (b) $A[c] \rightarrow B[b] \, C[c]$;
   (c) $A[a] \rightarrow a$.

Note that in the binary productions in (ii)a and (ii)b, the lexical item associated with the left-hand-side nonterminal is always inherited from the nonterminals in the right-hand side. Note also that the start symbol $S[\$]$ is a lexicalized nonterminal, that is, $S \in V_D$ and $\$ \in V_T$. As a convention, we assume that $\$$ is a dummy lexical item at the end of the input string (end marker) that does not appear anywhere else in G, and disregard it in the definition of $L(G)$. Symbol $S[\$]$ should then rewrite into a pair of lexicalized nonterminals, with the first lexicalized nonterminal functioning as a sentential phrase marker and the second lexicalized nonterminal rewriting into $\$$.

In current practice, the set of delexicalized nonterminals V_D is kept separate from set V_T. More specifically, set V_D usually encodes syntactic and structural information as bar-level, subcategorization requirements, features as number, tense, and the like, and any additional information that does not explicitly refer to individual lexical items, as for instance contextual constraints for parent node category (Charniak, 1997; Johnson, 1998) or constraints on the constituent's yield, expressed through information about distribution of some lexical elements (Collins, 2003).

As already mentioned, in a production of the form in (ii)a in the definition of 2-LCFG, two occurrences of lexical elements from V_T are involved, allowing fine-grained control on selection of complements and modifiers of a given constituent. In this perspective, we have that a 2-LCFG encodes, through its productions, certain binary relations defined on the lexical elements of the grammar. Accordingly, we say that the grammar has a degree of lexicalization of two, or equivalently that the grammar is 2-lexical. One might easily think of specializations of CFGs to a degree of lexicalization of $k > 2$. In this chapter, however, we focus on degree of lexicalization of two, since this class of grammars is the most widely adopted model in statistical natural language parsing.

4.4 Parsing for 2-LCFGs

The cost of the expressiveness of a 2-LCFG is a very large production set, since the size of set P usually grows with the square of the size of V_T, and in practical applications V_T may contain hundred thousands lexical elements. Standard context-free parsing algorithms, which run in time linear in the size of the input grammar, are inefficient in such cases. To provide an example, let us consider the CKY algorithm as presented in figure 4.1. This algorithm works in time $O(|P| n^3)$, as already discussed. We observe that the number of binary productions in P is bounded by $|V_N|^3$. Since in practice the processing of the productions of the form $A \rightarrow a$ in P does not dominate the time complexity of the algorithm, the CKY algorithm runs in time $\mathcal{O}(|V_N|^3 \cdot n^3)$. For a 2-LCFG, however, the number of binary productions in P can grow as large as $|V_D|^3 \cdot |V_T|^2$, which is very large for the size of V_T used in practical applications. Therefore, a first goal in the design of a parsing algorithm for 2-LCFGs is the one of achieving running time sublinear with respect to the grammar size.

A common practice is to use standard CFG parsing algorithms and to select only those productions from the 2-LCFG whose nonterminals have heads occurring in the input sentence. In the case of the CKY algorithm, one considers only productions $A[b] \rightarrow B[b] \ C[c]$ and $A[c] \rightarrow B[b] \ C[c]$ such that at least one occurrence of b and at least one occurrence of c are contained in the input string w. In this way, the parsing algorithm works with a number of binary production from the original grammar that is bounded by $|V_D|^3 \cdot n^2$. We thus obtain a running time of $\mathcal{O}(|V_D|^3 \cdot \min(n, |V_T|)^2 \cdot n^3)$. In practical applications we always have $n \ll |V_T|$. Then, in this chapter, we restrict our analysis to the (infinite) set of input instances of the parsing problem that satisfy relation $n < |V_T|$ (set V_T is arbitrary). With this assumption, the asymptotic time complexity of the CKY algorithm becomes $\mathcal{O}(|V_D|^3 \cdot n^5)$. In other words, it is a factor of n^2 slower than a comparable algorithm running with a nonlexicalized CFG.

To get a better understanding of this increase in the complexity, let us take a second look at the CKY algorithm in figure 4.1, particularized to 2-LCFG. In this case we can use items of the form

$$[\langle h, A \rangle, i, j]$$

to represent a nonterminal $A[a]$ spanning the substring $w_{i,j}$ of the input string w and with head $a = w_h$, with $i + 1 \le h \le j$. The adapted algorithm is reported in figure 4.2. Note that we now have two distinguished steps dealing with binary productions, one for each of the two kinds of binary productions in a 2-LCFG. Let us consider rule (4.6) in figure 4.2. This rule can be executed for every possible value of the delexicalized nonterminals A, B, and C in V_D, every possible value of variables i, k and j with $0 \le i < k < j \le n$, and every possible value of the variables h and h' with $i + 1 \le h \le k$ and $k + 1 \le h' \le j$. Then the number of possible executions of rule (4.6) is bounded by $\mathcal{O}(|V_D|^3 \cdot n^5)$. A similar analysis holds for rule (4.7). As in the case of the original CKY algorithm, the dominating step in the complexity

$$\frac{}{[\langle h, A \rangle, h-1, h]} \quad \begin{cases} (A[a] \to a) \in P \\ a = w_h \end{cases} \tag{4.5}$$

$$\frac{[\langle h, B \rangle, i, k]}{[\langle h, A \rangle, i, j]} \quad \begin{cases} (A[b] \to B[b]\, C[c]) \in P \\ b = w_h, \ c = w_{h'} \end{cases} \tag{4.6}$$

$$\frac{[\langle h', B \rangle, i, k]}{[\langle h, A \rangle, i, j]} \quad \begin{cases} (A[c] \to B[b]\, C[c]) \in P \\ b = w_{h'}, \ c = w_h \end{cases} \tag{4.7}$$

FIGURE 4.2 The CKY recognition algorithm particularized for a 2-LCFG.

of the algorithm is represented by the processing of binary productions. We thus conclude that the running time of the algorithm in figure 4.2 is $\mathcal{O}(|V_D|^3 \cdot n^5)$.

We now discuss a recognition algorithm that achieves an asymptotic improvement on the preceding time complexity. This algorithm has been originally presented in Eisner and Satta (1999). The basic idea underlying the algorithm is to split the processing of binary productions into several steps, each step dealing with the processing of some specific information within the representation of parsed constituents, that is, our items. We start by adding to the inventory of items used in figure 4.2 the items defined in what follows.

- $[\langle h, A \rangle, -, j]$ represents a lexicalized nonterminal $A[a]$ with head $a = w_h$. $A[a]$ spans a substring $w_{i,j}$ of w for some index i, which is not known.

- $[\langle h, A \rangle, i, -]$ has a symmetrical meaning with respect to item $[\langle h, A \rangle, -, j]$, representing a lexicalized nonterminal $A[a]$ with head $a = w_h$ and spanning a substring $w_{i,j}$ for some unknown index j.

- $[\langle h, A \rangle, i, -, C, k]$ represents a lexicalized nonterminal $A[a]$ with head $a = w_h$ and with two children. The left child of $A[a]$ spans substring $w_{i,k}$. We do not know the lexicalized nonterminal at the root of the left child. The right child of $A[a]$ has root labeled by lexicalized nonterminal $C[a]$ and spans a substring $w_{k,j}$ for some unknown index j. Note that the head of $A[a]$, that is, the lexical element w_h in w, is inherited by $A[a]$ from its right child, so that $h \geq k + 1$.

- $[\langle h, A \rangle, -, j, B, k]$ has a symmetrical meaning with respect to item $[\langle h, A \rangle, i, -, C, k]$, representing a lexicalized nonterminal $A[a]$ with head $a = w_h$ and with two children. The right child spans substring $w_{k,j}$ and we do not know the lexicalized nonterminal at its root. The left child of $A[a]$ has root labeled by lexicalized nonterminal $B[a]$ and spans substring $w_{i,k}$ for some unknown index i. In this case, the head of $A[a]$, that is, the lexical element w_h in w, is inherited by $A[a]$ from its left child, so that $h \leq k$.

$$\frac{}{[\langle h, A\rangle, h-1, h]} \quad \left\{ \begin{array}{l} (A[a] \to a) \in P \\ a = w_h \end{array} \right. \tag{4.8}$$

$$\frac{[\langle h, A\rangle, i, j]}{[\langle h, A\rangle, -, j]} \tag{4.9}$$

$$\frac{[\langle h, A\rangle, i, j]}{[\langle h, A\rangle, i, -]} \tag{4.10}$$

$$\frac{\begin{array}{c} [\langle h, B\rangle, -, k] \\ [\langle h', C\rangle, k, j] \end{array}}{[\langle h, A\rangle, -, j, B, k]} \quad \left\{ \begin{array}{l} (A[b] \to B[b] \ C[c]) \in P \\ b = w_h, \ c = w_{h'} \end{array} \right. \tag{4.11}$$

$$\frac{\begin{array}{c} [\langle h, B\rangle, i, k] \\ [\langle h, A\rangle, -, j, B, k] \end{array}}{[\langle h, A\rangle, i, j]} \tag{4.12}$$

$$\frac{\begin{array}{c} [\langle h', B\rangle, i, k] \\ [\langle h, C\rangle, k, -] \end{array}}{[\langle h, A\rangle, i, -, C, k]} \quad \left\{ \begin{array}{l} (A[c] \to B[b] \ C[c]) \in P \\ b = w_{h'}, \ c = w_h \end{array} \right. \tag{4.13}$$

$$\frac{\begin{array}{c} [\langle h, C\rangle, k, j] \\ [\langle h, A\rangle, i, -, C, k] \end{array}}{[\langle h, A\rangle, i, j]} \tag{4.14}$$

FIGURE 4.3 Enhanced recognition algorithm for a 2-LCFG.

The algorithm is presented in figure 4.3. We now discuss each of its steps, that is, each of the deduction rules in its specification. Rule (4.8) is the same as rule (4.5) in the algorithm in figure 4.2. Rule (4.9) constructs a single item $[\langle h, A \rangle, -, j]$ out of all items of the form $[\langle h, A \rangle, i, j]$ with $0 \leq i \leq h$. This rule performs a sort of item projection, removing information which, at some later step in the processing, is not relevant to our parsing goal. An other way of looking at this is that through item $[\langle h, A \rangle, -, j]$ we may be able to process at once all the items of the form $[\langle h, A \rangle, i, j]$ with $0 \leq i \leq h$ that have been previously constructed by the algorithm. Rule (4.10) works symmetrically.

The core of the algorithm is represented by rules (4.11) and (4.12), and by the rules (4.13) and (4.14), which are symmetrical with respect to rules (4.11) and (4.12). We discuss here rules (4.11) and (4.12), which implement what was done in a single step by rule (4.6) in the algorithm in figure 4.2. The basic idea here is that the two indices h' and i in rule (4.6) can be processed independently one of the other. We can thus split rule (4.6) into two substeps. Rule (4.11) is executed first. It combines two lexicalized nonterminals according to some binary production in which the head is inherited from the left child. Note that in this combination the crucial information is represented by the two indices h and h', referring to the heads of the left and the right child, respectively. Meanwhile, the index representing the left boundary of the left child is not needed here (this information can be resumed at some later step). As we will see, this is the key to the reduction of the time complexity of the algorithm. The outcome of this step is an item representing a derivation starting with a binary production, but with missing information about the index representing its left boundary.

Rule (4.12) is executed after rule (4.11). Its main purpose is to restore the missing information about the left boundary. Note that at this point the head of the right child, which was the basic information in the processing of rule (4.11), is of no use and is no longer present in the items involved in this step. Again, this is a key to the reduction of the time complexity of the algorithm. The output of this step is the same item that would have been obtained in a single application of rule (4.6) in the algorithm in figure 4.2.

Let us now analyze the time complexity of the algorithm in figure 4.3. The complexity is dominated by the execution of rules (4.11) and (4.12) (and their symmetrical rules). The analysis is very similar to that of rule (4.6) in the algorithm in figure 4.2. We notice that, in the worst case, the total number of executions of rule (4.11) depends on the possible values of the delexicalized nonterminals A, B, and C in V_D, and the possible values of variables k, j, h, and h' with $0 < h \leq k < h' \leq j \leq n$. Then there are $\mathcal{O}(|V_D|^3 \cdot n^4)$ possible executions of rule (4.6). As for rule (4.12), we have a total number of executions depending on the possible values of the delexicalized nonterminals A and B in V_D, and the possible values of variables i, k, j, and h with $0 \leq i < h \leq k < j \leq n$. This results in a total number of executions in $\mathcal{O}(|V_D|^2 \cdot n^4)$. Thus, the most expensive step is represented by rule (4.11) (and by the symmetrical rule (4.13)). Since every rule in the algorithm can be implemented to run in constant time per single execution, we can conclude that the total running time of the algorithm in figure 4.3 is $\mathcal{O}(|V_D|^3 \cdot n^4)$. This is an asymptotic improvement over the time complexity of the algorithm in figure 4.2.

4.5 Parsing for Tree-Adjoining Grammars

In this second part of this chapter, we show how ideas similar to those developed in the previous section for 2-LCFGs can be adapted to other lexicalized formalisms that are generatively more powerful than CFGs. Specifically, we consider the case of lexicalized tree-adjoining grammars, that have been extensively discussed in this book. Before considering the problem of parsing for lexicalized tree-adjoining grammars in the next section, we briefly introduce here a basic algorithm for parsing based on tree-adjoining grammars (Joshi et al., 1975; Joshi, 1985) and provide an analysis of its computational complexity. This will serve as the basis for the discussion of the algorithm presented in the next section.

We denote a **tree-adjoining grammar** (TAG) as a 5-tuple $G = (V_N, V_T, S, I, A)$, where V_N is a finite set of nonterminals, V_T is a finite set of terminals, or lexical elements, with $V_T \cap V_N = \emptyset$, $S \in V_N$ is a special symbol called the start symbol, I is a finite set of trees called initial trees and A is a finite set of trees called auxiliary trees, with $I \cap A = \emptyset$. Set $I \cup A$ is also called the set of elementary trees. We assume the reader is already familiar with the notion of foot node of an auxiliary tree and with the basic operations of adjunction and substitution that are used in TAGs to rewrite trees. An elementary tree that has been rewritten by means of zero or more adjunction or substitution operations is called a **derived tree**. Let γ be a subtree of a derived tree. If tree γ includes a foot node, its yield is a pair of strings u, v in V_T^*; if γ does not include a foot node, its yield is a single string u. Accordingly, we say that γ spans, respectively, string pair u, v or string u. The language generated by G is denoted by $L(G)$.

We adopt the following notation. If γ is an elementary tree, its root node is denoted $Root(\gamma)$. If γ is an auxiliary tree , its foot node is denoted $Foot(\gamma)$. A node η from γ has label $Labl(\eta)$. The (possibly empty) string of all nodes that are children of η, in left to right order, is denoted $Childr(\eta)$. The selectional constraints $Adj(\eta)$ and $Sbst(\eta)$ represent (possibly empty) sets of elementary trees that can be adjoined or substituted, respectively, at η. If adjunction at η can be dispensed with, then the special symbol "nil" is contained in $Adj(\eta)$. We define the size of η as $1 + |Adj(\eta)| + |Sbst(\eta)|$ and the size of γ, written $|\gamma|$, as the sum of the sizes of all nodes from γ. The size of a TAG G is defined as

$$|G| = \sum_{\gamma \in (I \cup A)} |\gamma|. \qquad (4.15)$$

The basic parsing algorithm we present for TAG assumes that each elementary tree in the input grammar is in binary form, that is, every internal node has exactly two children, and that no leaf node is labeled by ε. Let $G = (V_N, V_T, S, I, A)$ be such an input TAG and let $w = a_1 a_2 \cdots a_n$ be an input string, with $n \geq 1$ and $a_i \in V_T$ for $1 \leq i \leq n$. The tabular algorithm keeps a record of each complete subtree of a derived tree that matches some portion of w, as explained in what follows. We use items of the form

$$[\eta_X, i, j, f_1, f_2],$$

where η is the root of the complete subtree, i and j are indices for w, and f_1 and f_2 are either indices for w or may take the special value "$-$". In case f_1 and f_2 are indices, the yield of the subtree is composed by the two strings w_{i,f_1} and $w_{f_2,j}$, to the left and to the right, respectively, of the foot node. In case $f_1 = f_2 = -$, the subtree does not include a foot node and has yield $w_{i,j}$. Finally, $X \in \{\bot, \top\}$ records whether an adjunction at node η has been parsed ($X = \top$) or not ($X = \bot$).

$$\frac{}{[\eta_\bot, i-1, i, -, -]} \ \{ Labl(\eta) = w_i \tag{4.16}$$

$$\frac{}{[\eta_\bot, f_1, f_2, f_1, f_2]} \ \begin{cases} \eta = Foot(\beta), \ \beta \in A \\ 0 \le f_1 < f_2 \le n \end{cases} \tag{4.17}$$

$$\frac{\begin{array}{c} [\eta'_\top, i, k, -, -] \\ [\eta''_\top, k, j, f_1, f_2] \end{array}}{[\eta_\bot, i, j, f_1, f_2]} \ \{ Childr(\eta) = \eta'\eta'' \tag{4.18}$$

$$\frac{[\rho_\top, i, j, -, -]}{[\eta_\top, i, j, -, -]} \ \begin{cases} \rho = Root(\alpha) \\ \alpha \in Sbst(\eta) \end{cases} \tag{4.19}$$

$$\frac{\begin{array}{c} [\rho_\top, i', j', i, j] \\ [\eta_\bot, i, j, f_1, f_2] \end{array}}{[\eta_\top, i', j', f_1, f_2]} \ \begin{cases} \rho = Root(\beta) \\ \beta \in Adj(\eta) \end{cases} \tag{4.20}$$

$$\frac{[\eta_\bot, i, j, f_1, f_2]}{[\eta_\top, i, j, f_1, f_2]} \ \{ nil \in Adj(\eta) \tag{4.21}$$

FIGURE 4.4 Abstract specification of a basic recognition algorithm for TAG.

The basic steps of the algorithm are reported in figure 4.4. Again, we specify each step of the algorithm by means of a deduction rule. Rules (4.16) and (4.17) have the purpose of initializing the parse table, by constructing all items that match single lexical elements in w and by guessing the span of the foot nodes of the auxiliary trees of G, respectively. Rule (4.18) combines two subtrees whose root nodes are siblings, accounting for the case in which node η'' dominates the foot node. Note how the information about the spanning of the foot node is inherited by node η from node η''. Two additional versions of rule (4.18) are not displayed, corresponding to the case in which node η' dominates the foot node and to the case in which node η does not dominate a foot node. Rule (4.19) substitutes at some node η an initial tree α that has been successfully parsed. Rule (4.20) adjoins at node η an auxiliary tree β that has been successfully parsed, if this is compatible with the selectional constraints at η. In this rule, f_1 and f_2 may be indices for w, in case η dominates a foot node, or else $f_1 = f_2 = -$, in case η does not dominate a foot node. Rule (4.21) skips adjunction at some node η, again if this is compatible with the selectional constraints at that node. The algorithm accepts w if and only if it can construct an item of the form $[\eta_\top, 0, n, -, -]$ for some node η which is the root of an initial tree and is labeled by the start symbol of G.

We can implement the algorithm in figure 4.4 using data structures similar to those exploited in the case of CFG parsing in section 4.2. Items should be stored into a parsing table and an agenda. The parsing table can be implemented as a 4-dimensional array with $n + 2$ entries on each dimension (this is the maximum size of the range of an index, including the special value "−"). Each entry is a bit vector of size equal to the number of nodes in the elementary trees of G plus one bit for the special values "⊥" and "⊤". In this way, each single execution of a rule of the algorithm takes constant time. It is not difficult to see that the time complexity of the algorithm is dominated by rule (4.20). In the worst case, this rule can be executed for every possible value of the variables i', j', i, j, f_1, f_2, every node η in some elementary tree of G and every auxiliary tree in the selectional constraints of η. This accounts for a total number of executions in $\mathcal{O}(|G| \cdot n^6)$, which is also a bound on the running time of the algorithm.

4.6 Parsing for 2-lexical Tree-Adjoining Grammars

Lexicalized Tree-Adjoining Grammars (LTAGs) have been introduced in Schabes et al. (1988) and Joshi and Schabes (1997) as a variant of TAGs, and they have been extensively discussed in this book. In this section, we develop a recognition algorithm for this class that improves upon the complexity results discussed in the previous section. We use the following terminology for LTAGs. Given an elementary tree γ, we call **head** of γ the unique lexical element $a \in V_T$ that projects γ. We also say that a heads γ.

LTAGs are generatively more powerful than the 2-LCFGs introduced in section 4.3. This follows from the fact that the same property holds for the unlexicalized versions of these formalisms. Apart form generative capacity, we observe here that LTAGs can be more expressive than 2-LCFGs, as explained in what follows. As already discussed in section 4.3, in a 2-LCFG we can implement certain binary relations defined on the lexical elements of the grammar. More specifically, in the context of a given production of a 2-LCFG, a given lexical element can take as argument/modifier some other lexical element, through the constituents that these lexical elements project. However, in a 2-LCFG it is not possible to encode similar relations involving three or more lexical elements. In contrast, in a LTAG we could in principle encode relations of arbitrary arity defined over the lexical elements of the grammar. As an example, we could define a lexicalized elementary tree γ of the grammar in such a way that the choice of the lexicalized elementary trees that can be adjoined/substituted at some node of γ depends not only on the head of γ, but also on the choice of the lexicalized trees that can be adjoined/substituted at each other node of γ itself. In natural language applications, however, this is not the standard practice. Accordingly, we take here the assumption that, for every elementary tree γ of the grammar, the choice of the lexicalized trees that can be adjoined at some node is fixed by the head of γ itself. We will define this notion more precisely.

Given an LTAG G, a **delexicalized elementary tree** of G is obtained by taking a lexicalized elementary tree γ of G and by removing the node with γ's head (along with its incoming arc) and the selectional constraints at each of the nodes of γ. We call **2-lexical tree-adjoining grammar** (2-LTAG) any LTAG G satisfying the following condition:

> Let $\gamma_1, \gamma_2, \ldots, \gamma_n$ be all the lexicalized elementary trees of G that are headed by a lexical element a. Then the delexicalized elementary trees obtained from $\gamma_1, \gamma_2, \ldots, \gamma_n$ are pairwise different.

It is not difficult to see that, given this, once a lexical element a and a delexicalized elementary tree γ are fixed, there is only one possible choice for the selectional constraints at the nodes of γ that results in an elementary tree of G headed by a. In the remainder of this section, we will focus our attention on 2-LTAGs and discuss the parsing problem for this formalism.

As we have seen in section 4.5, parsing for TAGs can be carried out in time $\mathcal{O}(|G| \cdot n^6)$, where G is the input grammar and w is the input string. When we consider 2-LTAGs, the size of G is prohibitively large for large vocabulary applications, because these grammars include specific lexicalized elementary trees for each lexical element, and because each node in such trees records selectional adjoining constraints for adjunction/substitution by lexicalized elementary trees. A common practice consists in restricting the grammar to the only lexicalized elementary trees that are headed by a lexical element from the input sentence. In what follows, we provide a computational analysis of such parsing strategy.

We start with some additional notation. For a fixed 2-LTAG G, we define g as the maximum number of elementary trees that a lexical element can head. We define t as the maximum number of nodes in an elementary tree of G. We assume, for each lexical element a, some arbitrary ordering for the lexicalized elementary trees headed by a. We also assume, for each lexicalized elementary tree, some arbitrary order for its nodes, with the root node always being the first. In this way, when some input string w is understood, the pair $\langle h, p \rangle$ denotes the p-th lexicalized elementary tree headed at w_h, and the triple $\langle h, p, q \rangle$ denotes its q-th node, for $1 \leq h \leq n$, $1 \leq p \leq g$, and $1 \leq q \leq t$. Similarly, $\langle h, p, 1 \rangle$ denotes the root node in such tree.

As already discussed in section 4.5, the most time expensive step in tabular parsing for TAG is the adjunction at nodes dominating a foot-node. We now reconsider this step in view of the processing of an LTAG using the selective parsing strategy outlined above. As in the case of 2-LCFG parsing, we restrict our analysis to the (infinite) set of input instances of the parsing problem that satisfy relation $n < |V_T|$. Say that we have recognized a complete subtree of a derived tree, and such a subtree is rooted at the internal node $\langle h, p, q \rangle$ of some lexicalized auxiliary tree. Let us assume that node $\langle h, p, q \rangle$ dominates the foot node of the auxiliary tree, so that our subtree spans substrings w_{i,f_1} and $w_{f_2,j}$. Say also that we have recognized a derived tree obtained from a lexicalized elementary tree β with root node $\langle h', p', 1 \rangle$, spanning substrings $w_{i',i}$ and $w_{j,j'}$. In the algorithm in figure 4.4 these two analyses are represented, respectively, by the two items $[\langle h, p, q \rangle_\perp, i, f_1, f_2, j]$ and $[\langle h', p', 1 \rangle_\top, i', i, j, j']$.

Adjunction of β at the node $\langle h, p, q \rangle$ would then be carried out by means of the following instantiation of rule (4.20) in figure 4.4:

$$\frac{[\langle h', p', 1 \rangle_\top, i', i, j, j']}{[\langle h, p, q \rangle_\perp, i, f_1, f_2, j]} \quad \{\langle h', p' \rangle \in Adj(\langle h, p, q \rangle) \quad (4.22)$$

Item $[\langle h, p, q \rangle_\top, i', f_1, f_2, j']$ represents a new subtree spanning w_{i',f_1} and $w_{f_2,j'}$, and no further adjunction is possible at the root of this subtree.

Variables i', j', i, j, f_1 and f_2 above may take values in a range bounded by $\mathcal{O}(n^6)$. Furthermore, variable h' can freely range within (the possible indices for) substrings $w_{i',i}$ and $w_{j,j'}$, and variable h can freely range within substrings $w_{0,i'}$, w_{i,f_1}, $w_{f_2,j}$ and $w_{j',n}$, since the head w_h of the tree $\langle h, p \rangle$ might not be dominated by node $\langle h, p, q \rangle$. Finally, p, p' and q can assume any value within their respective ranges. We then have that the possible number of executions of rule (4.20) is bounded by $\mathcal{O}(tg^2 \cdot n^8)$. Again, it is not difficult to see that when the algorithm in figure 4.4 runs on a 2-LTAG, the dominating step in its time complexity is represented by rule (4.20). We thus conclude that the algorithm runs in time $\mathcal{O}(tg^2 \cdot n^8)$.

Using ideas similar to those developed in section 4.4 for parsing based on 2-LCFG, we can improve upon the above time upper bound. The algorithm we will present has been originally presented in Eisner and Satta (2000). The result is achieved by splitting rule (4.20) into substeps. We start by observing that in (4.22) we simultaneously carry out two tests on the trees under analysis:

- we check that the tree $\langle h', p' \rangle$ is found in the selectional constraint $Adj(\langle h, p, q \rangle)$; and

- we check that the tree yield $w_{i',i}$, $w_{j,j'}$ "wraps" around the tree yield w_{i,f_1}, $w_{f_2,j}$, that is, the two copies of i match and likewise j.

To some extent, the two computations can be carried out independent of each other. More precisely, the result of the check on the selectional constraint does not depend on the value of variables f_1 and f_2. Furthermore, once the check has been carried out, we can do away with the head index h', since this information is not used by the wrapping test and is not referred to in the result of (4.22).

In order to implement this idea, we define two new kinds of item:

- $[\langle h, p, q \rangle_\perp, i, j]$ represents a subtree with root node $\langle h, p, q \rangle$ such that no adjunction has been performed yet at the root node. In case the root node does not dominate a foot node, the subtree spans the substring $w_{i,j}$; otherwise, the subtree spans two substrings w_{i,f_1} and $w_{f_2,j}$ for some indices f_1 and f_2, which are not known.

- $[\langle h, p, q \rangle_\top, i', i, j, j']$ represents a subtree with root node $\langle h, p, q \rangle$, such that adjunction of some lexicalized auxiliary tree β has been performed at the root node, with β spanning the two substrings $w_{i',i}$ and $w_{j,j'}$. In case the root node $\langle h, p, q \rangle$ does not dominate a foot node, the subtree spans $w_{i',j'}$; otherwise, the subtree spans two substrings w_{i',f_1} and $w_{f_2,j'}$ for some indices f_1 and f_2, which are not known.

The new algorithm is reported in figure 4.5. Rules (4.23), (4.24), (4.25), (4.26) and (4.30) are specialized versions for 2-LTAGs of similar steps in the algorithm in figure 4.4. Rules (4.27), (4.28) and (4.29) implement the new steps that replace rule (4.20) in the algorithm in figure 4.4, using the new items defined above. More specifically, for a fixed node $\langle h, p, q \rangle$ and fixed indices i, j, rule (4.27) 'projects' all items of the form $[\langle h, p, q \rangle_\perp, i, j, f_1, f_2]$ into items of the form $[\langle h, p, q \rangle_\perp, i, j]$. This allows the check on the selectional constraints at node $\langle h, p, q \rangle$ to be carried out at rule (4.28) independently of the two variables f_1 and f_2, which are not relevant. The information about variables f_1 and f_2 is restored afterward by rule (4.29).

A computational analysis similar to the one carried out in section 4.5 shows the following overall time costs: rule (4.27) takes time $\mathcal{O}(tg \cdot n^5)$, rule (4.28) takes time $\mathcal{O}(tg^2 \cdot n^6)$, and rule (4.29) takes time $\mathcal{O}(tg \cdot n^7)$. All the remaining steps can easily be accommodated within the indicated time upper bounds. We then conclude that the algorithm reported in figure 4.5 has worst case running time in $\mathcal{O}(tg \cdot n^6 \cdot \max\{g, n\})$.

In our analysis for the worst case time complexity of 2-LTAG parsing, we have made a rather drastic assumption. We have implicitly assumed that, for an input string w, the total number of *distinguishable* lexicalized elementary trees that are headed by lexical elements in w is $g \cdot n$. However, it should be noted here that in standard applications, elementary trees are not specialized for each individual lexical element of the grammar, but rather for certain lexical categories that are appropriately defined. Examples of these lexical categories taken from the XTAG project (XTAG Group, 2001) are for instance "transitive verb", "ditransitive verb with PP", and so on. As a consequence, we find that the set of elementary trees that are headed by one of the two lexical elements w_i and w_j with $i \neq j$ are often not disjoint. In practice, the total number of distinguishable lexicalized elementary trees headed by the lexical elements in w is quite smaller than the $g \cdot n$ theoretical bound. In addition, many application systems use several techniques for reducing this number ahead of parsing, as described at length in chapters 5, 6 and 7. Thus it seems more realistic to assume that the total number of distinguishable elementary trees that are headed by lexical elements occurring in w is bounded by $g' \cdot n$, where

$$\frac{}{[\langle h,p,q\rangle_\perp, h-1, h, -, -]} \quad \{Labl(\langle h,p,q\rangle) = w_h \tag{4.23}$$

$$\frac{}{[\langle h,p,q\rangle_\perp, f_1, f_2, f_1, f_2]} \quad \begin{cases} \langle h,p,q\rangle = Foot(\beta), \ \beta \in A \\ 0 \le f_1 < f_2 \le n \\ 0 < h \le f_1 \lor f_2 < h \le n \end{cases} \tag{4.24}$$

$$\frac{[\langle h,p,q'\rangle_\top, i, k, -, -] \quad [\langle h,p,q''\rangle_\top, k, j, f_1, f_2]}{[\langle h,p,q\rangle_\perp, i, j, f_1, f_2]} \quad \{Childr(\langle h,p,q\rangle) = \langle h,p,q'\rangle\langle h,p,q''\rangle \tag{4.25}$$

$$\frac{[\langle h',p',1\rangle_\top, i, j, -, -]}{[\langle h,p,q\rangle_\top, i, j, -, -]} \quad \begin{cases} \langle h',p',1\rangle = Root(\alpha) \\ \alpha \in Sbst(\langle h,p,q\rangle) \end{cases} \tag{4.26}$$

$$\frac{[\langle h,p,q\rangle_\perp, i, j, f_1, f_2]}{[\langle h,p,q\rangle_\perp, i, j]} \tag{4.27}$$

$$\frac{[\langle h',p',1\rangle_\top, i', j', i, j] \quad [\langle h,p,q\rangle_\perp, i, j]}{[\langle h,p,q\rangle_\top, i', j', i, j]} \quad \{\langle h',p'\rangle \in Adj(\langle h,p,q\rangle) \tag{4.28}$$

$$\frac{[\langle h,p,q\rangle_\top, i', j', i, j] \quad [\langle h,p,q\rangle_\perp, i, j, f_1, f_2]}{[\langle h,p,q\rangle_\top, i', j', f_1, f_2]} \tag{4.29}$$

$$\frac{[\langle h,p,q\rangle_\perp, i, j, f_1, f_2]}{[\langle h,p,q\rangle_\top, i, j, f_1, f_2]} \quad \{nil \in Adj(\langle h,p,q\rangle) \tag{4.30}$$

FIGURE 4.5 Enhanced recognition algorithm for 2-LTAG.

$g' < g$ is a real constant that depends on the system at hand, along with the choice of lexical categories adopted by the input grammar. In most natural language processing applications, we have $g' < n$. Thus we can rewrite the previous time complexity upper bound for the algorithm reported in figure 4.5 as $\mathcal{O}(tg' \cdot n^7)$.

4.7 Related Work

Several parsing algorithms have been presented in the literature for lexicalized formalisms other than the 2-LCFGs and the 2-LTAGs discussed in this chapter. We briefly overview here some of these works. To simplify the presentation, we disregard the size of the input grammar in the parsing problem, treating it as a constant. Thus, complexity results are expressed as functions of the length of the input string w only, which we assume to be some integer $n \geq 1$.

Link grammars have been presented in Sleator and Temperley (1993). This lexicalized formalism is strictly related to dependency grammars (Mel'čuk, 1988), allowing direct combination of lexical items and with no internal definition of extra symbols, as for instance the delexicalized nonterminals in 2-LCFGs. Standard assumptions are taken in link grammars that allow the formalism to encode relations on lexical elements of arity not greater than two. In this case, a parsing algorithm for the formalism running in time $O(n^3)$ has been presented in Sleator and Temperley (1993). To our knowledge, this is the first cubic time parsing algorithm that has been presented in the literature for a lexicalized formalism that is able to encode binary relations on lexical items. The algorithm uses techniques quite different from those presented in this chapter, related to computational geometry.

Head automaton grammars (Alshawi, 1996) are a lexicalized formalisms strictly related to 2-LCFGs. A head automaton grammar associates each lexical element of the formalism with a head automaton (HA). A single HA is an acceptor for a language of string pairs, which roughly corresponds in generative capacity to a so-called linear CFG, that is, a CFG that does not allow more than one nonterminal in the right-hand side of its productions. As in the case of 2-LCFGs, standard parsing algorithms applied to head-automaton grammars achieve $O(n^5)$ running time for an input string of length n. A construction translating from head automaton grammars to 2-LCFGs has been provided in Eisner and Satta (1999). This means that we can parse head automaton grammars in time $O(n^4)$, using the results in section 4.4.

A class of lexicalized formalisms called split grammars has been presented in Eisner (1997), motivated by certain grammar models in which left and right arguments/modifiers of a lexical element do not depend on each other. Parsing algorithms for split grammars have been presented in Eisner (1997) and Eisner and Satta (1999), running in time $\mathcal{O}(n^3)$.

We conclude by pointing out that the definition of 2-LTAG presented in section 4.6 imposes that the selectional constraints at each node in an elementary tree only depend on the tree's head and the internal structure of the tree itself. Grammars satisfying this requirement have been called node-dependent or SLG(2) in Carroll and Weir (1997), and bilexical in Eisner (1997); Eisner and Satta (1999, 2000).

Notes

1. Most of the content of this chapter is based on results that have been originally presented in Eisner and Satta (1999) and in Eisner and Satta (2000).

References

Ades, A. E. and Steedman, M. J. (1982). On the order of words. *Linguistics and Philosophy*, 4:517–558.

Aho, A. V. and Ullman, J. D. (1972). *The Theory of Parsing, Translation and Compiling*, vol. 1. Prentice-Hall.

Alshawi, H. (1996). Head automata and bilingual tiling: Translation with minimal representations. In *Proc. of the 34th ACL*, Santa Cruz, CA.

Carroll, J. and Weir, D. J. (1997). Encoding frequency information in lexicalized grammars. In *Proceedings of the 5th Int. Workshop on Parsing Technologies*, Cambridge, MA.

Charniak, E. (1997). Statistical parsing with a context-free grammar and word statistics. In *Proc. of AAAI-97*, Menlo Park, CA.

Charniak, E. (2000) A maximum-entropy-inspired parser. In *Proc. of the 1st NAACL*, Seattle.

Chelba, C. and Jelinek, F. (1998). Exploiting syntactic structure for language modeling. In *Proc. of the 36th ACL*, Montreal.

Chiang, D. (2000). Statistical parsing with an automatically-extracted tree adjoining grammar. In *Proc. of the 38th ACL*, Hong Kong.

Clark, S., Hockenmaier, J., and Steedman, M. J. (2002). Building deep dependency structures with a wide-coverage CCG parser. In *Proc. of the 40th ACL*, Philadephia.

Collins, M. (2003). Head-driven statistical models for natural language parsing. *Computational Linguistics*, 29(4): 589–637.

Eisner, J. M. (1996). Three new probabilistic models for dependency parsing: An exploration. In *Proc. of the 16th COLING*, pages 340–345, Copenhagen.

Eisner, J. M. (1997). Bilexical grammars and a cubic-time probabilistic parser. In *Proceedings of the 5th Int. Workshop on Parsing Technologies*, Cambridge, MA.

Eisner, J. M. and Satta, G. (1999). Efficient parsing for bilexical context-free grammars and head automaton grammars. In *Proc. of the 37th ACL*, College Park, MD.

Eisner, J. M. and Satta, G. (2000). A faster parsing algorithm for lexicalized tree-adjoining grammars. In *Proceedings of the 5th International Workshop on Tree Adjoining Grammars*, Paris.

XTAG-Group. (2001). A lexicalized tree adjoining grammar for english. Technical Report IRCS-01-03, IRCS, University of Pennsylvania.

Harrison, M. A. (1978). *Introduction to Formal Language Theory*. Addison-Wesley.

Hwa, R. (1998). An empirical evaluation of probabilistic lexicalized tree insertion grammars. In *Proc. of the 36th ACL*, Montreal.

Johnson, M. (1998). PCFG models of linguistic tree representations. *Computational Linguistics*, 24(4):613–632.

Joshi, A. K. (1985). Tree adjoining grammars: How much context-sensitivity is required to provide reasonable structural descriptions? In D. R. Dowty, L. Karttunen, and A. M. Zwicky, editors, *Natural Language Parsing: Psychological, Computational and Theoretical Perspectives*, pages 206–250. Cambridge University Press.

Joshi, A. K. and Schabes, Y. (1997). Tree-adjoining grammars. In G. Rozenberg and A. Salomaa, editors, *Handbook of Formal Languages. Vol 3: Beyond Words*, chapter 2, pages 69–123. Springer-Verlag.

Joshi, A. K., Levy, L. S., and Takahashi, M. (1975). Tree adjunct grammars. *J. Comput. Syst. Sci.*, 10(1).

Lafferty, J., Sleator, D., and Temperley, D. (1992). Grammatical trigrams: A probabilistic model of link grammar. In *Proc. of the AAAI Conf. on Probabilistic Approaches to Nat. Lang.*.

Manning, C. D. and Carpenter, B. (1997). Left-corner language models and parsing. In *Proceedings of the 5th Int. Workshop on Parsing Technologies*, Boston.

Mel'čuk, I. (1988). *Dependency Syntax: Theory and Practice*. State University of New York Press.

Ratnaparkhi, A. (1997). A linear observed time statistical parser based on maximum entropy models. In *Second Conference on Empirical Methods in Natural Language Processing*, Brown University, Providence, Rhode Island.

Roark, B. (2001). Probabilistic top-down parsing and language modeling. *Computational Linguistics*, 27(2):249–276.

Schabes, Y., Abeillé, A., and Joshi, A. K. (1988). Parsing strategies with "lexicalized" grammars: Application to tree adjoining grammars. In *Proc. of the 12th COLING*, Budapest.

Schabes, Y. and Waters, R. C. (1995). Tree insertion grammar: A cubic-time parsable formalism that lexicalizes context-free grammar without changing the trees produced. *Computational Linguistics*, 21(4):479–515.

Shieber, S. M., Schabes, Y., and Pereira, F. (1995). Principles and implementation of deductive parsing. *Journal of Logic Programming*, 24:3–36.

Sleator, D. and Temperley, D. (1993). Parsing English with a link grammar. In *Proceedings of the 3rd Int. Workshop on Parsing Technologies*, Tilburg, Durbuy, Germany.

Steedman, M. J. (2000). *The Syntactic Process*. MIT Press.

Younger, D. H. (1967). Recognition and parsing of context-free languages in time n^3. *Information and Control*, 10:189–208.

Combining Supertagging and Lexicalized Tree-Adjoining Grammar Parsing

Anoop Sarkar

5.1 Introduction

In this chapter, we study two particular applications of the idea that it is possible to combine Supertagging with Lexicalized Tree-Adjoining Grammar (LTAG) parsing. A Supertagger (Srinivas and Joshi, 1999) is a statistical model that can be used to assign probabilistically to the word sequence (which makes up the input string) a sequence of elementary trees from some LTAG grammar. An LTAG parser, on the other hand, has to attach the various possible elementary trees for each word in the input string to provide a complete derivation tree for the input (see Joshi and Schabes (1992) for more information on the LTAG formalism and LTAG parsing).

The first argument to combine Supertagging with LTAG parsing comes from parsing efficiency. Because of the highly lexicalized nature of the grammar formalism, we experimentally show that notions other than sentence length play a factor for speeding up observed parse times when finding all derivations for a given input string. In particular, *syntactic lexical ambiguity* and *sentence complexity* (both are terms we define more precisely later on in this paper) are the dominant factors that affect parsing efficiency. We then show how a Supertagger can be used to drastically reduce the syntactic lexical ambiguity for a given input, and so can be used in combination with an LTAG parser to improve parsing efficiency radically. All of these ideas are tested out experimentally by parsing sentences from Penn Treebank Wall Street Journal corpus (Marcus et al., 1993).

The second argument to combine Supertagging with LTAG parsing comes from the need for two distinct statistical models that use (preferably) conditionally independent features in assigning probabilities to their input, while at the same time producing the same output. This enables the use of the cotraining algorithm (Blum and Mitchell, 1998) to bootstrap new labeled data instances from raw unlabeled data. In this case, however, the combination of a Supertagger and an LTAG parser permits the use of the cotraining algorithm to assign a complex label, a structured description to the input, rather than the typical case of a binary or multiclass classifier.

There is a third alternative perspective on combining a Supertagger with a parser that uses the same lexicalized structures and that is to improve the efficiency of a statistical parser. However this idea has been thoroughly explored in Clark (2002) and Clark and Curran (2004); these use this same idea in a very related area of parsing for the Combinatory Categorial Grammar (CCG) formalism which also can exploit highly lexicalized structures as in the LTAG formalism. Because this perspective is discussed in these related publications, we will not discuss it here. One thing to note is that a statistical parser can use tricks such as beam search to improve parsing efficiency not available to a parser that finds all derivations. However, based on the experimental evidence presented in these publications, it seems as if the notions of syntactic lexical ambiguity and sentence complexity apply to this case as well.

5.2   Parsing Efficiency

The time taken by a parser to produce derivations for input sentences is typically associated with the length of those sentences. The longer the sentence, the more time the parser is expected to take. However, complex algorithms such as parsers are typically affected by several factors. A common experience is that parsing algorithms differ in the number of edges inserted into the chart while parsing. Here, we will explore some of these constraints from the perspective of lexicalized grammars and explore how these constraints might be exploited to improve parser efficiency.

We will show how Supertagging can effectively cut down on the observed time taken by an LTAG parser. First, we will show that various factors other than sentence length affect parsing complexity, and then we will show that based on this hypothesis Supertagging can be used to effectively speed up an all-paths LTAG parser that produces a derivation forest. We show this experimentally, using parsing experiments on the Penn Treebank corpus. We also describe how this approach can be useful for bootstrapping an LTAG statistical parser from labeled and unlabeled data.

We concentrate on the problem of parsing using *fully* lexicalized grammars by looking at parsers for Lexicalized Tree-Adjoining Grammar (LTAG). By a fully lexicalized grammar we mean a grammar in which there are one or more syntactic structures associated with each lexical item. In the case of LTAG each structure is a tree (or, in general, a directed acyclic graph). For each structure there is an explicit structural slot for each of the arguments of the lexical item. The various advantages of defining a lexicalized grammar formalism in this way are discussed in Joshi and Schabes (1991).

The particular experiments that we report on in this paper were chosen to discover certain facts about LTAG parsing in a practical setting. Specifically, we wanted to discover the importance of the worst-case results for LTAG parsing in practice. Let us take Schabes's Earley-style TAG parsing algorithm (Schabes, 1994), which is the usual candidate for a practical LTAG parser. The parsing time complexity of this algorithm for various types of grammars are as follows (for input of length n):

$O(n^6)$ - arbitrary TAGs
$O(n^4)$ - unambiguous TAGs
$O(n)$ - bounded state TAGs e.g. the usual grammar G shown below (see Joshi et al., 1975), where $L(G) = \{a^n b^n c^n d^n \mid n \geq 0\}$

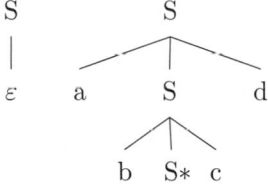

The grammar factors are as follows: Schabes's Earley-style algorithm takes:

$O(|A| \cdot |I \cup A| \cdot N \cdot n^6)$ worst case time, and
$O(|A \cup I| \cdot N \cdot n^4)$ worst case space

where n is the length of the input, A is the set of auxiliary trees, I is the set of initial trees, and N is maximum number of nodes in an elementary tree.

Given these worst-case estimates we wish to explore what the observed times might be for a TAG parser. It is not our goal here to compare different TAG parsing algorithms; rather, it is to discover what kinds of factors can contribute to parsing time complexity. Of course, a natural-language grammar that is large and complex enough to be used for parsing real-world text is typically neither unambiguous nor bounded in state size. It is important to note that here we are not concerned with *parsing accuracy*; rather, we want to explore *parsing efficiency*. This is why we do not pursue any pruning while parsing using statistical methods. Instead, we produce a shared derivation forest for each sentence that stores, in compact form, all derivations for each sentence. This helps us evaluate our TAG parser for time and space efficiency. The experiments reported here are also useful for statistical parsing using TAG, since discovering the source of grammar complexity in parsing can help in finding the right *figures-of-merit* for effective pruning in a statistical parser (Caraballo and Charniak, 1998).

An example LTAG is shown in figure 5.1. To parse the sentence *Ms. Haag plays Elianti*, the parser has to combine the trees selected by each word in the sentence by using the operations of substitution and adjunction (the two composition operations in LTAG) producing a valid derivation for the sentence. The result is shown in figure 5.2 where one possible derivation is shown. The derived tree or parse tree contains the constituency information (in practice, when using the Penn Treebank annotation style, we use an operation called sister-adjunction to generate the

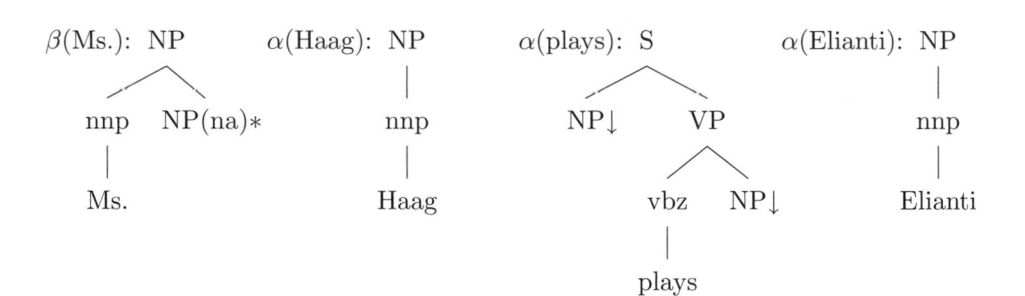

FIGURE 5.1 Example lexicalized elementary trees taken from a fragment of a lexicalized Tree-Adjoining Grammar extracted from the Penn Treebank. They are shown using the usual notation: ↓ denotes a *substitution* node; ∗ denotes a footnode in an auxiliary tree that has the same root label and footnode label enabling it to rewrite an internal node in any elementary tree (called the *adjunction* operation); and *na* is the *null adjunction* constraint, which states that no adjunction is permitted at that node.

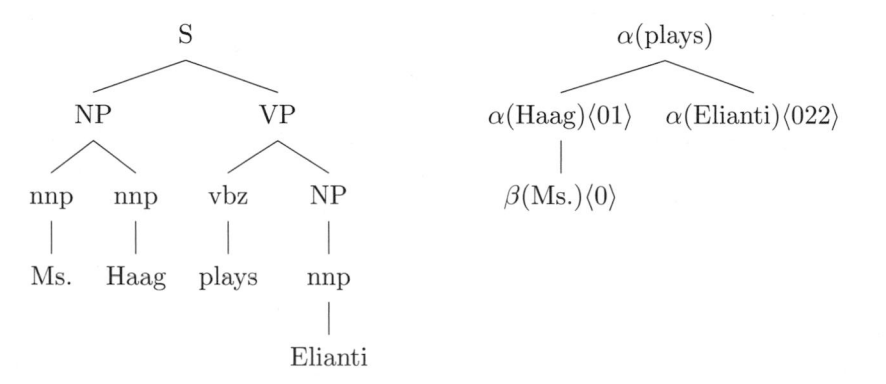

FIGURE 5.2 The parse tree and the derivation tree produced for the sentence *Ms. Haag plays Elianti*. The Gorn tree address of the attachment point in the parent node is provided within ⟨⟩ in the derivation tree. Note that the parser suppresses the printing of certain nodes in the elementary trees, for example, the node marked *na* in this grammar to enable the parser to produce parse trees that are identical to the trees in the Treebank.

relatively flat trees from the Treebank (see Schabes and Shieber, 1994 and Chiang, 2000) for more information on this slight modification to adjunction). The derivation tree is the history of how the elementary trees were combined to form the derived tree, and hence is the more basic representation of an LTAG parse. For all-paths parsing, all possible derivation trees for an input can be compactly encoded in polynomial space as a derivation forest (Vijay-Shanker and Weir, 1993).

Notice that as a consequence of this kind of lexicalized grammatical description, there might be several different factors that affect parsing complexity. Each word can select many different trees; for example, the word *plays* in figure 5.1 might select several trees for each syntactic context in which it can occur. The verb *plays* can be used in a relative clause, a wh-extraction clause, among others. While grammatical notions of argument structure and syntax can be processed in abstract terms just as in other kinds of formalisms, the crucial difference in LTAG is that all of this information is compiled into a finite set of trees *before* parsing. Each of these separate lexicalized trees is now considered by the parser. This compilation is repeated for other argument structures: for example, the verb *plays* could also select trees that are intransitive, thus increasing the set of lexicalized trees it can select. The set of trees selected by different lexical items is what we term *lexical syntactic ambiguity*.

The importance of this compilation into a set of lexicalized trees is that each predicate-argument structure across each syntactic context has its own lexicalized tree. Most grammar formalisms use feature structures to capture the same grammatical and predicate-argument information. In LTAG, this larger set of lexicalized trees directly corresponds to the fact that recursive feature structures are not needed for linguistic description. Feature structures are typically atomic, with a few instances of reentrant features.

Thus, in contrast with LTAG parsing, parsing for formalisms like HPSG or LFG concentrates on efficiently managing the unification of large feature structures and also the packing of ambiguities when these feature structures subsume each other (see Oepen and Carroll, 2000 and references cited there). We argue here that the result of having compiled out abstract grammatical descriptions into a set of lexicalized trees allows us to predict the number of edges that will be proposed by the parser even before parsing begins. This allows us to explore novel methods of dealing with parsing complexity that are difficult to consider in formalisms that are not fully lexicalized.

Furthermore, as the sentence length increases, the number of lexicalized trees increase proportionally increasing the attachment ambiguity. Each sentence is composed of several clauses. In a lexicalized grammar, each clause can be seen as headed by a single predicate tree with its arguments and associated adjuncts. We will see that empirically the number of clauses grows with increasing sentence length only up to a certain point. For sentences greater than a certain length, the number of clauses does not keep increasing.

Based on these intuitions, we identify the following factors that affect parsing complexity for lexicalized grammars:

Syntactic Lexical Ambiguity The number of trees selected by the words in the sentence being parsed. We show that this is a better indicator of parsing time than sentence length. This is also a predictor of the number of edges that will be proposed by a parser, allowing us to better handle difficult cases *before* parsing.

Sentence Complexity The clausal complexity in the sentences to be parsed. We observe that the number of clauses in a sentence stops growing in proportion to the sentence length after a point. We show that before this point parsing complexity is related to attachment of adjuncts rather than attachment of arguments.

5.3 LTAG Treebank Grammar

The grammar we used for our experiments was a LTAG Treebank Grammar that was automatically extracted from Sections 02–21 of the Wall Street Journal Penn Treebank II corpus (Marcus et al., 1993). The extraction tool (Xia, 1999) converted the *derived* trees of the Treebank into *derivation* trees in LTAG that represent the attachments of lexicalized elementary trees. There are $6,789$ tree templates in the grammar with $47,752$ tree nodes. Each word in the corpus selects some set of tree templates. The total number of lexicalized trees is $123,039$. The total number of word types in the lexicon is $44,215$. The average number of trees per word type is 2.78. However, this average is misleading, since it does not consider the frequency with which words that select a large number of trees occur in the corpus. In figure 5.3 we see that many frequently seen words can select a large number of trees.

Another objection that can be raised against a Treebank grammar that has been automatically extracted is that any parsing results using such a grammar might not be indicative of parsing using a hand-crafted linguistically sophisticated grammar. To address this point, Xia and Palmer (2000), compare this Treebank grammar with the XTAG grammar (XTAG-Group, 1998), a large-scale hand-crafted LTAG grammar for English. The experiment shows that 82.1% of template tokens in the Treebank grammar matches with a corresponding template in the XTAG grammar; 14.0% are covered by the XTAG grammar, but the templates in two grammars look different because the Treebank and the XTAG grammar havc adopted different analyses for the corresponding constructions; 1.1% of template tokens in the Treebank grammar are not linguistically sound due to annotation errors in the original Treebank; and the remaining 2.8% are not currently covered by the XTAG grammar. Thus, a total of 96.1% of the structures in the Treebank grammar match up with structures in the XTAG grammar.

5.4 Experimental Setup

5.4.1 Parsing algorithm

The parser used here implements a chart-based head-corner algorithm. The use of head-driven prediction to enchance efficiency was first suggested by Kay (1989)

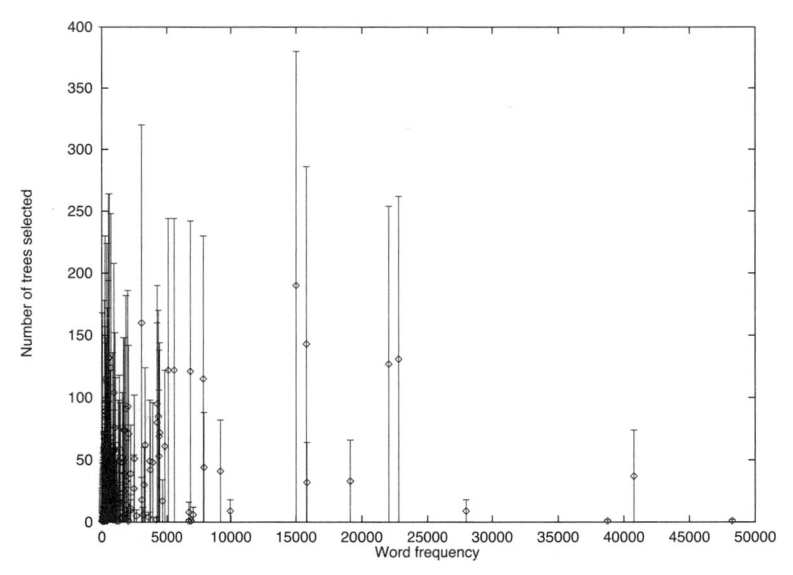

FIGURE 5.3 Number of trees selected plotted against words with a particular frequency. (x-axis: words of frequency x; y-axis: number of trees selected, error bars indicate least and most ambiguous word of a particular frequency x)

for CF parsing (see Sikkel, 1997 for a more detailed survey). Lavelli and Satta (1991) provided the first head-driven algorithm for LTAGs, a chart-based algorithm that lacked any top-down prediction. van Noord (1994) describes a Prolog implementation of a head-corner parser for LTAGs that includes top-down prediction. Significantly, van Noord (1994) uses a different closure relation from Lavelli and Satta (1991). The head-corner traversal for auxiliary trees starts from the footnode rather than from the anchor.

The parsing algorithm we use is a chart-based variant of the van Noord (1994) algorithm. We use the same head-corner closure as proposed there. We do not give a complete description of our parser here, since the basic idea behind the algorithm can be grasped by reading van Noord (1994). Our parser differs from the algorithm in van Noord (1994) in some important respects: our implementation is chart-based, and explicitly tracks *goal* and *item* states, and does not perform any implicit backtracking or selective memoization: we do not need any additional variables to keep track of which words are already "reserved" by an auxiliary tree (which van Noord (1994) needs to guarantee termination), and we have an explicit *completion* step.

5.4.2 Parser implementation

The parser is implemented in ANSI C. The implementation optimizes for space at the expense of speed, e.g. the recognition chart is implemented as a sparse array

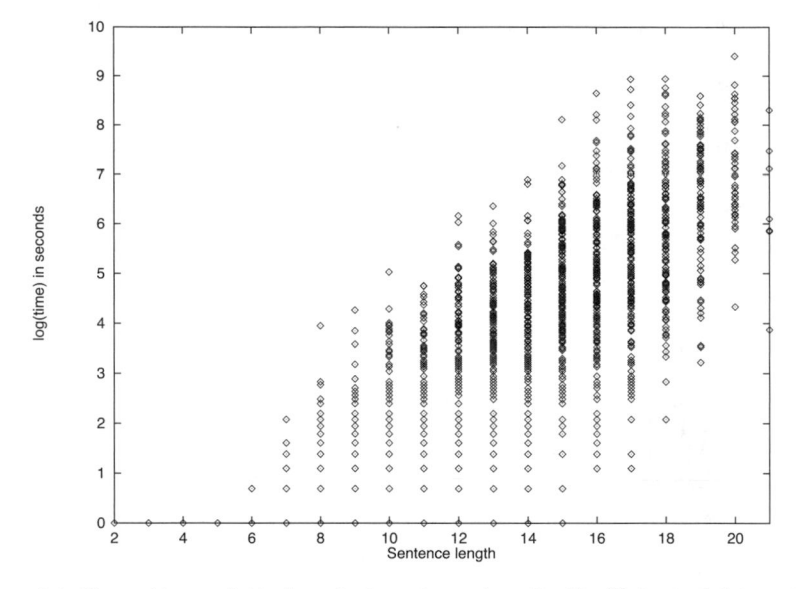

FIGURE 5.4 Parse times plotted against sentence length. Coefficient of determination: $R^2 = 0.65$. (x-axis: Sentence length; y-axis: log(time in seconds))

thus taking considerably less than the worst case n^4 space and the lexical database is read dynamically from a disk-based hash table. For each input sentence, the parser produces as output a shared derivation forest that is a compact representation of all the derivation trees for that sentence. We use the definition of derivation forests for TAGs represented as CFGs, taking $O(n^4)$ space as defined in Vijay-Shanker and Weir (1993) and Lang (1994).

5.4.3 Input data

To test the performance of LTAG parsing on a realistic corpus using a large grammar (described above) we parsed 2, 250 sentences from the Wall Street Journal using the lexicalized grammar described in section 5.3.[1] The length of each sentence was 21 words or less. The average sentence length was 12.3, and the total number of tokens was 27, 715. These sentences were taken from the same sections (02–21) of the Treebank from which the original grammar was extracted. This was done to avoid the complication of using default rules for unknown words.

5.4.4 Parsing setup

In this section we examine the performance of the parser on the input data (described in section 5.4.3).[2] Figure 5.4 shows the time taken in seconds by the parser plotted against sentence length.[3] We see a great deal of variation in timing for the same sentence length, especially for longer sentences. This is surprising since all time complexity analyses reported for parsing algorithms assume that the only

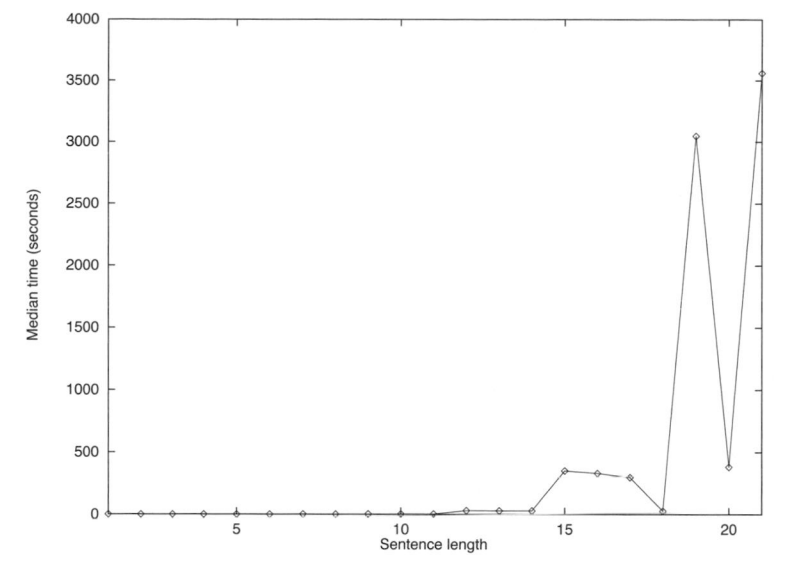

FIGURE 5.5 Median running times for the parser. (x-axis: Sentence length; y-axis: Median time in seconds)

relevant factor is the length of the sentence. In this paper, we will explore whether sentence length is the only relevant factor.[4]

Figure 5.5 shows the median of time taken for each sentence length. This figure shows that for some sentences the time taken by the parser deviates by a large magnitude from the median case for the same sentence length. Next we considered each set of sentences of the same length to be a sample, and we computed the standard deviation for each sample. This number ignores the outliers and gives us a better estimate of parser performance in the most common case. Figure 5.6 shows the plot of the standard deviation points against parsing time. The figure also shows that these points can be described by a linear function.

5.5   Syntactic Lexical Ambiguity

In a fully lexicalized grammar such as LTAG, the combinations of trees (by substitution and adjunction) can be thought of as *attachments*. It is this perspective that allows us to define the parsing problem in two steps (Joshi and Schabes, 1991):

1. Assigning a set of lexicalized structures to each word in the input sentence.

2. Finding the correct attachments between these structures to get all parses for the sentence.

In this section we will try to find which of these factors determines parsing complexity when finding all parses in an LTAG parser.

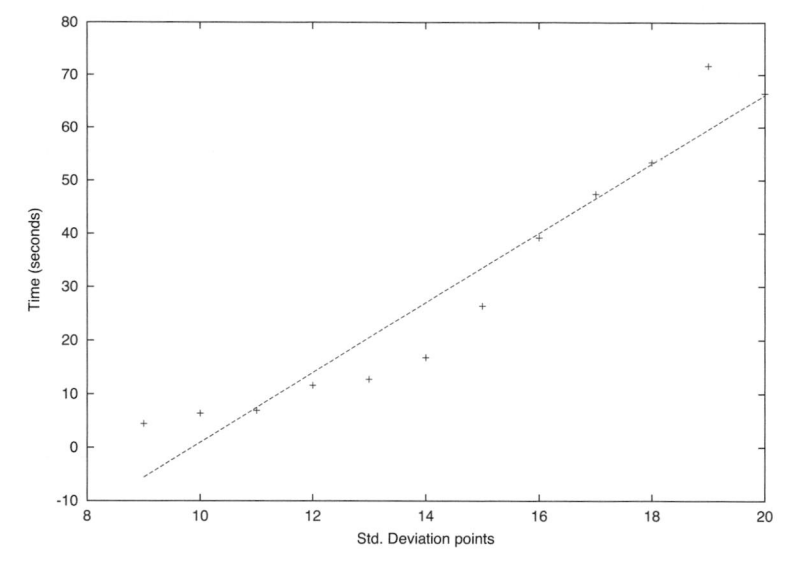

FIGURE 5.6 Least Squares fit over standard deviation points for each sentence length. Error was 9.078% and 13.74% for the slope and intercept respectively. We ignored sentences shorter than 8 words due to round-off errors; cf. Figure 5.4 (x-axis: Std. deviation points; y-axis: Time in seconds)

In all of the experiments reported here, the parser produces all parses for each sentence. It produces a shared derivation forest for each sentence that stores, in compact form, all derivations for each sentence.

We found that the observed complexity of parsing for LTAG is dominated by factors other than sentence length.[5] Figure 5.4 shows the time taken in seconds by the parser plotted against sentence length. We see a great deal of variation in timing for the same sentence length, especially for longer sentences.

We wanted to find the relevant variable other than sentence length that would be the right predictor of parsing time complexity. There can be a large variation in syntactic lexical ambiguity which might be a relevant factor in parsing time complexity. To draw this out, in figure 5.7 we plotted the number of trees selected by a sentence against the time taken to parse that sentence. By examining this graph we can visually infer that the number of trees selected is a better predictor of increase in parsing complexity than sentence length. We can also compare numerically the two hypotheses by computing the coefficient of determination (R^2) for the two graphs. We get a R^2 value of 0.65 for figure 5.4 and a value of 0.82 for figure 5.7. Thus, we infer that it is the syntactic lexical ambiguity of the words in the sentence which is the major contributor to parsing time complexity. Note that Supertagging directly addresses this issue of syntactic lexical ambiguity and we will show how Supertagging can help parsing efficiency in section 5.7.

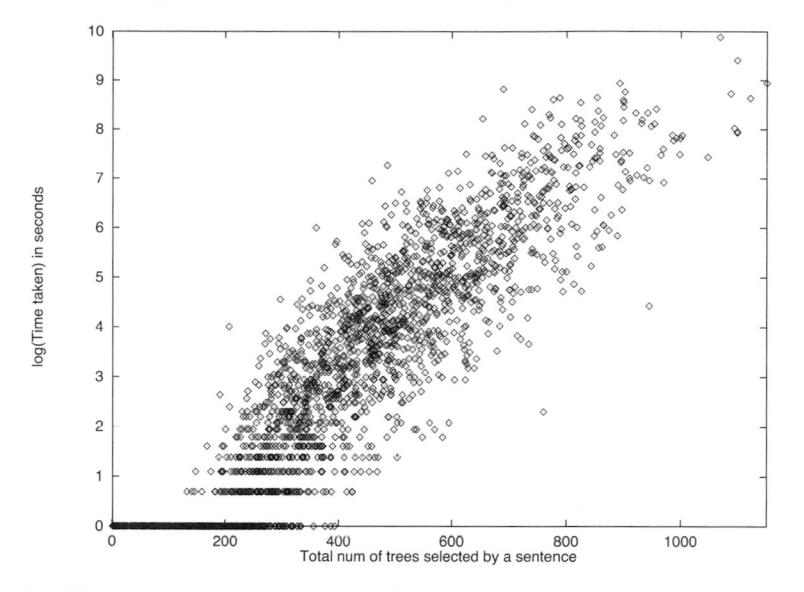

FIGURE 5.7 The impact of syntactic lexical ambiguity on parsing times. Log of the time taken to parse a sentence plotted against the total number of trees selected by the sentence. Coefficient of determination: $R^2 = 0.82$. (x-axis: Total number of trees selected by a sentence; y-axis: log(time) in seconds).

One might be tempted to suggest that instead of number of trees selected, the number of derivations reported by the parser might be a better predictor of parsing time complexity. We tested this hypothesis by plotting the number of derivations reported for each sentence plotted against the time taken to produce them (shown in figure 5.8). The figure shows that the final number of derivations reported is clearly not a valid predictor of parsing time complexity.

5.6 Sentence Complexity

There are many ways of describing sentence complexity,[6] which are not necessarily independent of each other. In the context of lexicalized tree-adjoining grammar (and in other lexical frameworks, perhaps with some modifications) the complexity of syntactic and semantic processing is related to the number of predicate-argument structures being computed for a given sentence.

In this section, we explore the possibility of characterizing sentence complexity in terms of the number of clauses which is used as an approximation to the number of predicate-argument structures to be found in a sentence.

The number of clauses of a given sentence in the Penn Treebank is counted using the bracketing tags. The count is computed to be the number of S/SINV/SQ/RRC nodes which have a VP child or a child with -PRD function tag. In principle, number of clauses can grow continuously as the sentence length increases. However, it is

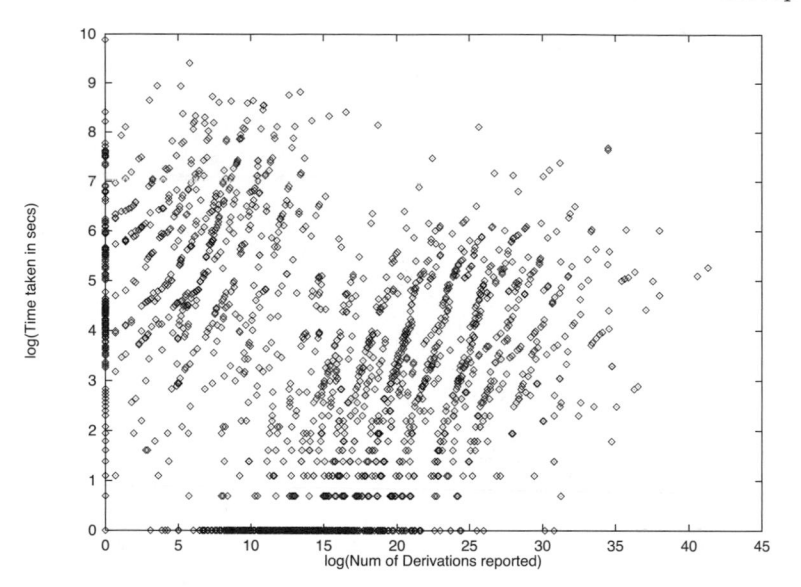

FIGURE 5.8 Number of derivations reported for each sentence plotted against the time taken to produce them (both axes are in log scale). (x-axis: log(Number of derivations reported); y-axis: log(Time taken) in seconds)

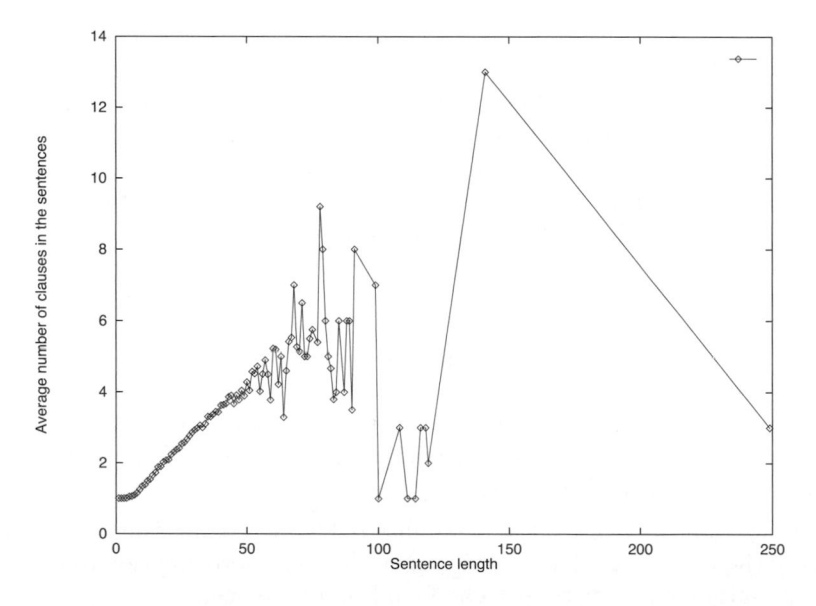

FIGURE 5.9 Average number of clauses plotted against sentence length.

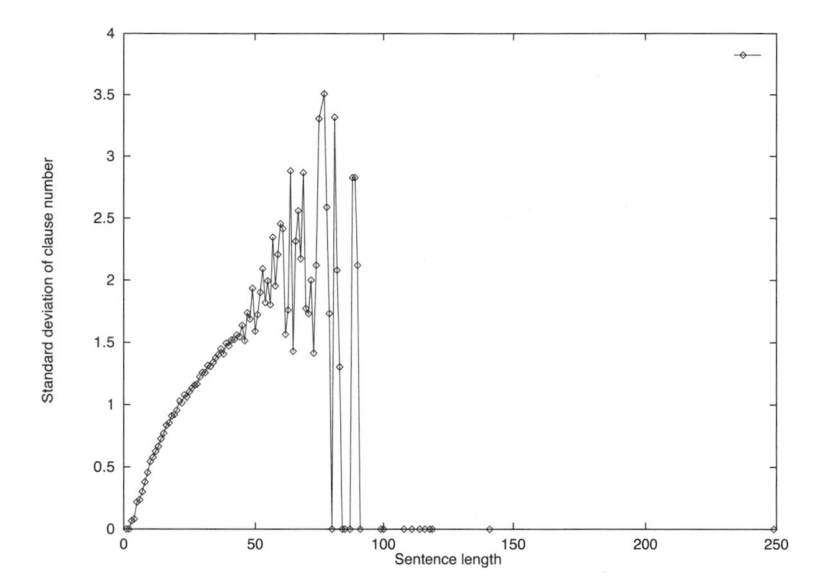

FIGURE 5.10 Standard deviation of number of clauses against sentence length.

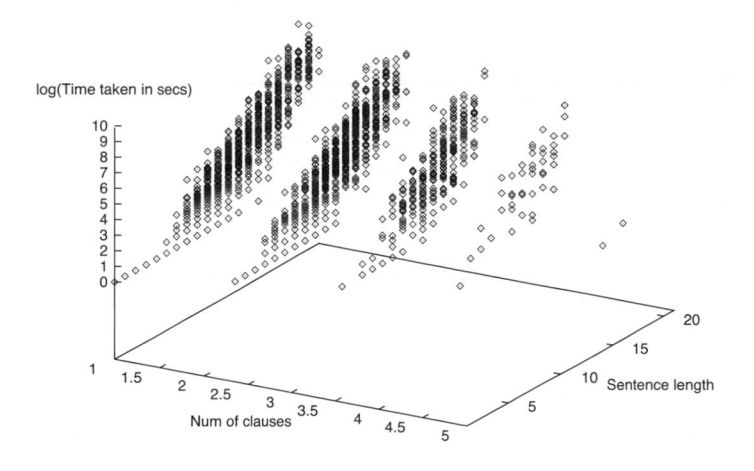

FIGURE 5.11 Variation in times for parsing plotted against length of each sentence while identifying the number of clauses.

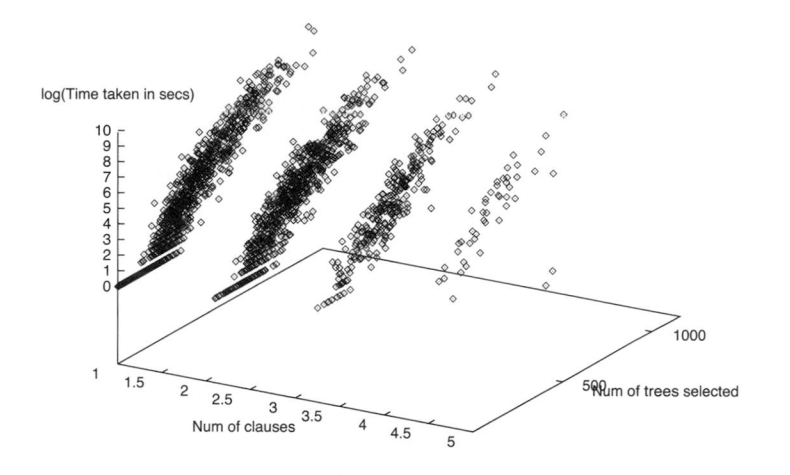

FIGURE 5.12   Variation in times for parsing plotted against the number of trees selected
by each sentence while identifying the number of clauses.

interesting to note that 99.1% of sentences in the Penn Treebank contain 6 or fewer clauses.

Figure 5.9 shows the average number of clauses plotted against sentence length. For sentences with no more than 50 words, which account for 98.2% of the corpus, we see a linear increase in the average number of clauses with respect to sentence length. But from that point on, increasing the sentence length does not lead to a proportional increase in the number of clauses. Thus, empirically, the number of clauses is bounded by a constant. For some very long sentences, the number of clauses actually decreases because these sentences include long but flat coordinated phrases.

Figure 5.10 shows the standard deviation of the clause number plotted against sentence length. There is an increase in deviation for sentences longer than 50 words. This is due to two reasons: first, quite often, long sentences either have many embedded clauses or are flat with long coordinated phrases; second, the data become sparse as the sentence length grows, resulting in high deviation.[7]

In figure 5.11 and figure 5.12 we show how parsing time varies as a function of the number of clauses present in the sentence being parsed. The figures are analogous to the earlier graphs relating parsing time with other factors (see figure 5.4 and figure 5.7). Surprisingly, in both graphs we see that when the number of clauses is small (in this case less than 5), an increase in the number of clauses has no effect on the parsing complexity. Even when the number of clauses is 1, we find the same pattern of time complexity that we have seen in the earlier graphs when we ignored

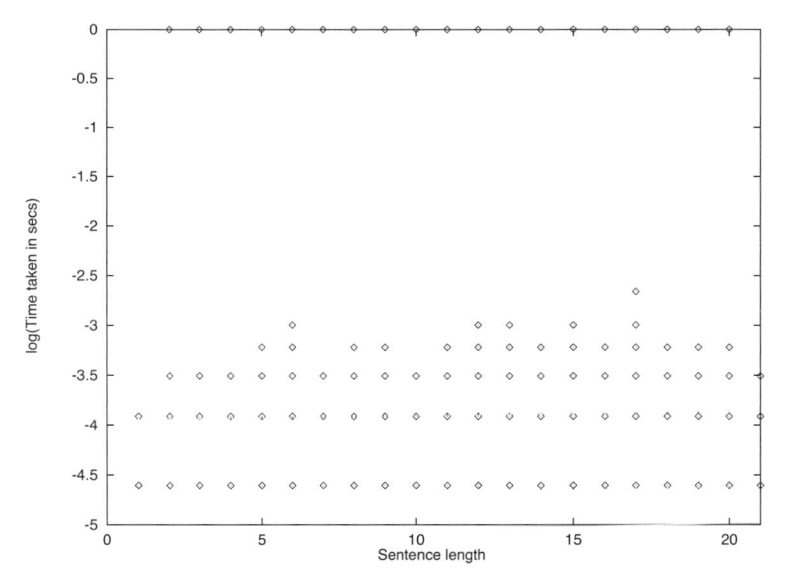

FIGURE 5.13 An oracle experiment: parse times when the parser gets the correct tree for each word in the sentence (eliminating any syntactic lexical ambiguity). The parsing times for all the 2250 sentences for all lengths never goes above 1 second. Total time was reduced from 548K seconds to 31.2 seconds. (x-axis: Sentence length; y-axis: log(time) in seconds)

clause complexity. Thus, when the number of clauses is small parsing complexity is related to attachment of adjuncts rather than arguments. It would be interesting to continue increasing the number of clauses and the sentence length and then compare the differences in parsing times.

We have seen that beyond a certain sentence length, the number of clauses does not increase proportionally. We conjecture that a parser can exploit this observed constraint on clause complexity in sentences to improve its efficiency. In a way similar to methods that account for low attachment of adjuncts while parsing, we can introduce constraints on how many clauses a particular node can dominate in a parse. By making the parser sensitive to this measure, we can prune out unlikely derivations previously considered to be plausible by the parser. There is also an independent reason for pursuing this measure of clausal complexity. It can be extended to a notion of syntactic and semantic complexity as they relate to both the representational and processing aspects (Joshi, 2000). The empirical study of clausal complexity described in this section might shed some light on the general issue of syntactic and semantic complexity.

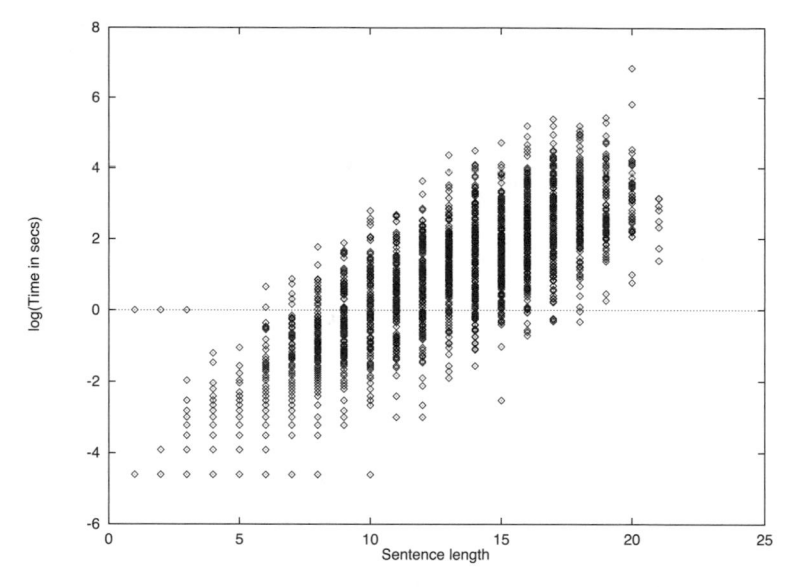

FIGURE 5.14 Time taken by the parser after n-best Supertagging ($n = 60$). Total time was reduced from 548K seconds to 21K seconds. (x-axis: Sentence length; y-axis: log(time) in seconds)

5.7   Supertagging Helps Parsing Efficiency

Since we can easily determine the number of trees selected by a sentence before we start parsing, we can use this number to predict the number of edges that will be proposed by a parser when parsing this sentence, allowing us to handle better difficult cases *before* parsing.

We test the preceding hypothesis further by parsing the same set of sentences, but this time using an oracle that tells us the correct elementary lexicalized structure for each word in the sentence. This eliminates lexical syntactic ambiguity but does not eliminate attachment ambiguity for the parser. The graph comparing the parsing times is shown in figure 5.13. As the comparison shows, the elimination of lexical ambiguity leads to a drastic increase in parsing efficiency. The total time taken to parse all $2,250$ sentences went from 548K seconds to 31.2 seconds.

Figure 5.13 shows us that a model that disambiguates syntactic lexical ambiguity can potentially be extremely useful in terms of parsing efficiency. Thus disambiguation of tree assignment or Supertagging (Srinivas, 1997) of a sentence before parsing it might be a way of improving parsing efficiency. This gives us a way to reduce the parsing complexity for precisely the sentences that were problematic: the ones that selected too many trees. To test whether parsing times are reduced after Supertagging, we conducted an experiment in which the output of an n-best Supertagger was taken as input to the parser. In our experiment we set n to be 60.[8]

The time taken to parse the same set of sentences was again dramatically reduced (the total time taken was 21K seconds). However, the disadvantage of this method was that the coverage of the parser was somewhat reduced. This was because some crucial tree was missing in the n-best output. Such coverage issues can be fixed fairly easily by having a LTAG grammar with sister adjunction, so that even with a small set of trees in the initial set, sister adjunction can be used to create parse trees for all input strings, with only a slight penalty in accuracy. The results are graphed in figure 5.14. The total number of derivations for all sentences went down to 1.01e+10 (the original total number was 1.4e+18) indicating (not surprisingly) that some attachment ambiguities persist although the number of trees are reduced.

5.8   Bootstrapping an LTAG Parser Using a Supertagger

In this section we provide another application to the ideas presented in section 5.7. Consider the derivation tree in figure 5.2. The probability of a sequence of elementary trees $t_0, t_1, \ldots, t_n$ assigned to the n words in the sentence $S = w_0, \ldots, w_n$ is computed using a statistical model for Supertagging (Srinivas and Joshi, 1999) that is the probability of generating a Supertag sequence and the input word sequence. We can think of the probability distribution over Supertag sequences given the input string as a particular instantiation of a scoring function f_A over such sequences.

$$f_A = P(t_0, t_1, \ldots, t_n, S)$$

Models for Supertagging are described in great detail elsewhere in this book.

In a similar fashion, the derivation tree itself can be assigned a probability. Let S be the input sentence and T be the derivation tree for that sentence. A statistical parsing model defines $P(T \mid S)$. Using this model, we can find the best parse T^*:

$$T^* = \operatorname*{argmax}_T P(T \mid S) = \frac{P(T, S)}{P(S)} \approx P(T, S)$$

So the best parse will be $T^* = \operatorname{argmax}_T P(T, S)$. A statistical model for LTAG (Schabes, 1992) computes $P(T, S)$. As before, we can think of the probability distribution over derivations given the input string as an instantiation of a scoring function over derivations, which we will call f_B.

$$f_B = P(T, S) = P(\alpha_0) \cdot \prod_{i=1\ldots n-1} P(\beta_i \mid \gamma, \eta)$$

for all the n trees in the derivation tree, where either the tree is at the root of the derivation and generated with probability $P(\alpha_0)$ or it is not the root, in which case the tree β_i is generated with probability $P(\beta_i \mid \gamma, \eta)$, which is the probability of β_i substituting or adjoining into some tree γ at node η. This is a generative model, so any tree γ previously generated can be used in the conditioning context to generate another tree in the derivation until all the trees in the LTAG derivation tree are generated. This is analogous to the probability distribution over parse trees defined in a probabilistic context-free grammar.

A is a statistical n-best Supertagger, and
B is a statistical LTAG parser.
M_A^i and M_B^i are models of A and B at step i.
U is a large pool of unlabeled sentences.
U^i is a small cache holding subset of U at step i.
L is the manually labeled seed data.
L_A^i and L_B^i are the labeled training examples for A and B at step i.

Initialize:
$$L_A^0 \leftarrow L_B^0 \leftarrow L$$
$$M_A^0 \leftarrow Train(A, L_A^0)$$
$$M_B^0 \leftarrow Train(B, L_B^0)$$
Loop:
$U^i \leftarrow$ Add unlabeled sentences from U.

M_A^i and M_B^i parse each sentences in U^i and assign scores to n-best Supertags
and most likely LTAG derivation using scoring functions f_A and f_B.

For each sentence in U_i, parse the n-best Supertags using the LTAG parser (cf. §5.7).

For each sentence in U_i, select most likely "parse" for Supertagger by choosing
the parse from the LTAG parser output forest that has the highest f_A score.

Select new parses $\{P_A\}$ and $\{P_B\}$ from parsed U_i according to selection method S,
which uses scores from f_A and f_B.

L_A^{i+1} is L_A^i augmented with $\{P_B\}$
L_B^{i+1} is L_B^i augmented with $\{P_A\}$
$$M_A^{i+1} \leftarrow Train(A, L_A^{i+1})$$
$$M_B^{i+1} \leftarrow Train(B, L_B^{i+1})$$
Return:
M_A^T and M_B^T after T rounds of cotraining.

FIGURE 5.15 Pseudo-code for the cotraining algorithm

A key issue is how to estimate all of the above probability distributions. The supervised learning solution is to estimate these probility distributions using maximum likelihood estimation from hand annotated data: the correct Supertag sequence for each sentence in training data to estimate probabilities for the Supertagger, and the correct LTAG derivation for each sentence in the training data to estimate probabilities for the LTAG statistical parser. There are standard heuristic methods to convert the Treebank parse trees into LTAG derivations (Xia, 1999; Chiang, 2000; Chen and Vijay-Shanker, 2000) and see also section 5.3. Training in the supervised setting simply amounts to relative frequency counts that are normalized to provide the probabilities needed.[9]

Instead of supervised learning, we consider here the setting of a model trained on small amount of seed labeled data combined with a model trained on larger amounts of unlabeled or raw data, where the correct annotations are not provided. This setting is attractive for several reasons:

- Annotating sentences is an expensive process. A parser that can be trained on a small amount of labeled data will reduce this annotation cost.
- Creating statistical parsers for novel domains and new languages will become easier.
- Combining labeled data with unlabeled data allows exploration of unsupervised methods that can now be tested using evaluations compatible with supervised statistical parsing.

The idea presented in this section is to combine a Supertagger and an LTAG statistical parser. However, instead of feeding the output of the Supertagger to an LTAG parser as we did in section 5.7, we instead use the each model to create newly parsed data for the other model. This newly parsed data is treated as new labeled data, which is used to retrain each model in an iterative augmentation process.

The pair of probabilistic models, a Supertagger and an LTAG statistical parser, can be exploited to bootstrap new information from unlabeled data. Since both of these steps ultimately have to agree with each other, we can utilize an iterative method called cotraining (Blum and Mitchell, 1998) that attempts to increase agreement between a pair of statistical models by exploiting mutual constraints between their output. Cotraining has some good generalization properties when the features or views used by the two models are conditionally independent of each other (Dasgupta et al., 2002), and it can be formulated to be a greedy search for agreement in the feature space of the two models, even if the two models are not conditionally independent (Abney, 2002). In the experiments reported here, however, we will use the simple greedy algorithm provided by Blum and Mitchell (1998), extended to handle the multiple views provided by a Supertagger and an LTAG parser.

Previous approaches that use cotraining were on tasks that involved identifying the right label from a small set of labels (typically 2–3), and in a relatively small parameter space. Compared to these earlier models, a statistical parser has a very large parameter space, and the labels that are expected as output are parse trees that have to be built up recursively. Cotraining can be informally described in the following manner:

- Pick two (or more) "views" of a classification problem.
- Build separate models for each of these "views" and train each model on a small set of labeled data.
- Sample an unlabeled data set and to find examples that each   model independently labels with high confidence. Nigam and Ghani (2000)
- Confidently labeled examples can be picked in various ways. Collins and Singer (1999); Goldman and Zhou (2000)
- Take these examples as being valuable as training examples and iterate this procedure until the unlabeled data is exhausted.

Effectively, by picking confidently labeled data from each model to add to the training data, one model is labeling data for the other model.

The pseudo-code for the cotraining algorithm we used to bootstrap an LTAG parser using a Supertagger is shown in figure 5.15. Note that f_A is the probability model for a Supertag sequence used by a statistical Supertagger, f_B is the probability model for LTAG derivations used by the LTAG parser, and the selection method S used here is simple *top-k* selection where the k labeled outputs from U_i with the highest scores are selected. Other variants are explored in Steedman et al. (2003b,a), and Hwa et al. (2003).

Experiments using this approach were reported in Sarkar (2001). The experiments used the Penn Treebank WSJ Corpus (Marcus et al., 1993). The various settings for the cotraining algorithm (cf. Figure 5.15) are as follows:

- L was set to sections 02–06 of the Penn Treebank WSJ (9625 sentences)
- U was 3,0137 sentences (section 07–21 of the Treebank stripped of all annotations).
- We used a tag dictionary of all lexicalized trees from *labeled* and *unlabeled* for unseen words.
- Novel trees were treated as unknown tree tokens.
- The cache U^i was set to be 3,000 sentences.

While it might seem expensive to run the parser over the cache multiple times, we use the pruning capabilities of the parser to good use here. During the iterations, we set the beam size to a value that is likely to prune out all derivations for a large portion of the cache except the most likely ones. This allows the parser to run faster, hence avoiding the usual problem with running an iterative algorithm over thousands of sentences. In the initial runs, we also limit the length of the sentences entered into the cache, since we select parses based on their probability, and shorter sentences tend to receive higher probability than longer sentences. The beam size is reset when running the parser on the test data to allow the parser a better chance at finding the most likely parse.

We scored the output of the parser on section 23 of the Wall Street Journal Penn Treebank. The following are some aspects of the scoring that might be useful for comparision with other results: No punctuations are scored, including sentence final punctuation. Empty elements are not scored. We used EVALB (written by Satoshi Sekine and Michael Collins), which scores based on PARSEVAL (Black et al., 1991), with the standard parameter file (as per standard practice, part of speech brackets were not part of the evaluation). Also, we used Adwait Ratnaparkhi's part-of-speech tagger (Ratnaparkhi, 1996) to tag unknown words in the test data.

We obtained 80.02% and 79.64% labeled bracketing precision and recall respectively (as defined in Black et al., 1991). The baseline model, which was only trained on the 9,695 sentences of labeled data, performed at 72.23% and 69.12% precision and recall. These results show that training a statistical parser using our cotraining method to combine labeled and unlabeled data strongly outperforms training only on the labeled data.

It is important to note that unlike previous studies which aim to infer a grammar in an unsupervised setting (de Marcken, 1995), our method is a step toward unsupervised parsing, but the output results are directly compared to the output of supervised parsers.

5.9 Conclusion

We identified syntactic lexical ambiguity and sentence complexity as factors that contribute to parsing complexity in fully lexicalized grammars. We conducted various experiments by parsing the Penn Treebank WSJ corpus using an LTAG grammar extracted from the annotated corpus. The experiments led to make the following conclusions.

We showed that lexical syntactic ambiguity has a strong effect on parsing time and that a model that disambiguates syntactic lexical ambiguity can potentially be extremely useful in terms of parsing efficiency. Assigning each word in the sentence with the correct elementary tree showed that parsing times were reduced by several orders of magnitude.

We showed that even as sentence length increases, the number of clauses is empirically bounded by a constant. The number of clauses in 99.1% of sentences in the Penn Treebank was bounded by 6. We discussed how this finding affects parsing efficiency and showed that for when the number of clauses is smaller than 4, parsing efficiency is dominated by adjunct attachments rather than argument attachments. We conducted an experiment in which the output of an n-best Supertagger was taken as input to the parser. The time taken to parse the same set of sentences was again dramatically reduced.

We also showed how the combination of a Supertagger with a LTAG parser can be effectively used in a cotraining approach for situations in which there is insufficient training data.

Notes

1. Some of these results appear in Sarkar (2000). In this section we present some additional data on the previous results and also the results of some new experiments that do not appear in the earlier work.

2. The data was split into 45 equal sized chunks and parsed in parallel on a Beowulf cluster of Pentium Pro 200Mhz servers with 512MB of memory running Linux 2.2.

3. From the total input data of 2250 sentences, 315 sentences did not get a parse. This was because the parser was run with the start symbol set to the label S. Of the sentences that did not parse 276 sentences were rooted at other labels such as FRAG, NP, and so on. The remaining 39 sentences were rejected because a tokenization bug did not remove a few punctuation symbols that do not select any trees in the grammar.

4. A useful analogy to consider is the run-time analysis of *quicksort*. For this particular sorting algorithm, it was detemined the distribution of the order of the numbers in the input array to be sorted was an extremely important factor to guarantee sorting in time $\Theta(nlogn)$. An array of numbers that is already completely sorted has time complexity $\Theta(n^2)$.

5. Note that the precise number of edges proposed by the parser and other common indicators of complexity can be obtained only while or after parsing. We are interested in *predicting* parsing complexity.

6. This section is based on some joint work with Fei Xia and Aravind Joshi, previously published as a workshop paper (Sarkar et al., 2000).

7. For some sentence lengths (e.g., length = 250), there is only one sentence with that length in the whole corpus, resulting in zero deviation.

8. Chen et al. (1999) show that to get greater than 97% accuracy using Supertagging, the value of n must be quite high ($n > 40$). They use a different set of Supertags, and so we used their result simply to get an approximate estimate of the value of n.

9. There are issues about smoothing these distributions that are not pertinent to our discussion here.

References

Abney, S. P. (2002). Bootstrapping. In *Proceedings of the 40th Annual Meeting of the Association for Computational Linguistics*, Philadelphia.

Black, E., Abney, S. P., Flickinger, D., Gdaniec, C., Grishman, R., Harrison, P., Hindle, D., Ingria, R., Jelinek, F., Klavans, J., Liberman, M., Marcus, M. P., Roukos, S.,

Santorini, B., and Strzalkowski, T. (1991). A procedure for quantitatively comparing the syntactic coverage of English grammars. In *Proceedings of the DARPA Speech and Natural Language Workshop*, Morgan Kaufmann.

Blum, A. and Mitchell, T. (1998). Combining Labeled and Unlabeled Data with Co-Training. In *Proceedings of the 11ᵗʰ Annual Conf. on Comp. Learning Theory (COLT)*.

Caraballo, S. A. and Charniak, E. (1998). New figures of merit for best-first probabilistic chart parsing. *Computational Linguistics*, 24(2):275–298.

Chen, J., Bangalore, S., and Vijay-Shanker, K. (1999). New models for improving supertag disambiguation. In *Proceedings of the 9th Conference of the European Chapter of the Association for Computational Linguistics*, Bergen, Norway.

Chen, J. and Vijay-Shanker, K. (2000). Automated Extraction of TAGs from the Penn Treebank. In *Proceedings of the 6ᵗʰ International Workshop on Parsing Technologies (IWPT-2000), Italy*.

Chiang, D. (2000). Statistical Parsing with an Automatically-Extracted Tree Adjoining Grammar. In *Proceedings of ACL-2000*.

Clark, S. (2002). Supertagging for combinatory categorial grammar. In *Proceedings of the 6th International Workshop on Tree Adjoining Grammars and Related Frameworks (TAG+6)*, Venice, Italy.

Clark, S. and Curran, J. R. (2004). The importance of supertagging for wide-coverage ccg parsing. In *Proceedings of the 20th International Conference on Computational Linguistics (COLING-04)*, Geneva, Switzerland.

Collins, M. and Singer, Y. (1999). Unsupervised Models for Named Entity Classification. In *Proceedings of WVLC/EMNLP-99*.

Dasgupta, S., Littman, M., and McAllester, D. (2002). PAC generalization bounds for co-training. In Dietterich, T. G., Becker, S., and Ghahramani, Z., eds., *Advances in Neural Information Processing Systems 14*, MIT Press.

de Marcken, C. (1995). Lexical heads, phrase structure and the induction of grammar. In Yarowsky, D. and Church, K., eds., *Proceedings of the Third Workshop of Very Large Corpora*, MIT Press.

Goldman, S. and Zhou, Y. (2000). Enhancing supervised learning with unlabeled data. In *Proceedings of ICML'2000*, Stanford University.

Hwa, R., Osborne, M., Sarkar, A., and Steedman, M. J. (2003). Corrected co-training for statistical parsers. In *Proceedings of the ICML Workshop on The Continuum from Labeled to Unlabeled Data in Machine Learning and Data Mining at the 20th International Conference on Machine Learning (ICML-2003)*, Washington DC.

Joshi, A. K. (2000). Some aspects of syntactic and semantic complexity and underspecification. Talk given at *Syntactic and Semantic Complexity in Natural Language Processing Systems, Workshop at ANLP-NAACL 2000*, Seattle.

Joshi, A. K., Levy, L. S., and Takahashi, M. (1975). Tree Adjunct Grammars. *Journal of Computer and System Sciences*.

Joshi, A. K. and Schabes, Y. (1991). Tree adjoining grammars and lexicalized grammars. In Nivat, M. and Podelski, A., eds., *Tree automata and languages*. North-Holland.

Joshi, A. K. and Schabes, Y. (1992). Tree-adjoining grammar and lexicalized grammars. In Nivat, M. and Podelski, A., eds., *Tree automata and languages*. Elsevier Science.

Kay, M. (1989). Head driven parsing. In *Proceedings of IWPT '89*, Pittsburgh.

Lang, B. (1994). Recognition can be harder than parsing. *Computational Intelligence*, 10(4).

Lavelli, A. and Satta, G. (1991). Bidirectional parsing of Lexicalized Tree Adjoining Grammars. In *Proceedings 5th EACL*, Berlin, Germany.

Marcus, M. P., Santorini, B., and Marcinkiewicz, M. A. (1993). Building a large annotated corpus of english. *Computational Linguistics*, 19(2):313–330.

Nigam, K. and Ghani, R. (2000). Analyzing the effectiveness and applicability of co-training. In *Proceedings of the Ninth International Conference on Information and Knowledge (CIKM-2000)*.

Oepen, S. and Carroll, J. (2000). Ambiguity packing in constraint-based parsing – practical results. In *Proceedings of the 1st Meeting of the North American ACL, NAACL-2000*, Seattle, Washington.

Ratnaparkhi, A. (1996). A Maximum Entropy Part-Of-Speech Tagger. In *Proceedings of the Empirical Methods in Natural Language Processing Conference*, University of Pennsylvania.

Sarkar, A. (2000). Practical experiments in parsing using tree adjoining grammars. In *Proceedings of the Fifth Workshop on Tree Adjoining Grammars*, Paris, France.

Sarkar, A. (2001). Applying co-training methods to statistical parsing. In *Proceedings of NAACL 2001*, Pittsburgh.

Sarkar, A., Xia, F., and Joshi, A. K. (2000). Some experiments on indicators of parsing complexity for lexicalized grammars. In *Efficiency in Large-Scale Parsing Systems Workshop held at COLING 2000*, Luxembourg.

Schabes, Y. (1992). Stochastic lexicalized tree-adjoining grammars. In *Proceedings of COLING '92*, Nantes, France.

Schabes, Y. (1994). Left to right parsing of lexicalized tree adjoining grammars. *Computational Intelligence*, 10(4).

Schabes, Y. and Shieber, S. M. (1994). An alternative conception of tree-adjoining derivation. *Computational Linguistics*, 20(1):91–124.

Sikkel, K. (1997). *Parsing Schemata*. Springer-Verlag.

Srinivas, B. (1997). Performance Evaluation of Supertagging for Partial Parsing. In *Proceedings of Fifth International Workshop on Parsing Technology*, Boston, USA.

Srinivas, B. and Joshi, A. K. (1999). Supertagging: An approach to almost parsing. *Computational Linguistics*, 25(2).

Steedman, M. J., Hwa, R., Clark, S., Osborne, M., Sarkar, A., Hockenmaier, J., Ruhlen, P., Baker, S., and Crim, J. (2003a). Example selection for bootstrapping statistical parsers. In *The Human Language Technology Conference and the 4th Meeting of the North Amcrican Association for Computational Linguistics: HLT-NAACL 2003*, Edmonton, Canada.

Steedman, M. J., Osborne, M., Sarkar, A., Clark, S., Hwa, R., Hockenmaier, J., Ruhlen, P., Baker, S., and Crim, J. (2003b). Bootstrapping statistical parsers from small datasets. In *Proceedings of the 11th Conference of the European Association for Computational Linguistics: EACL 2003*, Budapest, Hungary.

van Noord, G. (1994). Head-corner parsing for TAG. *Computational Intelligence*, 10(4).

Vijay-Shanker, K. and Weir, D. J. (1993). The use of shared forests in TAG parsing. In *Proceedings of the 6th Meeting of the EACL*, Utrecht, The Netherlands.

Xia, F. (1999). Extracting Tree Adjoining Grammars from Bracketed Corpora. In *Proceedings of NLPRS-99*, Beijing, China.

Xia, F. and Palmer, M. (2000). Evaluating the Coverage of LTAGs on Annotated Corpora. In *Proceedings of LREC Satellite Workshop Using Evaluation within HLT Programs: Results and Trends*.

XTAG-Group (1998). A Lexicalized Tree Adjoining Grammar for English. Technical Report IRCS 98-18, University of Pennsylvania.

6

Discriminative Learning of Supertagging

LIBIN SHEN

6.1 Introduction

In Lexicalized Tree-Adjoining Grammar (LTAG) (Joshi and Schabes, 1997), each word in a sentence is associated with an elementary tree, or a supertag (Joshi and Bangalore, 1994). Supertagging is the process of assigning the correct supertag to each word of an input sentence. Supertags contain more linguistic information than Part of Speech (POS) tags.

Although correct supertags are able to encode rich syntactic dependence, supertags automatically generated by a supertagger may contain more noise than useful information, since the supertagger cannot always assign the correct supertag to each word. If we use supertags as input in some NLP application, noise in supertags may result in decrease in the overall performance. So the question is whether supertags provide more useful information than noise.

In order to answer this question, we focus on NP chunking (Ramshaw and Marcus, 1995) as an application for supertags. Our experiments show that, by using the supertags generated by a trigram supertagger as input, the NP chunker obtains worse chunking accuracy, compared to a similar chunking system that takes POS tags as input. It is not surprising because a supertagger trained with local information in fact does not take full advantage of complex information available with supertag representation.

For the purpose of exploiting rich syntactic dependencies in a larger context, we propose a new model of supertagging that is based on discriminative learning. We apply discriminative classifier to sequential models via the Projection-base Markov Model (PMM) used in Punyakanok and Roth (2000). What is special with our approach is that we construct a SNoW classifier (Roth, 1998) for each POS tag. For each word of an input sentence, its POS tag, instead of the supertag of the previous word, is used to select the corresponding SNoW classifier. This method helps to avoid the sparse data problem and forces the local discriminative classifiers to focus on difficult cases in the context of supertagging task.

We evaluate the new supertagger on both the hand-coded supertags used in Chen et al. (1999) as well as the supertags extracted from Penn Treebank (PTB) (Xia, 2001; Marcus et al., 1994). On the dataset used in Chen et al. (1999), our supertagger achieves an accuracy of 92.41%.

We then apply the new supertagger to NP chunking. In this case, the use of the supertags gives rise to almost 1% absolute increase (from 92.03% to 92.95%) in F-score over the baseline under Transformation Based Learning (TBL) approach. This confirms our claim that using supertagging as a labeling system helps to increase the overall performance of NP chunking. The supertagger presented here provides an opportunity for advanced machine learning techniques to improve their performance on chunking tasks by exploiting more syntactic information encoded in the supertags.

6.2   Background

6.2.1   Supertagging

In Bangalore (1997), trigram models were used for supertagging, in which Good-Turing discounting technique and Katz's back-off model were employed. The supertag for each word was determined by the lexical preference of the supertag, as well as by the contextual preference of the previous two supertags. The model was tested on WSJ section 20 of PTB, and trained on section 0 through 24 except section 20. The accuracy on the test data is 91.37%. [1]

The trigram model often fails in capturing the cooccurrence dependence between a head word and its dependents. Consider the phrase "will *join* the board *as* a nonexecutive director". The occurrence of *join* has influence on the supertag selection of *as*. But *join* is outside the window of trigram. Bangalore (1997) proposed a head trigram model in which the supertag of a word depended on the supertags of the previous two *head* words, instead of the supertags of the two words immediately leading the word of interest. But the performance of this model was worse than the traditional trigram model because it discarded local information.

Chen et al. (1999) combined the traditional trigram model and head trigram model in their trigram *mixed* model. In their model, context for the current word was determined by the supertag of the previous word and context for the previous word according to six heuristic rules. The *mixed* model achieved an accuracy of 91.79% on the same dataset as that of Bangalore (1997). In Chen et al. (1999), three other models were proposed, but the *mixed* model achieved the highest accuracy. In addition, they combined all their models with *pairwise voting*, yielding an accuracy of 92.19%.

The *mixed* trigram model achieves better results on supertagging because it can capture both local and long distance dependencies to some extent. However, we think that a better way to find useful context is to use machine learning techniques. One approach is to switch to models like PMM, which can not only take advantage of generative models but also utilize the information in a larger contexts through flexible feature sets. This is the basic idea guiding the design of our supertagger.

6.2.2 NP chunking

Abney (1991) proposed a two-phase parsing model that includes chunking and attaching. Ramshaw and Marcus (1995) approached chunking by using Transformation Based Learning. Many machine learning techniques have been successfully applied to chunking tasks, such as Regularized Winnow (Zhang et al., 2001), SVMs (Kudo and Matsumoto, 2001), CRF (Sha and Pereira, 2003), Perceptron (Collins, 2002), Memory Based Learning (Sang, 2002), and SNoW (Muñoz et al., 1999).

The previous best result on chunking in literature was achieved by Regularized Winnow in Zhang et al. (2001), which took some of the parsing results given by an English Slot Grammar–based parser as input to the chunker. The use of parsing results contributed 0.62% absolute increase in F-score. However, this approach conflicts with the purpose of chunking. Ideally, a chunker generates n-best results, and an attacher uses chunking results to construct a parse.

The dilemma is that syntactic constraints are useful in the chunking phase, but they are unavailable until the attaching phase. The reason is that POS tags are not a good labeling system to encode enough linguistic knowledge for chunking. However, another labeling system, supertagging, can provide a great deal of syntactic information.

6.2.3 Using supertag in NP chunking

In Bangalore (1997), supertagging was used for NP chunking, and it achieved an F-score of 92.4%. Chen (2001) reported a similar result with a trigram supertagger. In their approaches, they first supertagged the test data and then used heuristic rules to detect NP chunks. But it is hard to say whether it is the use of supertags or the heuristic rules that makes their system achieve these good results.

A better way to evaluate the contribution of supertags in NP chunking is to use TBL, a well-known algorithm in the community of text chunking, as the learning tool for the NP chunking task, and compare it with Ramshaw and Marcus's original work, the de facto baseline of NP chunking. However, the use of supertags with TBL can be easily extended to other machine learning algorithms.

As a first attempt, we use *fast TBL* (Ngai and Florian, 2001), a TBL program, to repeat Ramshaw and Marcus's experiment on the standard dataset. Then we use the supertagger described in Bangalore (1997) to supertag both the training and test data. We run the *fast TBL* for the second round by using supertags instead of POS tags in the dataset. With POS tags we achieve an F-score of 92.01%, but with supertags we only achieve an F-score of 91.66%. This is not surprising, because supertag in Bangalore (1997) were trained only with a trigram model. Although supertags are able to encode rich syntactic dependence, supertaggers trained with local information in fact do not take full advantage of their strong capability in representing linguistic information. So we must use long-distance dependencies to train supertaggers to take full advantage of the information in supertags.

6.3   Discriminative Learning

6.3.1   Multiclass classifier

Various discriminative learning algorithms have been used in natural language processing recently, such as Perceptrons, Winnows, Boosting and SVMs. In this research, we will use Sparse Network of Winnow (SNoW) (Roth, 1998) as the local classifier.

SNoW is a learning architecture that is specially tailored for learning in the presence of a very large number of features where the decision for a single sample depends on only a small number of features. Furthermore, SNoW can also be used as a general purpose multi-class classifier, which is suitable for supertagging.

It is noted in Muñoz et al. (1999) that one of the important properties of the sparse architecture of SNoW is that the complexity of processing an example depends only on the number of features active in it, n_a, and is independent of the total number of features, n_t, observed over the life time of the system and this is important in domains in which the total number of features in very large, but only a small number of them is active in each example.

As far as supertagging is concerned, word context forms a very large space. However, for each word in a given sentence, only a small part of features in the space are related to the decision on supertag. Specifically, the supertag of a word is determined by the appearances of certain words, POS tags, or supertags in its context. In the case of supertagging, the feature space is very large, yet there are only a few features in each sample that play a crucial role in classification. Therefore, SNoW is suitable for the supertagging task.

6.3.2   Sequential inference

Supertagging can be viewed in terms of the sequential model, which means that the selection of the supertag for a word is influenced by the decisions made on the previous few words. Punyakanok and Roth (2000) proposed three methods of using classifiers in sequential inference, which are HMM, PMM, and CSCL. Among these three models, PMM is the most suitable for our task. Like PMM, we also use Viterbi decoding to find the best sequence of supertags.

The basic idea of PMM is as follows. Given an observation sequence O, we find the most likely state sequence S given O by maximizing

$$P(S|O) = [\prod_{t=2}^{n} P(s_t|s_1, ..., s_{t-1}, O)]P_1(s_1|O) \qquad (6.1)$$

In this model, the output of SNoW is used to estimate $P(s|s', O)$ and $P_1(s|O)$, where s is the current state, s' is the previous states, and O is the whole observation. $P(s|s', O)$ is separated to many sub-functions $P_{s'}(s|O)$ according to previous states s'. In practice, O is limited in a local window of the observed sequence, and s' is just the previous state according to the conditional independence assumption. Then the problem is how to map the SNoW results into probabilities. Furthermore, in Punyakanok and Roth (2000), the sigmoid function $1/(1 + e^{-(act-T)})$ is defined as *confidence*, where T is the threshold for SNoW, act is the dot product of the weight vector and the feature vector. The *confidence* is normalized by summing to 1 and used as the distribution mass $P_{s'}(s|O)$.

6.4 Modeling Supertagging

6.4.1 Sequential model for supertagging

First, we have to decide how to treat POS tags. One approach is to assign POS tags at the same time that we do supertagging. The other approach is to assign POS tags with a traditional POS tagger first, and then use them as input to the supertagger. Supertagging an unknown word becomes a problem due to the huge size of the supertag set, so we use the second approach. We first run the Brill POS tagger (Brill, 1995) on both the training and the test data, and use POS tags as part of the input.

Let $W = w_1 w_2 ... w_n$ be the sentence, $Q = q_1 q_2 ... q_n$ be the POS tags, and $T = t_1 t_2 ... t_n$ be the supertags respectively. Given W, Q, we can find the most likely supertag sequence T given W, Q by maximizing

$$P(T|W, Q) = \prod_{i=1}^{n} P(t_i|t_{1...i-1}, W, Q)$$

We decompose $P(t_i|t_{1...i-1}, W, Q)$ into sub-classifiers. However, in our model, we divide it with respect to POS tags as follows

$$P(t_i|t_{1...i-1}, W, Q) \equiv P_{q_i}(t_i|t_{1...i-1}, W, Q) \qquad (6.2)$$

There are several reasons for decomposing $P(t_i|t_{1...i-1}, W, Q)$ with respect to the POS tag of the current word, instead of the supertag of the previous word.

- To avoid sparse-data problem. There are 479 supertags in the set of hand-coded supertags, and almost 3,000 supertags in the set of supertags extracted from Penn Treebank.

- Supertags related to the same POS tag are more difficult to distinguish than supertags related to different POS tags. Thus by defining a classifier on the POS tag of the current word but not the POS tag of the previous word forces the learning algorithm to focus on difficult cases.

- Decomposition of the probability estimation can decrease the complexity of the learning algorithm and allows the use of different parameters for different POS tags.

For each POS q, we construct a SNoW classifier M_q to estimate distribution $P_q(t|t', W, Q)$ according to the previous supertags t'. Following the estimation of distribution function in Punyakanok and Roth (2000), we define confidence with a sigmoid function

$$C_q(t|t', W, Q) \equiv \frac{1}{1 + \alpha\, e^{-(M_q(t|t', W, Q) - s)}},$$
(6.3)

where s is the threshold of M_q, and α is set to 1.

The distribution mass is then defined with normalized confidence

$$P_q(t|t', W, Q) \equiv \frac{C_q(t|t', W, Q)}{\sum_t C_q(t|t', W, Q)}$$
(6.4)

6.4.2   Label bias problem

In Lafferty et al. (2001), it is shown that PMM and other nongenerative finite-state models based on next-state classifiers share a weakness, which they called the *label bias problem*: the transitions leaving a given state compete only against each other, rather than against all other transitions in the model. They proposed Conditional Random Fields (CRF) as solution to this problem.

Collins (2002) proposed a new algorithm for parameter estimation as an alternate to CRF. The new algorithm was similar to maximum-entropy model except that it skipped the local normalization step. Intuitively, it is the local normalization that makes distribution mass of the transitions leaving a given state incomparable with all other transitions.

It is noted in Muñoz et al. (1999) that SNoW's output provides, in addition to the prediction, a robust confidence level in the prediction, which enables its use in an inference algorithm that combines predictors to produce a coherent inference. In that paper, SNoW's output is used to estimate the probability of *open* and *close* tags. In general, the probability of a tag can be estimated as follows

$$P_q(t|t', W, Q) \equiv \frac{M_q(t|t', W, Q) - s}{\sum_t (M_q(t|t', W, Q) - s)}.$$
(6.5)

However, this makes probabilities comparable only within the transitions of the same history t'. An alternative to this approach is to use the SNoW's output directly in the prediction combination, which makes transitions of different history comparable, since the SNoW's output provides a robust confidence level in the prediction. Furthermore, in order to make sure that the confidences are not too sharp, we use the *confidence* defined in (6.3).

In addition, we use two supertaggers, one scans from left to right and the other scans from right to left. Then we combine the results via *pairwise voting* as in van Halteren et al. (1998); Chen et al. (1999) as the final supertag. This approach of voting also helps to cope with the *label bias problem*, because we can utilize the history information on both sides of the context to some extent.

6.4.3   Contextual model

$P_q(t|t', W, Q)$ is estimated within a 5-word window plus two head supertags before the current word. For each word w_i, the basic features are $W = w_{i-2,...,i+2}$, $Q = q_{i-2,...,i+2}$, $t' = t_{i-2,i-1}$ and $hd_{-2,-1}$, the two head supertags before the current word. Thus

$$P_{q_i}(t_i|t_{1...i-1}, W, Q)$$
$$= P_{q_i}(t_i|t_{i-2,i-1}, w_{i-2...i+2}, q_{i-2...i+2}, hd_{-2,-1}).$$

A basic feature is called *active* for word w_i if and only if the corresponding word/POS-tag/supertag appears at a specified place around w_i. For our SNoW classifiers, we use unigram and bigram of basic features as our feature set. A feature defined as a bigram of two basic features is active if and only if the two basic features are both active. The value of a feature of w_i is set to 1 if this feature is active for w_i, or 0 otherwise.

6.4.4   Related work

Chen (2001) implemented an MEMM model for supertagging which is analogous to the POS tagging model of Ratnaparkhi (1996). The feature sets used in the MEMM model were similar to ours. In addition, prefix and suffix features were used to handle rare words. Several MEMM supertaggers were implemented based on distinct feature sets.

In Muñoz et al. (1999), SNoW was used for text chunking. The IOB tagging model in that paper was similar to our model for supertagging, but there are some differences. They did not decompose the SNoW classifier with respect to POS tags. They used two-level deterministic (beam-width = 1) search, in which the second level IOB classifier takes the IOB output of the first classifier as input features.

6.5   Experiments on Supertagging

In our experiments, we use the default settings of the SNoW promotion parameter, demotion parameter and the threshold value given by the SNoW system. We train our model on the training data for two rounds, only counting the features that appear for at least five times. We skip the normalization step in test, and we use beam search with the width of 5.

model	acc%
Bangalore(97) trigram	91.37
Chen(99) trigram mix	91.79
Chen(99) voting	92.19
Chen(01) width=5	91.83
Chen(01) Viterbi	92.25
SNoW left-to-right	92.02
SNoW right-to-left	91.43
SNoW	92.41

TABLE 6.1 Comparison with previous work. Training data is WSJ section 00 thorough 24 except section 20 of PTB. Test data is WSJ section 20. Size of tag set is 479. acc% = percentage of accuracy. The number of Bangalore(97) is based on footnote 1 of Chen et al. (1999). The number of Chen(01) width=5 is the result of a beam search on model 8 with the width of 5.

In our first experiment, we use the same dataset as that of Chen et al. (1999) for our experiments. We use WSJ section 00 through 24 expect section 20 as training data, and section 20 as test data. Both training and test data are first tagged by Brill's POS tagger (Brill, 1995). We use the same pairwise voting algorithm as in Chen et al. (1999). We run supertagging on the training data and use the supertagging result to generate the mapping table used in pairwise voting.

By using beam search with width = 5, the SNoW supertagger scanning from left to right achieves an accuracy of 92.02%, and the one scanning from right to left achieves an accuracy of 91.43%. By combining the results of these two supertaggers with pairwise voting, we achieve an accuracy of 92.41%. Table 6.1 shows the comparison with previous work. Our algorithm, which is coded in Java, takes about ten minutes to supertag the test data with a PIII 1.13GHz processor.

The supertagger in Chen et al. (1999) achieved an accuracy of 92.19% by combination of five distinct supertaggers. However, our result is achieved by combining outputs of two homogeneous supertaggers, which only differ in scan direction. The MEMM supertagger in Chen (2001) achieved an accuracy of 92.25% by searching the whole space, but it is very slow. Using width = 5 in beam search as we do, the MEMM supertagger achieved an accuracy of 91.83%.

Our next experiment is with the set of supertags abstracted from PTB with LexTract (Xia, 2001). Xia extracted an LTAG-style grammar from PTB and repeated the experiment in Bangalore (1997) on her supertag set. There are 2,920 elementary trees in Xia's grammar G_2, so that the supertags are more specialized and hence there is much more ambiguity in supertagging. We have experimented with our model on G_2 and her dataset. We train our left-to-right model on WSJ section 02 through 21 of PTB, and test on section 22 and 23. We achieve an average error reduction of 13.0%. The reason why the accuracy is rather low is that systems

model	acc%(22)	acc%(23)
Xia(01) trigram	83.60	84.41
SNoW left-to-right	86.01	86.27

TABLE 6.2 Results on auto-extracted LTAG grammar. Training data is WSJ section 02 thorough 21 of PTB. Test data is WSJ section 22 and 23. Size of supertag set is 2920. acc% = percentage of accuracy.

tag set	size	norm?	acc%(20/22/23)
auto	2920	yes	NA / 85.77 / 85.98
auto	2920	no	NA / 86.01 / 86.27
hand	479	yes	91.98 / NA / NA
hand	479	no	92.02 / NA / NA

TABLE 6.3 Experiments on normalized and unnormalized models using left-to-right SNoW supertagger. size = size of the tag set. norm? = normalized or not. acc% = percentage of accuracy on section 20, 22 and 23. auto = auto-extracted tag set. hand − hand coded tag set.

using G_2 have to cope with much more ambiguities due the large size of the supertag set. The results are shown in table 6.2.

We test on both normalized and unnormalized models with both hand coded supertag set and auto-extracted supertag set. We use the left-to-right SNoW model in these experiments. The results in table 6.3 show that skipping the local normalization improves performance in all the systems. The effect of skipping normalization is more significant on auto-extracted tags. We think this is because sparse data is more vulnerable to the label bias problem.

6.6 Experiments on NP Chunking

Now we come back to the NP chunking problem. The standard dataset of NP chunking consists of WSJ section 15–18 as train data and section 20 as test data. In our approach, we substitute the supertags for the POS tags in the dataset. The new data look as follows.

```
For     B_Pnxs  O
the     B_Dnx   I
nine    B_Dnx   I
months  A_NXN   I
```

The first field is the word, the second is the supertag of the word, and the last is the IOB tag.

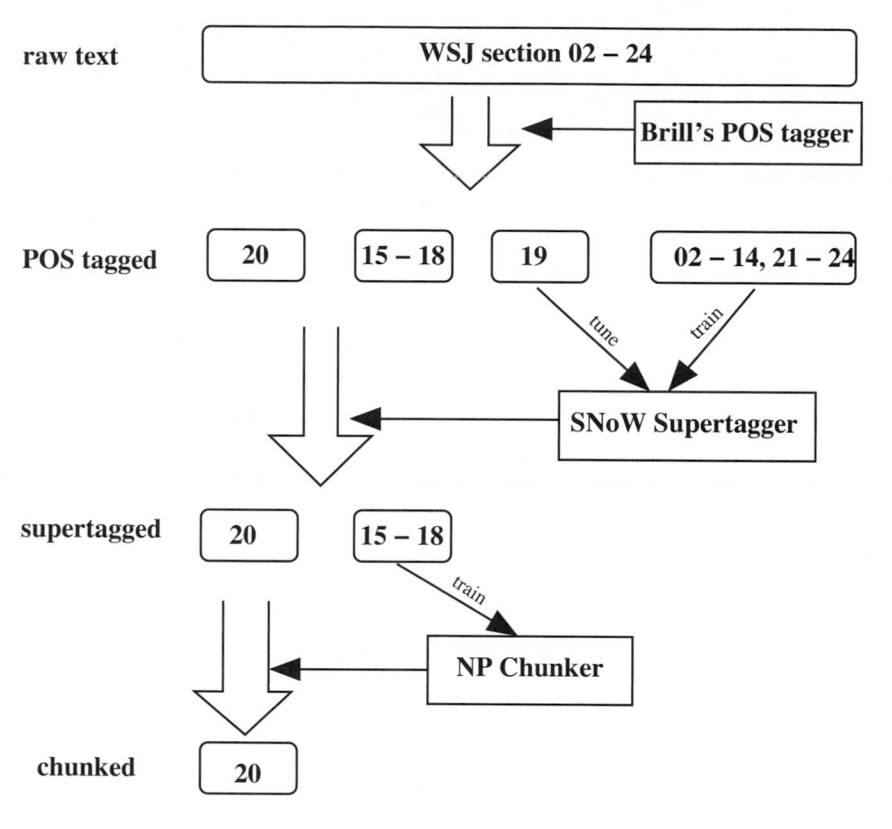

FIGURE 6.1 Procedure of the NP chunking with supertag dataset.

We first use the *fast TBL* to repeat Ramshaw and Marcus' experiment, and then apply the same program to our new dataset. Since section 15–18 and section 20 are in the standard data set of NP chunking, we need to avoid using these sections as training data for our supertagger. We have trained another supertagger that is trained on 776K words in WSJ sections 02–14 and 21–24, and it is tuned with 44K words in WSJ section 19. We use this supertagger to supertag section 15–18 and section 20. We train an NP chunker on section 15–18 with *fast TBL*, and test it on section 20. The whole procedure of using supertag in NP chunking is shown in figure 6.1.

There is a small problem with the supertag set that we have been using, as far as NP chunking is concerned. Two words with different POS tags may be tagged with the same supertag. For example both determiner (DT) and number (CD) can be tagged with B_Dnx. However this will be harmful in the case of NP chunking. As a solution, we use augmented supertags that have the POS tag of the lexical item specified. An augmented supertag can also be regarded as concatenation of a supertag and a POS tag. It should be noted that to use the POS tag and the

model	A	P	R	F
RM95	–	91.80	92.27	92.03
Brill-POS	97.42	91.83	92.20	92.01
Tri-STAG	97.29	91.60	91.72	91.66
SNoW-STAG	97.66	92.76	92.34	92.55
SNoW-STAG2	97.70	92.86	93.05	92.95
GOLD-POS	97.91	93.17	93.51	93.34
GOLD-STAG	98.48	94.74	95.63	95.18

TABLE 6.4 Results on NP Chunking. Training data is WSJ section 15–18 of PTB. Test data is WSJ section 20. A = Accuracy of IOB tagging. P = NP chunk Precision. R = NP chunk Recall. F = F-score. Brill-POS = *fast TBL* with Brill's POS tags. Tri-STAG = *fast TBL* with supertags given by Bangalore's trigram-based supertagger. SNoW-STAG — *fast TBL* with supertags given by our SNoW supertagger. SNoW-STAG2 = *fast TBL* with augmented supertags given by our SNoW supertagger. GOLD-POS = *fast TBL* with gold standard POS tags. GOLD-STAG = *fast TBL* with gold standard supertags.

supertag as two distinct features may help to improve the performance. However, for the purpose of comparing it to the baseline system, we use the combination of those two as a single feature.

For	B_Pnxs(IN)	O
the	B_Dnx(DT)	I
nine	B_Dnx(CD)	I
months	A_NXN(NNS)	I

The results are shown in Table 6.4. The system using augmented supertags achieves an F-score of 92.95%, or an error reduction of 11.8% below the baseline of using Brill POS tags. Although these two systems are both trained with the same TBL algorithm, we implicitly employ more linguistic knowledge as the learning bias when we train the learning machine with supertags. Supertags encode more syntactical information than POS tag do.

For example, in the sentence *Three leading drug companies ...*, the POS tag of *leading* is VBG, or present participle. Based on the local context of *leading*, *Three* can be the subject of *leading*. However, the supertag of *leading* is B_An, which represents a modifier of a noun. With this extra information, the chunker can easily solve the ambiguity. We find many instances like this in the test data.

It is important to note that the accuracy of supertag itself is much lower than that of POS tag while the use of supertags helps to improve the overall performance. On the other hand, since the accuracy of supertagging is rather lower, there is more room left for improvement.

If we use gold standard POS tags in the previous experiment, we can only achieve an F-score of 93.34%, which is only slightly higher than using supertags automatically generated by our supertagger. However, if we use gold standard supertags in our previous experiment, the F-score is as high as 95.18%. This tells us how much room there is for further improvements. Improvements in supertagging may give rise to further improvements in chunking.

6.7 Conclusions

We have proposed a novel supertagger based on discriminative learning. The new supertagging algorithm takes advantage of rich feature sets, avoids the sparse-data problem, and forces the learning algorithm to focus on the difficult cases. Being aware of the fact that our algorithm may suffer from the *label bias problem*, we have used two methods to cope with this problem, and achieved results comparable to the state-of-the-art.

We have tested our algorithms on both the hand-coded tag set used in Chen et al. (1999) and supertags extracted for Penn Treebank (Xia, 2001). On the same dataset as that of Chen et al. (1999), our new supertagger achieves an accuracy of 92.41%. Compared with the supertaggers with the same decoding complexity (Chen, 2001), our algorithm achieves an error reduction of 7.1%.

In order to demonstrate the new supertagger provides more useful syntactic information than noise, we focus on NP chunking as a case study. We repeat the Transformation Based NP chunking (Ramshaw and Marcus, 1995) experiment by substituting supertags for POS tags in the dataset. The use of supertags in NP chunking gives rise to almost 1% absolute increase (from 92.03% to 92.95%) in F-score under Transformation Based Learning frame, or an error reduction of 11.8%.

The accuracy of 92.95% with our individual TBL chunker is close to results of some POS-tag-based systems using advanced machine learning algorithms, such as 93.34% by voted MBL chunkers (Sang, 2002), 92.8% by SNoW chunker (Muñoz et al., 1999). The benefit of using a supertagger is obvious. The supertagger provides an opportunity for advanced machine learning techniques to improve their performance on chunking tasks by exploiting more syntactic information encoded in the supertags.

To sum up, the discriminative learning based supertagger proposed here provides an effective and efficient way to employ syntactic information that is unavailable with POS tag representation.

Acknowledgments

We thank Vasin Punyakanok for help on the use of SNoW in sequential inference, and John Chen for help on dataset and evaluation methods.

Notes

1. According to footnote 1 in Chen et al. (1999), a few supertags were grouped into equivalence classes for evaluation.

References

Abney, S. P. (1991). Parsing by chunks. In *Principle-Based Parsing*. Kluwer Academic.

Bangalore, S. (1997). Performance evaluation of supertagging for partial parsing. In *Proceedings of the International Workshop on Parsing Technologies*.

Brill, E. (1995). Transformation-based error-driven learning and natural language processing: A case study in part-of-speech tagging. *Computational Linguistics*, 21(4):543–565.

Chen, J. (2001). *Towards Efficient Statistical Parsing using Lexicalized Grammatical Information*. PhD thesis, University of Delaware.

Chen, J., Bangalore, S., and Vijay-Shanker, K. (1999). New models for improving supertag disambiguation. In *Proceedings of the Conference of the European Chapter of the Association for Computational Linguistics*.

Collins, M. (2002). Discriminative training methods for Hidden Markov Models: Theory and experiments with perceptron algorithms. In *Proceedings of the 2002 Conference of Empirical Methods in Natural Language Processing*.

Joshi, A. K. and Bangalore, S. (1994). Disambiguation of super parts of speech (or supertags): Almost parsing. In *Proceedings of COLING '94: The 15th Int. Conf. on Computational Linguistics*.

Joshi, A. K. and Schabes, Y. (1997). Tree-adjoining grammars. In Rozenberg, G. and Salomaa, A., eds., *Handbook of Formal Languages*. Springer.

Kudo, T. and Matsumoto, Y. (2001). Chunking with support vector machines. In *Proceedings of the 2nd Meeting of the North American Chapter of the Association for Computational Linguistics*.

Lafferty, J., McCallum, A., and Pereira, F. (2001). Conditional random fields: Probabilistic models for stgmentation and labeling sequence data. In *Proceedings of the 18th International Conference on Machine Learning*.

Marcus, M. P., Santorini, B., and Marcinkiewicz, M. A. (1994). Building a large annotated corpus of English: the Penn Treebank. *Computational Linguistics*, 19(2):313–330.

Muñoz, M., Punyakanok, V., Roth, D., and Zimak, D. (1999). A learning approach to shallow parsing. In *Proceedings of the 1999 Conference of Empirical Methods in Natural Language Processing*.

Ngai, G. and Florian, R. (2001). Transformation-based learning in the fast lane. In *Proceedings of the 2nd Meeting of the North American Chapter of the Association for Computational Linguistics*.

Punyakanok, V. and Roth, D. (2000). The use of classifiers in sequential inference. In *Proceedings of the 14th Annual Conference Neural Information Processing Systems*.

Ramshaw, L. and Marcus, M. P. (1995). Text chunking using transformation-based learning. In *Proceedings of the 3rd Workshop on Very Large Corpora*.

Ratnaparkhi, A. (1996). A maximum entropy part-of-speech tagger. In *Proceedings of the 1st Conference of Empirical Methods in Natural Language Processing*.

Roth, D. (1998). Learning to resolve natural language ambiguities: A unified approach. In *Proceedings of the 16th National Conference on Artificial Intelligence.*

Sang, E. F. T. K. (2002). Memory-based shallow parsing. *Journal of Machine Learning Research*, 2:559–594.

Sha, F. and Pereira, F. (2003). Shallow parsing with conditional random fields. In *Proceedings of the 2003 Human Language Technology Conference of the North American Chapter of the Association for Computational Linguistics.*

van Halteren, H., Zavrel, J., and Daelmans, W. (1998). Improving data driven wordclass tagging by system combination. In *Proceedings of the 36th Annual Meeting of the Association for Computational Linguistics and 17th Int. Conf. on Computational Linguistics.*

Xia, F. (2001). *Automatic Grammar Generation from Two Different Perspectives.* PhD thesis, University of Pennsylvania.

Zhang, T., Damerau, F., and Johnson, D. (2001). Text chunking using Regularized Winnow. In *Proceedings of the 39th Annual Meeting of the Association for Computational Linguistics (ACL).*

A Nonstatistical Parsing-Based Approach to Supertagging

PIERRE BOULLIER

7.1 Introduction

Joshi and Bangalore (1994) introduces the idea of supertagging in order to improve the efficiency of parsers for lexicalized formalisms by selecting, for each word, its appropriate descriptions given its context in a sentence. In NLP, numerous grammatical formalisms are lexicalized. In this chapter, we will concentrate on supertagging of lexicalized tree-adjoining grammars (LTAGs) (see Schabes, Abeillé and Joshi, 1988 and Joshi and Schabes, 1997). In LTAGs, each elementary tree contains at least one lexical item called an *anchor*. All the arguments of this anchor are instantiated at places (nodes) through either a substitution or an adjunction operation. Thus, an elementary tree may be seen as a description of the context (or *domain of locality*), of its anchor, including long-distance dependencies. Since an elementary tree (either initial or auxiliary) defines its anchor precisely, it is called a *supertag*, because it conveys much more information than the standard part-of-speech tag. As a consequence, in the LTAG context, the lexical ambiguity of a word (i.e., the number of supertags associated with it) is generally much greater than its number of standard part-of-speech tags.

Many LTAG parsers work in two phases: for each word in a sentence, the first phase selects the appropriate supertags, while the second phase combines the selected supertags through substitutions and adjunctions. The first phase is called *supertagging*. *Supertag disambiguation* is the process by which local lexical ambiguity can be reduced or eventually even resolved, resulting in a single supertag per word. This selection of the most probable supertag(s) is usually performed using statistical distributions of supertag cooccurrences extracted from (large) annotated corpora of parsed text. In this context, the result of a supertagger is almost a parse in the sense that a parser only needs to link together its supertags into a single structure. If such a single structure cannot be built, we have a partial parser (see, for example, Bangalore, 2000). However, this approach, which assigns a single supertag per word, even if it is extended to produce the n-best supertags for each word, may well eliminate trees that are parts of valid parses (a detailed discussion on supertagging can be found in Bangalore and Joshi, 1999).

In this chapter, we will depart from the supertagging community on several points, our approach being:

1. nonstatistical,

2. strict,

3. parsing-based.

The first point means that supertag disambiguation will not be done in a statistical way, thus avoiding the need for training on annotated corpora, which are very costly to develop.

The second point means that we adopt a *strict* supertag disambiguation approach. A strict supertagger cannot eliminate supertags that could take part in *some* complete parse.

With the third point, contrasting to Bangalore and Joshi (1999), who estimate that only *"local techniques can be used to disambiguate supertags"* and that *"full parsing is contrary to the spirit of supertagging,"* we advocate that a supertagger can indeed be a parser. A potential advantage of this approach is that our supertaggers may use global information to take their decisions, while only local (statistical) information (n-gram model) is used in traditional supertaggers.[1] However, this parser must be "sufficiently" efficient. This means, of course, that it cannot be based upon the original LTAG. We thus assume that a supertagger relies upon a grammar which is not the original LTAG. For obvious reasons of reliability and development costs, we require that the grammars upon which our supertaggers are based must be automatically deduced from the original LTAG. In other words, our purpose is to reduce the supertags ambiguity in using only structural information which can be automatically extracted from any given LTAG.

This chapter is divided into three main parts. In sections 7.2, 7.3 and 7.4, we study how it is possible to define a context-free (CF) superset and a regular superset for any given tree-adjoining language (TAL). In sections 7.5 and 7.6, we study how general recognizers for these supersets can be transformed into supertaggers for the original LTAG. Finally, in section 7.8 we report on the experiments that have been performed with a wide-coverage English LTAG, on a large test set.

7.2 From TAG to CFG

The purpose of this section is to show how any TAG G that defines the TAL $\mathcal{L}(G)$ can be transformed into a CF grammar (CFG) G_{cf} whose language $\mathcal{L}(G_{cf})$ is a superset of $\mathcal{L}(G)$. The process shown here is a direct transformation from TAG to CFG and is reminiscent of Boullier's work in which such a transformation is performed in using the intermediate formalism of range concatenation grammars (RCG).[2]

We assume here that the reader is familiar with the TAG formalism (see Joshi, 1987 for an introduction). Let $G = (V_N, V_T, \mathcal{I}, \mathcal{A}, S)$ be a TAG. As it is classical, we assume that the nonterminal symbols $V_N^{\mathcal{I}}$ which label the roots of the initial trees are disjoint from the nonterminal symbols $V_N^{\mathcal{A}}$ which label the roots of the auxiliary trees (we have $V_N^{\mathcal{I}} \cap V_N^{\mathcal{A}} = \emptyset$ and $V_N^{\mathcal{I}} \cup V_N^{\mathcal{A}} = V_N$), that the start symbol S is an element of $V_N^{\mathcal{I}}$, that each internal node of $\mathcal{I} \cup \mathcal{A}$ is labeled by an element of $V_N^{\mathcal{A}}$, while each leaf of $\mathcal{I} \cup \mathcal{A}$ is labeled by an element of $V_N^{\mathcal{I}} \cup V_T \cup \{\varepsilon\}$, except that each foot node bears the same label as its root node. In some TAG, you may associate to each adjunction node an *adjunction constraint* which specify whether the adjunction operation of an auxiliary tree is allowed, mandatory or forbidden. We call A-node a node which is labeled by the nonterminal symbol $A \in V_N$. We call A-tree a tree whose root node is an A-node. The *tree language* of a TAG G is defined as the set of all *complete* derived trees that can be composed (by substitution and adjunction), starting from an initial S-tree, and in which no more substitution or mandatory adjunction can take place. Its *string language* $\mathcal{L}(G)$ is the set of terminal yields of its tree language.

We will see how each initial tree of $\mathcal{I}$ and each auxiliary tree of $\mathcal{A}$ can be transformed into CF productions to form a CFG $G_{\mathrm{cf}} = (N, T, P, S)$ such that $\mathcal{L}(G) \subseteq \mathcal{L}(G_{\mathrm{cf}})$.

G and G_{cf} have the same set of terminal symbols (i.e., $V_T = T$) and the same start symbol S. The set N of nonterminal symbols of G_{cf} is defined by $N = V_N^{\mathcal{I}} \cup \{A_i \mid i \in \{L, R\} \text{ and } A \in V_N^{\mathcal{A}}\}$. That is, nonterminal symbols which label either substitution nodes or the roots of initial trees are kept unchanged, while the nonterminal symbols, say A, which label adjunction nodes, roots and feet of auxiliary trees produce two CF nonterminal symbols A_L and A_R. The intended meaning of A_L is to capture the set of strings generated by the parts of the auxiliary A-trees that lie to the left of their spines, while A_R captures the set of strings generated by the parts of the auxiliary A-trees which lie to the right of their spines.

As in Boullier (2000), for each elementary tree τ, its *decoration string* σ_τ is an element of $(N \cup T)^*$ defined as follows. We perform on each τ a traversal that collects in σ_τ the labels of the traversed nodes. The traversal of each X-subtree starts by the top-down traversal of its X-node, followed by the traversals of its daughter subtrees one after the other from left-to-right, and completed by a bottom-up traversal of its X-node. Therefore, each X-node is traversed twice, once top-down at the beginning of its X-subtree traversal and once bottom-up at the end. If X labels a leaf, the bottom-up traversal of this X-leaf immediately follows its top-down traversal. The traversals (both top-down and bottom-up) of root nodes in initial trees leave no trace in σ_τ. For an auxiliary A-tree τ, the top-down traversal of its A-root initializes σ_τ with A_L. Upon completion of this traversal, the bottom-up visit of the A-root of τ will eventually complete σ_τ with A_R. If we except the foot nodes of auxiliary trees, the inside nodes and the leaf nodes of initial and auxiliary trees are equally processed. The top-down traversal, immediately followed by the bottom-up traversal of a nonfoot leaf node labeled l (i.e., this node is either a terminal node or a substitution node) results in appending l to σ_τ (if $l = \varepsilon$, σ_τ is left unchanged). The top-down traversal of an inside (adjunction) A-node results in appending A_L to σ_τ, while its bottom-up traversal (after the complete traversal of this A-tree) results in appending A_R to σ_τ. The top-down traversal of a foot node labeled A results in appending A_L to σ_τ. This top-down traversal is immediately followed by a bottom-up traversal that appends A_R to σ_τ. If τ is an auxiliary A-tree, let σ_τ^L be the prefix of σ_τ collected before the bottom-up traversal of its foot node (including A_L) and let σ_τ^R be the suffix of σ_τ collected after the top-down traversal of its foot node (starting with A_R). If at some place the adjunction operation is forbidden (*null adjunction constraint*), the top-down and bottom-up traversals of that node leave the decoration string σ_τ unchanged.

If τ is an initial A-tree and if $\sigma_\tau = X_1 \cdots X_p$ is its decoration string ($X_i \in V_T \cup N$), we associate to τ the single CF production

$$A \to X_1 \cdots X_p.$$

If τ is an auxiliary A-tree and if $\sigma_\tau = \sigma_\tau^L \sigma_\tau^R$ is its decoration string, we associate to τ the pair of CF productions called *sister productions*

$$A_L \to X_1 \cdots X_p$$
$$A_R \to Y_1 \cdots Y_q,$$

if we have $\sigma_\tau^L = X_1 \cdots X_p$ and $\sigma_\tau^R = Y_1 \cdots Y_q$. Moreover, by construction (and without any adjunction constraints), we have $p \geq 2$, $X_1 = X_p = A_L$ and $q \geq 2$, $Y_1 = Y_q = A_R$.[3]

We can remark that the same CF production can be produced by different elementary trees.

The productions generated by all elementary tree traversals are gathered into the set of productions P.

However, in the general case, this generated CFG is not proper[4] since nonterminal symbols of the form A_L or A_R cannot derive a terminal string. This happens because the recursive definition of these symbols is not completed. This can be easily fixed by adding to P, for each $A \in V_N^{\mathcal{A}}$, the pair of ε-productions

$$A_L \to \varepsilon$$
$$A_R \to \varepsilon,$$

which will terminate any sequence of adjunction operations by an *empty adjunction*.

However, in this schema, we have implicitly assumed that any adjunction operation is either allowed or disallowed. If mandatory adjunctions are specified in the input TAG, the previous process may be slightly changed as follows.

For each $A \in V_N^{\mathcal{A}}$, the pair of ε-productions is replaced by the following two pairs:

$$A_L^{\overline{M}} \to A_L$$
$$A_R^{\overline{M}} \to A_R$$
$$A_L^{\overline{M}} \to \varepsilon$$
$$A_R^{\overline{M}} \to \varepsilon,$$

where $\overline{M}$ stands for not mandatory.

Moreover, during the decoration strings construction, if an adjunction A-node bear an allowed adjunction constraint, during the top-down visit of this node, we append $A_L^{\overline{M}}$ instead of A_L to the current decoration string while, during the bottom-up visit, we append $A_R^{\overline{M}}$ instead of A_R. If the A-node bears a mandatory adjunction constraint, nothing is changed: A_L and A_R are appended during the top-down and bottom-up visits. By this means, we see that any mandatory adjunction at, say, an A-node is translated into two calls (to A_L and A_R) that do not correspond to empty adjunctions. This new G_{cf} may be not proper if, for example, all the A-nodes bear a mandatory adjunction constraint. In this case the two nonterminals $A_L^{\overline{M}}$ and $A_R^{\overline{M}}$ do not occur in right-hand sides, and the two previous pairs of productions are useless and may thus not be generated.

To illustrate this process, we show in figure 7.1 the translation of an auxiliary A-tree τ into a pair of CF sister productions.

It is not difficult to see that if $w \in \mathcal{L}(G)$, we have $w \in \mathcal{L}(G_{\mathrm{cf}})$.

We have defined the decoration string σ_τ of an elementary tree τ, but this definition can also be applied to any derived tree.[5]

If we consider a complete derived tree whose terminal yield is w (we have $w \in \mathcal{L}(G)$) and its decoration string σ ($\sigma \in (T \cup \{A_i \mid i \in \{L, R\}$ and $A \in V_N^{\mathcal{A}}\})^*$), this string σ can be also derived from S w.r.t. G_{cf} (i.e., $S \underset{G_{\mathrm{cf}}}{\overset{*}{\Rightarrow}} \sigma$).[6] Since the nonterminals of the form A_L and A_R can, by construction of G_{cf}, derive the empty string, we have $\sigma \underset{G_{\mathrm{cf}}}{\overset{*}{\Rightarrow}} w$. This shows our result: $\mathcal{L}(G) \subseteq \mathcal{L}(G_{\mathrm{cf}})$.

If G is lexicalized, this does not mean that its associated CFG G_{cf} is also lexicalized: the productions generated by initial trees are lexicalized, at least one production of the CF sister productions generated by auxiliary trees is lexicalized, but the other production of the pair may well be nonlexicalized, while the ε-productions are surely not lexicalized.

7.3 From CFG to FA

In this section, we examine how a CFG G_{cf} can be transformed into a regular grammar (or equivalently into a finite automaton (FA)) that defines a (regular) superset of $\mathcal{L}(G_{\mathrm{cf}})$.

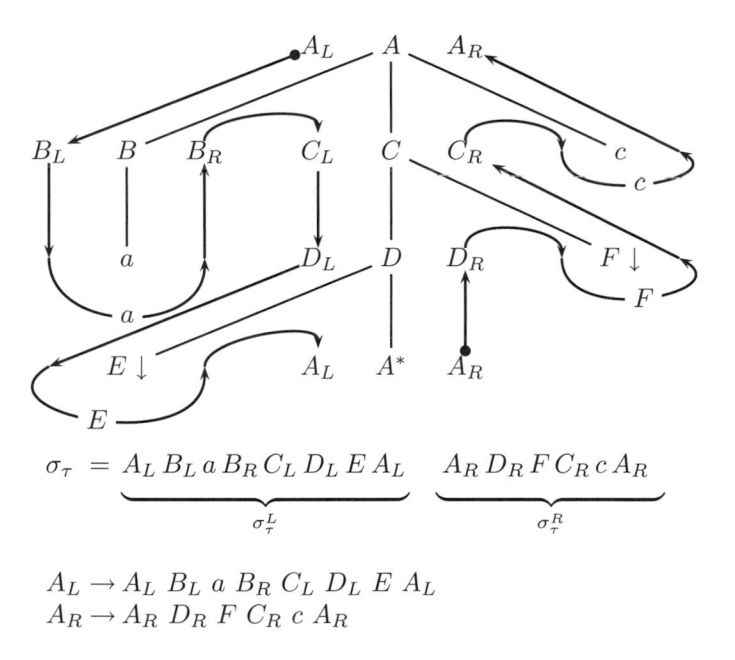

$$\sigma_\tau = \underbrace{A_L \, B_L \, a \, B_R \, C_L \, D_L \, E \, A_L}_{\sigma_\tau^L} \quad \underbrace{A_R \, D_R \, F \, C_R \, c \, A_R}_{\sigma_\tau^R}$$

$$A_L \to A_L \, B_L \, a \, B_R \, C_L \, D_L \, E \, A_L$$
$$A_R \to A_R \, D_R \, F \, C_R \, c \, A_R$$

FIGURE 7.1 Translation of an auxiliary A-tree τ into a pair of CF productions

The design of regular supersets (or more generally regular approximations) of CFLs is not new (see Nederhof, 2000, for example). The transformation of a CFG occurs either at the grammar level or at the pushdown automaton (PDA) level. In the first case, CFGs are transformed by exploiting some necessary condition for a CFG to define a regular language.[7] In the second case, a PDA is first built from the CFG, and then that PDA is approximated by an FA. However, in practice, for a real size CFG, the associated regular grammar or the associated FA is often too big.

Despite these rather discouraging results, we decided to investigate the FA method, which produces more precise approximations even if it is less easily tuned. The superset approximation process, which transforms a PDA into an FA always consists in reducing an infinite number of parse-stacks into a finite one, by defining an equivalence relation on parse-stacks which induces a finite partition. Each element of that partition is then mapped to a state of the FA. For example, we could say that two parse-stacks are equivalent if and only if they share their h topmost elements for a given integer h.[8] Of course, the precision of the PDA increases with h, but, for a large grammar (say more than 10,000 symbol occurrences), only the value $h = 1$ is practicable. For large CFGs, the challenge is thus to define regular supersets by means of FAs that are manageable.

We briefly describe below a method that has been successfuly used to improve the (practical) parse time of a CF Earley parser. The interested reader may consult Boullier (2003) where it is shown how to transform a CFG into a deterministic FA (DFA) called a *set automaton* (SA).

Consider an augmented[9] CFG $G_{cf} = (N', T, P', S')$, we define its set of *items* (dotted rules) as $I_{G_{cf}} = \{A \to \alpha.\beta \mid A \to \alpha\beta \in P'\}$.

If I and J are two subsets of $I_{G_{cf}}$, we define close-reduce(I, J) as the smallest set of items K such that $J \subseteq K \subseteq I_G$ by:

1. Initially $K = J$;
2. **closure**: If $A \to \alpha.B\gamma \in K$, then add $B \to .\beta$ to K for each $B \to \beta \in P$;
3. **reduce**: If $A \to \alpha. \in K$, and if there exists $B \to \beta.A\gamma \in (I \cup K)$ then add $B \to \beta A.\gamma$ to K;
4. Steps 2) and 3) are repeated until no new item is added to K.

The SA $\mathcal{A}_{G_{cf}} = (Q, T, \delta, q_0, F)$, associated to G_{cf} is a DFA. Its finite set of states is defined by $Q = \{[I, J] \mid I, J \in 2^{I_{G_{cf}}}\}$. For a state $q = [I, J]$, its first component I is a set of items called its *control* set, while its second component J is called its *active* set. The role of the active sets in the supertagging process will be explicited in the next section. The initial state q_0 is the pair $[I_0, I_0]$ with $I_0 = \text{close-reduce}(\emptyset, \{S' \to .S\})$. The set of final states is $F = \{[I, J] \mid S' \to S. \in J\}$. Let $[I, J]$ be a state in Q, for each $a \in T$, we write, for the (deterministic) transition function δ, $\delta([I, J], a) = [I', J']$ where $I' = I \cup J_a$, $J' = J_a$ and $J_a = \text{close-reduce}(I, \{A \to \alpha a.\beta \mid A \to \alpha.a\beta \in J\})$.

Informally, we see that in each state $[I, J]$, the active set J is responsible for the terminal transitions,[10] while the intent behind the control set I is to play the role of a *degenerated parse-stack*. If we follow a path from the initial state, we see that the control sets of the traversed states do not decrease. In fact, they (mainly) record the nonterminal items that have already been seen since the initial state. These nonterminal items are used during the reduce phase (see step 3 of close-reduce) to perform nonterminal A-transitions only on recorded A-items. By analogy with the notion of PDA, and by reference to the control and active sets, $\mathcal{A}_{G_{cf}}$ is called an SA.

For a given string $w = a_1 \cdots a_n \in T^*$, a *configuration* of an SA $\mathcal{A}_{G_{cf}} = (Q, T, \delta, q_0, F)$ is an element of $Q \times T^*$. The *initial configuration* c_0 is $c_0 = (q_0, w)$. A binary relation between configurations noted $\underset{\mathcal{A}_{G_{cf}}}{\vdash}$ is defined by $(q, tx) \underset{\mathcal{A}_{G_{cf}}}{\vdash} (q', x)$, if and only if $\delta(q, t) = q'$. The string w is *recognized* by $\mathcal{A}_{G_{cf}}$ if and only if we have $c_0 \underset{\mathcal{A}_{G_{cf}}}{\vdash} c_1 \cdots \underset{\mathcal{A}_{G_{cf}}}{\vdash} c_n$, with $c_n = (q_n, \varepsilon)$ and q_n is a final state in F.

It can be shown that $\mathcal{L}(\mathcal{A}_{G_{cf}})$, the language *accepted* by $\mathcal{A}_{G_{cf}}$ (i.e., the set of all its recognized strings) is a regular superset of $\mathcal{L}(G_{cf})$.

We remark here that this SA, which could be extremely large, is not (pre)constructed for a given CFG G_{cf}. Only the subautomaton selected by a given input $w = a_1 \cdots a_n \in T^*$ is constructed at run-time: that is the $n + 1$ states $q_0, q_1, \cdots, q_n$ needed by configurations $c_0, c_1, \cdots, c_n$.

7.4   From TAG to DFA

If G is a TAG, in section 7.2, we saw how to build a CFG G_{cf} that defines $\mathcal{L}(G_{\mathrm{cf}})$ a CF superset of the string language $\mathcal{L}(G)$ of G. In section 7.3, we saw how to build a DFA $\mathcal{A}_{G_{\mathrm{cf}}}$ that defines a regular superset of $\mathcal{L}(G_{\mathrm{cf}})$. In combining these two methods, we can transform any TAG G into a DFA $\mathcal{A}_{G_{\mathrm{cf}}}$ such that an input string w in the string language of G is recognized by $\mathcal{A}_{G_{\mathrm{cf}}}$.

7.5   Regular-Based Supertagging

This section presents how a supertagger can be based upon the previously developed methods.

However, the FA technology itself cannot be used as such, since the only recognition of an input string is not the purpose of a supertagger. We will show how an SA can be transformed into a finite transducer (FT) whose outputs are supertags.

Fortunately, SAs have the following property: if $w = a_1 \cdots a_n \in T^*$ is an input string, for each configuration $c_i = ([I_i, J_i], a_{i+1} \cdots a_n)$, $1 \le i \le n$, we are sure that in configuration $c_{i-1} = ([I_{i-1}, J_{i-1}], a_i \cdots a_n)$, the active set J_{i-1} contains items of the form $A \to \alpha.a_i\beta$. In other words, we can say that if a transition on some terminal t occurs between two configurations c_{i-1} and c_i, we have $a_i = t$ and, moreover, for each item of the form $A \to \alpha t.\beta$ in the active set of c_i, the CF production $A \to \alpha t\beta$ is anchored on a_i. That is, the production $A \to \alpha t\beta$ is a *CF supertag* w.r.t. G_{cf} for the ith word of w.

Therefore, if G is an LTAG, if G_{cf} is its associated CFG as defined in section 7.2, and if $\mathcal{A}_{G_{\mathrm{cf}}}$ is the SA associated with G_{cf} as defined in section 7.3, the FT based on $\mathcal{A}_{G_{\mathrm{cf}}}$, which outputs for each input word a subset of its CF supertags, is a *CF supertagger* for G_{cf}. To leave room to additional constraints that may lead to more accurate results, this definition allows us, for each word, to output only a subset of the associated CF supertags. In order to get a *supertagger* for the original LTAG G, we have only to exploit the reverse mapping, which records for each production r of G_{cf} the set of elementary trees τ of G from which r has been generated (see section 7.2).

If τ is an initial tree, there is a one-to-one mapping between τ and its associated (lexicalized) production, say r. Thus, if r is a CF supertag for some word a_i, we conclude that τ is a (TAG) supertag for a_i.

If τ is an auxiliary tree, it generates two sister productions, say r_L and r_R. The auxiliary tree τ can be part of some complete parse for G only if both r_L and r_R are themselves part of some complete parse for G_{cf} (for the same input w). With auxiliary trees, two cases may arise. First, if both r_L and r_R are lexicalized productions, if r_L is a CF supertag for some a_i, and if r_R is a CF supertag for some a_j, we may conclude that τ is a (candidate) supertag for both a_i and a_j. Second, if only one of r_L and r_R is a lexicalized production, say r_L, and if r_L is a CF supertag for some a_i, we may conclude that τ is a (candidate) supertag for a_i.

In this second case, we have concluded that τ is a supertag, even if r_R, the sister production of r_L, has not been recognized. This rather crude vision may be improved in adding the constraint that the recognition of a nonlexicalized sister production is mandatory to promote τ as a supertag.[11] To do that, the FT is extended as follows. It also looks into the active sets for complete items $A \to \alpha.$ of nonlexicalized productions $A \to \alpha$, $\alpha \in N^*$, and it records all these productions in a set R. Now, we say that τ is a (TAG) supertag for a_i only if r_L and r_R are both CF supertag for some a_i and a_j[12] or if r_L (resp. r_R) is a CF supertag for a_i and if r_R (resp. r_L) is in R. The previous (TAG) supertagger based on an SA is called $\mathcal{S}_{\mathrm{SA}}$ in the experiment of section 7.8.

One weakness of the previous method comes from the time when the discovery of a supertag happens. We have decided that the CF production $A \to \alpha t\beta$ is a CF supertag associated with $t = a_i$, the ith word of w, when its right-hand side $\alpha t\beta$ has been only partly recognized – more precisely, when the active set of c_i contains the item $A \to \alpha a_i.\beta$. This means that this decision only relies on the fact that a phrase of (a regular superset of) its prefix αt has been recognized while the phrases of its suffix β are not taken into account. In other words, only the left context of a word is used to find its supertags, while its right context is simply ignored. Of course, the precision of the supertagger could be improved if the β's parts of the rules are also considered. Taken the β's parts into account may be performed in several ways. We propose here to use the *mirror* SA of $\mathcal{A}_{G_{\mathrm{cf}}}$ (see Boullier, 2003).[13]

The mirror SA $\mathcal{A}_{\widetilde{G_{\mathrm{cf}}}}$ of $\mathcal{A}_{G_{\mathrm{cf}}}$ is an SA that uses the mirror grammar $\widetilde{G}_{\mathrm{cf}}$, which defines the mirror language of $\mathcal{L}(G_{\mathrm{cf}})$ (i.e., $\{a_n \cdots a_1 \mid a_1 \cdots a_n \in \mathcal{L}(G_{\mathrm{cf}})\}$). Of course, an interpreter of a mirror SA scans its input w from right to left. A supertagger that uses both an SA and its mirror proceeds in two passes. The first pass processes w from left to right with $\mathcal{A}_{G_{\mathrm{cf}}}$, while the second pass processes w from right to left with $\mathcal{A}_{\widetilde{G_{\mathrm{cf}}}}$. A production r of G_{cf} is a CF supertag for some word a_i, if and only if it is a CF supertag for a_i w.r.t. $\mathcal{A}_{G_{\mathrm{cf}}}$ and if $\tilde{r}$, its mirror production[14] is a CF supertag for a_i w.r.t. $\mathcal{A}_{\widetilde{G_{\mathrm{cf}}}}$. This supertagger, based on mirror SAs, which scans its input from left to right and from right to left, is called $\mathcal{S}_{\mathrm{LRSA}}$ in the experiment of section 7.8.

7.6 CF-Based Supertagging

In the previous section, in order to get a regular superset of a TAL, we built an intermediate CFG G_{cf} that defines a CF superset of this TAL. In this section, we will see how a general CF parser based on G_{cf} can be changed into a supertagger for G. Of course, doing that, we could expect on one hand a greater precision than the regular-based approach, but, on the other hand, we renounce the linear time behavior for a cubic time, at worst. However, since supertaggers typically handle short inputs (say sentences of a few dozen words), it could happen that the cubic run-time remains tractable. Since it exhibits good performances, we decided to use the guided[15] Earley recognizer of Boullier (2003) as a basis for a push-down transducer (PDT). As for the previous FTs, these PDTs will output for each input word at position i a set of CF productions of G_{cf} that have to be mapped back onto the original LTAG G in order to get our CF-parsing based supertaggers.

Since the regular languages upon which our FTs are based are themselves supersets of $\mathcal{L}(G_{\mathrm{cf}})$, the precision of a CF-based supertagger can not be less than the precision of a regular-based supertagger, even if mirror set automata are used.

If we consider the recognizer part of an Earley strategy, or more precisely its *Scanner* phase, we know that if an Earley item of the form $[A \to \alpha.t\beta, i]$ is in some table T_{j-1} and if the input $w = a_1 \cdots a_n$ is such that $a_j = t$, then the Earley item $[A \to \alpha t.\beta, i]$ is put in the next table T_j. This means that the production $A \to \alpha t\beta$ is a candidate CF supertag for the word a_j. However, as already noted in the regular-based case, we are not sure that the complete item $[A \to \alpha t\beta., i]$ will be eventually an element of some table T_k, $k \geq j$. In other words, it may happen that no β-phrase is a prefix of $a_{j+1} \cdots a_n$. Of course, such a premature supertag detection may spoil the precision. Thus we decide to postpone any association between an anchor $a_j = t$ and a supertag such as $A \to \alpha t\beta$ until the complete recognition of its right-hand side $\alpha t\beta$.

This supertagger is called $\mathcal{S}_{\mathrm{REC}}$ in the experiment described in section 7.8.

We can also remark that, even if the recognition of some lexicalized production $A \to \alpha t\beta$ has been completed in a table T_k (i.e., $\exists [A \to \alpha t\beta., i] \in T_k$, $i < k$), this does not mean that the corresponding subtree, say τ,[16] will necessarily be a part of some complete parse tree. Thus, we have built a second version of the CF supertagger, called $\mathcal{S}_{\mathrm{RED}}$, in which we postpone the association between an anchor $a_j = t$ and a supertag $A \to \alpha t\beta$ until we are sure that a subtree such as τ is a part of a complete parse tree.

We can note on one hand that $\mathcal{S}_{\mathrm{REC}}$ is very close to being an Earley recognizer, while, on the other hand, $\mathcal{S}_{\mathrm{RED}}$ is very close to being a complete Earley parser.

7.7   Precision of a Supertagger

Let G be an LTAG. We assume that, by definition, the output of a supertagger $\mathcal{S}$ on an input string $w = a_1 \cdots a_n \in T^*$ is a sequence of n sets of supertags. Each set, noted $\mathcal{S}_w^i$, $1 \leq i \leq n$ is the set of supertags anchored by a_i. We note $\mathcal{G}$ a TAG parser associated to G. For $\mathcal{G}$ and a sentence $w = a_1 \cdots a_n$, we note G_w^i the set of supertags anchored on the word a_i in the complete parse forest for w. Of course, no supertagger could do a more accurate job than a TAG parser and the sets G_w^i are taken as gold standard. We define, the *precision score* (precision for short) of $\mathcal{S}$ on the word a_i of some w by the quotient $\frac{|G_w^i|}{|\mathcal{S}_w^i|}$, the precision of $\mathcal{S}$ on a sentence w by the quotient $\frac{\sum_{1 \leq i \leq n} |G_w^i|}{\sum_{1 \leq i \leq n} |\mathcal{S}_w^i|}$,[17] and for a non-empty test set $\mathcal{T}$, the *average precision score for $\mathcal{T}$* by the quotient $\frac{\sum_{w \in \mathcal{T}} \sum_{1 \leq i \leq |w|} |G_w^i|}{\sum_{w \in \mathcal{T}} \sum_{1 \leq i \leq |w|} |\mathcal{S}_w^i|}$.

As a consequence of the strictness of our approach, the *recall score* of all our supertaggers is 100%: no supertag that is a part of a complete parse (w.r.t. $\mathcal{G}$) is left out.

7.8   Test Material and Experiment Results

Our experiment[18] is based upon a wide-coverage English grammar designed for the XTAG system (XTAG Research Group, 1995). This grammar consists of 1,132 tree templates that can be anchored on 476 anchors (i.e., $|T| = 476$). As explained in section 7.2, the XTAG grammar is first transformed into a CFG G_{cf}. In order to give an idea of the complexity of this grammar, the penultimate column of table 7.1 gives the size of G_{cf} ($|G_{\mathrm{cf}}|$ is the size of the grammar, that is the number of occurrences of its symbols in left and right-hand sides), while the last column gives the number of nonterminal symbols that occur in the right-hand side of the longest production.

$|N|$	$|T|$	$|P|$	$|G_{\mathrm{cf}}|$	max RHS #nt
33	476	1,131	17,129	26

TABLE 7.1 $G_{\mathrm{cf}} = (N, T, P, S)$ facts

Note that, rather surprisingly, the number of productions of G_{cf} is very close (one less) to the number of tree templates in G. This means that many auxiliary trees share identical tree parts that lie either to the left or to the right of their spines.

For our test set,[19] we have used sentences extracted from the Wall-Street Journal. We used 42,253 sentences for a total length of 1M words. An input word (inflected form) selects one or, more often, several terminal symbols (anchors). In this test set, a word selects about 11 anchors on average. The association between a word and its anchors is performed by means of a dictionary search. If an input word is not in the dictionary, we assign a default value to this *unknown word*: we assume that any unknown word is a noun and it thus selects the anchors associated with a noun. Out of 1M words, 68,407 are unknown. Each anchor, in turn, selects several supertags (tree templates in G). On average, a word selects about 66 supertags. This initial selection process is performed by a *lexer*. Of course, a lexer may itself be seen as a supertagger, its performances are reported in table 7.2 in the first column..

However, out of these 42,253 sentences, 964 are extragrammatical w.r.t. G_{cf}, and 715 others are extragrammatical w.r.t. G^{20}; thus, 1,679 input strings were left out of the actual test set, leaving 40,574 sentences for a total of 925,605 words. In this test set, the lengths of individual sentences show a great variation: with an average length of almost 23 words per sentence, there are single word sentences while the (two) longest ones contain 97 words. The distribution of our test set is shown in figure 7.2.

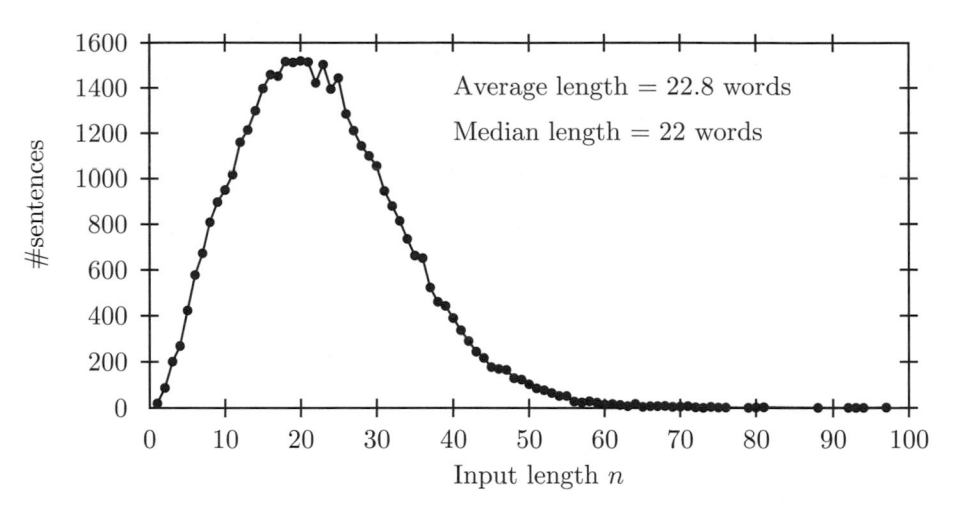

FIGURE 7.2 Distribution of the number of sentences according to their lengths

	Lexer	$\mathcal{S}_{\mathrm{SA}}$	$\mathcal{S}_{\mathrm{LRSA}}$	$\mathcal{S}_{\mathrm{REC}}$	$\mathcal{S}_{\mathrm{RED}}$	$\mathcal{G}$
#supertags	65.89	27.30	20.92	20.66	19.10	18.41
Precision (%)	27.94	67.43	87.99	89.10	96.39	100
Recall (%)	100	100	100	100	100	100

TABLE 7.2 Average number of supertags, average precision, and average recall per word

The performances of our supertaggers are displayed in table 7.2 while their precisions and run-times as a function of the input length are plotted in figures 7.3 and 7.4 respectively.

In figure 7.3, we note that the precision of each of our supertaggers seems to be largely independent of the sentence length, at least beyond a length of say 20 words. The high precision of $\mathcal{S}_{\mathrm{RED}}$ can be interpreted as follows: on the one hand, the English XTAG definition is close to being context-free and, on the other hand, our TAG to CFG transformation, together with its PDT interpretation are accurate enough to allow this closeness to be kept. Last, we can remark that the winnings of $\mathcal{S}_{\mathrm{REC}}$ over $\mathcal{S}_{\mathrm{LRSA}}$ are rather limited.

In figure 7.4, as expected, we note that both $\mathcal{S}_{\mathrm{SA}}$ and $\mathcal{S}_{\mathrm{LRSA}}$ seems to exhibit a linear run-time behaviour, while $\mathcal{S}_{\mathrm{REC}}$ and $\mathcal{S}_{\mathrm{RED}}$ show a superlinear behaviour (which should be cubic).

If we have to choose among these supertaggers, undoubtedly two candidates will emerge, $\mathcal{S}_{\mathrm{LRSA}}$ for its good trade-off between speed and precision and $\mathcal{S}_{\mathrm{RED}}$ for its high precision (if speed is not at a premium).

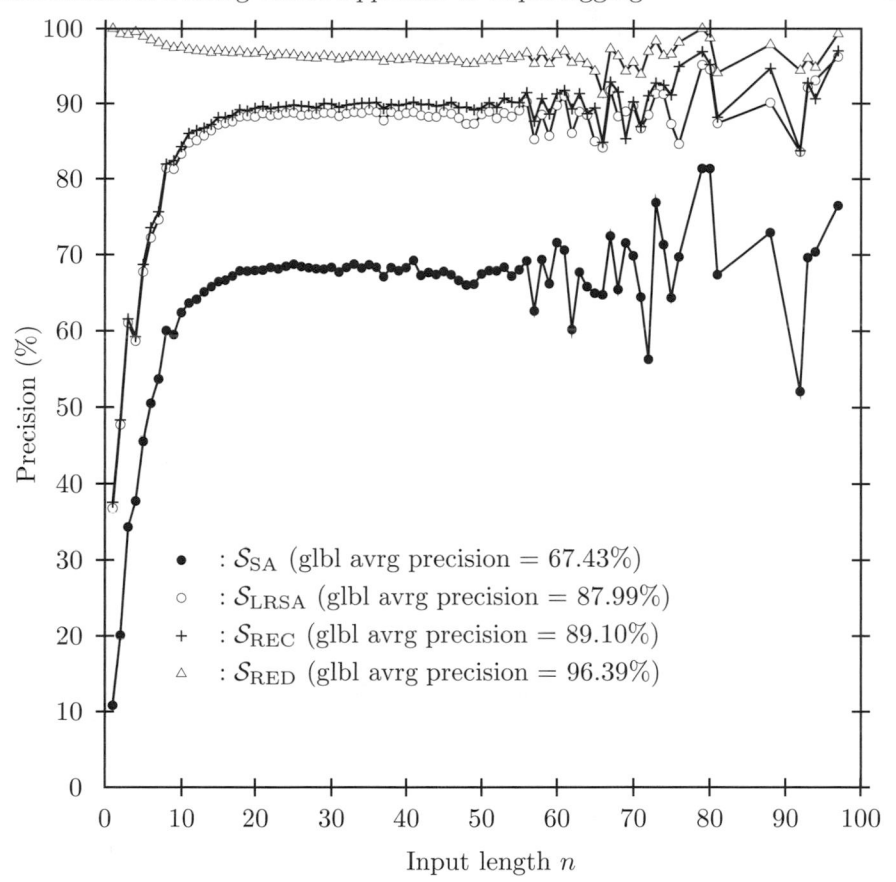

FIGURE 7.3 Supertaggers average precision score

However, if we look for a good compromise between speed and precision, it happens that the $\mathcal{S}_{\text{RED}}$ supertagger has, on small sentences, a very good precision and a rather low run-time, while the $\mathcal{S}_{\text{LRSA}}$ supertagger has, on long sentences, a good precision and a rather low run-time, which only increases linearly with n the sentence length. In the experiment conditions, the best compromise is in fact a pair of supertaggers $\mathcal{S}_{\text{RED}} + \mathcal{S}_{\text{LRSA}}$. $\mathcal{S}_{\text{RED}}$ is used when the length of the input sentences is less than or equal to some threshold value, while $\mathcal{S}_{\text{LRSA}}$ is used when the length exceeds this threshold value. Such a supertagger is called *composite*. Figures 7.5 and 7.6 show respectively the global average precision scores and the average run-times of a composite supertagger for the threshold value of 22. This supertagger reaches on the average a precision of 93% for an average run-time of 27ms per sentence. An other advantage of composite supertaggers comes from the fact that they are rather insensitive to the length of the input sentence, both in term of time and space. If the threshold value is well chosen, the cubic time and

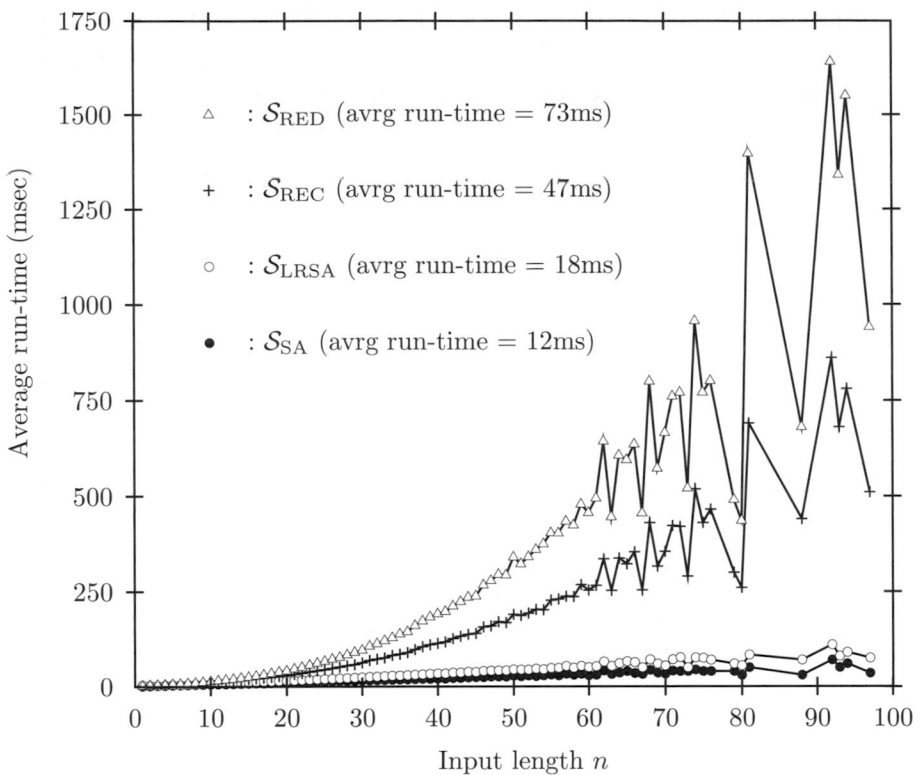

FIGURE 7.4 Supertaggers average run-times

space behavior of $\mathcal{S}_{\mathrm{RED}}$ may be controlled, while the linear time and space behavior of $\mathcal{S}_{\mathrm{LRSA}}$ allows the processing of (very) long sentences.

7.9   Conclusion

It is difficult to compare our results with previously published measures, both in terms of run-times and in terms of performance.

The practical run-times of other supertaggers are almost never addressed, though we may assume that, at least theoretically, they run in linear time.

In this chapter, we have presented two classes of supertaggers. In the first class, the two supertaggers $\mathcal{S}_{\mathrm{SA}}$ and $\mathcal{S}_{\mathrm{LRSA}}$ run in linear time with average run-times of, respectively, 12ms and 18ms per sentence on our test set. In the second class, the two supertaggers $\mathcal{S}_{\mathrm{REC}}$ and $\mathcal{S}_{\mathrm{RED}}$ run in cubic time. However, on typical small sentences that one usually handles in NLP, their run-times stay within reasonable limits: on average, $\mathcal{S}_{\mathrm{REC}}$ and $\mathcal{S}_{\mathrm{RED}}$ run respectively in 47ms and 73ms per sentence on our test set.

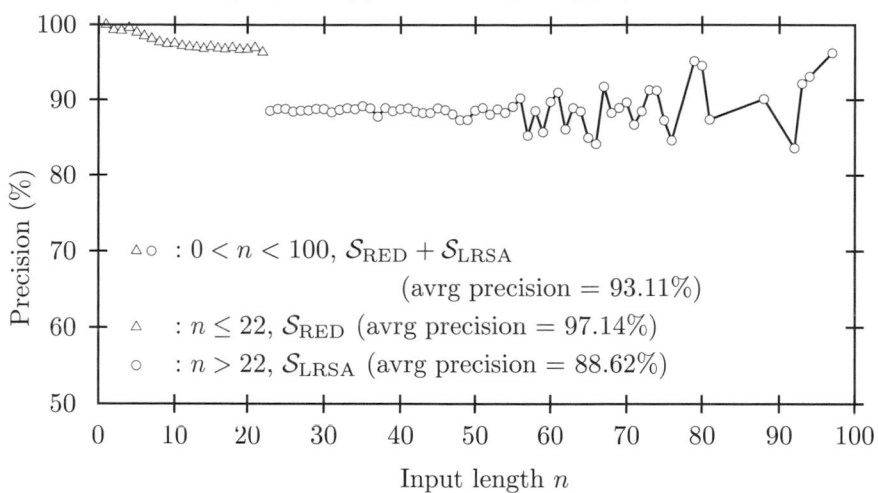

FIGURE 7.5 Composite supertagger average precision score ($\mathcal{S}_{\text{RED}} + \mathcal{S}_{\text{LRSA}}$ with threshold 22)

As performance concerns, the comparison of usual supertaggers with our work is also difficult, since their goals are different. Classical supertaggers try to assign the *best* supertag to each word,[21] whereas we have designed a method in which each word selects a set of supertags that does not exclude any supertag that will eventually be used in a valid complete derivation (i.e., we have designed a method whose recall score is 100%). In order to perform our precision score measures on a real-size application (both on a large scale grammar and on numerous unrestricted length sentences), we must have at our disposal a complete TAG parser to play the role of "gold supertagger." It seems that the only previously published measures that use the results of a TAG parser put considerable limits on the length of their input sentences.[22] These limits are due to the fact that the available TAG parsers, when working with a large grammar, are unable to process long sentences. To our knowledge, the only TAG parser that is capable of handling (almost) unrestricted length sentences has been described in Barthélemy et.al. (2001). It has been slightly modified and transformed into a gold supertagger that allows us to supertag 1M words of the WSJ corpus (more than 42,000 WSJ sentences, up to a length of almost 100 words). As already remarked,[23] the usage of TAG derivations to perform some evaluations is more severe than the usage of annotated corpora.

Nevertheless, we have reached very good precision scores: 88% for the linear time supertagger $\mathcal{S}_{\text{LRSA}}$ and more than 96% for the cubic time supertagger $\mathcal{S}_{\text{RED}}$. Moreover, if we look for a good compromise between speed and precision, we can use a composite supertagger with $\mathcal{S}_{\text{RED}}$ for short sentences and $\mathcal{S}_{\text{LRSA}}$ for long sentences, the threshold value being around 22 words. Such a composite supertagger has an average precision of 93% and a linear time behavior on long sentences.

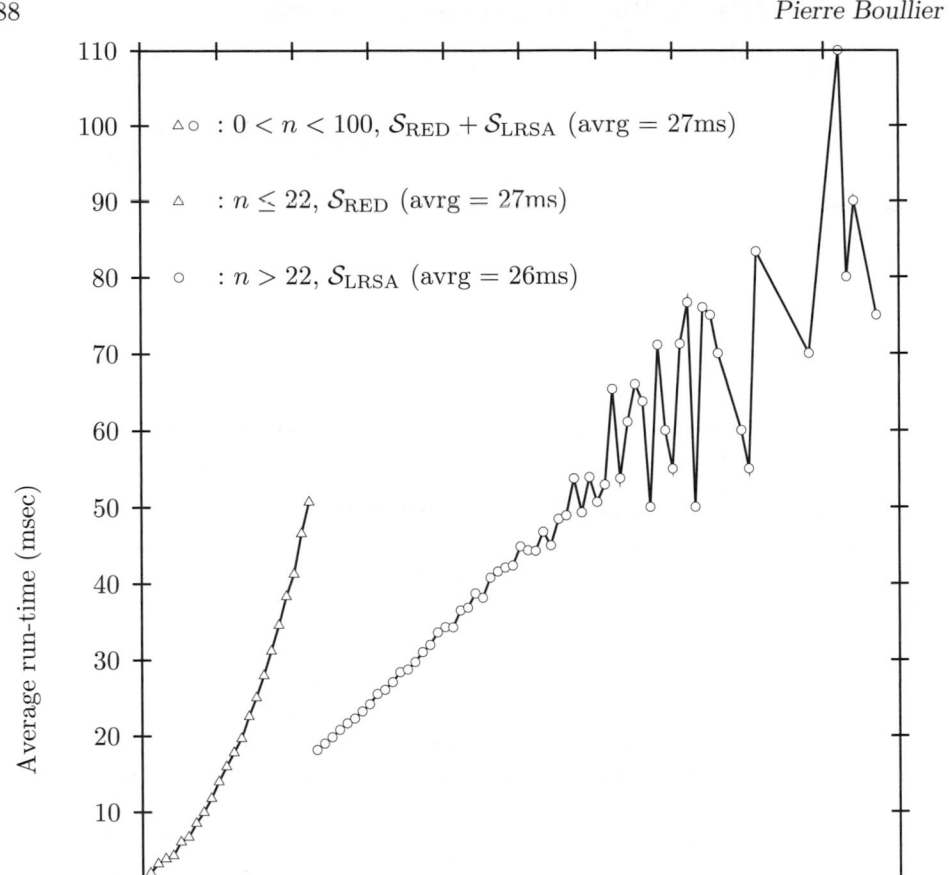

FIGURE 7.6 Composite supertagger average run-times ($\mathcal{S}_{\text{RED}} + \mathcal{S}_{\text{LRSA}}$ with threshold 22)

Moreover, in this conclusion, we want to stress that our supertagging methods are automatically deduced from the (TAG) grammar and do not need any training data. Our purpose was to build correctness-preserving supertaggers by using only structural information. We can note that such a correctness cannot be reached with statistical supertaggers, even if they select the top n supertags, for any value of n. In contrast to other approaches, our supertaggers may be safely used as neutral filters by other processors (no useful information is lost). These processors may well be classical statistical supertaggers or TAG parsers. Incidently, the complete TAG parser that we used as a gold supertagger in our experiments uses $\mathcal{S}_{\text{RED}}$ as a filter.[24]

Notes

1. The *dependency model* of Bangalore and Joshi (1999) does not put any limitation on the size of the window. However, they stopped their experiments because they "are constrained by the lack of a large corpus of LTAG parsed derivation structures that is needed to reliably estimate the various parameters of this model."

2. Following Boullier (2000) G is first transformed into an equivalent simple positive RCG (PRCG). Then, following Barthélemy et.al. (2001), this simple PRCG is transformed into a simple 1-PRCG which defines a CF superset. This simple 1-PRCG is in turn transformed into an equivalent CFG (see Boullier, 2000).

3. Note that G_{cf} is ambiguous since each of these productions is left and right recursive. This CF ambiguity, if we go back to the TAG level, reflects the fact that repeated adjunctions of the same auxiliary tree may occur either to the foot or to the root node. It is a standard practice in TAGs community to disallow adjuntion to foot nodes (foot nodes all bear a null adjunction constraint).

4. A CFG $G_{\text{cf}} = (N, T, P, S)$ is *proper* if each nonterminal symbol $A \in N$ is accessible from the axiom ($S \overset{*}{\underset{G_{\text{cf}}}{\Rightarrow}} \alpha A \beta$ where $\alpha, \beta \in (N \cup T)^*$) and if each nonterminal symbol $A \in N$ can generate a terminal string ($A \overset{*}{\underset{G_{\text{cf}}}{\Rightarrow}} x$, $x \in T^*$).

5. If an initial I-tree is substituted at some I-leaf, this leaf becomes an inside I-node. If we assume that no adjunction is allowed on that I-node, the traversals of I, both top-down and bottom-up, as the traversals of root nodes in initial trees, leave no trace in the decoration string.

6. In the general case, this derivation is neither leftmost, nor rightmost.

7. Recall that it is undecidable whether the language defined by a CFG is regular or not.

8. If the PDA is an LR automaton, for $h = 1$, we have the method described in Baker (1981), while for $h > 1$, we have the methods of Boullier (1984) and Bermudez and Schimpf (1990).

9. If (N, T, P, S) is a CFG, its *augmented* grammar is the CFG (N', T, P', S') where $N' = N \cup \{S'\}, S' \notin N, P' = P \cup \{S' \to S\}$.

10. Note how fresh leftmost terminals (i.e., $A \to \alpha.t\beta, \alpha \overset{*}{\underset{G_{\text{cf}}}{\Rightarrow}} \varepsilon$) are introduced by the close-reduce operation.

11. Note that two productions r_L and r_R may be recognized as sister productions without being part of the same auxiliary tree.

12. Of course, the obvious constraint $j > i$ may be added.

13. Our mirror SAs are reminiscent of bimachines from formal language theory (see Schutzenberger, 1961).

14. The mirror production of $A \rightarrow X_1 \cdots X_p$ is the production $A \rightarrow X_p \cdots X_1$.

15. Guiding is a technique that may improve nondeterministic processing times. A *guide* is a structure that contains only a (pertinent) subset of the full search space. Because they will surely lead to a failure, elements in the complement part will not be selected by the processor. This guide is generated during a preprocessing phase. If the nondeterministic processor is a CF parser, this preprocessor can be a FT which is, as in section 7.5, based on a regular superset.

16. that is, the subtree rooted at A whose daughter nodes are $\alpha t \beta$ and that spans the substring $a_{i+1} \cdots a_k$ of the input.

17. Note that multianchored supertags are counted several times in G_w^i and $\mathcal{S}_w^i$.

18. The measures presented in this section have been gathered on a 1.2GHz AMD Athlon PC running Linux. All programs are written in C and have been compiled with gcc without any optimization flag.

19. We use exactly the same test set as Boullier (2003).

20. Note that some of these input strings are considered to be "extragrammatical" only because they exhausted the memory resource available for that test. As an example, this happened for a 158 word sentence.

21. Or a small set of supertags as in Chen, Bangalore and Vijay-Shankar (1999).

22. In Bangalore (2000), the reported experiment uses the English XTAG parser on 1350 WSJ sentences, the lengths of which are less than 16.

23. From Bangalore (2000), we quote that "...evaluation against LTAG derivation trees is much more strict and hence more significant than the crossing bracket precision and recall figures measured against skeletally bracketed corpora".

24. In fact, $\mathcal{S}_{\text{RED}}$ is used as the guiding phase of our (guided) TAG parser (see Barthélemy et.al., 2001 and Boullier, 2003, for a notion of guided parsing).

References

Abney, S. (1991). Parsing by chunks. In *Principle-Based Parsing*. Kluwer Academic.

Baker, T. P. (1981). Extending lookahead for LR parsers. *Journal of Computer and System Sciences*, 22:243–259, 1981.

Bangalore, S. (2000). *Advances in Probabilistic and Other Parsing Technologies*, volume 16 of *Text, Speech and Language Technology*, pages 203–220. Kluwer Academic Publishers, 2000.

Bangalore, S. and Joshi, A. K. (1999). Supertagging: An approach to almost parsing. *Computational Linguistics*, 25(2):237–265, 1999.

Barthélemy, F., Boullier, P., Deschamp, P., and Clergerie, E. (2001). Guided parsing of range concatenation languages. In *Proceedings of the 39th Annual Meeting of the Association for Computational Linguistics (ACL'01)*, pages 42–49, University of Toulouse, France, July 2001.

Bermudez, M. E. and Schimpf, K. M. (1990). Practical arbitrary lookahead LR parsing. *Journal of Computer and System Sciences*, 41:230–250, 1990.

Boullier, P. (1984). *Contribution à la construction automatique d'analyseurs lexicographiques et syntaxiques*. PhD thesis, Université d'Orléans, France, 1984.

Boullier, P. (2000). A cubic time extension of context-free grammars. *Grammars*, 3(2/3):111–131, 2000.

Boullier, P. (2000). On TAG parsing. *Traitement Automatique des Langues (T.A.L.)*, 41(3):759–793, 2000.

Boullier, P. (2003). Guided Earley parsing. In *Proceedings of the 8th International Workshop on Parsing Technologies (IWPT 03)*, pages 43–54, Nancy, France, April 2003.

Chen, J., Bangalore, S., and Vijay-Shanker, K. (1999). New models for improving supertag disambiguation. In *Proceedings of the 9th Conference of the European Chapter of the Association for Computational Linguistics (EACL'99)*, pages 188–195, Bergen, Norway, June 1999.

Joshi, A. K. (1987). An introduction to tree adjoining grammars. In A. Manaster-Ramer, editor, *Mathematics of Language*, pages 87–114. John Benjamins, 1987.

Joshi, A. K. and Bangalore, S. (1994). Disambiguation of super parts of speech (or supertags): Almost parsing. In *Proceedings of the 17th International Conference on Computational Linguistics (COLING'94)*, Kyoto, Japan, 1994.

Joshi, A. K. and Schabes, Y. (1997). Tree-adjoining grammars. In G. Rozenberg and A. Salomaa, editors, *Handbook of Formal Languages*, pages 69–123. Springer-Verlag, 1997.

Nederhof, M.J. (2000). Practical experiments with regular approximation of context-free languages. *Computational Linguistics*, 26(1):17–44, 2000.

Schabes, Y., Abeillé, A., and Joshi, A. K. (1988). Parsing strategies with "lexicalized" grammars: Application to tree adjoining grammars. In *Proceedings of the 12th International Conference on Computational Linguistics (COLING'88)*, Budapest, Hungary, 1988.

Schützenberger, M. (1961). A remark on finite transducers. *Information and Control*, 4:185–187, 1961.

XTAG-Group. (1995). A lexicalized tree adjoining grammar for English. Technical Report IRCS 95-03, Institute for Research in Cognitive Science, University of Pennsylvania, Philadelphia,, March 1995.

Nonlexical Chart Parsing for TAG

ALEXIS NASR AND OWEN RAMBOW

8.1 Introduction: Supertags and Parsing

Over the last ten years, there has been a great increase in the performance of parsers. Current parsers use the notion of lexical head when generating phrase structure parses, and they use bilexical dependencies – probabilities that one particular head depends on another – to guide the parser. Current parsers achieve a score of about 90% to 92% when measuring just the accuracy of choosing these dependencies (Collins, 1997; Chiang, 2003; Charniak, 2000; Clark et al., 2002; Hockenmaier and Steedman, 2002); see also Yamada and Matsumoto (2003). Interestingly, the choice of formalism (headed CFG, TAG, or CCG) does not greatly change the parsers' accuracy, presumably because in all approaches, the underlying information is the same – word-word dependencies, with various types of backoff.

An alternative approach has been proposed in the literature: supertagging followed by "lightweight" parsing. The idea behind supertagging (Bangalore and Joshi, 1999) is to extend the notion of "tag" from a part of speech or a part of speech including morphological information to a tag that represents rich syntactic information as well, in particular active valency including subcategorization (who can/must be my dependents?), passive valency (who can be my governor?), and notions specific to particular parts of speech, such as voice for verbs. If words in a string can be tagged with this rich syntactic information, then, Bangalore and Joshi (1999) claim, the remaining step of determining the actual syntactic structure is trivial. They propose a "lightweight dependency parser" (LDA), which is a heuristically-driven, very simple program that creates a dependency structure from the tagged string of words. It uses no information gleaned from corpora at all, and it performs with an (unlabeled) accuracy of about 95%, given the correct supertag. While the supertagging only requires a notion of syntactically relevant features, the stage of determining a syntactic structure requires a grammar that uses these syntactically relevant features; Bangalore and Joshi (1999) use Tree-Adjoining Grammar (TAG) as a bridge between the features and the actual syntactic combinations. The approach does not rely on TAG, however,[1] and any lexicalized[2] (or lexicalist, in a wider sense) grammar formalism could be used.

There are several reasons why it is worthwhile to pursue an approach to parsing in which the sentence is first supertagged and then analyzed syntactically. The main point is that the models involved are potentially simpler than those in bilexical parsing. More precisely, the probabilistic models of the parser define a smaller number of parameters and are therefore less prone to data sparseness.[3] In particular, no bilexical or monolexical information is used in the parsing model. This holds the promise that when porting a supertagger-based parser to a new domain, a nonlexical structural model can be reused from a previous domain, and only a supertagged corpus in the new domain is needed (to train the supertagger), not a structurally annotated corpus. Furthermore, this approach uses an explicit lexicalized grammar. As a consequence, when porting a parser to a new domain, learned parser preferences in the supertagger can be overridden explicitly for domain-idiosyncratic words before the parse happens. For example, suppose that an application of a parser such as that of Collins (1997) trained on a news corpus is applied to a different genre, and that sentences such as *John put the book on the table*, unseen in training, are mostly analyzed with the PP attached to the noun, not to the verb (as is always required in the new domain). In the application, this would need to be fixed by writing special postprocessing code to rearrange the output of the parser, since there is no way to change the parser's behavior short of retraining it; in our approach, we could simply state that *put* should always (or with greatest probability) have a PP argument. And finally, we point out that is a different approach from the dominant bilexical one, and it is always worthwhile to pursue new approaches, especially as the performance of the bilexical parsers seems to be plateauing.

In this chapter, we follow the line of research started by Bangalore and Joshi (1999). Like their work, we in fact use a less powerful tree-rewriting formalism than TAG, namely TIG. We depart from their work in two ways.

- First, we use a chart parser with a statistical model derived from a corpus, which, however, is entirely nonlexical and just uses the supertags, not the words or lexemes found in the corpus. As we will see, when supertagging is combined with a full chart parser, the dependency accuracy is about 98% when given correct (gold-standard) supertags. We thus cut the error rate of the heuristic LDA by more than half. Our approach is still in the spirit of Bangalore and Joshi (1999), since the parser has no access to lexical information, only to information about the supertags. We differ from Bangalore and Joshi (1999) only in that we use, in addition to structural information contained in the supertag, probabilistic information about the relation between supertags, as derived from a corpus.

- Second, we use a grammar extracted automatically from the Penn Treebank (PTB) rather than a hand-crafted one mapped to the corpus (Chen, 2001; Xia et al., 2000; Chiang, 2003). We use a grammar derived from a treebank in order to achieve greater empirical coverage.

The overall goal of this chapter is to show that the use of a full probabilistic chart parser can improve on the results of the LDA, while retaining the intuition of localizing all lexical information in the supertagging stage. The specific goal of this paper is to present a nonlexical probabilistic model based on supertags alone; more specifically, we want to investigate different probabilistic models of adjunction at the same node.

We present results using the approach of Nasr and Rambow (2004b), but using actual supertagging (while Nasr and Rambow (2004b) uses gold-standard supertags). We explore using n-best results from two supertaggers, namely a standard n-gram supertagger, and a maximum entropy tagger, which performs better (Bangalore et al., 2005). (Note that the LDA can only take one supertag per word in input, so we are here making use of the chart parser.) We achieve about 85% accuracy on dependency arcs. While this performance is below the state of the art using other methods,[4] we believe that the work reported here can serve as a starting point for more research into this kind of parsing. In particular, in our architecture we can explore supertagging and parsing as separate processes, finding ways to improve the performance of either, or as interdependent processes.

The chapter is structured as follows. In section 8.2, we discuss related work. We concentrate on two lines of research which are very similar to ours in certain respects: the work on CCG parsing by Clark and Curran (2004), and the work on nonlexical CFG parsing by Klein and Manning (2003). These comparisons further help clarify the goals of our research. We present the underlying formalism in section 8.3. In section 8.4 we present the parser we use. We discuss the probabilistic models encoded in the automaton representation of the grammar in section 8.5, and how to extract a grammar which encodes such models from a corpus in section 8.6. In section 8.7, we present and discuss results. We conclude in section 8.8 with a summary of future avenues of research based on the preliminary study presented here.

8.2   Related Work

The work we describe in this paper is closely related in different ways to the work of Bangalore and Joshi (1999), Clark and Curran (2004), and Klein and Manning (2003). We have discussed the relation to the work of Bangalore and Joshi (1999) in section 8.1; we discuss the other two in turn in this section. In addition, there is work on probabilistic TAG parsing which does not use supertagging; see Sarkar and Joshi (2003) for a general overview. The advantage of using probabilistic TAG is that the bilexical model can be expressed very naturally. Our (nonlexical) work follows most current probabilistic TAG work in being based on the (very similar) models of Resnik (1992) and Schabes (1992). Of particular relevance to our work is Chiang (2003), which, while using a bilexical model, uses a TAG variant similar to the one we use, and also uses a similar horizontal markovization (section 8.5.3). We omit a general comparison to the growing literature on non-TAG dependency parsing, and refer to Nivre (2006) for a general overview.

8.2.1   CCG parsing

Clark and Curran (2004) present a CCG parser that uses a supertagger. It is the first full parser of any kind to successfully use a supertagger in conjunction with a parser. In CCG, the supertags correspond to lexical categories. The corpus used is the CCGbank (Hockenmaier and Steedman, 2002), which fixes the set of lexical categories to about 1,200, of which 400 occur more than 10 times. (Note that for our purposes, the CCGbank should be compared to a particular way of extracting a TAG from the PTB and the resulting annotated corpus, not directly to the PTB.) Clark and Curran (2004) use a maximum-entropy tagger that produces more than one result. The parser (described in Clark and Curran, 2004) is a discriminative log-likelihood chart parser, which uses lexical information as well, unlike our parser, for which all lexical information is relegated to the supertagging phase. There are several important results. First, they obtain an oracle parser results of almost 98%, which is comparable to our oracle result, that is, our result using the gold supertag. (But note that their parser is a bilexical parser, while ours is nonlexical.) Second, the performance of their n-best supertagger varies from 96.4% to 98.6%, depending on two parameters for choosing the n (which differs from word to word), which gives an average ambiguity per tag ranging from 1.4 to 3.5. This result is better than that of the supertagger we use, presumably because of their smaller tag set. Finally, using this supertagger in a parser, the best performance (unordered, unlabeled dependency recall/precision on the CCG derivation) is 92.5% (precision) and 91.1% (recall). Again, this performance is better than our parser, presumably because their supertagger performs better.

8.2.2   Nonlexical CFG parsing

Our approach is similar to that of Klein and Manning (2003) in that we do not use a bilexical or monolexical probability model. Rather, the generative probabilistic model that we use only models the relation between the elementary structures in the grammar. The second important similarity is that the grammars are extracted from the Penn Treebank, and the probability model is estimated at the same time using a maximum likelihood estimation. The principal difference is that Klein and Manning (2003) use a CFG as their underlying grammar formalism, while we use TAG. This difference has important repercussions: on one hand, the extracted TAG is much bigger than an extracted CFG, and the lexicon much more ambiguous (i.e., the tagging task is harder). On the other hand, the extended domain of locality of TAG makes the grammar more expressive. As a result, many of the techniques discussed in Klein and Manning (2003), which are aimed at changing the CFG in order to boost performance, are not relevant. Specifically:

- In vertical markovization, ancestor nodes are annotated in nonterminal nodes. In TAG (but not in CFG), each elementary structure contains the entire syntactic projection from the head. This is different from a fixed-length "vertical" history, but captures the same kind of information.

- There is no need for special modeling of unary rules. This is because unary context-free expansions will be part of a larger structure. Furthermore, many of the cases in which Klein and Manning (2003) deal with unary rules are in fact not unary because empty categories are explicitly included in the elementary structures of the grammar. This includes the traces left by *wh*-movement and by argument movement (for passive), and by empty arguments (including pro and PRO).

- Many groups of words which receive the same PTB part-of-speech tag are differentiated by their supertag. To take the example discussed in Klein and Manning (2003), demonstrative pronouns and demonstrative determiners have the same tag DT in the PTB, but they have different elementary trees in our grammar (an initial tree and an auxiliary tree, respectively). In general, a TAG subsumes the annotation of preterminals, as no elementary tree has only a preterminal and a terminal symbol.

However, the following techniques are also relevant to nonlexical TAG parsing:

- Horizontal markovization refers to the decomposition of flat rules into a sequence of rules conditioned on the context, and was first proposed by Collins (1997) and subsequently used by Klein and Manning (2003) and by Chiang (2003) for a TAG model, among others. We use horizontal markovization as well (see section 8.5.3). However, in our model (as in that of Chiang (2003), but unlike CFG-based models), the adjunction operation allows for explicitly modeling the argument/adjunct distinction, and the markovization only applies to adjuncts, and only to adjuncts adjoined at the same node, not to any expansion of the derived or derivation tree.

- Attachment errors and conjunction scope are problems that also affect our approach, though note that attachment errors include only those that are attachments to the same category (for example, attachment of a VP modifier to a higher or a lower clause), but not the classical NP-VP attachment ambiguities (which are disambiguated by the supertag). The technique proposed by Collins (1997), which Klein and Manning (2003) investigate, could also be used in TAG parsing (in appropriately modified form), but we do not investigate this question in this paper.

In summary, we could consider our approach as an alternate form of nonlexical parsing.

8.3 Generative Dependency Grammar (GDG)

The formalism we use can be presented in several different ways:

- As a generative string-rewriting system, GDG (Generative Dependency Grammar). We present this formalism in detail in Nasr and Rambow (2004a).

- As an implementation of Recursive Transition Networks (RTN).

- As a tree-rewriting formalism, namely Tree Insertion Grammar (Schabes and Waters, 1995).

Here, we choose the presentation as a RTN, and refer to the cited papers for the other views.

8.3.1 Informal definition

A GDG is a set of finite-state automata (FSMs) of a particular type, namely *lexicalized automata*. A lexicalized automaton with the anchor (word) m describes all possible dependents of m. Each automaton has a name, which defines not only the part-of-speech of m, but also the active valency of m (i.e., all word classes that can depend on it), as well as their linear order. Thus this name can be thought of as a *supertag* in the sense of Bangalore and Joshi (1999), and we will adopt the name "supertag" here to avoid confusion with simple part-of-speech tags. A sample lexicalized automaton is shown in Figure 8.1.[5] The transitions of the automaton are labeled with pairs $\langle f, c \rangle$, where f is a grammatical function (subject, object, different types of adjuncts, etc.), and c is a supertag, or by pairs $\langle \text{LEX}, m \rangle$, where m is an anchor of the automaton. For expository purposes, in these examples, the supertags c are simply standard part-of-speech tags, but one should think of the symbol N in figure 8.1, for example, as representing an initial tree whose anchor is of category N. This automaton indicates that the verb *eat* has a dependent that is its subject, obligatory and nonrepeatable, and whose category is noun or pronoun; a dependent that is its object which is optional and nonrepeatable; and an adjunct prepositional phrase that is optional and repeatable.

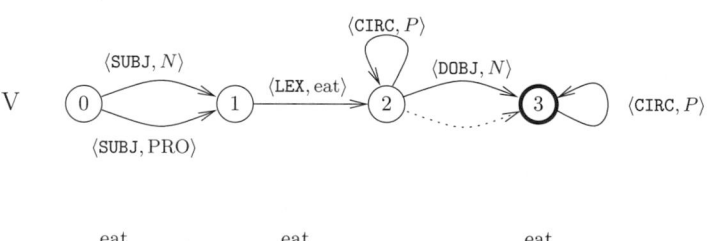

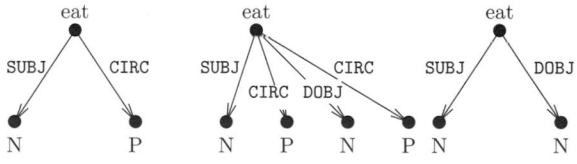

FIGURE 8.1 A lexicalized automaton and three elementary dependency trees that can be derived from it

Each word in the formal language theory sense, that is, each sentence (in the linguistic sense) accepted by an automaton, is a sequence of pairs $\langle f, c \rangle$. Each such sequence corresponds to a dependency tree of depth one, which we will call an *elementary dependency tree* of the grammar. Three sample elementary dependency trees can be seen in the lower part of figure 8.1. The word corresponding to the leftmost tree is: $\langle \text{SUBJ}, N \rangle$ $\langle \text{LEX}, \text{eat} \rangle$ $\langle \text{CIRC}, P \rangle$.

A GDG derivation is defined like a derivation in an RTN (Woods, 1970). It uses a stack, which contains pairs $\langle c, e \rangle$ where c is the name of an automaton from the grammar, and e is a state of c. When $\langle c, e \rangle$ is on the top of the stack, and a transition of type $\langle f, c' \rangle$ goes from state e to state e' in automaton c, $\langle c, e \rangle$ is popped and $\langle c, e' \rangle$ is pushed as well as the machine c' in its initial state $(\langle c', q \rangle)$. When we reach an accepting state q' in c', the pair $\langle c', q' \rangle$ is popped, uncovering $\langle c, e' \rangle$, and the traversal of automaton c resumes. We need to use a stack because, as we saw, during a derivation, several automata can be traversed in parallel, with one invoking the next recursively.

Since our automata are lexicalized, each traversal of a nonlexical arc (i.e., an arc of the form $\langle f, c \rangle$) corresponds to the establishment of a dependency between the lexical anchor of the automaton we are traversing, and that we then put on the stack (as governor), and the lexical anchor of the new automaton, which we start upon traversing the arc (as dependent). Thus, the result of a derivation can be seen as a sequence of transitions, which can be bijectively mapped to a dependency tree.

A probabilistic GDG, PGDG, is a GDG in which the automata of the grammar are weighted finite state automata. For each state in an automaton of the grammar, the weights of the outgoing arcs represent a probability distribution over possible transitions out of that state.

8.3.2   The sites of an automaton

The transitions of a lexicalized automaton do not all play the same role. We have already seen the lexical transitions that provide the words that anchor the automaton. In addition, we will distinguish the *argument transitions* that attach an argument as a dependent to the lexical anchor. All argument transitions that share the same grammatical function label constitute an *argument site* of the automaton. An example can be seen in figure 8.2, where site 1 is the subject site, while site 4 is the object site. Note that since we consider in this example the grammatical object of *eat* to be optional, the attachment in site 4 can be skipped using its ε -transition.

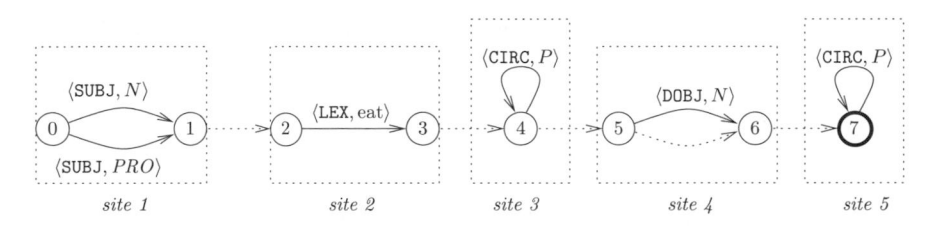

FIGURE 8.2 Sites of the automaton in figure 8.1

The transitions associated with adjuncts are called *adjunct transitions*. They are grouped into *adjunct sites*, such as sites 3 and 5 in figure 8.2. Each adjunct site corresponds to all adjunctions that can be made at one node of the tree, from one side. Some adjunct sites are repeatable, while others (such as determiners in some languages) are not. When several dependencies are generated by the same repeatable adjunct site, we distinguish them by their *adjunct position position*, which we mark with integers. The argument and adjunct sites are distinguished from the lexical transitions, which are called *lexical sites*.

8.4   Parsing with a GDG

The parsing algorithm is a simple extension of the chart parsing algorithm for context-free grammar (CFG). The difference is in the use of finite state machines in the items in the chart. In the following, we will call t-**FSM** an FSM M if its supertag is t. If T is the parse table for input sentence $W = w_1 \cdots w_n$ and GDG G, then $T_{i,j}$ contains (M, q) where M is a t-FSM, and q is one of the final states of M, iff we have a complete derivation of substring $w_i \cdots w_j$ such that the root of the corresponding dependency tree is the lexical anchor of M with supertag t. The main operation we use to fill the table is the following. If $T_{i,j}$ contains (M, q_1), if there is a transition in M from q_1 to q_2 labeled t, and if $T_{j+1,k}$ contains (M', q') where M' is a t-FSM and q' is a final state, then we add (M, q_2) to $T_{i,k}$. Note that because our grammars are lexicalized, this operation corresponds to establishing a dependency between the lexical anchor of M (as head) and the lexical anchor of M' (as dependent). The algorithm is extended to lattice input following Chappelier et al. (1999).

Before starting the parse, we create a tailored grammar by selecting those automata associated with the words in the input sentence. (Note that the crucial issue is how to associate automata with words in a sentence, which is the job of the supertagger; we do not discuss this issue here and refer to the literature on supertagging, for example, Bangalore and Joshi (1999). At the end of the parsing process, a shared parse forest has been built. The nonterminal nodes are labeled with pairs (M, q) where M is an FSM and q a state of this FSM. Obtaining the dependency trees from the packed parse forest is performed in two stages. In a first stage, a forest of binary phrase-structure trees is obtained from the packed forest and in a second stage, each phrase-structure tree is transformed into a dependency tree. An extended description of this algorithm can be found in Nasr (2004), and a more compact description in English can be found in Nasr and Rambow (2004b).

8.5   Probabilistic Models for GDG

The parser introduced in section 8.4 associates one or several analyses to a supertag sequence $S = S_1 \ldots S_n$. Each analysis $\mathcal{A}$ can be seen as a set of $n - 1$ attachment operations of one lexical node as an immediate dependent of another lexical node, and the selection of one supertag token as the root of the analysis (the single supertag that is not attached in another supertag). For the sake of uniformity, we will consider the selection of the root as a special kind of attachment, and $\mathcal{A}$ is therefore of cardinality n. In the following, for an attachment operation A, $O(A)$ returns its type (argument, adjunct, root), which in the case of argument and adjuncts is determined by the site at which it takes place. *Root* designates the unique event in $\mathcal{A}$ that selects the root.

From a probabilistic point of view, each attachment operation is considered as an event and an analysis $\mathcal{A}$ as the joint event $A_1, \ldots, A_n$. A large range of different models can be used to compute such a joint probability, from the simplest, which considers that all events are independent, to the model that considers that they are all dependent. The three models that we describe in this section vary in the way they model multiple adjuncts attaching at the same adjunct site. Put differently, the internal structure of repeatable adjunct sites is the only difference between the models. The three models described here consider that attachments at argument sites are independent of all the other attachments that make up an analysis. The general model (following Resnik, 1992; Schabes, 1992) is therefore:

$$P(\mathcal{A}) = P(Root)$$
$$\times \prod_{A \in \mathcal{A} | O(A) = argument} P(A)$$
$$\times \prod_{A \in \mathcal{A} | O(A) = adjunct} P(A)$$

What is important is that the three models we present in this section change the automata, but the changes are fully within sites; if we abstract to the level of sites, the automata are identical. Furthermore, while the automata implement different probabilistic models, the same parser described in section 8.4 can of course be used in conjunction with all of them.

The three models for adjunction will be illustrated on a simple example where two automata c_1 and c_2 are candidates for attachment at a given repeatable adjunct site (which we will simply refer to as a "site"). In the following models, we estimate parameters from the corpus obtained by running the TAG extraction algorithm over the PTB training corpus (see section 8.6). We can then easily count the relevant events.

8.5.1 Model 1: Independent attachments

In this model, an attachment at a site is considered independent from the other attachments that can take place at the same site. The probability of each attachment depends on the dependent automaton, on the governor automaton, and on the site of the governor automaton at which the attachment takes place. However, it is independent of the order of the attachments. The model does therefore not distinguish between attachments that only differ in their order. For example, the probability of the sequence $c_1 c_2 c_1 c_2$ being adjoined is modeled as follows (we use here and subsequently a simplified notation where $P(c_1)$ designates the probability of the attachment of c_1 at the relevant site in the relevant automaton):

$$P(c_1 c_2 c_1 c_2) = P(c_1)P(c_2)P(c_1)P(c_2).$$

It is clear that this probability is the same as that of the sequence $c_1 c_1 c_2 c_2$ adjoining, or of any other permutation.

8.5.2   Model 2: Positional model

This model adds to the first one the knowledge of the *order* of an attachment. But when modeling the probability that automaton c_1 attaches at a given site in order i, it does not take into account the attachments that happened for *order* $< i$. Such models also add a new parameter, which is the maximum number of attachment that are distinguished (from a probabilistic point of view). The automaton for a repeatable site with two positions is shown in figure 8.3. It consists of a series of transitions between consecutive pairs of states. The first "bundle" of transitions models the first attachment at the site, the second bundle, the second attachment, and so on, until the maximum number of attachments is reached. This limit on the number of attachments concerns only the probabilistic part of the automaton, more attachment can occur on this node, but their probabilities will not be distinguished. These attachments correspond to the loops on state 6 of the automaton. ϵ-transitions allow the attachments to stop at any moment by transitioning to state 7. (The ϵ-transitions are shown as dotted lines for reading convenience, they are formally regular transitions in the FSM.) Under model 2, the probability of the sequence $c_1 c_2 c_1 c_2$ being adjoined is:

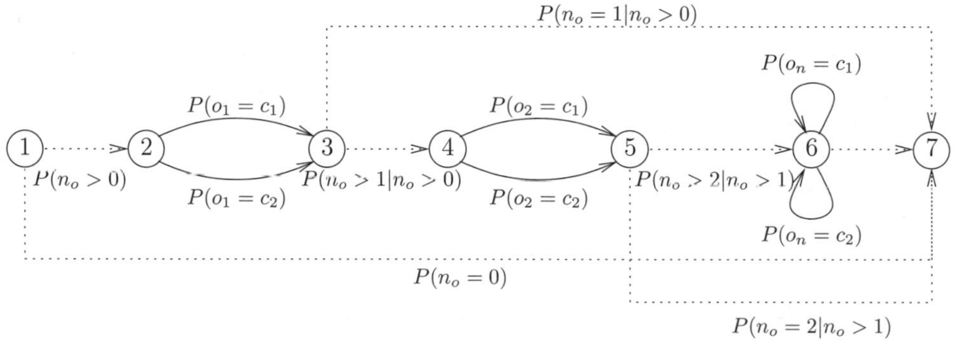

FIGURE 8.3 Positional model: a repeatable site with two positions

$$P(c_1 c_2 c_1 c_2) = P(o_1 = c_1) \times P(o_2 = c_2) \times P(o_n = c_1) \times P(o_n = c_2) \times P(n_o > 2)$$

Here, variables o_1 and o_2 represent the first and second order adjunctions. Variable o_n represents adjunctions of order higher than 2. Variable n_o represents the total number of adjunctions.

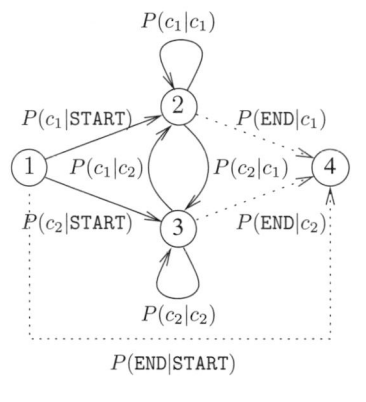

FIGURE 8.4 N-Gram model: repeatable site with bigram modeling

8.5.3   Model 3: *n*-gram model

The previous model takes into account the order of an attachment and disregards the nature of the attachments that happened before (or after) a given attachment. The model described here is the frequently used horizontal markovization (see section 8.2.2). Horizontal markovization is, in a sense, complementary to the positional model since it takes into account, in the probability of an attachment, the nature of the attachment that occurred just before and ignores the order of the current attachment. The probability of a series of attachments on the same side of the same node will be computed by an order-1 Markov chain, represented as a finite state automaton in figure 8.4. The transitions with probabilities $P(x|\text{START})$ (respect. $P(\text{END}|x)$) correspond to the occurrence of automaton x as the first (respectively the last) attachment at this node and the transition with probability $P(\text{END}|\text{START})$ corresponds to the null adjunction (the probability that no adjunction occurs at a node). The probability of the sequence $c_1 c_2 c_1 c_2$ being adjoined is now:

$$
\begin{aligned}
P(c_1 c_2 c_1 c_2) = {} & P(c_1|START) \\
& \times P(c_2|c_1) \\
& \times P(c_1|c_2) \\
& \times P(c_2|c_1) \\
& \times P(END|c_2)
\end{aligned}
$$

8.5.4 Finding the n-best parses

We extend our parser by augmenting entries in the parse table with probabilities. The algorithm for extracting parses is augmented to choose the best parse (or n-best parses) in the usual manner (Huang and Chiang, 2005). Note that the different models discussed in this section only affect the manner in which the TAG grammar extracted from the corpus is converted to an FSM; the parsing algorithm (and code) is always the same.

8.6 Extracting a GDG from a Corpus

We first describe the basic approach, we then show how we use the corpus to estimate probabilities, and finally we discuss the more complex models of adjunction we introduced in section 8.5.

8.6.1 Basic approach

To extract a GDG (i.e., a lexicalized RTN) from the Penn Treebank (PTB), we first extract a TAG and then convert it to a GDG. We make the detour via TAG for the following reason: we must extract an intermediate representation first in any case, as the automata in the GDG may refer in their transitions to any other automaton in the grammar. Thus, we cannot construct the automata until we have done a first pass through the corpus. We use TAG as the result of the first pass because this work has already been done, and we can reuse previous work, specifically the approach of Chen (2001) (which is similar to Xia et al., 2000 and Chiang, 2003).

We first briefly describe the work on TAG extraction, but refer the reader to the just cited literature for details. We use sections 02 to 21 of the Penn Treebank. We optimize the head percolation in the grammar extraction module to create meaningful dependency structures, rather than (for example) maximally simple elementary tree structures. For example, we include long-distance dependencies (*wh*-movement, relativization) in elementary trees, we distinguish passive transitives without *by*-phrase from active intransitives, and we include strongly governed prepositions (as determined in the PTB annotation, including passive *by*-phrases) in elementary verbal trees as secondary lexical heads. Generally, function words such as auxiliaries or determiners are dependents of the lexical head,[6] conjunctions (including punctuation functioning as conjunction) are dependent on the first conjunct and take the second conjunct as their argument, and conjunction chains are represented as right-branching rather than flat.

In the second step, we directly compile this TAG grammar into a set of FSMs that constitute the GDG and that are used in the parser. To derive a set of FSMs from a TAG, we do a depth-first traversal of each elementary tree in the grammar to obtain a sequence of nonterminal nodes. We exclude the root and foot nodes of adjunct auxiliary trees (its "passive valency structure"), because this structure merely tells us where and from which direction this tree can be adjoined, and we represent this information differently, namely in the structures into which this tree

can be adjoined. As usual, the elementary trees are tree schemas, with positions for
the lexical heads. Substitution nodes are represented by obligatory transitions, and
in the basic model, which assumes independent attachments, adjunction nodes are
represented by optional transitions (self-loops). Adjunction nodes are represented
by more complex structures in the other two models; we will return to them. Each
node in the TAG tree becomes two states of the FSM, one state representing the
node on the downward traversal on the left side (the **left node state**), the other
representing the state on the upward traversal, on the right side (the **right node
state**). For leaf nodes (and only for leaf nodes), the two states immediately follow
one another. The states are connected with transitions as described in the next
paragraph, with the left node state of the root node the start state, and its right
node state the final state (except for predicative auxiliary trees).

For each pair of adjacent states representing a substitution node, we add
transitions between them labeled with the names of all the trees that can substitute
there. For the lexical head, we add a transition on that head. For footnodes of
predicative auxiliary trees, which are left auxiliary trees (in the sense of Schabes
and Waters (1995), that is, all nonempty frontier nodes are to the left of the footnode
and it therefore adjoins from the left), we take the left node state as the final state.
Finally, in the basic model, in which adjunctions are modeled as independent (we
return to the other models below), we proceed as follows for nonleaf nodes. To each
nonleaf state, we add one self loop transition for each tree in the grammar that can
adjoin at that state from the specified direction (i.e., for a state representing a node
on the downward traversal, the auxiliary tree must be a left auxiliary tree and adjoin
from the left), labeled with the tree name. There are no other types of leaf nodes,
since we do not traverse the passive valency structure of adjunct auxiliary tees. The
result of this phase of the conversion is a set of FSMs, one per elementary tree of
the grammar, whose transitions refer to other FSMs. We give a sample grammar in
figure 8.5 and the result of converting it to FSMs in figure 8.6.

Note that the treatment of footnodes makes it impossible to deal with trees that
have terminal, substitution, or active adjunction nodes on both sides of a footnode.
It is this situation (iterated, of course) that makes TAG formally more powerful
than CFG; in linguistic uses, it is very rare, and no such trees are extracted from
the PTB. As a result, the grammar is weakly equivalent to a CFG. In fact, the
construction treats a TAG as if it were a Tree Insertion Grammar (TIG; Schabes
and Waters, 1995).

8.6.2 The basic probabilistic model

In the basic model, each event in constructing the derived tree is modeled as
independent. To determine the weights in the FSM, we use a maximum likelihood
estimation on the Penn Treebank with add-X smoothing.[7] We make use of a
representation of the PTB that we obtain from the TAG extraction process, which
provides the derivation tree for each sentence, using the extracted TAG. The
derivation tree shows not only which trees are associated with each word in the

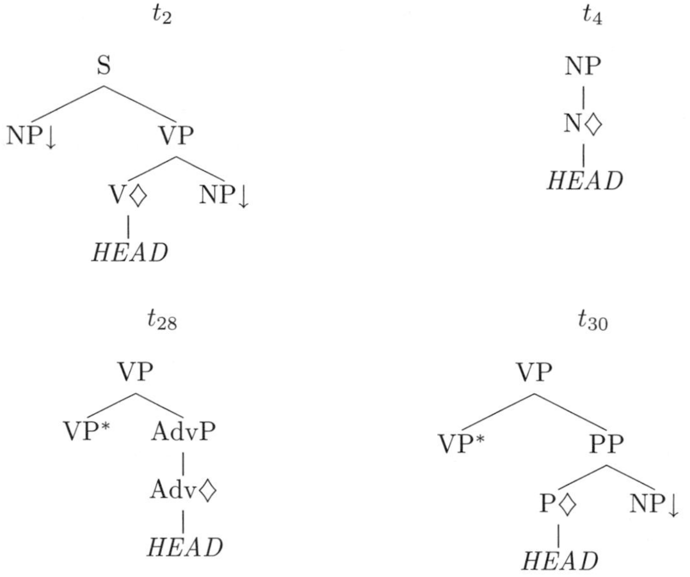

t_2

```
            S
          /   \
       NP↓     VP
              /  \
            V◊    NP↓
            |
          HEAD
```

t_4

```
       NP
       |
       N◊
       |
      HEAD
```

t_{28}

```
         VP
        /  \
     VP*    AdvP
             |
            Adv◊
             |
           HEAD
```

t_{30}

```
          VP
        /    \
     VP*      PP
             /  \
           P◊    NP↓
           |
          HEAD
```

FIGURE 8.5 Sample small grammar: trees for a transitive verb, a nominal argument, and two VP adjuncts from the right

sentence, but also into which other tree they are substituted or adjoined, and at which node (and, in the case of adjunction, from which direction). Given the previous construction, we can always map between tree location and corresponding substitution and adjunction sites in the FSM that corresponds to the tree. In the case of adjunction, we distinguish between left and right adjunction, which correspond to self-loops on the left and right node states, respectively.

Recall that there are three types of nodes in our FSMs, which we group into sites. In this model, each site consists of two nodes. The sites are connected by ε-transitions. The lexical sites contain a single obligatory transition on the lexical head (which is instantiated when an FSM is chosen for a particular word in the input sentence). This transition is given a weight of 1. In the case of substitution sites, we count all cases of substitution into the corresponding tree location, and we use these counts to estimate the probabilities of the transition between the left node state and the right node state of the substitution node. We perform smoothing, in order for formally possible substitutions that have not been seen in the corpus to have a nonzero probability. Since substitution is obligatory, there is no special case to consider. Adjunction is optional, so in the case of adjunction sites, we must also take into account the cases in which no adjunction occurred at that node. In the following, we assume we are considering a particular tree, a particular node in that tree, and either adjunction from the left or from the right to that node. We count the number of times each tree has been adjoined at that node from the relevant direction, and also how many times there is a "no adjunction" event. A

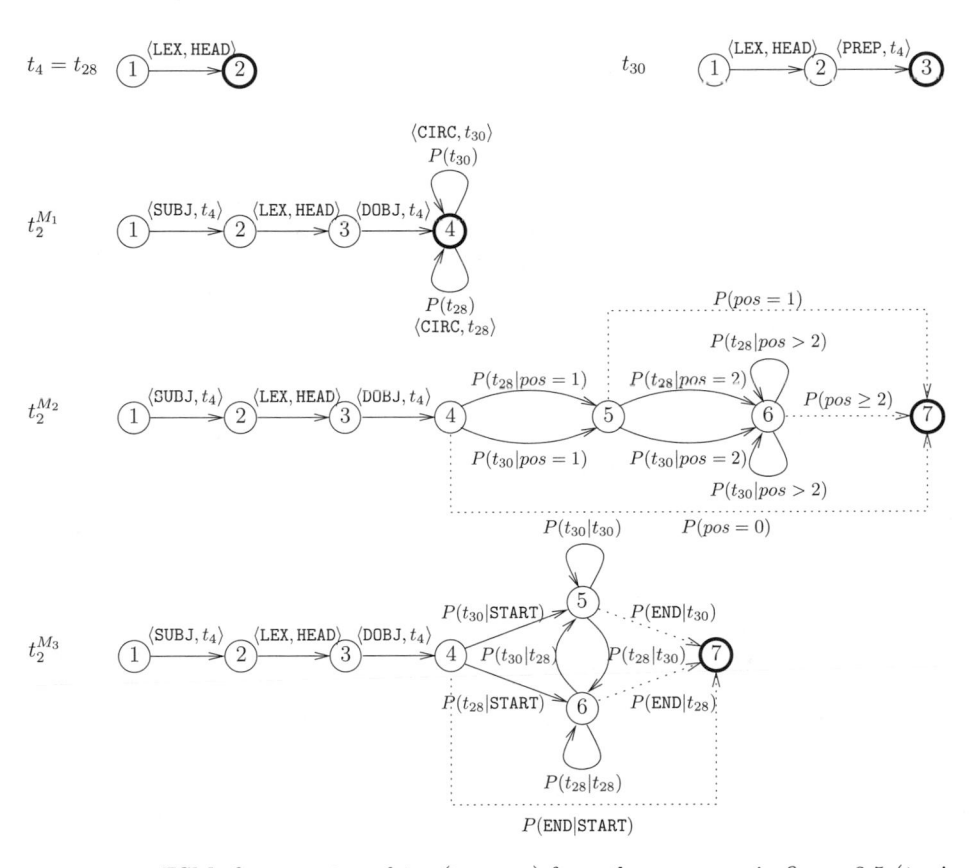

FIGURE 8.6 FSMs for trees t_4 and t_{30} (top row) from the grammar in figure 8.5 (t_{28} is similar to t_4), and three FSMs for tree t_2 derived according to the basic model (second row), the positional model (third row), and the *n*-gram model (bottom row)

Boys/t4 like/t2 cakes/t4
Parents/t4 bake/t2 cakes/t4 daily/t28 in/t30 kitchens/t4 with/t30 gusto/t4
Boys/t4 eat/t2 cakes/t4 beside/t30 dogs/t4 after/t30 snowstorms/t4
Parents/t4 allow/t2 binges/t4 reluctantly/t28

FIGURE 8.7 Sample corpus

"no adjunction" event means that no *further* adjunction occurs; it marks the end
of every sequence of adjunctions (including the empty sequence of adjunctions).
Thus, for every instance in the corpus of the governing supertag, and for each of its
adjunction nodes, there is exactly one "no adjunction" event for adjunction from the
left, and one from the right, independently of how many adjunctions occurred at
that node. We do not record how many adjunctions take place at a given node and
from a given direction, but rather consider the total number of events — adjunctions
and "no adjunction" events — for the node and direction. We then use counts of
the adjunctions to estimate the probability of the adjunction self-loops on the first
state of the adjunction site, while the probability of the ε-transition to the second
state is estimated based on the number of "no adjunction" events.

We illustrate this estimation with a simple (obviously made-up) example corpus,
shown in figure 8.7, in which a supertag is associated to every word. The elementary
trees corresponding to the supertags are represented in figure 8.5. We omit the tree
addresses at which the operations occur, as the grammar is so simple. We assume
there are no other trees in the grammar. For the two substitution nodes in t_2 and the
one in t_{30}, there is only one possible tree that can substitute, t_4, so its probability is
1. The interesting case are the arcs emerging from the fourth state of $t_2^{M_1}$, which is
the first state of its only adjunction site. There are six adjunctions at this node in
our corpus, two of t_{28} and four of t_{30}, as well as four "no-adjunction" events (since
there are four instances of t_2). We get probabilities of 0.2 for t_{28}, and of of 0.4 for
both t_{30} and for the ε-transition to the next (and final) state without smoothing.

8.6.3   The positional and n-gram probabilistic models

In section 8.4, we discussed two other models that treat adjunction in a more
complex manner. For the positional model, we create a new distribution for each
position, that is, for the first adjunct in that position, for the second adjunct, and
so on. Specifically, we count how often a particular tree was adjoined in position n,
and how often there were exactly $n - 1$ adjunctions (to estimate the probability of
no adjunction at position n). The positional model is parametrized for the number
of positions explicitly modeled; beyond this value of this parameter, we use the
basic model. (In fact, the basic model is the same as the positional model with no
positions explicitly modeled.) We show the probabilities for the middle model of
figure 8.4 in figure 8.8.

In the N-Gram model, we estimate the probabilities of bigrams for those trees
that can be adjoined at the same node. Note that we do not use bigrams to model

$P(pos = 0)$	0.250001
$P(t_{28}|pos = 1)$	0.499999
$P(t_{30}|pos = 1)$	0.250001
$P(pos = 1)$	0.333333
$P(t_{28}|pos = 2)$	0.000003
$P(t_{30}|pos = 2)$	0.666663
$P(pos \geq 2)$	0.666663
$P(t_{28}|pos > 2)$	0.000003
$P(t_{30}|pos > 2)$	0.333333

FIGURE 8.8 Transition probabilities on automaton $T_2^{M_2}$ for the positional model (see figure 8.6), given sample corpus in figure 8.7; figures may not add up to 1 due to rounding

the probabilities of *all* sister nodes in a dependency tree (as do some models), only those sister nodes that result from adjunctions at the same node in the governing tree. We estimate the probabilities by counting the number of bigrams found for a given tree, a given node in that tree, and a given adjunction direction. If fewer than N cases of the tree were found in the corpus, we use the category of the node instead. The probabilities are smoothed using linear interpolation of the unigram and bigram probabilities.

8.7 Results

In this section, we present results using three types of supertagged input: the gold supertag (i.e., the correct supertag); the output of a trigram HMM supertagger; the (better) output of a maximum entropy supertagger. All results reported in this section are based on unlabeled evaluation. (In our dependency representation, the only relevant labels are the arc labels, and we use labels that identify the deep subject, the deep object, the deep indirect object, and a single label for all adjuncts.)

Newer results using an improved supertagger and a reimplemented parser (including results for labeled dependency) can be found in Bangalore et al. (2009).

8.7.1 Using the Gold Supertag

In this evaluation, we are interested in exploring how parsing performs in the presence of the correct supertag. As a result, in the following, we report on data which has been correctly supertagged. We used Sections 02 to 21 of the Penn Treebank for training, the first 800 sentences of Section 00 for development, and Section 23 for testing only. The figures we report are accuracy figures: we evaluate how many dependency relations have been found. The root node is considered to depend on itself (a special dependency relation). There is no need to report recall and precision, as each sentence always has a number of dependency relations which is equal to the number of words (should a node remain unattached in a parse, it is given itself as governor). In the evaluation, we disregard true (non-conjunction)

Method	Accuracy on Sec 00	Accuracy on Sec 23
Baseline: LDA	94.35%	95.14%
Baseline: full parse with random choice	94.73%	94.69%
Model 1 (Independent Adjunction)	95.96%	
Model 2 (Positional Model): 1 position	97.54%	
Model 2 (Positional Model: 2 position	97.49%	
Model 2 (Positional Model: 3 position	97.57%	
Model 3 (N-Gram Model), using Supertag	97.73%	97.61%
Model 3 (N-Gram Model), using Category	97.29%	

FIGURE 8.9 Results (accuracy) for different models using the Gold-Standard supertag on development corpus (Section 00, first 800 sentences) with add-0.001 smoothing, and for the best performing model as well as the baselines on the test corpus (Section 23)

punctuation. The figures for the LDA are obtained by using the LDA as developed previously by Bangalore Srinivas, but using the same grammar we used for the full parser. Note that none of the numbers reported in this section can be directly compared to any numbers reported elsewhere, as this task differs from the tasks discussed in other research on parsing.

We use two different baselines. First, we use the performance of the LDA of Bangalore and Joshi (1999). The performance of the LDA on Section 00 is about 94.35%, on Section 23 95.14%. Second, we use the full chart parser, but randomly choose a parse from the parse forest. This baseline measures to what extent using a probabilistic model in the chart parser actually helps. The performance of this baseline is 94.73% on Section 00, 94.69% on Section 23. As we can see, the supertags provide sufficient information to result in high baselines. The results are summarized in figure 8.9.

There are several clear conclusions to be drawn from figure 8.9. First, a full parse has advantages over a heuristic parse, as even a random choice of a tree from the parse forest in the chart (i.e., without use of a probabilistic model) performs nearly as well as the heuristic LDA. Second, the use of even a simple probabilistic model using no lexical probabilities at all, and modeling adjunctions as entirely independent, reduces the error rate over the nonprobabilistic baseline by 22.8%, to 4.04%. Third, the modeling of multiple adjunctions at one node as independent is not optimal, and two different models can further reduce the error rate substantially. Specifically, we can increase the error reduction to 53.0% by modeling the first adjunction (from left to right) separately from all subsequent ones. However, presumably due to sparseness of data, there is no major advantage to using more than one position (and modeling the first and second adjunction separately). Furthermore, switching to the n-gram model in which an adjunction is conditioned on the previously adjoined supertag as well as the governing supertag, the error reduction is further increased slightly to 56.6%, with an error rate of 2.27%.

Number of paths	Stag. Acc.	Dep. Acc.
1	81.3%	71.1%
10	85.6%	76.4%
20	88.2%	77.9%
50	89.2%	78.4%
100	89.9%	79.4%
500	90.7%	79.9%
1000	90.8%	79.3%
1500	90.9%	79.5%
2000	90.9%	79.7%

FIGURE 8.10 Accuracy of the trigram tagger and the parser on the development corpus (first 800 sentences from Section 00) as a function of the number of supertagging paths taken into account: accuracy of the supertags of the best path among the n-best paths ("Stag. Acc.") and accuracy of the best dependency parse among the n-best paths ("Dep. Acc.")

This is the best result obtained on the development corpus using gold supertags. On the test corpus, the error rate increases to 2.39%.

8.7.2 Using supertags predicted by an HMM tagger

In this section, we present results on an initial subsection of section 00 of the PTB (800 sentences), using a standard trigram HMM tagger with backoff, where the parameters were calculated using the CMU Language Modeling Toolkit. An HMM tagger used in conjunction with a Viterbi decoder can be used to obtain n-best paths. Since our parser was extended to take lattices as input, we give the parser as input a lattice representing the n-best paths.

We show in figure 8.10 the results as a function of the number of paths. As we can see, beyond 100 paths, the results of both the supertagger and the parser fluctuate a bit, but presumably not at a statistically significant level. We assume (backed by the analysis of some cases) that this is due to the fact that the paths start to differ only in choices which do not affect the parse. Note that the LDA obtains a score of about 75% dependency accuracy on the 1-best path; to process multiple paths, it must be run multiple times, and there is no way to choose among multiple results.

8.7.3 Using supertags predicted by a maximum entropy tagger

In this subsection, we report results using two innovations: we use a better-performing tagger, and we use a much faster parser. We discuss these in turn.

Given the nonlocal nature of supertag dependencies, we move from an trigram-based HMM tagger to a tagger based on a standard maximum entropy (maxent)

Category	Dependency Accuracy	Number
Det	94.9%	3,989
Adj	91.8%	3,190
N	88.6%	15,675
P (no *to*)	73.6%	3677
Adv	81.5%	1554
V	83.2%	6262
Conj	68.3%	1124

FIGURE 8.11 Accuracy of choice of governor for words of different categories in the best parse on section 00; the third column shows the number of cases in the test corpus

model (Bangalore et al., 2005). The features used for the maxent model include: the lexical and part-of-speech attributes from the left and right context in a six-word window and the lexical, orthographic (e.g. capitalization, prefix, is digit) and part-of-speech attributes of the word being supertagged. Note there is no use of preceding supertags, which permits very fast (parallel) decoding of a sentence. However, as a result, we do not obtain n-best paths, but only n-best supertags (for each word). The 1-best accuracy of this supertagger is 85.7% and 85.5% on sections 00 and 23, respectively.

The use of a new tagger has an important consequence: since the tagger no longer emits n-best paths of supertags but n-best supertags per word, the number of possible paths increases exponentially with the sentence length, resulting in a performance problem for the original implementation of our parser. We therefore reimplemented the parser using the parsing approach of Boullier (2003), in which a context-free grammar is compiled into an Earley-type parser. In this approach, the plain GDG is transformed into a CFG, from which the Earley parser is compiled. The parser outputs a shared parse forest from which the search algorithm extracts the best parse, according to a given probabilistic model. Of course, we chose our best-performing model (the n-gram model). The main advantage of this parser is a significant speedup, which allows us to take more supertags into account when parsing, and to use a wider beam. All results that we report in this subsection were obtained using this reimplementation of the parser. These results represent the best performance of our parser at the present moment.

The new parser has two parameters: the beam width, and the number of supertags taken into account in the input. Suppose α is the beam width. Then if the highest confidence score for all supertags of a given word is s, we eliminate all supertags with a confidence score less than s/α. Using section 00, we determine the optimal values of these parameters to be 9 input supertags per word, and a beam width of 224. The tagger takes about 8.2 seconds for 1,000 words (when tagging an entire section of the Penn Treebank), while the parser takes about 7 seconds at these parameter settings, for a total of about 15.2 seconds per 1,000 words end-to-end. A

Length ≤ %	Corr. Sent.	Dep. Accuracy	Stag acc.	Number
5	81.94%	86.43%	78.68%	72
10	71.81%	89.49%	82.51%	259
15	57.28%	89.56%	82.78%	604
20	46.11%	88.55%	82.35%	989
25	39.20%	87.56%	81.62%	1306
30	33.97%	87.00%	81.12%	1572
35	30.69%	86.37%	80.53%	1756
40	29.37%	86.11%	80.21%	1835
45	28.68%	85.93%	80.08%	1883
50	28.39%	85.71%	79.87%	1902
80	28.17%	85.45%	79.59%	1917
300	28.11%	84.67%	78.84%	1921

FIGURE 8.12 Using Maxent supertagger, results for sentences of different maximum length in section 00: sentences with completely correct parses ("corr. Sent."), accuracy of the best dependency parse among the n-best paths ("Dep. Acc."), accuracy of the supertags of the best path among the n-best paths ("Stag. Acc."), and number of sentences of the specified length ("Number")

smaller beam or a smaller number of input supertags results in a faster parse, at the expense of accuracy.

Overall we obtain a dependency accuracy score of 84.7% and 84.8% on sections 00 and 23, respectively, of the Penn Treebank. This result is worse than that obtained by Clark and Curran (2004) (92.5% recall, 92.1% precision). However, their measure does not take into account the direction of the dependency arc, while our accuracy figure does. Furthermore, the gold dependency structures are different (ours are oriented toward the predicate-argument structure), so a direct comparison is difficult. Clark and Curran (2004) use recall/precision as some nodes may not be assigned governors. We use accuracy as all nodes are assigned governors, so for us recall, precision, and accuracy all have the same value.

We give some additional data for the results for section 00. First, we observe that the root is chosen correctly in 90.0% of cases. 99.5% of sentences have a complete analysis (i.e., analyses in which all nodes except a single root node are dependent on another node in the sentence, with no unattached subtrees), and 28.1% have a fully correct analysis. Figure 8.11 shows the distribution of attachment error rate for different part-of-speech categories. We see that determiners and adjectives, both nominal dependents with restricted syntax in English (and a simplified analysis in the PTB) do best, while conjunctions do worst. The relatively low performance on verbs reflects the difficulty of determining proper attachment for relative clauses.

Finally, figure 8.12 shows the results as a function of maximum sentence length. We see the expected deterioration with sentence length, except that very short

Type	Corpus	Stag accuracy	Parsing accuracy
HMM	Sec. 00 (800 sentences)	81.3%	79.7%
Maxent	Sec. 00	85.7%	84.7%
Maxent	Sec. 23	85.5%	84.8%
Gold	Sec. 00 (seen stags)	100.0%	97.7%

FIGURE 8.13   Summary of results for the 1-best supertagger and the resulting parser (which, except for the Gold case, is based on n-best supertags or supertag paths)

sentences do not perform as well as slightly longer sentences. We also note that the supertag accuracy on the best parses is worse than the accuracy of the supertagger.

8.7.4   Summary of Results

We summarize the results in figure 8.13. As we can see, increased performance in supertagging leads to increased performance in parsing, as we would expect. Given only three data points, with rather different characteristics, we do not wish to hazard generalizations, but the data suggests strongly that further research into improving supertagging will also directly improve parsing.

8.8   Conclusion

We have presented a nonlexical probabilistic chart parser for TIG which works in conjunction with a supertagger. It is implemented using finite-state automata. We have shown that this parser improves on the results of the Lightweight Dependency Analyzer, while retaining the intuition of localizing all lexical information in the supertagging stage. Furthermore, we have shown that the parser performance is roughly a linear function of the supertagger performance. This implies that research in further increasing the performance of a supertagger will also directly benefit parsing.

Acknowledgments

We would like to thank John Chen for letting us use his extracted grammar; Srinivas Bangalore, Patrick Haffner, and Ahmad Emami for the use of their supertagger; Pierre Boullier for for his patient and efficient assistance during the development of the new parser; and an anonymous reviewer for helpful comments.

Notes

1. The morpheme *tag* in *supertagging* is not the TAG of Tree-Adjoining Grammar, but the English word that means "label".

2. We use the term *lexicalized* to refer to a grammar formalism such that each of its elementary structures is associated with one lexical item (i.e., terminal symbol in the sense of formal grammar theory); we use the terms *nonlexical, monolexical,* and *bilexical* to refer to probabilistic models that take no, one or two lexical heads into account, respectively. The more common terms in the literature for these notions, *unlexicalized, lexicalized,* and *bilexical* are confusing and inconsistent.

3. Gildea (2001) shows that in fact the bilexical dependencies contribute little to performance of bilexical parsers, with lexical-structural dependencies being more important. While that finding is compatible with our results, we structure the parsing process in a completely different manner.

4. However, we point out that unlike many other dependency structures, our dependency structure is very "semantic," in that it directly represents predicate-argument structure. We give several examples: in the presence of an auxiliary, the subject still depends on the main verb, as does the auxiliary (which has no dependents); nominal, adjectival, and prepositional predicates are analyzed with the copula as auxiliary (i.e., the subject depends directly on the predicate, as does the auxiliary); a strongly governed preposition (for example, *to* in *give books to Mary*) does not govern a verbal argument (*Mary* in the example), but instead the verbal argument depends directly on the verb. Thus, our accuracy figures may not be comparable directly to other published results.

5. The initial state of an automaton is labeled 0, while its accepting states are indicated in boldface. The empty transitions are represented in dotted lines.

6. This is a linguistic choice and not forced by the formalism or the PTB. We prefer this representation as the resulting dependency tree is closer to predicate-argument structure.

7. After tuning on the development corpus, we chose $X = 0.00001$.

References

Bangalore, S., Boullier, P., Nasr, A., Rambow, O., and Sagot, B. (2009). MICA: A probabilistic dependency parser based on tree insertion grammars (application note). In *Proceedings of Human Language Technologies: The 2009 Annual Conference of the North American Chapter of the Association for Computational Linguistics, Companion Volume: Short Papers*, Association for Computational Linguistics, pages 185–188.

Bangalore, S., Haffner, P., and Emami, A. (2005). Factoring global inference by enriching local representations. Technical report, AT&T Labs – Reserach.

Bangalore, S. and Joshi, A. K. (1999). Supertagging: An approach to almost parsing. *Computational Linguistics*, 25(2):237–266.

Boullier, P. (2003). Guided Earley parsing. In *Proceedings of the 8th International Workshop on Parsing Technologies (IWPT03)*, Nancy, France, pages 43–54.

Chappelier, J.-C., Rajman, M., and Rozenknop, A. (1999). Lattice parsing for speech recognition. In *Traitement Automatqiues du Langage Naturel (TALN'99)*, Cargèse,

France.

Charniak, E. (2000). A maximum-entropy-inspired parser. In *1st Meeting of the North American Chapter of the Association for Computational Linguistics (NAACL'00)*, pages 132–139.

Chen, J. (2001). *Towards Efficient Statistical Parsing Using Lexicalized Grammatical Information*. PhD thesis, University of Delaware.

Chiang, D. (2003). Statistical parsing with an automatically extracted tree adjoining grammar. In Bod, R., Scha, R., and Sima'an, K., eds., *Data-Oriented Parsing*. CSLI Publications, Stanford.

Clark, S. and Curran, J. R. (2004). Parsing the WSJ using CCG and log-linear models. In *42nd Meeting of the Association for Computational Linguistics (ACL'04)*, Barcelona, Spain.

Clark, S., Hockenmaier, J., and Steedman, M. J. (2002). Building deep dependency structures with a wide-coverage CCG parser. In *40th Meeting of the Association for Computational Linguistics (ACL'02)*, pages 327–334.

Collins, M. (1997). Three generative, lexicalised models for statistical parsing. In *Proceedings of the 35th Annual Meeting of the Association for Computational Linguistics*, Madrid, Spain.

Gildea, D. (2001). Corpus variation and parser performance. In *Proceedings of the 2001 Conference on Empirical Methods in Natural Language Processing (EMNLP01)*, Pittsburgh, pages 167–202.

Hockenmaier, J. and Steedman, M. J. (2002). Generative models for statistical parsing with combinatory categorial grammar. In *40th Meeting of the Association for Computational Linguistics (ACL'02)*, pages 335–342.

Huang, L. and Chiang, D. (2005). Better k-best parsing. In *Proceedings of IWPT'05*, pages 53–64.

Klein, D. and Manning, C. D. (2003). Accurate unlexicalized parsing. In *41st Meeting of the Association for Computational Linguistics (ACL'03)*.

Nasr, A. (2004). Analyse syntaxique probabiliste pour grammaires de dépendances extraites automatiquement. Habilitation à diriger des recherches, Université Paris 7.

Nasr, A. and Rambow, O. (2004a). A simple string-rewriting formalism for dependency grammar. In *Recent Advances in Dependency Grammar: Proceedings of the Coling Workshop*.

Nasr, A. and Rambow, O. (2004b). Supertagging and full parsing. In *Proceedings of the Workshop on Tree Adjoining Grammar and Related Formalisms (TAG+7)*, Vancouver, Canada.

Nivre, J. (2006). *Inductive Dependency Parsing*. Springer.

Resnik, P. (1992). Probabilistic tree-adjoining grammar as a framework for statistical natural language processing. In *Proceedings of the Fourteenth International Conference on Computational Linguistics (COLING '92)*, Nantes, France.

Sarkar, A. and Joshi, A. K. (2003). Tree-adjoining grammars and its application to statistical parsing. In Bod, R., Scha, R., and Sima'an, K., eds., *Data-Oriented Parsing*. CSLI Publications, Stanford.

Schabes, Y. (1992). Stochastic lexicalized tree-adjoining grammars. In *Proceedings of the 15th International Conference on Computational Linguistics (COLING'92)*.

Schabes, Y. and Waters, R. C. (1995). Tree Insertion Grammar: A cubic-time, parsable formalism that lexicalizes Context-Free Grammar without changing the trees produced. *Computational Linguistics*, 21(4):479–514.

Woods, W. A. (1970). Transition network grammars for natural language analysis. *Commun. ACM*, 3(10):591–606.

Xia, F., Palmer, M., and Joshi, A. K. (2000). A uniform method of grammar extraction and its applications. In *Proc. of the EMNLP 2000*, Hong Kong.

Yamada, H. and Matsumoto, Y. (2003). Statistical dependency analysis with support vector machines. In *Proceedings of the 8th International Workshop of Parsing Technologies (IWPT2003)*, Nancy, France.

Part III

Supertags in Related Formalisms

9

Supertagging for Efficient Wide-Coverage CCG Parsing

Stephen Clark and James R. Curran

9.1 Introduction

Parsing with Combinatory Categorial Grammar (CCG), as with other lexicalized grammar formalisms such as Lexicalized Tree-Adjoining Grammar (LTAG), is a two-stage process: first, one or more elementary syntactic structures are assigned to each word in the sentence, and then the structures are combined by the parser. The original LTAG motivation for using a supertagger to achieve stage one was to reduce the number of structures assigned to each word and thereby increase parsing efficiency (Bangalore and Joshi, 1999). This motivation applies equally well to CCG.

In this chapter, we describe a CCG supertagger that uses an automatically extracted grammar and that is accurate enough to serve as a front end to a wide-coverage CCG parser. The use of the supertagger greatly increases the speed of the parser without adversely affecting its accuracy. The supertagger is based on standard maximum entropy tagging techniques (Ratnaparkhi, 1996). The accuracy of the supertagger when assigning a single category to each word is around 92%. In order to increase the number of words assigned the correct category, we develop a multitagger which uses the forward-backward algorithm to define a distribution over the lexical category set for each word in the sentence. These distributions are then used to assign a set of categories to each word.

A feature of this work is the way in which the supertagger is tightly integrated with the parser. To achieve maximum parsing speed, the supertagger initially assigns only a small number of CCG categories to each word, and the parser requests more categories from the supertagger only if it cannot provide a spanning analysis. We find that the supertagger is accurate enough, even when assigning a small number of categories to each word, to enable both highly efficient and accurate parsing.

A further advantage of the supertagger is that it allows conditional log-linear parsing models to be estimated using the automatically extracted grammar. The log-linear model parameters are estimated using a discriminative method, that is, one that requires all incorrect parses for a sentence as well as the correct parse. The supertagger is crucial in limiting the total number of parses for the training data to a manageable number.

The result of using the supertagger is a state-of-the-art CCG parsing system which is suitable for many large-scale NLP tasks. The rest of the chapter assumes a basic understanding of CCG; see Steedman (2000) for an introduction, and see Clark et al. (2002) and Hockenmaier (2003a) for an introduction to statistical parsing with CCG.

9.2 CCG Supertagging

The grammar used in this chapter is taken from CCGbank (Hockenmaier and Steedman, 2002a; Hockenmaier, 2003a), a CCG version of the Penn Treebank. Since the grammar is automatically extracted and has wide coverage, the number of possible derivations for a sentence can be extremely large. In order to enable practical parsing, a method is needed to reduce the size of the parse space. Hockenmaier's approach (Hockenmaier and Steedman, 2002b; Hockenmaier, 2003a,b) is to assign all possible lexical categories to a word during stage one of the parsing (from the word's entry in the lexicon), and then use a probabilistic beam search during stage two to limit the number of items that are added to the parsing chart. The approach taken here is to limit the size of the parse space during stage one, by using statistical tagging techniques to assign only the most probable lexical categories to each word. The number of categories assigned to each word can be greatly reduced in this way, with a correspondingly massive reduction in the number of derivations.

The original LTAG supertagger of Bangalore and Joshi (1999) was based on an HMM tagger. Here we use the maximum entropy tagger described in Curran and Clark (2003). An advantage of the maximum entropy approach is that it is easy to encode a wide range of potentially useful features; for example, it was shown in Clark (2002) that POS tags provide useful information for CCG supertagging. Section 9.2.2 describes the models used by the supertagger, and section 9.2.3 shows how these can be used to provide a CCG multitagger. Section 9.3 shows how the multitagger can be integrated with a CCG parser, leading to large increases in parsing speed. The next section describes the grammar used by the supertagger and parser.

9.2.1   The lexical category set

Obtaining a set of lexical category types from CCGbank simply involves reading the lexical categories off each derivation in the treebank. Figure 9.1 gives an example sentence together with the lexical categories. The categories can be thought of as fine-grained part-of-speech tags, primarily encoding subcategorization information; for example, the category (S[dcl]\NP)/NP is that of a transitive verb in English,

The	WSJ	is	a	publication
NP/N	N	(S[dcl]\NP)/NP	NP/N	N

that	I	enjoy	reading
(NP\NP)/(S[dcl]/NP)	NP	(S[dcl]\NP)/(S[ng]\NP)	(S[ng]\NP)/NP

FIGURE 9.1 Example sentence with CCG lexical categories

which in CCG is represented as a sentence missing a noun phrase to its right, and a noun phrase to its left (indicated by the directions of the slashes). The [dcl] feature on the S category indicates the sentence is declarative. (See Hockenmaier, 2003a for the complete list of sentence features used in CCGbank.)

In the example sentence, the CCG combinatory rule of type-raising is required for the categories to combine: the NP category for *I* is type-raised to S/(S\NP), which is then combined with (S[ng]\NP)/NP using the rule of forward composition. It would be possible to have the type-raised category as a preterminal in the derivation, and include type-raised categories in the set of lexical categories used by the supertagger. However, we follow the treatment of type-raised categories in CCGbank and leave the application of the type-raising rule to the parsing stage; thus, type-raised categories such as S/(S\NP) do not appear in the supertagger's lexical category set.

The lexical category set used by the supertagger is taken from sections 02–21 of CCGbank (version 1.2). The total number of lexical category types in these sections is 1,285. However, due to noise in the original Penn Treebank and some noise introduced in the treebank conversion process, not all instances of lexical categories in CCGbank are correct. To reduce the number of noisy categories in the set of lexical category types, a frequency cutoff is applied. Table 9.1 shows the reduction in the number of category types when a cutoff of 10 is used, and the coverage of the resulting set on both the training data (sections 02–21) and the development data (section 00). The table shows that the use of a frequency cutoff is highly effective in reducing the size of the category set, while retaining good coverage on unseen data. The resulting set of 425 category types was used in the experiments reported in the rest of this paper.

Clark (2002) compares the size of grammars extracted from CCGbank with automatically extracted LTAG grammars. The grammars of Chen and Vijay-Shanker (2000) contain between 2,000 and 9,000 tree frames, depending on the parameters used in the extraction process, significantly more elementary structures than the number of lexical categories derived from CCGbank. Why the CCGbank grammar is smaller than an automatically extracted LTAG grammar is an open question. One reason may be due to differences in the grammar formalisms themselves; in particular, various syntactic phenomena are treated differently in the two formalisms. For example, in LTAG each minimal construction in which a transitive verb can appear (for example, subject extraction, topicalization, subject relative,

frequency cutoff	# cat types	# cat tokens in 02–21 not in cat set	# sentences in 02–21 with missing cat	# cat tokens in 00 not in cat set	# sentences in 00 with missing cat
1	1,285	0	0	29 (0.1%)	17 (0.9%)
10	425	2,055 (0.2%)	1,815 (4.6%)	95 (0.2%)	72 (3.8%)

TABLE 9.1 Statistics for the lexical category set

object relative, passive) has associated with it a different elementary tree (Sarkar and Joshi, 2003). In contrast, in CCG, the lexical category of the transitive verb in each of those cases will be (S\NP)/NP.[1] Another difference is that, in the grammars of Chen and Vijay-Shanker (2000), punctuation marks can have a variety of elementary trees. In contrast, a comma in CCGbank, for example, is always assigned the category ",". Rules in the parser then determine the attachment of the comma.

Another reason may be due to differences in the grammar extraction processes. For example, Hockenmaier substantially cleaned up the Penn Treebank before converting it to CCG (Hockenmaier and Steedman, 2002a). Whatever the reasons for the differences in grammar sizes, we hypothesize that the relatively small size of the CCG lexical category set is a key factor in the higher accuracy reported for CCG supertagging compared with supertagging using an automatically extracted LTAG.

9.2.2   The maximum entropy tagging model

The supertagger uses conditional probabilities of the form $P(y|x)$, where y is a lexical category and x is a local context containing y. The conditional probabilities have the following log-linear form:

$$P(y|x) = \frac{1}{Z(x)} e^{\sum_i \lambda_i f_i(x,y)} \tag{9.1}$$

The feature functions $f_i(x,y)$ are binary-valued and return 1 or 0, depending on the lexical category y and the value of a particular contextual predicate given the context x. Contextual predicates identify elements of the context that might be useful for predicting the lexical category. For example, the following feature returns 1 if the previous word's POS tag is DT and the lexical category y is N; otherwise it returns 0:

$$f_j(x,y) = \begin{cases} 1 & \text{if prev\_pos\_is\_DT}(x) = true \ \& \ y = \mathsf{N} \\ 0 & \text{otherwise} \end{cases} \tag{9.2}$$

prev_pos_is_DT (x) is an example of a contextual predicate. Each feature f_i has an associated weight λ_i that is determined during training. $Z(x)$ is a normalization constant that ensures a proper probability distribution for each context.

Word templates	POS tag templates	Category templates
w_i	t_i	c_{i-1}
w_{i-1}	t_{i-1}	c_{i-2}, c_{i-1}
w_{i-2}	t_{i-2}	
w_{i+1}	t_{i+1}	
w_{i+2}	t_{i+2}	
	t_{i-1}, t_i	
	t_{i-2}, t_{i-1}	
	t_{i-1}, t_{i+1}	
	t_i, t_{i+1}	
	t_{i+1}, t_{i+2}	

TABLE 9.2 Contextual predicate templates for the context x_i

The conditional probability of a sequence of lexical categories, $y_1, \ldots, y_n$, given a sentence, $w_1, \ldots, w_n$, is defined as the product of the individual probabilities for each category:

$$P(y_1, \ldots, y_n | w_1, \ldots, w_n) = \prod_{i=1}^{n} P(y_i | x_i) \tag{9.3}$$

where x_i is the context for word w_i.

Clark (2002) describes experiments investigating various contextual predicates and window sizes for the context. Following Ratnaparkhi (1996), contextual predicates designed for predicting the category of unknown and rare words were considered; these contextual predicates pick out properties of the word to be tagged, such as suffixes of variable lengths, and whether the word contains a capital letter, numeric character or hyphen. Such features were found to be very useful for POS tagging. However, for supertagging it was found that, when the POS tags of the words in the window were included as features, the rare word features had no impact on accuracy.

It was also found that extending the context window beyond two words either side of the target word had a negligible impact on accuracy. Thus, the features used in this chapter are defined in terms of the words and POS tags in the 5-word window surrounding the target word, and the previous two lexical categories. Table 9.2 gives templates for the contextual predicates corresponding to context x_i; t_i is the POS tag of word w_i and c_i is its lexical category.

The feature weights are estimated by maximizing an objective function consisting of the likelihood function and a Gaussian prior, which is used to avoid overfitting. We use the L-BFGS optimisation algorithm to perform the estimation (Nocedal and Wright, 1999; Malouf, 2002). Sections 02–21 of CCGbank were used as training data.

9.2.3   From single tagging to multitagging

The most probable lexical category sequence can be found efficiently using a variant of the Viterbi algorithm for HMM taggers. We restrict the categories that can be assigned to a word by using a *tag dictionary*: for words seen at least k times in the training data, the tagger can only assign categories that have been seen with the word in the data. For words seen less than k times, an alternative based on the word's POS tag is used: the tagger can only assign categories that have been seen with the POS tag in the data. We have found the tag dictionary to be beneficial in terms of both efficiency and accuracy. A value of $k = 20$ was used in the experiments described here.

The accuracy of the supertagger on section 00 of CCGbank is 92.6%, with a sentence accuracy of 36.8%. Sentence accuracy is the percentage of sentences whose words are all tagged correctly. These figures include punctuation marks, for which the lexical category is simply the punctuation mark itself, and are obtained using gold standard POS tags. With automatically assigned POS tags, using the POS tagger of Curran and Clark (2003), the accuracies drop to 91.5 and 32.7. An accuracy of 91–92% may appear reasonable given the large lexical category set; however, the low sentence accuracy suggests that the supertagger may not be accurate enough to serve as a front end to a parser. Clark (2002) reports that a significant loss in coverage results if the supertagger is used as a front end to the parser of Hockenmaier and Steedman (2002b). In order to increase the number of words assigned the correct category, we develop a CCG multitagger, which is able to assign more than one category to each word.

The multitagger uses the following conditional probabilities:

$$P(y_i|w_1, \ldots, w_n) = \sum_{y_1, \ldots, y_{i-1}, y_{i+1}, \ldots, y_n} P(y_i, y_1, \ldots, y_{i-1}, y_{i+1}, \ldots, y_n|w_1, \ldots, w_n)$$

$$(9.4)$$

Here y_i is to be thought of as a constant category, whereas y_j $(j \neq i)$ varies over the possible categories for word j. In words, the probability of category y_i, given the sentence, is the sum of the probabilities of all sequences containing y_i. This sum can be calculated efficiently using a variant of the forward-backward algorithm.[2] For each word in the sentence, the multitagger then assigns all those categories whose probability according to (9.4) is within some factor, β, of the highest probability category for that word.

Table 9.3 gives the per-word accuracy on section 00 for various levels of category ambiguity, together with the average number of categories per word. The SENT column gives the percentage of sentences whose words are all supertagged correctly. The set of categories assigned to a word is considered correct if it contains the correct category. The table gives results when using gold standard POS tags and, in the final two columns, when using POS tags automatically assigned by the POS

CATS/		GOLD POS		AUTO POS	
WORD	β	WORD	SENT	WORD	SENT
1.0	1	92.6	36.8	91.5	32.7
1.2	0.1201	96.8	63.4	95.8	56.5
1.4	0.0337	97.9	72.1	96.9	64.8
1.6	0.0142	98.3	76.4	97.5	69.3
1.8	0.0074	98.4	78.3	97.7	71.0
2.0	0.0048	98.5	79.4	97.9	72.5
2.5	0.0019	98.7	80.6	98.1	74.3
3.0	0.0009	98.7	81.4	98.3	75.6
12.5	0	98.9	82.3	98.8	80.1

TABLE 9.3 Supertagging accuracy on section 00 for different levels of ambiguity

tagger described in Curran and Clark (2003). The drop in accuracy is expected given the importance of POS tags as features.

The table demonstrates the significant reduction in the average number of categories that can be achieved through the use of a supertagger. To give one example, the number of categories in the tag dictionary's entry for the word *is* is 45. However, in the sentence *Mr. Vinken is chairman of Elsevier N.V., the Dutch publishing group.*, the supertagger correctly assigns 1 category to *is* for all values of β.

These results are an improvement over our earlier work, since in Clark and Curran (2004a) the forward-backward algorithm was not used to estimate the probability in (9.4). Curran et al. (2006) investigates the improvement obtained from using the forward-backward algorithm. It also addresses the drop in supertagger accuracy when using automatically assigned POS tags. We show how to maintain some POS ambiguity through to the supertagging phase, using a multi-POS tagger, and also how POS tag probabilities can be encoded as real-valued features in the supertagger. The drop in supertagging accuracy when moving from gold to automatically assigned POS tags is reduced by roughly 50% on average across the various β values.

9.3 Integrating the Supertagger with a CCG Parser

9.3.1 The parser

The parser used in this chapter is described in detail in Clark and Curran (2004b). It takes POS tagged sentences as input with each word assigned a set of lexical categories. A packed chart is used to efficiently represent all of the possible analyses for a sentence, and the CKY chart parsing algorithm described in Steedman (2000) is used to build the chart.

In Clark and Curran (2004b) we evaluate a number of log-linear parsing models for CCG. In this paper we use the normal-form model, which defines probabilities with the conditional log-linear form in (9.1), where y is a derivation and x is a sentence. Features are integer-valued and defined in terms of local subtrees in the derivation, including lexical head information and word-word dependencies. The normal-form derivations in CCGbank provide the gold standard training data. The feature set we use is from the best performing normal-form model in Clark and Curran (2004b).

In Clark and Curran (2004a) we investigate increasing the speed of the parser by imposing constraints on the derivation, as well as using the supertagger. The first constraint is to allow categories to combine only if they have been seen to combine in sections 02–21 of CCGbank. This significantly reduces the number of categories created using the composition rules, since the derivations in CCGbank are normal-form and only contain instances of composition rules when necessary (for example, in object extraction cases and some cases of coordination). These constraints also prevent the creation of low-probability categories using rule combinations not seen in CCGbank.

The second set of restrictions also rule out some nonnormal-form derivations, and are taken from Eisner (1996). The idea is to restrict the combination of categories produced by composition; more specifically, any constituent that is the result of a forward composition cannot serve as the primary (left) functor in another forward composition or forward application. Similarly, any constituent which is the result of a backward composition cannot serve as the primary (right) functor in another backward composition or backward application. Eisner only deals with a grammar without type-raising, and so the constraints cannot guarantee a normal-form derivation when applied to the grammars used in this chapter. However, the constraints are still useful in restricting the derivation space. The experiments reported in the rest of this paper used both kinds of normal-form constraints.

9.3.2   Combining the supertagger with the parser

The philosophy in earlier work that combined the supertagger and parser (Clark et al., 2002; Clark and Curran, 2003) was to use an unrestrictive setting of the supertagger but still allow a reasonable compromise between speed and accuracy. The idea was to give the parser the greatest possibility of finding the correct parse, by initializing it with as many lexical categories as possible but still retain reasonable efficiency. However, for some sentences, the number of categories in the chart gets extremely large with this approach, and parsing is unacceptably slow. Hence a limit was applied to the number of categories in the chart, and a more restrictive setting of the supertagger was reverted to if the limit was exceeded.

In this chapter, we consider the opposite approach: start with a very restrictive setting of the supertagger, and only assign more categories if the parser cannot find an analysis spanning the sentence. In this way the parser interacts much more closely with the supertagger. In effect, the parser is using the grammar to decide if the categories provided by the supertagger are acceptable, and if not the parser requests more categories.

The advantage of this approach is that parsing speeds are much higher. We have also found that parsing accuracy is not reduced; in fact, given the current parsing model, accuracy has been found to increase with the new supertagging approach. See Clark and Curran (2004b) and Clark and Curran (2004a) for more discussion of the accuracy of the parser.

9.3.3 Parse times

The results in this section were obtained using a 3.2 GHz Intel Xeon P4. Table 9.4 gives parse times for the 2,407 sentences in section 23 of CCGbank. The final two columns give the number of sentences, and the number of words, parsed per second. For all of the figures reported on section 23, unless stated otherwise, the parser is able to provide an analysis for 99.6% of the sentences. The parse times and speeds include the failed sentences, but do not include the time taken by the supertagger; however, the supertagger is extremely efficient, taking less than 4 seconds to supertag section 23, most of which consists of load time for the Maximum Entropy model.

SUPERTAGGING/PARSING CONSTRAINTS	TIME SEC	SENTS /SEC	WORDS /SEC
$\beta = 0.005 \rightarrow \ldots \rightarrow 0.075$	394.2	6.1	140
$\beta = 0.075 \rightarrow \ldots 0.0001_{k=150}$	74.7	32.2	741
$\beta = 0.15$ (93.9% cov)	42.9	56.1	1 290
Oracle	13.2	181.9	4 185

TABLE 9.4 Parse times for section 23

The first row corresponds to the strategy of earlier work by starting with an unrestrictive setting of the supertagger. The first value of β is 0.0001; if the parser cannot find a spanning analysis, this is changed to $\beta = 0.0001_{k=150}$, which increases the average number of categories assigned to a word by increasing the tag-dictionary parameter. If the node limit is exceeded at $\beta = 0.0001$ (for these experiments the node limit is set at 1,000,000), β is changed to 0.005. If the node limit is still exceeded, β is changed to 0.001, then 0.03, and finally 0.075.

The second row corresponds to the new strategy of starting with the most restrictive setting of the supertagger ($\beta = 0.075$), and moving through the settings if the parser cannot find a spanning analysis. The table shows that the new strategy has a significant impact on parsing speed, increasing it by a factor of 5 over the earlier approach (given the parameter settings used in these experiments).

The 93.9% coverage row corresponds to using only one supertagging level with $\beta = 0.15$; the parser ignores the sentence if it cannot get an analysis at this level. The percentage of sentences without an analysis is now 6%, but the parser is extremely

β	CATS/ WORD	0.075 FIRST PARSES	%	0.005 FIRST PARSES	%
0.075	1.25	2312	96.1	0	0.0
0.03	1.42	28	1.2	5	0.2
0.01	1.71	28	1.2	10	0.4
0.005	1.99	6	0.2	2359	98.0
$0.0001_{k=150}$	6.98	23	1.0	23	1.0
NO SPAN		10	0.4	10	0.4

TABLE 9.5 Supertagger β levels used on section 00

fast, processing 56 sentences a second. This configuration of the system would be useful for obtaining data for lexical knowledge acquisition, for example, for which large amounts of data are required. The oracle row gives the parser speed when it is provided with only the correct lexical categories, showing the speeds which could be achieved given the perfect supertagger.

Table 9.5 gives the percentage of sentences which are parsed at each supertagger level, for both the new and old parsing strategies. The results show that, for the old approach, most of the sentences are parsed using the least restrictive setting of the supertagger ($\beta = 0.01$); conversely, for the new approach, most of the sentences are parsed using the most restrictive setting ($\beta = 0.1$). This suggests that, in order to increase the accuracy of the parser without losing efficiency, the accuracy of the supertagger at the $\beta = 0.1$ level needs to be improved, without increasing the number of categories assigned on average.

9.3.4   Estimating the log-linear parsing models

In Clark and Curran (2004b) a discriminative method is described for estimating a log-linear parsing model. The estimation method maximises an objective function consisting of a likelihood function and a Gaussian prior to avoid overfitting. The optimization is performed using L-BFGS (Noccdal and Wright, 1999), an iterative algorithm from the numerical optimization literature. The algorithm requires the gradient of the objective function, and the value of the objective function, at each iteration. Calculation of these values requires all derivations for each sentence in the training data. In Clark and Curran (2004b) efficient methods are described for performing the calculations using packed charts. However, a very large amount of memory is still needed to store the packed charts; in Clark and Curran (2004a) memory usage of up to 31 GB is reported. To deal with the large memory requirements, a parallel implementation of the estimation algorithm is used that runs on a Beowulf cluster.

The supertagger can be used to reduce the memory requirements by restricting the number of derivations for each sentence in the training data. While training the parser, the supertagger can be thought of as supplying a number of plausible but incorrect categories for each word; these, together with the correct categories (which are obtained from CCGbank), determine the parts of the parse space that are used in the estimation process. We would like to keep the packed charts as small as possible but not lose accuracy in the resulting parser.

Clark and Curran (2004a) shows that, in combination with the two types of normal-form constraints described earlier, the use of the supertagger can significantly reduce the memory requirements for training. The normal-form constraints reduce the memory usage from 31 GB to 16 GB, and use of a more restrictive setting on the supertagger allows a model to be estimated using only 4 GB (but with a slight loss of accuracy: 0.6 F-score over labelled dependencies; see Clark and Curran, 2004a).

Note that, even with a memory usage of 31 GB, the number of categories assigned to each word by the supertagger is still only around 3 on average. Thus it is only through use of the supertagger that we are able to estimate a log-linear parsing model at all, since without it the memory requirements would be far too great, even for the entire 64-node Beowulf cluster.

9.4   Related Work

The only other work we are aware of to investigate the impact of supertagging on parsing efficiency is the work of Sarkar et al. (2000), and Chen et al. (2002), for LTAG. Sarkar et al. did find that LTAG supertagging increased parsing speed, but at a significant cost in coverage: only 1,324 sentences out of a test set of 2,250 received a parse. A similar result is presented in Chen et al. (2002).

Nasr and Rambow (2004) investigate the parsing accuracy that could be achieved for LTAG *given a perfect supertagger*. They find that, in combination with a statistical parsing model, the perfect supertagger leads to over 97% accuracy on dependency recovery. A similar result is presented in Clark and Curran (2004b) in the context of CCG parsing.

For the LTAG supertagging task itself, the original work of Bangalore and Joshi (1999) reports per-word accuracies of around 92% on Penn Treebank data, using a manually constructed LTAG grammar containing 300 supertags. However, for automatically extracted LTAG grammars, the reported accuracies are much lower: Chen et al. (2002) report around 83% for a single tagger, and around 94% for a multitagger that assigns 8 supertags to each word.

9.5   Conclusions and Future Work

This chapter has described a CCG supertagger that uses an automatically extracted grammar and is accurate enough to serve as a front end to a parser. We have shown that, by tightly integrating the supertagger with the parser using a novel integration mechanism, fast CCG parse times can be achieved for WSJ text. A further advantage of the supertagger is that it can be used to reduce the size of the derivation space for training, allowing the discriminative estimation of a log-linear CCG parsing model.

The results suggest that further improvements — in both parsing accuracy and speed — can be obtained by improving the supertagger, which should be possible given the simple feature sets currently being used.

Another potential advantage of the supertagger lies in the context of porting the parser to a new domain. In Clark et al. (2004) we show how the supertagger can be ported to the question domain, in the context of a Question Answering system, by creating new training data at the lexical category level only. The creation of such data can be done relatively quickly, allowing rapid porting of the supertagger to the new domain. The combination of the new supertagger and the original parsing model leads to accurate question parsing. Clark and Curran (2006) takes this a step farther by showing how a dependency parsing model for CCG can be estimated using lexical category sequences alone.

9.6   Acknowledgments

This work was carried out while the authors were at the University of Edinburgh's School of Informatics, as part of Mark Steedman's wide-coverage CCG parsing project. Thanks to Mark for his advice and guidance during that project, and thanks also to Julia Hockenmaier for the use of CCGbank. This chapter has benefitted from a number of useful comments from an anonymous reviewer.

Notes

1. In the CCGbank grammar, a small number of those cases will be distinguished by a different feature on the S node.

2. In the implementation used here, the sum is limited to those sequences allowed by the tag dictionary. For efficiency purposes, a pruning strategy is also used to discard low probability subsequences.

References

Bangalore, S. and Joshi, A. K. (1999). Supertagging: An approach to almost parsing. *Computational Linguistics*, 25(2):237–265.

Chen, J., Bangalore, S., Collins, M., and Rambow, O. (2002). Reranking an N-gram supertagger. In *Proceedings of the TAG+ Workshop*, Venice, Italy, pages 259–268.

Chen, J. and Vijay-Shanker, K. (2000). Automated extraction of TAGS from the Penn Treebank. In *Proceedings of IWPT 2000*, Trento, Italy.

Clark, S. (2002). A supertagger for Combinatory Categorial Grammar. In *Proceedings of the TAG+ Workshop*, Venice, Italy, pages 19–24.

Clark, S. and Curran, J. R. (2003). Log-linear models for wide-coverage CCG parsing. In *Proceedings of the EMNLP Conference*, Sapporo, Japan, pages 97–104.

Clark, S. and Curran, J. R. (2004a). The importance of supertagging for wide-coverage CCG parsing. In *Proceedings of COLING-04*, Geneva, Switzerland, pages 282–288.

Clark, S. and Curran, J. R. (2004b). Parsing the WSJ using CCG and log-linear models. In *Proceedings of the 42nd Meeting of the ACL*, Barcelona, Spain, pages 104–111.

Clark, S. and Curran, J. R. (2006). Partial training for a lexicalized-grammar parser. In *Proceedings of the Human Language Technology Conference and North American Chapter of the Association for Computational Linguistics (HLT-NAACL-06)*, New York.

Clark, S., Hockenmaier, J., and Steedman, M. J. (2002). Building deep dependency structures with a wide-coverage CCG parser. In *Proceedings of the 40th Meeting of the ACL*, Philadelphia, PA, pages 327–334.

Clark, S., Steedman, M. J., and Curran, J. R. (2004). Object-extraction and question-parsing using CCG. In *Proceedings of the EMNLP Conference*, Barcelona, Spain, pages 111–118.

Curran, J. R. and Clark, S. (2003). Investigating GIS and smoothing for maximum entropy taggers. In *Proceedings of the 10th Meeting of the EACL*, Budapest, Hungary, pages 91–98.

Curran, J. R., Clark, S., and Vadas, D. (2006). Multi-tagging for lexicalized-grammar parsing. In *Proceedings of the Joint Conference of the International Committee on Computational Linguistics and the Association for Computational Linguistics (ACL-COLING-06)*, Sydney, Australia.

Eisner, J. M. (1996). Efficient normal-form parsing for Combinatory Categorial Grammar. In *Proceedings of the 34th Meeting of the ACL*, Santa Cruz, CA, pages 79–86.

Hockenmaier, J. (2003a). *Data and Models for Statistical Parsing with Combinatory Categorial Grammar*. PhD thesis, University of Edinburgh.

Hockenmaier, J. (2003b). Parsing with generative models of predicate-argument structure. In *Proceedings of the 41st Meeting of the ACL*, Sapporo, Japan, pages 359–366.

Hockenmaier, J. and Steedman, M. J. (2002a). Acquiring compact lexicalized grammars from a cleaner treebank. In *Proceedings of the Third LREC Conference*, Las Palmas, Spain, pages 1974–1981.

Hockenmaier, J. and Steedman, M. J. (2002b). Generative models for statistical parsing with Combinatory Categorial Grammar. In *Proceedings of the 40th Meeting of the ACL*, Philadelphia, pages 335–342.

Malouf, R. (2002). A comparison of algorithms for maximum entropy parameter estimation. In *Proceedings of the Sixth Workshop on Natural Language Learning*, Taipei, Taiwan, pages 49–55.

Nasr, A. and Rambow, O. (2004). Supertagging and full parsing. In *Proceedings of the TAG+7 Workshop*, Vancouver, Canada.

Nocedal, J. and Wright, S. J. (1999). *Numerical Optimization*. Springer, New York.

Ratnaparkhi, A. (1996). A maximum entropy part-of-speech tagger. In *Proceedings of the EMNLP Conference*, Philadelphia, pages 133–142.

Sarkar, A. and Joshi, A. K. (2003). Tree-adjoining grammars and its application to statistical parsing. In Bod, R., Scha, R., and Sima'an, K., eds., *Data-oriented parsing*. CSLI.

Sarkar, A., Xia, F., and Joshi, A. K. (2000). Some experiments on indicators of parsing complexity for lexicalized grammars. In *Proceedings of the COLING Workshop on Efficiency in Large-Scale Parsing Systems*, Luxembourg, pages 37–42.

Steedman, M. J. (2000). *The Syntactic Process*. The MIT Press, Cambridge, MA.

Constraint Dependency Grammars: SuperARVs, Language Modeling, and Parsing

MARY P. HARPER AND WEN WANG

10.1 Introduction

Over the past ten years, we have been investigating the use of Constraint Dependency Grammar (CDG). This effort began shortly after Maruyama introduced the concept of a CDG (Maruyama, 1990b,c). In Maruyama's original vision, grammar constraints were used to limit dependencies in the space of potential parses of a sentence to those that are valid. This vision of CDG was adapted by the speech group at Purdue University in order to address speech processing applications and by Menzel and his students at the University of Hamburg (Heinecke et al., 1998; Menzel, 1994, 1995, 1996; Schröder et al., 2000) for applications requiring grammar robustness, such as the diagnosis of grammar errors by second language learners. These two foci have had deep impacts on the way each of these labs has utilized CDG. This chapter focuses on our spoken language processing path.

Our goal was to build effective and efficient linguistically motivated language models (LMs) for large vocabulary continuous speech recognition (LVCSR) tasks. CDG was selected as the underlying grammar formalism for this language modeling work for several reasons. CDG is able to utilize a variety of knowledge sources in the constraints used in parsing, and these constraints can be ordered for efficiency, withheld, or even relaxed. Hence, CDG provides a flexible framework for combining multiple knowledge sources. A parse of a sentence in CDG is represented distributively as a set of values assigned to variables associated with each word in the sentence; hence, a CDG model can be highly lexicalized. Also, CDG can model languages with crossing dependencies and free word ordering; hence, the results of our efforts can be applied to languages with these phenomena.

This chapter first provides a brief overview of CDG. It then describes how a CDG can be extracted from a treebank of CDG annotated sentences. Next is a discussion of our statistical CDG parser in which we evaluate some of the factors contributing to its performance. Finally, two types of CDG-based language models are presented and evaluated.

10.2   Parsing with Constraint Dependency Grammar

Maruyama (1990b,c) defined a CDG as a four-tuple, $\langle \Sigma, R, L, C \rangle$, where $\Sigma = \{\sigma_1, \ldots, \sigma_c\}$ is a finite set of lexical categories (e.g., determiner), $R = \{r_1, \ldots, r_p\}$ is a finite set of uniquely named roles (e.g., governor, need1, need2), $L = \{l_1, \ldots, l_q\}$ is a finite set of labels (e.g., subject), and C is a constraint formula. The number of roles (per word) p in a CDG is the *degree* of the grammar. In CDG, a *sentence* $s = w_1 w_2 w_3 \ldots w_n$ has a length $n \geq 1$ and is an element of Σ^* (that is, the parser operates over lexical categories). Given a grammar of degree p, each $w_i \in \Sigma$ of a sentence s has p different roles, yielding $n * p$ roles for the entire sentence. Each *role* is a variable that is assigned a *role value*, which is a tuple consisting of a label $l \in L$ and a modifiee m (a position of a word in the sentence) and is depicted in parsing examples as *l-m*. The label l indicates a syntactic function for the word when its role is assigned that role value, and m specifies the position that the word is *modifying* when it takes on the function specified by l.

Given that $L(G)$ is the language generated by the CDG G, a sentence of length n, $s = w_1 w_2 w_3 \ldots w_n$, is in $L(G)$ if for every w_i there is at least one assignment of role values to each of the roles of w_i such that the constraints in C are satisfied. Hence, a parse is represented by an assignment of role values to all the roles in s that records the syntactic functions of the words and their dependents. Consider, for example, the parse for *clear the screen* depicted in figure 10.1. Each word has a single lexical category in Σ and a set of role value assignments that are used to represent the parse. Maruyama introduced two types of roles: governor and need roles. The governor role of a word is assigned a role value such that the word's modifiee is the position of that word's governor or head. For example, the role value assigned to the governor role (denoted G in examples) of *the* is det-**3**, where the label det indicates its grammatical function and the modifiee **3** is the position of its head, *screen*. The need roles (denoted N1, N2, and N3 in this example) are used to ensure that the grammatical requirements of a word are met. The use of need roles enables CDG to distinguish between complements and adjuncts. In the example shown in figure 10.1, the verb *clear* needs an object (and so the role value assigned to N2, S-**3**, has a modifiee that points to the object *screen*). Maruyama uses the label blank and a nil modifiee to indicate that a role value is not used for a particular role. Because the verb *clear* does not require a subject or another complement, the role values of its other need roles are set to blank-nil. In our CDG parser implementation, we have found that it is more parsimonious to indicate that a role value has no modifiee by using the word's position rather than nil (e.g., the N1 role value for *clear* in figure 10.1 would be blank-1 rather than blank-nil). This convention will be used henceforth in this chapter.

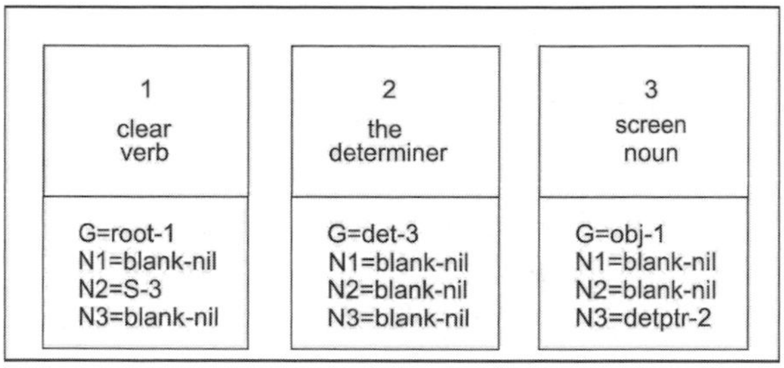

1	2	3
clear verb	the determiner	screen noun
G=root-1 N1=blank-nil N2=S-3 N3=blank-nil	G=det-3 N1=blank-nil N2=blank-nil N3=blank-nil	G=obj-1 N1=blank-nil N2=blank-nil N3=detptr-2

FIGURE 10.1 A CDG parse for *clear the screen* is represented by the assignment of role values to roles associated with each word in the sentence.

Maruyama framed the CDG parsing algorithm as a constraint satisfaction problem: the rules are the constraints and the solutions are the parses. During parsing, the grammaticality of a sentence is determined by applying C to all possible role value assignments, applying node and arc consistency so that assignments and assignment pairs are consistent with C, and then extracting a consistent parse assignment. Murayama defined C as a first-order predicate calculus formula over all roles; a valid assignment of role values to roles must be consistent with C. Each subformula P_i in C is a predicate involving $=$, $<$, or $>$, or predicates joined by the logical connectives and, or, if, or not. A subformula is called a *unary constraint* if it contains only a single variable (by convention x_1) and a *binary constraint* if it contains two variables (by convention x_1 and x_2). A unary constraint restricts assignments of role values to roles. A binary constraint limits pairs of assignments. See figure 10.2 for a parsing example with $\Sigma = \{$det, noun, verb$\}$, $R = \{$governor$\}$, $L = \{$DET, SUBJ, ROOT$\}$. The figure shows the steps used by a traditional CDG parser using the unary and binary constraints of C depicted in the figure. After arc consistency, parses are extracted from the remaining role values (see Maruyama, 1990c for more detail). A sentence s is said to be generated by the grammar G if there exists an assignment $\mathbf{A}$ that maps a role value to each of the roles for s such that C is satisfied. There may be more than one assignment of role values to the roles of a sentence that satisfies C, in which case there is ambiguity. A CDG has an *arity* parameter a, which indicates the maximum number of variables in the subformulas of C (e.g., the grammar in figure 10.2 has an arity of two).

Because Maruyama represents the problem of parsing a sentence in CDG as a constraint satisfaction problem (CSP), his parsing algorithm operates on sentences for which each word is assigned a single lexical class. Harper and Helzerman (1995a) expanded the scope of CDG to enable the analysis of sentences containing lexically ambiguous words, to support the inclusion of lexical features (e.g., subcategorization, number, case), and to operate on word graphs containing multiple alternative sentence hypotheses. To support this, they extended the constraint satisfaction problem; a MUSE CSP (*MU*ltiply *SE*gmented *C*onstraint *S*atisfaction *P*roblem) (Helzerman and Harper, 1996) is able to support problems that arise naturally in applications for which it can be quite difficult to segment

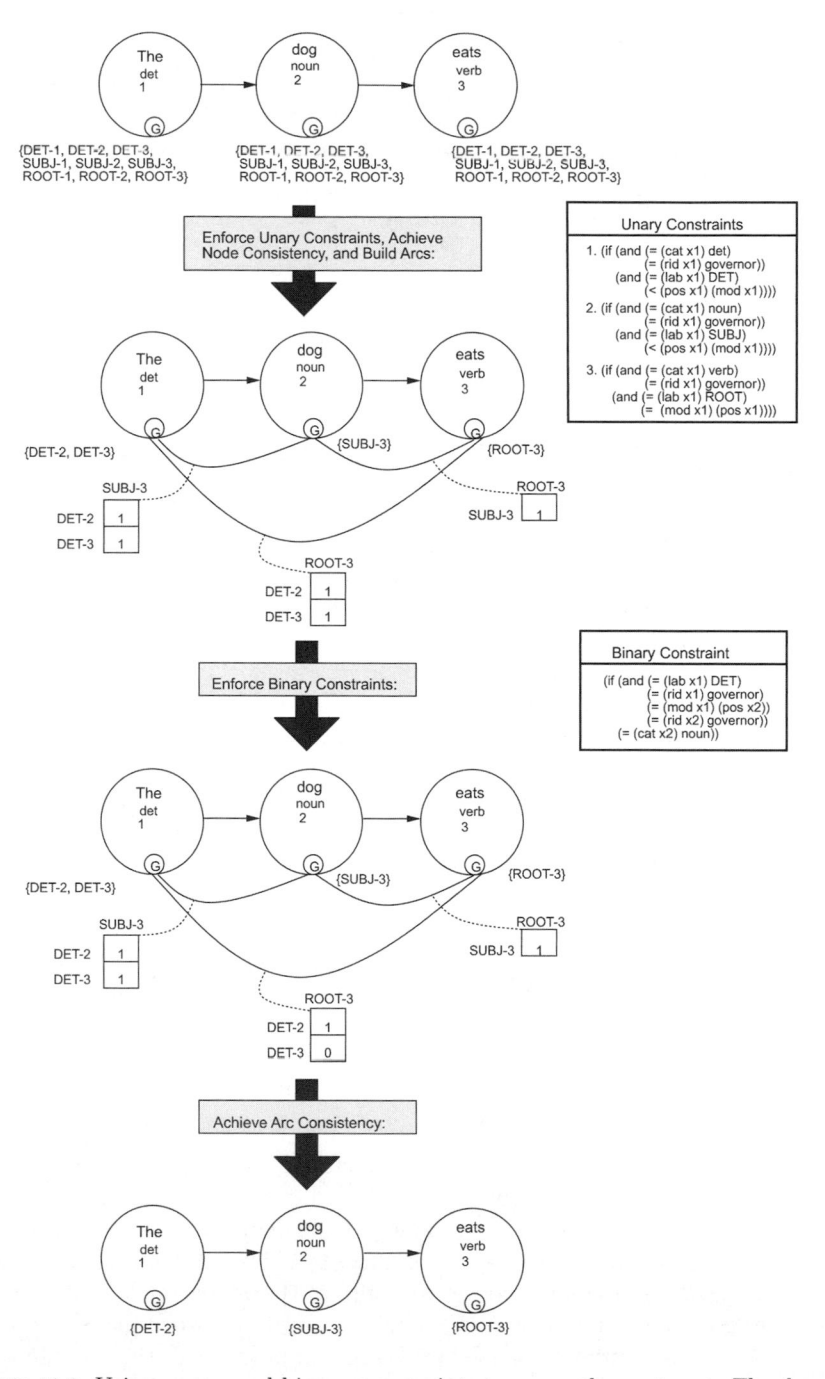

FIGURE 10.2 Using unary and binary constraints to parse the sentence: *The dog eats.*

the data in only one way (e.g., computer vision, speech processing, and handwriting recognition). To parse efficiently, algorithms for MUSE arc and path consistency were developed (Helzerman and Harper, 1996) and refined (Harper et al., 1999b). Methods for staging in feature constraints were also developed to control parse forest size and reduce parsing time (Harper et al., 1999a).

Given these modifications to support lexical ambiguity and features, a CDG is defined as a five tuple, $\langle \Sigma, R, L, C, T \rangle$, where Σ, R, L, and C are defined as previously, and T is a table that specifies which roles are used for each lexical category (most lexical classes need only one or two (Harper et al., 1999a), e.g., determiners use only the governor role, but others use additional roles, e.g., verbs), the set of labels that are supported for each role and lexical category, the domain of feature values for each feature type (if there are k feature types, the domains are denoted as $F_1, F_2, \ldots, F_k$), the feature types that are defined for each category in Σ, and the subset of feature values allowed by each category and feature type combination. A dictionary of lexical entries for words is also used for parsing. A lexical entry is made up of one lexical category $\sigma \in \Sigma$ and a single feature value for each feature supported by σ. Each word has one or more associated lexical entries. An example parse, given these modifications, appears in figure 10.3 for a sentence from the DARPA Naval Resource Management (RM) corpus (Price et al., 1988). This corpus has a vocabulary of around 1,000 different words drawn from queries in the form of *wh*-questions and yes/no-questions involving naval resources or commands for controlling an interactive database and graphics display. We constructed a conventional CDG for RM by hand with around 1,500 unary and binary constraints (that is, its arity is 2) that were designed to parse the sentences in this corpus. This CDG covers a wide variety of grammar constructs (including conjunctions and wh-movement) and has a fairly rich semantics. It uses 16 lexical categories, 4 roles (so its degree is 4), 24 labels, and 13 lexical feature types (agr, behavior [e.g., mass], case, conjtype, gap, inverted, mood, semtype, subcat, takesdet, type [e.g., interrogative, relative], voice, and vtype [e.g., progressive]). The parse shown at the top of figure 10.3 is an assignment of role values to roles that is consistent with the unary and binary constraints of this grammar.

In order to derive C directly from CDG annotated sentences, we then developed a method to extract grammar relations using information derived directly from annotated sentences (Harper et al., 2000). Using relative position information, unary constraints can be represented as a finite set of *abstract role values* (ARVs). Formally, an ARV for a particular grammar $G = \langle \Sigma, R, L, C, T \rangle$ is an element of the set: $\mathcal{A}_1 = \Sigma \times R \times L \times F_1 \times \ldots \times F_k \times \text{UC}$, where k is the number of feature types defined in T, F_i represents the set of feature values for that type, and UC encodes the three possible positional relations between the position (denoted $\text{P}x_1$) and modifiee (denoted $\text{M}x_1$) of a role value assigned to the role of a word ($\text{M}x_1$ and $\text{P}x_1$ can be related by $<$, $>$, or $=$). The box under the parse in figure 10.3 shows an example of an ARV for the role value assigned to the governor role of the word *the* obtained from the parsed sentence. Note that an ARV can be extended to include information about the lexical category and features of the modifiee, that is, $\mathcal{A}'_1 = \Sigma \times R \times L \times F_1 \times$

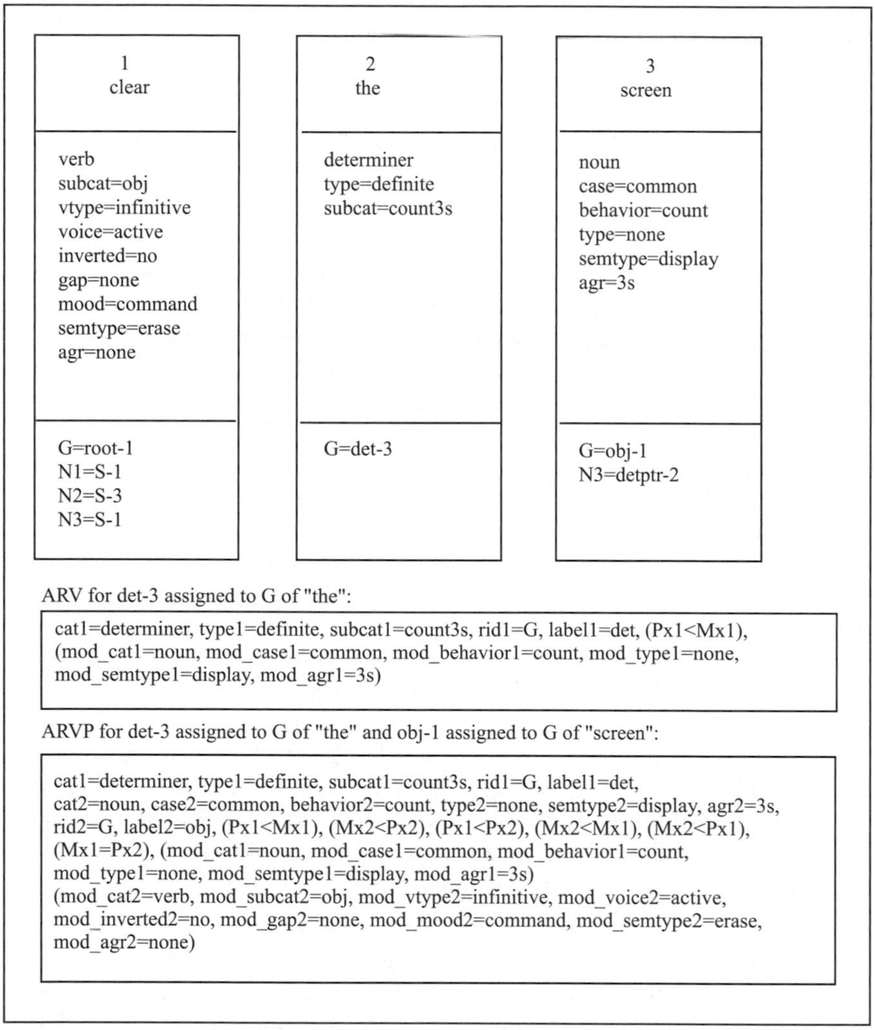

```
┌──────────────────────────────────────────────────────────────────────┐
│  ┌──────────────────┐  ┌──────────────────┐  ┌──────────────────┐     │
│  │        1         │  │        2         │  │        3         │     │
│  │      clear       │  │       the        │  │     screen       │     │
│  ├──────────────────┤  ├──────────────────┤  ├──────────────────┤     │
│  │ verb             │  │ determiner       │  │ noun             │     │
│  │ subcat=obj       │  │ type=definite    │  │ case=common      │     │
│  │ vtype=infinitive │  │ subcat=count3s   │  │ behavior=count   │     │
│  │ voice=active     │  │                  │  │ type=none        │     │
│  │ inverted=no      │  │                  │  │ semtype=display  │     │
│  │ gap=none         │  │                  │  │ agr=3s           │     │
│  │ mood=command     │  │                  │  │                  │     │
│  │ semtype=erase    │  │                  │  │                  │     │
│  │ agr=none         │  │                  │  │                  │     │
│  ├──────────────────┤  ├──────────────────┤  ├──────────────────┤     │
│  │ G=root-1         │  │ G=det-3          │  │ G=obj-1          │     │
│  │ N1=S-1           │  │                  │  │ N3=detptr-2      │     │
│  │ N2=S-3           │  │                  │  │                  │     │
│  │ N3=S-1           │  │                  │  │                  │     │
│  └──────────────────┘  └──────────────────┘  └──────────────────┘     │
```

ARV for det-3 assigned to G of "the":

> cat1=determiner, type1=definite, subcat1=count3s, rid1=G, label1=det, (Px1<Mx1),
> (mod_cat1=noun, mod_case1=common, mod_behavior1=count, mod_type1=none,
> mod_semtype1=display, mod_agr1=3s)

ARVP for det-3 assigned to G of "the" and obj-1 assigned to G of "screen":

> cat1=determiner, type1=definite, subcat1=count3s, rid1=G, label1=det,
> cat2=noun, case2=common, behavior2=count, type2=none, semtype2=display, agr2=3s,
> rid2=G, label2=obj, (Px1<Mx1), (Mx2<Px2), (Px1<Px2), (Mx2<Mx1),
> (Mx1=Px2), (mod_cat1=noun, mod_case1=common, mod_behavior1=count,
> mod_type1=none, mod_semtype1=display, mod_agr1=3s)
> (mod_cat2=verb, mod_subcat2=obj, mod_vtype2=infinitive, mod_voice2=active,
> mod_inverted2=no, mod_gap2=none, mod_mood2=command, mod_semtype2=erase,
> mod_agr2=none)

FIGURE 10.3 A CDG parse for *clear the screen*, shown in the top portion of this figure, is represented by the assignment of role values to roles associated with a word that has a specific lexical category and one feature value per feature. ARVs and ARVPs (see an example of each in the bottom two boxes) represent grammatical relations that can be extracted from a sentence's parse.

$\ldots \times F_k \times \mathrm{UC} \times (\Sigma \times F_1 \times \ldots \times F_k)$. This added information is equivalent to modifiee constraints investigated in Harper et al. (1999a); these constraints when included in unary constraints (and equivalently ARVs) do not change grammar coverage and help to improve parse times by eliminating ungrammatical role values during the less costly unary constraint enforcement stage of parsing. The ARV in figure 10.3 contains modifiee constraints that appear surrounded by parentheses.

Similarly, binary constraints are represented as a finite set of abstract role value pairs (ARVPs), which are members of the domain $\mathcal{A}_2 = \Sigma \times R \times L \times F_1 \times \ldots \times F_k \times \Sigma \times R \times L \times F_1 \times \ldots \times F_k \times \mathrm{BC}$, where BC encodes for a pair of role values the positional relations among their positions ($\mathrm{P}x_1$ and $\mathrm{P}x_2$) and modifiees ($\mathrm{M}x_1$ and $\mathrm{M}x_2$) (there are six ways to pair the position and modifiee of two role values, each of which can be related in three different ways; Harper et al., 2000; White, 2000). The box under the example ARV in figure 10.3 shows an example of an ARVP obtained from the parsed sentence. Modifiee constraints can also be added to the ARVPs, that is, $\mathcal{A}_2' = \Sigma \times R \times L \times F_1 \times \ldots \times F_k \times \Sigma \times R \times L \times F_1 \times \ldots \times F_k \times \mathrm{BC} \times (\Sigma \times F_1 \times \ldots \times F_k) \times (\Sigma \times F_1 \times \ldots \times F_k)$. However, since the ARVP space is larger than the ARV space, using this information could generate a very large, overly specific grammar. The ARVP in figure 10.3 contains two sets of modifiee constraints, each surrounded by parentheses.

An enumeration of the positive ARV/ARVPs can be used to represent the CDG constraints, C, thus simplifying the process of writing constraints. A role value would be supported by the ARVs only if it appears in the set of ARVs for the grammar. Similarly, a role value pair would be supported by the ARVPs only if it appears in the set of ARVPs. A fast table lookup method was developed (Harper et al., 2000; White, 2000) to determine whether a role value (or role value pair) is allowed (rather than propagating thousands of constraints) to speed up parsing.

Given Maruyama's initial research and our extensions, CDG offers a flexible and powerful parsing framework. First, the set of languages accepted by a CDG is a superset of the set of languages that can be accepted by context-free grammars (CFGs). Maruyama (1990a,b) proved that any arbitrary CFG converted to Griebach Normal form can be converted into a CDG with a degree of two and an arity of two that accepts the same language as the CFG. In addition, CDG can recognize languages that CFGs cannot, for example, $a^n b^n c^n$ (where a, b, and c are terminal symbols) or ww (where w is some string of terminal symbols). Note that grammars recognizing these languages utilize crossing dependencies, not supported by a CFG, to represent the positional correspondences. Harbusch (1997) has shown also that every language recognized by a tree-adjoining grammar (TAG) can also be generated by a CDG, but not vice versa (e.g., $L_6 = a^n b^n c^n d^n e^n f^n$). Like other dependency grammars (Holan et al., 1998; Järvinen and Tapanainen, 1998; Polguère and Kahane, 1998; Tesnière, 1959), free-order languages can be handled without enumerating all permutations (Harper and Helzerman, 1995a). In addition, the CDG parser uses sets of constraints that operate on role values assigned to roles to determine whether or not a string of terminals is in the grammar. These constraints can make use of syntactic, prosodic, semantic, and context-dependent knowledge

(Harper and Helzerman, 1995a,b; Menzel, 1995, 1996). Constraints can be ordered for efficiency, withheld, or even relaxed. The presence of ambiguity can trigger the use of stricter constraints to further refine the parse for a sentence (Harper and Helzerman, 1995b). This flexibility can be utilized to create a smart language processing system: one that decides when and how to use its constraints based on the state of the parse. Furthermore, a CDG parser can be parallelized to speed up parsing (Helzerman and Harper, 1992). Finally, grammar constraints can be derived by reading them from a corpus of CDG parses (Harper et al., 2000), as was described in this section.

10.3   Grammar Induction Experiments

Before developing a statistical parsing model for CDG, we carried out a series of grammar induction experiments. We did this work prior to building statistical models in order to evaluate the learnability of various types of CDG constraints and their importance for reducing parse ambiguity. For this effort, we developed a CDG treebank for the 2,844 sentences in the RM corpus. This corpus was chosen for several reasons: it provided a good source of both training and testing materials; we already developed a CDG by hand for the domain; the sentences have syntactic variety and a definable semantics; the scope of the problem was limited enough to enable systematic investigation of a wider variety of grammar development techniques than would be possible with larger corpora; it is a domain-specific task that enabled investigation of semantics; and the underlying grammar that we were trying to learn was well defined, which is important for evaluating the learnability of CDG from corpora.

Although there had been some previous work carried out on corpus-based learning of other grammar formalisms, in particular on CFGs, these prior results provided only limited guidance for our task of investigating whether a CDG could be learned from a corpus of sentences and what would be needed to successfully learn a high-quality grammar. CFGs appear to have a different learning bias than a CDG. For example, consider the CFG and CDG (only unary constraints are depicted) that would be obtained from the parsed sentence shown in figure 10.4. Once the CFG has learned an NP rule, it can be used in any context, making the grammar more general than the CDG on the basis of this single example. By contrast, the CDG is unable to parse the new sentence given the rules obtained from the dependency parse. The CDG must see an example of a pronoun being governed by a verb to its left in order to allow that relation. Hence, it appears that CDGs learned from a corpus of sentences would need a larger training corpus or require more careful training to achieve the desired level of generality.

In our investigations, we considered two important characteristics of learned grammars: generality and selectivity (Allen, 1995). Ideally, a learned grammar should be general enough that it covers unseen sentences in the target language but restrictive enough that it does not generate a large number of spurious parses. There is clearly a trade-off between these two attributes, and yet both attributes are

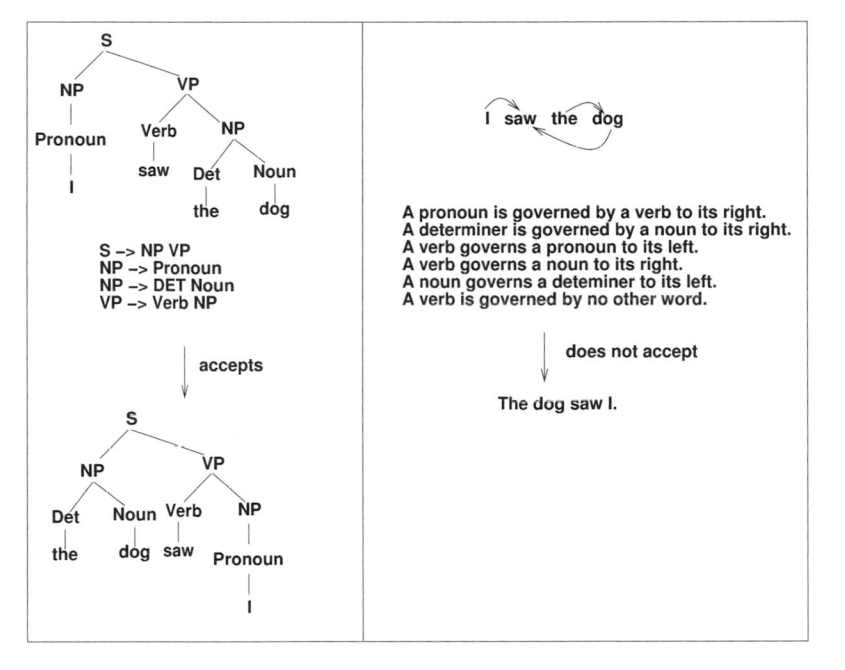

FIGURE 10.4 Comparing CFG and CDG generality on a simple example.

important for developing high-quality statistical CDG-based parsing and language models.

We have investigated a variety of methods for deriving C directly from sentences in the RM corpus annotated with CDG parse relations (Harper and Wang, 2001; Harper et al., 2000; Wang, 2003; White, 2000). Since the number of distinct ARVs tend to be more limited than the number of distinct ARVPs (see White, 2000), in all the grammars we have investigated, ARVs include all the information that can be extracted from the parse concerning a single role assignment: the role, the label of its assigned role value, the category and feature values of its word, a UC relation, and the modifiee's lexical category and feature values. To obtain ARVPs that are closest in spirit to the binary constraints of Maruyama, they would include lexical category, role, label, modifiee, and feature information for all pairs of role values from the annotated sentences. When ARVPs are extracted in this way, they are called Full grammars. Modifiee constraints can also be added to the ARVPs, but since the ARVP space is larger than the ARV space, using this information could generate a very large, overly specific grammar. We examined Full grammars with and without modifiee constraints (Full Mod versus Full) in order to explore the impact of this added information. In a series of experiments described in several documents (Harper and Wang, 2001; Harper et al., 2000; Wang, 2003; White, 2000), we investigated the generality and selectivity of CDGs extracted from CDG-annotated treebanks. Two important factors impacting grammar generality were investigated: increasing the size of the corpus (either directly or by enhancing what can be learned from annotations) and selectively relaxing grammar constraints.

To examine the first factor, we constructed a treebank for the RM sentences in two different ways. The first treebank involved a set of sentences annotated using the CDG annotation tool SENATOR (Harper et al., 2000; White, 2000) together with an active learning, selective sampling procedure similar to Thompson et al. (1999). The second treebank was composed of the same sentences updated to include subgrammar invocations (e.g., dates, years, times, numbers, and latitude and longitude coordinates) in place of some of the word strings (Harper and Wang, 2001; Harper et al., 2000; Wang, 2003) in an attempt to enhance what could be learned from a sentence in the corpus. We compared the Full and Full Mod grammars extracted from the sentence and subgrammar-expanded treebanks on grammar size, learning rate, the generality and parse ambiguity on an independent set of 4,946 sentences generated from the underlying grammar model used to create the original Resource Management corpus sentences (called RM domain sentences) and the reranking of sentence recognition hypotheses output by a speech recognition system trained on the RM speech corpus (Harper and Wang, 2001; Harper et al., 2000; White, 2000). The coverage and parse ambiguity for the Full and Full Mod grammars extracted from the standard sentence treebank can be compared in the baseline curves in figure 10.5(a) and figure 10.5(b), respectively; the modifiee constraints reduce parse coverage for the test set significantly, while reducing ambiguity only slightly. The coverage improves dramatically for the Full and Full Mod grammars when using the subgrammar-expanded treebank as can be observed in the baseline curve in figure 10.6(a); whereas, ambiguity only increases slightly (see figure 10.6(b)). In general, the Full Mod grammars are larger than the Full grammars regardless of the treebank type, and the subgrammar-expansion process increases the grammar size for the Full Mod grammar (178.65% increase) more dramatically than the Full grammar (67.51% increase) (Harper and Wang, 2001; Wang, 2003). The Full and Full Mod grammars trained using the subgrammar-expanded treebank achieve a greater coverage with a lower percentage of the corpus observed and generalize better to unseen test sentences than their corresponding sentence grammars with only a minor increase in ambiguity (Harper and Wang, 2001; Wang, 2003). They also perform much better when reranking the sentence hypotheses output by the speech recognizer (Harper and Wang, 2001; Wang, 2003). This suggests that annotation of subgrammar-expanded sentences is an effective method for intelligently increasing the size of a training set for developing high-quality domain-specific CDGs (e.g., radiology reports).

Even though higher quality grammars are obtained by taking the extra effort to identify and use subgrammars within sentences (Harper and Wang, 2001; Harper et al., 2000; Wang, 2003; White, 2000), this approach requires more effort than simply learning grammars from sentences; hence, we also investigated the impact of selective constraint relaxation to balance generality and selectivity (Harper and Wang, 2001; Harper et al., 2000; Wang, 2003; White, 2000). Relaxing CDG constraints is a double-edged sword: it can improve the generality of the grammars, but at the cost of allowing the incorrect acceptance of ill-formed sentences or spuriously increasing the amount of parse ambiguity. The features used in our grammars are important for enhancing the selectivity of a CDG; however, in many cases the features associated with a pair of role values may be irrelevant to the pair (e.g., for many transitive verbs, the number of the object noun should not prevent it from acting as its direct object) making the grammar less general than it should be. We have investigated the impact of fairly straightforward global relaxation methods: reducing grammar degree (that is, the full grammar versus one that uses only the governor role), relaxing specific features (e.g., semantics), or relaxing both (Wang, 2003). We also investigated the impact of relaxing constraints on role value pairs based on whether or not they are linked by a modifiee relation (that is, one role value has a modifiee pointing to the other or they share a modifiee) (Harper and Wang, 2001; Harper et al., 2000; Wang, 2003; White, 2000). The rationale for this constraint relaxation method is that role value pairs that are not linked should be much less important to the parse and so their violation should not cause the parse to fail. In one variation, we ignore feature information when there is no modifiee relation (denoted Feature), and in the other (denoted Direct), we allow any role value pair to exist when they are not directly linked by a modifiee link, that is, the only pairs that can be eliminated by the grammar constraints are those directly linked by a modifiee (the others would need to be deleted by the arc consistency algorithm). We also examined a knowledge-based (KB) feature relaxation approach (Wang, 2003); the fundamental idea is that for a particular role value pair, only some features are relevant to the relation. See Wang (2003) for more details.

Each of these constraint relaxation methods was evaluated by parsing the RM domain sentences after learning the grammar based on our original CDG treebank or based on the subgrammar-expanded treebank. First, we examine the impact of relaxing constraints on role value pairs based on whether or not they are linked by a modifiee relation. As can be seen in the baseline curve in figures 10.5(a) and 10.6(a), the Full grammars are less general than Feature grammars, which are slightly less general than the Direct variant. The fact that the Direct and Feature grammars had a far greater generality than the Full grammar, with only a limited increase in parse ambiguity (see the baseline curve in figures 10.5(b) and 10.6(b)), suggests that focusing on learning specific feature information for role values that share a modifiee link is an effective strategy, a strategy that we exploited in developing our statistical parsing model. The grammars with modifiee constraints tend to be less general than their counterparts without modifiee constraints while being slightly more selective (less parse ambiguity) when extracted from the standard treebank; however, modifiee constraints offer a good balance between coverage and ambiguity containment when using the subgrammar-expanded treebank.

Considering the global relaxation methods of reducing the grammar degree to governor only, eliminating semantic constraints, and the combination of both, we find in figures 10.5 and 10.6 that these methods improve coverage, but at a cost of increased parse ambiguity. Degree relaxation has less impact on coverage and ambiguity than relaxation of semantics, although their combination results in a slight increase in coverage and a large increase in parse ambiguity compared to relaxation of semantics alone. Based on these results, it appears that semantics is difficult to learn together with parse rules, and that the use of multiple roles helps to contain some of the ambiguity when the semantic information is ignored.

We next examine the effect of the more specific knowledge-based relaxation approach. As can be seen in figures 10.5 and 10.6, the global relaxation methods were less effective at containing parse ambiguity than the knowledge-based approach. The knowledge-based method relaxes the features for role value pairs to those that were identified as being important for selectivity (e.g., the agr feature is important for a subject and verb pair, but not an object and a preposition). Considering the grammar coverage and parse ambiguity plots in figures 10.5 and 10.6, we observe that KB Feature Relaxation improves generality of all grammar extraction variations while only increasing parse ambiguity slightly relative to the baseline grammar. Although the Direct and Feature grammars are much less general when they also encode modifiee information, if they are combined with KB feature relaxation, they achieve a good balance between generality and selectivity. Overall, KB Feature Relaxation produced grammars with a good trade-off between generality and selectivity for both sentence grammars and subgrammar-expanded sentence grammars.

We have investigated the impact of corpus enrichment and selective constraint relaxation on improving grammar quality by balancing generality and selectivity (Harper and Wang, 2001; Harper et al., 2000; Wang, 2003; White, 2000). This research was important for several reasons. First, CDG has a different inductive bias than CFG, suggesting that we will need to work more effectively with and/or identify additional training data when constructing the statistical models. It is critical to identify materials that cover the phenomena we wish to model. Second, although features have proven to be an effective way to reduce the number of roles needed to represent grammar relations in CDG (White, 2000), the inclusion of feature information in ARVPs dramatically increases the size of the ARVP space (Harper and Helzerman, 1995b), making it more challenging to obtain training data with sufficient coverage. Some features are more relevant for some relationships among words than for others; exploiting this insight should be very important especially when modeling modifiee constraints in our statistical models. Third, we have found that focusing on ARVPs that involve modification links provides a good balance between selectivity and generality. It is infeasible to integrate all the ARVPs of a Full model into a statistical CDG parsing model; fortunately, the grammar induction results suggest that an effective statistical CDG parsing model can be constructed by focusing on those parsing relations involving direct modifiee links.

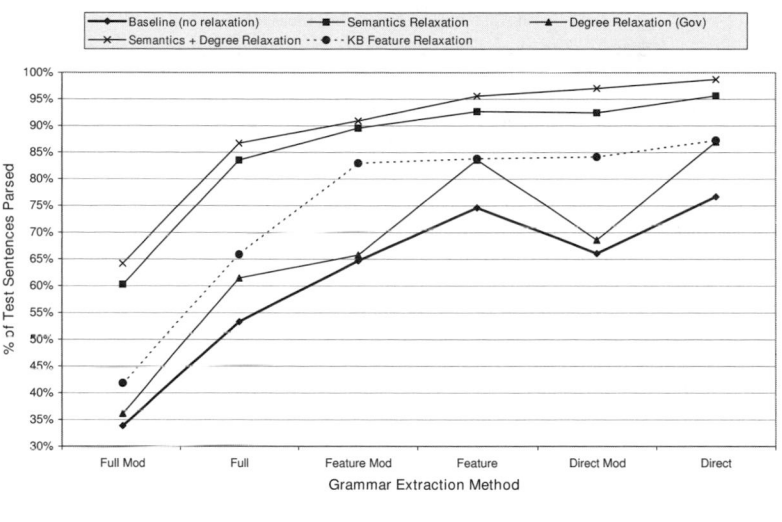

(a)

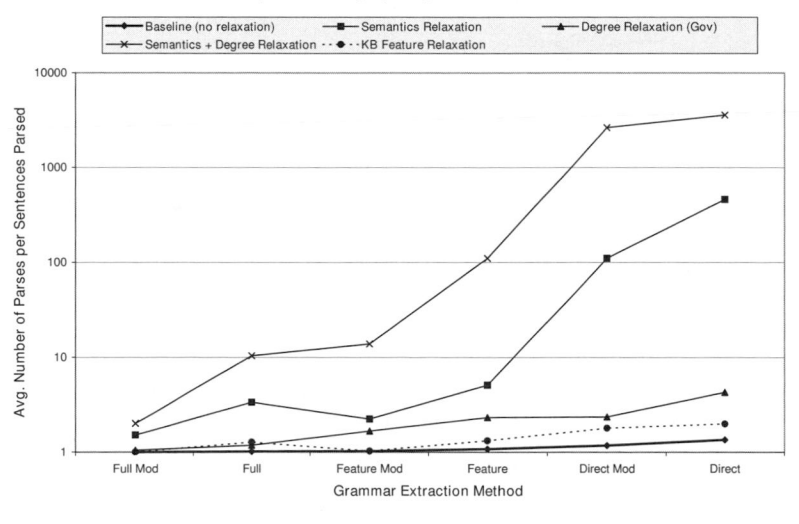

(b)

FIGURE 10.5 Percentage of RM domain sentences parsed for each grammar extraction method (shown in subplot a) and the corresponding parse ambiguity (shown in subplot b) given the indicated relaxation on sentence grammars.

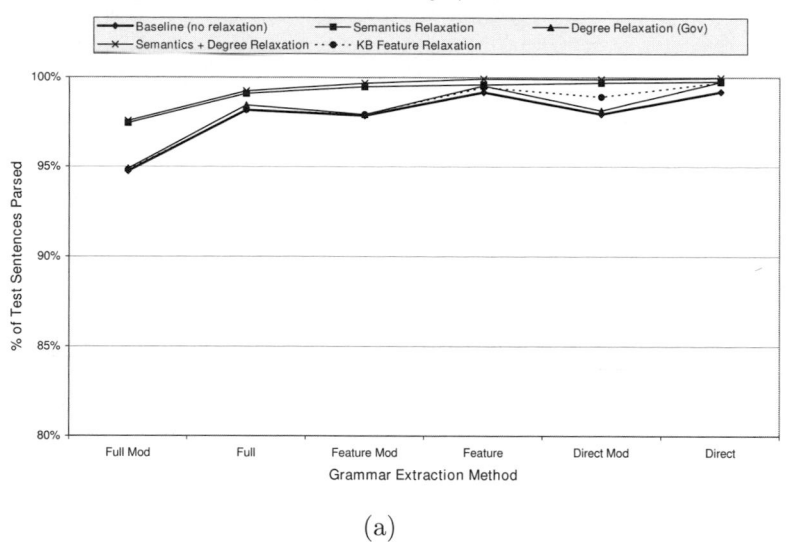

(a)

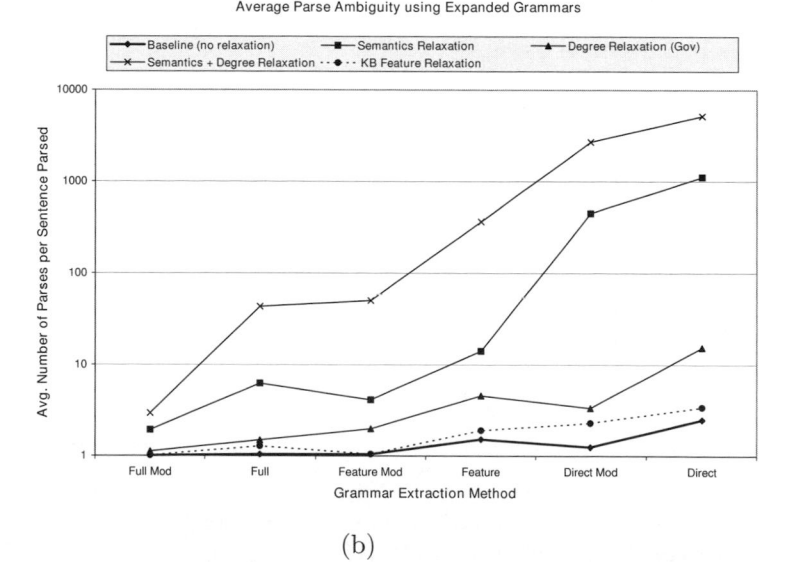

(b)

FIGURE 10.6 Percentage of RM domain sentences parsed for each grammar extraction method (shown in subplot a) and the corresponding parse ambiguity (shown in subplot b) given the indicated relaxation on subgrammar-expanded grammars.

10.4 Statistical CDG: SuperARVs and Modifiees

This section first describes the concept of the Super Abstract Role Value (SuperARV), the data structure central to our statistical modeling efforts. Next, we discuss our statistical CDG parser together with the factors contributing to its performance. Finally, two types of CDG-based language models are presented and evaluated.

10.4.1 The SuperARV

CDG parse information can be easily lexicalized at the word level by combining the information associated with a word in a CDG parse into a structure that we call a Super Abstract Role Value (SuperARV). A SuperARV combines the lexical category of a word, a rich set of lexical features, and the syntactic constraints represented by all its role value assignments and how their modifiees interrelate. It is super in the sense that it includes all of the information associated with the word (except its word string) in a parse. The concept of a SuperARV was inspired by the supertag concept from Lexicalized Tree-Adjoining Grammar (LTAG) (Joshi et al., 1975; Schabes, 1992; Schabes et al., 1988). A supertag encodes lexical dependencies as well as syntactic and semantic constraints in a representation of supertag-based classes that are more fine-grained than part-of-speech (POS) based classes (Joshi and Srinivas, 1994; Srinivas, 1996).

The concept of a SuperARV is central to our development of statistical CDG-based parsing and language models. A SuperARV is formally defined as a four-tuple for a word, $\langle C, F, (R, L, UC, MC)+, DC \rangle$, where C is the lexical category of the word, $F = \{Fname_1 = Fvalue_1, \ldots, Fname_f = Fvalue_f\}$ is a feature vector representing the lexical feature values for the word (where $Fname_i$ is the name of a feature and $Fvalue_i$ is its corresponding value), (R, L, UC, MC)+ is a list of one or more four-tuples, each representing an abstraction of a role value assignment, where R is a role variable (e.g., governor), L is a label (e.g., np), UC represents the relative positional relation for a word and its modifiee dependent, MC encodes modifiee constraints for the dependent (e.g., the lexical category and/or lexical features of the modifiee), and DC represents binary constraint (ARVP) information concerning the relative ordering of the positions of the corresponding word and all its modifiees. Since modifiee constraints can make the grammar quite specific, they need to be added with care; hence, in initial studies, we included only the lexical category of the modifiee.

The gray box in figure 10.7 shows an example of a SuperARV for the word *clear* derived from the CDG parse for the sentence *clear the screen*. Note that the SuperARV structure provides an explicit way to organize all the information concerning one consistent set of dependency links for the word *clear* that can be directly derived from its parse assignments. The SuperARV aggregates the four ARVs (unary constraints) that would be extracted for that word in the parse in a factored form; the lexical category and feature information is shared across these ARVs in the SuperARV representation. In addition, the representation aggregates information from six ARVPs; these ARVPs would be extracted over the pairs of role value assignments for the word *clear* and essentially add additional information on the relative positions of the word and each of its dependents. Based on this, a SuperARV can be thought of as providing a set of admissibility constraints on syntactic and lexical environments in which the word may be used. It encodes lexical information as well as syntactic constraints in a uniform fine-grained representation.

Like ARVs and ARVPs, SuperARVs can be extracted from a corpus of CDG annotated sentences. Once the SuperARVs are extracted, it is common for words to have more than one SuperARV to indicate different uses. The average number of SuperARVs for words of different lexical categories varies, with verbs having the greatest SuperARV ambiguity. This is mostly due to the wide variety of feature values and variations on complement types and positions found for verbs. It should be noted that the set of lexical features used in our statistical models include agr, behavior, case, gap, inverted, mood, type, voice, and vtype. We eliminated semtype based on the grammar induction experiments; learning semantic distinctions while learning syntactic constraints requires greater resources than are currently available for CDG. We also eliminated features that were redundant given information encoded by the need roles (e.g., subcat).

As in Joshi and Srinivas (1994), a sentence can be tagged with SuperARVs to provide an almost-parse for the sentence; to produce a parse all that remains is to specify the precise position of each modifiee. SuperARVs inherit an important characteristic from CDG that has proven useful for constructing probabilistic models: the addition of more knowledge sources tightens constraints but ignoring knowledge sources loosens them. Selective constraint relaxation can be implemented by eliminating one or more component from the SuperARV structure. This provides us with a very flexible framework not only for modeling natural language but also for supporting smoothing (that is, we can build backoff models for smoothing using SuperARVs that encode less specific information).

10.4.2   Statistical CDG parsing

Our Statistical CDG (SCDG) parser is a probabilistic generative model described in detail in Wang (2003) and Wang and Harper (2004). For all sentences s and all parses D, the parser assigns a probability $P(s, D) = P(D)$ for all D with yield s. For s, the parser returns the parse D that maximizes its probability, as follows:

$$argmax_d P(D|s) = argmax_D P(s, D)$$
$$= argmax_D P(D) \qquad (10.1)$$

The parser can be viewed as consisting of two components: SuperARV tagging and modifiee determination. These two steps can be either loosely or tightly integrated. To simplify discussion, we describe the loosely integrated algorithm, but we have implemented and evaluated both strategies. The basic parsing algorithm for the loosely integrated case is summarized in figure 10.8, with the algorithm's symbols

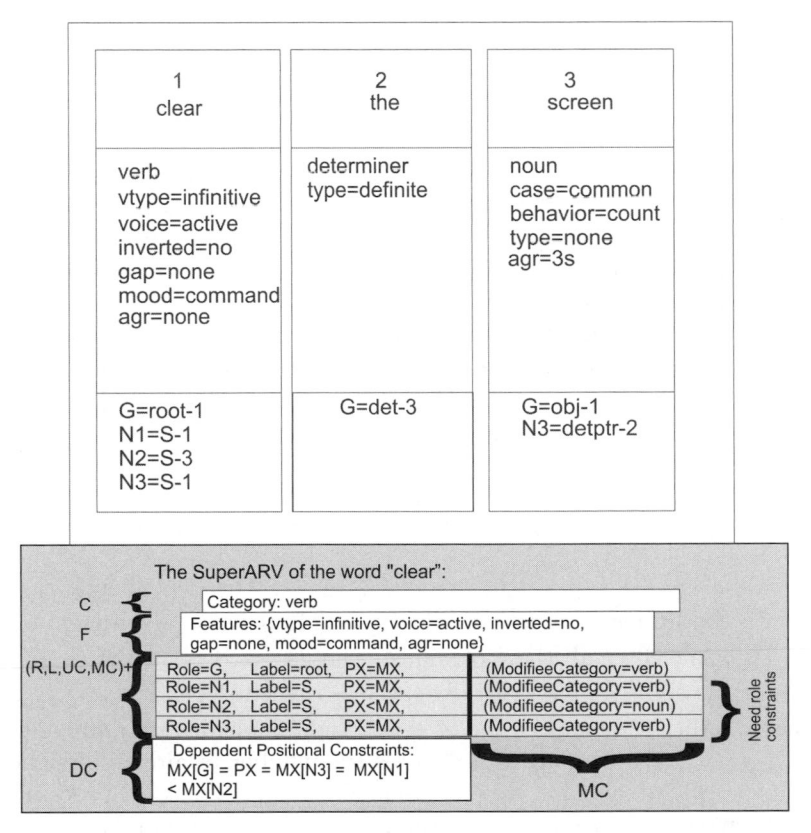

FIGURE 10.7 An example of a CDG parse and the SuperARV for the word "clear" from the sentence *clear the screen*. Note: *G* represents the governor role; the need roles, *N1*, *N2*, and *N3*, are used to ensure that the grammatical requirements of the word are met. PX and MX([R]) represent the position of a word and its modifiee (for role R), respectively.

defined in table 10.1. Later in this section, we will describe additions to this basic model.

In the first step of parsing (item 1 in figure 10.8), the top n-best SuperARV assignments are generated for an input sentence $w_1, \ldots, w_n$ using token-passing (Young et al., 1997) on a Hidden Markov Model with trigram probabilistic estimations for both transition and emission probabilities. Each SuperARV sequence for the sentence is represented as a sequence of tuples: $\langle w_1, s_1 \rangle, \ldots, \langle w_n, s_n \rangle$, where $\langle w_k, s_k \rangle$ represents the word w_k and its SuperARV assignment s_k. The parse probability for each sequence is initialized to the tag assignment probability. Each sequence is then stored on the stack ranked in non-increasing order by this probability.

During the second step of parsing (item 2 in figure 10.8), the modifiees are statistically specified in a left-to-right manner. Modifiee specification is conducted on each tag assignment in the stack, which maintains the record of all partial CDG parses determined for the sentence prefix. Note that the algorithm utilizes modifiee lexical category constraints to filter out candidates with mismatched lexical categories. When processing the word $w_k, k = 1, \ldots, n$, the algorithm first attempts to determine the left dependents of w_k from the closest to the farthest (see step a in item 2). The dependency assignment probability when choosing the $(c+1)^{\text{th}}$ left dependent (with its position denoted $dep(k, -(c+1))$) of w_k, s_k is defined as:

$$P(\text{link}(s_{dep(k,-(c+1))}, s_k, -(c+1)|syn, \mathcal{H})),$$

where $\mathcal{H} = \langle w, s \rangle_k, \langle w, s \rangle_{dep(k,-(c+1))}, \langle w, s \rangle_{dep(k,-1)}^{dep(k,-c)}$. The dependency assignment probability is conditioned on the word identity and SuperARV assignment to w_k and $w_{dep(k,-(c+1))}$, as well as all the c previously chosen left dependents $\langle w, s \rangle_{dep(k,-1)}^{dep(k,-c)}$ for w_k. After the algorithm statistically specifies the left dependents for w_k, it then determines whether w_k could be the $(d+1)^{\text{th}}$ right dependent of a previously seen word $w_p, p = 1, \ldots, k-1$ (where d denotes the number of already assigned right dependents of w_p), as shown in step b in item 2 of figure 10.8. After processing word w_k in each partial parse on the stack, the partial parses are reranked according to their updated probabilities (see the last step under item 2). Step 2 is iterated until all the words in the sentence are processed. The top parse in the stack is then selected as the parse for the sentence.

CDG differs from traditional dependency grammars in that CDG utilizes multiple roles to specify symmetric grammatical dependencies that are necessary for grammaticality. For example, the verb-object relationship involves two role value assignments in CDG: a governor dependency from the object to the verb and a need dependency based on subcategorization from the verb to the object. Hence, if a noun w_i is dependent on a verb w_j as an object, then the expectation of the verb w_j for an object should be simultaneously satisfied by w_i. In our model, we use a Boolean random variable *syn* to capture the synergistic relationship between certain role value pairs. This mechanism allows us to elevate, for example, the probability that

TABLE 10.1 Definitions of symbols used in the basic parsing algorithm.

Term	Denotes
$\mathcal{L}(s_k)$, $\mathcal{R}(s_k)$	all dependents of s_k to the left and right of w_k, respectively
$N(\mathcal{L}(s_k))$, $N(\mathcal{R}(s_k))$	the number of left and right dependents of s_k, respectively
$dep(k, -c)$, $dep(k, c)$	c^{th} left dependent and right dependent of s_k, respectively
$dep(k, -1)$, $dep(k, 1)$	the position of the closest left dependent and right dependent of s_k, respectively
$dep(k, -N(\mathcal{L}(s_k)))$ $dep(k, N(\mathcal{R}(s_k)))$	the position of the farthest left dependent and right dependent of s_k, respectively
$\text{Cat}(s_k)$	the lexical category of s_k
$\text{ModCat}(s_k, -c)$ $\text{ModCat}(s_k, c)$	the lexical category of s_k's c^{th} left and right dependent (encoded in the SuperARV structure), respectively
$\text{link}(s_i, s_j, k)$	the dependency relation between SuperARV s_i and s_j with w_i assigned as the kth dependent of s_j, e.g., $\text{link}(s_{dep(k,-(c+1))}, s_k, -(c+1))$ indicates that $w_{dep(k,-(c+1))}$ is the $(c+1)^{\text{th}}$ left dependent of s_k
$D(\mathcal{L}(s_k))$, $D(\mathcal{R}(s_k)))$	the number of left and right dependents of s_k already assigned, respectively
$\langle w, s \rangle_{dep(k,-1)}^{dep(k,-c)}$	words and SuperARVs of s_k's closest left dependent up to its cth left dependent
$\langle w, s \rangle_{dep(k,1)}^{dep(k,c)}$	words and SuperARVs of s_k's closest right dependent up to its cth right dependent
syn	a random variable denoting the synergistic relation between some dependents

BASIC PARSING ALGORITHM

1. Using SuperARV tagging on word sequence $w_1, \ldots, w_n$, obtain a set of n-best SuperARV sequences with each element consisting of n (word, SuperARV) tuples, denoted $\langle w_1, s_1 \rangle, \ldots, \langle w_n, s_n \rangle$, which we will call an assignment. Initialize the stack of parse prefixes with these assignments, ranked in nonincreasing order by their probability.

2. /* From left-to-right, process each $\langle word, tag \rangle$ of the assignment and generate parse prefixes. */

   for $k := 1$ to n do

       for each item on the stack

           /* Step a: */

           /* Decide left dependents of $\langle w_k, s_k \rangle$ from the nearest to the farthest. */

           for $c := 0$ to $N(\mathcal{L}(s_k)) - 1$ do

               /* Choose a position for the $(c+1)^{\text{th}left}$ dependent of $\langle w_k, s_k \rangle$ from the set possible positions $\mathcal{C} = \{1, \ldots, dep(k, -c) - 1\}$. The position choice is denoted $dep(k, -(c+1))$. */

               /* In the following equations, different left dependent assignments will generate different parse prefixes, each of which is stored in the stack. */

               for each $dep(k, -(c+1))$ from positions $\mathcal{C} = \{1, \ldots, dep(k, -c) - 1\}$

                   /* Check whether the lexical category of the choice matches the modifiee lexical category of the $(c+1)^{\text{th}}$left dependent of $\langle w_k, s_k \rangle$. */

                   if $\text{Cat}(s_{dep(k, -(c+1))}) == \text{ModCat}(s_k, -(c+1))$ then

                   $P(D) := P(D) \times P(\text{link}(s_{dep(k, -(c+1))}, s_k, -(c+1)|syn, \mathcal{H}))$

                   where $\mathcal{H} = \langle w, s \rangle_k, \langle w, s \rangle_{dep(k, -(c+1))}, \langle w, s \rangle_{dep(k, -1)}^{dep(k, -c)}$

           /* End of choosing left dependents of $\langle w_k, s_k \rangle$ for this parse prefix. */

           /* Step b: */

           /* For the word/tag pair $\langle w_k, s_k \rangle$, check whether it could be a right dependent of any previously seen word within a parse prefix of $\langle w_1, s_1 \rangle, \ldots, \langle w_{k-1}, s_{k-1} \rangle$. */

           for $p := 1, k - 1$ do

               /* If $\langle w_p, s_p \rangle$ still has right dependents left unspecified, then try out $\langle w_k, s_k \rangle$ as a right dependent. */

               if $D(\mathcal{R}(s_p)) \neq N(\mathcal{R}(s_p))$ then

               $d := D(\mathcal{R}(s_p))$

               /* If the lexical category of $\langle w_k, s_k \rangle$ matches the modifiee lexical category of the$(d+1)^{\text{th}}$ right dependent of $\langle w_p, s_p \rangle$, then s_k might be $\langle w_p, s_p \rangle$'s $(d+1)^{\text{th}}$right dependent. */

               if $\text{Cat}(s_k) == \text{ModCat}(s_p, d + 1)$ then

               $P(D) := P(D) \times P(\text{link}(s_k, s_p, d + 1)|syn, \mathcal{H})$,

               where $\mathcal{H} = \langle w, s \rangle_p, \langle w, s \rangle_k, \langle w, s \rangle_{dep(p, 1)}^{dep(p, d)}$

   Sort the parse prefixes in the stack according to $logPr(D)$ and apply pruning using the thresholds.

3. After processing $w_1, \ldots, w_n$, pick the parse with the highest $logPr(T)$ in the stack as the parse for that sentence.

FIGURE 10.8   The basic loosely coupled parsing algorithm.

the subject of a sentence w_i is governed by a tensed verb w_j when the need role value of w_j points to w_i as its subject. Note that this is a much simpler mechanism than the *trigger* approach used by Rosenfeld (2000) to model synergistic features. The values of *syn* for a dependency relation were determined heuristically based on the lexical category, role name, and label information of the two dependent words (Wang, 2003; Wang and Harper, 2004).

For the tightly coupled parser, the first step of SuperARV tagging is removed, and the SuperARV assignment for each word and the corresponding decisions on specifying its modifiees are integrated into a single step that updates the conditional probabilities for modifiee specification and adds each SuperARV possibility to the conditions for dependency assignment probability estimations. For both versions, the parsing algorithm is implemented as a simple best-first search using a stack to store partial parses.

To control time and memory complexity, we used two pruning thresholds: maximum stack depth (maximum number of partial parses allowed in the stack) and maximum difference between the log probabilities of the top and bottom partial parses in the stack. The latter is defined as a percentage, that is, the bottom partial parse cannot have its probability lower than $\sigma\%$ of that of the top partial parse (a negative value due to the use of log probabilities). These two pruning thresholds were tuned based on the trade-off between time and memory complexity and parsing accuracy on a heldout set, and they both had hard limits.

Note that the maximum likelihood estimation of the dependency assignment probabilities in the basic loosely coupled parsing algorithm presented in figure 10.8 is likely to suffer from data sparsity, and the estimates for the tightly coupled algorithm are likely to suffer even more so. Hence, we smooth the probabilities using Jelinek-Mercer smoothing (Jelinek, 1997). To simplify the presentation, we describe the smoothing procedure for the loosely coupled case, where the $+$ prefix represents items related to right dependents and the $-$ prefix, left dependents:

$$
P(\text{link}(s_{dep(k,\pm(c+1))}, s_k, \pm(c+1))|syn, \mathcal{H})
$$
$$
= \sum_{i=1}^{c} \eta_i \cdot P(\text{link}(s_{dep(k,\pm(c+1))}, s_k, \pm(c+1))|syn, \delta_i)
$$
$$
+ \lambda_1 \cdot P(\text{link}(s_{dep(k,\pm(c+1))}, s_k, \pm(c+1))|syn, \mathcal{H}_1)
$$
$$
+ \lambda_2 \cdot P(\text{link}(s_{dep(k,\pm(c+1))}, s_k, \pm(c+1))|syn, \mathcal{H}_2)
$$
$$
+ \lambda_3 \cdot P(\text{link}(s_{dep(k,\pm(c+1))}, s_k, \pm(c+1))|syn, \mathcal{H}_3)
$$
$$
+ \lambda_4 \cdot P(\text{link}(s_{dep(k,\pm(c+1))}, s_k, \pm(c+1))|syn, \mathcal{H}_4)
$$
$$
+ \lambda_5 \cdot P(\text{link}(s_{dep(k,\pm(c+1))}, s_k, \pm(c+1))|syn, \mathcal{H}_5)
$$
$$
+ \lambda_6 \cdot P(\text{link}(s_{dep(k,\pm(c+1))}, s_k, \pm(c+1))|syn, \mathcal{H}_6),
$$

where:

$$\mathcal{H} = \langle w, s \rangle_k, \langle w, s \rangle_{dep(k, \pm(c+1))}, \langle w, s \rangle_{dep(k, \pm 1)}^{dep(k, \pm c)}$$

$$\delta_i = \langle w, s \rangle_k, \langle w, s \rangle_{dep(k, \pm(c+1))}, \langle w, s \rangle_{\pm 1}^{\pm i}$$

$$\mathcal{H}_1 = \langle w, s \rangle_k, w_{dep(k, \pm(c+1))}, s_{dep(k, \pm 1)}^{dep(k, \pm c)}$$

$$\mathcal{H}_2 = \langle w, s \rangle_k, s_{dep(k, \pm(c+1))}, s_{dep(k, \pm 1)}^{dep(k, \pm c)}$$

$$\mathcal{H}_3 = s_k, \langle w, s \rangle_{dep(k, \pm(c+1))}, s_{dep(k, \pm 1)}^{dep(k, \pm c)}$$

$$\mathcal{H}_4 = s_k, s_{dep(k, \pm(c+1))}, s_{dep(k, \pm 1)}^{dep(k, \pm c)}$$

$$\mathcal{H}_5 = s_k, s_{dep(k, \pm(c+1))}, POS_{dep(k, \pm 1)}^{dep(k, \pm c)}$$

$$\mathcal{H}_6 = POS_k, POS_{dep(k, \pm(c+1))}, POS_{dep(k, \pm 1)}^{dep(k, \pm c)}.$$

Note that POS_k denotes the part of speech of word w_k. The η_i and λ values are determined using the EM algorithm described by Jelinek (1990) on a held-out data set.

Additions to the basic model

Next, we describe a set of additions to the basic model presented in section 10.4.2 that should help improve parsing accuracy.

- **Modeling crossing dependencies:** The basic parsing algorithm was implemented to preclude crossing dependencies; however, it is important to allow them in order to model certain *wh*-movement structures in our model. Hence, we investigated the impact of modeling crossing dependencies during parsing, relying on the dependency statistics of the SuperARVs to determine when they are allowed.

- **Distance between dependents:** Distance between two dependent words (e.g., the distance value 0 means the two words are adjacent) is an important factor in determining the modifiees of a word. Collins found that for the Wall Street Journal Penn Treebank (WSJ PTB) corpus, 74.2% of the dependent words of a particular word abut that word, 86.3% of the dependencies are within a trigram window, and 95.6% of the dependencies are within a 5-gram window (Collins, 1996). Since distance plays an important role in statistically determining the modifiees of a word, we evaluated an alternative model that includes distance by adding $\Delta_{dep(k, \pm(c+1)), k}$ to $\mathcal{H}$. To avoid data sparsity problems, distance was bucketed as: $[0]$, $[1]$, $[2, 4]$, $[5, 9]$, $[10, \infty)$, that is, a discrete random variable with five possible ranges was used to model distance.

- **Barriers between dependents:** Punctuation and verbs provide useful information for restricting dependencies. For example, words do not tend to modify words to the left of a verb they follow unless there is *wh*-movement or to modify words on the other side of a punctuation mark unless there is an apposition or a parenthetical comment. Hence, we added several boolean random variables to our model representing questions related to these barriers as conditions to the conditional dependency assignment probability estimations (as in Collins, 1996). This allows us to capture some of the binary constraints that were part of our hand-developed CDG.

1. Is there a verb between the dependencies?
2. Are there 0, 1, 2, or more commas or colons between the dependents?
3. Is there a comma immediately following the first of two dependents, or is there a comma immediately preceding the second of the two dependents?

- **Additional modifiee constraints:** In the basic model, the modifiee constraints of the SuperARV were limited to the lexical category of the dependent. In our previous work (Harper and Wang, 2001), we found that modifiee lexical features play an important role in strengthening selectivity of a CDG; however, for many dependencies, only a subset of the possible lexical features are relevant to the dependency relation. For example, a noun's number feature is often irrelevant in many of its grammatical roles (e.g., as a possessive noun) and yet it is a very important constraint when the noun acts as a subject of a sentence with a present-tensed verb. Since the knowledge-based feature relaxation approach discussed in section 10.3 provided a good trade-off between grammar generality and selectivity, we have utilized a knowledge-based method to incorporate selective relevant lexical features into modifiee constraints of a SuperARV structure (Wang, 2003).

Parsing evaluation

In order to train an SCDG parser, we had to either identify or create corpora annotated with CDG parse relations. Because of lack of availability of CDG annotated treebanks, we chose to convert an existing CFG annotated corpus, namely, the Wall Street Journal Penn Treebank (WSJ PTB) into CDG annotations. Dependency structures were generated by headword percolation together with a rule-based method to determine lexical features and need role values for words; details appear in Wang (2003). Note that the soundness of the CFG-to-CDG transformer was evaluated by examining a subset of the CDG parses generated from the transformer on the WSJ PTB development set to ensure that they were correct. The SCDG parser was evaluated using this converted treebank with the traditional data setup (that is, sections 02–21 for training, section 23 for testing, and section 24 for development). As in Charniak (2000), Collins (1999), and Ratnaparkhi (1999), it was evaluated on all sentences with length $\leq$ 40 words (2,245 sentences) and length $\leq$ 100 words (2,416 sentences).

Since our parser was trained using a CFG-to-CDG transformer (Wang, 2003), which maps a CFG parse tree to a unique CDG parse, we chose to evaluate our parser's accuracy using "gold standard" CDG parse relations. The alternative would be to map back to a CFG tree; however, this mapping would add noise to our evaluation. In addition, when there are crossing dependencies, then no tree can be generated for that set of dependencies. Consequently, we defined a dependency-based metric adapted from Eisner (1996), namely role value labeled precision (RLP) and role value labeled recall (RLR):

$$RLP = \frac{\text{correct modifiee assignments}}{\text{number of modifiees our parser found}}$$

$$RLR = \frac{\text{correct modifiee assignments}}{\text{number of modifiees in the gold test set parses}},$$

where a modifiee assignment for a word w_i in the test parse for a sentence is correct only when the three-tuple ⟨role id, role label, modifiee word position⟩ (that is, a role value) for w_i is the same as the three-tuple role value for the corresponding role id of w_i in the gold test parse.

In a first experiment (Wang, 2003; Wang and Harper, 2004), we evaluated the basic loosely coupled model that uses a trigram SuperARV tagger to generate 40-best SuperARV sequences prior to modifiee specification and examined the impact of the model improvements described previously on this loosely coupled model. Table 10.2 shows the results for each of the models, including SuperARV tagging accuracy (%) and parsing accuracy (%) based on RLP and RLR. Allowing crossing dependencies improves the overall parsing accuracy, but using distance information together with barrier heuristics produces an even greater improvement especially on the longer sentences. The accuracy is further improved by adding additional modifiee lexical feature constraints to the SuperARVs to enforce feature constraints on dependencies, highlighting the importance of selective enhancement of grammar specificity. Overall, using a distance model and modifiee lexical features provides the greatest improvement. Note that RLR is lower than RLP in these investigations; this is possibly due to errors in SuperARV tagging and the use of a tight stack pruning threshold.

In a second experiment (Wang, 2003; Wang and Harper, 2004), we evaluated the impact of increasing the context of the SuperARV tagger (3-gram to 4-gram) and increasing the length of the n-best list (40-best to 100-best) passed from the tagger to the modifiee specification step of our best loosely coupled model (that is, with all of the model enhancements). We also evaluated a model that tightly integrates SuperARV prediction with modifiee specification. As can be seen in Table 10.3, a stronger SuperARV tagger and a larger search space of SuperARV sequences produces improvements in parse accuracy; however, the best results were achieved by the tightly integrated model. Note that SuperARV tagging accuracy and parse accuracy improve in tandem, consistent with the observations of Collins (1999) and Eisner (1996).

Given this framework of tightly integrated, multiple knowledge sources, with special attention to modeling distance, barriers, and modifiee constraints, we have achieved a solid parsing accuracy on the WSJ PTB corpus. We have also compared

TABLE 10.2 Results on section 23 of the WSJ PTB for four loosely coupled model variations. The evaluation metrics, RLR and RLP, are our dependency-based role value labeled recall and precision.

Models	Configuration	$\leq$ 40 words (2,245 sentences)				
		Tagging Acc.	governor only		all roles	
			RLP	**RLR**	**RLP**	**RLR**
(1)	basic model	94.7	90.6	90.3	86.8	86.2
(2)	(1)+crossing dependencies	95.0	90.7	90.5	87.0	86.5
(3)	(2)+distance and barrier model	95.7	91.1	90.9	87.4	87.0
(4)	(3)+modifiee lexical features	96.2	91.5	91.2	88.0	87.4
Models	**Configuration**	$\leq$ 100 words (2,416 sentences)				
		Tagging Acc.	governor only		all roles	
			RLP	**RLR**	**RLP**	**RLR**
(1)	basic model	94.0	89.7	89.3	86.0	85.5
(2)	(1)+crossing dependencies	94.2	89.9	89.6	86.2	85.8
(3)	(2)+distance and barrier model	94.7	90.4	90.2	86.8	86.3
(4)	(3)+modifiee lexical features	95.4	90.9	90.5	87.5	86.8

TABLE 10.3 Results on Section 23 of the WSJ PTB comparing models that utilize different SuperARV taggers and n-best sizes with the tightly coupled implementation.

Models		≤ 40 words (2,245 sentences)				
		Tagging Acc.	governor only		all roles	
			RLP	RLR	RLP	RLR
Loose Basic	trigram, 40-best	94.7	90.6	90.3	86.8	86.2
Loose Plus	trigram, 40-best	96.2	91.5	91.2	88.0	87.4
	trigram, 100-best	96.7	91.9	91.5	88.3	87.7
	4-gram, 40-best	96.9	92.2	91.7	88.6	88.1
	4-gram, 100-best	97.2	92.4	92.3	89.1	88.6
Tight		97.4	93.2	92.9	89.8	89.2
Models		≤ 100 words (2,416 sentences)				
		Tagging Acc.	governor only		all roles	
			RLP	RLR	RLP	RLR
Loose Basic	trigram, 40-best	94.0	89.7	89.3	86.0	85.5
Loose Plus	trigram, 40-best	95.4	90.9	90.5	87.5	86.8
	trigram, 100-best	95.8	91.3	90.8	87.7	87.0
	4-gram, 40-best	96.0	91.7	91.2	88.0	87.4
	4-gram, 100-best	96.3	91.8	91.5	88.5	87.8
Tight		96.6	92.6	92.2	89.1	88.5

the SCDG parser to other statistical parsing algorithms (Wang, 2003; Wang and Harper, 2004) and found that it performed similarly to and in some cases better than those models using our dependency metric. We have also evaluated the parser on the Switchboard corpus (Wang, 2003) and obtained substantially lower recall and precision results. It should be noted that the Switchboard Treebank is quite small for training an SCDG parsing model, and the corpus contains many typos that could seriously degrade the quality of the training data produced by the CFG-to-CDG conversion process. In addition, the SCDG parser that was used did not directly model some of the more challenging phenomena that occur in spontaneous speech (e.g., speech repairs).

10.4.3 Language modeling

We have also developed and evaluated two types of CDG-based language models (LMs) that we will summarize here, an almost-parsing LM and a full parser-based LM. It should be noted that the design of these LMs gained significantly from the insight obtained from our initial CDG grammar induction experiments. The SuperARV almost-parsing LM is trained, like the SCDG parser, using information derived from a corpus of CDG parses, but unlike the parser, it does not construct a full parse, which should help make the model more robust and more efficient than a full parser model. The full CDG parser-based LM utilizes complete parse information obtained by adding the modifiee links to the SuperARVs assigned to each word in a sentence in order to capture important long-distance dependency constraints. Clearly there is a synergy between these two language models and our SCDG parser. Indeed, we have found that the insights that improve one usually positively impact the others.

The SuperARV LM

The SuperARV language model is implemented using a joint probabilistic model framework so that word form information is tightly integrated at the model level. Without loss of generality, given a word sequence w_1^N and their SuperARV tags t_1^N, a trigram version of the SuperARV language model is:

$$
\begin{aligned}
P(w_1^N t_1^N) &= \prod_{i=1}^{N} P(w_i t_i \mid w_1^{i-1} t_1^{i-1}) \\
&= \prod_{i=1}^{N} P(t_i \mid w_1^{i-1} t_1^{i-1}) \cdot P(w_i \mid w_1^{i-1} t_1^{i}) \\
&\approx \prod_{i=1}^{N} P(t_i \mid w_{i-2}^{i-1} t_{i-2}^{i-1}) \cdot P(w_i \mid w_{i-2}^{i-1} t_{i-2}^{i})
\end{aligned}
\tag{10.2}
$$

Note that the model does not encode word identity directly at the data structure level since this could dramatically increase the number of parameters and cause serious data sparsity problems. Instead, the SuperARV language model combines the knowledge of word identity with SuperARVs at the model level by the joint prediction shown in equation (10.2). A SuperARV class-based language model leads to a linguistically compact model that not only makes the use of higher order n-grams feasible but also enables the joint modeling of lexical features and syntactic constraints. Because a word can have multiple SuperARVs, this class-based language model uses soft class membership.

SuperARVs are accumulated from a corpus annotated with CDG relations and associated words, so we can learn their joint frequency of occurrence. As discussed previously, the CDG treebanks used in this work were derived from CFG trees (Wang, 2003). To estimate the probability distributions in equation (10.2), we used recursive linear interpolation among probability estimations of different orders as discussed in Wang (2003) and Wang and Harper (2002), with the best performance among smoothing algorithms achieved using the modified Kneser-Ney smoothing algorithm (Chen and Goodman, 1998). Table 10.4 enumerates the n-grams utilized and their interpolation order for smoothing the two distributions. The SuperARV LM hypothesizes categories for out-of-vocabulary words using the leave-one-out technique (Niesler and Woodland, 1996). The SuperARV LM is most closely related to the almost-parsing-based LM developed by Srinivas (1997). By comparison, the SuperARV LM incorporates direct word dependencies, more lexical feature information than the supertag LM, uses joint instead of conditional probability estimations, and uses modified Kneser-Ney rather than Katz smoothing.

TABLE 10.4 The enumeration and order of n-grams for smoothing the distributions in equation (10.2).

n-grams	$\hat{P}(t_i \mid w_{i-2}^{i-1}t_{i-2}^{i-1})$	$\hat{P}(w_i \mid w_{i-2}^{i-1}t_{i-2}^{i})$
highest	$\hat{P}(t_i \mid w_{i-2}^{i-1}t_{i-2}^{i-1})$	$\hat{P}(w_i \mid w_{i-2}^{i-1}t_{i-2}^{i})$
	$\hat{P}(t_i \mid w_{i-1}t_{i-2}^{i-1})$	$\hat{P}(w_i \mid w_{i-2}^{i-1}t_{i-1}^{i})$
	$\hat{P}(t_i \mid w_{i-2}^{i-1}t_{i-1})$	$\hat{P}(w_i \mid w_{i-1}t_{i-2}^{i})$
	$\hat{P}(t_i \mid t_{i-2}^{i-1})$	$\hat{P}(w_i \mid w_{i-1}t_{i-1}^{i})$
	$\hat{P}(t_i \mid w_{i-1}t_{i-1})$	$\hat{P}(w_i \mid w_{i-1}t_i)$
	$\hat{P}(t_i \mid t_{i-1})$	$\hat{P}(w_i \mid t_{i-1}^{i})$
lowest	$\hat{P}(t_i)$	$\hat{P}(w_i \mid t_i)$

We conducted a variety of experiments using this model, and some of the most interesting results are summarized as follows:

- We compared the perplexity of the joint probabilistic trigram SuperARV LM (as in Heeman, 1998) on the WSJ PTB task (Wang, 2003; Wang and Harper, 2002) to a trigram word-based LM, a joint part-of-speech class-based LM, a conditional trigram SuperARV LM, and the parser-based LMs of Chelba (2000), Xu et al. (2002), Roark (2001), and Charniak (2001). The joint probabilistic SuperARV LM achieved a lower perplexity than all of the models. Although the parser-based models benefitted from interpolation with the word-based trigram, the joint SuperARV LM did not. In fact, we found that since the SuperARV LM is highly correlated with the word-based LM, unless the word model is based on additional materials not used to train the SuperARV LM, then the SuperARV LM does not benefit from interpolation with that word-based model. The conditional version of the SuperARV LM is less correlated with the word-based LM and so benefited from interpolation; however, the interpolated model was unable to achieve the performance of the joint SuperARV LM. Similar results were found for the DARPA WSJ continuous speech recognition task (WSJ CSR) (Wang, 2003; Wang and Harper, 2002).

- The rescoring effectiveness of our SuperARV LM was compared to several other LMs on the 1993 20K open vocabulary DARPA Hub1 WSJ CSR lattices (denoted 93–20K) used in Chelba (2000). The word error rate (WER) was 12.83% for the SuperARV LM, 13.72% for the trigram word-based LM, 13.51% for the joint part-of-speech (POS) class-based LM, 12.89% for Chelba's parser-based LM (Chelba, 2000), and 12.3% for Xu and Chelba's model (Xu et al., 2002). The SuperARV LM was superior to the word-based and POS LMs and performed similarly to Chelba's parser-based model, but did not perform as well as Xu and Chelba's LM, which utilized substantially more context than our LM. We will discuss our full parser based LM in section 10.4.3.

TABLE 10.5 Comparing perplexity results for each language model on the WSJ CSR test sets. The language models appear in decreasing order of perplexity.

language model	92–5K	93–5K	92–20K	93–20K
3gram	45.61	50.51	106.52	109.22
POS	44.21	30.26	98.79	96.64
SARV-fmn	45.01	27.42	96.23	93.16
SARV-fm	43.42	27.22	95.10	91.33
SARV-f	42.33	27.06	94.87	90.20
SARV-mn	40.38	26.96	90.23	89.54
SARV-n	35.02	26.08	87.32	88.04
SARV-L	28.76	25.71	82.45	84.82
SARV-m	26.86	25.58	80.24	83.12
SARV	**21.35**	**23.42**	**69.95**	**74.22**

- The tight integration of lexical category, lexical features, and structural dependency constraints is important to the SuperARV LM's performance. We found in experiments in which we relax the knowledge sources that the performance of the LM decreases (that is, perplexity and WER increase) (Wang, 2003; Wang and Harper, 2002). See the perplexity results in Table 10.5 in which the indicated types of information were relaxed, that is, modifiee constraints (-m), need roles (-n), lexical category (-c), lexical features (-f), and label (-L) in the role value assignment from the full SuperARV LM (denoted SARV in the table). Clearly, the fully constrained SuperARV LM achieved the lowest perplexity, suggesting that each of these knowledge sources provides important information to the model such that if any of it is relaxed, the model performs less well. It is interesting that ignoring lexical features produced an even greater increase in perplexity than eliminating the need roles and the modifiee constraints. Similar results were found when rescoring WSJ CSR lattices.

- We investigated the use of the SuperARV LM on the DARPA Hub4 (Broadcast News) CSR task (Wang, 2003; Wang et al., 2003). The challenge for building a SuperARV LM for this domain was that, in contrast to the DARPA WSJ CSR task, there was no corpus of CFG parse trees available for deriving CDG annotations for training. To circumvent this problem to some extent, we generated a set of training parse trees by using available probabilistic parsers (Charniak, 2000; Collins, 1999), and then converted the trees into CDG annotations. Fortunately, much of the Hub4 training data corresponds to planned speech that is similar to the material that appears in the WSJ PTB, and so we were able to train the parsers using that treebank.

The language model training data sources for the SuperARV and baseline LMs consisted of two sets of Hub4 training data, that is, the 130 million

(M) word loosely transcribed Broadcast News corpus for language model training and the 380,000 word closely transcribed material for acoustic training, and two sets of non-Hub4 training data, that is, the North American Business News (NABN) corpus and the Switchboard-I corpus (Stolcke et al., 2003); the former was chosen for additional business and politics coverage, and the latter for its conversational speech characteristics. A baseline word-based LM, with a vocabulary size of 48K, was constructed for the Hub4 task by interpolating the 5-gram word-based LMs for each Hub4 training set together with the trigram LMs for each non-Hub4 training set. Each LM was estimated by the SRILM toolkit (Stolcke, 2002) using the modified Kneser-Ney smoothing algorithm. A 4-gram SuperARV LM was trained using an automatically constructed CDG treebank for each data set, and parameter tuning was done on a heldout data set of 20% of the training data. Since spontaneous speech characteristics (such as disfluencies) are not well represented in the training data for the SuperARV LM, we also interpolated the SuperARV LM with the baseline LM.

The language models were evaluated by rescoring n-best lists (of up to 2,000 hypotheses per utterance), generated by SRI's 1997 Broadcast News System (Sankar et al., 1998) for the 1996 Hub4 development test set using a log linear combination of two types of acoustic models (crossword and within-word triphones), word insertion penalty, and language model. The WER was computed for the hypotheses with the highest combined scores. The WER for the SuperARV LM alone was 26.1% compared to 26.9% for the baseline LM. When the SuperARV and word-based LMs were interpolated, the WER dropped slightly to 26.0% (possibly because that spontaneous speech characteristics such as disfluencies were not accurately represented in the training data for the SuperARV LM). This result is exciting because these levels of performance were obtained using a potentially errorful method to automatically construct the needed treebanks for the language model training data. It should be noted that efforts to generate more consistent and accurate treebanks also contributed to LM performance (Wang, 2003; Wang et al., 2003).

- We also investigated the use of the SuperARV LM on the Hub5 CSR task (Wang, 2003; Wang et al., 2004) using an approach quite similar to that used for Hub4. To create training material for the SuperARV LM, we parsed the sentences in the LM training data using available probabilistic parsers (Charniak, 2000; Collins, 1999) to generate CFG parse trees and then transformed those trees to CDG parses.

The baseline and SuperARV LMs were trained on the acoustic training transcripts (that is, Switchboard-1 corpus, the Credit Card corpus, the CallHome English corpus, transcribed Switchboard Cellular data released by LDC, and the Switchboard-2 data transcribed by CTRAN and released by BBN, for a total of 418 hours of speech), as well as the 1996 Broadcast News Hub4 LM training corpus (130M words). An additional 191M words of LM training data were retrieved from the Web through the Google search engine by searching for conversational n-grams extracted from the conversational telephone speech (CTS) transcripts (Bulyko et al., 2003). Furthermore, 102M words of data relevant to the topics of the Switchboard-2 and LDC Fisher data collections were selected from Google newsgroups, in an attempt to better match the unseen CTS test data drawn from those collections (Stolcke et al., 2003).

We evaluated the SuperARV LM in the context of the SRI 2003 CTS system (Stolcke et al., 2003). Baseline language models of increasing orders were used for initial decoding and lattice generation, lattice expansion and rescoring, and finally n-best rescoring. The system employed computationally inexpensive decoding steps first to generate intermediate results that constrain the search space, followed by rescoring with more sophisticated acoustic and language models. A bigram class-conditioned mixture LM (Bulyko et al., 2003) was used during the first pass of acoustic decoding, and a trigram class-conditioned mixture LM was used for lattice expansion. A 4-gram class-conditioned mixture LM was employed for rescoring n-best hypotheses. For the baseline 2-gram, 3-gram, and 4-gram LMs, separate LMs were built for each data source; all source-specific LMs, with the exception of the web-topic LM, were then combined by class-conditioned interpolation (Bulyko et al., 2003), and the resulting mixture LM was interpolated with the topic-related LM using fixed weighting of $(0.8, 0.2)$. The interpolation of word n-gram was static and resulted in a single combined backoff n-gram model, as described in Stolcke (2002).

To train the SuperARV LM, similarly to our procedure on the Hub4 Broadcast News CSR task, we parsed the sentences in the LM training data to generate their CFG parse trees and then transformed the trees to CDG parses. Just as for the baseline LM, a separate SuperARV 4-gram LM was trained for each available source and the resulting source-specific LMs were then combined into a single model, with the weights obtained by minimizing the perplexity on a held-out development set. To enable efficient integration of the SuperARV LM into the recognition system, we generated an ARPA-style backoff LM based on the SuperARV word probability estimates. Note that the SuperARV language model, as a class-based LM, is theoretically able to estimate probabilities for any word sequence; however, to keep the generated word LM to a reasonable size, n-gram pruning similar to Stolcke (1998) is applied. The pruning threshold was tuned on a development set to achieve a satisfactory balance between LM size and perplexity. The word 4-gram SuperARV LM thus obtained was used in the n-best rescoring stages of our system. As an expedient to leverage the SuperARV LM in the earlier stages of the recognition system, we used the "LM rescoring" feature of the SRILM toolkit (Stolcke, 2002). We replaced bigram and trigram probability estimates in the baseline LMs (for the initial decoding and lattice expansion stages) with SuperARV LM probability estimates (backing off as needed for lack of full 4-gram word contexts). Following this replacement, backoff weights were recomputed to normalize the LM.

Comparing the SRI DARPA RT-03 Spring CTS system (which used the baseline LMs) with a modified system that uses the SuperARV LM on the DARPA RT-02 CTS evaluation set, we found that the use of the SuperARV LM provided a significant reduction in word error rate, reducing the final result on the complete RT-02 set (that is, tuning and test sets) by 1.6% (from 25.8% to 24.2%). Note that later stages benefited from both the improved LM and the better quality of adaptation hypotheses in earlier stages. By converting the SuperARV LM into the standard word n-gram form, no additional computational effort was incurred at recognition time, so the model could be used in all stages of a multipass CSR system, giving 6.2% relative WER reduction on a standard CTS recognition task.

The SCDG parser-based LM

Like other parser-based LMs, an SCDG parser LM estimates a string's probability by summing the probabilities of all CDG parses for the string produced by the parser. Given the set of partial CDG parses for a sentence prefix w_1^{i-1} is D_1^{i-1}, the probability $P(w_i|w_1^{i-1})$ is calculated as:

$$P_{\text{SCDG}}(w_i|w_1^{i-1}) = \frac{\sum_{d \in D_1^i} P(d)}{\sum_{d' \in D_1^{i-1}} P(d')} \tag{10.3}$$

where $P(d)$ is the probability of a partial CDG parse d for the sentence prefix w_1^i in question. In section 10.4.2, we described the implementation of the underlying SCDG parser, where we already discussed, in particular, how to calculate $P(d)$ in equation (10.3).

The SCDG parser-based LM was evaluated on the 1993 20K open vocabulary DARPA Hub1 WSJ CSR task in order to compare to other parser-based LMs on this task (Chelba, 2000; Roark, 2001; Xu et al., 2002). The LM training data for this task was composed of the 1987–1989 files containing 37,243,300 words. Since this is a speech corpus, this material contains no punctuation or case information. All words outside the provided vocabulary were mapped to $\langle UNK \rangle$. We evaluated all LMs on the 1993 20K open vocabulary DARPA WSJ CSR evaluation set (denoted 93–20K), which consists of 213 utterances and 3,446 words. For consistency, we rescored the same lattices as those used by Chelba (2000), Roark (2001), and Xu et al. (2002). Note that, for the parser-based LMs, we split the contractions in the word lattices so that they could be processed properly. The SCDG parser LM was trained using constraint dependency grammar parses for the complete (that is, 37+ M word) WSJ CSR LM training data, obtained using the CFG-to-CDG transformer (as in Wang and Harper, 2002 and Wang, 2003) to transform the CFG parses from the WSJ Penn Treebank (Marcus et al., 1993) and the BLLIP Treebank (Charniak et al., 2000), which together cover the entire LM training set.

We compared several variations of our SCDG parser LM to a variety of other LMs: the baseline trigram provided by LDC for the task, the joint probabilistic part-of-speech LM (Wang and Harper, 2002), the best SuperARV LM described in Wang and Harper (2002), Chelba's (2000) parser-based LM (trained on a 20M word subset of the WSJ CSR LM training data), Chelba's parser-based LM retrained using the entire training set (Wang and Harper, 2002), and Xu and Chelba's (Xu et al., 2002) revised parser-based LM (trained on a 20M word subset of the WSJ CSR LM training data due to time and space constraints on the model). All models were trained on the complete 37+ M word LM training data using the 20K open vocabulary, unless otherwise indicated. Note that we did not compare to Roark's model (2001) since it was trained on the much smaller WSJ PTB corpus. Note that (Xu et al., 2002) rescored 50-best lists generated from Chelba's (2000) lattices, whereas, Chelba (2000) performed lattice rescoring.

Models		WER(SAC) (%)	Interp. Weight
3gram		13.72(36.18)	N/A
POS		13.51(37.96)	1.0
SuperARV		12.83(43.86)	1.0
Loose SCDG LM	(1): basic model	12.79(44.25)	0.8
	(2): (1)+crossing dependencies	12.71(45.86)	0.8
	(3): (2)+distance and barrier model	12.59(48.33)	0.8
	(4): (3)+modifiee lexical features	12.44(49.02)	0.8
Tight SCDG LM using (4)		12.18(53.66)	0.9
Chelba (rerun)		12.89(41.66)	0.6
Chelba (2000)		13.0(−)	0.6
Xu and Chelba (2002)		12.3(−)	0.6
Lattice Accuracy		3.41 (68.86)	N/A

TABLE 10.6 Comparing WER and SAC (%) after rescoring lattices or n-best lists using each LM on the DARPA WSJ CSR 1993 20K open vocabulary evaluation test set. The lattice WER and SAC that define the best accuracy possible for a set of lattices given perfect knowledge is also provided.

Table 10.6 shows the word error rate (WER) and sentence accuracy (SAC) after rescoring with each LM. Note that Lattice WER/SAC shows the best possible accuracy for the set of lattices used given perfect knowledge. As can be seen from the table, all the SCDG parser LMs outperformed the trigram, POS, SuperARV, and Chelba's parser-based LMs. As was found for the SCDG parser, model enrichment improved the performance of the loosely coupled SCDG parser-based LM. Also, the tightly coupled SCDG parser-based LM outperformed each of the loosely coupled SCDG LMs, which verifies our belief that this tight integration benefits both tagging and modifiee determination. Furthermore, the tightly coupled LM performed slightly better than Xu and Chelba's revised structured LM (Xu et al., 2002).

It should be noted that Xu et al. (2002) trained their LM on a subset of the WSJ CSR training data and rescore using 50-best lists derived from the same set of lattices. Consequently, to more directly compare our tightly coupled SCDG parser-based LM to this state-of-the-art LM, we retrained it on the smaller set of training data used by Xu et al. (2002) and then used the resulting LM to rescore 50-best lists. In this case, we obtained a WER of 12.5%, higher than the 12.3% reported by Xu and Chelba. However, when the tightly coupled SCDG parser LM was trained on the complete data set, we obtained a comparable WER of 12.3% given 50-best rescoring. In prior work on CDG induction (Harper and Wang, 2001), we found that CDGs tend to have a greater selectivity and lower generality than CFGs learned from the same corpus, which is further confirmed by these findings. Although it is possible to relax grammar constraints to increase generality, we have found that a selective SCDG parser LM trained on more data performs better than a more general SCDG model.

Table 10.6 also shows the interpolation weight λ for combining each corresponding model with the baseline trigram (optimized on the same development set). As discussed in section 10.4.3 and in Wang and Harper (2002), the POS and almost-parsing SuperARV LMs were not improved by interpolation because they already contain word cooccurrence knowledge in their models. By contrast, the parser-based LMs of Chelba (2000) and Xu et al. (2002) obtained a decrease in WER when interpolated with word n-gram LMs. Because of their focus on modeling syntactic knowledge with nonterminals, these parser-based LMs may not capture all the local word cooccurrence information available to the trigram. Our SCDG parser-based LM tightly integrates word and parse structure information; however, all the SCDG parser-based LMs, whether loosely or tightly coupled with SuperARV tagging, obtained an improved performance given interpolation with the trigram, possibly due to pruning. The lower interpolation weight of the loosely coupled SCDG parser-based LM indicates that it received a greater level of compensation from the word n-gram than its tightly coupled counterpart.

The SCDG parser-based LM tightly integrates multiple knowledge sources such as word identity, syntactic constraints, and lexical features. The model utilizes long-distance dependency information and subcategorization information to make word predictions. When evaluated on the WSJ CSR task, the model outperformed the almost-parsing SuperARV LM and produced a recognition accuracy comparable to or exceeding state-of-the-art parser-based LMs.

10.5   Conclusions and Future Directions

We have developed and investigated annotation and extraction approaches to learn CDGs from annotated corpora. From these investigations, we have gained insights into the contributions of different types of constraints to grammar quality and a better understanding concerning the inductive bias of a CDG learned from a corpus. Using these insights, we have developed high-quality statistical CDG-based parsing models and language models built on the concept of a SuperARV, which is an abstraction of the joint assignment of dependencies for a word that provides a mechanism for lexicalizing CDG parsing rules.

The SuperARV framework was originally developed for read and planned speech, which tends to exhibit more standard grammatical structures. The models described in this chapter did not include any provisions for dealing with the special features of conversational speech, such as incomplete sentences and disfluencies, and future work will be aimed at modeling these features. Conversational speech raises many challenges to our models. Effective automatic identification of speech repairs is important for building higher quality treebanks automatically, for improving parsing accuracy, and for building higher quality language models for spontaneous speech. Most current parsers assume that sentence boundaries are given and parse at the sentence level; however, speech recognizers produce only words as output. Although recognizers do work on segments of speech, these rarely correspond to a sentence in text. Because this can cause serious problems for a parser-based language model, understanding the impact of segmentation on parser-based LMs is important to obtaining further improvements to these models (Harper et al., 2005).

Another interesting direction for future work is applying our models to languages other than English. Since CDG is the formal basis of our models, there is sufficient grammar power to model a variety of other languages. Foth et al. (2000), Heinecke et al. (1998), Menzel (1994), Menzel (1995), and Schröder et al. (2000) have used CDG to parse spoken and newswire German test sets. Building on the insights of this prior work, we should be able to construct an SCDG parser and language models for German. The availability of the Prague Dependency Treebank (Hajic, 1998) and the research conducted at the 1998 Johns Hopkins Summer Workshop (Hajic et al., 1998) makes Czech an attractive option. Another possible direction is to model Asian languages such as Chinese. Since there are few inflectional and grammatical markers in the Chinese language, an approach that combines syntactic and semantic knowledge is likely to be important for producing a high-quality model.

10.6 Acknowledgments

We thank Srinivas Bangalore, Eugene Charniak, Ciprian Chelba, Jason Eisner, Yang Liu, Andreas Stolcke, and Peng Xu for valuable input to and support of the research described in this chapter. This research has been supported by Purdue Research Foundation, the National Science Foundation (NSF) under grant number 9980054-BCS, the Advanced Research and Development Activity (ARDA) under contract number MDA904-03-C-1788, and by the Defense Advanced Research Projects Agency (DARPA) under contract number MDA972-02-C-0038. Any opinions, findings, and conclusions expressed in this paper are those of the authors and do not necessarily reflect the views of Purdue, NSF, ARDA, or DARPA.

References

Allen, J. (1995). *Natural Language Understanding*. Benjamin/Cummings, 2nd edition.

Bulyko, I., Ostendorf, M., and Stolcke, A. (2003). Getting more mileage from web text sources for conversational speech language modeling using class-dependent mixtures. In *Proceedings of the Joint Conference on Human Language Technology and North American Chapter of Association for Computational Linguistics (HLT-NAACL)*, volume 2, Edmonton, Alberta, Canada, pages 7–9.

Charniak, E. (2000). A maximum-entropy-inspired parser. In *Proceedings of the First Annual Meeting of the North American Association for Computational Linguistics*.

Charniak, E. (2001). Immediate-head parsing for language models. In *Proceedings of the Annual Meeting of the Association for Computational Linguistics*.

Charniak, E., Blaheta, D., Ge, N., Hall, K., and Johnson, M. (2000). BLLIP WSJ Corpus. CD-ROM. Linguistics Data Consortium.

Chelba, C. (2000). *Exploiting Syntactic Structure for Natural Language Modeling*. PhD thesis, CLSP, The Johns Hopkins University.

Chen, S. F. and Goodman, J. (1998). An empirical study of smoothing techniques for language modeling. Technical report, Harvard University, Computer Science Group.

Collins, M. (1996). A new statistical parser based on bigram lexical dependencies. In *Proceedings of the Annual Meeting of the Association for Computational Linguistics*, pages 184–191.

Collins, M. (1999). *Head-Driven Statistical Models for Natural Language Parsing*. PhD thesis, University of Pennsylvania.

Eisner, J. M. (1996). An empirical comparison of probability models for dependency grammar. Technical report, University of Pennsylvania, CIS Department, Philadelphia PA 19104-6389.

Foth, K. A., Menzel, W., Pop, H. F., and Schröder, I. (2000). An experiment in incremental parsing using weighted constraints. In *Proceedings of the 18th International Conference on Computational Linguistics*, Saarbürcken, Germany, pages 1026–1030.

Hajic, J. (1998). Building a syntactically annotated corpus: The Prague Dependency Treebank. In *Issues of Valency and Meaning (Festschrift for Jarmila Panevova)*, pages 106–132. Carolina, Charles University, Prague.

Hajic, J., Brill, E., Collins, M., Hladka, B., Jones, D., Kuo, C., Ramshaw, L., Schwartz, O., Tillmann, C., and Zeman, D. (1998). Core natural language processing technology applicable to multiple languages – Workshop '98. Technical report, Johns Hopkins University.

Harbusch, K. (1997). The realtion between tree-adjoining grammars and constraint dependency grammars. In *Proceedings of the Fifth Meeting on the Mathematics of Language*, pages 38–45.

Harper, M. P., Dorr, B., Hale, J., Roark, B., Shafran, I., Lease, M., Liu, Y., Snover, M., Yung, L., Krasnyanskaya, A., and Stewart, R. (2005). 2005 Johns Hopkins Summer Workshop final report on parsing and spoken structural event detection. Technical report, Johns Hopkins University.

Harper, M. P. and Helzerman, R. A. (1995a). Extensions to constraint dependency parsing for spoken language processing. *Computer Speech and Language*, 9:187–234.

Harper, M. P. and Helzerman, R. A. (1995b). Managing multiple knowledge sources in constraint-based parsing spoken language. *Fundamenta Informaticae*, 23(2,3,4):303–353.

Harper, M. P., Hockema, S. A., and White, C. M. (1999a). Enhanced constraint dependency grammar parsers. In *Proceedings of the IASTED International Conference on Artificial Intelligence and Soft Computing*.

Harper, M. P. and Wang, W. (2001). Approaches for learning constraint dependency grammar from corpora. In *Proceedings of the Grammar and Natural Language Processing Conference*, Montreal, Canada.

Harper, M. P., White, C. M., Helzerman, R. A., and Hockema, S. A. (1999b). Faster MUSE CSP arc consistency algorithms. In *Proceedings of the IASTED International Conference on Artificial Intelligence and Soft Computing*.

Harper, M. P., White, C. M., Wang, W., Johnson, M. T., and Helzerman, R. A. (2000). Effectiveness of corpus-induced dependency grammars for post-processing speech. In *Proceedings of the 1st Annual Meeting of the North American Association for Computational Linguistics*, pages 102–109.

Heeman, P. A. (1998). POS tagging versus classes in language modeling. In *Proceedings of the 6th Workshop on Very Large Corpora, Montreal*.

Heinecke, J., Kunze, J., Menzel, W., and Schröder, I. (1998). Eliminative parsing with graded constraints. In *Proceedings of the International Conference on Computational Linguistics and the Annual Meeting of the Association for Computational Linguistics*.

Helzerman, R. A. and Harper, M. P. (1992). Log time parsing on the MasPar MP-1. In *Proceedings of the Sixth International Conference on Parallel Processing*, volume 2, pages 209–217.

Helzerman, R. A. and Harper, M. P. (1996). MUSE CSP: An extension to the constraint satisfaction problem. *Journal of Artificial Intelligence Research*, 5:239–288.

Holan, T., Kuboň, V., Oliva, K., and Plátek, M. (1998). Two useful measures of word order complexity. In Polguère, A. and Kahane, S., eds., *Processing of Dependency-Based Grammars: Proceedings of the Workshop*, pages 21–28.

Järvinen, T. and Tapanainen, P. (1998). Towards an implementable dependency grammar. In Polguère, A. and Kahane, S., eds., *Processing of Dependency-Based Grammars: Proceedings of the Workshop*, pages 1–10.

Jelinek, F. (1990). Self-organized language modeling for speech recognition. In Waibel, A. and Lee, K.-F., eds., *Readings in Speech Recognition*. Morgan Kaufmann, San Mateo, CA.

Jelinek, F. (1997). *Statistical Methods For Speech Recognition*. MIT Press.

Joshi, A. K., Levy, L. S., and Takahashi, M. (1975). Tree adjunct grammars. *Journal of Computer and System Sciences*, 10:136–163.

Joshi, A. K. and Srinivas, B. (1994). Disambiguation of super parts of speech (or supertags): Almost parsing. In *Proceedings of the 1994 International Conference on Computational Linguistics*.

Marcus, M. P., Santorini, B., and Marcinkiewicz, M. A. (1993). Building a large annotated corpus of English: The Penn Treebank. *Computational Linguistics*, 19(2):313–330.

Maruyama, H. (1990a). Constraint Dependency Grammar. Technical Report #RT0044, IBM, Tokyo, Japan.

Maruyama, H. (1990b). Constraint Dependency Grammar and its weak generative capacity. *Computer Software*.

Maruyama, H. (1990c). Structural disambiguation with constraint propagation. In *The Proceedings of the Annual Meeting of Association for Computational Linguistics*, pages 31–38.

Menzel, W. (1994). Parsing of spoken language under time constraints. In *11th European Conference on Artificial Intelligence*, pages 560–564.

Menzel, W. (1995). Robust processing of natural language. In *Proceedings of the 19th Annual German Conference on Artificial Intelligence.*

Menzel, W. (1996). Constraint satisfaction for robust processing of spoken language. In *Proceedings of the European Conference on Artificial Intelligence Workshop on Non-Standard Constraint Processing.*

Niesler, T. R. and Woodland, P. C. (1996). Variable-length category-based N-gram language model. In *Proceedings of the International Conference of Acoustics, Speech, and Signal Processing*, pages 164–167.

Polguère, A. and Kahane, S., eds. (1998). *Processing of Dependency-Based Grammars: Proceedings of the Workshop.* Association For Computational Linguistics, New Brunswick, NJ.

Price, P. J., Fischer, W., Bernstein, J., and Pallett, D. (1988). A database for continuous speech recognition in a 1000-word domain. In *Proceedings of the International Conference on Acoustics, Speech, and Signal Processing*, pages 651–654.

Ratnaparkhi, A. (1999). Learning to parse natural language with maximum entropy models. *Machine Learning*, 34:151–175.

Roark, B. (2001). Probabilistic top-down parsing and language modeling. *Computational Linguistics*, 27(2):249–276.

Rosenfeld, R. (2000). Two decades of statistical language modeling: Where do we go from here? *Proceedings of the IEEE*, 88:1270–1278.

Sankar, A., Weng, F., Rivlin, Z., Stolcke, A., and Gadde, R. (1998). Development of SRI's 1997 Broadcast News transcription system. In *Proceedings of DARPA Broadcast News Transcription and Understanding Workshop*, Lansdowne, VA, pages 91–96.

Schabes, Y. (1992). Stochastic Lexicalized Tree Adjoining Grammars. In *Proceedings of the International Conference on Computational Linguistics*, pages 75–80.

Schabes, Y., Abeillé, A., and Joshi, A. K. (1988). Parsing strategies with 'lexicalized' grammars: Application to Tree Adjoining Grammars. In *Proceedings of the International Conference on Computational Linguistics*, pages 578–583.

Schröder, I., Menzel, W., Foth, K. A., and Schulz, M. (2000). Modeling dependency grammars with restricted constraints. *International Journal Traitement Automatique des Langues (T.A.L.). Special Issue on Grammaires de dèpendance*, 41(1):97–126.

Srinivas, B. (1996). 'Almost parsing' technique for language modeling. In *Proceedings of the International Conference on Spoken Language Processing*, volume 2, pages 1173–1176.

Srinivas, B. (1997). *Complexity of lexical descriptions and its relevance to partial parsing.* PhD thesis, University of Pennsylvania.

Stolcke, A. (1998). Entropy-based pruning of backoff language models. In *Proceedings DARPA Broadcast News Transcription and Understanding Workshop*, pages 270–274.

Stolcke, A. (2002). SRILM – An extensible language modeling toolkit. In *International Conference on Spoken Language Processing*, volume 2, pages 901–904.

Stolcke, A., Franco, H., Gadde, R., Graciarena, M., Precoda, K., Venkataraman, A., Vergyri, D., Wang, W., Zheng, J., Huang, Y., Peskin, B., Bulyko, I., Ostendorf, M., and Kirchhoff, K. (2003). Speech-to-text research at SRI-ICSI-UW. In *DARPA RT-03 Workshop*, Boston.

Tesnière, L. (1959). *Éléments de Syntaxe Structurale.* Klincksiek.

Thompson, C. A., Califf, M. E., and Mooney, R. J. (1999). Active learning for natural language parsing and information extraction. In *Proceedings of the International Conference on Machine Learning)*, pages 406–414.

Wang, W. (2003). *Statistical Parsing and Language Modeling Based on Constraint Dependency Grammar*. PhD thesis, School of Electrical and Computer Engineering, Purdue University.

Wang, W. and Harper, M. P. (2002). The SuperARV language model: Investigating the effectiveness of tightly integrating multiple knowledge sources. In *Proceedings of Conference of Empirical Methods in Natural Language Processing*, pages 238–247.

Wang, W. and Harper, M. P. (2004). A statistical constraint dependency grammar (CDG) parser. In *Proceedings of the Association for Computational Linguistics Workshop on Incremental Parsing–Bringing Engineering and Cognition Together*.

Wang, W., Harper, M. P., and Stolcke, A. (2003). The robustness of an almost-parsing language model given errorful training data. In *Proceedings of the International Conference of Acoustics, Speech, and Signal Processing*, volume 1, Hong Kong, pages 240–243.

Wang, W., Stolcke, A., and Harper, M. P. (2004). The use of a linguistically motivated language model in conversational speech recognition. In *Proceedings of the International Conference of Acoustics, Speech, and Signal Processing*, Montreal, Canada.

White, C. M. (2000). *Rapid Grammar Development and Parsing: Constraint Dependency Grammars with Abstract Role Values*. PhD thesis, School of Electrical and Computer Engineering, Purdue University.

Xu, P., Chelba, C., and Jelinek, F. (2002). A study on richer syntactic dependencies for structured language modeling. In *Proceedings of the Annual Meeting on Computational Linguistics*.

Young, S. J., Odell, J., Ollason, D., Valtchev, V., and Woodland, P. C. (1997). *The HTK Book*. Entropic Cambridge Research Laboratory, Ltd.

Guiding a Constraint Dependency Parser with Supertags

Kilian Foth, Tomas By, and Wolfgang Menzel

11.1   Introduction

Supertagging is based on the combination of two powerful and influential ideas of natural language processing. On one hand, parsing is (at least) partially reduced to a decision on the optimal sequence of categories, a problem for which a large number of efficient and easily trainable procedures exist. On the other hand, supertagging exploits complex categories, that is, tree fragments — instead of atomic ones, which much better reflect the mutual compatibility conditions between neighboring lexical items than say part-of-speech tags.

Bangalore and Joshi (1999) derived the notion of supertag within the framework of Lexicalized Tree-Adjoining Grammars (LTAG) (Schabes and Joshi, 1991). They considered supertagging a process of almost parsing, since all that needs to be done after having a sufficiently reliable sequence of supertags available is to decide on their combination into a spanning tree for the complete sentence. Thus, the approach lends itself easily for preprocessing sentences or filtering parsing results with the goal of guiding the parser or reducing its output ambiguity.

Assuming that a correct supertag assignment would be available, indeed a major contribution of this information to the parsing process can be expected. Nasr and Rambow (2004) estimated that perfect supertag information already provides for a parsing accuracy of 98%. Unfortunately, perfectly reliable supertag information cannot be expected. Usually this uncertainty is compensated by running the tagger in multitagging mode, expecting that the reliablility can be increased by not forcing the tagger to take unreliable decisions but allow it to offer a set of alternatives from which a subsequent processing component can choose.

Bangalore and Joshi (1999) inherited both the decomposition of trees into tree fragments as well as the fundamental distinction between complements and adjuncts from LTAG. If, however, the idea is to be transferred to other lexicalized grammar formalisms, the question of a suitable definition of supertags with respect to their purpose needs to be raised.

A grammar formalism that seems particularly well suited to decompose structural descriptions into lexicalized tree fragments is dependency grammar. Wang and Harper (2002) define their supertags following Constraint Dependency Grammar (CDG) by abstracting away adjunct related information. Since attachment information in CDG is encoded as a number of role values for the modifiee as well as for the modifiers, supertags describe generalized, hence abstract, role values called SuperARVs. Dependency-based supertags seem to be particularly attractive because they allow us to define supertags on different levels of granularity (White, 2000), thus facilitating a fine-grained analysis of how the different aspects of supertag information influence the parsing behavior. In the following, we are going to use these characteristics to study in more detail the utility of different kinds of supertag information for guiding the parsing process.

Supertags are usually integrated into a rule-based parser by filtering, that is, parsing hypotheses that are not compatible with the supertag predictions are simply discarded. Drawing on the ability of Weighted Constraint Dependency Grammar (WCDG) (Schröder et al., 2000) to deal with defeasible constraints, here we try another option for making available supertag information: Using a *score* to estimate the general reliability of unique supertag decisions, the information can be combined with evidence derived from other constraints of the grammar in a soft manner. It makes it possible to rank parsing hypotheses according to their plausibility and allows the parser even to override supertag decisions. Thus, it can be assumed that wrong supertag assignments will not always have fatal consequences.

Starting from a range of possible supertag models, section 11.2 explores the reliability with which dependency-based supertags can be determined on the different levels of granularity. Then, section 11.3 describes how the supertags are integrated into the existing parser for German. The complex nature of the supertags as we define them makes it possible to separate the different structural predictions made by a single supertag into components and study their contributions independently (c.f. section 11.4). We can show that indeed the parser is robust enough to tolerate supertag errors and that even with a fairly low tagger performance it can profit from the additional, though unreliable information.

11.2   Supertagging German Text

In defining the nature of supertags for dependency parsing, a trade-off has to be made between expressiveness and accuracy. A simple definition that leads to a very small number of supertags will not be able to capture the full variety of syntactic contexts that actually occur, while an overly expressive definition may lead to a tag set that is so large that it cannot be accurately predicted from the available training data. Similar to Wang and Harper (2002), we distinguish between different featues of the local context of a word that could be encoded in a supertag:

- morphosyntactic features of ambiguous word forms
- the edge label of the word
- the attachment direction of the word
- the occurrence of obligatory dependents[1] of the word
- the occurrence of all dependents of the word
- whether each predicted dependent occurs to the right or to the left of the word
- the relative order among different dependents

Because we foresee severe data sparsity if we modeled the rich morphosyntax of German (regular adjectives can have up to 26 homonyms), we disregard this feature from the outset. The simplest useful task that could then be asked of a supertagger for dependency parsing would be to predict the dependency relation that each word enters. In terms of the CDG formalism, this means associating each word at least with one of the syntactic labels that decorate dependency edges, such as SUBJ or DET; in other words, the supertag set would be identical to the label set. The example sentence

"Es mag sein, daß die Franzosen kein schlüssiges Konzept für eine echte Partnerschaft besitzen."

(Perhaps the French management does not have a viable concept for a true partnership.)

if analyzed as in figure 11.1, would then be described by a supertag sequence beginning with EXPL S AUX ...

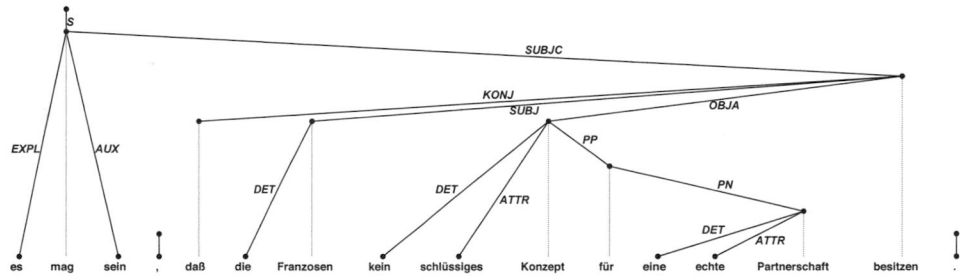

FIGURE 11.1 Dependency tree for the last sentence in our test set.

Of course, to describe a dependency relation fully, the regent as well as the dependent must be named. It is hardly feasible to consider the regent word itself a feature, since this would lead to impractically large supertag sets. Even the relative position of the regent and dependent word might be considered too large a degree of freedom, since it is theoretically unbounded. Following Wang and Harper (2002), we classify dependencies merely into Left (L), Right (R), and No attachments (N), depending on whether the regent (if any) is found to the left or to the right of the dependent. We combine the label with the attachment direction to obtain composite

supertags. The sequence of supertags describing the example sentence would then
begin with EXPL/R S/N AUX/L ....

Although this kind of supertag gives information about the role of each word in
a sentence, it still does not specify the entire local context; for instance, it associates
the information that a word functions as a subject only with the subject and not
with the verb that takes the subject. In other words, it does not predict the relations
under a given word. Greater expressivity is reached by also encoding the labels of
these relations into the supertag.

For instance, the word *mag* in the example sentence is modified by an expletive
(EXPL) on its left side and by an AUX (auxiliary) and a SUBJC (subject clause)
dependency on its right side. To capture this extended local context, these labels
must be encoded into the supertag. We add the local context of a word to the
end of its supertag, separated with the delimiter +. This yields the expression
S/N+AUX,EXPL,SUBJC. If we also want to express that the EXPL precedes the
word but the AUX follows it, we can instead add two new fields to the left and to the
right of the supertag, which leads to the new supertag EXPL+S/N+AUX,SUBJC.

			Supertag model	
Word	A	B	H	J
es	EXPL	EXPL/R	EXPL/R+	+EXPL/R+
mag	S	S/N	S/N+AUX,EXPL, SUBJC	EXPL+S/N+AUX, SUBJC
sein	AUX	AUX/L	AUX/L+	+AUX/L+
,		/N	/N+	+/N+
daß	KONJ	KONJ/R	KONJ/R+	+KONJ/R+
die	DET	DET/R	DET/R+	+DET/R+
Franzosen	SUBJ	SUBJ/R	SUBJ/R+DET	DET+SUBJ/R+
kein	DET	DET/R	DET/R+	+DET/R+
schlüssiges	ATTR	ATTR/R	ATTR/R+	+ATTR/R+
Konzept	OBJA	OBJA/R	OBJA/R+ATTR, DET,PP	ATTR,DET+OBJA/R+PP
für	PP	PP/L	PP/L+PN	+PP/L+PN
eine	DET	DET/R	DET/R+	+DET/R+
echte	ATTR	ATTR/R	ATTR/R+	+ATTR/R+
Partnerschaft	PN	PN/L	PN/L+ATTR,DET	ATTR,DET+PN/L+
besitzen	SUBJC	SUBJC/L	SUBJC/L+KONJ, OBJA,SUBJ	KONJ, OBJA, SUBJ+SUBJC/L+
.		/N	/N+	+/N+

TABLE 11.1 Annotation of the example sentence under different supertag models.

Table 11.1 shows the complete annotation of the example using different
supertag models. Note that the notation **+EXPL/R+** explicitly represents the
fact that the word labeled EXPL has no dependents of its own, while the simpler
EXPL/R makes no assertion of this kind. The extended context specification with
two + delimiters expresses the complete set of dependents of a word and whether
to find each of them to its left or right. However, it does not distinguish the order of
the left or right dependents among each other; instead the labels on either side

are always ordered alphabetically for consistency. Also, duplicate labels among the dependents on either side are not represented. For instance, a verb with two postmodifying prepositions would still list PP only once in its right context. This ensures that the set of possible supertags is finite.

The full set of different supertag models we used is given in table 11.2. Note that the most complicated models G–J predict all dependents of each word, while the models C–F predict obligatory dependents only, which should be an easier task.

Supertag model	Prediction of				#tags	Supertag accuracy	Component accuracy
	label	direction	dependents	order			
A	yes	no	none	no	35	84.1%	84.1%
B	yes	yes	none	no	73	78.9%	85.7%
C	yes	no	obligatory	no	914	81.1%	88.5%
D	yes	yes	obligatory	no	1336	76.9%	90.8%
E	yes	no	obligatory	yes	1465	80.6%	91.8%
F	yes	yes	obligatory	yes	2026	76.2%	90.9%
G	yes	no	all	no	6858	71.8%	81.3%
H	yes	yes	all	no	8684	67.9%	85.8%
I	yes	no	all	yes	10762	71.6%	84.3%
J	yes	yes	all	yes	12947	67.6%	84.5%

TABLE 11.2 Definition of all supertag models used.

To obtain and evaluate supertag predictions, we used the NEGRA and TIGER corpora (Brants et al., 1997, 2002). Both treebanks were automatically transformed into dependency format with the freely available tool DepSy described in Daum et al. (2004). As our test set, we used sentences 18,602 through 19,601 of the NEGRA corpus, for comparability to earlier work. All other sentences were used as the training set; this amounts to 59,622 sentences with 1,032,091 words. For each word in its training set, the local context was extracted and expressed in our supertag notation.

The word/supertag pairs were then used to train the statistical part-of-speech tagger TnT (Brants, 2000), which performs trigram tagging efficiently and allows easy retraining on different data. However, a few of TnT's limitations had to be worked around: since it cannot deal with words that have more than 510 different possible tags, we systematically replaced the rarest tags in the training set with a generic *OTHER* tag until the limit was met. Also, in tagging mode it can fail to process sentences with many unknown words in close succession. In such cases, we simply ran it to shorter fragments of the sentence until no error occurred. Fewer than 0.5% of all sentences were affected by this problem even with the largest tag set.

A more serious problem arises when using a stochastic process to assign tags that partially predict structure: the tags emitted by the model may contradict each other. Consider, for instance, the following supertagger output for the previous example sentence:

```
es      +EXPL/R+
mag     +S/N+AUX,SUBJC
sein    PRED+AUX/L+
...
```

The supertagger predicts that the first word is labeled as EXPL, the second as S, and the third as AUX (which is entirely correct). However, it also predicts that the word *sein* (to be) has a preceding PRED complement. This is to be expected, since most instances of *sein* do in fact have such a dependent. However, in this case the supertagger contradicts its earlier prediction that the two preceding words are labeled EXPL and S, that is, neither of them can be the predicted PRED complement. Although such contradictory information is not fatal in a robust system, it is nevertheless likely to cause unnecessary work for the parser when some rules demand the impossible. We therefore decided simply to ignore context predictions when they contradict the basic label predictions made for the same sentence; in other words, we pretend that the prediction for the third word was just +AUX/L+ rather than PRED+AUX/L+. Up to 13% of all predictions were simplified in this way for the most complex supertag model.

The last columns of table 11.2 give the number of supertags extracted from the training set and the performance of the retrained TnT on the test set in single-tagging mode. Although the number of occurring tags rises and the accuracy of supertag predictions falls with the complexity of the supertag definition, note that the correlation is not absolute. Thus, it seems markedly easier to predict supertags that include complements but no direction information (C) than supertags that include direction information but no complements (B), although the tag set is larger by an order of magnitude. In fact, the prediction of attachment direction turns out to be much more difficult than that of undirected supertags in every case; this is not surprising in a language with semifree word order such as German. The greater tag set size when predicting complements of each words is at least partly offset by the contextual information available to the n-gram model, since it is much more likely that a word will have, for instance, a SUBJ complement when an adjacent SUBJ supertag is present.

For the simplest model A (no direction, no dependents, no order), all 35 possible supertags actually occur, while in the most complicated model J (with direction, all dependents, with order), only 12,947 different supertags are observed in the training data (out of a theoretically possible 10^{24} for set of 35 edge labels). Note that this is still considerably larger than most other reported supertag sets. The prediction quality falls to rather low values with the more complicated models; however, our goal here is not to optimize the supertagger, but to show that a supertagger can be immediately useful even without extensive tuning. Altogether most results fall into a range of 70–80% of accuracy; as we will see later, this is in fact enough to provide a benefit to automatic parsing.

Although supertag accuracy is usually determined by simply counting matching and nonmatching predictions, a more accurate measure should take into account how

many of the individual predictions that are combined into a supertag are correct
or wrong. For instance, a word that is attached to its left as a subject is preceded
by a preposition and an attributive adjective: followed by an apposition, it would
bear the supertag ATTR,PP+SUBJ/L+APP. Since the prepositional attachment
is notoriously difficult to predict, a supertagger might miss it and emit the slightly
different tag ATTR+SUBJ/L+APP. Although technically this supertag counts as
an error, it is in fact much more right than wrong: of the four predictions of label,
direction, following dependents, and preceding dependents, three are correct and
only the fourth is wrong. We therefore define the *component accuracy* for a given
model as the ratio of correct predictions among the possible ones. This results
in a value of 0.75 rather than 0 for the example prediction, since it gets the
label, subordination direction and right context right, but not the left context. By
this measure, for instance, the component accuracy of the supertag model J is in
fact 84.5% rather than 67.6%. We would expect the component accuracy to match
the effect on parsing more closely than the supertag accuracy.

11.3 Using Supertag Information in WCDG

Weighted Constraint Dependency Grammar (WCDG) is a formalism in which
declarative constraints can be formulated that describe well-formed dependency
trees in a particular natural language. A grammar composed of such constraints can
be used for parsing by feeding it to a constraint-solving component that searches
for structures that satisfy the constraints.

Each constraint carries a numeric score or *penalty* between 0 and 1 that indicates
its importance. The penalties of all instances of constraint violations are multiplied
to yield a score for an entire analysis; hence, an analysis that satisfies all rules of
the CDG bears the score 1, while lower values indicate small or large aberrations
from the language norm. A constraint penalty of 0, then, corresponds to a hard
constraint, since every analysis that violates such a constraint will always bear the
worst possible score of 0. This means that of two constraints, the one with the *lower*
penalty is more important to the grammar.

Since constraints can be soft as well as hard, parsing in the WCDG formalism
amounts to solving a multidimensional optimization problem. Of two possible
analyses of an utterance, the one that satisfies more (or more important) constraints
is always preferred. All knowledge about grammatical rules is encoded in the
constraints that (together with the lexicon) constitute the grammar. Although the
parsing problem in WCDG is computationally infeasible in general, good success
has been achieved with approximative heuristic algorithms that try to compute the
global optimum through local optimization.

A grammar of German is available (Foth et al., 2004) that achieves state-
of-the-art accuracy on written German input. Despite its good results, it seems
probable that the information provided by a supertag prediction component could
improve the accuracy further. While the grammar rules deal mainly with structural

compatibility, a supertagger exploits patterns in the sequence of words in its input, so that both analyzers can contribute complementary information.

Also, the rules in the grammar as it stands were derived from the personal judgment of native speakers. Although this leads to a consistent grammar model without large obvious errors, there is reason to believe that it fails to make many of the distinctions that a stochastically induced model would contain: the existing constraints predominantly describe the possible relations between words on the level of syntactic *categories*, but it is quite clear that human readers also base their understanding on the particular *words* that occur.

For instance, the German sentence "Diese Zahlen gaben die Minister gestern Abend in Genf bekannt" can mean either "These figures announced the ministers last evening in Geneva" or, "The ministers announced these figures last evening in Geneva." Since verb complements can be freely redistributed in German, both meanings are grammatical; in fact, the first version is the unmarked word order. Nevertheless, the second reading will be much preferred because it agrees with readers' conceptions of politicians and figures. Few constraints capture such distributional evidence, since it is virtually impossible to write a rule, for instance, about each possible noun in a language, or even about every semantic class. A lexicalized supertagger could be a useful approximation of such information.

More generally, handwritten rules are good at describing the obvious structures and forbidding the clear errors, but it is much more difficult to capture regularities that are less pronounced but nevertheless critical for language understanding; and in fact a large proportion of the remaining errors that the model now makes result from analyses that are perfectly grammatical but are still dispreferred by humans for distributional reasons.

To make the information from the supertag sequence available to the parser, we treat the complex supertags as a set of up to four predictions and write constraints to prefer those analyses that satisfy them. The prediction of the label made by model A as well as the predictions of label and direction made by model B are mapped onto two corresponding constraints that demand that each word in the analysis should exhibit the predicted label and direction. The more complicated supertag models constrain the local context of each word further. Effectively, they predict that the specified dependents of a word occur, and that no other dependents occur. The former prediction equates to an existence condition, so constraints are added that demand the presence of the predicted relation types under that word (one for left dependents and one for right dependents). The latter prediction disallows all other dependents; it is implemented by two constraints that test the edge label of each word-to-word attachment against the set of predicted dependents of the regent (again, separately for left and right dependents). Altogether, six new constraints are added to the grammar that refer to the output of the supertagger on the current sentence.

Note that in contrast to most other approaches we do not perform multisupertagging; exactly one supertag is assumed to correspond to each word. To deal with alternative supertags would require us to compute the logical disjunctions of the predictions made by each alternative supertag, and then weaken the new constraints accordingly. This is considerably more complicated than just to translate a single supertag.

11.4 Experiments

We tested the effect of supertag predictions on a full parser by adding the new constraints to the CDG of German described in Foth et al. (2004) and reparsing the same 1,000 sentences from the NEGRA corpus. Although the heuristic parsing algorithm we employ does not guarantee that it always retrieves the numerically optimal analysis of a sentence, it does guarantee to return a complete dependency tree in every case. Together with the syntax model of structure as word-to-word dependencies this means that the parser output always contains exactly the same number of attachments as the reference tree, and each of them is either correct or incorrect. In other words, there is no difference between *precision* and *recall*; both coincide with the *dependency accuracy*, the ratio of correctly computed to annotated dependencies. However, we do distinguish *unlabeled accuracy*, which compares only the subordination of a word, from the stricter *labeled accuracy*, which compares both the subordination and the edge label. The unlabeled accuracy without any supertags is 89.6%; this compares favorably to other results on the same data set (Dubey and Keller, 2003; Schiehlen, 2004).

To determine the best trade-off between complexity and prediction quality, we tested all ten supertag models against the baseline case of no supertags at all. The results are given in table 11.3.

Model	Supertag accuracy	Component accuracy	Parsing accuracy unlabeled	labeled
baseline	–	–	89.6%	87.9%
A (no direction, no dependents, no order)	84.1%	84.1%	90.8%	89.4%
B (with direction, no dependents, no order)	78.9%	85.7%	90.6%	89.2%
C (no direction, only obligatory dependents, no order)	81.1%	88.5%	91.0%	89.6%
D (with direction, only obligatory dependents, no order)	76.9%	90.8%	91.1%	89.8%
E (no direction, only obligatory dependents, with order)	80.6%	91.8%	90.9%	89.6%
F (with direction, only obligatory dependents, with order)	76.2%	90.9%	91.4%	90.0%
G (no direction, all dependents, no order)	71.8%	81.3%	90.8%	89.4%
H (with direction, all dependents, no order)	67.9%	85.8%	90.8%	89.4%
I (no direction, all dependents, with order)	71.6%	84.3%	91.8%	90.4%
J (with direction, all dependents, with order)	67.6%	84.5%	91.8%	90.5%

TABLE 11.3 Influence of supertag integration on parsing accuracy.

Two observations can be made about the effect of the supertag model on parsing. Firstly, all types of supertag prediction — even the very basic model A, which predicts only edge labels — improve the overall accuracy of parsing, although the baseline is already quite high. Second, the richer models of supertags appear to be more suitable for guiding the parser than the simpler ones, even though their own accuracy is markedly lower; almost one third of the supertag predictions according to the most complicated definition J are wrong, but nevertheless their inclusion reduces the remaining error rate of the parser by over 20%.

We hypothesized earlier that if supertags are integrated as individual constraints, their component accuracy would be more important for parsing success than the supertag accuracy. This turns out to be only partially true. While the supertag accuracy is almost inversely correlated to parsing accuracy, the component accuracy reaches its highest value for intermediate supertag definitions, but even this does not explain why it is the most complex supertags that lead to the best parsing accuracy. Apparently the decreasing accuracy of more complex supertags is more than counterbalanced by the additional information that they contribute to the analysis. Obviously, this trend cannot continue indefinitely; a supertag definition that predicted even larger parts of the dependency tree would certainly lead to much lower accuracy by even the most lenient supertag measure, and a prediction that is mostly wrong must ultimately start to degrade parsing performance as well. Since the most complex model J (with order among dependents) shows little parsing improvement over its successor I (without order among dependents), this point might already have been reached.

The use of supertags in WCDG is comparable to previous work which integrated POS tagging and chunk parsing. Foth and Hagenström (2002); Daum et al. (2003) showed that the correct balance between the new knowledge and the existing grammar is crucial for successful integration. Since statistically computed supertags are inherently an uncertain knowledge source that introduces some errors, they should not be given full confidence; this would risk overconstraining the parser so that no solution can be found at all. Note also that in our approach, a supertag can impose up to six additional constraints on each word. If they were given too much weight, they could easily dominate the entire grammar because all scores are multiplied. The experiments described so far used a value of 0.9, which is otherwise used for preferences rather than important rules. This factor seemed reasonable for an uncertain knowledge source. Nevertheless, a different weighting of the two competing language models could lead to a better overall performance. We repeated the previous experiment, using the most successful supertag model J and different values for the integration of the new supertag constraints into the grammar.

Table 11.4 shows the effect of different constraint penalties. As expected, making supertag constraints hard (with a value of 0.0) overconstrains most parsing problems, so that hardly any analyses can be computed. Other values near 0 avoid this problem but still lead to much worse overall performance, since wrong or even impossible predictions too often overrule the normal syntax constraints. The previously used value of 0.9 actually yields the best results with this particular grammar.

Constraint penalty	Parsing accuracy	
	unlabeled	labeled
0.0	3.7%	3.7%
0.05	85.2%	83.5%
0.1	87.6%	85.7%
0.2	88.9%	87.3%
0.5	91.2%	89.5%
0.7	91.5%	90.1%
0.9	91.8%	90.5%
0.95	91.1%	89.8%
1.0	89.6%	87.9%

TABLE 11.4 Parsing accuracy depending on different strength of supertag integration.

The fact that a statistical model can improve parsing performance when superimposed on a sophisticated handwritten grammar is of particular interest because the statistical model we used is so simple, and in fact not particularly accurate; it certainly does not represent the state of the art in supertagging. This gives rise to the hope that as better supertaggers for German become available, parsing results will continue to see additional improvements, that is, future supertagging research will directly benefit parsing. The obvious question is how great this benefit might conceivably become under optimal conditions. To obtain this upper limit of the utility of supertags, we simulated the hypothetically perfect supertagger by reading the supertags off the reference trees; in other words, we gave the parser access to the actual local environment in each sentence to be parsed.

Table 11.5 again gives the unlabeled and labeled parsing accuracy for all ten different supertag models with the integration strengths of 0 and 0.9. (Note that since all our models predict the edge label of each word, hard integration of perfect predictions eliminates the difference between labeled und unlabeled accuracy.) As expected, an improved accuracy of supertagging would lead to improved parsing accuracy in each case. In fact, knowing the correct supertag would solve the parsing problem almost completely with the more complex models. This confirms earlier findings for English (Nasr and Rambow, 2004).

Since perfect supertaggers are not available, we have to make do with the imperfect ones that do exist. One method of avoiding some errors introduced by supertagging would be to reject supertag predictions that tend to be wrong. To this end, we ran the supertagger on its training set and determined the average component accuracy of each occurring supertag. The supertags whose average precision fell below a variable threshold were then excluded from the process of adding constraints, as if the supertagger had not made a prediction. This means that a threshold of 100% corresponds to the baseline of not using supertags at all, while a threshold of 0% prunes nothing, so that these two cases duplicate the first and last line from table 11.2.

	Constraint penalty	
Supertag model	0.9	0.0
A (no direction, no dependents, no order)	92.7% / 92.2%	94.0% / 94.0%
B (with direction, no dependents, no order)	94.3% / 93.7%	96.0% / 96.0%
C (no direction, only obligatory dependents, no order)	92.8% / 92.4%	94.1% / 94.1%
D (with direction, only obligatory dependents, no order)	94.3% / 93.8%	96.0% / 96.0%
E (no direction, only obligatory dependents, with order)	93.1% / 92.6%	94.3% / 94.3%
F (with direction, only obligatory dependents, with order)	94.6% / 94.1%	96.1% / 96.1%
G (no direction, all dependents, no order)	94.2% / 93.7%	95.8% / 95.8%
H (with direction, all dependents, no order)	95.2% / 94.7%	97.4% / 97.4%
I (no direction, all dependents, with order)	97.1% / 96.8%	99.5% / 99.5%
J (with direction, all dependents, with order)	97.1% / 96.8%	99.6% / 99.6%

TABLE 11.5 Unlabeled and labeled parsing accuracy with a simulated perfect supertagger.

As table 11.6 shows, pruning supertags that are wrong more often then than they are right results in a further small improvement in parsing accuracy: unlabeled syntax accuracy rises up to 92.1% against the 91.8% if all supertags of model J are used. However, the effect is not very noticeable, so that it would be almost certainly more useful to improve the supertagger itself rather than second-guess its output.

	Parsing accuracy	
Threshold	unlabeled	labeled
0%	91.8%	90.5%
20%	91.8%	90.4%
40%	91.9%	90.5%
50%	92.0%	90.7%
60%	92.1%	91.0%
80%	91.4%	90.0%
100%	89.6%	87.9%

TABLE 11.6 Parsing accuracy with empirically pruned supertag predictions.

11.5   Related Work

Supertagging was originally suggested (Joshi and Srinivas, 1994; Bangalore and Joshi, 1999) as a method to reduce the lexical ambiguity, and thereby the amount of disambiguation work done by the parser, in Lexicalized Tree-Adjoining Grammar. Sarkar et al. (2000) report that this increases the speed of their LTAG parser by a factor of 26 (from 548k to 21k seconds), but at the price of only being able to parse 59% of the sentences in their test data (of 2,250 sentences), because too often the correct supertag is missing from the output of the supertagger. Chen et al. (2002) investigate different supertagging methods as preprocessors to a Tree-Adjoining Grammar parser, and they claim a 1-best supertagging accuracy of 81.47%, and a 4-best accuracy of 91.41%. With the latter, they reach the highest parser coverage, about three quarters of the 1,700 sentences in their test data.

Clark and Curran (2004a) describe a combination of supertagger and parser for parsing Combinatory Categorial Grammar, where the tagger is used to filter the parses produced by the grammar, before the computation of the model parameters, and the parser uses an incremental method, where the supertagger first assigns a small number of categories to each word, and the parser requests more alternatives only if the analysis fails. They report 91.4% precision and 91.0% recall of unlabeled dependencies and a speed of 1.6 minutes to parse 2,401 sentences (Clark and Curran, 2004b). A speedup factor of 77 thanks to supertagging (Clark and Curran, 2004a) is claimed.

The supertagging approach that is closest to ours in terms of linguistic representations is probably Wang and Harper (2002) whose "Super Abstract Role Values" are very similar to our model F supertags (with direction, only obligatory dependents, with order; see table 11.2). It is interesting to note that they have a relatively low number of these SuperARVs: between 328 and 791 for different corpora, whereas we have 2026 category F supertags. Part of the explanation for this difference is that we use a larger set of labels: 35 (the same as the number of model A supertags; see table 11.2) whereas they have 24 (White, 2000, :50). Also, we are not using the same corpus data. In addition to determining the optimal sequence of SuperARVs in a separate procedure, Wang and Harper (2002) also combine the SuperARV n-gram probabilities with a dependency assignment probability into a dependency parser for English. A maximum tagging accuracy of 96.3% (for sentences up to 100 words) is achieved using a 4-gram n-best tagger producing the 100 best SuperARV sequences for a sentence. The tightly integrated model is able to determine 96.6% of SuperARVs correctly. The parser itself reaches a labeled precision of 92.6% and a labeled recall of 92.2% (Wang and Harper, 2004).

In general, the effect of supertagging in the other systems mentioned here is to reduce the ambiguity in the input to the parser and thereby increase its speed, in some cases dramatically. For us, supertagging decreases the speed slightly (because the heuristic search is driven by constraint violations, additional constraints tend to lead to more search steps being made). On the other hand, it gives us better parsing accuracy. Using a constraint penalty of 0.0 for the supertagger integration (see table 11.5) does speed up our parser several times, but would only be practical with very high tagging accuracy. An important point is that for some other systems, like Sarkar et al. (2000) and Chen et al. (2002), parsing is not actually feasible without the supertagging speedup.

Using the supertagging predictor as one of several prediction components a hybrid system for parsing unrestricted German text has been implemented that achieves a competitive parsing accuracy (Foth and Menzel, 2006). Although parsing results for German have been published a number of times, a direct comparison is difficult for a number of reasons, in particular if different syntactic representations are used. For phrase structure parsing, the state of the art is defined by the probabilistic parser of Dubey (2005) who combined treebank transformation techniques with a suffix analysis, and reached a labeled F-score of 76.3% for a subset of the sentences used here (and elsewhere), but with a maximum length of 40 words.

For dependency parsing, a labeled accuracy of 87.34% and an unlabeled one of 90.38% has been achieved by applying the dependency parser described in McDonald et al. (2005) to German data.[2] This system is based on a procedure for online large margin learning and considers a huge number of locally available features, which allows it to determine the optimal attachment fully deterministically. Despite the fact that a similar source of text has been used for this evaluation (newspaper), even those numbers cannot be directly compared to our results, since both the test set and the annotation guidelines differ from the ones used in our experiments and the parsing task has been defined in a slightly different way.

11.6   Conclusions and future work

We have shown that a statistical supertagging component can significantly improve the parsing accuracy of a general-purpose dependency parser for German. The error rate among syntactic attachments can be reduced by 24% over an already competitive baseline. Although the statistical model is rather simple-minded, it clearly captures at least some distributional characteristics of German text that the handwritten rules do not.

A crucial factor for success is the defeasible integration of the supertagging predictions via soft constraints. Rather than pursue a strict filtering approach where supertagging errors are partially compensated by an n-best selection, we commit to only one supertag per word but reduce its influence. Treating supertag predictions as weak preferences yields the best results.

Of the investigated supertag models, the ones that express the most complex local context proved to guide the parser best, although their own accuracy is not the best one, even when measured by the more pertinent component accuracy. Since purely statistical parsing methods do not reach comparable parsing accuracy on the same data, we assume that this trend does not continue indefinitely but would stop at some point, perhaps already reached by us.

The simple-minded approach to supertagging suggests that a better-written supertagger could aid parsing even more. Control experiments with simulated supertags confirm that there is almost no limit to the benefit that complex supertags can provide to this parser as they get better. As an alternative, the accuracy of label, direction, and context predictions implied by the output of the real supertagger could be measured separately, and correspondingly different weights could be assigned to the six new constraints, in order to attune the integration better to the strengths and weaknesses of supertagging.

It remains to be investigated whether a model of supertags can be found that usefully captures even more local context to help the parser further. It is also possible that even better results could be achieved through judicious multisupertagging. In such an approach, different supertags for the same word have to be amalgamated into more general constraints that allow all alternative configurations. Such an approach would be particularly useful if it could compensate supertagger errors enough so that the supertagging constraints can be made hard, since this is the only configuration that holds promise for improving the speed as well as the accuracy of parsing.

Notes

1. The model of German used here considers the objects of verbs, prepositions, and conjunctions to be obligatory and most other relations as optional. This corresponds closely to the set of needs roles of Wang and Harper (2002).

2. See http://nextens.uvt.nl/~conll.

References

Bangalore, S. and Joshi, A. K. (1999). Supertagging: an approach to almost parsing. *Computational Linguistics*, 25(2):237–265.

Brants, S., Dipper, S., Hansen, S., Lezius, W., and Smith, G. (2002). The TIGER treebank. In *Proceedings of the Workshop on Treebanks and Linguistic Theories*, Sozopol.

Brants, T. (2000). TnT — a statistical part-of-speech tagger. In *Proceedings of the 6th Applied NLP Conference, ANLP-2000*.

Brants, T., Hendriks, R., Kramp, S., Krenn, B., Preis, C., Skut, W., and Uszkoreit, H. (1997). Das NEGRA-Annotationsschema. Negra project report, Universität des Saarlandes, Computerlinguistik, Saarbrücken, Germany.

Chen, J., Bangalore, S., Collins, M., and Rambow, O. (2002). Reranking an N-gram supertagger. In *Proceedings of the Sixth International Workshop on Tree Adjoining Grammar and Related Frameworks*.

Clark, S. and Curran, J. R. (2004a). The importance of supertagging for wide-coverage CCG parsing. In *Proceedings of the 20th International Conference on Computational Linguistics*.

Clark, S. and Curran, J. R. (2004b). Parsing the WSJ using CCG and log-linear models. In *Proceedings of the 42nd Meeting of the Association for Computational Linguistics*.

Daum, M., Foth, K. A., and Menzel, W. (2003). Constraint based integration of deep and shallow parsing techniques. In *Proc. 11th Conference of the European Chapter of the ACL*, Budapest, Hungary.

Daum, M., Foth, K. A., and Menzel, W. (2004). Automatic transformation of phrase treebanks to dependency trees. In *Proc. 4th Int. Conf. on Language Resources and Evaluation*, Lisbon, Portugal, pages 99–106.

Dubey, A. (2005). What to do when lexicalization fails: parsing German with suffix analysis and smoothing. In *Proc. 43rd Annual Meeting of the ACL*, Ann Arbor, MI.

Dubey, A. and Keller, F. (2003). Probabilistic parsing for German using sister-head dependencies. In *Proc. 41st Annual Meeting of the Association of Computational Linguistics, ACL-2003*, Sapporo, Japan, pages 96–103.

Foth, K. A., By, T., and Menzel, W. (2006). Guiding a constraint dependency parser with supertags. In *Proc. 21st Int. Conf. on Computational Linguistics, Coling-ACL-2006*, Sydney.

Foth, K. A., Daum, M., and Menzel, W. (2004). A broad-coverage parser for German based on defeasible constraints. In *KONVENS 2004, Beiträge zur 7. Konferenz zur Verarbeitung natürlicher Sprache*, Vienna, Austria, pages 45–52.

Foth, K. A. and Hagenström, J. (2002). Tagging for robust parsers. In *2nd Workshop on Robust Methods in Analysis of Natural Language Data, ROMAND2002*, Frascati, Italy, pages 21–32.

Foth, K. A. and Menzel, W. (2006). Hybrid parsing. In *Proc. 21st Int. Conf. on Computational Linguistics, Coling-ACL-2006*, Sydney.

Joshi, A. K. and Srinivas, B. (1994). Disambiguation of super parts of speech (or supertags): Almost parsing. In *Proceedings of the 15th International Conference on Computational Linguistics*.

McDonald, R., Pereira, F., Ribarov, K., and Hajic, J. (2005). Non-projective dependency parsing using spanning tree algorithms. In *Proc. Human Language Technology Conference / Conference on Empirical Methods in Natural Language Processing, HLT/EMNLP-2005*, Vancouver, BC.

Nasr, A. and Rambow, O. (2004). A simple string-rewriting formalism for dependency grammar. In Kruijff, G.-J. M. and Duchier, D., eds., *COLING 2004 Recent Advances in Dependency Grammar*, Geneva, Switzerland, pages 17–24.

Sarkar, A., Xia, F., and Joshi, A. K. (2000). Some experiments on indicators of parsing complexity for lexicalized grammars. In *Proceedings of the COLING Workshop on Efficiency in Large-Scale Parsing Systems*.

Schabes, Y. and Joshi, A. K. (1991). Parsing with lexicalized tree adjoining grammar. In Tomita, M., ed., *Current Issues in Parsing Technologies*. Kluwer Academic.

Schiehlen, M. (2004). Annotation strategies for probabilistic parsing in german. In *Proc. 20th International Conference on Computational Linguistics, COLING 2004*, Geneva, Switzerland, pages 390–396.

Schröder, I., Menzel, W., Foth, K. A., and Schulz, M. (2000). Modeling dependency grammar with restricted constraints. *Traitement Automatique des Langues (T.A.L.)*, 41(1):97–126.

Wang, W. and Harper, M. P. (2002). The SuperARV language model: Investigating the effectiveness of tightly integrating multiple knowledge sources. In *Proc. Conf. on Empirical Methods in Natural Language Processing, EMNLP-2002*, Philadelphia, pages 238–247.

Wang, W. and Harper, M. P. (2004). A Statistical Constraint Dependency Grammar (CDG) Parser. In Keller, F., Clark, S., Crocker, M., and Steedman, M., eds., *Proceedings of the ACL Workshop Incremental Parsing: Bringing Engineering and Cognition Together*, Barcelona, Spain, Association for Computational Linguistics, pages 42–49.

White, C. M. (2000). *Rapid Grammar Development and Parsing: Constraint Dependency Grammar with Abstract Role Values*. PhD thesis, Purdue University.

Extraction of Type-Logical Supertags from the Spoken Dutch Corpus

Richard Moot

12.1 Introduction

The Spoken Dutch Corpus assigns 1 million of its 9 million total words a syntactic annotation in the form of dependency graphs. We will look at strategies for automatically extracting a lexicon of type-logical supertags from these dependency graphs and investigate how different levels of lexical detail affect the size of the resulting lexicon as well as the performance with respect to supertag disambiguation.

12.2 Type-Logical Grammars

Combinatory categorial grammars and type-logical grammars extend the simple but very limited AB grammars (Ajdukiewicz, 1935; Bar-Hillel, 1964) in different ways. Whereas CCGs (Steedman, 2001) choose to add combinators allowing types to combine in more flexible ways, type-logical grammars, as pioneered by Lambek (1958) and further developed by — among many others — Morrill (1994), Moortgat and Oehrle (1994) choose to extend the system to a full logic. That is, they add to the AB calculus, which contains only rules telling us how to *use* complex formulas, the symmetric rules of *proof* which allow us to show we can derive a complex formula from an expression.

My introduction to type-logical grammars in this section will be necessarily brief, but I hope it will be enough for the reader to understand the applications in the following sections.

12.2.1 The nonassociative Lambek calculus

We will start by looking at the nonassociative Lambek calculus, NL (Lambek, 1961). Formulas in this calculus are either atomic formulas, from a fixed set determined by the grammar — for example, we typically find np for noun phrase, n for common noun and s for sentence — or complex formulas. If A and B are formulas, then

- $B\backslash A$ (B under A) is a formula looking to its left for a B formula to give an A as a result; an example would be $np\backslash s$ for an intransitive verb, which looks for a subject np to its left to form a sentence,

- A/B (A over B) is a formula looking to its right for a B formula to give an A as a result; an example would be np/n for a determiner, which looks for a common noun to its right to form a noun phrase or $(np\backslash s)/np$ for a transitive verb, which looks to the right for an object np to form an intransitive verb.

- finally, we have $A \bullet B$ (A and B), which is simply an expression of type A next to an expression of type B.

Note that we follow Lambek's notation where the result category is always above the slash and the argument below it.

A *statement* is a pair of the form $X \vdash A$, where X is a non-empty, binary branching tree with words as its leaves and where A is a formula. It states that we have shown X to be an expression of type A.

To save space, we will usually write the tree X in flat notation, using an infix operator "∘". In this notation, the tree

will be written as ('*t ∘ eten*) ∘ (*is ∘ koud*).

A *lexicon* is a set of statements which assign formulas to single words. A Dutch example, with English translations for the words, is given in table 12.1.

'*t* $\vdash np/n$	the
eten $\vdash n$	food
is $\vdash (np\backslash s)/(n/n)$	is
koud $\vdash n/n$	cold

TABLE 12.1 Example lexicon

The rules of NL, which allow us to combine these lexical statements into derivations, are given in table 12.2.

A simple consequence of these rules is that type-lifting is now derivable: if X is an expression of type B it is necessarily also an expression of type $A/(B\backslash A)$. Figure 12.1 shows a proof of this.

$$\frac{X \vdash A \bullet B \quad \begin{matrix} \mathrm{x} \vdash A \quad \mathrm{y} \vdash B \\ \vdots \\ Z[\mathrm{x} \circ \mathrm{y}] \vdash C \end{matrix}}{Z[X] \vdash C}\,[\bullet E] \qquad \frac{X \vdash A \quad Y \vdash B}{X \circ Y \vdash A \bullet B}\,[\bullet I]$$

$$\frac{X \vdash A/B \quad Y \vdash B}{X \circ Y \vdash A}\,[/E] \qquad \frac{\begin{matrix} \mathrm{x} \vdash B \\ \vdots \\ X \circ \mathrm{x} \vdash A \end{matrix}}{X \vdash A/B}\,[/I]$$

$$\frac{Y \vdash B \quad X \vdash B\backslash A}{Y \circ X \vdash A}\,[\backslash E] \qquad \frac{\begin{matrix} \mathrm{x} \vdash B \\ \vdots \\ \mathrm{x} \circ X \vdash A \end{matrix}}{X \vdash B\backslash A}\,[\backslash I]$$

TABLE 12.2 Natural deduction rules for the nonassociative Lambek calculus NL

$$\cfrac{\cfrac{X \vdash B \quad \mathrm{x} \vdash B\backslash A}{X \circ \mathrm{x} \vdash A}\,[\backslash E]}{X \vdash A/(B\backslash A)}\,[/I]$$

FIGURE 12.1 General derivability of lifting

12.2.2   Multimodal extensions

Because NL generates only context free languages, it is inadequate as a formalism for linguistic analysis. In this section we will look at some refinements of the calculus that allow it to expand its expressiveness without losing its essential logical nature. Moortgat (1997) gives a modern and more detailed description of these extensions.

Unary modalities

As a first extension, we no longer require the trees on the left-hand side of a statement to be binary branching. If we add the possibility of unary branching as well as different *modes i* of unary branching, indicated on the flat term as $\langle X \rangle^i$, we are led — by analogy to the binary rules — to the rules shown in table 12.3. Kurtonina and Moortgat (1997) provide a good introduction to these unary modalities and give several interesting applications.

$$\frac{X \vdash \Diamond_i A \quad Z[\langle \mathrm{x} \rangle^i] \vdash C}{Z[X] \vdash C} \; [\Diamond E] \qquad \frac{X \vdash A}{\langle X \rangle^i \vdash \Diamond_i A} \; [\Diamond I]$$

where the left premise has the subderivation
$$\begin{array}{c} \mathrm{x} \vdash A \\ \vdots \end{array}$$

$$\frac{X \vdash \Box_i^{\downarrow} A}{\langle X \rangle^i \vdash A} \; [\Box^{\downarrow} E] \qquad \frac{\langle X \rangle^i \vdash A}{X \vdash \Box_i^{\downarrow} A} \; [\Box^{\downarrow} I]$$

TABLE 12.3   Natural deduction rules for the unary modalities

One of the typical applications of the unary modalities is to use them to implement linguistic features. For example $\langle X \rangle^n$ could mean "I'm an X constituent but I carry nominative case," whereas $\langle X \rangle^a$ could mean "I'm an X constituent, but I carry accusative case." Note that a and n are simply used as mnemonics and we might just as well have use more abstract modes like 1 and 2 two distinguish between the two cases.

Let us look at the rules in table 12.3 with the intended implementation of features in mind. The $[\Box^{\downarrow} E]$ rule states that if structure X is of type $\Box_i^{\downarrow} A$ then $\langle X \rangle^i$ is of type A. The $[\Box^{\downarrow} E]$ rule *adds* feature information to a structure. Inversely, the $[\Box^{\downarrow} I]$ rule *verifies* if the antecedent structure has the proper form $\langle X \rangle^i$ and then *removes* this feature information.

The $[\Diamond I]$ rule states that if X is of type A then $\langle X \rangle^i$ is of type $\Diamond_i A$. Like the $[\Box^{\downarrow} E]$ rule, we add feature information to the previous structure. The final rule is perhaps the most difficult to explain; the $[\Diamond I]$ rule tell us what to do when we have derived a structure X to be of type $\Diamond_i A$. In order to remove this diamond formula, we start a subderivation using a structure x of type A demanding at the end of this subderivation that the variable x has the unary brackets $\langle \; \rangle^i$ around it. Finally, we continue the derivation replacing the structure $\langle x \rangle^i$ by X, that is, the structure we had computed for $\Diamond_i A$ before. In other words, we verify that an A constituent has the correct feature information, then remove this feature information and continue with a $\Diamond_i A$ constituent. This "check then remove" behavior is similar to the $[\Box^\downarrow I]$ rule.

Two useful derivability patterns are shown in figure 12.2. On the left we show that for every mode i and structure X of type A, this same structure is also of type $\Diamond_i \Box_i^\downarrow A$. Conversely, as shown on the right of the figure, if X is of type $\Diamond_i \Box_i^\downarrow A$, then it is also of type A.

$$\frac{\dfrac{X \vdash A}{\langle X \rangle^i \vdash \Diamond_i A}\,[\Diamond I]}{X \vdash \Box_i^\downarrow \Diamond_i A}\,[\Box^\downarrow I] \qquad \frac{X \vdash \Diamond_i \Box_i^\downarrow A \quad \dfrac{x \vdash \Box_i^\downarrow A}{\langle x \rangle^i \vdash A}\,[\Box^\downarrow E]}{X \vdash A}\,[\Diamond E]$$

FIGURE 12.2 Derivability patterns for the unary modalities

Table 12.4 shows how we can exploit these patterns when adding basic case information to the lexicon. Heylen (1999) gives a much more detailed treatment of feature information for categorial grammars. The personal pronouns, such as *hij* (he) and *hem* (him), are specified in the lexicon for nominative and accusative case respectively.

$$
\begin{aligned}
hij &\vdash \Box_n^\downarrow \Diamond_n np & &\text{he} \\
hem &\vdash \Box_a^\downarrow \Diamond_a np & &\text{him} \\
Vincent &\vdash np & &\text{Vincent} \\
Peru &\vdash np & &\text{Peru} \\
slaapt &\vdash \Box_n^\downarrow \Diamond_n np \backslash s & &\text{sleeps} \\
bezoekt &\vdash (\Box_n^\downarrow \Diamond_n np \backslash s)/\Box_a^\downarrow \Diamond_a np & &\text{visits}
\end{aligned}
$$

TABLE 12.4 Lexicon with basic case information

Since Dutch proper nouns do not change their form to indicate their case, we would prefer to assign them only a single form that is underspecified for case. But this is exactly what the standard np type allows us to do, given that we have just seen that any structure of type np is also a structure of type $\Box_n^\downarrow \Diamond_n np$ and a structure of type $\Box_a^\downarrow \Diamond_a np$. The resulting grammar correctly predicts that *hij bezoekt hem* is a grammatical sentence but that *hem bezoekt Peru* is not.

Structural Rules

By themselves, the unary modalities do not extend the generative capacity of type-logical grammars. A second extension, in the form of structural rules, allows us to do this. Adding structural rules to NL is not a new idea. For example, adding the structural rule of associativity to NL gives us an alternative formulation of the associative Lambek calculus L.

The advantage of a multimodal calculus is that rather than having structural rules apply *globally*, we can "anchor" them to specific modes, which in turn are obtained from the lexical types.

Consider for example a permutation mode p, which allows us to move constituents that have been lexically specified as being of type $\Diamond_p \Box_p^{\downarrow} A$. As we have seen in figure 12.2 on the right, such a constituent can play the role of an A when needed. However, the structural rules shown in figure 12.3 show us how we can move a constituent marked as $\langle X \rangle^p$ from one right branch in a tree to another. The rule MA, for "mixed associativity", takes an embedded x_3, which is a sister of the x_2 node and moves it upwards to be a sister of the node one level up, regrouping x_1 and x_2 together. It is an associativity rule since it only changes the grouping of the nodes but not their order. The rule MC, for "mixed commutativity" *does* change the order. Before application of the rule, the x_3 node is between the x_1 and x_2 nodes. After the rule, x_1 and x_2 are adjacent.

Observe that as long as the top of the binary tree has not been reached, exactly one of these two rules will apply, depending on whether the parent node of $\langle x_3 \rangle^p$ is on a left or a right branch.

We can use these structural rules to given an account of extraction in type-logical grammar. Let us look at the following examples.

(1)   *leest Proust Tsjechov ?*
      reads Proust Tsjechov ?

      "does Proust read Chekov?"

(2)   *wie leest Proust ?*
      who reads Proust ?

      ambiguous between "who reads Proust?" and "who does Proust read?"

If we were to assign *wie* the formula $wh/(s/np)$ in our lexicon, only the second reading would be available to us. However, if we would assign it the formula $wh/(s/\Diamond\Box^{\downarrow}np)$ it would say: I'm looking to my right for a sentence that is missing an np anywhere on a right branch to give a wh question. Figure 12.4 shows how this allows us to find both readings for this sentence.

The first reading simply uses the fact that a structure of type $\Diamond_p \Box_p^{\downarrow} np$ can be used as an np, after which we simply have an NL derivation. The second reading is more interesting, since it requires us to use the structural rule of mixed commutativity. The $[\Diamond E]$ and $[\Box^{\downarrow} E]$ rules introduce a constituent $\langle y \rangle^p$, our moving np. Combining this np with *leest* and *Proust* gives a configuration to which the mixed commutativity rule can be applied. We have the bottom left tree of figure 12.3 with $x_1 = leest$, $x_3 = y$ and $x_2 = Proust$. After this structural rule we can finish the $[\Diamond E]$ rule, replacing $\langle y \rangle^p$ by x, then conclude our derivation as we would in NL.

$$\frac{Z[X_1 \circ (X_2 \circ \langle X_3 \rangle^p) \vdash C}{Z[(X_1 \circ X_2) \circ \langle X_3 \rangle^p] \vdash C}\ [MA]$$

$$\frac{Z[(X_1 \circ \langle X_3 \rangle^p) \circ X_2] \vdash C}{Z[(X_1 \circ X_2) \circ \langle X_3 \rangle^p] \vdash C}\ [MC]$$

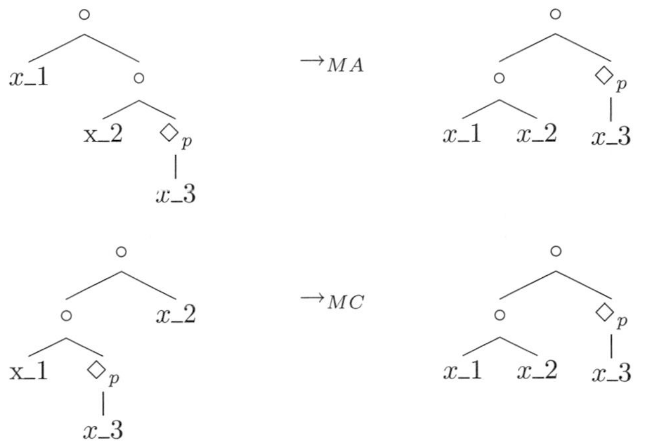

FIGURE 12.3 The structural rules of mixed associativity and mixed commutativity in flat representation and as tree rewrites

$$\dfrac{wie \vdash wh/(s/\Diamond_p\Box_p^{\downarrow}np) \qquad \dfrac{\dfrac{\dfrac{leest \vdash (s/np)/np \quad Proust \vdash np}{leest \circ Proust \vdash s/np}\,[/E] \qquad \dfrac{\mathrm{x} \vdash \Diamond_p\Box_p^{\downarrow}np \quad \dfrac{\mathrm{y} \vdash \Box_p^{\downarrow}np}{\langle \mathrm{y} \rangle^p \vdash np}\,[\Box^{\downarrow}E]}{\mathrm{x} \vdash np}\,[\Diamond E]}{(leest \circ Proust) \circ \mathrm{x} \vdash s}\,[/E]}{leest \circ Proust \vdash s/\Diamond_p\Box_p^{\downarrow}np}\,[/I]}{wie \circ (leest \circ Proust) \vdash wh}\,[/E]$$

$$\dfrac{wie \vdash wh/(s/\Diamond_p\Box_p^{\downarrow}np) \qquad \dfrac{\dfrac{\mathrm{x} \vdash \Diamond_p\Box_p^{\downarrow}np \qquad \dfrac{\dfrac{\dfrac{leest \vdash (s/np)/np \quad \dfrac{\mathrm{y} \vdash \Box_p^{\downarrow}np}{\langle \mathrm{y} \rangle^p \vdash np}\,[\Box^{\downarrow}E]}{leest \circ \langle \mathrm{y} \rangle^p \vdash s/np}\,[/E] \quad Proust \vdash np}{(leest \circ \langle \mathrm{y} \rangle^p) \circ Proust \vdash s}\,[/E]}{(leest \circ Proust) \circ \langle \mathrm{y} \rangle^p \vdash s}\,[MC]}{(leest \circ Proust) \circ \mathrm{x} \vdash s}\,[\Diamond E]}{leest \circ Proust \vdash s/\Diamond_p\Box_p^{\downarrow}np}\,[/I]}{wie \circ (leest \circ Proust) \vdash wh}\,[/E]$$

FIGURE 12.4 Two derivations for the ambiguous sentence “wie leest Proust”

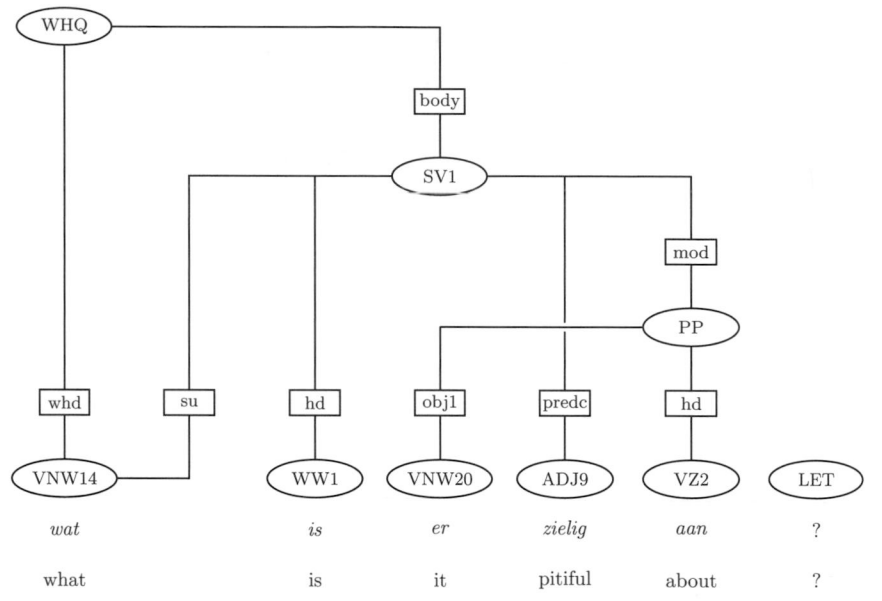

FIGURE 12.5 What is pitiful about it?

Adding unary modalities and structural rules gives us a flexible logic, able to handle the harsh reality of linguistic phenomena, to which we will now turn.

12.3   Treebank Extraction

In this section, I will show how to generate a type-logical treebank from the syntactic annotation files of the Spoken Dutch Corpus and some methods for reducing the size of the generated lexicon.

12.3.1   Syntactic annotation for the spoken Dutch corpus

The Spoken Dutch Corpus (Corpus Gesproken Nederlands, or CGN) contains 9 million words of contemporary spoken Dutch with various forms of linguistic annotation. Orthographic transcription and part-of-speech tagging have been provided for all 9 million words. A core corpus of 1 million word has, in addition, been provided with a syntactic annotation in the form of dependency graphs.

For the CGN syntactic annotation, the annotation tools developed for the German NEGRA Corpus (Brants, 1999) have been used to produce semiautomatically syntactic annotation graphs of the form shown in figure 12.5.

I will briefly discuss some properties of these annotation graphs. More details on the annotation format and philosophy can be found in Hoekstra et al. (2002).

The annotation graphs are directed, acyclic graphs, where every leaf is labeled with a part-of-speech tag (such as WW1 for a singular, inflected verb) and all other vertices are labeled with a grammatical constituent (such as SV1 for a verb-initial sentence). Edges are labeled with a dependency relations (such as *hd* for head and *obj1* for a direct object).

The POS tags used for the syntactic annotation are a simplification of the morphologically richer tags that have been used for POS tagging the Spoken Dutch Corpus. The WW1 tag for the verb, for example, is a simplification of the T301 tag, which also indicates the verb is in present tense and does not end with the *t* suffix for verb inflection.

Some other properties are:

- Annotation structures are flat. A new node is only introduced when necessitated by a lexical head. This means, for example, that we have no separate *vp* nodes.
- We can have multiple dependencies, sometimes called "secondary edges". These are used both for the treatment of ellipsis and for long-distance dependencies. In the example, we have a long-distance dependency, where VNW14 (*wat*) is both the head of the *wh* phrase and the subject of the verb-initial sentence.
- Constituents can be discontinuous. For example, *er aan* is a PP in the example sentence, even though the ADJ9 (*zielig*) is positioned between these two words.
- Annotation graphs are allowed to be disconnected. In our example the LET constituent is an isolated vertex.

12.3.2   Preprocessing

Given that we are using a spoken corpus, we have to deal with a number of artifacts which would not normally be present in written language. Words indicating speaker hesitation, such as "uh," for example, occur frequently and are almost never assigned a grammatical function. They appear as isolated vertices in the annotation graph. Some annotators choose to give them a role in incomplete phrases, but this is relatively rare (192 out of 23,289 occurrences). The same can be said for interpunction marks, which, as shown in figure 12.5, are generally annotated as an isolated LET vertex. Only 634 out of 114,221 occurrences are assigned a grammatical function. Figure 12.6 shows an example.

To prevent these "easy" word categories from giving a too-flattering impression of the performance of the supertagger, I cleaned up the data, filtering out all isolated vertices, including hesitation marks and interpunction symbols but also partial repeats (see 3, where *het/'t is* occurs twice) and self-corrections, as in 4 where the speaker corrects the gender of the article he is using.

(3)   *ja*   het is 't is nog wel   erger   geweest ...
      yes it   is it is still even worse been   ...

      "yes, still it has been even worse ..."

(4)   ... dat 't   de   huidige regelgeving ...
      ... that the-NEU the-MSC/FEM current legislation   ...

      ... "that the current legislation"

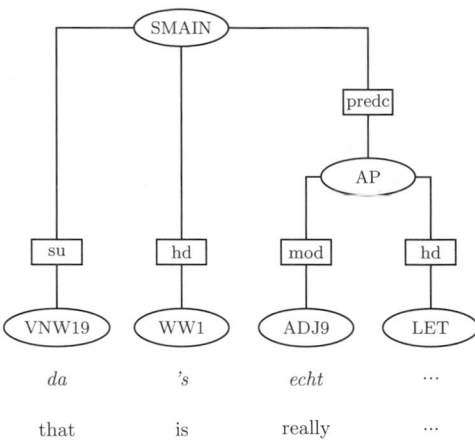

FIGURE 12.6 Incomplete phrase with grammatical role for an interpunction symbol

In cases like these, the first occurrences of the repeated or corrected words are usually not assigned a grammatical role.

Removing all these isolated vertices gives a filtered corpus contains 87,404 sentences (out of 114,801, most of the removed sentences being single-word utterances like "yes") and 794,872 words (out of 1,002,098).

We will look a way of filtering the corpus without looking at the syntactic annotation in section 12.4.4.

12.3.3   Extraction algorithm

The algorithm used for extracting a treebank is essentially the one proposed in Moortgat and Moot (2002), which is parametric for three functions:

1. a function from vertex labels (or ⟨*vertex label, edge label*⟩ pairs) to formulas,
2. a function identifying the head of every grammatical constituent,
3. a function identifying the modifiers of every grammatical constituent.

We will discuss different functions assigning formulas to vertex labels, since this has a great influence on the number of different lexical entries we extract. The other two functions have been kept constant.

The current implementation identifies the functor from a set of daughters by their edge labels using a list in order of preference. For most vertex labels this will just be *hd*, but, because the algorithm requires finding a head for every syntactic category, there are typically some strange items further down the list to make sure we can find a head even for incomplete utterances.

The function identifying modifiers marks only constituents with edge label *mod* as modifier for most syntactic categories. Siblings of the head that are not modifiers will be its arguments.

The algorithm operates by performing a basic depth-first search from the different root nodes of a corpus graph assigning a *primary* formula f to every node in the graph as well as a list $g_1, \ldots, g_n$ of *secondary* formulas. The list of secondary formulas is necessary for nodes with multiple parents and will contain a formula for each additional parent of the node, that is, every node will have one formula for every role if fulfills in the syntactic structure. The corresponding formula is $(\ldots (f \bullet \Diamond_p \Box_p^\downarrow g_1) \ldots \bullet \Diamond_p \Box_p^\downarrow g_n)$. For most nodes, however, this list will be empty, and the primary formula f will directly correspond to the assigned type.

To divide an annotation graph into lexical formulas for all words in it, we begin by finding all root nodes in the annotation graph and looking up the corresponding formula f in the table. We determine for each of the children if they are the unique head, a modifier or an argument. We descend the modifiers assigning their vertex f/f or $f\backslash f$, depending on their position with respect to the head. For the arguments, we look up the corresponding formulas $a_1, \ldots, a_n$ in the table and assign it to their vertex. Finally, the head child will be assigned the complex formula

$$(a_i \backslash \ldots (a_1 \backslash ((f/a_n) \ldots /a_{i+1}))),$$

which first selects the arguments $a_{i+1}, \ldots, a_n$ to the right of it then the arguments $a_1, \ldots, a_i$, to its left. When we arrive at a node via a secondary edge we append the formula to the list of secondary formulas.

In every case, after assigning a type to a vertex we will descend recursively until we reach the leaves, in which case the formula will be added to the lexicon for that word.

The operation of the algorithm is perhaps most clearly demonstrated by an example. If our vertex label to formula mapping assigns *wh* to WHQ and *s* to SV1 and we make, like the CGN annotation, the choice of *whd* as head of a *wh* question then, returning to figure 12.5, we are compelled to assign the formula *s* to the SV1 and *wh/s* to the VNW14 node, as shown in figure 12.7.

Now it is the turn of the SV1 node to be split. It has four children, the WW1, reached by the *hd* label, being the head and the PP, reached by the *mod* label, a modifier. Because it is to the right of the head, it will be assigned the modifier category $s\backslash s$. The other two children are arguments and we look up the formulas that correspond to them: *np* for VNW14 and *ap* for ADJ9. Therefore, the formula assigned to the verb will be $(s/ap)/np$.

Because we now arrive at the relative pronoun via a secondary edge, we add an *np* formula to the list of secondary formulas. As shown in the figure, this corresponds to assigning it the formula $(wh/s) \bullet \Diamond \Box^\downarrow np$.

There is only one nonterminal left to be split, which is the PP node. We have the preposition VZ2 as its head and the pronoun VNW20 as its argument. Again, the type for the argument is *np*, so the type for the head will be $np\backslash(s\backslash s)$.

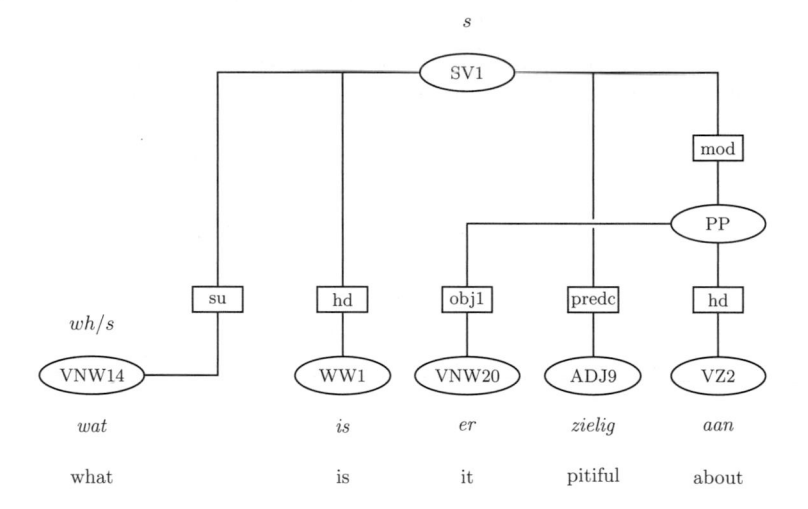

FIGURE 12.7 Lexicon extraction: removing the WHQ node

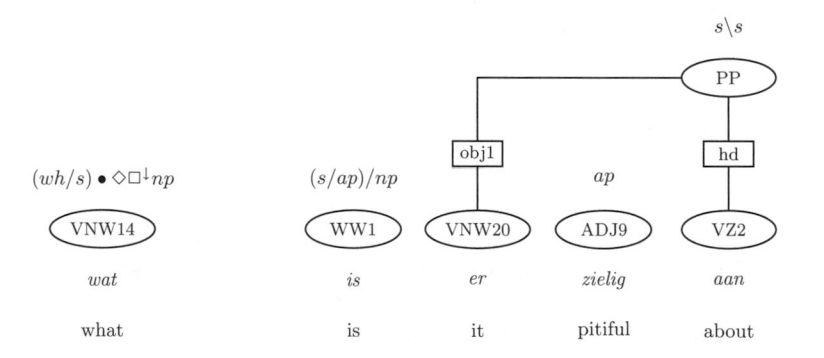

FIGURE 12.8 Lexicon extraction: removing the SV1 node

The final extracted lexicon is shown in figure 12.9. We note that if we specialize the product type for *wat*, we will produce the type $wh/(s/\diamond\square^{\downarrow}np)$ which is identical to the one proposed for the manually generated lexicon of table 12.5.

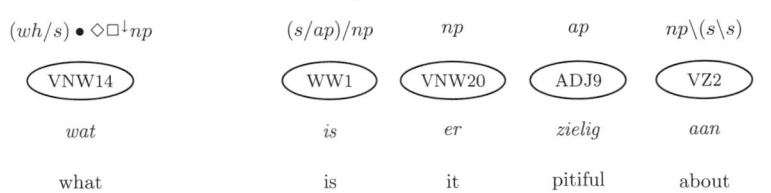

FIGURE 12.9 Final lexicon

$$
\begin{aligned}
wie &\vdash wh/(s/\diamond_p\square^{\downarrow}_p np) &&\text{who} \\
leest &\vdash (s/np)/np &&\text{reads (interrogative)} \\
Proust &\vdash np &&\text{Proust} \\
Tsjechov &\vdash np &&\text{Chekov}
\end{aligned}
$$

TABLE 12.5 Lexicon for the treatment of *wh* questions in Dutch

The algorithm for corpus extraction only exploits the fact that we have a dependency-based annotation. Given the three functions we discussed at the beginning of this section, we could directly use the current algorithm to extract a type-logical grammar from other corpora employing dependency structures for their annotation format, such as the French TALANA treebank (Abeillé et al., 2000), the German TIGER treebank (Brants et al., 2002), and the Prague dependency treebank (Hajic, 1998).

12.3.4 Refinement

Some of the vertex labels of the Spoken Dutch Corpus, like DU (discourse unit), CONJ (conjunction), LIST and MWU (merged word unit, a category assigned to multi-word names and fixed expressions) are not really grammatical categories.

An example of a discourse unit is shown in figure 12.10. Often it is just an ordinary sentence introduced by a tag like "yes" or (as in the example) "no" or an element linking it to the previous sentence like "and". Examples of the other categories are shown in the following.

(5) *wij hadden nog* [*meetkunde en   algebra*]$_{CONJ}$
     we had   still [geometry   and algebra]$_{CONJ}$

     "we still had geometry and algebra"

(6) *koffie* [*geen melk geen suiker*]$_{LIST}$
     coffee [no   milk no   sugar]$_{LIST}$

"coffee, no milk, no sugar"

(7) [*boulimia   nervosa*]$_{MWU}$ *heet 't*
     [boulimia   nervosa]$_{MWU}$ called it

"it is called boulimia nervosa"

Rather than use a type *conj* or *list* in the lexicon, we give a conjunction the type of it first conjoint and a list the type of its first list item. A discourse unit is assigned the type of its nucleus, if there is one, and the type of its first discourse element otherwise. We simply assign *np* to merged-word units.

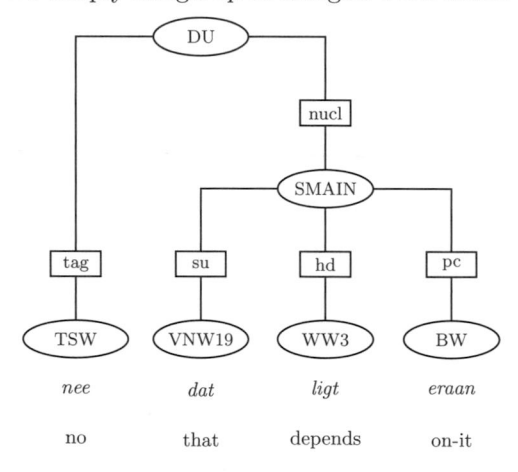

FIGURE 12.10 Discourse unit

12.4   Supertagging

Now that we have a generic method of extracting supertags from the Spoken Dutch Corpus, it is time to extract different grammars and evaluate the size of the lexicon as well as the performance of supertag disambiguation for these lexicons.

12.4.1   The extracted grammars

The most basic way of applying the algorithm of the previous section is simply to keep syntactic categories of the CGN annotation (22 in total when we exclude DU, CONJ, LIST, and MWU) and map the part-of-speech tags of the leaves to these categories (adjectives to AP, pronouns to NP, and so on). This leaves us with a rather large lexicon, the *basic* treebank, containing 6,817 different formulas.

To reduce the size of the lexicon, we have merged a number of these formulas: no longer distinguishing between the different sentence types SMAIN (declarative sentence, which is verb second), SV1 (interrogative sentence, with the verb first), and SSUB (subordinate clause, with the verb last) and mapping them all simply to *s*. Though we can still determine the sentence type from the directionality of the implications, this will make a big difference for the sentence modifiers, which now no longer need to distinguish between the different sentence types. Other changes include mapping AP to noun modifier. This reduces the size of the lexicon to 3,539, giving us the *compact* treebank.

Another simplification is obtained by removing external discourse unit nodes. This removes the need to analyze a discourse unit containing several different parts, which are often elliptical or only loosely related like 8, 9, or 10, where any decision as to what would be modifiers, arguments or head would be rather artificial.

(8)   *deze* onderaan   hier
       this at the bottom here

       "this one at the bottom here"

(9)   *mama* dronken
       mother drunk

       "mother (is) drunk"

(10)   *positief* tenzij
       positive unless

       "I am of positive opinion, unless ..."

The resulting *split* treebank contains 2,201 lexical entries.

For comparison, I added three other strategies to reduce the size of this treebank. While these grammars will provide much coarser linguistic descriptions, it is perhaps useful to look at the effect of the reduced lexicon size on the performance of the supertagger.

- The first collapses even more lexical categories than before, by for example replacing the *pp* category by $s \backslash s$, which causes a preposition that modifies a verb to have the same type as a preposition which is the argument of the verb, with only the verb type differing in the two cases. This is the *very compact* treebank, containing 1,962 entries.
- The second removes all multiple dependencies from the grammar. This makes the grammar a simple AB grammar, needing only elimination rules to find a derivation. This is useful if we are interested in parsing the supertagged sentence afterwards, given that we can use chart parsing techniques for these grammars. The *AB* treebank contains 1,761 lexical formulas.
- The third removes all directionality from the implications, making it a grammar for the Lambek-van Benthem calculus LP. For example, it no longer distinguishes between verbs in initial, second or final position. If we are interested only in the semantic type, however, this information would suffice. The *LP* treebank is the smallest we will consider, containing 1,137 formulas.

Other strategies for extracting type-logical grammars from structured data and reducing the size of the lexicon exist. Buszkowski and Penn (1990) propose a strategy for learning AB grammars from structures and using unification of type variables to reduce the lexical ambiguity. An advantage of this method is that it can be used to find the optimal way of mapping vertex labels to formulas. Unfortunately, the algorithm for finding this mapping is exponential, and therefore the current choice of requiring the extraction algorithm to know the formulas corresponding to the different labels seems more practical, giving us an algorithm for extracting our grammars in time linear to the size of the corpus.

Moortgat (2001) proposes a strategy for reducing the lexical ambiguity for automatically extracted grammars by introducing modal operators and structural reasoning to replace different lexical type assignments by a single one that is at least as general as the types it replaces. If we can avoid overgeneralisation, this would allow us to reduce our treebank to a corpus of a size that would ideally be comparable to the LP treebank without collapsing to full commutativity. This seems challenging to achieve, however.

12.4.2   Experiments and results

All experiments have used the 72 part-of-speech tags instead of the 324 morphology tags, which contain too detailed morphology information, actually hindering performance because of the resulting data sparseness. The single exception is the SPEC (special) tag, which we split into the seven different versions used by the morphology tagger, giving us a total of 78 part-of-speech tags for our experiments. The choice to split up the special tags was made because it comprises words in different groups like: inaudible, broken off, foreign, part-of-whole (as in multiword proper names) and background noise.

We have trained our models using a supertagger based on the Edinburgh maximum entropy tools, making a decision for the lexical formula of the words based on:

- the current word and POS tags, as well the two previous/following words and POS tags

- the previous two supertags.

Only features which were seen 5 times or more in the training data have been selected for training.

All models were trained using 100 iterations on 69,923 sentences of the filtered corpus (635,764 words), whereas the other 17,480 sentences (159,086 words, every fifth sentence of the corpus) were kept for testing the performance.

Table 12.6 summarizes the results for the different corpora.

The Split corpus assigns lexical formulas which are closest to those provided by a manually generated lexicon and offers a good compromise between performance and descriptive adequacy. Compared to the Compact corpus, which differs only in that it does not split up root discourse unit nodes, there is a big improvement both in lexicon size and performance.

	Experiment	Formulas	Result
1	Basic	6,817	70.61%
2	Compact	3,539	72.06%
3	Split	2,201	77.13%
4	Very compact	1,962	77.83%
5	AB	1,761	77.52%
6	LP	1,137	80.50%

TABLE 12.6 Combined results of the different extraction procedures

The AB corpus, in spite of its reduced lexicon size, actually performs worse than the Very Compact corpus, presumably because not treating the secondary edges forces us to assign unusual types to verbs.

The LP corpus has the best performance, both in lexicon size and in correct supertag assignments, though at the price of a significant loss in the information the supertags provide.

12.4.3   Analysis of the extracted lexicon

To give a better idea of the form of the extracted lexicon, I will now discuss some of the frequently occurring verb forms as well as the most frequent product types which are extracted in the case of multiple dependencies. All discussion in this section will be about the Split treebank.

Table 12.7 lists the supertags that have been extracted more than 1,000 times for finite, singular verbs, together with the percentage of the total extracted verb forms these formulas account for. So, the nine formulas shown in the table, when taken together, account for 72.09% of the total verbs forms.

	Formula	Occurrences	Total Coverage
1	$(np\backslash s)/(np\backslash s)$	9,487	14.66%
2	$(np\backslash s)/np$	9,401	29.18%
3	$np\backslash s$	7,187	40.28%
4	$(s/(np\backslash s))/np$	6,019	49.58%
5	s/np	4,698	56.84%
6	$(np\backslash s)/(np/np)$	3,893	62.85%
7	$(s/np)/np$	3,050	67.57%
8	$np\backslash(np\backslash s)$	1,660	70.07%
9	$(s/(np/np))/np$	1,268	72.09%

TABLE 12.7 All supertags that have been extracted more than 1,000 times for finite verbs

The type assigned to auxiliaries $(np\backslash s)/(np\backslash s)$ is the most frequent, closely followed by the type for transitive verb with the verb occurring in second position,

Word	Transl.	Freq.	# st	Most Frequent
's	is	1,919	42	$(np\backslash s)/(np/np)$
ben	am	1,474	90	$(np\backslash s)/(np\backslash s)$
denk	think	1,851	61	$(np\backslash s)/s$
had	had	2,104	112	$(np\backslash s)/(np\backslash s)$
heb	have	4,049	126	$(np\backslash s)/(np\backslash s)$
is	is	14,212	313	$(np\backslash s)/np$
kan	can	2,731	93	$(np\backslash s)/(np\backslash s)$
moet	has to	3,340	91	$(np\backslash s)/(np\backslash s)$
vind	find	1,353	82	$((np\backslash s)/(np/np))/np$
was	was	4,467	176	$(np\backslash s)/np$
weet	know	2,362	78	$(np\backslash s)/np$
wil	want	1,137	65	$(np\backslash s)/(np\backslash s)$
zeg	say	1,095	61	s
zit	sit	1,018	62	$np\backslash s$
zou	would	1,688	57	$(np\backslash s)/(np\backslash s)$

TABLE 12.8 All verb forms occurring more than 1,000 times

as it will in a nontopicalized declarative sentence. In total, there are 724 different supertags assigned to these verbs, though only 396 are assigned more than once.

As can be seen from the formulas in the table, the types assigned are quite construction-specific, as they would be in an extracted LTAG grammar. For example, several frequently occurring type differ only in the order of the arguments. For intransitive verbs, we see both s/np and $np\backslash s$, and for transitive verbs we see all three possibilities: verb-initial $(s/np)/np$, verb-second $(np\backslash s)/np$, and verb-final $np\backslash(np\backslash s)$. Even the type $(s/(np\backslash s))/np$ is just the sentence-initial version of the standard auxiliary verb type. While it seems we can gain something using a unique type in these cases and derive the other possibilities using structural rules, the improvement in supertag performance is relatively small, with less than one percent improvement in the number of supertags that are correctly assigned to verbs. Apparently, the trigrams give us enough context to decide on the proper direction of the arguments of verbs and, given that this information is useful for parsing, I have decided not to collapse types which differ only in the direction of the arguments.

Table 12.8 lists all singular, declarative verb forms which occur more than 1,000 times, together with the number of supertags with which they have been found as well as indicating the most common one. Unsurprisingly, forms of "be", "have", and other auxiliaries dominate here, both in number of occurrences and in the number of assigned supertags. Some remarks on the most frequently assigned supertags: "vind", as indicated by the type $((np\backslash s)/(np/np))/np$ is most often seen in constructions of the type "find movies interesting," whereas the s type for "zeg" is due to the

	Occurrences	Type	Simplified Type
1	3,672	$((np \backslash np)/s) \bullet \Diamond_p \Box_p^{\downarrow} np$	$(np \backslash np)/(s/\Diamond_p \Box_p^{\downarrow} np)$
2	3,174	$(wh/s) \bullet \Diamond_p \Box_p^{\downarrow} np$	$wh/(s/\Diamond_p \Box_p^{\downarrow} np)$
3	1,796	$np \bullet \Diamond_p \Box_p^{\downarrow} np$	

TABLE 12.9 Frequent long-distance dependencies

frequently occurring interjection "zeg maar," which corresponds roughly to "so to say."

Product types for long-distance dependencies are a frequent occurrence as well. Table 12.9 shows the three most frequent ones, with their number of occurrences, formula and (where possible) the corresponding product-less formula. Unsurprisingly, the two most frequently occurring formulas are the type of the relativizer, as extracted for words such as *die* (that) and the question type for words such as *wat* (what), as we have already seen it in section 12.3.3. The final type is perhaps more surprising. It is a result of the treatment of ellipsis in the Spoken Dutch Corpus.

For example, in the sentence

(11) *die* ouwe krant   of de nieuwe
      that old   newspaper or the new

"that old newspaper or the new one"

the word *krant* will be assigned the type $np \bullet \Diamond_p \Box_p^{\downarrow} np$, since it is considered to be the head noun of both conjuncts. From a type-logical point of view, this is not an entirely satisfactory solution. We would like to keep a simple np type in these cases and analyze the construction differently, for example along the lines proposed by Hendriks (1995). However, it is unclear if we can keep the lexicon extraction fully automatic when reanalyzing these constructions in the treebank.

12.4.4   Detecting isolated vertices automatically

While we have cleaned up the training data using information from the syntactic annotation itself, it is useful to see how well we do if we perform this step using only the information we would have for the 8 million that have only part-of-speech tag information.

To verify if training with the filtered dataset has actually gained us something we performed the following final experiment. We repeated the Split extraction procedure, this time using the nonfiltered corpus and divided this into a set of training data and test data. As before, every fifth sentence has been reserved for test data.

We trained three models using these data: one assigning supertags directly, one indicating only if a word is isolated or not and a final model using the filtered version of the training data. Our goal is to compare the performance of the first model against the two others applied in series. That is to say: a word correctly tagged as isolated is considered to have the correct tag, a word incorrectly tagged as isolated is considered to have an incorrect tag, and a word tagged as nonisolated is considered to have the correct tag if the model trained on the filtered corpus produces the correct result for it.

For deciding whether a word is an isolated vertex in the graph or not, a simple experiment was performed, using only word and part-of-speech tag information of the current word and the two words preceding and following it. Additionally, we used information about words that are labeled as being broken off or a repeat of the current word or part-of-speech tag in the previous five words. This simply strategy received a 98.35% success rate on the test data.

Table 12.10 shows a comparison between the two strategies. We note that the performance on both tasks is better than the supertagging performance on the filtered corpus, even when we do not count interpunction symbols. This is because, as already noted in section 12.3.2, word categories such as hesitation marks ("uh") are almost always correctly tagged as isolated (in the combined experiment) or assigned the correct category based on their unigram information (in the nonfiltered experiment).

Experiment	Result
Nonfiltered, with interpunction	81.26%
Nonfiltered, without interpunction	78.85%
Combined supertagger, with interpunction	81.50%
Combined supertagger, without interpunction	79.11%

TABLE 12.10 Comparison between the combined and the nonfiltered supertaggers

We also note that the combined experiment performs slightly better than the direct method: filtering out words that do not contribute to the syntactic structure of the phrase means that we get somewhat cleaner trigrams to train our models.

Finally, these experiments show that it is possible to remove the isolated nodes from the corpus automatically, without negatively affecting the performance.

12.4.5   Comparison

Chen and Vijay-Shanker (2000) propose a method of automatically extracting LTAGs from the Penn Treebank and investigate the effect of different extraction strategies. Their results appear to be a bit better than the results presented here, between 77.79% and 78.90% depending on the extraction strategy, even though we obtain a more compact lexicon. It stands to reason, however, that these differences are due to spoken corpora being inherently more noisy.

Semiautomatically extracted supertag sets, as used by Clark (2002), and manually crafted supertag sets, as used by Srinivas (1997), appear to fare significantly better, producing both a more compact lexicon and better performance for supertag disambiguation, which suggests there is a trade-off to be made between manual effort and performance.

12.5 Conclusions

We have seen how we can automatically extract a type-logical treebank from the CGN syntactic annotation. Depending on the level of detail we choose to maintain in our lexicon, the number of different formulas varies between 6.817 and 1.137, whereas the correctness of supertag disambiguation varies between 72.06% and 80.50%.

References

Abeillé, A., Clément, L., and Kinyon, A. (2000). Building a treebank for French. In *Proceedings of the Second International Language Resources and Evaluation Conference*, Athens, Greece.

Ajdukiewicz, K. (1935). Die syntaktische Konnexität. *Studies in Philosophy*, 1:1–27.

Bar-Hillel, Y. (1964). *Language and Information. Selected Essays on their Theory and Application.* Addison-Wesley.

Brants, S., Dipper, S., Hansen, S., Lezius, W., and Smith, G. (2002). The TIGER treebank. In *Proceedings of the Workshop on Treebanks and Linguistic Theories*, Sozopol.

Brants, T. (1999). *Tagging and Parsing with Cascaded Markov Models - Automation of Corpus Annotation.* PhD thesis, German Research Center for Artificial Intelligence and Saarland University.

Buszkowski, W. and Penn, G. (1990). Categorial grammars determined from linguistic data by unification. *Studia Logica*, 49:431–454.

Chen, J. and Vijay-Shanker, K. (2000). Automated extraction of TAGs from the Penn treebank. In *Proceedings of the 6th International Workshop on Parsing Technologies*, Trento, Italy.

Clark, S. (2002). Supertagging for combinatory categorial grammar. In *Proceedings of the 6th International Workshop on Tree Adjoining Grammars and Related Formalisms*, Venice, pages 19–24.

Hajic, J. (1998). Building a syntactically annotated corpus: The Prague dependency treebank. In *Issues of Valency and Meaning*, pages 106–132. Karolinum, Prague, Czech Republic.

Hendriks, P. (1995). Ellipsis and multimodal categorial type logic. In Morril, G. and Oehrle, R. T., eds., *Proceedings of Formal Grammar 1995*, Barcelona, Spain, pages 107–122.

Heylen, D. (1999). *Types and Sorts: Resource Logic for Feature Checking.* PhD thesis, Utrecht Institute of Linguistics OTS, Utrecht University.

Hoekstra, H., Moortgat, M., Renmans, B., Schuurman, I., and van der Wouden, T. (2002). Syntactic analysis in the Spoken Dutch Corpus (CGN). In *Proceedings of the Third International Language Resources and Evaluation Conference*, Las Palmas, Spain.

Kurtonina, N. and Moortgat, M. (1997). Structural control. In Blackburn, P. and de Rijke, M., eds., *Specifying Syntactic Structures*, pages 75–113. CSLI, Stanford.

Lambek, J. (1958). The mathematics of sentence structure. *American Mathematical Monthly*, 65:154–170.

Lambek, J. (1961). On the calculus of syntactic types. In Jacobson, R., ed., *Structure of Language and its Mathematical Aspects, Proceedings of the Symposia in Applied Mathematics*, volume XII, American Mathematical Society, pages 166–178.

Moortgat, M. (1997). Categorial type logics. In van Benthem, J. and ter Meulen, A., eds., *Handbook of Logic and Language*, chapter 2, pages 93–177. Elsevier/MIT Press.

Moortgat, M. (2001). Structural equations in language learning. In de Groote, P., Morrill, G., and Retoré, C., eds., *Logical Aspects of Computational Linguistics*, volume 2099 of *Lecture Notes in Artificial Intelligence*, pages 1–16. Springer.

Moortgat, M. and Moot, R. (2002). Using the Spoken Dutch Corpus for type-logical grammar induction. In *Proceedings of the Third International Language Resources and Evaluation Conference*, Las Palmas, Spain.

Moortgat, M. and Oehrle, R. T. (1994). Adjacency, dependency and order. In *Proceedings 9th Amsterdam Colloquium*, pages 447–466.

Morrill, G. (1994). *Type Logical Grammar*. Kluwer Academic, Dordrecht.

Srinivas, B. (1997). Performance evaluation of supertagging for partial parsing. In *Proceedings of Fifth International Workshop on Parsing Technology*, Boston.

Steedman, M. J. (2001). *The Syntactic Process*. MIT Press.

Extracting Supertags from HPSG-Based Treebanks

GÜNTER NEUMANN AND BERTHOLD CRYSMANN

13.1 Introduction

In recent years, several approaches have been proposed to improve the performance of Natural Language systems, which are based on the linguistic theory of Head-Driven Phrase Structure Grammars (HPSG) (Kasper et al., 1995; van Noord, 1997; Makino et al., 1998; Torisawa et al., 2000; Kiefer et al., 2002; Toutanova et al., 2002; Toutanova and Manning, 2002). Common to all these approaches is that the coverage of the original general grammar is not affected. Thus, if the original grammar is defined domain-independently, it might also define a great many theoretically valid analyses covering a wide range of plausible linguistic constructions, including the rarest cases. However, in building real-world applications, it has been shown to be a fruitful compromise to focus on frequency and plausibility of linguistic structures with respect to a certain domain. A number of attempts have been made to adapt a general grammar to a corpus automatically in order to achieve efficiency through domain adaptation, e.g., using PATR-style grammars (Briscoe and Carroll, 1993; Samuelsson, 1994; Rayner and Carter, 1996) or lexicalized TAGs (Srinivas, 1997).

In Neumann and Flickinger (2002) and Neumann (2003), we applied the idea of a data-oriented approach for achieving domain adaptation to HPSG.[1] We called this approach *HPSG-DOP*, because it had some strong corresponding relationships to the framework of Data-Oriented Parsing (DOP), see Bod et al. (2003). The basic idea of HPSG-DOP is to parse all sentences of a representative training corpus using an HPSG grammar and parser in order to acquire automatically from the parsing results a stochastic lexicalized tree grammar (SLTG) such that each resulting parse tree is recursively decomposed into a set of subtrees. The decomposition operation is guided by the head feature principle of HPSG. Each extracted tree is automatically lexically anchored, and each node label of the extracted tree compactly represents a set of relevant features by means of a simple symbol (these are specific category labels defined as part of the HPSG source grammar; see section 13.3). For each extracted tree, a frequency counter is used to estimate the probability of a tree, after all parse trees have been processed.

Processing of an SLTG is performed by a two level parser. In a first step, a new sentence is completely parsed using the extracted SLTG, followed by a second step where the SLTG-valid parse trees are expanded *offline* by applying the corresponding feature constraints of the original HPSG-grammar. Our approach has many advantages:

- An SLTG has context-free power and meets the criteria of a lexicalized context-free grammar.

- The offline step guarantees that no information of the original grammar is lost (including semantics).

- Since the SLTG learning phase is driven by the HPSG principles of the source grammar, the whole extraction process is simple and transparent.

- Our approach allows a proper embedding of statistical information into HPSG structures, which supports preference-based and robust processing.

- The whole approach has an important application impact, for example, for controlled language processing or information extraction, making use of rich and linguistically motivated information from HPSG. Furthermore, the same mechanism can also be applied to NL generation (see Neumann, 1997), as well as to efficient interleaved parsing and generation (see Neumann, 1998b).

A major drawback of this approach was that nonheaded constructions were not factored out consequently; for example, recursive modifier constructions were restricted by the number of the largest embedding found in the corpus. However, in Hwa (1998), Neumann (1998a), Xia (1999), Chen and Vijay-Shanker (2000), and Chiang (2000), a number of approaches for the automatic extraction of Tree-Adjoining Grammars (TAGs) from treebanks are presented, which treat the factorization of modifier constructions by interpreting the head/argument rules exploited by Magerman (1995) and Collins (1997) as a heuristic for reconstructing full structural descriptions from partial ones rather than as a means for rearranging information in the training data.

In this chapter, we extend HPSG-DOP by extending it with these TAG-related approaches and apply it on a linguistically rich HPSG treebank for German that is based on the recently developed Redwoods treebank (see Oepen et al., 2002 and section 13.3). To our knowledge, our approach is the first time that a rich linguistic theory together with a stochastic TAG is applied to the German language. This is not a trivial task; recently Dubey and Keller (2003) and Levy and Manning (2004) have shown that treebank parsing for German (using the rather shallow NEGRA Treebank) yields substantial lower performance compared to English Penn Treebank parsing, probably because differences in both languages and treebank annotation may be involved (see section 13.7). To give our new approach a name, we call it

HPSG-Supertag following Srinivas (2003) who defines the elementary structures of a lexicalized TAG as *supertags*.

The rest of the chapter is structured as follows. We begin by summarizing the formalism of the used tree structures. The HPSG treebank and details concerning the German HPSG are described in section 13.3; in section 13.4, the method for the induction of the stochastic grammar from the HPSG treebank is described. This also includes a description of the HPSG-based head/argument rules used for the grammar reconstruction process. In sections 13.5 and 13.6 we describe experiments using the standard PARSEVAL measurement. In section 13.7 important related work is discussed. We conclude in section 13.8 by giving an outline of future work.

13.2   Stochastic Lexicalized Tree Grammars

The set of lexically anchored trees extracted via the original HPSG-DOP method already characterizes a lexical tree-substitution grammar, that is, a tree-adjoining grammar with no auxiliary trees, see Schabes (1990). In Neumann (1998a) and subsequently in Xia (1999), Chen and Vijay-Shanker (2000), and Chiang (2000), it is shown how tree-adjoining grammars can be extracted from the Penn Treebank by performing a reconstruction of the derivations using head-percolation rules. Here we follow the approach developed in Chiang (2000), because his approach requires only a minimal amount of treebank preprocessing, which makes it easier to adapt it to other kind of treebanks.[2]

For efficiency reasons, a restricted form of lexicalized tree-adjoining grammars is considered, namely lexicalized tree insertion grammars (LTIGs). LTIG has been introduced in Schabes and Waters (1995) as a TAG-formalism in which all auxiliary trees are either left or right auxiliary trees. No elementary wrapping auxiliary trees or elementary empty auxiliary trees are allowed. Furthermore, left (right) auxiliary trees cannot be adjoined to a node that is on the spine of an elementary right (left) auxiliary tree; and there is no adjunction allowed to the right (left) of the spine of an elementary left (right) auxiliary tree (see figure 13.1).

There is an additional tree composition operation called sister-adjunction used by Chiang (2000), which is based on the extended notion of TAG derivation introduced in Schabes and Shieber (1994). In sister-adjunction, the root of a modifier tree is added as a new daughter to any other node, and multiple trees may be sister-adjoined at the same position. The main motivation for introducing this operation is its potential for deriving the flat structures found in the Penn treebank (see figure 13.2). Note that in our case the HPSG-derivations are deeply nested binary trees, so that sister-adjunction is actually not effective; however, we leave it here for completeness.

The parameters of a probabilistic TAG that control the combination of trees by the substitution and adjunction operations are:

$$\sum_\alpha P_i(\alpha) = 1$$

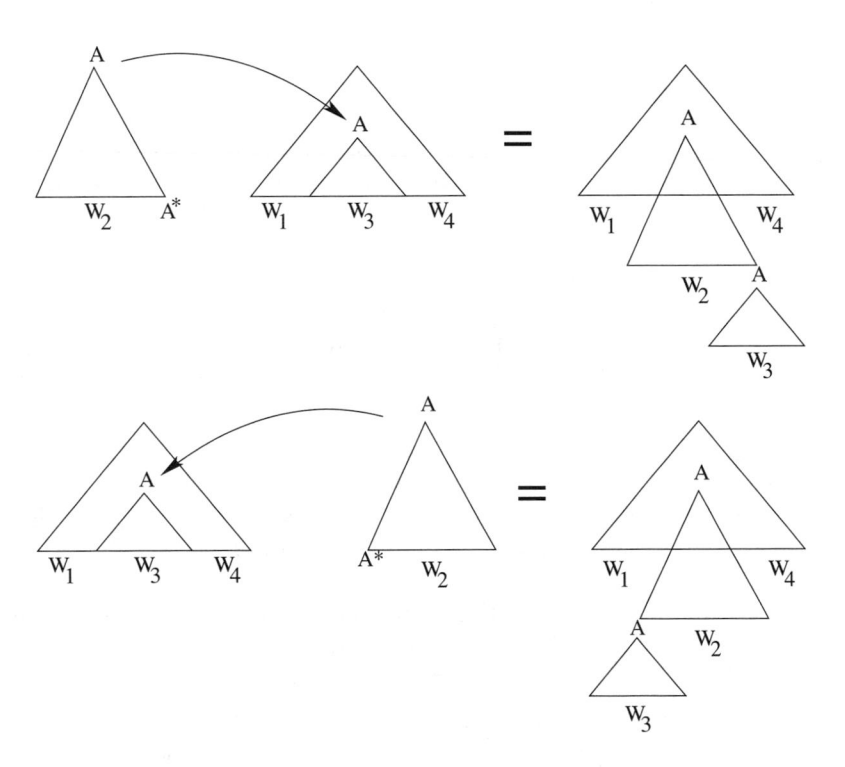

FIGURE 13.1 Left and right adjunction.

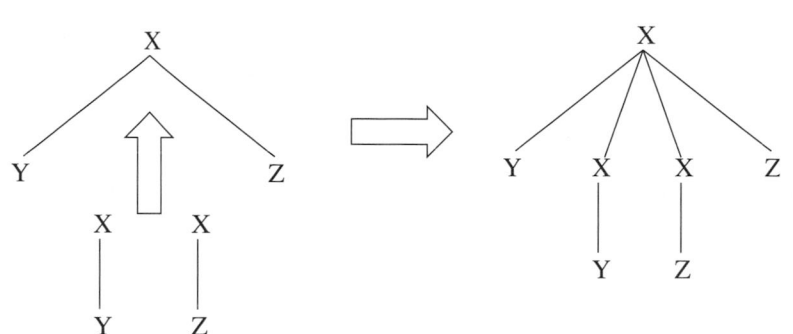

FIGURE 13.2 Sister-adjunction.

$$\sum_{\alpha} P_s(\alpha \mid \eta) = 1$$

$$\sum_{\beta} P_a(\beta \mid \eta) + P_a(\text{NONE} \mid \eta) = 1$$

$$\sum_{\alpha} P_{sa}(\beta \mid \eta, i, X) + P_{sa}(\text{STOP} \mid \eta, i, X) = 1$$

, where α ranges over initial trees, β over auxiliary trees, and η over nodes. $P_i(\alpha)$ is the probability of beginning a derivation with α; $P_s(\alpha \mid \eta)$ is the probability of substituting α at η; $P_a(\beta \mid \eta)$ is the probability of adjoining β at η; $P_a(\text{NONE} \mid \eta)$ is the probability of nothing adjoining at η; $P_{sa}(\beta \mid \eta, i, X)$ is the probability of sister-adjoining; and $P_{sa}(\text{STOP} \mid \eta, i, X)$ is the probability of no further sister-adjunction. X is the root label of the previous tree to sister-adjoin at the site (η, i), or START if none. The probability of a derivation can then be expressed as the product of the probabilities of the individual operations of the derivation (see Chiang, 2004 for more details).

LTIGs have context-free power and can be parsed in $\mathrm{O}(n^3)$. For the experiments reported in section 13.5, we are using a CKY-style bottom-up parser based on Schabes and Waters (1993) written by David Chiang. Basically, the parser starts by placing each foot node and each frontier node that is labeled with the empty string in every cell $C[i, i]$ of an $n \times n$ array C (n is the length of the input sentence $a_1 \ldots a_n$) with probability one. This indicates that they each cover the empty string at all positions (a node η covers a string if and only if the string can be derived starting from η). The initialization adds each terminal node η in every cell $C[i, i+1]$ where η is labeled a_{i+1} with probability one (scanning). Then all possible ways of combining matching substrings into longer matched substrings are considered by filling the upper diagonal portion of the array $C[i, k]$ ($0 \le i \le k \le n$) for increasing values of $k - i$. This process repeats until all the S-rooted derivations have been determined. Chiang has adapted this schema, in that, his CKY-parser implements sister-adjunction, and uses a beam search, computing the score of an item $[\eta, i, j]$ by multiplying it by the prior probability $P(\eta)$. All items with score less than a given threshold compared to the best item in a cell are pruned (see Chiang, 2000 and section 13.5 on details concerning the used parser settings).

13.3   HPSG Treebank

The HPSG treebank (codename *Eiche*) we use in our study is based on a subset of the Verbmobil corpus, that has been automatically annotated with a German HPSG grammar. The analyses provided by the grammar have then been manually disambiguated using the Redwoods treebanking technology (Oepen et al., 2002) .

The underlying HPSG grammar itself has originally been developed as a large-scale competence grammar of German by Stefan Müller and Walter Kasper in the context of the Speech-to-Speech machine translation project Verbmobil (see Müller and Kasper, 2000), and has subsequently been ported to the LKB (Copestake, 2001) and PET (Callmeier, 2000) processing platforms. In 2002, grammar development has been taken over by Berthold Crysmann. Since then, the grammar has undergone several major changes, most importantly the treatment of verb placement in clausal syntax (Crysmann, 2003).

13.3.1   Some basic properties of German syntax

The syntax of German features a variety of phenomena that make syntactic analysis much harder than that of more configurational languages. Chief among these is the relative free word order in which syntactic arguments of a verb can appear within the clausal domain.

(12)   a. *weil   der Lehrer   dem Schüler   das Buch   schenkte*
           because the teacher.NOM the pupil.DAT the book.ACC donated

           "because the teacher gave the book to the pupil as a present"

       b. *weil der Lehrer das Buch dem Schüler schenkte*

       c. *weil dem Schüler der Lehrer das Buch schenkte*

       d. *weil dem Schüler das Buch der Lehrer schenkte*

       e. *weil das Buch der Lehrer dem Schüler schenkte*

       f. *weil das Buch dem Schüler der Lehrer schenkte*

Almost anywhere between the arguments modifiers can be interspersed quite freely.

(13)   *weil   (gestern)   der Lehrer   (gestern)   dem Schüler*
       because (yesterday) the teacher.NOM (yesterday) the pupil.DAT
       (gestern)   das Buch   (gestern)   schenkte
       (yesterday) the book.ACC (yesterday) donated

       "because yesterday the teacher gave the book to the pupil as a present"

This situation is further complicated by the combined effects of verb cluster formation and argument composition, which permit permutation even among the arguments of different verbs within the cluster.

(14) a. *weil   der Lehrer   das Buch   zu kaufen versprach*
          because the teacher.NOM the book.ACC to buy   promised

      "because the teacher promised him to buy the book."

      b. *weil   das Buch   der Lehrer   zu kaufen versprach*
          because the book.ACC the teacher.NOM to buy   promised

      "because the teacher promised him to buy the book."

Furthermore, realization of the verb cluster is often discontinuous, typically in matrix clauses.

(15) a. *da   versprach der Lehrer.NOM das Buch   zu kaufen*
          there promised the teacher.NOM the book.ACC to buy

      "There, the teacher promised him to buy the book."

      b. *da   versprach das Buch   der Lehrer   zu kaufen*
          there promised the book.ACC the teacher.NOM to buy

      "There, the teacher promised him to buy the book."

Assuming continuous constituents only, the argument structure is therefore only partially known in bottom-up parsing, until the other member of the discontinuous verb cluster is found. In German matrix clauses, the finite verb typically surfaces in second position, the first position being occupied by some fronted, that is, extracted, constituent. Thus, in contrast to English, presence of nonlocal dependencies is the norm, rather than the exception.

Taken together, permutation of arguments, modifier interspersal, discontinuous complex predicates, and the almost categorial presence of nonlocal dependencies give rise to a considerable degree of variation in tree structure. As a consequence, we expect data-driven approaches to parsing to be more prone to the problem of data-sparseness. In the context of grammar induction from treebanks, it has already been observed (e.g., by Dubey and Keller, 2003) that methods that are highly successful in a more configurational language, such as Collins PCFG parser for English (see Collins, 1997), give less optimal results when applied to German.

This problem is further enhanced by the fact that German is a highly inflectional language, with four distinct cases, three gender and two number distinctions, all of which enter into agreement relations. The same holds for the verbal domain, where up to five person/number combinations are clearly distinguished.

13.3.2   The grammar

In the spirit of HPSG as a highly lexicalized grammatical theory, most of the information about an items combinatorial potential is encoded in the lexical entries itself, in terms of typed feature structures (see figure 13.3 for an example lexicon entry). Syntactic composition is then performed by means of highly general rule schemata, again, implemented as typed feature structures, which specify the flow of information within syntactic structure, see figure 13.4. As a result, the DFKI German HPSG specifies only 87 phrase structure schemata, as compared to some 280+ leaf types for the definition of parameterised[3] lexical entries, augmented by 56 lexical rules and 286 inflectional rules.

The rule schemata, which make up the phrase structure backbone of the HPSG grammar, correspond quite closely to principles of syntactic composition: by themselves they encode basic functional relations between daughter constituents, such as head-subject, head-complement, or head-adjunct, rather than intrinsic properties of the node itself. Thus, a rule like h-comp can be used to saturate a subcategorised complement of a preposition, a verb, or, a noun. Similarly, which constituents can function as the complement daughter of the h-comp rule is mainly determined by the information represented on the SUBCAT list of the lexical head. The rule schemata merely ensure that the subcategorisation constraints formulated by the head will actually be imposed on the complement daughter, and that the saturated valence requirement will be canceled off.

Since the underlying processing platforms (LKB/PET) do not currently support the segregation of immediate dominance and linear precedence, some rule schemata are further specialized according to the position of the head: alongside h-adjunct, h-subj and h-comp rules for verb-initial clauses and *pre*positional phrases, the grammar also defines their head-final counterparts (adjunct-h, subj-h, comp-h), required for verb-final clauses, adjectival phrases and *post*positional phrases. Within NPs some modifiers, e.g. adjectives are licensed by adjunct-h structures, whereas PPs are licensed in posthead position only. To summarize, the rules of the context-free backbone provide crucial information about the position of the syntactic head, as well as the functional status of the nonhead daughter (figure 13.5).

Scrambling of complements is licensed in the German grammar by special lexical rules that permute the elements on a head's SUBCAT list. Modifier interspersal and scrambling across the subject are accounted for by permitting the application of h-subj, h-comp, and h-adjunct rules in any order.

Argument composition and scrambling of arguments from different verbs is captured by shuffling the SUBCAT lists of the upstairs and downstairs verb (e.g., vcomp-h-0 ... vcomp-h-4). Discontinuous verb clusters are modeled by means of simulated verb movement (Müller and Kasper, 2000), expanding an earlier idea proposed by Kiss and Wesche (1991). Essentially, the subcategorization requirements of the initial verb are percolated down the tree to be shuffled with those of the final verb.

Finally, extraction is implemented in a fairly standard way using slash feature percolation. Slash introduction is performed, at the gap site, by a unary rule. For subjects and complements, slash introduction saturates an argument requirement of

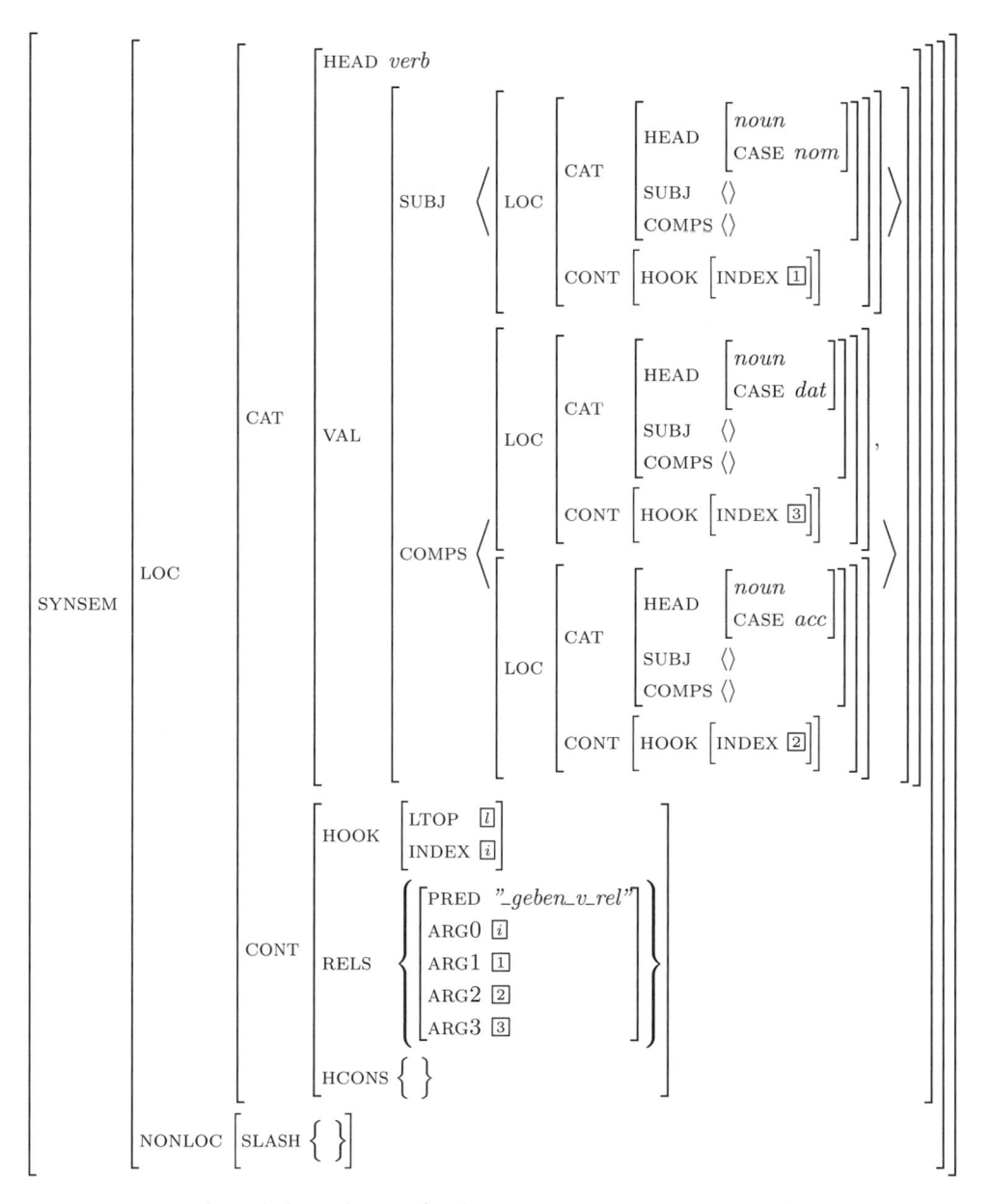

FIGURE 13.3 Sample lexical entry for ditransitive verb *geben* "give", including case requirements and semantic linking

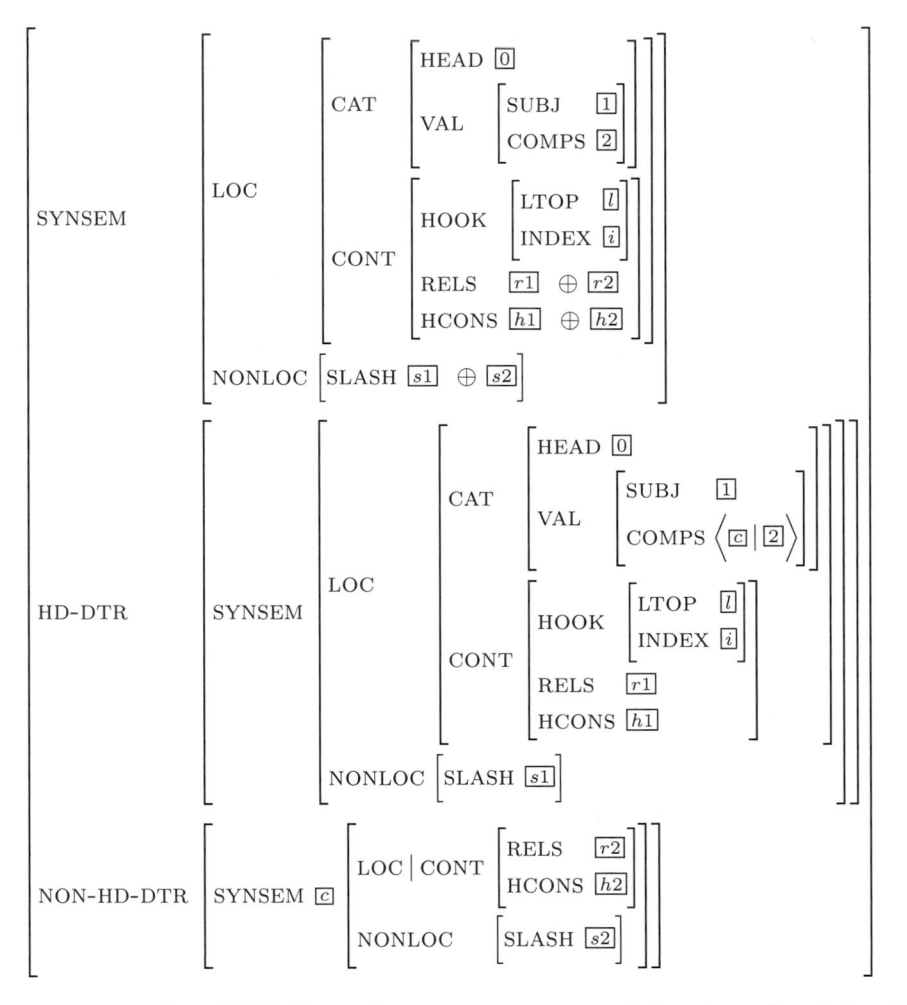

FIGURE 13.4 HPSG HEAD-COMPLEMENT SCHEMA: Saturation of head daughter's
subcategorization requirement on COMPS under unification (⌐c⌐). Percolation of not yet
saturated valencies (⌐1⌐, ⌐2⌐), semantic composition (concatenation of relations (RELS)
and scope constraints (HCONS), identification of semantic head (⌐i⌐, ⌐1⌐)), percolation of
nonlocal features (SLASH), and head feature principle (⌐0⌐). Constraints on semantic
composition, head, and slash percolation are inherited from principles, encoded as types.

the head by inserting its LOCAL value into the SLASH list. For adjuncts, the slash introduction also inserts a *local* object into SLASH, but since there is no valency to be saturated, it only semantically attaches the extracted modifier to the head. At the filler-site, SLASH specifications are retrieved, under unification: for semantic reasons, the grammar crucially distinguishes here between *wh*-fillers (wh-h rule) and non-*wh*-fillers (filler-h rule).

Besides these more basic constructions, the grammar also provides rule schemata for different types of coordinate structures, extraposition phenomena (Crysmann, 2005), dislocation, as well as some constructions more specific to German, such as auxiliary flip and partial VP fronting.

13.3.3 The treebank

The version of the HPSG formalism underlying the LKB and PET processing systems assumes continuous constituents only. Thus, the derivation tree of a sentence analysed by the grammar corresponds to a context-free phrase structure tree. Given a grammar, the full HPSG analysis of a sentence can therefore always be reconstructed deterministically, once the derivation tree is stored together with the unique identifiers of the lexical entries on the terminal nodes. This fact is actually exploited by the Redwoods treebanking infrastructure to provide a compact representation format. From the fully reconstructed feature structure representation of a parse, it is possible to extract additional derived structures: one such auxiliary structure that deserves particular mentioning is an isomorphic constituent tree decorated with more conventional node labels, such as S, NP, VP, PP, and so on (see figure 13.5). Note that these traditional labels are actually abbreviations (or names) of corresponding feature structures, for example,

pp-label := label-sign &
    [SYNSEM.LOC.CAT [HEAD prep-head,
                 SUBCAT <! !>,
                 VCOMP <>
          ],
     LABEL-NAME "PP"].

These labels are obtained by testing the unifiability of a feature structure description against the AVM associated with the node, and assigning the label of the first matching description. Since these derived trees are isomorphic to the derivation history, the "functional" decorations provided by the rule backbone can be enriched straightforwardly with "categorial" information, providing for a very rich annotation.

As already mentioned, the primary data used for the construction of the *Eiche* treebank are taken from the Verbmobil test corpora. In order to minimize duplication of annotation effort, only unique sentence strings have been incorporated into the treebank. Thus, redundancy in the data is limited to partial structures.

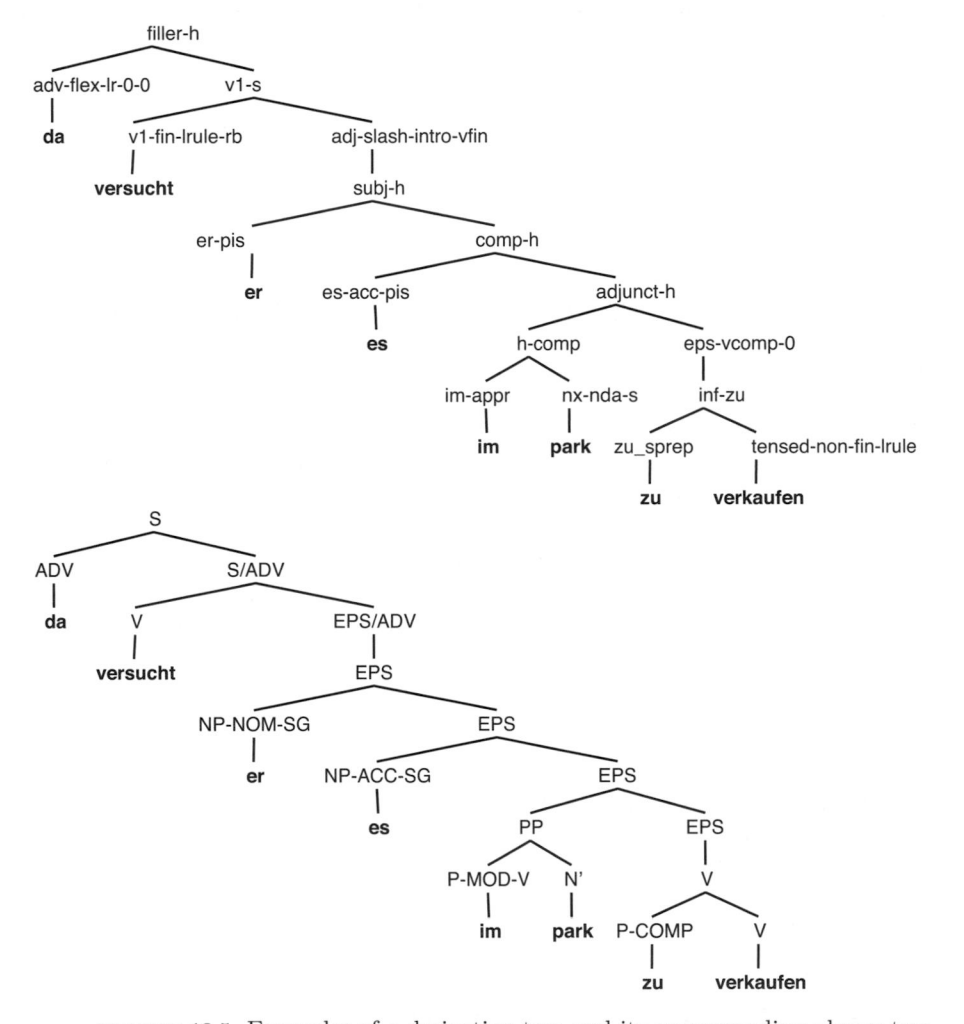

FIGURE 13.5 Examples of a derivation tree and its corresponding phrase tree representation for the sentence "*Then tries he it in the park to sell*" (literal reading, meaning "Then he tries to sell it in the park"). See text for an explanation of the different symbols.

13.4 HPSG-Supertag Extraction from the Treebank

The main purpose of the grammar extraction process is twofold: (1) extract automatically all possible supertags, that is, an LTIG, and (2) to obtain a maximum-likelihood estimation of the parameters of the extracted LTIG. The grammar extraction process actually reconstructs TAG derivations underlying the parse trees and is quite similar to the head-driven decomposition operation used in HPSG-DOP, but now adapted for the case of LTIG extraction.

13.4.1 The extraction method

Similar to Magerman (1995) and Chiang (2000), we use head-percolation and argument rules that classify for each node η exactly one child of η as the head and the others as either argument or modifier. However, as we will discuss, our rules are based on HPSG and as such, are much more smaller in number and less heuristic in nature as those defined in Chiang (2000). Using these rules, the derivations are reconstructed using the method described in Chiang (2000), and summarized here for convenience:

- If η is an adjunct, excise the subtree rooted at η to form a modifier tree.

- If η is an argument, excise the subtree rooted at η to form an initial tree, leaving behind a substitution node.

- If η has a right corner θ that is an argument with the same label as η (and all intervening nodes are heads), excise the segment from η down to θ to form an auxiliary tree.

From the determined structures, supertags are generated in two steps: first the tree template (that is, the elementary tree minus its anchor), then the anchor. From there, the probabilities are decomposed accordingly, and three back-off levels are computed, as described in Chiang (2000). Furthermore, all words seen n or fewer times in training are treated as a single symbol UNKNOWN, in order to handle unknown words.

13.4.2 The rule definition

Tables 13.1 and 13.2 contain the HPSG-based head and argument rules currently in use:

Parent:	Child:
SUBJ-H	last *
ADJUNCT-H	last *
COMP-H	last *
FILLER-II	last *
WH-H	last *
POS-ES	last *
DET-NBAR	last *
NP-NBAR	last *
VCOMP-H-0	last *
VCOMP-H-1	last *
VCOMP-H-2	last *
VCOMP-H-3	last *
VCOMP-H-4	last *
BINARY-COORD	last *
RECURSIVE-EV-COORD	last *
RECURSIVE-NOM-COORD	last *
**	first *

Table 13.1: Head rules for the HPSG treebank. The symbol * stands for any label.

Parent:	Child:
SUBJ-H	first *
H-SUBJ	last *
COMP-H	first *
H-COMP	last *
H-COMP-EXTRAPOSED	last *
H-SUBJ-EXTRAPOSED	last *

Table 13.2: Arg rules for the HPSG treebank. The symbol * stands for any label.

The list of rules is processed in the order specified, and the first rule that fires is applied. A rule fires if the label of the current node matches with one of the parent node labels specified in the rule list. A head rule such as "SUBJ-H last *" determines that the last child of a parent node with label **SUBJ-H** is the head, regardless of the child's label. The head rule "* first *" means that for a parent with an arbitrary node label its leftmost child is chosen as the head daughter. This rule plays the role of a default head rule. The argument rules work in the same way. For an explanation of the linguistic content of these rules, see section 13.3.

13.5   Experiments

We performed a tenfold cross-validation over a corpus of 3,528 sentences from the Verbmobil domain with an average sentence length of 7.2 words. We used "evalb"[4] to compute the standard PARSEVAL scores for our results, and focused on the Labeled Precision (LP) and Labeled Recall (LR) scores, as they are commonly used to rank parsing systems. During the experiments we used the same settings for the parser as used by Chiang (2000) for his Penn Treebank experimentations: (a) beam size set to 10^{-5}, (b) unknown word threshold set to 4.

The anchors of the extracted supertags consist of the preterminals of the derivation trees and are lexical labels. These are much more fine-grained than Penn Treebank preterminal tags, covering information about POS, morphosyntactic, valence, and other information. The input to the parser is then a sequence of pairs (LEX-LABEL WORDFORM) (we also ignore upper and lower case). For example for the sentence *Wann hätten Sie denn dann noch Zeit?* ("When would you have still time, then?"), the input to the parser is (see appendix 13.9 for the corresponding derivation and phrase tree representations):

(WANN-
ADV WANN) (HABEN-T HAETTEN) (SIE_SH-PIS SIE) (DENN_SCADV-ADV
DENN) (DANN_SCADV-VVPP DANN) (NOCH_PADV-ADV NOCH) (ZEIT-N
ZEIT)

Since, we do not have any HPSG-based lexical tagger available, we used the (LEX-LABEL WORDFORM) sequence of each sentence extracted from the parse trees of the test corpus (that is, from the 10% blind data used in each iteration of the cross-validation step). Note that the UNKNOWN symbol relates only to corresponding words in the training set (it maps words seen fewer than N times to this symbol), that is, stems that occur only in the test set, but not in the training set, are not covered by the grammar. Hence, the parser will deliver no result for sentences that contain "out-of-vocabulary" stems.

We trained and tested our method on the full encoding of the symbols, which among others encode values for gender, number, person, case, tense, and mood. Furthermore, the symbols also encode the valency of verbs. The number of different node labels is 2,069; appendix 13.10 shows the top most frequent symbols in the corpus (together with the frequency count).

It seems clear that using lexical labels as anchors will effect at least the coverage and recall. In order to test this, we also run an experiment, where we used only the Part-of-Speech (POS) of the lexical labels, which are retrieval from the yield of the corresponding phrase tree (but note, that the labels of all nonterminal nodes are labels from the derivation trees). This will lead to a much more coarse-grained classification of word forms, but probably also to a less restrictive tree selection.

Table 13.1 presents our current results, where we computed the average values for the labeled recall and precision results determined in all ten iterations:

Anchor	Cov.	LR(tot.)	LP(tot.)	LR(cov.)	LP(cov.)
Lexical label	77.47	57.68	77.07	77.33	78.27
POS	98.12	76.42	78.36	77.92	78.44

TABLE 13.1 Labeled recall and precision results

where LR(tot.)/LP(tot.) is measured over all sentences, and LR(cov.)/LP(cov.) over the parsed sentences, that is, for sentences without out-of-vocabulary stems.

13.6   Discussion

In Neumann (2003), we discussed initial results for our HPSG-DOP approach using an English HPSG grammar and a less detailed analysis. For example instead of a cross-validation analysis, we used 1,000 Verbmobil sentences for training, and another 1,000 for testing. We did not measure recall and precision, but checked whether it was possible to expand each one, by unifying the feature constraints of the original HPSG grammar. Thus seen, we consider a sentence analysis as valid, if it is consistent with respect to the HPSG constraints (including all lexical constraints, of course). Following this way, 704 sentences were recognized, which corresponds to a coverage of 70.4% .

Our current results suggest that the HPSG-Supertag method is superior compared to our earlier work. It should be clear, that the moderate coverage is basically due to the very specific nature of the tree anchors. The size of the current corpus is small compared to the Penn Treebank, so we assume that it will improve for larger corpora. Note also, that the redundancy in the corpus is limited to partial structures (see also section 13.3.3), which also affects the performance.

Nevertheless, our current results are encouraging, if we compare them with other recent approaches of probabilistic parsing for German. To date, there is only little work on full probabilistic parsing of German from treebanks — mainly using the NEGRA treebank (Skut et al., 1997) — and the PARSEVAL measurement.

The first probabilistic treebank parser for German (using the NEGRA treebank) is presented in Dubey and Keller (2003). They obtain (for sentence length of $\leq$ 40): LR=71.32% and LP=70.93% (coverage = 95.9%). Müller et al. (2003) also present a probabilistic parser for NEGRA. They study the consequences that the NEGRA implies for probabilistic parsing, and concentrate on the role of two factors (1) lexicalization and (2) grammatical functions. The results they report: LR=71.00% and LP=72.85% (coverage = 100%). Furthermore, Levy and Manning (2004) present experiments on probabilistic parsing using NEGRA concentrating on nonlocal dependency reconstruction. Their results also suggest that current state-of-the-art statistical parsing is far better on Penn Treebank than on the NEGRA treebank.

Clearly, one cannot directly compare the results obtained for the NEGRA treebank with the results, we have achieved for the Redwoods treebank. A comparison between the English and German treebank parsers shows a significant reduction for German. These results should not be overestimated as well, because the treebank representation (e.g., the degree of information that is encoded in the symbols) might be too difficult to compare.

13.7 Related Work

Here, we will briefly mention and discuss other relevant work, in addition to the already discussed work done for LTAG and German treebank parsing.

Our approach is also related to approaches of grammar specialization based on Explanation-based Learning (EBL) (Samuelsson, 1994; Srinivas and Joshi, 1995; Rayner and Carter, 1996), and other grammar approximation methods. For example, Krieger (2005), presents an approximation method that specialized an English HPSG-grammar to a probabilistic context-free grammar. In Keselj and Cercone (2002), an interesting approach called "just-in-time subgrammar extraction" is presented, which has some ideas in common with our HPSG-DOP approach but differs in that they perform a subgrammar extraction in form of a PCFG online for a piece of text, rather than offline for a specific domain.

In Foth et al. (2004) a broad-coverage parser for German based on weighted constraint dependency grammar is presented and analyzed using the NEGRA treebank. In order to evaluate their parsing result with the NEGRA parse trees, the phrase-based trees are mapped to dependency trees. Then the accuracy is measured by counting the number of correctly computed dependency edges. Using the same subset of NEGRA sentences for testing as done by Dubey and Keller (2003), they report an labeled edge accuracy of 87%.

Current stochastic approaches for HPSG basically focus on parse tree disambiguation using the English Redwoods treebank (Oepen et al., 2002). For example, Toutanova et al. (2002), present a parse selection method using conditional log-linear models built over the levels of derivation tree, phrase structure tree, and semantic dependency graph in order to analyze the effect of different information levels represented in the Redwoods treebank. The best reported result (in terms of accuracy) is obtained for the derivation tree representation and by implementing an extended PCFG that conditions each node's expansion on several of its ancestors in the derivation tree (with a manually specified upper bound of four ancestors). They report an exact parse accuracy of 81.80% for such an extended PCFG, which was only slightly improved when combining it with a PCFG based on the semantic dependency graph representation (82.65%). In Toutanova and Manning (2002) this work is extended by the integration of automatic feature selection methods based on decision trees and ensembles of decision trees. Using this mechanism, they are able to improve the parse selection accuracy for the derivation tree based PCFG from 81.82% to 82.24%.

13.8   Conclusion and Future Work

We have presented an approach of extracting supertags from a HPSG-based treebank, and have evaluated the performance of the grammar using a stochastic LTIG parser. In future work, we will consider the following aspects. First, we will explore how the current results can be improved by either adding more information to the tree labels or by generalizing those tree labels which are currently too specific. Second, we will investigate how this technology can be used to provide the n-best derivation trees and to use them as input for the deterministic feature structure expansion step using the HPSG-source grammar. In this way, a preference-based parsing schema for HPSG using a treebank model will function as a filter.

Acknowledgments

The work presented here was partially supported by a research grant from the German Federal Ministry of Education, Science, Research and Technology (BMBF) to the DFKI project Quetal (FKZ: 01 IW C02) and the EC-funded project DeepThought. We thank very much David Chiang for making available to us his TIG training and parsing system. We also thank the Redwoods treebank team for making their tools open-source, and especially Stephan Oepen for his kind support.

13.9 Appendix

The treebank representation of the derivation tree and the phrase tree for the sentence *Wann hätten Sie denn dann noch Zeit?* ("When would you have still time, then?"):

```
(1347 WH-H -2.03203 0 7 (44 PX-ALL_INFL_RULE 1.98206 0 1
 (8 WANN-ADV 0 0 1 ("wann" 0 1)))
 (1137 ADJ-SLASH-INTRO-VINI -3.15029 1 7
  (1133 H-COMP -1.90074 1 7
   (610 H-ADJUNCT 4.23003 1 6
    (492 H-ADJUNCT 6.68481 1 4
     (171 H-SUBJ 2.84761 1 3
      (40 V1-FIN-LRULE-NO-RB 2.49282 1 2
       (39 PERS-SILR-LRULE 3.79787 1 2
        (38 VX-PAST-CONJ-PL-1-3_INFL_RULE 3.79787 1 2
        (21 HABEN-T 0 1 2 ("haetten" 1 2)))))
      (98 PX-ALL_INFL_RULE -2.2774 2 3
       (27 SIE_SH-PIS 0 2 3 ("sie" 2 3))))
     (46 PX-ALL_INFL_RULE 1.63737 3 4
      (29 DENN_SCADV-ADV 0 3 4 ("denn" 3 4))))
    (54 ADJUNCT-H 2.2854 4 6
     (50 PX-ALL_INFL_RULE 1.63737 4 5
      (32 DANN_SCADV-VVPP 0 4 5 ("dann" 4 5)))
     (48 PX-ALL_INFL_RULE 1.63737 5 6
      (33 NOCH_PADV-ADV 0 5 6 ("noch" 5 6)))))
   (860 EMPTY-DET-SG -5.40906 6 7
    (96 NX-FEM-SG_INFL_RULE -1.66928 6 7
     (35 ZEIT-N 0 6 7 ("zeit" 6 7))))))))

(S (ADV
 (ADV (wann)))
 (S/ADV
  (S
   (V (V (V (V (V (V (V (haetten)))))
    (NP-NOM-PL (NP-NOM-PL (sie))))
     (ADV (ADV (denn))))
   (ADV (ADV (ADV (dann)))
    (ADV (ADV (noch)))))
  (NP-ACC-SG (N' (N' (zeit))))))))
```

13.10   Appendix

The top fully encoded symbols together with their frequency counts:

Label	Freq.
PX-ALL_INFL_RULE	13143
H-COMP	4095
ADJUNCT-H	3499
PERS-SILR-LRULE	3475
H-ADJUNCT	2768
FILLER-H	2293
NX-MAS-NDA-SG_INFL_RULE	1943
DET-NBAR	1940
V1-FIN-LRULE-NO-RB	1890
V1-S	1284
V1-FIN-LRULE-RB	1284
SUBJ-SLASH-INTRO	1244
H-SUBJ	1228
ADV-FLEX-LR-0-0	1167
EMPTY-DET-SG	1157
FULL-PREP-NOUN-TO-VERB-MOD-LRULE	1096
DET-D-DET	1093
EPS-VCOMP-0	1027
ICH-PIS	988
SUBJ-H	982
EMPTY-NOUN-MODIFIER-RULE	895
COMP-H	892
NX-FEM-SG_INFL_RULE	887
NON-FIN-SILR-LRULE	822
VX-PAST-CONJ-SG-1-3_INFL_RULE	803
ADJ-SLASH-INTRO-VINI	775
DX-INFL-EN_INFL_RULE	748
VX-PRES-PL-1-3_INFL_RULE	747
TENSED-NON-FIN-LRULE	741
VX-SUP-BARE_INFL_RULE	727
WIR-PIS	722
INTERJECTION-RULE	711
AX-POS-NULL_INFL_RULE	684
DEF-PREP-NOUN-TO-VERB-MOD-LRULE	661
DAS-NP-NEU-SG-NA	600
CARDINAL_INFL_RULE	519
VX-PRES-IND-SG-3_INFL_RULE	511

Notes

1. A first initial approach for applying data-oriented methods to HPSG is described in Neumann (1994), where an approach for memory-based processing with HPSG based on Explanation-Based Learning is described.

2. His approach can be seen as a substantial improvement of the initial work we had laid out and described in Neumann (1998a).

3. Lexical entries may get further specialized beyond the information encoded in the lexical leaf type: typically, this includes subcategorisation for lexical case, selection of prepositional complements and verb particles, specification of auxiliary type (*have* vs. *be*), as well as sortal restrictions on complements.

4. http://nlp.cs.nyu.edu/evalb/.

References

Bod, R., Sima'an, K., and Scha, R., eds. (2003). *Data Oriented Parsing*. Center for Study of Language and Information (CSLI) Publications, Stanford:CA, USA.

Briscoe, E. J. and Carroll, J. (1993). Generalized probabilistic lr parsing of natural language (corpora) with unification-based grammars. *Computational linguistics*, 19(1):25–59.

Callmeier, U. (2000). PET — a platform for experimentation with efficient HPSG processing techniques. *Natural Language Engineering*, 6(1):99–108.

Chen, J. and Vijay-Shanker, K. (2000). Automated extraction of tags from the Penn treebank. In *6th International Workshop on Parsing Technologies (IWPT'2000)*, Trento, Italy.

Chiang, D. (2000). Statistical parsing with an automatically-extracted tree adjoining grammar. In *38th ACL*, Hong Kong.

Chiang, D. (2004). *Evaluating Grammar Formalisms for Applications to Natural Language Processing and Biological Sequence Analysis*. PhD thesis, University of Pennsylvania.

Collins, M. (1997). Three generative, lexicalised models for statistical parsing. In *ACL*.

Copestake, A. (2001). *Implementing Typed Feature Structure Grammars*. CSLI Publications.

Crysmann, B. (2003). On the efficient implementation of German verb placement in HPSG. In *RANLP 2003*.

Crysmann, B. (2005). Relative clause extraposition in German: An efficient and portable implementation. *Research on Language and Computation*, 3(1):61–82.

Dubey, A. and Keller, F. (2003). Probabilistic parsing for German using sister-head dependencies. In *ACL*.

Foth, K. A., Daum, M., and Menzel, W. (2004). A broad-coverage parser for German based on defeasible constraints. In *Konvens, Vienna*, pages 45–52.

Hwa, R. (1998). An empirical evaluation of probabilistic lexicalized tree insertion grammars. In *Proceedings of the 36th ACL and 17th Coling*, Montreal.

Kasper, R., Kiefer, B., Netter, K., and Vijay-Shanker, K. (1995). Compilation of HPSG into TAG. In *33rd Annual Meeting of the Association for Computational Linguistics*, Cambridge, MA.

Keselj, V. and Cercone, N. (2002). Just-in-time subgrammar extraction for HPSG. In *Proceedings of the Conference Pacific Association for Computational Linguistics, PACLING'01, Kitakyushu, Japan*.

Kiefer, B., Krieger, H., and Prescher, D. (2002). A novel disambiguation method for unification-based grammars using probabilistic context-free approximations. In *COLING 2002*.

Kiss, T. and Wesche, B. (1991). Verb order and head movement. In Herzog, O. and Rollinger, C., eds., *Text Understanding in LILOG*. Springer.

Krieger, H. (2005). Grammar approximation as a speed-up technique for unification-based parsing. In Fernau, H., ed., *Invited talks on Learning of Automata and Grammars at the TAGI Workshop*, pages 10–21.

Levy, R. and Manning, C. D. (2004). Deep dependencies from context-free statistical parsers: Correcting the surface dependency approximation. In *ACL*.

Magerman, D. M. (1995). Statistical decisiontree models for parsing. In *ACL*, pages 276–283.

Makino, T., Yoshida, M., Torisawa, K., and Tsujii, J. (1998). LiLFeS – towards a practical HPSG parser. In *Proceedings of the 36th ACL and 17th Coling*, Montreal, pages 807 – 811.

Müller, K., Prescher, D., and Sima'an, K. (2003). Grammatical functions and parsing the German NEGRA treebank. In *Slides from CLIN 2003 presentation, http://staff.science.uva.nl/ kmueller/Onlinepapers/ CLIN03_slides.pdf*.

Müller, S. and Kasper, W. (2000). HPSG analysis of German. In Wahlster, W., ed., *Verbmobil: Foundations of Speech-to-Speech Translation*, Artificial Intelligence, pages 238–253. Springer-Verlag, Berlin Heidelberg New York.

Neumann, G. (1994). Application of explanation-based learning for efficient processing of constraint-based grammars. In *Proceedings of the 10th IEEE Conference on Artificial Intelligence for Applications, March 1-4*, San Antonio, TX, pages 208–215.

Neumann, G. (1997). Applying explanation-based learning to control and speeding-up natural language generation. In *35th Annual Meeting of the Association for Computational Linguistics/8th Conference of the European Chapter of the Association for Computational Linguistics*, Madrid, Spain.

Neumann, G. (1998a). Automatic extraction of stochastic lexicalized tree grammars from treebanks. In *TAG+ workshop*, Philadelphia, PA, USA.

Neumann, G. (1998b). Interleaving natural language parsing and generation through uniform processing. *Artifical Intelligence*, 99:121–163.

Neumann, G. (2003). Data-driven approaches to head-driven phrase structure grammar. In Bod, R., Scha, R., and Sima'an, K., eds., *Data Oriented Parsing*. CSLI Publications, Stanford:CA, USA.

Neumann, G. and Flickinger, D. (2002). HPSG-DOP: Data-oriented parsing with HPSG. In *HPSG-2002*, Kyung Hee University, Seoul.

Oepen, S., Toutanova, K., Shieber, S. M., Manning, C. D., Flickinger, D., and Brants, T. (2002). The lingo redwoods treebank: Motivation and preliminary applications. In *COLING*.

Rayner, M. and Carter, D. (1996). Fast parsing using pruning and grammar specialization. In *34th Annual Meeting of the Association for Computational Linguistics*, Morristown, NJ.

Samuelsson, C. (1994). Grammar specialization through entropy thresholds. In *ACL*, pages 188–195.

Schabes, Y. (1990). *Mathematical and Computational Aspects of Lexicalized Grammars.* PhD thesis, University of Pennsylvania, Philadelphia.

Schabes, Y. and Shieber, S. M. (1994). An alternative conception of tree-adjoining derivation. *Computational Linguistics*, 20(1):91–124.

Schabes, Y. and Waters, R. C. (1993). Stochastic lexicalized context-free grammar. In *IWPT'93*.

Schabes, Y. and Waters, R. C. (1995). Tree insertion grammar: A cubic-time parsable formalism that lexicalizes context-free grammar without changing the trees produced. *Computational Linguistics*, 21:479–513.

Skut, W., Krenn, B., Brants, T., and Uszkoreit, H. (1997). An annotation scheme for free word order languages. In *ANLP, Washington, DC*, pages 88–95.

Srinivas, B. (1997). *Complexity of Lexical Restrictions and Its Relevance to Partial Parsing.* PhD thesis, University of Pennsylvania. IRCS Report 97–10.

Srinivas, B. (2003). Localizing dependencies and supertagging. In Bod, R., Scha, R., and Sima'an, K., eds., *Data Oriented Parsing*. CSLI Publications, Stanford:CA, USA.

Srinivas, B. and Joshi, A. K. (1995). Some novel applications of explanation-based learning to parsing lexicalized tree-adjoining grammars. In *33rd Annual Meeting of the Association for Computational Linguistics*, Cambridge, MA.

Torisawa, K., Nishida, N., Miyao, Y., and Tsujii, J. (2000). An HPSG parser with CFG filtering. *Natural Language Engineering*, 6(1):63–80.

Toutanova, K. and Manning, C. D. (2002). Feature selection for a rich HPSG grammar using decision trees. In *Proceedings of the Sixth Conference on Natural Language Learning (CoNLL)*.

Toutanova, K., Manning, C. D., Shieber, S. M., Flickinger, D., and Oepen, S. (2002). Parse disambiguation for a rich HPSG grammar. In *First Workshop on Treebanks and Linguistic Theories (TLT2002)*, pages 253–263.

van Noord, G. (1997). An efficient implementation of the head-corner parser. *Computational Linguistics*, 23:425–456.

Xia, F. (1999). Extracting tree adjoining grammars from bracketed corpora. In *Proceedings of the 5th Natural Language Processing Pacific Rim Symposium(NLPRS-99)*, Beijing, China.

Probabilistic Context-Free Grammars with Latent Annotations

Takuya Matsuzaki, Yusuke Miyao and Jun'ichi Tsujii

14.1 Introduction

Variants of PCFGs form the basis of several broad-coverage and high-precision parsers (Collins, 1999; Charniak, 2000; Klein and Manning, 2003). In those parsers, the strong conditional independence assumption made in vanilla treebank PCFGs is weakened by annotating nonterminal symbols with many "features" (Goodman, 1997; Johnson, 1998). Examples of such features are head words of constituents, labels of ancestor and sibling nodes, and subcategorization frames of lexical heads. Effective features and their good combinations are normally explored using trial and error.

We introduce a generative model of parse trees that we call PCFG with latent annotations (PCFG-LA). This model is an extension of PCFG models in which nonterminal symbols are annotated with latent variables. The latent variables work just like the features attached to nonterminal symbols. A fine-grained PCFG is automatically induced from parsed corpora by training a PCFG-LA model using an EM-algorithm, which replaces the manual feature selection used in previous research.

As is the case of most statistical parsing models, we can formulate parsing with PCFG-LA as an optimization problem where the most probable parse (MPP) is searched given an input sentence. The MPP T of a sentence w is defined as $T = \mathrm{argmax}_{T'} P(T'|w)$, where $P(T'|w)$ is the probability with which the model predicts T' as the correct parse tree for w.

Unfortunately, it turned out to be an NP-hard problem to find the MPP of a given input sentence in the case of PCFG-LA.[1] Some kind of approximation is therefore inevitable in parsing with PCFG-LA. We empirically compared three different approximation methods: a reranking-style method, a method based on the

Viterbi algorithm, and a method inspired by approximate inference algorithms for graphical models (Jordan et al., 1999). The last method gave a performance of 86.6% (F_1, sentences $\leq$ 40 words) on the standard test set of the Penn WSJ corpus.

Utsuro et al. (1996) proposed a method that automatically selects a proper level of generalization/specialization of nonterminal symbols of a PCFG, but they did not report the results of parsing with the obtained PCFG. Henderson's parsing model (Henderson, 2003) has a similar motivation as ours in that a derivation history of a parse tree is compactly represented by induced hidden variables (hidden layer activation of a neural network), although the details of his approach are quite different from ours.

14.2   Probabilistic Model

In PCFG-LA model, an observed parse tree is considered as an incomplete data, and the corresponding complete data is a tree with *latent annotations*. Each nonterminal node in the complete data is labeled with a complete symbol of the form $A[x]$, where A is the nonterminal symbol of the corresponding node in the observed tree and x is a *latent annotation symbol*, which is an element of a fixed set H.

A complete/incomplete tree pair of the sentence, "*the cat grinned*," is shown in figure 14.1. The complete parse tree, $T[\mathbf{X}]$ (left), is generated through a process just like the one in ordinary PCFGs, but the nonterminal symbols in the CFG rules are annotated with latent symbols, $\mathbf{X} = (x_1, x_2, \dots)$. Thus, the probability of the complete tree ($T[\mathbf{X}]$) is

$$
\begin{aligned}
P(T[\mathbf{X}]) = {} & \pi(S[x_1]) \times \beta(S[x_1] \to NP[x_2]VP[x_5]) \\
& \times \beta(NP[x_2] \to DT[x_3]N[x_4]) \\
& \times \beta(DT[x_3] \to the) \times \beta(N[x_4] \to cat) \\
& \times \beta(VP[x_5] \to V[x_6]) \times \beta(V[x_6] \to grinned),
\end{aligned}
$$

where $\pi(S[x_1])$ denotes the probability of an occurrence of the symbol $S[x_1]$ at a root node and $\beta(r)$ denotes the probability of a CFG rule r. The probability of the observed tree $P(T)$ is obtained by summing $P(T[\mathbf{X}])$ for all the assignments to latent annotation symbols, $\mathbf{X}$:

$$
P(T) = \sum_{x_1 \in H} \sum_{x_2 \in H} \cdots \sum_{x_6 \in H} P(T[\mathbf{X}]) = \sum_{\mathbf{X} \in H^6} P(T[\mathbf{X}]). \tag{14.1}
$$

Using dynamic programming, the theoretical bound of the time complexity of the summation in equation 14.1 is reduced to be proportional to the number of nonterminal nodes in a parse tree. However, the calculation at node n still has a cost that exponentially grows with the number of n's daughters because we must sum the probabilities of $|H|^{d+1}$ combinations of latent annotation symbols for a node with d daughters. We thus took a kind of transformation/detransformation approach, in which a tree is binarized before parameter estimation and restored to its original form after parsing. Some nodes that are located close to each other in a original tree (e.g., sibling nodes) might grow apart from each other in the binarized tree.

Probabilistic dependency among those nodes is, however, to some extent retained by introducing latent annotations because any two nodes can "interact" through latent annotation symbols on the path connecting them. The details of the binarization are explained in section 14.4.

The parameters of a PCFG-LA model is estimated by an EM algorithm using syntactically annotated corpora as training data. The algorithm is a special variant of the inside-outside algorithm of Pereira and Schabes (1992). Several recent works also use similar estimation algorithms as ours, namely, inside-outside reestimation on parse trees (Chiang and Bikel, 2002; Shen, 2004).

The rest of this section precisely defines PCFG-LA models and briefly explains the estimation algorithm. The derivation of the estimation algorithm is largely omitted; see Pereira and Schabes (1992) for details.

14.2.1   Model definition

We define a PCFG-LA $\mathcal{M}$ as a tuple $\mathcal{M} = \langle N_{\mathrm{nt}}, N_{\mathrm{t}}, H, R, \pi, \beta \rangle$, where

N_{nt} : a set of observable nonterminal symbols

N_{t} : a set of terminal symbols

H : a set of latent annotation symbols

R : a set of observable CFG rules

$\pi(A[x])$: the probability of the occurrence

of a complete symbol $A[x]$ at a root node

$\beta(r)$: the probability of a rule $r \in R[H]$.

We use $A, B, \ldots$ for nonterminal symbols in N_{nt}; $w_1, w_2, \ldots$ for terminal symbols in N_{t}; and $x, y, \ldots$ for latent annotation symbols in H. $N_{\mathrm{nt}}[H]$ denotes the set of complete nonterminal symbols, that is, $N_{\mathrm{nt}}[H] = \{A[x] \mid A \in N_{\mathrm{nt}}, x \in H\}$. Note that latent annotation symbols are not attached to terminal symbols.

In the preceding definition, R is a set of CFG rules of observable (i.e., not annotated) symbols. For simplicity of discussion, we assume that R is a CNF grammar, but extending to the general case is straightforward. $R[H]$ is the set of CFG rules of complete symbols, such as $V[x] \rightarrow grinned$ or $S[x] \rightarrow NP[y]VP[z]$. More precisely,

$$R[H] = \{(A[x] \rightarrow w) \mid (A \rightarrow w) \in R;\ x \in H\}$$
$$\cup \{(A[x] \rightarrow B[y]C[z]) \mid (A \rightarrow BC) \in R;\ x, y, z \in H\}.$$

We assume that nonterminal nodes in a parse tree T are indexed by integers $i = 1, \ldots, m$, starting from the root node. A complete tree is denoted by $T[\mathbf{X}]$, where $\mathbf{X} = (x_1, \ldots, x_m) \in H^m$ is a vector of latent annotation symbols and x_i is the latent annotation symbol attached to the i-th nonterminal node.

We do not assume any structured parametrizations in β and π; that is, each $\beta(r)$ $(r \in R[H])$ and $\pi(A[x])$ $(A[x] \in N_{\mathrm{nt}}[H])$ is itself a parameter to be tuned. Therefore, an annotation symbol, say, x, generally does not express any commonalities among the complete nonterminal symbols annotated by x, such as $A[x], B[x], etc.$ The parameters β and π satisfy the normalization constraints:

$$\sum_{\alpha \in \{\alpha' \mid (A[x] \to \alpha') \in R[H]\}} \beta(A[x] \to \alpha) = 1 \ \text{ for } \ \forall A[x] \in N_{\text{nt}}[H]$$

$$\sum_{A[x] \in N_{\text{nt}}[H]} \pi(A[x]) = 1.$$

The probability of a complete parse tree $T[\mathbf{X}]$ is defined as

$$P(T[\mathbf{X}]) = \pi(A_1[x_1]) \prod_{r \in D_{T[\mathbf{X}]}} \beta(r), \tag{14.2}$$

where $A_1[x_1]$ is the label of the root node of $T[\mathbf{X}]$ and $D_{T[\mathbf{X}]}$ denotes the multiset of annotated CFG rules used in the generation of $T[\mathbf{X}]$. We have the probability of an observable tree T by marginalizing out the latent annotation symbols in $T[\mathbf{X}]$:

$$P(T) = \sum_{X \in H^m} P(T[\mathbf{X}]), \tag{14.3}$$

where m is the number of nonterminal nodes in T.

14.2.2   Forward-backward probability

The sum in equation 14.3 can be calculated using a dynamic programming algorithm analogous to the backward algorithm for HMMs. For a sentence $w_1 w_2 \ldots w_n$ and its parse tree T, backward probabilities $b_T^i(x)$ are recursively computed for the i-th nonterminal node and for each $x \in H$. In the definition that follows, $N_i \in N_{\text{nt}}$ denotes the nonterminal label of the i-th node.

- If node i is a preterminal node above a terminal symbol w_j, then

$$b_T^i(x) = \beta(N_i[x] \to w_j).$$

- Otherwise, let j and k be the two daughter nodes of i. Then

$$b_T^i(x) = \sum_{x_j, x_k \in H} \beta(N_i[x] \to N_j[x_j] N_k[x_k]) \, b_T^j(x_j) \, b_T^k(x_k).$$

Using backward probabilities, $P(T)$ is calculated as

$$P(T) = \sum_{x_1 \in H} \pi(N_1[x_1]) \, b_T^1(x_1).$$

We define forward probabilities $f_T^i(x)$, which are used in the estimation described later, as follows:

- If node i is the root node (i.e., $i = 1$), then

$$f_T^i(x) = \pi(N_i[x]).$$

- If node i has a right sibling k, let j be the mother node of i. Then

$$f_T^i(x) = \sum_{x_j, x_k \in H} \beta(N_j[x_j] \to N_i[x]N_k[x_k]) \, f_T^j(x_j) \, b_T^k(x_k).$$

- If node i has a left sibling, $f_T^i(x)$ is defined analogously.

14.2.3 Estimation

We now derive the EM algorithm for PCFG-LA, which estimates the parameters $\theta = (\beta, \pi)$. Let $\mathbf{T} = \{T_1, T_2, \dots\}$ be the training set of parse trees and $N_1^i, \dots, N_{m_i}^i$ be the labels of nonterminal nodes in T_i. Like the derivations of the EM algorithms for other latent variable models, the update formulas for the parameters, which update the parameters from θ to $\theta' = (\beta', \pi')$, are obtained by constrained optimization of $Q(\theta'|\theta)$, which is defined as

$$Q(\theta'|\theta) = \sum_{T_i \in \mathbf{T}} \sum_{\mathbf{X}_i \in H^{m_i}} P_\theta(\mathbf{X}_i|T_i) \log P_{\theta'}(T_i[\mathbf{X}_i]),$$

where P_θ and $P_{\theta'}$ denote probabilities under θ and θ', and $P(\mathbf{X}|T)$ is the conditional probability of latent annotation symbols given an observed tree T, i.e., $P(\mathbf{X}|T) = P(T[\mathbf{X}])/P(T)$. Using the Lagrange multiplier method and rearranging the results using the backward and forward probabilities, we obtain the update formulas in figure 14.2.

14.3 Parsing with PCFG-LA

In theory, we can use PCFG-LAs to parse a given sentence w by selecting the most probable parse:

$$T_{\text{best}} = \underset{T \in G(w)}{\operatorname{argmax}} P(T|w)$$

$$= \underset{T \in G(w)}{\operatorname{argmax}} P(T) \tag{14.4}$$

$$= \underset{T \in G(w)}{\operatorname{argmax}} \sum_{X \in H^m} P(T[\mathbf{X}]), \tag{14.5}$$

where $G(w)$ denotes the set of possible parses for w under the observable grammar R and m is the number of nonterminal nodes in T. While the optimization problem in equation 14.4 can be efficiently solved for PCFGs using dynamic programming techniques, the sum-of-products form of $P(T)$ in PCFG-LA models makes it difficult to apply such techniques to solve equation 14.5.

Actually, the optimization problem in equation 14.5, namely, finding the most probable observable tree, is NP-hard for general PCFG-LA models. The NP-hardness is caused by the fact that when we "hide" the latent annotation symbol of a node by marginalizing it out, the nonterminal symbols of its daughter nodes are no longer conditionally independent of the nonterminal symbol of the grandparent node (and more distant ancestors) because the information on the ancestor nodes represented in the latent annotation symbol, given which the distribution of the

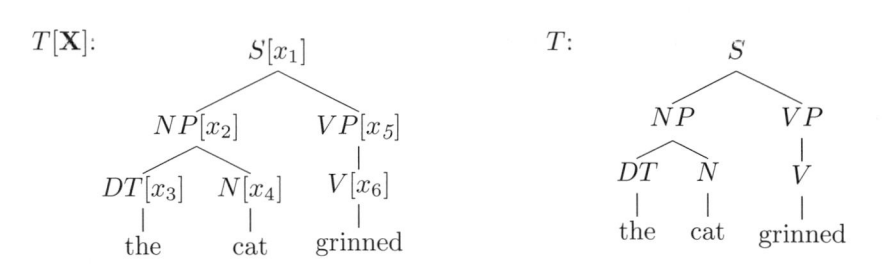

FIGURE 14.1 Tree with latent annotations $T[\mathbf{X}]$ (complete data) and observed tree T (incomplete data).

$$\beta'(A[x] \to B[y]C[z]) = \frac{1}{Z_{A[x]}} \sum_{T_i \in \mathbf{T}} \frac{1}{P(T_i)} \sum_{(j,k,l) \in \mathrm{Covered}(T_i, A \to BC)} f_{T_i}^j(x)\, \beta(A[x] \to B[y]C[z])\, b_{T_i}^k(y)\, b_{T_i}^l(z)$$

$$\beta'(A[x] \to w) = \frac{1}{Z_{A[x]}} \sum_{T_i \in \mathbf{T}} \frac{1}{P(T_i)} \sum_{j \in \mathrm{Covered}(T_i, A \to w)} f_{T_i}^j(x)\, \beta(A[x] \to w)$$

$$\pi'(A[x]) = \frac{1}{|\mathbf{T}|} \sum_{T_i \in \mathrm{Root}(\mathbf{T}, A)} \frac{1}{P(T_i)} \pi(A[x])\, b_{T_i}^1(x)$$

$$Z_{A[x]} = \sum_{T_i \in \mathbf{T}} \frac{1}{P(T_i)} \sum_{j \in \mathrm{Labeled}(T_i, A)} f_{T_i}^j(x)\, b_{T_i}^j(x)$$

$$\mathrm{Covered}(T_i, A \to BC) = \{(j,k,l) \mid N_j^i \to N_k^i N_l^i \in D_{T_i}; (N_j^i, N_k^i, N_l^i) = (A, B, C)\}$$

$$\mathrm{Covered}(T_i, A \to w) = \{j \mid (N_j^i \to w) \in D_{T_i}; N_j^i = A\}$$

$$\mathrm{Labeled}(T_i, A) = \{j \mid N_j^i = A\}$$

$$\mathrm{Root}(\mathbf{T}, A) = \{T_i \in \mathbf{T} \mid N_1^i = A\}$$

FIGURE 14.2 Parameter update formulas.

daughter symbols are conditionally independent of ancestor symbols, is hidden. Although we omit the details, we can prove the NP-hardness by observing that a stochastic tree substitution grammar (STSG) can be represented by a PCFG-LA model in a similar way to one described by Goodman (1996a), and then using the NP-hardness of STSG parsing (Sima'an, 2002).

The difficulty of the exact optimization in equation 14.5 forces us to use some approximations of it. The rest of this section describes three different approximations, which are empirically compared in the next section. The first method simply limits the number of candidate parse trees T compared in equation 14.4; we first create n-best parses using a PCFG and then, within the n-best parses, select the one with the highest probability according to the PCFG-LA model. The other two methods are a little more complicated, and we explain them in separate subsections.

14.3.1 Approximation by Viterbi complete trees

The second approximation method selects the best *complete* tree $T'[\mathbf{X}']$, that is,

$$T'[\mathbf{X}'] = \operatorname*{argmax}_{T \in G(w), \mathbf{X} \in H^{|\mathbf{X}|}} P(T[\mathbf{X}]). \tag{14.6}$$

We call $T'[\mathbf{X}']$ a Viterbi complete tree. Such a tree can be obtained in $O(|w|^3)$ time by regarding the PCFG-LA as a PCFG with annotated symbols.[2]

The observable part of the Viterbi complete tree $T'[\mathbf{X}']$ (i.e., T') does not necessarily coincide with the best observable tree T_{best} in equation 14.4. However, if T_{best} has a "dominant" assignment $\mathbf{Y}$ to its latent annotation symbols such that $P(T_{\text{best}}[\mathbf{Y}]) \approx P(T_{\text{best}})$, then $P(T') \approx P(T_{\text{best}})$ because $P(T_{\text{best}}[\mathbf{Y}]) \leq P(T'[\mathbf{X}'])$ and $P(T'[\mathbf{X}']) \leq P(T') \leq P(T_{\text{best}})$, and thus T' and T_{best} are almost equally "good" in terms of their marginal probabilities.

14.3.2 Viterbi parse in approximate distribution

In the third method, we approximate the true distribution $P(T|w)$ by a cruder distribution $Q(T|w)$. The approximate distribution Q is defined to be in a simple form so that the tree with the highest $Q(T|w)$ is easily found.

We first create a packed representation of $G(w)$ for a given sentence w.[3] Then, the approximate distribution $Q(T|w)$ is created using the packed forest, and the parameters in $Q(T|w)$ are adjusted so that $Q(T|w)$ approximates $P(T|w)$ as closely as possible. The form of $Q(T|w)$ is that of a product of the parameters, just like the form of a PCFG model, and thus we can find the tree with the highest $Q(T|w)$ by using the Viterbi algorithm.

A packed forest is defined as a tuple $\langle I, \delta \rangle$. The first component, I, is a multiset of chart items of the form $\langle A, b, e \rangle$. A chart item $\langle A, b, e \rangle \in I$ indicates that there exists a parse tree in $G(w)$ that contains a constituent with the nonterminal label A that spans from the b-th to e-th word in w. The second component, δ, is a function on I that represents dominance relations among the chart items in I; $\delta(i)$ is a set of possible daughters of i if i is not a preterminal node, and $\delta(i) = \{w_k\}$ if i is a preterminal node above w_k. Two parse trees for a sentence $w = w_1w_2w_3$ and a packed representation of them are shown in figure 14.3.

We require that each tree $T \in G(w)$ has a unique representation as a set of connected chart items in I. A packed representation satisfying the uniqueness condition is obtained by using the CKY algorithm with the observable grammar R.

The approximate distribution, $Q(T|w)$, is defined as a PCFG, whose CFG rules R_w is defined as $R_w = \{(i \to \eta) \mid i \in I; \eta \in \delta(i)\}$. Thus, the PCFG derives only the input sentence w. We use $q(r)$ to denote the rule probability of rule $r \in R_w$ and $q_r(i)$ to denote the probability with which $i \in I$ is generated as a root node. We thus define $Q(T|w)$ as

$$Q(T|w) = q_r(i_1) \prod_{k=1}^{m} q(i_k \to \eta_k),$$

where the set of connected items $\{i_1, \ldots, i_m\} \subset I$ is the unique representation of T. In the example in figure 14.3, the approximated probability of the left tree, T_1, is

$$\begin{aligned}
Q(T_1|w) = {} & q_r(\langle A, 1, 3\rangle) \\
& \times q(\langle A, 1, 3\rangle \to \langle B, 1, 2\rangle\langle E, 3, 3\rangle) \\
& \times q(\langle B, 1, 2\rangle \to \langle C, 1, 1\rangle\langle D, 2, 2\rangle) \\
& \times q(\langle C, 1, 1\rangle \to w_1)\ q(\langle D, 2, 2\rangle \to w_2)\ q(\langle E, 3, 3\rangle \to w_3).
\end{aligned}$$

In this example, most of qs and q_rs equal to one because all the chart items except for i_1 have unique daughter items (i.e., $|\delta(i) = 1|$), and hence $Q(T_1|w)$ is simplified to be

$$Q(T_1|w) = q(\langle A, 1, 3\rangle \to \langle B, 1, 2\rangle\langle E, 3, 3\rangle).$$

Note that I is a *multiset* of chart items; two chart items i_1 and i_2, which have the same nonterminal symbol and the same span, can both exist in I. By having such duplicated chart items, an effect similar to "parent-annotation" (Johnson, 1998) represented in the original distribution P is retained through the approximation; if i_1 and i_2 have the same nonterminal symbol but are dominated by different parent nodes, different rule probabilities $q(i_1 \to \eta)$ and $q(i_2 \to \eta)$ are assigned even if they share a common sequence of daughters η.

As suggested, we can choose the degree of approximation by changing the "packedness" of the packed representation; a more loosely packed representation (i.e., a packed chart that contains more duplicated chart items) gives a more accurate approximation. The packedness can be controlled by using R with different levels of ancestor annotations; for example, R with grandparent annotation makes a more loosely packed structure than R with parent annotation does.

To measure the closeness of approximation by $Q(T|w)$, we use the "inclusive" KL-divergence, $KL(P||Q)$ (Frey et al., 2000):

$$KL(P||Q) = \sum_{T \in G(w)} P(T|w) \log \frac{P(T|w)}{Q(T|w)}.$$

Minimizing $KL(P||Q)$ under the normalization constraints on q_r and q yields closed form solutions for q_r and q as follows:

- If $i_1 \in I$ is not a preterminal node, for each $\eta = i_2 i_3 \in \delta(i_1)$, let A, B, and C be nonterminal symbols of i_1, i_2, and i_3, then,

$$q(i_1 \to \eta) = \frac{\sum\limits_{x \in H} \sum\limits_{y \in H} \sum\limits_{z \in H} P_{\text{out}}(i_1[x]) \beta(A[x] \to B[y]C[z]) P_{\text{in}}(i_2[y]) P_{\text{in}}(i_3[z])}{\sum\limits_{x \in H} P_{\text{out}}(i_1[x]) P_{\text{in}}(i_1[x])}.$$

- If $i \in I$ is a preterminal node above word w_k, then $q(i \to w_k) = 1$.
- If $i \in I$ is a root node, let A be the nonterminal symbol of i, then,

$$q_r(i) = \frac{1}{P(w)} \sum_{x \in H} \pi(A[x]) P_{\text{in}}(i[x]).$$

P_{in} and P_{out} are defined analogously as ordinary inside/outside probabilities. We define P_{in} as follows:

- If $i = (A, k, k) \in I$ is a preterminal node above w_k, then

$$P_{\text{in}}(i[x]) = \beta(A[x] \to w_k).$$

- Otherwise,

$$P_{\text{in}}(i[x]) = \sum_{jk \in \delta(i)} \sum_{y \in H} \sum_{z \in H} \beta(A[x] \to B_j[y] C_k[z]) P_{\text{in}}(j[y]) P_{\text{in}}(k[z]),$$

where B_j and C_k denote nonterminal symbols of chart items j and k.

The outside probability, P_{out}, is calculated using P_{in} and PCFG-LA parameters along the packed structure, as follows:

- If $i = (A, 1, |w|)$ is a root node,

$$P_{\text{out}}(i[x]) = \pi(A[x]).$$

- Otherwise,

$$P_{\text{out}}(i[x]) = \sum_{(j,k)} \sum_{y \in H} \sum_{z \in H} \beta(B_j[y] \to A[x] C_k[z]) P_{\text{out}}(j[y]) P_{\text{in}}(k[z])$$

$$+ \sum_{(h,l)} \sum_{y \in H} \sum_{z \in H} \beta(B_h[y] \to C_l[z] A[x]) P_{\text{out}}(h[y]) P_{\text{in}}(l[z]),$$

where $(j,k)/(h,l)$ in the first/second sum runs over (parent, right/left daughter) pairs of chart items that have i as the left/right daughter.

Once we have computed $q(i \to \eta)$ and $q_r(i)$, the parse tree T that maximizes $Q(T|w)$ is found using a Viterbi algorithm, as in PCFG parsing.

Several parsing algorithms that also use inside-outside calculation on packed chart have been proposed (Goodman, 1996b; Sima'an, 2003; Clark and Curran, 2004). Those algorithms optimize some evaluation metric of parse trees other than the posterior probability $P(T|w)$, for example, (expected) labeled constituent recall or (expected) recall rate of dependency relations contained in a parse. It is in contrast with our approach, where (approximated) posterior probability, $Q(T|w)$ is optimized.

14.4   Experiments

We conducted four sets of experiments. In the first set of experiments, the degree of dependency of trained models on initialization was examined since EM-style algorithms yield different results with different initial values of parameters. In the second set of experiments, we examined the relationship between model types and their parsing performances. In the third set of experiments, we compared the three parsing methods described in the previous section. Finally, we show the result of a parsing experiment using the standard test set.

We used sections 2 through 20 of the Penn WSJ corpus as training data and section 21 as heldout data. The heldout data was used for early stopping; that is, the estimation was stopped when the rate of increase in the likelihood of the heldout data became lower than a certain threshold. Section 22 was used as test data in all parsing experiments except in the final one, in which section 23 was used. We stripped off all function tags and eliminated empty nodes in the training and heldout data, but any other preprocessing, such as comma raising or base-NP marking (Collins, 1999), was not done except for binarizations.

14.4.1   Dependency on initial values

To see the degree of dependency of trained models on initializations, four instances of the same model were trained with different initial values of parameters.[4] The model used in this experiment was created by **CENTER-PARENT** binarization (explained shortly) and $|H|$ was set to 16. Table 14.1 lists training/heldout data log-likelihood per sentence (LL) for the four instances and their parsing performances on the test set (section 22). The parsing performances were obtained using the approximate distribution method in section 14.3.2. Different initial values were shown to affect the results of training to some extent.

14.4.2   Model types and parsing performance

We compared four types of binarization shown in figure 14.4. In the first two methods, called **CENTER-PARENT** and **CENTER-HEAD**, the head-finding rules of Collins (1999) were used. Note that latent symbols are attached both to "original" nodes (e.g., A) and to "artificial" nodes (e.g., $\langle A \rangle$). We obtained an observable grammar R for each model by reading off grammar rules from the binarized training trees. For each binarization method, PCFG-LA models with different numbers of latent annotation symbols, $|H| = 1, 2, 4, 8$, and 16, were trained.

The relationships between the number of parameters in the models and their parsing performances are shown in figure 14.5. Note that models created using

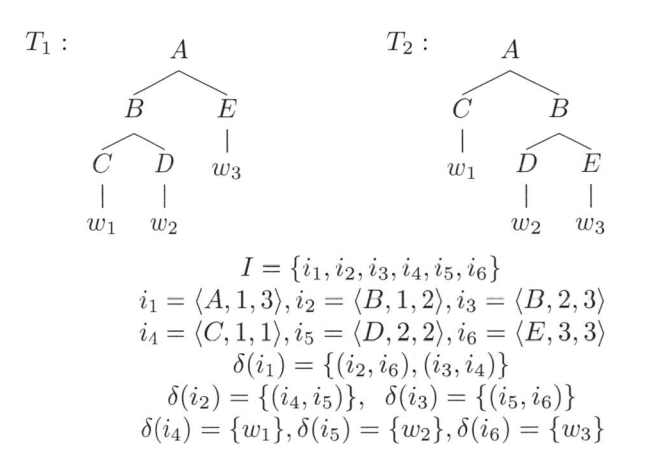

$$I = \{i_1, i_2, i_3, i_4, i_5, i_6\}$$
$$i_1 = \langle A, 1, 3 \rangle, i_2 = \langle B, 1, 2 \rangle, i_3 = \langle B, 2, 3 \rangle$$
$$i_4 = \langle C, 1, 1 \rangle, i_5 = \langle D, 2, 2 \rangle, i_6 = \langle E, 3, 3 \rangle$$
$$\delta(i_1) = \{(i_2, i_6), (i_3, i_4)\}$$
$$\delta(i_2) = \{(i_4, i_5)\}, \quad \delta(i_3) = \{(i_5, i_6)\}$$
$$\delta(i_4) = \{w_1\}, \delta(i_5) = \{w_2\}, \delta(i_6) = \{w_3\}$$

FIGURE 14.3 Two parse trees and packed representation of them.

TABLE 14.1 Dependency on initial values.

	1	2	3	4	average $\pm\ \sigma$
training LL	-115	-114	-115	-114	-114 $\pm$ 0.41
heldout LL	-114	-115	-115	-114	-114 $\pm$ 0.29
LR	86.7	86.3	86.3	87.0	86.6 $\pm$ 0.27
LP	86.2	85.6	85.5	86.6	86.0 $\pm$ 0.48

different binarization methods have different numbers of parameters for the same $|H|$. The parsing performances were measured using F_1 scores of the parse trees that were obtained by reranking of 1000-best parses by a PCFG.

We can see that the parsing performance gets better as the model size increases. We can also see that models of roughly the same size yield similar performances regardless of the binarization scheme used for them, except the models created using LEFT binarization with small numbers of parameters ($|H| = 1$ and 2). Taking into account the dependency on initial values at the level shown in the previous experiment, we cannot say that any single model is superior to the other models when the sizes of the models are large enough.

The results shown in figure 14.5 suggest that we could further improve parsing performance by increasing the model size. However, both the memory size and the training time are more than linear in $|H|$, and the training time for the largest ($|H| = 16$) models was about 15 hours for the models created using CENTER-PARENT, CENTER-HEAD, and LEFT and about 20 hours for the model created using RIGHT. To deal with larger (e.g., $|H| = 32$ or 64) models, we therefore need to use a model search that reduces the number of parameters while maintaining the model's performance, and an approximation during training to reduce the training time.

14.4.3   Comparison of parsing methods

The relationships between the average parse time and parsing performance using the three parsing methods described in section 14.3 are shown in figure 14.6. A model created using CENTER-PARENT with $|H| = 16$ was used throughout this experiment.

The data points were made by varying configurable parameters of each method, which control the number of candidate parses. To create the candidate parses, we first parsed input sentences using a PCFG,[5]using beam thresholding with beam width α. The data points on a line in the figure were created by varying α with other parameters fixed. The first method reranked the N-best parses enumerated from the chart after the PCFG parsing. The two lines for the first method in the figure correspond to $N = 100$ and $N = 300$. In the second and the third methods, we removed all the dominance relations among chart items that did not contribute to any parses whose PCFG-scores were higher than $\gamma P_{\max}$, where $P_{\max}$ is the PCFG-score of the best parse in the chart. The parses remaining in the chart were the candidate parses for the second and the third methods. The different lines for the second and the third methods correspond to different values of γ.

The third method outperforms the other two methods unless the parse time is very limited (i.e., < 1 sec is required), as shown in the figure. The superiority of the third method over the first method seems to stem from the difference in the number of candidate parses from which the outputs are selected.[6] The superiority of the third method over the second method is a natural consequence of the consistent use

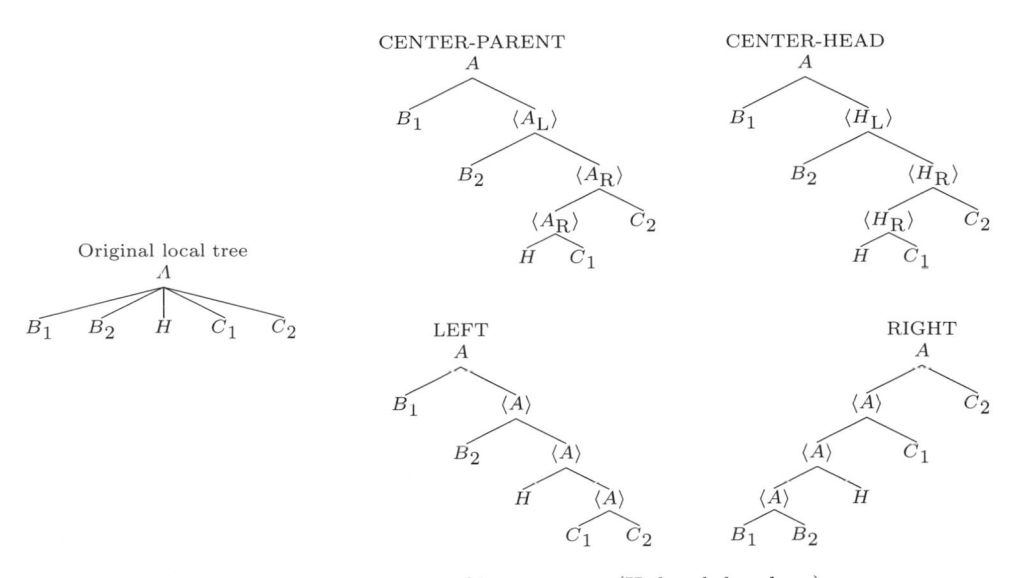

FIGURE 14.4 Four types of binarization (H: head daughter).

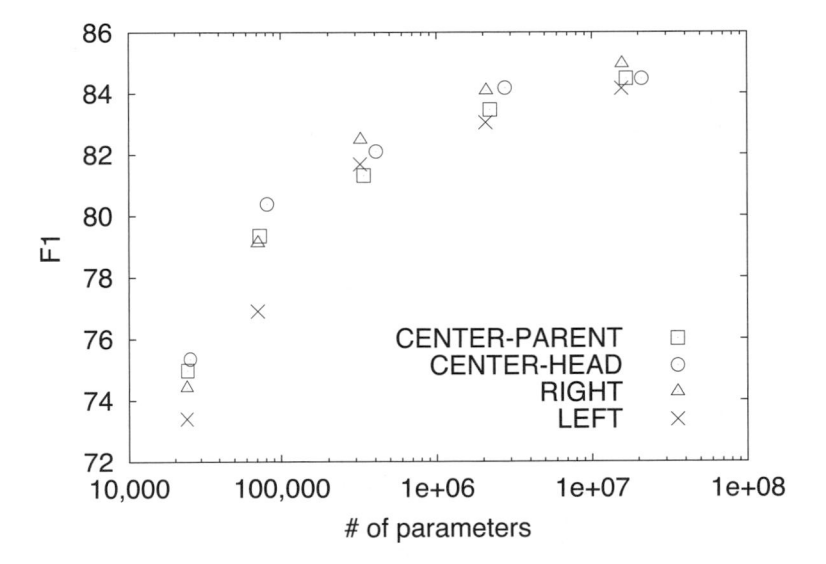

FIGURE 14.5 Model size vs. parsing performance.

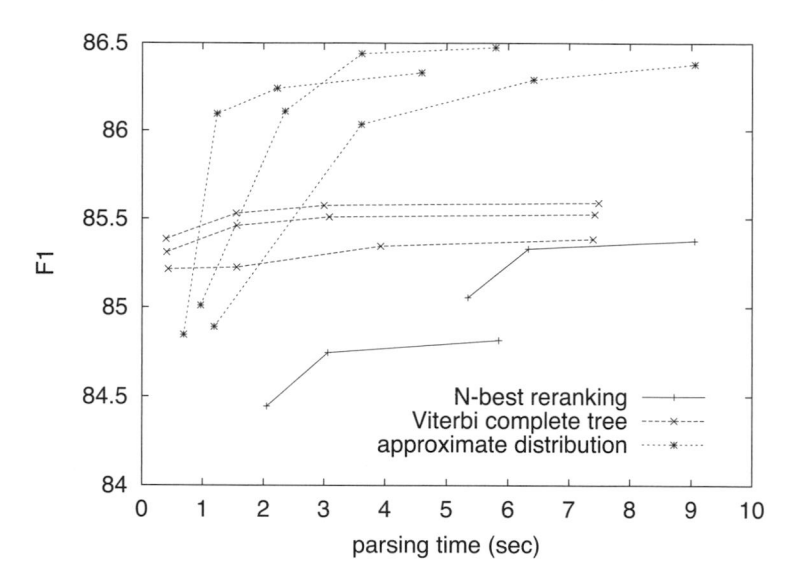

FIGURE 14.6   Comparison of parsing methods.

of $P(T)$ both in the estimation (as the objective function) and in the parsing (as the score of a parse).

14.4.4   Comparison with related work

Parsing performance on section 23 of the WSJ corpus using a PCFG-LA model is shown in table 14.2. We used the instance of the four compared in the second experiment that gave the best results on the development set. Several previously reported results on the same test set are also listed in table 14.2.

TABLE 14.2   Comparison with other parsers.

$\leq$ 40 words	LR	LP	CB	0 CB
This chapter	86.7	86.6	1.19	61.1
Klein and Manning (2003)	85.7	86.9	1.10	60.3
Collins (1999)	88.5	88.7	0.92	66.7
Charniak (2000)	90.1	90.1	0.74	70.1
$\leq$ 100 words	LR	LP	CB	0 CB
This chapter	86.0	86.1	1.39	58.3
Klein and Manning (2003)	85.1	86.3	1.31	57.2
Collins (1999)	88.1	88.3	1.06	64.0
Charniak (2000)	89.6	89.5	0.88	67.6

Our result is lower than the state-of-the-art lexicalized PCFG parsers (Collins, 1999; Charniak, 2000), but comparable to the unlexicalized PCFG parser of Klein and Manning (2003). Klein and Manning's PCFG is annotated by many linguistically motivated features that they found using extensive manual feature selection. In contrast, our method induces all parameters automatically, except that manually written head rules are used in binarization. Thus, we could say that our method extracts a considerable amount of hidden regularity from parsed corpora. However, our result is worse than the lexicalized parsers, even though our model has access to words in the sentences. It suggests that certain types of information used in those lexicalized parsers are difficult to learn for our approach.

14.5   Conclusion and Future Directions

We have introduced an extension of PCFG in which nonterminal symbols are augmented by latent variables. An EM-algorithm for the model and three approximate parsing algorithms have also been described. A main advantage of our approach is that it does not require manual feature selection or any special skill on translating linguistic notions to a form of probability model. The approach gives 86.0% F_1 score on the standard test set, which indicates that a considerable amount of information traditionally "hard-coded" in probability models as features can automatically be induced from parsed corpora.

A possible future direction of our approach is to develop a method that systematically selects a proper level of subdivision for each nonterminal symbol by adjusting the number of values of latent variables attached to each nonterminal symbol. In our current approach, all nonterminal symbols have the same number of possible latent annotation. We could, by relaxing this ad-hoc restriction, further improve the expressiveness of the model and hence its parsing performance. Utsuro et al. (1996) proposed a method with similar objective. However, its different nature limits direct application of their method to ours. Especially, we might need special attention to keep the computational cost required in such a method within a realistic level.

Notes

1.   This is not surprising, since the model is designed to overcome the wrong Markov assumption made in PCFG and what facilitates to find MPPs in the case of PCFG is the markov assumption itself.

2.   It is not necessary to parse an input sentence with $R[H]$. In the experiments in section 14.4, we first parsed an input sentence with observable grammar R to make a packed parse forest for the sentence and then found a Viterbi complete tree by selecting the most probable annotation symbol for each node in the packed forest in a bottom-up direction.

3. In practice, fully constructing a packed representation of $G(w)$ has an unrealistically high cost for most input sentences. Alternatively, we can use a packed representation of a subset of $G(w)$, which is obtained by parsing with beam thresholding, for instance. An approximate distribution $Q(T|w)$ on such subsets can be derived in almost the same way as one for the full $G(w)$, but the conditional distribution, $P(T|w)$, is renormalized so that the total mass for the subset sums to 1.

4. The initial value for an annotated rule probability, $\beta(A[x] \rightarrow B[y]C[z])$, was created by randomly multiplying the maximum likelihood estimation of the corresponding PCFG rule probability, $P(A \rightarrow BC)$, as follows:

$$\beta(A[x] \rightarrow B[y]C[z]) = Z_{A[x]}^{-1} e^{\gamma} P(A \rightarrow BC),$$

where γ is a random number that is uniformly distributed in $[-\log 3, \log 3]$ and $Z_{A[x]}$ is a normalization constant.

5. The PCFG used in creating the candidate parses is roughly the same as the one that Klein and Manning (2003) call a "markovised PCFG with vertical order = 2 and horizontal order = 1" and was extracted from sections 02–20. The PCFG itself gave a performance of 79.6/78.5 LP/LR on the development set. This PCFG was also used in the experiment in section 14.4.4.

6. Actually, the number of parses contained in the packed forest is more than 1 million for over half of the test sentences when $\alpha = 10^{-4}$ and $\gamma = 10^{-3}$, while the number of parses for which the first method can compute the exact probability in a comparable time (around 4 sec) is only about 300.

References

Charniak, E. (2000). A maximum-entropy-inspired parser. In *Proc. NAACL*, pages 132–139.

Chiang, D. and Bikel, D. M. (2002). Recovering latent information in treebanks. In *Proc. COLING*, pages 183–189.

Clark, S. and Curran, J. R. (2004). Parsing the WSJ using CCG and log-linear models. In *Proc. ACL*, pages 104–111.

Collins, M. (1999). *Head-Driven Statistical Models for Natural Language Parsing*. PhD thesis, University of Pennsylvania.

Frey, B. J., Patrascu, R., Jaakkola, T., and Moran, J. (2000). Sequentially fitting "inclusive" trees for inference in noisy-OR networks. In *Proc. NIPS*, pages 493–499.

Goodman, J. (1996a). Efficient algorithms for parsing the DOP model. In *Proc. EMNLP*, pages 143–152.

Goodman, J. (1996b). Parsing algorithms and metric. In *Proc. ACL*, pages 177–183.

Goodman, J. (1997). Probabilistic feature grammars. In *Proc. IWPT*.

Henderson, J. (2003). Inducing history representations for broad coverage statistical parsing. In *Proc. HLT-NAACL*, pages 103–110.

Johnson, M. (1998). PCFG models of linguistic tree representations. *Computational Linguistics*, 24(4):613–632.

Jordan, M. I., Ghahramani, Z., Jaakkola, T., and Saul, L. K. (1999). An introduction to variational methods for graphical models. *Machine Learning*, 37(2):183–233.

Klein, D. and Manning, C. D. (2003). Accurate unlexicalized parsing. In *Proc. ACL*, pages 423–430.

Pereira, F. and Schabes, Y. (1992). Inside-outside reestimation from partially bracketed corpora. In *Proc. ACL*, pages 128–135.

Shen, L. (2004). Nondeterministic LTAG derivation tree extraction. In *Proc. TAG+7*, pages 199–203.

Sima'an, K. (2002). Computational complexity of probabilistic disambiguation. *Grammars*, 5(2):125–151.

Sima'an, K. (2003). On maximizing metrics for syntactic disambiguation. In *Proc. IWPT*.

Utsuro, T., Kodama, S., and Matsumoto, Y. (1996). Generalization/specialization of context free grammars based-on entropy of non-terminals. In *Proc. JSAI (in Japanese)*, pages 327–330.

15

Computational Paninian Grammar Framework

Akshar Bharati and Rajeev Sangal

15.1 Introduction

This chapter presents the Computational Paninian Grammar (CPG) framework and its comparision with Tree-Adjoining Grammar and Supertagging. Paninian framework is explicated through its application to modern Indian languages. These languages have free word order and a rich system of case endings and postpositions.

In the Paninian framework, a sentence is analyzed in terms of dependency relations, more specifically modifier-modified relations.[1] A verb is related to its arguments through karaka relations (pronounced "kaaraka"), which are syntactico-semantic relations. Other relations are verb-verb relations indicating simultaneity, precedence, and the like; and noun-noun relations; and so forth.

Paninian grammar framework is an elegant account of modern Indian languages, and a computational account as well. As a result, the theory has elements that allow a system to be built for derivation and representation of meaning.

Section 15.2 goes into details of CPG for modern Indian languages. Section 15.3 presents some surprising similarities between CPG and Tree-Adjoining Grammar (TAG). Relation with supertagging also follows naturally. Section 15.4 gives details of a constraint parser for CPG.

15.2 CPG for Indian languages

The Paninian framework considers *information* as central to the study of language. When a writer (or a speaker) uses language to convey some information to the reader (or the hearer), he codes the information in the language string.[2] Similarly, when a reader (or a hearer) receives a language string, he extracts the information coded in it. The Computational Paninian Grammar framework (CPG) is primarily concerned with how the information is coded and how it can be extracted.

Two levels of representation can be readily seen in language use: One, the actual language string (or sentence), two, what the speaker has in his mind. The latter can also be called as the meaning. Paninian framework has two other important levels: *karaka* and *vibhakti* (figure 15.1).

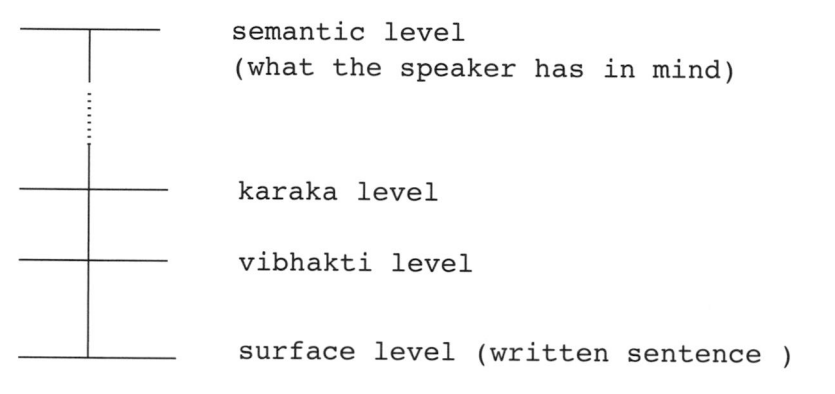

```
                    semantic level
                    (what the speaker has in mind)



                    karaka level

                    vibhakti level

                    surface level (written sentence )
```

FIGURE 15.1 Levels of representation/analysis in the Paninian model

The surface level is the uttered or the written sentence. The vibhakti level is the level at which there are local word groups together with case endings, prepositions or postposition markers.[3]

At the karaka level, we have karaka relations, verb-verb relations, and so on. Karaka relations are syntactico-semantic (or semantico-syntactic) relations between the verbs and other related constituents (typically nouns) in a sentence. They capture a certain level of semantics that is close to thematic relations but different from it. But this is the level of semantics that is important syntactically and that is reflected in the surface form of the sentence(s).

The vibhakti level abstracts away from many minor (including orthographic and idiosyncratic) differences among languages. The topmost level relates to what the speaker has in mind. This may be considered to be the ultimate meaning level. Between this level and vibhakti level is the karaka level. It includes karaka relations and a few additional relations such as taadaarthya (purpose). One can imagine several levels between the karaka and the ultimate level, each containing more semantic information. Thus, karaka is one in a series of levels, but one that has relationship to semantics on one hand and syntax on the other.

As mentioned earlier, vibhakti for verbs can be defined similar to that for the nouns. A head verb may be followed by auxiliary verbs (which may remain as separate words or may combine with the head verb). Such information, consisting of the verb ending, the auxiliary verbs, and the like, is collectively called vibhakti for the verb. The vibhakti for a verb gives information about tense, aspect, and modality (TAM) and is therefore also called the TAM label. TAM labels are purely syntactic, determined from the verb form and the auxiliary verbs.

The grammar gives the mapping between the levels. For example, CPG specifies a mapping between the karaka level and the vibhakti level, and the vibhakti level and the surface form.

It has been shown earlier (Bharati et al., 1995) that the Paninian grammar is particularly suited to free-word-order languages. It gives a mapping between karaka relations and vibhakti, and uses position information only secondarily. As the Indian languages have (relatively) free word order and vibhakti, they are eminently suited to be described by Paninian grammar.

15.2.1 Karaka-vibhakti mapping

The most important insight regarding the karaka-vibhakti mapping is that it depends on the verb and its tense aspect modality (TAM) label. The mapping is represented by two structures: verb karaka frame (earlier called karaka chart) and karaka frame transformation. The basic karaka frame for a verb or a class of verbs specifies the vibhakti permitted for each of the nouns, which are its karaka relations.[4] In other words, when the verb in a sentence has the basic TAM label, then vibhakti is specified by the karaka frame for each of its related nouns in the sentence.

The basic karaka frame for three of the karakas is given in figure 15.2. This

Karaka	*Vibhakti*	*Presence*
Karta	ϕ	mandatory
Karma	ko or ϕ	mandatory
Karana	se or dvaaraa	optional

FIGURE 15.2 Default karaka frame

explains the vibhaktis in sentences (1)a and (1)b.

Take for example, the following modifier-modified structure: Using the karaka

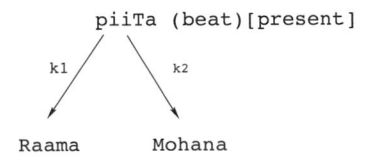

frame, we get the following vibhaktis:

raama [φ], mohana [ko], piiTa [taa_hei]

which yield the following sentences:

(1)   a. *raama mohana ko   piiTataa hei.*
          Ram   Mohan -ko beat   is

          Ram beats Mohan.

       b. *mohana ko   raama piiTataa hei.*
          Mohan -ko Ram   beat   is

          Ram beats Mohan.

Note that no order is specified by the grammar among the nouns.

The basic TAM label chosen for Hindi is *taa_hei* and roughly corresponds to present indefinite tense. For TAM labels other than basic, there are karaka frame transformation rules that need to be used first. For a given verb in a sentence, appropriate karaka-vibhakti mapping can be obtained in a two step procedure: First, using the basic karaka frame for the verbal root, and applying the transformation rule depending on its TAM label, a transformed karaka frame is obtained for the verb. Second, the transformed karaka frame determines the karakas of the verb using the vibhakti information. (Note that any other TAM label could have been chosen as basic without any problem. Moreover, the TAM labels are purely syntactic in nature and can be determined by looking at the verb form and the associated auxiliary verbs.)

It is important to reemphasize that the transformation depends on the TAM label, which is purely syntactic, and not on tense/time, aspect, and modality which are semantic. The TAM label can be determined for Hindi and other Indian languages by syntactic forms of the verb and its auxiliaries without the need to refer to any semantic aspects. The specification for obtaining TAM labels can be given by a finite state machine (Bharati et al., 1995, Chapter 4).

Paninian theory (i.e., karaka frames and karaka frame transformations) can be used to generate (or analyze) sentences such we have seen. However, there are additional constraints that would disallow the following sentences to be generated, for example[5]:

(2)   a. **ladake ne   raama ne laDakii ko   kitaaba dii.*
          boy   -ne Ram   -ne girl   -ko book   gave

          *The Ram the boy gave a book to the girl.

       b. **laDake ne   laDakii ko   kitaaba phoola dii.*
          boy   -ne girl   -ko book   flower gave

          *The boy gave a book a flower to the girl.

The constraints are

1. Each mandatory karaka in the karaka frame for each verb group, is expressed *exactly once*. (In other words, a given mandatory karaka generates only one noun group with the specified vibhakti in its karaka frame unlike in (2)a.)
2. Each optional karaka in the karaka frame for each verb group, is expressed *at most once*.

3. Each source word group satisfies some karaka relation with some verb (or some other relation). In other words, there should no unconnected source word group in a sentence, otherwise, the sentence becomes bad as in (2)b.

Karaka frames are based on the idea of aakaankshaa and yogyataa. A karaka frame for a verb expresses its aakaankshaas, or demands, and specifies the vibhaktis that must be used (i.e., yogyataa) with word groups that satisfy the demands. The same ideas can be used to handle noun-adjectives, noun-noun relations, verb-verb relations, and so on each of which can be viewed as a demand-satisfaction pair.

15.2.2   Complex sentences

Let us now consider the generation of sentences with more than one verb group. We begin with an example. Suppose the speaker (or writer) wants to express the fact that

(3)   a. *raama ne   mohana ko   phala khaakara   bulaaya*
        Ram   erg. Mohan dat fruit having-eaten called

   Ram called Mohan having eaten the fruit.

This can be expressed by the structure at the karaka level shown in figure 15.3.

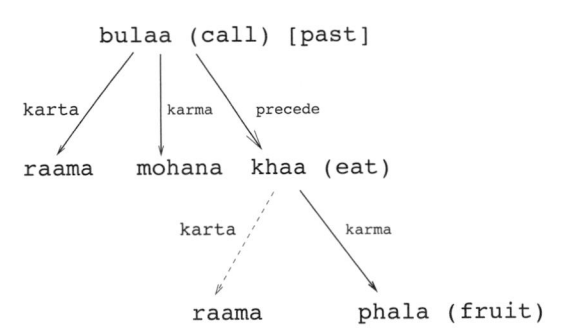

FIGURE 15.3 Modifier-modified relations for a complex sentence (shared karakas shown by dotted lines)

One way of realizing it in a sentence is to choose *kara* TAM label for *khaa* (eat). This label specifies the temporal precedence relation with its parent node *bulaa* (call).[6]

The vibhaktis for the nouns can now be generated using the karaka frame (i.e., the basic karaka frame together with karaka frame transformation rule for *kara* shown in figure 15.4). In this example, the transformed karaka frame shows that the karta of *khaa* is not expressed. The vibhaktis for the nouns in figure 15.3 are as follows:

   raama [φ], mohana [ko], phala [φ], khaa [kara], bulaa [taa_hei]

The generated sentence reads as:

raama mohana ko phala khaakara bulaataa hei.

The karaka frame transformation rules are given in figure 15.4.

TAM label	Transformation
kara	Karta must not be expressed.
	Karma is optional.
naa	Karta and karma are optional.
taa_huaa	Karta and karma are optional.

FIGURE 15.4 Transformation rules for complex sentences

The karaka-sharing rule is given in Rule S1.

Rule S1: The karta of a verb with TAM label *kara* is the same as the karta of the verb modified by the verb.

15.2.3 Some additional constraints

Three additional constraints are included to handle some more grammatical constructions (Bharati et al., 2002). They are introduced along with example constructions in this subsection.

Sentential Argument of Verb

Some verbs take a sentence as their argument. For example,

(4) a. *raama ne   kahaa ki   vaha ghara jaaegaa*
         Ram   erg. said that he   home will   go.

      Ram said that he will go home.

Here *vaha ghara jaaegaa* (he will go home) is the karma or k2 argument of *kahaa* (say). In other words, the argument of the verb is a verb. In the preceding sentence, that argument appears to the right of the verb rather than to the left in case of normal arguments.

Consequently, two additional information can be specified in the karaka frame:

- ltype: type of lexical category (noun, verb, etc.)
- posn : Position of source word (*l* for left, *r* for right)

Here, is an example karaka frame for *kahaa* (or say) where *sampradaana* stands for beneficiary. When the values of ltype and posn are left blank, they stand for "noun" and *l* (or left) respectively by default.

Karaka	Vibh	Pres	ltype	posn
Karta	ϕ	m		
Karma	ki or ϕ	m	v	r
Sampradana	se or dvaaraa	opt		

FIGURE 15.5 Example karaka frame for 'kahaa'(say)

Adjectives

In case of adjectives, there is a demand frame associated with them, and they require a noun. However, the noun is the parent of the adjective. Therefore, an additional information to indicate the directionality of relation can also be given. For example, for adjectives, the demand frame is given in figure 15.6, where "p" says that the

Karaka	Vibh	Pres	ltype	posn	reln
nmod		m	n		p

FIGURE 15.6 Example demand frame for adjective

noun is the parent of the adjective. Spaces left blank are filled by defaults. (The default for vibhakti is any vibhakti without any constraint; other defaults were given earlier.)

15.3 Lexicalized Representation: Correspondence with TAG

The karaka frames of a verb are elementary lexicalized grammatical structures in CPG, much like supertags. There is a direct correspondence between derivation trees on one hand and modifier-modified trees on the other. As an example, the TAG derivation tree for the sentence

The boy saw a girl.

is shown in figure 15.7.

Similarly, the modifier-modified tree in CPG for the following sentence in Hindi:

(5) a. *usa ladake ne   eka ladakii ko   dekhaa*
         that boy   ergative a   girl   accusative saw
      That boy saw a girl.

is shown in figure 15.8

The similarities are too obvious to be missed. Note also the correspondence between tree addresses in elementary trees of TAG (e.g., address (1) and (2.2) in α_{saw}) and the karaka label of demand word in CPG (e.g., karta and karma of *dekhaa* (saw)).

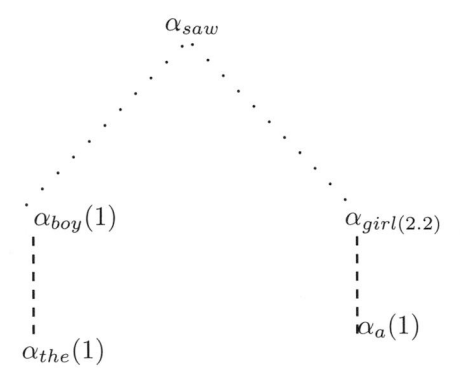

FIGURE 15.7 A TAG derivation tree.

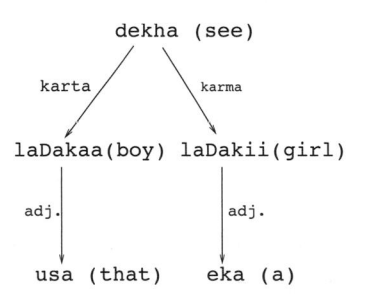

FIGURE 15.8 A CPG modifier-modified tree

Addresses where substitution takes place in an elementary tree indicate its arguments; similarly, the karakas indicate the "arguments" of a verb or a demand word. For example, address 1 of α_{saw}, a formal object at this level of analysis, can be mapped to an appropriate theta role such as agent at the next level of analysis. In the case of CPG, the label karta, again a formal relation at this level of analysis, can be mapped to agent theta role at the next level of analysis.

If one compares the elementary trees (i.e., initial trees and auxiliary trees) in TAG with karaka frames in CPG, one again finds a similarity. An initial tree for a verb anchor (or a demand word) is like a karaka frame (or a demand frame). The initial tree for a verb specifies (along with initial trees for noun) how the nouns "fit" in with the verb anchor. This "fitting" is primarily in terms of word order. The karaka frame in CPG, on the other hand, specifies what vibhaktis must occur with the nouns, for them to "fit" in with the verb. This fitting is in terms of constraints on vibhaktis. All this is perfectly reasonable: Position works for positional languages, and vibhakti works for free-word-order languages. (See Bharati et al. 1997, where CPG has also been applied to English.)

Choosing a karaka frame out of the possible frames for a verb is like supertagging. Just as in TAG, supertagging helps select the elementary trees; similarly, in CPG, selection of the karaka frame would be helped using supertagging. As the grammar for Hindi in CPG framework becomes more extensive with several karaka frames for each verb, choosing the right karaka frame would help speed up parsing, much like how supertagging helps in parsing using TAG. Experimental studies will be carried out after a more extensive grammar is available.

15.4 Constraint-Based Parsing

The Paninian theory outlined herein can be used for building a parser. The first stage of the parser takes care of morphology. For each word in the input sentence, a dictionary or a lexicon is looked up, and the associated grammatical information is retrieved. In the next stage, local word grouping takes place, in which, based on local information, certain words are grouped together, yielding noun groups and verb groups. These are the word groups at the vibhakti level (i.e., typically each word group is a noun or verb with its vibhakti, TAM label, etc.). These involve grouping postpositional markers with nouns, auxiliary verbs with main verbs, and so forth. Rules for local word grouping are given by finite state machines. Finally, the karaka relations among the elements are identified in the last stage, called the *core parser* (Bharati et al., 1995, Chapter 6).

The task of the core parser is to identify karaka relations. It requires karaka frames and transformation rules. For a given sentence after the word groups have been formed, each of the noun groups is tested against each row (called *karaka restriction*) in each karaka frame for each of the verb groups (provided the noun group is to the left of the verb group whose karaka frame is being tested). When testing a noun group against a karaka restriction of a verb group, vibhakti information is checked, and if found satisfactory, the noun group becomes a candidate for the karaka of the verb group.

This can be shown in the form of a constraint graph. Nodes of the graph are the word groups, and there is an arc labeled by a karaka from a verb group to a noun group, if the noun group satisfies the karaka restriction in the karaka frame of the verb group. (There is an arc from one verb group to another, if the karaka frame of the former shows that it takes a sentential or verbal karaka.) The verb groups are called demand groups, since they make demands about their karakas, and the noun groups are called source groups because they satisfy demands.

As an example, consider a sentence containing the verb *khaa* (eat):

(6)   a. *baccaa haatha se kelaa   khaataa hi*
          child   hand   -se banana eats

       The child eats the banana with his hand.

Its word groups are marked, and *khaa* (eat) has the same karaka frame as in figure 15.2. Its constraint graph is shown in figure 15.9.

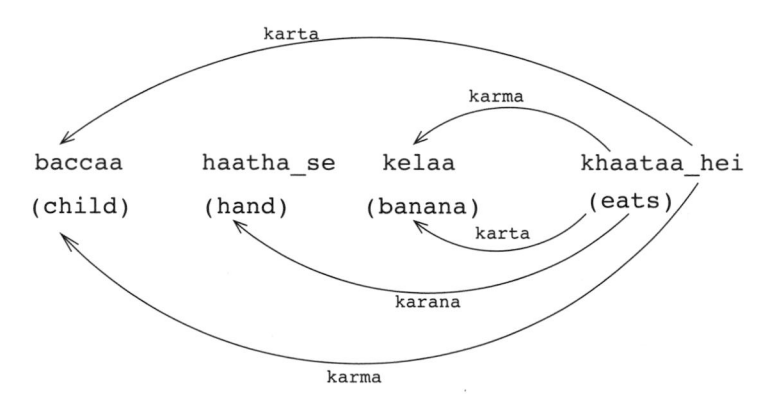

FIGURE 15.9 Constraint graph for sentence (6)

A parse is a sub-graph of the constraint graph containing all the nodes of the constraint graph and satisfying the following conditions:

C1. For each of the mandatory karakas in a karaka frame for each demand group, there should be *exactly one* outgoing edge labeled by the karaka from the demand group.

C2. For each of the desirable or optional karakas in a karaka frame for each demand group, there should be *at most one* outgoing edge labeled by the karaka from the demand group.

C3. There should be *exactly one* incoming arc into each source group.

If several subgraphs of a constraint graph satisfy these conditions, it means that there are multiple parses and the sentence is ambiguous. If no subgraph satisfies the above constraints, the sentence does not have a parse and is probably illformed.

For the example sentence (6), and its constraint graph in figure 15.9, its subgraphs which are solution parses, are given in figure 15.10. Note that only one karta and one karma relations occur in each of the two parses (to satisfy constraint C1), and all the other constraints are also satisfied.

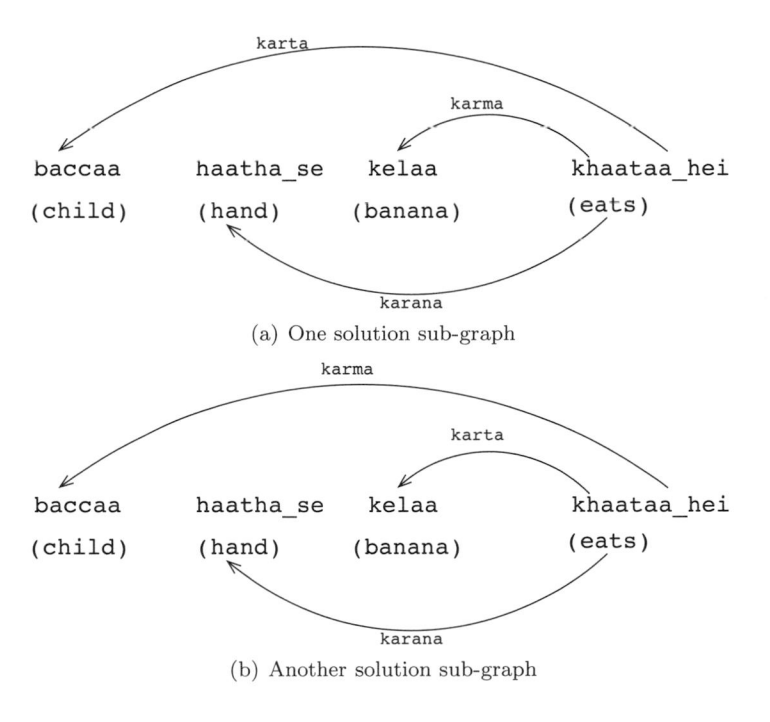

(a) One solution sub-graph

(b) Another solution sub-graph

FIGURE 15.10 Two parses for sentence (6)

15.4.1   Integer programming constraints

A parse can be obtained from the constraint graph using integer programming. A constraint graph is converted into an integer programming problem by introducing a variable x for an arc from node i to j labeled by karaka k in the constraint graph such that for every arc there is a variable. The variables take their values as 0 or 1. A parse is an assignment of 1 to those variables whose corresponding arcs are in the parse subgraph, and 0 to those that are not. Equality and inequality constraints in integer programming problem can be obtained from the conditions (C1, C2, and C3) listed earlier, as follows respectively:

1. For each demand group i, for each of its mandatory karakas k, the following equalities must hold:

$$M_{i,k} : \sum_j x_{i,k,j} = 1$$

Note that $M_{i,k}$ stands for the equation formed, given a demand word i and karaka k (given that the karaka frame has already been selected like in supertagging). Thus, there will be as many equations as combinations of i and k.

2. For each demand group i, for each of its optional or desirable karakas k, the following inequalities must hold:

$$O_{i,k} : \sum_j x_{i,k,j} \leq 1$$

3. For each of the source groups j, the following equalities must hold:

$$S_j : \sum_{i,k} x_{i,k,j} = 1$$

Thus, there will be as many equations as there are source words.

The cost function to be minimized is the sum of all the variables.

15.4.2   Constraint parser using matching and assignment

With the constraints (C1, C2, and C3) specified earlier, the parsing problem reduces to bipartite graph matching[7] and assignment problems (Bharati et al., 1995, chapter 6). These have efficient solutions even in the worst case.

To perform the reduction of the problem of finding a solution graph to finding a matching, first a bipartite graph may be constructed.

A *bipartite graph* G(V,U,E) is defined as:

U: set of nodes $u_1, u_2, ..., u_n$
V: set of nodes $v_1, v_2, ..., v_m$
E: edges between U and V, and $U \bigcap V = \phi$.

The bipartite graph is constructed in three stages:

1. For every source node s in the constraint graph, form a node s in U.

2. For every demand node d in the constraint graph and every mandatory karaka k in the karaka chart for d, form a node v in V. (Thus, for every pair (d,k) there is a node in V.)

3. For every edge (d,s) labeled by karaka k in the constraint graph, create an edge between node (d,k) in V to s in U.

For example, for the constraint graph in figure 15.9 (but assuming that the optional karana karaka is mandatory) we have the bipartite graph in figure 15.11.

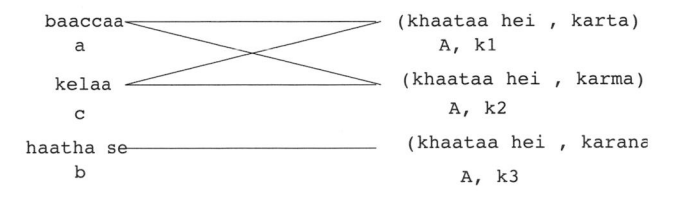

FIGURE 15.11 Bipartite graph for constraint graph in figure 15.9

A *matching* M of a bipartite graph $G = (U, V, E)$ is a subset of edges with the property that no edges of M share the same node. The matching problem is to find a *maximal* matching of G, that is, a matching with the largest number of edges. A maximal matching is called a *complete* matching, if every node in U and V has an edge.

There are two maximal complete matchings of the graph in figure 15.11. They are shown in figure 15.12. They correspond to the parses shown in figure 15.10.

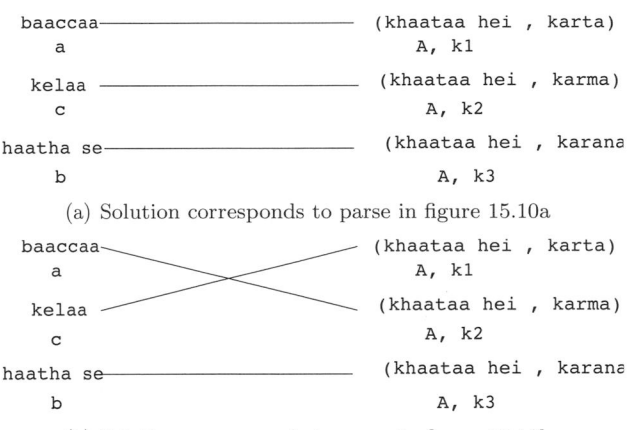

(a) Solution corresponds to parse in figure 15.10a

(b) Solution corresponds to parse in figure 15.10b

FIGURE 15.12 Maximal (complete) matchings of bipartite graph of figure 15.11

Now we show that finding a maximal matching in a bipartite graph is the same as finding a parse in a constraint graph. Let M be a maximal matching of a bipartite graph G. If M is complete, it represents a parse. The proof is easy. For an edge between a node (d,k) in V and a node S in U, it represents the demand for karaka k of the demand node d being satisfied by the source node s. Since all the nodes in V have exactly one edge in M, the original constraint C1 is satisfied. Since all the nodes in U have exactly one edge in M, constraint C3 is satisfied. (And since there are no optional karakas, C2 is satisfied trivially.)

If M is not complete, that is, it does not have an edge on at least one node in U or V, then G does not have a parse. If a node in V does not have an edge, it is a violation of constraint C1, otherwise, it is a violation of constraint C3. Therefore, M is not a parse. Let the cardinality of M be m. Clearly $|U| > m$ or $|V| > m$. Since M is a maximal matching, there is no matching on G with a larger number of edges. Therefore, any other maximal matching (which might choose a different set of edges) will cover exactly m nodes in U and m nodes in V. Consequently, some node in U or V would again not have an edge. Thus, any other maximal matching would also not give us a parse.

The converse is left as an exercise.

To find a maximal matching of a bipartite graph, there is the well-known augmenting path algorithm. (See Papadimitrou and Steiglitz 1982 and Ahuja et al. 1993 for a description.)[8]

This works when all the karakas are mandatory. To handle optional karakas as well, the problem can be reduced to assignment problem, which has a known solution by the Hungarian method with the time complexity $O(n^3)$. See Bharati et al. (1995, section. 6.4.2) to see the reduction.

15.5   Conclusions

In this chapter, we have introduced Computational Paninian Grammar (CPG) formalism, which gives an elegant account for Indian languages. It uses demand frames based on root, transformation of frames based on TAM (tense-aspect-modality), and so on. There are also well developed karaka sharing rules. CPG has also been applied to English elsewhere (Bharati et al., 1997).

There are remarkable similarities between the tree-adjoining grammar (TAG) and the Computational Paninian grammar (CPG). Derivation trees in TAG and modifier-modified trees in CPG have a one-to-one correspondence. It should be noted that the existing TAG and CPG are both lexicalized and have good locality. CPG has optional arguments and sentential arguments of verbs as a part of its karaka frame.

It should be further mentioned here that a dependency treebank for Hindi (based on the Paninian framework) is being created. The framework covers all the relations given here, but it also includes participial and relative clause constructions. Once such a treebank is available, it will be used for conducting experiments pertaining to supertagging as well as full parsing.

15.6   Acknowledgments

The development of the Computational Paninian Grammar (CPG) framework has major inputs from Vineet Chaitanya, who really should be the principal author.

The work also owes a debt of gratitude to K.V. Ramakrishnamacharyulu of Rashtriya Sanskrit Vidyapeetha, Tirupati, who helped with many discussions and clarifications. Amba Kulkarni did work on the development of ideas as well as on implementation of the Paninian framework. The authors were supported by Satyam Computers from 1998 to 2002, which is gratefully acknowledged.

This chapter combines material available in different sources. It includes material from Bharati and colleagues (1995, 2002) on Paninian grammar and parsing.

Notes

1. Paninian theory was formulated by Panini 2,500 years ago for Sanskrit. It evolved with the contributions of grammarians that followed.

2. By string we mean any word, phrase, sentence, paragraph, and the like.

3. For positional languages such as English, it would also include position or word order information.

4. What karaka relations are applicable for a verb obviously depends on the particular verb. Not all verbs will take all possible karaka relations. For example, akarmaka (roughly, intransitive) verbs do not take karma karaka.

5. A '*' before a sentence indicates that it is not a good sentence.

6. However, it comes packaged, so to say, with the karaka sharing constraint that karta of *khaa* must be the same as that of its parent. Since this constraint is satisfied, the choice of TAM as *kara* is acceptable. More on this later.

7. We are indebted to Somnath Biswas for suggesting the reduction.

8. The fastest known algorithm has asymptotic time complexity of $O(|V|^{1/2}.|E|)$ and is based on max flow problem (Hopcroft and Karp, 1973). The reduction itself can be carried out in linear time on number of nodes and edges.

References

Ahuja, R., Magnanti, T.L., and Orlin, J. (1993). Network Flows:Theory, Algorithms, and Applications Prentice Hall.

Bendapudi, P. (1992). *Algorithmic Aspects of Natural Language Parsing Using Paninian Framework.* M.Tech. thesis, Dept. of CSE, IIT Kanpur.

Bharati, A., Bhatia, M., Chaitanya, V., and Sangal, R. (1997). Paninian Grammar Framework Applied to English. South Asian Language Review.

Bharati, A., Chaitanya, V., and Sangal, R. (1994). Anusaraka or Language Accessor: A Short Introduction. In *Automatic Translation*, Thiruvananthpuram, Int. School of Dravidian Linguistics.

Bharati, A., Chaitanya, V., and Sangal, R. (1995). Natural Language Processing: A Paninian Perspective. Prentice-Hall.

Bharati, A., and Sangal, R., (1993). Parsing Free Word Order Languages in the Paninian Framework. In *Proceedings of Annual Meeting of Association for Computational Linguistics*, pp. 105–111.

Bharati, A., Sangal, R., and Reddy, T.P. (2002). A Constraint Based Parser Using Integer Programming. In *Recent Advances in NLP, Proc. of International Conference on NLP-2002*.

Bhatia, M. (1995). Paninian Theory Applied to English. Dept. of CSE, IIT Kanpur, 1995. Bachelor's thesis.

Bhatt, R. (1993). Paninian Theory for English. Dept. of CSE, IIT Kanpur, 1993. Bachelor's thesis.

Papadimitrou, C., and Steiglitz, K. (1982). Combinatorial Optimization: Algorithms and Complexity. Prentice Hall.

Part IV

Linguistic and Psycholinguistic Issues

Lexicalized Syntax and Phonological Merge

ROBERT FRANK

16.1 Whither Syntax in a Lexicalized Grammar?

It is recognized across a wide range of frameworks that lexical information plays a fundamental role in determining the properties of syntactic structure (Chomsky, 1981; Bresnan, 1982; Pollard and Sag, 1994; Steedman, 2000b; Frank, 2002). For instance, lexically specified properties of a predicate are widely agreed to determine the number and configurations of syntactic arguments, the case properties of these arguments, associated inflectional morphology, and so on. This connection between lexical properties and syntactic structure takes its most extreme form in lexicalized grammatical frameworks, such as Categorial Grammar and Tree-Adjoining Grammar, where lexical items are associated directly with pieces of syntactic structure, and where syntactic derivation consists exclusively in composing these pieces of structure, which I will refer to as *elementary structures*, adapting slightly the terminology from the TAG literature. In lexicalized grammars, no syntactic operations or structural constraints on syntactic configurations are involved in the specification of the properties of global syntactic structure apart from those responsible for determining the properties of elementary structures. As a result, lexicalized grammars deny the existence of syntactic movement operations, templates or schemata for grammatical constructions, and the like.

The viability of lexicalized grammars as a framework for linguistic theory depends on a basic hypothesis about the kinds of constraints that natural language grammars impose. Specifically, what I will refer to as the *Syntactic Lexicalization Hypothesis* (SLH) states that syntactic relations entered into by a lexical item L must be expressed within the elementary structure that is associated with L.[1] If the SLH is correct, one might question what role is being played by the *syntactic* combination of elementary structures, since by hypothesis there can be no new syntactic relations created via such combination. It is of course true that the representations of sentences will require that elementary structures or something like them be combined in some fashion. On one hand, a representation of a sentence needs to include a phonological form, establishing the ordering among the lexical items of the constituent elementary structures. In addition, the meaning of a sentence cannot be determined on the basis of an unstructured set of elementary structures, as that would leave us unable to distinguish, say, the interpretation of *The dog bites the postman* from that of *The postman bites the dog*. Rather, some representation or process must determine the semantic relations that hold between predicates and their arguments, operators and their scope, and so on.

Such phonological and semantic representations are often taken to derive from or be read off of a complex syntactic object that is constructed by the grammar, and indeed this might be taken to constitute motivation for a syntactic derivation that combines elementary structures. However, in light of the previous discussion, I would like to propose an alternative conception, in which the only syntactic representations are those of the elementary structures. I assume that it is these elementary structures that are the object of phonological and semantic interpretation, yielding a pairing of local phonological and semantic representations. What has traditionally been thought of as a syntactic derivation will then involve the subsequent and direct combination of these phonological and semantic representations.[2]

The idea that aspects of phonological and semantic interpretation apply not to a global syntactic object but rather to a small piece of structure has been explored in the Minimalist framework (Uriagereka, 1999; Chomsky, 2001; Erteschik-Shir, 2005; Fox and Pesetsky, 2005) (see also Bresnan, 1971 for an earlier exploration of similar ideas). In this line of work, the syntactic derivation builds structure by iteratively merging lexical items and their combinations. At some point in the derivation, the operation of spell-out applies, which interprets the derived syntactic object for the phonological and semantic interfaces. This point of spell-out is referred to as a *phase*, and it has most often been taken to be delimited by the occurrence of one of a fixed set of syntactic categories. There has been a range of opinion concerning what spell-out accomplishes and how its results are integrated with the rest of the sentence. For Fox and Pesetsky (2005), the effect of spell-out is to annotate a syntactic structure with further information relevant to the phonology, specifically an encoding of linear order among the terminals. The resulting augmented structure may then continue to participate in the syntactic derivation. In the work of Uriagereka (1999), the result of spell-out is no longer a syntactic structure, but rather an object analogous to a lexical item. The internal properties of such an object are inaccessible to subsequent syntactic derivation, but this object may itself be incorporated into a subsequent syntactic derivation in a manner analogous to other lexical items. Both of these approaches have their shortcomings, I believe. If spell-out simply annotates syntactic structure, it cannot provide an account of the differing constituencies that appear to hold in the syntax and in the phonology. As illustrated in (1), right branching syntactic structure appears not to be matched by the flat iterated structure of the associated prosodic groupings.

(1)   a. This is (the cat that killed (the rat that ate (the malt that lay in (the house that Jack built))))

    b. (This is the cat) (that killed the rat) (that ate the malt) (that lay in the house) (that Jack built)

Assuming this divergence to be real, the "annotation" approach to spell-out will force us to posit an additional operation that is responsible for the deformation of the hierarchical structure appropriate for the representation of syntactic constituency into one appropriate for the representation of prosodic groupings. In contrast, the view of spell-out as producing an object analogous to a lexical item does have the potential to deal with divergences of the sort just discussed. However, as we will see, the mode of combination of spelled-out domains is insufficiently flexible to accommodate the range of phenomena discussed below.

The conception I will argue for in this chapter shares with the phase approach the idea that syntactic structure is spelled out locally. However, I will assume that the syntactic domain over which spell-out applies is analogous to that of a TAG elementary tree.[3] Specifically, I adopt the view of elementary trees advocated in Frank (2002) according to which they must satisfy two basic principles:

(2)   Condition of Elementary Tree Minimality (CETM): The syntactic heads in an elementary tree and their projections must form an extended projection of a single lexical head.

(3)   Theta criterion:

    a. If H is the lexical head of elementary tree T, H assigns all of its θ-roles in T.

    b. If A is a frontier nonterminal node of elementary tree T, A must be assigned a θ-role in T.

The CETM bounds the size of an elementary tree to the domain determined by a lexical head, while the theta criterion delimits the kind of nonterminal nodes that can decorate the frontier of an elementary tree. The following structures all constitute elementary trees under this conception:

(4)

In the TAG framework, these syntactic objects may be combined via the operations of substitution and adjoining to produce a complex structure for a sentence such as *The bassist composed a simple tune*. This approach raises the question however of why there should be two levels of syntactic organization, the hierarchical structure within elementary trees and that resulting from the combination of elementary trees. Stated another way, why are elementary trees reified as distinct types of syntactic objects?

The approach I advocate here avoids this question. Rather each of the structures in (4), is spelled out separately, resulting in a pairing (π, λ) of a phonological and semantic representation. No subsequent syntactic combination of the elementary trees takes place after spell-out, since the elementary trees qua syntactic objects cease to exist. Instead, I assume that two operations, Phonological and Semantic Merge , combine these (π, λ) pairings directly.

In this chapter, I begin an exploration of this perspective, focusing my attention on the phonological side. I first explore the nature of the combinatorial operation of Phonological Merge. As we shall see, this operation permits rather flexible sorts of combination of phonological representations, in a manner that is somewhat reminiscent of the TAG operations for syntactic structure building. Then I will turn my attention to the nature of the spell-out process in this model, and to the explanatory possibilities that are afforded by decomposing sentences in the way envisioned here. During the discussion, I consider consequences of this approach in a number of empirical domains, including object shift in Scandinavian, Spanish determiner allomorphy, English *do*-support, and English and German phrasal stress.

Though my focus here is phonological, there is one assumption about semantic composition that will play an important role: the requirement that combination of phonological and semantic representations will take place in a synchronous fashion (Shieber and Schabes, 1990; Shieber, 1994). That is, alongside each combination over phonological representations of the sort discussed in this chapter, there will be a corresponding combination of semantic representations. This will ensure that there is a sensible correspondence between the semantic and phonological representations that are constructed for a sentence.

A final note before proceeding: Note that my goal here is to demonstrate the interest and potential of a novel approach to grammatical derivation. The current discussion should be seen as only the beginning of the much larger enterprise of developing this approach. As a result, I leave for future work the analysis of a vast array of issues that have been investigated in the syntax literature over the past half-century that appear to require a syntactic representation of the sort I am denying here. My current belief is that these can be handled in terms of either morphophonology or semantics. And while the proof of the pudding is in the eating, my goal here is to convince the reader that it will be worth the wait.

16.2   Phonological Merge

Consider the following elementary tree headed by the verb *compose*:

(5)

```
                        TP
                     ／      ＼
                  DP           T
                           ／      ＼
                        T           VP
                        |         ／    ＼
                       past      V       DP
                                 |
                              compose
```

I assume that the phonological output of spell-out when it is fed such a structure will be a representation of (at least) prosodic constituency. Thus, given (5), spell-out might produce a structure like the following:

(6)

```
                        U
                        |
                        I
                     ／  |  ＼
                   X    φ    Y
                        |
                        ω
                        |
                     composed
```

The constituents in this structure correspond to levels in the prosodic hierarchy (Selkirk, 1978; Nespor and Vogel, 1986). At the lowest level is the Phonological Word ω, then the Phonological Phrase ϕ, then the Intonational Phrase I, and finally the Utterance U. These different levels have been postulated in order to account for the different loci of various phonological processes, either within a certain type of constituent or at its edge. The Phonological Phrase is taken to be a domain that typically includes a pitch accent, whose boundaries are marked by boundary tones, and which is the locus for processes such as French liaison, Italian raddoppiamento sintattico and English stress retraction. As an illustration of the latter, we see in (7a) that the stress on the final syllable of *kangaroo* shifts to the initial syllable in the context of a following word *life* with stress on the initial (and only) syllable, in order to avoid a "stress clash" between adjacent syllables. In contrast, in (7b) where the following word is separated from the word-final stress by a phonological phrase boundary, word-final stress remains.

(7)   a. [$_\phi$ the kángaroo's life] is full of surprises.

       b. John persevéres [$_\phi$ gladly and diligently]

The Intonation Phrase is the domain to which intonational contours are associated and is also the domain within which processes like the flapping of *t* in American English occur (Nespor and Vogel, 1986). As seen in (8), when a word final *t* precedes a word beginning with a vowel, it can be pronounced as a flapped *t* (indicated here by underlining), even when separated by a phonological phrase boundary.

(8)   a. John [$_I$ [$_\phi$ me<u>t</u>] [$_\phi$ Anne and Sue]]

       b. Anne and Sue [$_I$ [$_\phi$ me<u>t</u>] [$_\phi$ anonymously and anxiously]]

In contrast, when the word final *t* occurs at the right edge of a intonational phrase, such as the one that is formed by the parenthetical in (9), it does not undergo flapping.

(9)   [$_I$ Roger] [$_I$ alias the rat/*ra<u>t</u>] [$_I$ eats only cheese]

Selkirk (1984) proposes that prosodic constituents differ from their syntactic counterparts in a significant respect in that they obey what she labels the Strict Layer Hypothesis: constituents of a given type embed constituents of the next lowest type in the prosodic hierarchy. Thus, while phonological phrases constitute the immediate subconstituents of intonational phrases, intonational phrases may not constitute immediate subparts of phonological phrases. Among other things, this has the effect of preventing recursion in phonological structure.

The prosodic structure in (6) contains two constituents labeled X and Y in addition to those categorized with some prosodic type. These constituents are what I will refer to as *phonological variables*, whose content will be instantiated during the application of the Phonological Merge (PMerge) operation. PMerge combines one phonological structure with another containing a phonological variable. Thus, given the verbally-headed prosodic structure in (6) and the prosodic counterpart of a DP structure, PMerge accomplishes the structural combination in (10), replacing the variable Y.

(10)

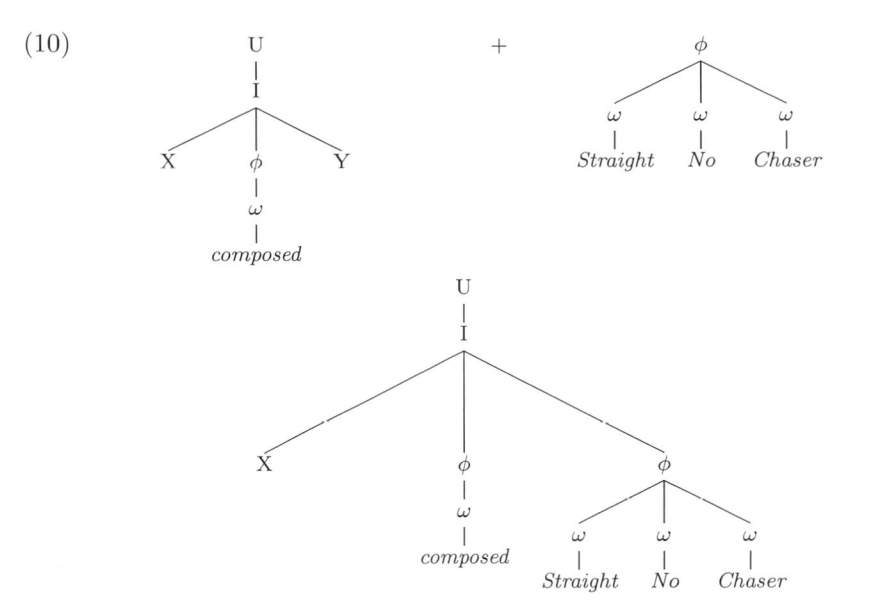

Note that the Strict Layer Hypothesis allows us to uniquely identify the prosodic category of phonological variables on the basis of the context in which they occur. For instance, since both X and Y in (6) are immediate subconstituents of an intonation phrase, each must be a phonological phrase. I assume that PMerge is constrained to respect the representation of prosodic structure present in the elementary structures, so that its results will also abide by the Strict Layer Hypothesis. As a result, if a phonological constituent does not match in type with that of a phonological variable, PMerge cannot apply. This is instantiated in the following (preliminary) definition of PMerge:

(11) $\mathrm{PMerge}(A_{C_i}, B_{C_j}) = B[A/X]$ for some variable X of category C_i.

(The notation A_{C_i} indicates a structure of prosodic category C_i, and $B[A/X]$ indicates the replacement of X in structure B by the structure A.) As a result of this definition, only phonological representations that are full phonological phrases can be merged into the the phonological variables in (6). In the case of a DP elementary tree headed by a demonstrative pronoun for instance, its prosodic representation need not project to an independent phonological phrase but may project only to a phonological word as shown in (12). Consequently, PMerge of such a structure into the postverbal position Y in (6) will not be possible.

(12)

$$\begin{array}{c} \omega \\ | \\ that \end{array}$$

Thus far I have been silent about the way in which an elementary tree is mapped onto prosodic structure. A wide array of proposals have been made to accomplish this mapping (Selkirk, 1986, 1996; Nespor and Vogel, 1986; Zec and Inkelas, 1990; Truckenbrodt, 1995), but it is beyond the scope of this chapter to choose among them and not crucial that we do so. What is important for present purposes is the locus of the information that is necessary to compute this mapping. As we have just seen, weak pronominal objects project to prosodic constituents different from those of full DPs. More generally, phonologically weightier elements will parse as prosodic constituents higher in the prosodic hierarchy. In addition, the discourse status of the entities denoted by the various constituents is also significant in determining prosodic constituency. In (13a), where both the subject and predicate are given in the discourse, the object is parsed into an independent intonational phrase. In contrast, in (13b) only the subject is given, and the remaining material is parsed into a single prosodic constituent.

(13)   a. Who did John meet?
            [$_I$ John met] [$_I$ Alice]

        b. What did John do?
            [$_I$ John] [$_I$ me*t* Alice]

The difference in intonational boundary position can be diagnosed by the possibility of flapping: only in (13b) can the *t* at the end of *met* be flapped. Note, however, that neither phonological weight nor focus structure are represented in the verbally-headed elementary tree in (5): this structure simply encodes the fact that we have a transitive verb that takes a DP subject and object, but says nothing about the phonological weight of the arguments or their discourse status.[4] As a result, the spell-out operation must be nondeterministic, permitting multiple possible outputs for a single syntactic representation. Alongside (6) then, spell-out might produce any of the following prosodic representations for the elementary tree in (5) (among others).

(14)   a.

        b.

c.

```
        U
        |
        I
       / \
      X    φ
          / \
         ω    Y
         |
      composed
```

d.

```
        U
        |
        I
       / \
      X    φ
           |
           ω
          / \
     composed  Y
```

The prosodic structure in (14a) would be appropriate in the context given in (13b), where only the subject is semantically given. The structure in (14b) corresponds to the context in (13a), where the subject and verb are given, but the object consists of new information. The structure in (14c) involves a prosodically reduced object, forming a single prosodic phrase together with the verb. Such a structure would license PMerge of a prosodic structure like the one in (12), representing a demonstrative, at the variable corresponding to the object position. Finally, the prosodic structure in (14d) involves an object that is even further prosodically reduced, so that the verb and object together form a single phonological word. Richards (2004) suggests that weak object pronouns, which he takes to project only a foot, participate in just such a structure.

16.2.1 Merger of adjuncts

As noted earlier, elementary trees do not include a representation of modifiers of the lexical head. In the TAG context, this entails that modifiers are introduced into a sentence during the course of the syntactic derivation. Under the current proposal, where combination of the lexical content of the elementary trees takes place over phonological representations, this combination will fall to the PMerge operation. As yet, however, because there is no representation of the modifier in the elementary tree, there will be nothing in the structure that can be translated into a phonological variable in the prosodic structure into which a modifier may PMerge. In order to overcome this difficulty, I propose to revise the formulation of the PMerge operation as follows:

(15) $\text{PMerge}(A_{C_i}, B_{C_j}) = B[A/X]$ for a variable X of category C_i; or
$$B[A > C_i]$$
(where $B[A > C]$ denotes the result of concatenating A to some category C within B)

The latter clause of this definition permits the insertion of a prepositional phrase into the clausal structure in (10) by concatenating the prosodic representation of the PP to some phonological phrase in the clause's prosodic representation.[5]

(16)

The concatenation portion of PMerge is ill defined in the sense that it does not uniquely determine where structure gets inserted. I assume that the elements that are merged may have some morphophonological specification that indicates whether they attach to the left or to the right of a constituent of the appropriate sort, and perhaps we might additionally require that concatenation take place at the edge of a still larger prosodic constituent. However, even such constraints may still underdetermine the locus of attachment in case an elementary prosodic structure includes more than one constituent of the relevant type. For now, I put this issue aside, but return to it later.

This approach to modifier placement allows us to derive the result that modifiers such as adverbs and PPs may not intervene between the verb and its object. In (16), there is no ϕ boundary at this position to which the PP/adverb could be attached. If the object of the verb were assigned a prosodically weightier representation, for instance an independent intonational phrase, the adverb could be inserted between the verb and object. This yields a derivation of so-called heavy NP shift via the interleaving of prosodic constituents that is possible with PMerge rather than a syntactic movement process.[6]

(17)

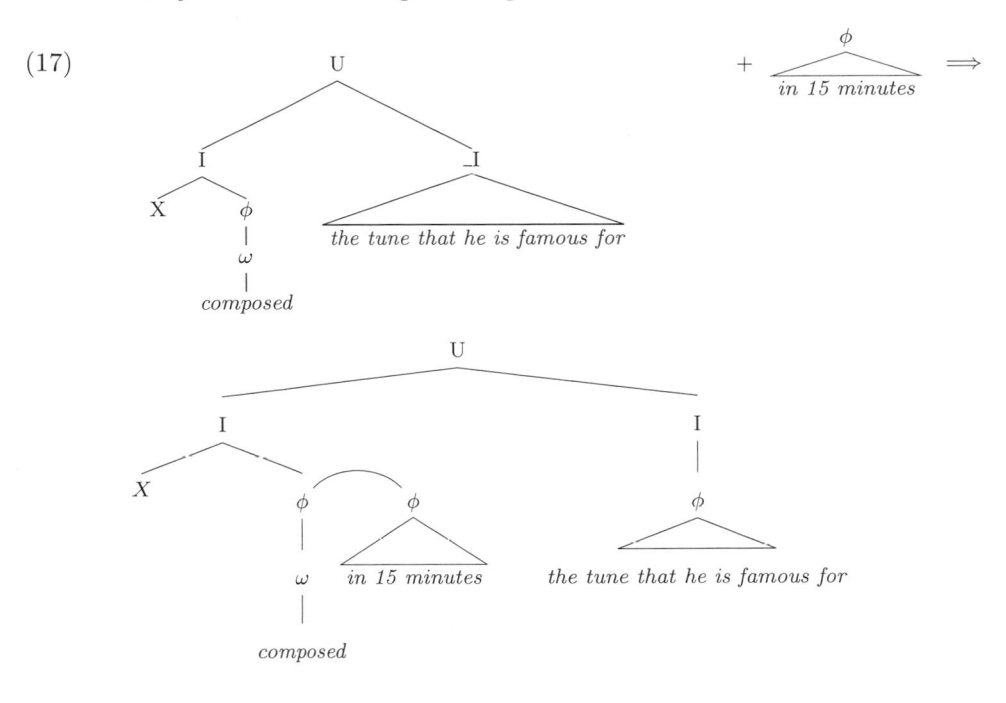

Observe that this analysis does not extend to cases of heavy NP shift with ditransitive verbs, as in (18).[7]

(18)   Alice explained [to him] [the problem with the solution].

In such cases, if we take both arguments to be generated as part of the verb's elementary tree, they will both give rise to phonological variables whose order is determined within the derivation of the elementary tree and is fixed at spell-out. Any effect of heavy NP shift would therefore not derive in this case from the possibility of interposing an adverb, but rather from some reordering within the original elementary tree. If this analysis is correct, we should expect to find distributional differences between these two types of heavy NP shift, a matter I leave open for future work.

   The formulation of PMerge given thus far requires a slight modification if it is to deal with cases involving complex arguments, which are broken up into multiple prosodic constituents. Take, for instance, a sentence such as the following:

(19)   He composed ($_\phi$ Straight No Chaser) ($_\phi$ Round Midnight) ($_\phi$ and Brilliant Corners).

I assume that the conjoined object will be derived via the concatenation of three separate phonological phrases. We must allow for the insertion of such a concatenated structure into one of the slots specified by a phonological variable. Since all of the concatenated phrases will be constituents at the same level of the prosodic hierarchy, the insertion of many such constituents will not induce a violation of the strict layer hypothesis. On the semantic side of the derivation, we will, however, require that these concatenated constituents contribute a unitary interpretation for the verb's internal argument.

16.2.2   Object shift

The line of analysis just suggested for the insertion of modifiers also provides a analysis of the phenomenon of object shift in a manner that is similar in certain respects to the proposals made by Erteschik-Shir (2005), Vogel (2004), and Richards (2004). Before developing this analysis, I will provide some background on the phenomenon.

In the Scandinavian languages, as the following Swedish example illustrates, verbs precede their objects.

(20)   *Jag har   inte kysst   Marit.*
        I   have not kissed Marit.

In sentences with an auxiliary verb such as this one, the lexical verb must follow negative elements like *inte* and certain adverbial elements, which are usually assumed to mark the left edge of VP. This suggests that the lexical verb remains in situ in such cases. When there is no auxiliary verb however, the lexical verb precedes negation and adverbials.

(21)   *Jag kysste inte Marit.*
        I   kissed not Marit

This pattern has been taken to show that finite main verbs (in matrix clauses) undergo movement to a higher position, often assumed to be the head of CP. The subject or some other element must then move to fill the specifier of this CP projection, giving rise to the verb second effect.

So far this is fairly straightforward. Where things get interesting is when the object of the verb is a pronoun. In such cases, the pronoun appears to move out of the VP along with the verb, surfacing to the left of the negation.

(22)   *Jag kysste henne inte.*
        I   kissed her   not

This movement of the object pronoun is known as *object shift* (OS). As first noted by Holmberg (1986), OS is only possible when the verb has left the VP. Otherwise, the pronoun must remain within the VP.

(23)   a.   * *Jag har   henne inte kysst.*
                I   have her   not kissed

        b.   Jag har inte kysst henne.

This correlation between verb movement and the possibility of OS has come to be known as Holmberg's generalization. However, as Holmberg (1986) also observes, OS is blocked not only by the failure to move the verb, but also by the failure to move anything else out of the VP that precedes the base position of the object, such as a particle or an indirect object.

(24) a. * *Dom kastade me inte ut.*
           they threw   me not out.

      b. *Dom kastade inte ut me.*

(25) a. * *Jag gav den inte Elsa.*
           I   gave it   not Elsa

      b. *Jag gav inte Elsa den.*

Holmberg (1999) thus characterizes the generalization on OS as a prohibition against movement across any phonologically visible category, with the crucial exception of adverbs and negation. This restriction has the consequence that OS is possible so long as it does not reorder any of the elements within the verb phrase. This is a surprising property for an instance of syntactic movement to have, since the raison d'être of movement has been to account for displacement. Moreover, it remains a puzzle why adverbs and negation are exempt from the prohibition against reordering.[8]

To avoid these curious restrictions on movement, I propose instead that OS derives not from syntactic movement but rather from the interaction of the PMerge operation and the prosodic constituency that is assigned to clausal structures. Since PMerge lacks the ability to reorder elements present in an elementary tree and because I assume that the grammar of Swedish does not permit the elementary trees in which the object precedes the verb, examples (23a), (24a) and (25a) cannot be generated. To see how cases of OS can be generated, consider the structure for a simple Swedish sentence:

(26)

As before, a number of prosodic constituencies are possible when this structure is spelled out, among which are the following:

(27)   a.

        b.

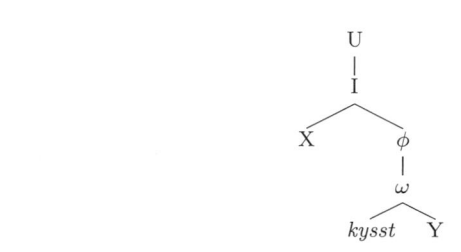

In the first of these, the object is spelled out as an independent phonological phrase, while in the latter, it is spelled out as part of the same phonological word as the verb as in the case of a weak pronominal object.[9] Let us assume that the negation *inte* is generated as an independent elementary tree, whose phonological spell-out is (at least) an independent phonological word. Observe now that if we attempt to PMerge *inte* with (27a), the negation may intervene between the verb and the variable Y, as shown in (28a). In contrast, PMerge of *inte* with the structure in (27b) will not tolerate such intervention. The negation may only precede or follow the phonological counterpart of the entire VP. When the negation is PMerged to the right of the "VP," this yields the structure in (28b).

(28)   a.

b.

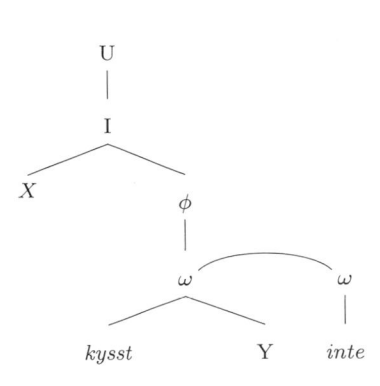

When the phonological variables X and Y are instantiated through further applications of PMerge, the two structures in (28) will give rise to the orderings with unshifted and shifted structure respectively.

The discussion thus far does not address the significant issue of how the precise position of the PMerged negation is determined. In both of the structures in (28), the PMerge operation permits the attachment of *inte* to the left of the phonological word to which it attached as well as to the right. To rule out the former possibility, we might stipulate that *inte* is lexically specified as being an enclitic, so that it must attach to a phonological word to its right. Other adverbial elements, particularly those that project higher levels of prosodic structure, might not show such directional dependence, and we will therefore get insertion either to the left or the right of prosodic constituents of the appropriate sort. However, even with such stipulations, an important question remains open about the difference in placement of negation between simple and compound tenses. In compound tenses, negation must precede both the verb and the object.

(29) a. *Jag har inte kysst henne.*
          I   have not kissed her

  b. * *Jag har kysst henne inte.*

  c. * *Jag har kysst inte henne.*

The last of these examples is ruled out for reasons already discussed. However, nothing in what we have said rules out the order in (29b), particularly since the verb and object will surely form the same type of prosodic constituent as before. There is, however, one significant difference between the prosodic structure of this case and the one with the simple tense: in the context of the compound tense, I will assume that there is another phonological word boundary in the prosodic structure associated with the elementary tree, to the right of the auxiliary verb. Assuming this to be the case, we can constrain PMerge to apply in a leftmost fashion, so that instances of PMerge (for at least a certain class of elements) must go to the linearly first site that is phonologically permissible.[10] A second source of constraint on the locus of PMerge might stem from the semantic side of the derivation. Recalling that applications of PMerge will proceed in synchrony with semantic compositional operations, we must ensure that the negation PMerges with a constituent whose corresponding semantics are appropriate for the application of sentential negation. From this perspective, it might be possible to rule out example (29b) if the semantics corresponding to the rightmost phonological phrase *kysst henne* could not be the argument of sentential negation, as the latter plausibly requires tense in its scope. A similar argument will have to be made for embedded clauses, which show the same pattern as compound tenses: negation must precede the verb.

(30)   ... *att   jag inte kysste henne*
           that I   not kissed her

(31)   *... *att   jag kysste henne inte*
           that I   kissed her   not

In this case, just as in English, the complementizer and subject form a prosodic constituent that provides the crucial attachment site. If we assume that tense is associated with the C head, the semantic constraint on attachment would apply as well.

Thus far, all of the examples of OS we have considered involve pronominal objects. This was no accident: in the mainland Scandinavian languages, OS is possible only with pronouns. Happily, the analysis just presented provides a simple explanation for the restriction of OS to pronominal objects: it is only weak pronominals by virtue of their reduced phonological character, that can be inserted into the slot Y in (28b): pronouns are the only DPs that can be parsed phonologically as a proper subpart of a phonological word. Consequently, apparent OS, now understood as the result of tight phonological constituency between the verb and object, is blocked with full DP objects.[11]

In contrast, a non-OS structure like (28a) requires that the object be a phonologically weightier constituent (represented there as a phonological phrase, though see note 9) that is parsed separately from the element preceding it. My analysis leads us to the expectation that OS of unstressed pronouns should be obligatory: if such pronouns may not project to the level of a phonological phrase, they cannot be inserted into a structure that licenses the interpolation of negation. This expectation is borne out for all the Scandinavian languages except for Swedish. Only in Swedish can pronouns fail to precede negation.

(32)   a.   *Hun såv ham ikke.* (Danish)
            she   saw him not
            She didn't see him.

       b. * *Hun såv ikke ham.*

(33)   a.   *Jag kysste henne inte.* (Swedish; Sells, 2001)
            I   kissed her   not

       b.   *Jag kysste inte henne.*

Under the current proposal this distinctive property of Swedish OS should be related to a difference in prosodic outputs. Specifically, we can assume that Swedish pronouns may project to larger prosodic constituents than other Scandinavian pronouns, thereby allowing them to be PMerged with the variable Y in (28b). If Swedish pronouns are indeed more phonologically independent than the rest of their Scandinavian counterparts, we should expect to find not only an absence of OS, but more freedom in general regarding the placement of adverbials to the left and right of the pronouns.[12] This is in fact what we see in the phenomenon of adverbial intermingling (examples from Kaiser, 1997 via Sells, 2001): an object pronoun can surface in any position within a sequence of adverbials.

(34)   a. *Igår   läste han dem ju   alltså tolingen inte.*
         yesterday read he   them as you know thus   probably not
         Yesterday, as you know he probably did not read them thus.

     b. *Igår läste han ju dem alltså tolingen inte.*

     c. *Igår läste han ju alltså dem tolingen inte.*

     d. *Igår läste han ju alltså tolingen dem inte.*

     e. *Igår läste han ju alltså tolingen inte dem.*

Note however that adverbial intermingling is impossible in other Scandinavian languages, as the following Danish examples illustrate:

(35)   a. *Peter læste den uden   tvivl   ikke.* (Vikner, 1989)
         Peter read it   without doubt not.

     b. **Peter læste uden tvivl den ikke.*

     c. **Peter læste uden tvivl ikke den.*

Since adverbial intermingling requires the insertion of some set of adverbs to the left of the pronominal object, it follows that these orderings should be possible only with pronouns with a certain degree of phonological independence, as I hypothesized for Swedish.[13] The examples in (34) point to another argument in favor of the prosodic approach to OS over the movement approach: if we assume that adverbs occupy fixed positions in clausal structure (Cinque, 1999), these cases would require multiple landing sites for OS. In contrast, if the PMerge operation is responsible for adverb insertion, the relative ordering of the pronoun and the adverbs will be determined by prosodic constituency. Of course much more needs to be said in order to account for the restrictions on adverbial ordering that Cinque (1999) discusses. However, assuming that this can be addressed, it might be possible to deal with variation in the positioning of participles across Romance varieties that Cinque documents in a prosodically-based manner.

    The account of OS that I am giving here bears a certain resemblance to an analysis that is considered (and rejected) by Hellan (1994) in which the phenomenon of OS derives from the cliticization of the object pronoun onto the preceding verb. Under this analysis, cliticization feeds syntactic verb movement, allowing the cliticized object pronoun to get a "free ride" past the negation. A significant problem for this analysis, and the reason it was ultimately rejected by Hellan, arises in sentences in which an adverbial occupies the sentence initial topic position. When the verb raises to C, a cliticized object should necessarily raise along, moving past the subject to yield the order Adv-V-O-S (with an adverb initial sentence). Although such long OS is to some extent possible in Swedish as shown in (36a) (subject to considerable restrictions, on which see Josefsson, 2003), it is not possible in the other Scandinavian languages as seen in the Danish example in (36b) .

(36) a. I hallen mötte honom en hemsk syn. (Swedish)
          in the hall met   him   a   horrible view
          'In the hall he met a horrible sight.'

      b. * Hvorfor læste den studenterne ikke? (Danish)
            why   read it   the students not
            'Why didn't the students read it?'

Instead, the ordering that surfaces for such sentences is Adv-V-S-O, with the object obligatorily shifted past the negation but not past the subject:

(37) Hvorfor læste studenterne den ikke? (Danish; Vikner, 1989)
      why   read the students it   not

Hellan points out that if an object pronoun must undergo syntactic cliticization to the verb, such sentences cannot be generated. Observe though that this ordering is unproblematic on the analysis I am proposing. Displacement of the verb to C will take place within the elementary tree, prior to the formation of prosodic constituents, yielding a structure like (38) in which the verb precedes both the subject and (in-situ) object.

(38)

When this structure is spelled out, the direct object will continue to follow the subject. In the case of Swedish long OS, I assume that there is a syntactic process that applies within the elementary tree that accomplishes the displacement. In order to accomplish the "short" OS of the direct object pronoun past the negation in (37), I will assume that the elementary tree may map to a prosodic structure in which the verb, subject and object may form a single prosodic constituent. As before, an appropriate representation will be necessary to license the insertion of a weak object pronoun, and we may assume that the verb-subject-object prosodic constituent is possible only when the object is prosodically weak. As a result of this prosodic constituency, PMerge will be unable to insert negation between the subject and object, yielding the impossibility of (39).[14]

(39)   * Hvorfor læste studenterne ikke den ?
        why   read the students not it

More generally, the PMerge analysis of OS leads to the expectation that negation and adverbs may surface only in front of a phonologically weighty constituent present in the elementary tree. This expectation is borne out in a number of contexts. Engdahl et al. (2004) observe that in Swedish, postverbal subjects may be preceded by negation or adverbs only when they are phonologically heavy. Thus, while stressed pronominal subjects may either precede or follow adverbs, unstressed pronouns must precede them .

(40)   a. Då kommer vi/VI tyvärr   för sent.
            then come we   unfortunately late
            'Unfortunately we'll be late then.'

        b. Då kommer tyvärr   *vi/VI för sent.
            then come unfortunately we   late
            'Then it's unfortunately us that will be late.'

Furthermore, expletive subjects, which cannot be stressed, must appear before an adverb.

(41)   a. *Här regnar det/*DET aldrig.*
            here rains it(expl)   never
            'It never rains here.'

        b. * *Här regnar aldrig det/DET.*
            here rains   never it(expl)

Secondly, in clauses with ditransitive verbs, negation may precede the indirect object-direct object sequence so long as the indirect object is a full DP, independent of the properties of the direct object:

(42)   a. *Jeg lånte ikke Marie bogerne.* (Danish; Christensen, 2003)
            I   lent not Marie the books
            'I didn't lend Marie the books.'

        b. *Jeg lånte ikke Marie dem.*
            I   lent not Marie them.

I propose that in such examples it is a prosodic break prior to the indirect object which licenses the PMerge of the negation. In example (42b), the direct object *dem* is a weak pronoun that I take to form a single prosodic constituent with the preceding indirect object. Given the prosodic break after the verb, the negation must be PMerged before the indirect object-direct object grouping, yielding the absence of object shift.[15] Under a view of OS in which pronouns move to a VP external position to satisfy some syntactic requirement, the well-formedness of examples like (42b) are surprising: this structure would fail to satisfy whatever syntactic requirement it is that motivates OS.

As noted earlier, OS of weak pronominal objects is obligatory in the Scandinavian languages other than Swedish. However, when the pronominals are stressed, they may remain in situ. This is unsurprising in the current context: I take stress on the pronoun to indicate that it projects a larger prosodic constituent, thereby licensing the PMerge of negation before it. Interestingly, Svenonius (2005) notes that the effects of stress on a pronoun are even more profound. In a Norwegian ditransitive clause containing a sequence of three pronouns, the negation may be inserted anywhere within the sequence so long as the pronoun immediately following it is stressed.

(43)   a.   *Vanligvis gir   ikke HAN meg den.* (Norwegian)
               usually   gives not he   me it
               'Usually he doesn't give me it.'

        b.   *Vanligvis gir han ikke MEG den.*

        c.   *Vanligvis gir han meg ikke DEN.*

        d.   *Vanligvis gir han meg den ikke.*

Once again, if take the presence of stress to indicate the left periphery of a phonological constituent at least as large as a phonological word, the analysis I am advocating leads us to expect that negation can be inserted at this point.

Finally, it is interesting to observe that OS applies to subcategorized pronominal adverbials as well, as Josefsson (2003) observes for Swedish:

(44)   *Därför   bor Sten där   inte längre.*
        therefore lives Sten there not anymore
        Therefore Sten doesn't live there anymore.

Such subcategorized adverbs cannot precede negation when they are not pronominal.

(45)   *Därför   bor Sten (*i Lund) inte (i Lund) längre.*
        therefore lives Sten (*in Lund) not (in Lund) anymore

Since these adverbials will be represented in the verbally-headed elementary tree in virtue of being subcategorized, they will be spelled out during the same process as object DPs. As a result, there will be the possibility of forming during spell-out a single prosodic constituent containing subject DP and the adverbial, thereby forcing the insertion of negation below this unit.

16.3 Spelling out spell-out

The discussion in the last section focused on the combinatorics of the phonology once the spell-out operation has applied to the individual elementary trees. In this section, I turn to the nature of the spell-out operation itself, considering the kind of computations that are carried out during the transformation of syntactic into phonological representations. I will discuss three operations which I take to apply during spell-out: resolution of allomorphy, morphological merger and assignment of phrasal stress. The central point of my argument in each case will center on one property of elementary trees, namely that they lack a representation of adjuncts. Consequently, we should expect that spell-out-related processes should be insensitive to the presence of such elements.

16.3.1 Allomorphy

Spanish definite determiners are usually taken to come in two forms: masculine *el* and feminine *la*. Interestingly, in certain circumstances feminine nouns like *agua* 'water', but not ones like *torre* 'tower', surface with the determiner *el* (Harris, 1989; Hayes, 1990).

(46)　a.　*el/la tórre*

　　　b.　*el/*la água*

The relevant property that distinguishes these classes of feminine nouns is whether they begin with stressed *a*. Only those that do so permit the *el* form of the determiner. Thus, we might be tempted to characterize the alternation in terms of a morphological rule of the following form:

(47)　*la* → *el* / ___ *á*

This rule does not however capture a crucial fact about this *el/la* alternation. The stressed *a* that triggers the change cannot be on a prenominal adjective that is adjacent to the determiner, but must occur on the noun itself.

(48)　*el/la álta torre*
　　　the　high tower

Recall that adjectives are not present in the elementary trees, and must therefore be integrated to the nominal structure via PMerge. Therefore, we can straightforwardly explain this pattern of *el/la* allomorphy via the assumption that the process that resolves the rule applies at the point of spell-out of the nominal elementary tree.

One additional complication in this pattern of facts stems from the fact that the head noun beginning with the stressed *a* must be adjacent to the determiner in order for the *el* form to be possible. That is, if a prenominal adjective is inserted prior to a noun like *agua*, the *el* form is no longer possible.[16]

(49)   *el/la misma agua*
    the   same   water

This pattern fits into the analysis just sketched if we make more precise the assumptions about the prosodic structure of DPs. I will assume that the nominally-headed elementary tree in (50) may be spelled out in one of two ways, depicted in (51).

(50)

$$
\begin{array}{c}
\text{DP} \\
\diagup\diagdown \\
\text{D}\quad\text{NP} \\
|\qquad| \\
\text{la}\quad\text{N} \\
| \\
\text{agua}
\end{array}
$$

(51)

$$
\begin{array}{ccc}
\phi & & \phi \\
\diagup\diagdown & \text{OR} & | \\
\omega\quad\omega & & \omega \\
|\qquad| & & \diagup\diagdown \\
\text{la}\quad\text{agua} & & \text{la}\quad\text{agua}
\end{array}
$$

Let us further suppose that the the allomorphy rule in (47) may only apply within the domain of a prosodic word.

(52) $la \rightarrow el \; / \; (_\omega \underline{\quad} \; \text{'a} \;)$

The result of this prosodic constraint on the rule's application is that the *el* form of the feminine determiner will surface only when the second of the two spell out options in (51) is chosen. Furthermore, because the determiner and noun will be tightly bound together in a prosodic constituent in such a case, subsequent PMerge of an adjective between them will be impossible. In contrast, when the first spell out option is chosen, the allomorphy rule does not apply, resulting in the retention of the *la* form of the determiner. Why then don't we find the surface form *la agua*? I assume here that such an output is blocked because of the nature of this phonological representation. That is, even though *la* is parsed into an independent phonological word during spell out of the elementary tree, it cannot surface as such. As a result, some element must undergo PMerge into the phonological word to support the determiner. Assuming that determiners are phonologically proclitic, this will require the insertion of an element between the determiner and noun.

Of course, not all cases of allomorphy will be resolved in this way. The form of the English indefinite article is determined on the post-PMerge structure, since it is sensitive only to whether it is strictly adjacent to a vowel:

(53) a. a/*an book/rotten apple

  b. *a/an apple/old book

Similarly, the form of the Italian masculine definite determiner varies on the basis of the word the immediately follows:

(54) a. *il/*lo tipo/grande scoiattolo*
    the   guy/large   squirrel

  b. **il/lo scoiattolo/strano tipo*
    the   squirrel/strange guy

Hence, there must still be some rules of allomorphy that apply post-cyclically, that is after the conclusion of the phonological derivation.

16.3.2 Morphological merger

Another process that appears to apply at the point of spell out of the individual elementary trees is morphological merger. As observed first by Chomsky (1957), the merger of V and finite inflection requires a certain sort of adjacency between these two elements. When this adjacency is disturbed as a result of the presence of negation or because of subject-aux inversion, a semantically empty verb *do* is inserted to bear the inflectional features.

(55) a. Lila *[3sg,pres]* not *give* interesting talks. →
    Lila does not give interesting talks.

  b. *[3sg,pres]* Lila *give* interesting talks? →
    Does Lila give interesting talks?

One puzzling complication arises in the presence of adverbs: when an adverb intervenes between T and V, morphological merger appears to go through without any problem.

(56) Lila *T[3sg,pres]* always *give* interesting talks. →
    Lila always *gives* interesting talks.

This has led to a variety of proposals to account for the apparent invisibility of adverbs (Bobaljik, 1995, 2002; Ochi, 1999). On the approach taken here, this array of facts follow straightforwardly from the assumption that T-V merger applies under adjacency at the point of spell out, since at this point the adverb has not yet been integrated into the clausal structure. Examples like those in (55) will be ruled out since T and V are not adjacent in the elementary tree, under the assumption that negation is present in the verbally-headed elementary tree in English. English negation would differ in a crucial respect from its Scandinavian counterpart under this analysis. It is tempting to try to collapse this distinction between types of negation with the traditional dichotomy between phrasal and head negation, though I leave this for the future.

16.3.3   Assignment of phrasal stress

Let me turn finally to another process that I take to apply during the spell-out operation: the assignment of phrasal stress. As before, since elementary trees lack a representation of adjuncts, we should expect the assignment of prosodic prominence to be insensitive to the presence or absence of these elements (Feng, 2002).[17]

This conclusion appears to be correct. Gussenhoven (1992) argues extensively that arguments and adjuncts pattern quite differently with respect to stress assignment. In contexts of wide focus (i.e., where the entire sentence expresses new information), for instance, the primary stress in a transitive sentence in both verb-medial languages like English and verb-final languages like German and Dutch appears on the object itself, and not on the verb.

(57)   a. She sang the whole ária.

　　　 b. *Sie hat die ganze Árie gesungen.*
　　　　 she has the whole aria sung

In contrast, in the case of intransitive verbs with an adverbial modifier, the pattern is quite different: stress appears both on the verb and on the modifier.

(58)   a. She sáng the whole dáy.

　　　 b. *Sie hat den ganzen Tág gesúngen.*
　　　　 she has the whole   day sung

To account for this pattern, Gussenhoven proposes the following rule for assigning prosodic prominence to syntactic structures:

(59)   Sentence Accent Assignment Rule (SAAR): If focused, every predicate, argument, and modifier must be accented, with the exception of a predicate that, discounting unfocused constituents, is adjacent to an argument.

If we assume that each prosodic phrase can include only a single accent, the SAAR can be interpreted as saying that predicates (i.e., verbs) may form prosodic constituents only with their arguments, thereby allowing the retraction of stress from the verb onto the argument as in (57). The SAAR also tells us that verbs and modifiers may not form such constituents and therefore retraction is impossible in such contexts, as the examples in (58) demonstrate.

Gussenhoven provides no principled reason for this distinction between arguments and adjuncts with respect to prosodic constituency and stress retraction. However, in the context of the proposal in this chapter, we can understand the pattern of sentence accents directly. Specifically, if we assume that prominence is assigned at the point of spell-out, the possibility of forming a prosodic constituent comprising the verb and its object, and consequently the retraction of stress from the verb, will be unavailable for verb-modifier combinations, thereby forcing prominence on some element within the verbally headed elementary tree (the verb). To ensure that an accent appears on the modifier as well, I will assume then that any elementary tree containing some focused element must include at least one accent.[18]

The approach adopted here diverges somewhat from the SAAR in cases where the object is separated from the verb by a modifier. Under the SAAR, the intervention of the adverb should prevent the formation of a prosodic constituent consisting of the verb and object, with the result that retraction of stress from the verb should be impossible. However, as Baart (1987) notes (see also Féry and Herbst, 2004), the intervention of a modifier does not affect the possibility of having an unaccented verb, whether the modifier is focused (as in (60a)) or not (as in (60b)).

(60)   a. *We bestellen vandáag de ríngen (dan kunnen we ons morgen*
       we order   today   the rings then can   we us tomorrow
       verloven). (Dutch)
       marry
       If we order the rings today, then we can get married tomorrow.

     b. *(Warum will   Malte in Finnland wohnen?) Weil   Halina tángos in*
       why   wants Malte in Finland live   because Halina tangos in
       Finnland komponiert. (German)
       Finland   composed.
       Why does Malta want to live in Finland? Because Halina composed tangos in Finland.

If we assume instead that accent placement is determined during spell-out of individual elementary trees, we can understand why inserted adverbial elements have no effect on stress placement. Note, however, that it will be crucial that the prosodic constituent inside of which stress retraction takes place must be large enough to permit PMerge of the adverb, thereby allowing for no accent on the verbs in (60). Since I am leaving open the details of the process of stress assignment, I leave to the future the problem of determining the nature of this constituent.

16.4 Conclusions

This chapter has begun to explore a model of grammatical derivation that relieves the syntax of the burden of constructing recursive structure. Instead, it is only the phonological and semantic representations that can grow without bound. I have sketched out a number of consequences in the phonological portion of the derivation, and I hope to have convinced the reader of the explanatory force that this kind of approach might have.

This said, a great many issues remain open for future work. The crucial assumptions I have made about prosodic constituency have not always been sufficiently justified on independent phonological grounds, and this remains an important area for future work. Furthermore, while I have discussed one kind of structural combination at some length, namely that of modifiers with the material they modify, I have said little about the prosodic integration of predicates and their (clausal) arguments. One important area for future study is that of so-called reduced complements, such as Germanic and Romance restructuring infinitivals, where some of the evidence in favor of monoclausal syntax derives from phonological considerations. Perhaps the division between phonological and semantic combination I advocate will shed light on this important issue.

As noted at the outset, since I am denying the existence of a global syntactic representation, any phenomena whose explanation has been tied to properties of such a structure will need to be reanalyzed. Examples that spring to mind here are unbounded displacement (e.g., wh-movement and raising) as well as anaphoric and scopal dependencies. Concerning the former, it is tempting to try to treat such displacement in a manner familiar from work in the TAG framework, exploiting the similarity between the function of the adjoining and PMerge operations. As for the latter, recent work has suggested that conditions on anaphora and scope can be recast in semantic terms (see, among others, Butler, 2003; Jacobson, 2003; Schlenker, 2005). Depending upon the assumptions that are made about the system for semantic combinatorics in the current system, it may be straightforward to integrate these results.

This brings to the fore the need to make explicit the semantic side of the derivation: it remains to be clarified just what character the local semantic representations should have, what the combinatory operations over these representations will be, what kind of correspondences should be posited between the phonological and semantic elementary structures, and the proper formulation of the isomorphism condition for the two derivations. Past work on semantic interpretation in the TAG framework (Shieber, 1994; Schabes and Shieber, 1994; Shieber and Schabes, 1990; Kallmeyer and Joshi, 2003; Joshi et al., 2007) will play a helpful role in guiding these investigations, but there are certain to be novel questions given the differences between the syntactic representation assumed in the TAG work and the phonological representations assume here.

Acknowledgments

For helpful discussion, comments, and objections, I am grateful to Adam Albright, Arto Anttila, Rajesh Bhatt, Tony Kroch, David Pesetsky, Lisa Selkirk, Paul Smolensky, Ken Wexler, and an anonymous reviewer for this volume, as well as audiences at MIT, UPenn, and the Mediterranean Syntax Meeting, Rhodes.

Notes

1. The SLH is a restatement in the more general context of lexicalized grammars of the "Fundamental TAG hypothesis" proposed in Frank (2002).

2. Observe that in this context, the problem of assigning a syntactic "parse" to a sentence therefore requires only the determination of the elementary structures

associated with the lexical items in the sentence, with the task of composing such structures left to some other component. This is precisely the division proposed in the supertagging model of Bangalore and Joshi (1999), and thus the current conception is resonant with that work.

3. In what follows, I will assume familiarity with TAG. For background on the linguistic and formal properties of this formalism, see Frank (2002) and Joshi and Schabes (1997) respectively.

4. Cardinaletti and Starke (1999) suggest that the distinction between weak pronoun and full DP is in fact syntactically represented, in terms of the category level of the phrase, and such a syntactic distinction could be used to drive a difference in prosodic structure. Even if this approach is correct, it remains implausible that all relevant properties, such as number of syllables, will be syntactically represented. It has also been suggested that the partition between focused and unfocused material is represented in syntactic structure, either as a feature on focused elements (Selkirk, 1995) or more directly through nonstandard syntactic constituency (Steedman, 2000a). For the purposes of the present chapter, I put aside these options and explore instead the consequences of having a syntactic representation that significantly underdetermines prosodic structure.

5. These dual modes of combination recall the operations of Tree-Adjoining Grammar, and especially those of the mixed grammars studied by Joshi (1973).

6. Note that we will also need to require that the concatenation of the adverb/PP take place at the right edge of an intonation phrase, so as to prevent insertion even when the object is a separate phonological phrase, though not if it is an independent intonational phrase. Such an edge requirement might be central in accounting for the phenomenon of verb raising (Emonds, 1978; Pollock, 1989) in prosodic terms. Supposing French permits the insertion of adverbs/PPs at the edge of any phonological phrase, and not only at intonational phrase boundaries, we can explain why it is possible for adverbs to intervene between the verb and object in French, but not in English. Alternatively, this phenomenon might have its roots in the distinct syntactic representations in the elementary trees for the two languages, under the assumption that this syntactic difference gives rise to a difference in prosodic structure.

7. Thanks to Ken Wexler for pointing this out.

8. Fox and Pesetsky (2005) attempt to answer this objection by providing a principled grounding for the restriction against reordering on the basis of a system of cyclic spell-out that fixes the ordering of words within a certain derivational domain, but permits their subsequent movement so long as this order is maintained. If adverbs and negation are outside of the VP-containing phase, this proposal explains why OS can cross these elements.

9. If we assume that insertion of negation/adverbs must be at the edge of a phonological phrase, in order to block OS it would be sufficient for the object to be part of the same phonological phrase as the verb. Note that what is crucial is that object shift be associated with a tighter prosodic constituency between the object and the preceding constituent (here the verb), and not the details of labels of the prosodic constituents, whose identity will need to wait for further study of the relevant phonological processes.

10. This follows a similar constraint proposed by (Erteschik-Shir, 2005, p.61) on the linearization of negation and adverbial elements.

11. Icelandic differs from the Mainland Scandinavian languages in permitting OS to occur with full DP objects. Under the present analysis, this will necessarily derive from a difference in how Icelandic syntactic structure is mapped onto prosodic representations. I leave open here the question of what distinctive property the grammar of Icelandic possesses that underlies this difference.

12. Alternatively, Swedish might be distinguished from the other Scandinavian languages in the prosodic status of its negation and adverbial elements. If these can be spelled out as small enough prosodic constituents, PMerge could in principle insert them between a verb and a somewhat phonologically reduced object. This line of analysis would lead us to expect that such intercalation, and hence lack of OS, would be impossible with heavy adverbials. I do not know whether such a distinction is observed. There is, however, suggestive evidence that the prosodic weight of the pronoun is significant in determining the possibility of OS, as would be predicted under the proposal made in the text. In Josefsson's (2003) survey of acceptability of shifted and unshifted pronominal objects in Swedish, she notes that speakers preferred the shifted version of sentences with the monosyllabic pronoun *den* (it) as compared to the unshifted version, but preferred the unshifted version of sentences with the disyllabic pronoun *honom* (him). This dependence on phonological weight suggests that the prosodic independence of the pronoun is playing a significant role in determining the viability of OS.

13. The astute reader will have noted that these cases of adverbial intermingling constitute apparent counterexamples to the idea that PMerge applies in a leftmost fashion. I leave open the resolution of this puzzle. Note also that if adverbial intermingling requires only a certain degree of phonological independence of the objects, we should also expect to find it with full DP objects. This is essentially what we find in English in cases like the following (modeled on similar Icelandic examples in Thráinsson, 1986):

(i)   Gianni (rarely) puts (*rarely) the butter (rarely) in his pocket (rarely).

The impossibility of placing the adverb between the verb and direct object is related to factors of VP-internal prosodic constituency discussed earlier.

14. Erteschik-Shir (2005) proposes an analysis of object shift that shares certain properties with the one I am proposing. Specifically, although she assumes adjuncts to be present in the syntactic structure, she takes their surface position to be the result of a linearization process that is subject to phonological constraints. Certain elements, such as weak object pronouns, must undergo a process of *prosodic incorporation* (PI) with an adjacent word, and it is the necessity of doing this that is taken to block the occurrence of negation between the verb and pronominal object. From Erteschik-Shir's discussion, it appears that the process of PI can precede the linearization of adverbs, and thus it is also necessary for her to stipulate that these adverbs cannot themselves serve as the hosts for PI. Such a stipulation is unnecessary on the conception proposed here, since the determination of prosodic constituency (and hence the formation of a verb-object unit) necessarily precedes the insertion of the adverb.

15. We also need to rule out the possibility of PMerging negation after the IO-DO unit, giving rise to the appearance of OS for both the IO and DO:

(i)   * *Jeg lånte Marie dem ikke.* (Danish)
       I   lent   Marie them not.

I assume that this example is ill-formed for the same reason that blocks OS of full DP objects with transitive verbs.

(ii)   * *Jag kysste Marit inte.* (Swedish)
        I   kissed Marit not

In both cases, we must prevent negation from PMerging into a position further to the right than the appropriate one. One possibility is to invoke the leftmost condition on PMerge inherited from (Erteschik-Shir, 2005, p.61) that was mentioned earlier. Additionally, the requirement that the semantic derivation take place in synchrony with the phonological derivation might have the effect of blocking examples like (i) if the semantics corresponding to the rightmost phonological phrase consisting of *Marie dem* could not be the argument of sentential negation. Similarly, (ii) would be ruled out assuming that the semantics associated with *Marit* were not appropriate for negation.

16. Adam Albright (p.c.) has pointed out to me that the empirical situation is slightly more complex. He notes that with the gender-invariant adjective *gran* (large) in prenominal position, the *el* determiner is apparently possible for at least some speakers: *el gran águila* (the big eagle) registers 293 hits on Google, while *la gran águila* yields 1,120 hits (search conducted on August 11, 2005). (By way of comparison, *el misma agua* shows only 11 hits in comparison to 5,390 hits for *la misma agua*, a pattern that suggests the impossibility of the former.) It is possible that these examples were generated by speakers for whom the noun *águila* has been reanalyzed as masculine. If not, it remains to be explained why uninflected forms

like *gran* behave differently from inflected forms like *misma*. One possibility lies in another distinction between these two classes of adjectives: *gran*, in virtue of having no gender inflection is monosyllabic, and therefore may project a smaller prosodic constituent than the disyllabic *misma*, and therefore might allow for the possibility of PMerge between the determiner and noun in a prosodic structure even where these form a tight prosodic constituent. If this is the correct generalization, we should expect that polysyllabic uninflected adjectives should pattern with *misma*. I leave the investigation of this question open for future work.

17. Feng (2002) makes the same point in the context of a TAG-based theory of the phonology-syntax interface. As in the current proposal, Feng assumes that prosodic prominence is computed over elementary trees. His proposal diverges from what I suggest here, however, in that the computation of prominence yields as output not a phonological object, but rather an elementary tree whose nodes are annotated as prosodically weak or strong. These annotations constrain the insertion of subsequent elementary trees during the TAG derivation in a similar fashion to the way that prosodic structure constrains application of the PMerge operation. Feng also applies this idea to an analysis of the distribution of *ba*-NPs in Chinese.

18. As before, I leave open the proper characterization of the function that assigns prosodic constituency to elementary trees, as well as the principle that assigns prosodic prominence.

References

Baart, J.L.G. (1987). Focus, syntax and accent placement. PhD dissertation, University of Leiden.

Bangalore, S. and Joshi, A. K. (1999). Supertagging: An approach to almost parsing. *Computational Linguistics* 25:237–265.

Bobaljik, J. D. (1995). Morphosyntax: the syntax of verbal inflection. PhD dissertation, MIT.

Bobaljik, J. D. (2002). A-chains at the PF-interface: Copies and "covert" movement. *Natural Language and Linguistic Theory* 20:197–267.

Bresnan, J. (1971). Sentence stress and syntactic transformations. *Language* 47:257–281.

Bresnan, J., ed. (1982). *The mental representation of grammatical relations*. Cambridge, MA: MIT Press.

Butler, A. (2003). Predicate logic with barriers and its locality effects. In *Proceedings of Sinn und Bedeutung 7*, ed. Matthias Weisgerber, Abreitspaper nr. 114, 70–80. Fachbereich Sprachwissenschaft der Universität Konstanz. URL http://ling.uni-konstanz.de/pages/conferences/sub7.

Cardinaletti, A. and Starke, M. (1999). The typology of structural deficiency: A case study of the three classes of pronouns. In *Clitics in the languages of Europe*, ed. Henk van Riemsdijk, volume 8 of *Empirical Approaches to Language Typology*, 145–233. Berlin: Mouton de Gruyter.

Chomsky, N. (1957). *Syntactic structures*. The Hague: Mouton.

Chomsky, N. (1981). *Lectures on government and binding*. Dordrecht: Foris.

Chomsky, N. (2001). Derivation by phase. In *Ken Hale: a life in language*, ed. Michael Kenstowicz, 1–52. Cambridge: MIT Press.

Christensen, K. R. (2003). Obj-shift, neg-shift & double objects. Manuscript, University of Aarhus.

Cinque, G. (1999). *Adverbs and functional heads: A cross-linguistic perspective*. New York: Oxford University Press.

Emonds, J. (1978). The verbal complex V′–V in French. *Linguistic Inquiry* 9:151–175.

Engdahl, E., Andréasson, M. and Börjars, K. (2004). Word order in the Swedish midfield – an OT approach. In *Proceedings of the 20th Scandinavian Conference of Linguistics*, ed. Fred Karlsson. University of Helsinki, Department of General Linguistics.

Erteschik-Shir, N. (2005). Sound patterns of syntax: Object shift. *Theoretical Linguistics* 31:47–93.

Feng, S. (2002). *Prosodic syntax and morphology in Chinese*. Munich: LINCOM Europa.

Féry, C. and Herbst, L. (2004). German sentence accent revisited. In *Interdisciplinary studies on information structure 1*, ed. Shinichiro Ishihara, Michaela Schmitz, and Anne Schwarz, 43–75. SFB 632, University of Potsdam.

Fox, D. and Pesetsky, D. (2005). Cyclic linearization of syntactic structure. *Theoretical Linguistics* 31:1–46.

Frank, R. (2002). *Phrase structure composition and syntactic dependencies*. Cambridge, MA: MIT Press.

Gussenhoven, C. (1992). Sentence accents and argument structure. In *Thematic structure: Its role in the grammar*, ed. I.M. Roca, 79–106. Dordrecht:Foris.

Harris, J. (1989). The stress erasure convention and cliticization in Spanish. *Linguistic Inquiry* 20:339–363.

Hayes, B. (1990). Precompiled phrasal phonology. In Inkelas and Zec (1990), 85–108.

Hellan, L. (1994). On pronominal clitics in Norwegian. In *Proceedings of the XIVth Scandinavian Conference of Linguistics, Special Session on Scandinavian Syntax*, ed. Celia Hedlund and Anders Holmberg, number 70 in Gothenburg Papers in Theoretical Linguistics. Department of Linguistics, Gothenburg University.

Holmberg, A. (1986). Word order and syntactic features in the Scandinavian languages and English. PhD Dissertation, University of Stockholm.

Holmberg, A. (1999). Remarks on Holmberg's generalization. *Studia Linguistica* 53:1–39.

Inkelas, S. and Zec, D., eds. (1990). *The phonology-syntax connection*. Chicago: University of Chicago Press.

Jacobson, P. (2003). Binding without pronouns (and pronouns without binding). In *Resource-sensitivity, binding and anaphora*, ed. Geert-Jan Kruijff and Richard T. Oehrle. Berlin: Springer Verlag.

Josefsson, G. (2003). Four myths about Object Shift in Swedish — and the truth . . . . In *Grammar in focus II: Festschrift for Christer Platzack*, ed. Lars-Olof Delsing, 199–207. Stockholm: Wallin and Dalholm.

Joshi, A. K. (1973). A class of transformational grammars. In *The formal analysis of natural languages*, ed. Maurice Gross, Morris Halle, and Marcel-Paul Schützenberger. The Hague: Mouton.

Joshi, A. K., Kallmeyer, L., and Romero, M. (2007). Flexible composition in LTAG: Quantifier scope and inverse linking. In *Computing meaning 3*, eds. Harry Bunt and Reinhard Muskens. Dordrecht:Kluwer.

Joshi, A. K., and Schabes, Y. (1997). Tree-adjoining grammars. In *Handbook of formal languages, volume 3: Beyond words*, ed. G. Rozenberg and A. Salomaa, 69–124. New York: Springer.

Kaiser, L. (1997). The morphological cliticization of object-shifted weak pronouns in Swedish. In *Yale a-morphous linguistics essays*, ed. Lizanne Kaiser, 99–129. Department of Linguistics, Yale University.

Kallmeyer, L. and Joshi, A. K. (2003). Factoring predicate argument and scope semantics: Underspecified semantics with LTAG. *Research on Language and Computation* 1:3–58.

Nespor, M. and Vogel, I. (1986). *Prosodic phonology*. Dordrecht: Foris.

Ochi, M. (1999). Multiple spell out and PF-adjacency. In *Proceedings of the 29th Annual Meeting of the North Eastern Linguistics Society*, ed. Pius Tamanji, Masako Hirotani, and Nancy Hall, 293–306. Graduate Linguistics Students Association, University of Massachusetts, Amherst.

Pollard, C and Sag, I. A. (1994). *Head-driven phrase structure grammar*. Stanford, CA: CSLI Publications.

Pollock, J. (1989). Verb movement, universal grammar, and the structure of IP. *Linguistic Inquiry* 20:365–424.

Richards, M. (2004). Object shift and scrambling in North and West Germanic: A case study in symmetrical syntax. PhD dissertation, University of Cambridge.

Schabes, Y. and Shieber, S. M. (1994). An alternative conception of tree adjoining derivation. *Computational Linguistics* 20:91–124.

Schlenker, P. (2005). Non-redundancy: Towards a semantic reinterpretation of binding theory. *Natural Language Semantics* 13:1–92.

Selkirk, E. (1978). On prosodic structure and its relation to syntactic structure. In *Nordic prosody II*, ed. T. Fretheim, 111–140. Trondheim: TAPIR.

Selkirk, E. (1984). *Phonology and syntax: The relation between sound and structure*. Cambridge, MA: MIT Press.

Selkirk, E. (1986). On derived domains in sentence phonology. *Phonology* 3:371–405.

Selkirk, E. (1995). Sentence prosody: intonation, stress, and phrasing. In *The handbook of phonological theory*, ed. John Goldsmith, 550–569. Cambridge, MA: Blackwell.

Selkirk, E. (1996). The prosodic structure of function words. In *Signal to syntax: Bootstrapping from speech to grammar in early acquisition*, ed. James Morgan and Katherine Demuth, 187–213. Mahwah, NJ: Lawrence Erlbaum Associates.

Sells, P. (2001). *Structure, alignment and optimality in Swedish*. Stanford, CA: CSLI Publications.

Shieber, S. M. and Schabes, Y. (1990). Synchronous tree adjoining grammars. In *Proceedings of the 13th International Conference on Computational Linguistics*, volume 3, 253–258. Helsinki.

Shieber, S. M. (1994). Restricting the weak-generative capacity of synchronous tree-adjoining grammars. *Computational Intelligence* 10:371–385.

Steedman, M. J. (2000a). Information structure and the syntax-phonology interface. *Linguistic Inquiry* 34:649–689.

Steedman, M. J. (2000b). *The syntactic process*. Cambridge, MA: MIT Press.

Svenonius, P. (2005). How phonological is object shift? *Theoretical Linguistics* 31:215–228.

Thráinsson, H. (1986). On auxiliaries, AUX and VPs in Icelandic. In *Topics in scandinavian syntax*, ed. Lars Hellan and Kirsti Koch Christensen, 235–265. Dordrecht: Reidel.

Truckenbrodt, H. (1995). Phonological phrases: Their relation to syntax, focus, and prominence. PhD dissertation, MIT.

Uriagereka, J. (1999). Multiple spell-out. In *Working minimalism*, ed. Samuel David Epstein and Norbert Hornstein, 217–250. Cambridge, MA: MIT Press.

Vikner, S. (1989). Object shift and double objects in Danish. *Working Papers in Scandinavian Syntax* 44:141–155.

Vogel, R. (2004). Weak function word shift. Manuscript, University of Potsdam.

Zec, D and Inkelas, S. (1990). Prosodically constrained syntax. In Inkelas and Zec (1990), 365–405.

Constraining the Form of Supertags with the Strong Connectivity Hypothesis

ALESSANDRO MAZZEI, VINCENZO LOMBARDO, AND PATRICK STURT

17.1 Introduction

This chapter introduces a TAG-based dynamic approach to syntax and explores the consequences of this approach in a realistic setting. In particular, we focus on the problem of how the lexicon increases when we incorporate an eager derivation procedure into the formalism. We start by discussing in section 17.1 some experimental psycholinguistic data that support an eager approach to the syntactic process and that can be implemented through an adequate use of the adjoining operation. The dynamic framework we introduce in section 17.2, called Dynamic Version of TAG (DVTAG), involves the critical notion of predicted heads, which guarantees the satisfaction of an eager treatment of the incoming words. Predicted heads lead to an expansion of the elementary trees in comparison with their LTAG counterparts, which obey the CETM principle only (Frank, 2002). In section 17.3 we propose a method for the automatic extraction of a wide coverage DVTAG from a treebank. Finally, in section 17.4 we analyze the basic properties of a DVTAG automatically extracted from the Penn Treebank. In particular, we show that the predicted heads do not result in an explosion of the dynamic lexicon.

17.2 TAG Adjoining and Psycholinguistic Evidence

How eager is the computation of the syntactic structure in human sentence processing? From a theoretical point of view, we can consider a large space of possibilities in relation to the eagerness of structure building, depending on which parsing strategy one assumes. For example, a strongly bottom up parsing strategy, such as the shift-reduce strategy, leads to delays in the building of right-branching structure, because smaller constituents are combined into larger constituents only when they become complete (see Abney and Johnson, 1991 for discussion). In contrast, strategies such as left-corner or recursive descent result in an increased eagerness of structure building, because portions of structure can be predicted before the relevant constituent is completed, resulting in a minor delay in structure building.

A second factor that affects the eagerness of structure building is the grammar formalism. One reason for this is that formalisms differ in the definition of constituency: formalisms where constituency is rigidly defined (such as those based on context-free grammar) will tend to result in more delays to structure building than those that allow flexible constituency, such as Combinatory Categorial Grammar (Steedman, 2000). Another reason is that formalisms differ in the types of combinatorial operations they allow. Here, we will consider the consequences of the *adjoining* operation of Tree-Adjoining Grammar (henceforth TAG) (Joshi et al., 1975), with respect to eagerness. The elementary structures of TAG consist of a set of *initial trees*, like the tree in figure 17.1a, which do not contain recursive structure, and *auxiliary trees*, like the tree in figure 17.1b, which implements a factorization of recursion. The *adjoining* operation involves inserting an auxiliary tree into another

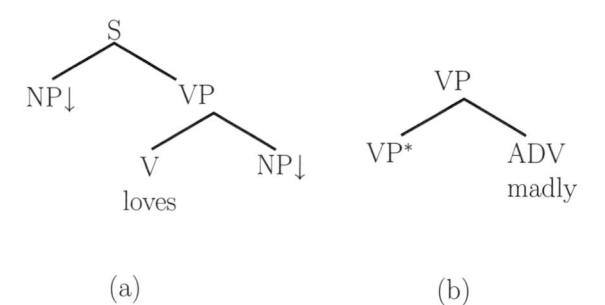

(a)   (b)

FIGURE 17.1 (a) Initial tree, (b) Auxiliary tree.

elementary tree, to form a larger structure incorporating recursion. So, for example, combining (a) and (b) above could result in the tree in figure 17.2. The adjoining operation therefore allows a potentially complete constituent (like *John loves Mary*) to be modified by the attachment of new material (like the elementary tree of *madly*) in the middle of the original structure. In practice, this feature of the TAG formalism allows one to model a high degree of eagerness in the processing of postmodifiers and coordination (Sturt and Lombardo, 2005).

A number of recent psycholinguistic studies examine the time course with which syntactic structure is computed in human sentence processing (Kamide et al., 2003; Aoshima et al., 2004; Sturt and Lombardo, 2005). These studies all show evidence for the immediate creation of syntactic structure, and they fail to show evidence for

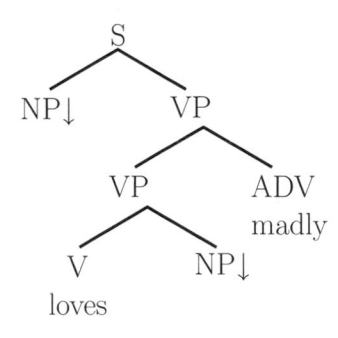

FIGURE 17.2 The structure following adjoining.

the systematic delays that are predicted by less eager strategies, such as head-driven strategies.

The experiment reported in Sturt and Lombardo (2005) has contrasted the predictions of two hypotheses concerning the eagerness of the computation of verb phrase coordination structures in an eyetracking experiment. One of the experiments used sentences like (1):

1 The pilot [$_{\text{VP}}$ [$_{\text{VP}_1}$ embarrassed John] and [$_{\text{VP}_2}$ put himself in a very awkward situation]].

Note that, if binding constraints are ignored, *himself* can potentially have two referents (*the pilot* and *John*). However, only one of them (*the pilot*) is in the relevant structural relation with *himself* for binding to occur (Chomsky, 1981). According to the *bottom-up* hypothesis, the two VP conjuncts (VP$_1$ and VP$_2$) can only be combined into the higher VP when both conjuncts are complete. This is because a pure bottom-up parsing strategy can only build higher structure out of complete subconstituents. As pointed out by Schneider (1998), this is the case even when one considers flexible categorial grammar (Steedman, 2000). In contrast, in the *adjunction* hypothesis, the conjunction schema [$_{\text{VP}}$ VP and VP] can be immediately adjoined to the structure of the sentence *The pilot embarrassed John*, and the content of VP$_2$ can then be incorporated directly into the resulting structure.

The results of the experiment (Sturt and Lombardo, 2005) showed clear evidence for a very early incorporation of the second conjunct into the structure—in the experimental design, sentences like (1) were contrasted with sentences like (2):

2 The pilot embarrassed John and put herself in a very awkward situation.

In (2), the feminine morphology on *herself* clashes with the stereotypical male gender bias of *pilot*. This results in processing difficulty on the word *herself* in (2) compared with *himself* in (1). The difference was detectable in the first eye fixation on the word *himself/herself* well before the point at which the second VP conjunct could be judged to be complete. This effect was interpreted by Sturt and Lombardo (2005) as evidence to show that *himself/herself* and *the pilot* had both been incorporated into a single structure by the time the reflexive was first read, since it is usually assumed that the relation between a reflexive and its antecedent relies on structural relations (for example, c-command or co-argumenthood). In contrast, there is no obvious reason why the bottom-up hypothesis would have predicted the effect so early. Because smaller constituents need to be complete before they can be combined into larger constituents, the second VP should not have been incorporated into the overall structure as early as the reflexive, because the second VP cannot be complete at that point.[1]

Given the apparent lack of delays in the computation of syntactic structure in the experimental literature, theoretically the most parsimonious approach is arguably to assume that structure building is *never* delayed. This implies that each input token (that is, each word) is immediately incorporated into a fully connected syntactic representation. Since a number of different forms of "connectivity" have been proposed and analyzed in a number of works (Stabler, 1994; Abney and Johnson, 1991; Shieber and Johnson, 1993; Sturt and Crocker, 1996; Lombardo and Sturt, 2002a), we call this proposal the *strong connectivity hypothesis* (SCH).

17.3   DVTAG

The psycholinguistics literature reports a number of proposals that implement SCH in the design of the parsing method, leaving the definition of the well-formed structures to the grammar component. In these models, the competence grammar is usually a standard context-free formalism (Roark, 2001), or a generative syntactic theory based on a context-free backbone (Crocker, 1992), or a categorial approach such as Combinatory Categorial Grammar[2] (CCG) (Steedman, 2000).

In these approaches the parsing method defines what legal partial syntactic structures are actually built during processing and in what order. As stated in section 17.2, different algorithms result in different spaces of partial structures. For example, a bottom-up algorithm cannot account for SCH because each nonterminal node is instantiated only after all its daughters, and so it leaves a number of partial structures disconnected during processing. On the contrary, a top-down parsing algorithm, which expands nonterminal nodes down to leaves, is compliant with SCH, as the partial syntactic structure is always fully connected (Shieber and Johnson, 1993). Moreover, left-corner parsing algorithm is a more practical strategy that partially accounts for SCH in its *arc-eager* version (Stabler, 1994).

The approach followed here assigns the responsibility of defining the space of partial structures to the competence grammar component. The derivation process is constrained by the SCH, and the parsing algorithm cannot go beyond such competence restrictions. The SCH becomes part of competence, and the definition of syntactic phenomena, such as constituency, as well as interpretation, must take into account the legal partial structures as constrained by the derivation process (Kempson et al., 2000; Phillips, 2003; Milward, 1994). Phillips proposed a syntactic theory that accounts for SCH: this theoretical model is able to explain some otherwise contradictory results of constituency tests. Milward described a new computational framework for syntax called *dynamic grammar*, such that the incremental derivation rules are defined by the grammar, in contrast with standard generative paradigm. Milward's model fulfills SCH and gives a clear explanation of the nonconstituency coordination. Moreover, a number of other syntactic phenomena can be elegantly accounted for in a system where syntax is defined in terms of the incremental growth of semantic structures during a left-to-right derivation (Kempson et al., 2000). In this chapter, we illustrate a TAG-based grammatical framework that accounts for the SCH, and we explore the empirical consequences of extracting a wide coverage grammar from a treebank. The formalism is a Dynamic Version of Lexicalized Tree-Adjoining Grammar (DVTAG), introduced in Lombardo and Sturt (2002b).

17.3.1 Extended projection and the strong connectivity hypothesis

When we express a linguistic theory using a grammar formalism, we have to define linguistic constraints on the elementary objects of the formalism. Because of its extended domain of locality and factoring of recursion, TAG offers a particularly restrictive constraint, which is an assumption shared by all TAG-based linguistic theories (Frank, 2002):

Definition 17.1 THE FUNDAMENTAL TAG HYPOTHESIS: *Every syntactic dependency is expressed locally within a single elementary tree.*

Moreover, linguistic theories based on TAG have tended to be highly lexicalized, where the lexicon simply consists of a set of elementary trees. Frank suggested a general principle with the aim to limit the size of the elementary trees, and, therefore, indirectly to guarantee the finiteness of the lexicon (Frank, 2002):

Definition 17.2 CONDITION ON ELEMENTARY TREE MINIMALITY (CETM)*: The syntactic heads in an elementary tree and their projections must form an extended projection of a single lexical head.*

The *extended projection* of a lexical item includes the projection of all those functional heads that depend on the lexical item (Grimshaw, 1991). For instance, the tree in figure 17.1a is the extended projection of the lexical item *loves*. Starting from this assumption and from the related notion of the *Theta Criterion*, Frank sketches one syntactic theory based on LTAG. This theory explains several linguistic phenomena, such as subject raising and the *wh*-dependencies in English (Frank, 2002). An appealing consequence of the CETM is that it provides a natural way to capture compositional semantics within LTAG, such that the meaning of the sentence can be computed from the meaning of the elementary trees.

In the following sections, we will consider the consequences of adding an extra condition on the form of the elementary trees; namely, we will require not only that the elementary tree of a lexical item includes its extended projection, but also that it includes any predicted material necessary to allow a fully connected left-to-right derivation, that is, a derivation that satisfies the SCH. Consider the following sentence fragment:

3 John thinks his ....

Assuming that *thinks* subcategorizes for a clause, the sentence prefix in (3) can be given a fully connected analysis only if we allow extra *predicted projections* (i.e. nodes projected by predicted heads), to be included in the structure. This is because *his* must form the left corner of a noun phrase, and this noun phrase must form the left corner of the subcategorized clause (figure 17.3). Therefore, if we constrain the form of elementary trees to allow for fully connected left-to-right derivations, the elementary tree for *his* must include extra predicted heads to the right (that is, the predicted head of the NP and the predicted head of the S), or by predicting the embedded clause structure in the elementary tree of *thinks* (see the discussion in note 6).

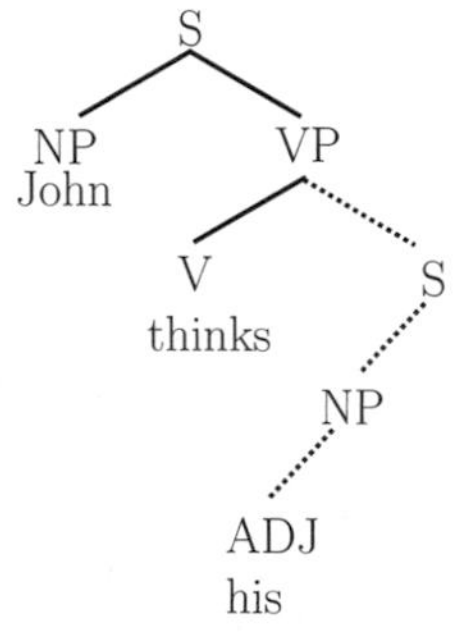

FIGURE 17.3 In the fragment sentence *John thinks his*, the word *his* is a left corner.

This example shows that if we pose the extra condition on the form of elementary trees to reflect SCH compliant derivations, we increase the size of the elementary trees, and also increase the amount of syntactic predictions that they encode—while the CETM entails that subcategorized arguments will be predicted, strong connectedness implies also that certain heads will be predicted, in order to maintain a fully connected derivation.

It is worth noticing that this is not the case in adjoining. The SCH does not necessitate adjoining to take place in advance, since modifiers are incorporated into a structure licensed by some other element. However, when arguments need to be substituted into a predicted argument structure (for example, in Japanese where the direct object precedes the verb), or modifiers need to adjoin before the modified head arrives (for example, in English, where the adverb precedes the verb), the implementation of SCH must rely on the arbitrary insertion of predicted projections.

In other words, the derivation process makes a prediction of lexical heads to come. The grammar becomes larger because the elementary trees must go beyond the CETM to account for predicted projections.[3]. However, such predicted projections must plausibly be limited in number.

The goal of this chapter is to test the validity of these ideas in an empirical manner, namely, by extracting a dynamic grammar from a treebank and to see what are the requirements of predicted projections in order to satisfy the SCH.

17.3.2   Informal DVTAG, predicted heads, and the finiteness of the lexicon

The idea of syntax as a dynamic process governed by a competence framework is not new. One known example of a previous approach is Milward (1994), who developed a dynamic dependency grammar expressed in functional terms. Working in the LTAG framework (Joshi and Schabes, 1997), the dynamic process encodes the SCH in a partial structure called "left context," which spans a left fragment of the sentence and is expanded by inserting elementary structures anchored by the words that occur at the immediately right of the left context.

In figure 17.4 and in figure 17.5, we can see the DVTAG derivations of *John loves Mary madly* and *Bill often pleases Sue* respectively. Like LTAG (Joshi and Schabes, 1997), a DVTAG consists of a set of elementary trees, divided into initial trees and auxiliary trees, and attachment operations for combining them. Lexicalization is expressed through the association of a lexical *anchor* with each elementary tree. In standard LTAG, the lexical dependencies are directly represented in the derivation tree and are established when the two heads involved are both introduced into the syntactic structure. In DVTAG, in contrast, the introduction of predicted projections carries constraints on head dependencies that are yet to come. So, in order to represent such constraints, we have to augment each node with a feature indicating the lexical head that projects that particular node. The head variable is a variable in logic terms: $\_v_3$ is unified with the constant *loves* and $\_v_2$ with the constant *Mary* in the derivation of figure 17.4; $\_v_1$ is unified with the constant *pleases* and $\_v_2$ with the constant *Sue* in the derivation of figure 17.5. The derivation process in DVTAG builds a constituency tree by combining the elementary trees via some operations that are illustrated below. DVTAG implements the incremental process by constraining the *derivation process* to be a series of steps in which an elementary tree is combined with the partial tree spanning the left fragment of the sentence. The result of each step is an updated partial structure. Specifically, at processing step i, the elementary tree anchored by the i-th word in the sentence is combined with the partial structure spanning the words from position 1 to position $i - 1$; the result is a partial structure spanning the words from 1 to i. In DVTAG, the derivation process starts from an elementary tree anchored by the first word in the sentence, one that does not require any attachment that would introduce lexical material on the left of the anchor (such as in the case that a Substitution node is on the left of the anchor). This elementary tree becomes the first left context, and

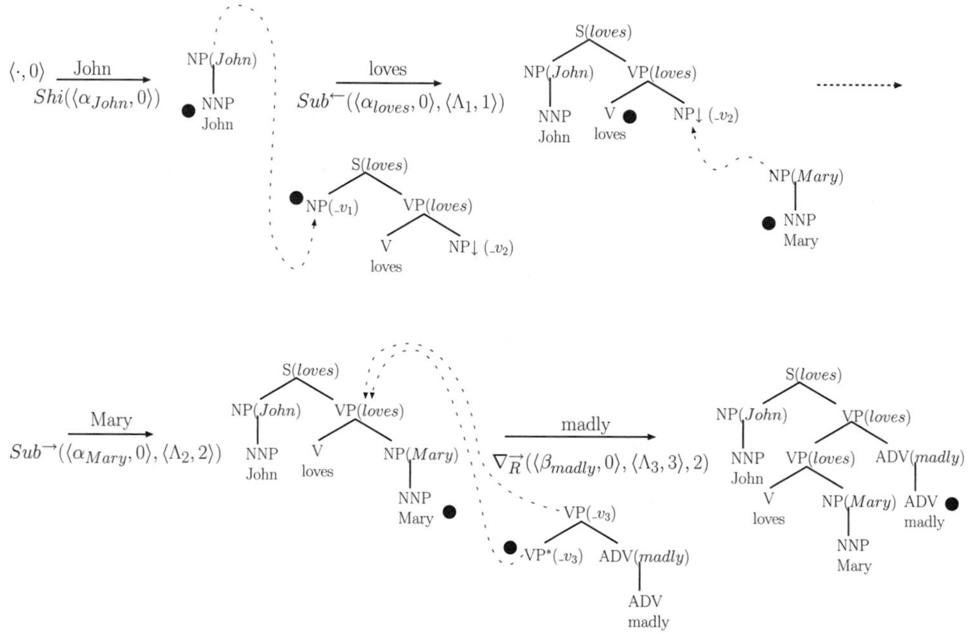

FIGURE 17.4 The DVTAG derivation of the sentence *John loves Mary madly*. The operations used in this derivation are shift (*Shi*), inverse substitution (*Sub*$^{\leftarrow}$), substitution (*Sub*$^{\rightarrow}$) and adjoining from the right ($\nabla_R^{\rightarrow}$). The abbreviation under the arrows denotes the elementary dotted tree, the left context, and eventually the adjoining node (Gorn address) involved the operation.

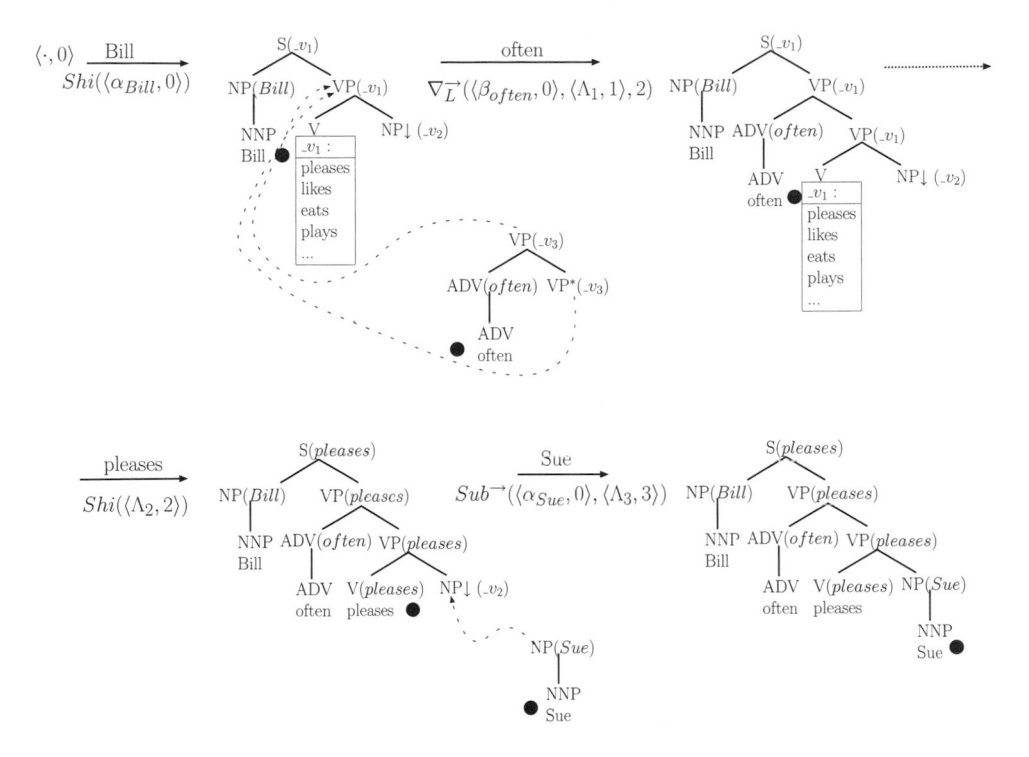

FIGURE 17.5 The DVTAG derivation of the sentence *Bill often pleases Sue*. The operations used in this derivation are shift (*Shi*), adjoining from the left ($\nabla_L^{\rightarrow}$), shift (*Shi*) and substitution (*Sub*$^{\rightarrow}$).

it will subsequently have to be combined with some elementary tree on the right. At the end of the derivation process, the left context spans the whole sentence and is called the *derived tree*: the last trees in figures 17.4 and 17.5 are the derived trees of *John loves Mary madly* and *Bill often pleases Sue* respectively.

In DVTAG we always combine a left context with an elementary tree. There are seven attachment operations.[4] Three operations — substitution, adjoining from the left, and adjoining from the right — are called *forward operations* because they insert the current elementary tree into the left context; three other operations — inverse substitution, inverse adjoining from the left, and inverse adjoining from the right — are called *inverse operations* because they insert the left context into the current elementary tree; the seventh operation — shift — does not insert new structural material.

The *substitution* operation is similar to the LTAG substitution, where an initial tree is inserted into a substitution node in the left context. In figure 17.4 we have a substitution of the elementary tree anchored by *Mary*.

Standard LTAG adjoining is split into two operations: *adjoining from the left* and *adjoining from the right*. The type of adjoining depends on the position of the lexical material introduced by the auxiliary tree in relation to the material currently dominated by the adjoined node (which is in the left context). In figure 17.4 we have an adjoining from the right in the case of the right auxiliary tree anchored by *madly*, and in figure 17.5 we have an adjoining from the left in the case of the left auxiliary tree anchored by *often*.

Inverse operations account for the insertion of the left context into the elementary tree. In the case of *inverse substitution*, the left context replaces a substitution node in the elementary tree. In figure 17.4 we have an inverse substitution in the case of the initial tree anchored by *John*.

In the case of *inverse adjoining from the left*, and *inverse adjoining from the right*, the left context acts like an auxiliary tree, and the elementary tree is split because of the adjoining of the left context at some node.

Finally, the *shift* operation either scans a lexical item which has been already introduced in the structure or derives a lexical item from some predicted heads. The grounding of the variable $\_v_1$ in Fig. 17.5 is an example of shift.

It is important to notice that, during the derivation process, not all the nodes in the left context and the elementary tree are accessible for performing operations: given the i-1-th word in the sentence we can compute a set of accessible nodes in the left context (the *left context fringe*); also, given the lexical anchor of the elementary tree, which in the derivation process matches the i-th word in the sentence, we can compute a set of accessible nodes in the elementary tree (the *elementary tree fringe*). To take into account this feature, the elementary tree in DVTAG is a dotted tree, that is, a pair $\langle \gamma, i \rangle$ formed by a tree γ and an integer i denoting the accessible fringe[5] of the tree (Mazzei, 2005).

The DVTAG derivation process requires the full connectivity of the left context at all times and hence satisfies SCH. The extended domain of locality provided by LTAG elementary trees appears to be a desirable feature for implementing full connectivity. However, each new word in a string has to be connected with the preceding left context, and there is no a priori limit on the amount of structure that may intervene between that word and the preceding context. For example, in a DVTAG derivation of *John said that tasty apples were on sale*, the adjective *tasty* cannot be directly connected with the S node introduced by *that*; there is an intervening NP symbol that has not yet been predicted in the structure. Another example is the case of an intervening modifier between an argument and its predicative head, like in the example *Bill often pleases Sue* (see figure17.5). The elementary tree *Bill* is linguistically motivated up to the NP projection; the rest of the structure depends on connectivity. These extra nodes are called *predicted nodes*. A predicted nonterminal node is referred by a set of lexical items, that represent a *predicted head*. So, the extended domain of locality available in LTAG has to be further extended. In particular, some structures have to be predicted as soon as there is some evidence from arguments or modifiers on the left.[6]

In DVTAG there is no theoretical limit on the number of predicted projections. Predicted heads arise because of a particular mixture of leftward and rightward dependencies. If we neglect the predicted heads that arise from trivial left recursion (because of adjoining), then the theoretical maximum is related to the number of possible ways of obtaining the mixture of leftward and rightward dependencies, which for "nontrivial" left recursion is unbounded. By "nontrivial" left recursion we mean a kind of left recursion that cannot be accounted for by adjoining. Indeed, adjoining allows us to modify the immediate dominance relations but not the dominance relations. However, elementary tree structures allow for a kind of left-recursion that changes the dominance relations. We can schematize this left recursion with the example depicted in figure 17.6a: this is a case of recursion that is not treatable with DVTAG. Figure 17.6b depicts the derivation of the string $z_1 a_1 z_2 a_2$, and figure 17.6c depicts the derivation of the string $z_1 a_1 b_1 a_2 z_2 b_2$. It is worth noticing that there is no way to transform the derived tree in figure 17.6b into the derived tree of figure 17.6c by using DVTAG operations. The key point is that substitution and adjoining cannot modify dominance relations, so there is no way to change the dominance relation between z_2 and the node X.[7]

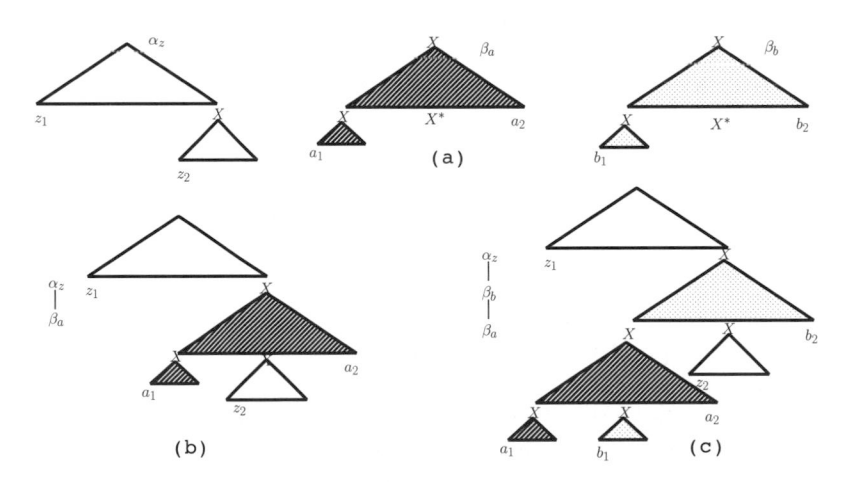

FIGURE 17.6 A LTAG (a) deriving a kind of recursion (b,c) that cannot be derived in DVTAG.

As a consequence it seems hard to define linguistic principles with the aim to constrain the shape of the trees, and thus to guarantee the finiteness of the lexicon. This means that the notion of predicted heads is crucial for the linguistic appeal of the formalism. Moreover, from a different point of view, several works have shown that the most important factor in TAG parsing complexity is the size of the grammar (Sarkar et al., 2000; Mazzei and Lombardo, 2004a), and for a wide-coverage DVTAG, predicted projections could produce a very huge grammar (Lombardo et al., 2004). Therefore, the notion of predicted heads is crucial for the applicability of the formalism too.

However, an empirical limit on the number of predicted heads can be estimated through the observation of empirical data. Recent work in psycholinguistics has shown that there are severe limitations on the number of predictions of syntactic heads that can be maintained at any given time during incremental parsing (Gibson, 1998). It therefore seems likely that there will be a similar limit on the number of predicted heads that are necessary in any given DVTAG elementary tree if we induce a DVTAG from a parsed corpus.

In order to assess the theoretical adequacy and applicability of DVTAG, we therefore need to know how frequently such predictions are necessary, and how many such predictions are needed in the elementary trees.[8] The observation is based on a simulation of strong connectivity in a treebank that employs DVTAG operations and elementary trees. A number of related works have confirmed that the number of predicted heads needed to guarantee the strong connectivity and the finiteness of the lexicon is bounded by four (Lombardo and Sturt, 2002a). In the next sections, we address the problem of building a wide-coverage DVTAG for English by automatic grammar extraction from a treebank. We present a number of exploratory experiments that empirically verify the hypothesis about the limitations on the number of predicted heads, and their low frequency.

17.4   Empirical Plausibility of SCH: Building a Wide-Coverage DVTAG

Here we propose a method for extracting a large DVTAG from a treebank. Our main goal is to prove that a wide-coverage DVTAG involves a limited number of predicted heads for any given elementary tree, and that such predicted heads occur with low frequency.

In order to extract a wide-coverage DVTAG grammar from a treebank we propose a three-step procedure. In the first step, we extract an LTAG from the treebank. In the second step, we transform the extracted LTAG into a trivial DVTAG, that is, a DVTAG without predicted heads that does not cover the treebank. In the third step, we transform the trivial DVTAG into a DVTAG that covers the treebank by increasing the number of predicted heads into the elementary dotted trees. The set of tree languages generated by DVTAG is a proper subset of the tree languages generated by LTAG (Mazzei et al., 2005); thus, DVTAG cannot generate the tree language generated by the LTAG of figure 17.6a. Since our aim is to produce a DVTAG that covers a treebank, we assume as a working hypothesis that the difference in generative power between LTAG and DVTAG is not substantially relevant for this task.[9] We will describe the details of the LTAG extraction, the conversion from the LTAG to the trivial DVTAG, and the procedure to increase in the number of the predicted heads in the DVTAG.

Now we describe the basic features of the algorithm proposed in Xia (2001) (henceforth LexTract) for the extraction of a wide-coverage LTAG from Penn Treebank. LexTract has two stages. In the first stage, each constituency tree T of the treebank TB is converted into a set of elementary trees $\gamma_1^T...\gamma_n^T$. By using a head-table and a modifier-table, the algorithm identifies the head and modification relations between the nodes of the constituency tree. The algorithm uses the head-modifier annotation together with a set of prototypical tree templates (a sort of extended projection skeleton) to extract the elementary trees $\gamma_1^T...\gamma_n^T$ that derive the constituency tree T. In the second stage by using the elementary trees $\gamma_1^T...\gamma_n^T$ produced in the first stage each constituency tree T of the treebank is converted into a derivation tree D^T, that is, $derived(D_T) = T$. The derivation tree plays a key role in the definition of a probabilistic model for the treebank grammar (Joshi and Sarkar, 2003), and it will play a key role in the third step too. Figure 17.7 depicts a binarized tree[10] from the Penn Treebank; in figures 17.8a and 17.8b, there are the LTAG elementary trees and the corresponding derivation tree extracted by LexTract.

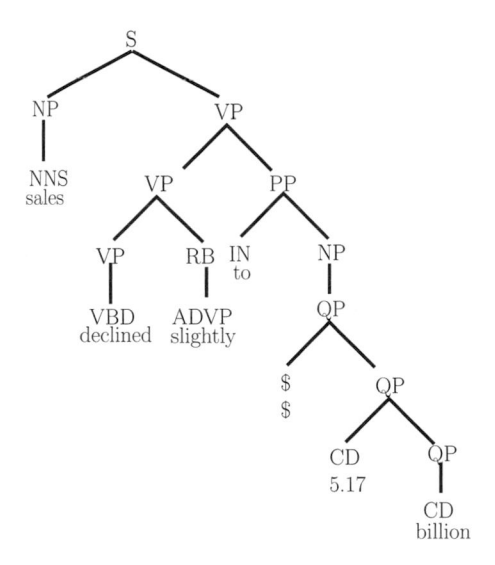

FIGURE 17.7 A binarized tree from the Penn Treebank.

In the second step of the procedure, we build the dotted trees $\langle\gamma_1^T,0\rangle...\langle\gamma_n^T,0\rangle$ augmenting each non terminal node in γ_i with $i \in \{1...n\}$ (extracted in the first step) with a head feature that contains the lexical item projecting the node (figure 17.9). Note that the DVTAG $\langle\gamma_1^T,0\rangle...\langle\gamma_n^T,0\rangle$ does not contain any predicted heads, and as a consequence it cannot (in general) derive T.

In the third step we use an operation called *left-association*. Left-association takes as input two DVTAG elementary trees, called the *base tree* and the *raising tree* respectively, and returns a new DVTAG elementary tree, the *raised tree*.[11] The operation produces the raised tree by grafting the base tree into the raising tree, and by replacing the anchor of the raising tree with a new head-variable. The raised tree produced by left-association displays one more predicted head compared to

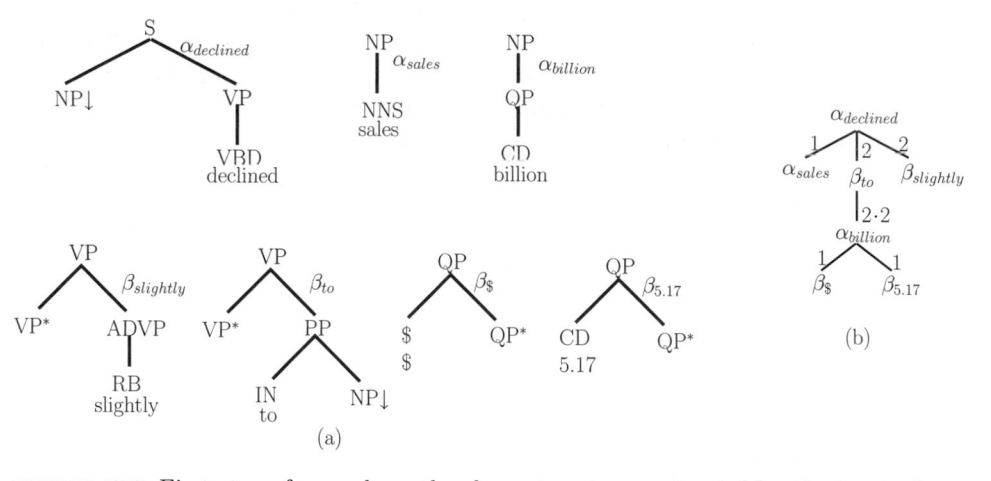

FIGURE 17.8 First step of procedure: the elementary trees extracted by the tree in figure
17.7a, and the corresponding derivation tree (b).

the base tree; such a predicted head implies a number of predicted projections (see
figure 17.10). We transform the trivial DVTAG produced in the second step by
iterating left-association on $\langle \gamma_1^T, 0 \rangle ... \langle \gamma_n^T, 0 \rangle$. However a weak-restricted application
of left-association allows for an explosion in the number of elementary dotted trees.
In Mazzei (2005), we applied left-association to the XTAG (1,101 templates) (Doran
et al., 2000), and by using a restriction based only on the nonrepeatability of the
root labels, we obtained a huge number (6,094,503) of dotted templates. Here we
use a stronger restriction that takes into account the occurrence of a predicted
projection in the treebank.

For each tree T in the treebank, we define a relation called *left-corner* on the nodes
belonging to D_T. We say that γ_k^T and γ_l^T are in the left-corner relation if γ_k^T is
the leftmost child (i.e., the child such that its anchor is in the leftmost position in
the derived sentence) of γ_l^T. We can distinguish a number of branches in D^T that
are in left-corner relation, that is $\gamma_{k_1}^T ... \gamma_{k_m}^T$ such that $\gamma_{k_i}^T$ is the left-corner of $\gamma_{k_{i+1}}^T$.
We build the final DVTAG by using these branches. For each word w_{k_1} in the tree
$T \in TB$, we consider the maximal left-corner branch $\gamma_{k_1}^T ... \gamma_{k_m}^T$ such that the root
label of γ_{k_i} is different from the root label of $\gamma_{k_j} \forall i, j \in \{1...m\}$. Then we iterate
left-association on $\langle \gamma_{k_1}^T, 0 \rangle ... \langle \gamma_{k_m}^T, 0 \rangle$ producing a final dotted tree $\langle \gamma_{k_1...m}^T, 0 \rangle$ that
has exactly $m - 1$ predicted-heads. In this way $\forall T \in TB$ we produce a set of dotted
trees $\langle \gamma_{k_{1...m}k}^T, 0 \rangle$ deriving T.[12]

For example, in order to convert the automatically extracted LTAG shown in
figure 17.8, we have to apply left-association to all the trees that are in left-corner
relation with respect to the derivation depicted in figure 17.8b. In particular, the
tree $\beta_\$$ is a left-corner of $\alpha_{billion}$, and the tree α_{sales} is a left-corner of $\alpha_{declined}$.
In the first case we apply left-association between the base tree $\langle \beta_\$, 0 \rangle$ and the

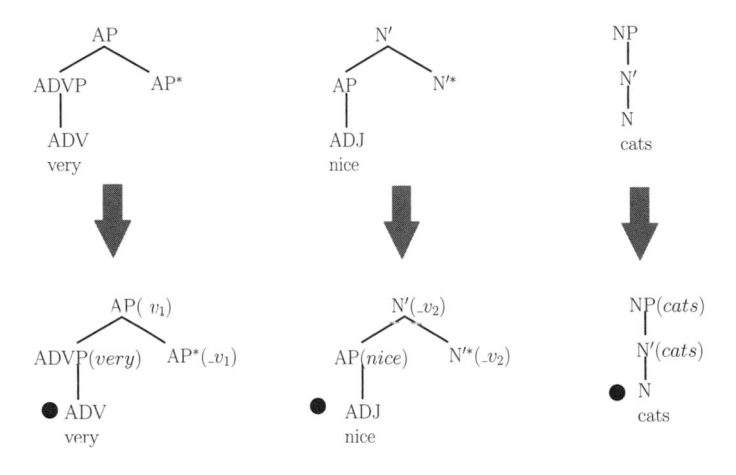

FIGURE 17.9 Second step of procedure: each node is augmented with a head variable.

raising tree $\langle \alpha_{billion}, 0 \rangle$, obtaining the first raised tree of figure 17.11. In the second case, we apply left-association between the base tree $\langle \alpha_{sales}, 0 \rangle$ and the raising tree $\langle \alpha_{declined}, 0 \rangle$, obtaining the second raised tree of figure 17.11.

17.5 Results: The Number of Predicted Heads

In this section we report on the application of the conversion procedure described above to the Penn Treebank. The goal is to verify the hypothesis of a limited increase of the dynamic lexicon due to the notion of predicted heads. The comparison baseline is provided by the *Connection Path Grammars* (CPG) that have been introduced in an empirical work on the Penn Treebank (Lombardo and Sturt, 2002a). CPG is representative of a family of dynamic approaches that apply SCH through the parsing method while adopting the standard CF competence grammar. Works from psycholinguistics literature (see Crocker, 1992) and from computational linguistics literature (see Roark, 2001; Collins and Roark, 2004) build the partial structures that CPG licenses as a competence grammar.

Both DVTAG and CPG are dynamic constituency-based grammatical formalisms that use the notion of predicted heads. The difference between DVTAG and CPG is that DVTAG uses linguistically motivated elementary trees and CPG uses elementary structures motivated uniquely by the constraint of strong incrementality. For example, in a DVTAG derivation for the fragment sentence *John thinks his ...* (figure 17.3), the elementary tree left anchored by the anchor *his* has to predict the arguments of the predicted verb projecting the S node (i.e. the verb subcategorization frame). In contrast, in a CPG derivation for this fragment the elementary structure anchored by the anchor *his* only predicts the NP and S nodes. In other words, the CPG does not fulfill the CETM principle while DVTAG does.

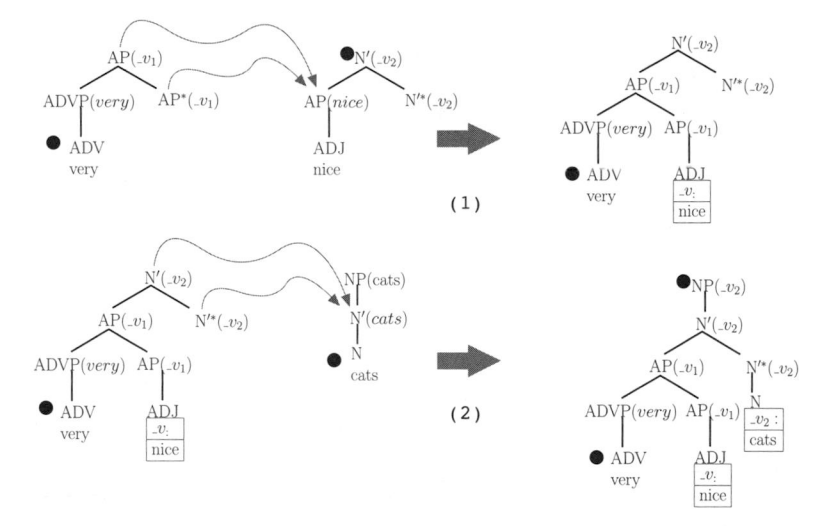

FIGURE 17.10 Third step of procedure: iteration of left-association.

By applying LexTract[13] on sections 02–21 of the Wall Street Journal part of the Penn Treebank II (39,832 sentences, 950,026 words), we have obtained 841,316 LTAG (nondistinct) elementary tree tokens,[14] corresponding to 5,268 (distinct) templates. The DVTAG conversion algorithm on these LTAG elementary trees produces a DVTAG (henceforth DVPenn) with 840,450 (nondistinct) elementary dotted trees corresponding to 12,026 (distinct) dotted templates. In table 17.1, we have reported the number of dotted trees with respect to the number of left-associations in DVPenn. Moreover we have reported also the percentage of CPG with respect to the number of *headless projections*.[15] Comparing the percentage of dotted trees in DVPenn to the percentage of connection path in the CPG extracted from Penn, we note that both the grammars have really few elementary structures with more than two predicted heads (~0.001% and 0.13% for DVPenn and CPG respectively). Moreover, most of the structures do not use predicted heads (90.95% and 82.27% for DVPenn and CPG respectively). In table 17.2 we have reported the number of dotted templates with respect to the number of left-associations in DVPenn. As a consequence of the fulfilment of the CETM principle, the number of templates with zero predicted heads is greater in DVTAG in comparison to CPG. However the maximum percentage of dotted templates (52.63 %) are left-associated once, and the same is true for CPG (43.09 %).

Note that there are 5,212 total connection path templates for CPG, there are 5,268 total tree templates for LTAG, and there are 12,026 dotted tree templates for DVTAG. The number of templates in DVTAG is greater compared with both LTAG and CPG. The motivations for the difference with CPG lie on the presence of rightward predicted symbols in the DVTAG templates. The motivations for the

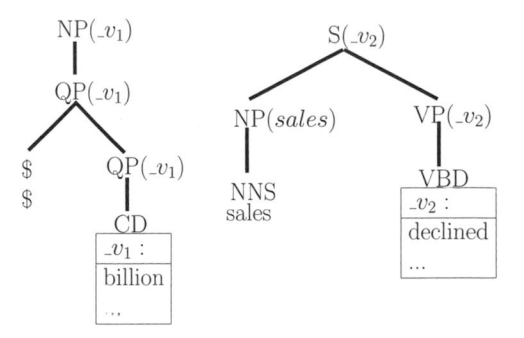

FIGURE 17.11 Elementary dotted trees

# of iterations of left-association	# DVPenn dotted trees	% DVPenn dotted trees	# Connection paths	% Connection paths
0	764,359	90.95	691,420	82.27
1	75,125	8.94	128,870	15.33
2	959	0.11	19,103	2.27
3	7	0.00	990	0.12
4	0	0.00	13	0.00
Total:	840,450		840,396	

TABLE 17.1 Number of (nondistinct) DVTAG elementary dotted trees with respect to the number of left-associations for the DVPenn grammar.

difference with LTAG lie on the presence of the extra material required to satisfy SCH. However, these numbers are of the same order of magnitude.

This is an empirical proof that the number of structures necessary to fulfill both strong connectivity and CETM principle is not unmanageably large, but more experiments on the properties of the extracted grammars are necessary. For example, to assess the quality of the grammars it is necessary to test their *coverage* (see Mazzei and Lombardo, 2004b). However, the results of the experiment show that for the Penn Treebank, few dotted trees have more than two predicted heads, in accord with earlier tests performed with CPG on two smaller samples of the Penn Treebank (∼100,000 words) (Lombardo and Sturt, 2002a).

17.6 Conclusions

We have described the basic features of the DVTAG formalism, and we have explored the empirical plausibility of a wide-coverage DVTAG with respect to the

# of iteration of left-association	# DVPenn dotted templates	% DVPenn dotted templates	# Connection paths	% Connection paths
0	4,947	41.13	1,527	29.30
1	6,329	52.63	2,246	43.09
2	743	6.18	1,166	22.37
3	7	0.06	262	5.03
4	0	0.00	11	0.21
Total:	12,026		5,212	

TABLE 17.2   Number of DVTAG templates with respect to the number of left-associations for the DVPenn grammar.

grammar size. DVTAG is a dynamic formalism that fulfills the hypotheses of strong connectivity in the competence by using the adjoining operation and predicted heads. We have analyzed the theoretical and applicative problems related to the notion of predicted heads. Moreover, we have defined an algorithm to extract a DVTAG from a treebank based on an LTAG extractor, and we have used this algorithm to produce a wide-coverage DVTAG for English. Analyzing this grammar, we have found as a side result that the DVTAG elementary trees extracted from the treebanks have an empirical bound on the number of predicted heads.

Considering that one of the motivations for DVTAG is psycholinguistic adequacy, one question that arises is the degree to which a large treebank-extracted grammar can be considered representative of human linguistic knowledge. It may be possible to devise an efficient representation of this knowledge through the sharing of common substructures (e.g. underspecification Toussenel, 2004). Actually, CPG structures, which lack the rightward predictions, implement a sort of underspecification (see Roark, 2001). Moreover, one may assume a model of language acquisition in which smaller elementary structures are progressively enlarged (here implemented through left-association) as a result of the chunking of successful structures (Miller, 1956).

A more reliable way to test psychological plausibility of a DVTAG is to examine its usage in parsing. The main question is about the efficiency of a DVTAG parser in comparison with a LTAG parser, and whether the efficiency gain is balanced by the effect of the larger lexicon. We are still investigating the feasibility of a practical polynomial parser for DVTAG, however some speculation can be made. In particular, we notice that an Earley parser for LTAG needs to predict right adjoining without any lexical cue; in contrast, a DVTAG parser should predict this operation only when the next word to process is the anchor of the right auxiliary tree. This property seems computationally appealing in the parsing of a number of linguistic cases concerning left-recursion (e.g., genitive constructions in English).

From another point of view, in future work we want to extend the analysis of the extracted grammars by exploring the issue of their coverage.

Notes

1. Further pilot experimental work has extended this result to cases where there are even stronger grammatical constraints forcing second VP to continue beyond the reflexive.

2. As pointed out by an anonymous reviewer, CCG differs from the other approaches mentioned here in that its flexible constituency permits a much wider range of incremental parses that match grammatical derivations. However, there are some cases where this is not enough to fulfill SCH.

3. We might think that the expansion in the size of the elementary trees would lead us to expect grammatical dependencies over larger domains than those that are permitted under the CETM, and this can have important advantages from computational point of view. One linguistic case is the subject quantifier in an embedded clause, which can project the subject noun as well as the main verb (e.g., *every* in the sentence *I think every dog barks.*) This would provide the necessary structure to state the usual semantics for the quantifier. We thank an anonymous reviewer for this valuable comment: we plan to investigate this linguistic issue in future work.

4. With the aim to simplify the exposition, we omit the *dynamic wrapping* operation defined in Mazzei (2005); Mazzei et al. (2005).

5. In the picture we represent the integer using a dot. Note that *fringe* and *dotted tree* are two concepts borrowed from parsing (Sikkel, 1997) as a consequence of the dynamic nature of DVTAG.

6. In contrast with the elementary tree anchored by *Bill*, the elementary tree anchored by *John* does not introduce any predicted head. In these derivations, we have decided to use the expanded tree only when it is necessary in order to guarantee the connectivity, that is, we have decided to delay until necessary the prediction of the heads in the left-to-right derivation of the sentence. One of the consequences of this choice is a difference in elementary trees involved in main and embedded clauses.

7. A linguistic example with a kind of recursion similar to figure 17.6a is the *partitive construction* of the XTAG grammar (Doran et al., 2000).

8. We thank an anonymous reviewer for this comment.

9. We have manually checked on a sample of the Penn Treebank that the recursion depicted in figure 17.6 is not present.

10. Binarization is necessary to extract LTAG trees, since it allows for insertion of a word in any position by adjoining.

11. There are some similarities between left-association and the CCG type-raising operation (Steedman, 2000), because in both cases some root category X is raised to some higher category Y. Here we are considering left-association *offline*, but similarly to type-raising it can be performed online too (see the SPARSE model described in Schneider, 1998).

12. Notice that we do not allow for repetition of root labels, since adjoining can take account of this recursion. However there are some cases in which adjoining cannot account for it, such as the recursion of figure 17.6b: in our experiment, we neglect these cases.

13. We wish to thank Fei Xia, who kindly let us use her program.

14. The number of elementary trees is differentm in comparison with the number of token words, because LexTract does not extract trees anchored by punctuation.

15. We used the CPG extraction algorithm described in Lombardo and Sturt (2002a). In this work the samples used were ~100,000 words large.

References

Abney, S. P. and Johnson, M. (1991). Memory requirements and local ambiguities of parsing strategies. *Journal of Psycholinguistic Research*, 20(3):233–250.

Aoshima, S., Phillips, C., and Weinberg, A. (2004). Processing filler-gap dependencies in a head-final language. *Journal of Memory and Language*, 51:23–54.

Chomsky, N. (1981). *Lectures on Government and Binding*. Foris.

Collins, M. and Roark, B. (2004). Incremental parsing with the perceptron algorithm. In *ACL04*, Barcelona, pages 111–118.

Crocker, M. W. (1992). *A Logical Model of Competence and Performance in the Human Sentence Processor*. PhD thesis, Dept. of Artificial Intelligence, University of Edinburgh.

Doran, C., Hockey, B. A., Sarkar, A., Srinivas, B., and Xia, F. (2000). Evolution of the XTAG system. In Abeillé, A. and Rambow, O., eds., *Tree Adjoining Grammars*, pages 371–405. University of Chicago Press.

Frank, R. (2002). *Phrase Structure Composition and Syntactic dependencies*. MIT Press.

Gibson, E. A. F. (1998). Linguistic complexity: Locality of syntactic dependencies. *Cognition*, 68(1):1–76.

Grimshaw, J. (1991). Extended projection. Unpublished manuscript, Brandeis University.

Joshi, A. K., Levy, L. S., and Takahashi, M. (1975). Tree adjunct grammars. *Journal of the Computer and System Sciences*, 10(1):136–163.

Joshi, A. K. and Sarkar, A. (2003). Tree adjoining grammars and their application to statistical parsing. In Bod, R., Scha, R., and Sima'an, K., eds., *Data-Oriented Parsing*, pages 255–283. CSLI Publications.

Joshi, A. K. and Schabes, Y. (1997). Tree-adjoining grammars. In Rozenberg, G. and Salomaa, A., eds., *Handbook of Formal Languages*, pages 69–123. Springer.

Kamide, Y., Altmann, G. T. M., and Haywood, S. L. (2003). The time-course of prediction in incremental sentence processing: Evidence from anticipatory eye movements. *Journal of Memory and Language Language*, 49:133–156.

Kempson, R., Meyer-Viol, W., and Gabbay, D. (2000). *Dynamic Syntax: the Flow of Language Understanding*. Blackwell.

Lombardo, V., Mazzei, A., and Sturt, P. (2004). Competence and performance grammar in incremental parsing. In *Incremental Parsing: Bringing Engineering and Cognition Together, Workshop at ACL-2004*, Barcelona, pages 1–8.

Lombardo, V. and Sturt, P. (2002a). Incrementality and lexicalism: A treebank study. In Stevenson, S. and Merlo, P., eds., *Lexical Representations in Sentence Processing*. John Benjamins.

Lombardo, V. and Sturt, P. (2002b). Towards a dynamic version of TAG. In *TAG+6*, pages 30–39.

Mazzei, A. (2005). *Formal and empirical issues of applying dynamics to Tree Adjoining Grammars*. PhD thesis, Dipartimento di Informatica, Università degli studi di Torino.

Mazzei, A. and Lombardo, V. (2004a). Building a large grammar for Italian. In *LREC04*, Lisbon, pages 51–54.

Mazzei, A. and Lombardo, V. (2004b). A comparative analysis of extracted grammars. In *16th European Conference on Artificial Intelligence, ECAI04*, Valencia, pages 601–605.

Mazzei, A., Lombardo, V., and Sturt, P. (2005). Strong connectivity hypothesis and generative power in TAG. In *Proceedings of the 10th conference on Formal Grammar and the 9th Meeting on Mathematics of Language*, Edinburgh, pages 169–184.

Miller, G. (1956). The magical number seven, plus or minus two. *Psychological Review*, 63.

Milward, D. (1994). Dynamic dependency grammar. *Linguistics and Philosophy*, 17(6):561–604.

Phillips, C. (2003). Linear order and constituency. *Linguistic Inquiry*, 34(1):37–90.

Roark, B. (2001). Probabilistic top-down parsing and language modeling. *Computational Linguistics*, 27(2):249–276.

Sarkar, A., Xia, F., and Joshi, A. K. (2000). Some experiments on indicators of parsing complexity for lexicalized grammars. In *COLING00*.

Schneider, D. (1998). *Parsing and incrementality*. PhD thesis, University of Delaware, Newark.

Shieber, S. M. and Johnson, M. (1993). Variations on incremental interpretation. *Journal of Psycholinguistic Research*, 22(2):287–318.

Sikkel, K. (1997). *Parsing Schemata: A Framework for Specification and Analysis of Parsing Algorithms*. Springer.

Stabler, E. P. (1994). The finite connectivity of linguistic structure. In Clifton, C., Frazier, L., and Reyner, K., eds., *Perspectives on Sentence Processing*, pages 303–336. Lawrence Erlbaum Associates.

Steedman, M. J. (2000). *The Syntactic Process*. MIT Press.

Sturt, P. and Crocker, M. W. (1996). Monotonic syntactic processing: a cross-linguistic study of attachment and reanalysis. *Language and Cognitive Processes*, 11(5):449–494.

Sturt, P. and Lombardo, V. (2005). Processing coordinated structures: Incrementality and connectedness. *Cognitive Science*, 29(2):291–305.

Toussenel, F. (2004). Why supertagging is hard. In *TAG+7*.

Xia, F. (2001). *Automatic Grammar Generation from Two Different Perspectives*. PhD thesis, Computer and Information Science Department, Pensylvania University.

Part V

Applications of Supertagging

Semantic Labeling and Parsing via Tree-Adjoining Grammars

JOHN CHEN

18.1   Introduction

The PropBank (Palmer et al., 2005) superimposes an annotation of semantic predicate-argument structures on top of the Penn Treebank (PTB). Consequently, it becomes possible to experiment with statistical models for semantic parsers. In Chen and Rambow (2003), we find that models that take advantage of deep linguistic features to predict semantic labels are more effective than those that rely on surface-syntactic representations. These deep linguistic features are easily obtained given that a tree-adjoining grammar (TAG) is used as the basis for the models. Furthermore, we show that a lightweight parser based on such models can achieve comparable performance to a full statistical parser based on models that use less predictive features. A caveat to the work in Chen and Rambow (2003), however, is that we use a pre-release version of the PropBank where only the most common verbs were semantically annotated.

In order to verify the validity of our results, in this work we repeat our experiments on a fully-annotated, full-release version of the PropBank. We show again that deep linguistic features are preferable to surface syntactic features for semantic labeling, as well as useful for semantic parsing when used in conjunction with a lightweight parser. Besides replicating previous experiments, we conduct new experiments on semantic parsing. We show that a lightweight, fast TAG parser can approach the performance of a full statistical TAG parser in certain situations on the task of semantic parsing. We also show that a unified syntactic and semantic TAG parser is preferable to a pipelined syntactic TAG parser and semantic labeler.

This work is comprised as follows. In section 18.2 we introduce the PropBank and describe the problem of predicting semantic roles. After briefly describing related work in section 18.3, we present an overview of typically used surface syntactic features for semantic role prediction in section 18.4 as well as our contrasting set of deeper syntactic features for semantic role prediction. In section 18.5 we describe how these deeper syntactic features are extracted from the PropBank. Section 18.6 describes the training and test data used in our experiments. Following this, section 18.7 is devoted to models that predict semantic role labels given syntax-only information as input, while section 18.8 describes experiments with semantic parsers. Section 18.9 summarizes this work and hints at future directions.

18.2   The PropBank and the Labeling of Semantic Roles

The PropBank (Palmer et al., 2005) adds a layer of semantic predicate argument information to the syntactically annotated Penn Treebank. Each word corresponding to a predicate is assigned a sense tag, and each complement and adjunct is assigned a semantic label. Complement labels consist of numbers ranging from 0 to 5 that are used consistently across syntactic alternations for the same verb meaning (See figure 18.1). Adjuncts are given special tags such as TMP or LOC derived from labels found in the Penn Treebank.

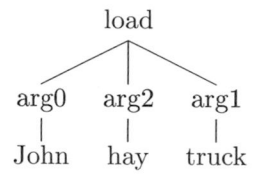

FIGURE 18.1 PropBank-style semantic representation for both *John loaded the truck with hay* and *John loaded hay into the truck.*

In addition to the annotated corpus, PropBank provides a lexicon that lists, for each meaning of each annotated verb, its *roleset*, that is, the possible arguments in the predicate and their labels. For example, the entry for the verb *kick*, is given in figure 18.2. The notion of "meaning" used is fairly coarse-grained, typically motivated from different syntactic behavior. Meaning and roleset are often used interchangeably because each verb meaning corresponds to exactly one roleset.

In our work, we focus on the prediction of complement labels only. We do not predict adjunct labels, since, as discussed previously, they are basically derived from Penn Treebank labels, for which there is already previous work. We also do not predict rolesets, though perhaps roleset disambiguation is not the most difficult task; our preliminary investigations show that the majority of predicate tokens in the training corpus (53.4%) are unambiguous with respect to roleset, and furthermore a simple strategy of assigning the most common roleset given an input predicate yields an accuracy of 88.3% on the training set.[1]

ID	kick.01	
Name	drive or impel with the foot	
VN/Levin classes	11.4-2, 17.1, 18.1, 23.2 40.3.2, 49	
Roles	Number	Description
	0	Kicker
	1	Thing kicked
	2	Instrument (defaults to foot)
Example	[John]$_i$ tried [*trace*$_i$]$_{\text{ARG0}}$ to kick [the football]$_{\text{ARG1}}$	

FIGURE 18.2 The unique roleset for *kick*.

18.3 Related Work

There is related work in semantic labeling and parsing. On the task of semantic labeling, Gildea and Palmer (2002) show that semantic role labels can be predicted given syntactic features derived from the PTB with fairly high accuracy. They perform modeling using an interpolated smoothing model using a backoff lattice. Gildea and Hockenmaier (2003) also use a backoff lattice, but they use features derived from a combinatory categorial grammar (CCG). Their CCG-derived path feature is roughly equivalent to Chen and Rambow (2003)'s surface subcat feature. They show that these features can aid in the prediction of semantic labels, although the ultimate performance of their models is hindered by mismatches between the PropBank and their CCG training data. Xue and Palmer (2004) introduce a syntactic frame feature which is similar to Chen and Rambow (2003)'s surface subcat and surface role feature taken together, except that the syntactic frame feature may be lexicalized. Pradhan et al. (2003) use the same features as Gildea and Palmer (2002), but they show that using SVMs instead of a backoff lattice results in an increase in accuracy. They also get a performance boost by dividing the semantic labeling task into a detection task and a labeling task.

The shared task for CoNLL-2004 concerns semantic role labeling using partial syntactic information, namely words, part of speech tags, base chunks, clauses, and named entities (Carreras and Márquez, 2004). The shared task for CoNLL-2005 concerns semantic role labeling using the output of full syntactic parsers (Carreras and Márquez, 2005). The highest performing systems combine outputs of multiple syntactic parsers, and then use a variety of features to label semantic roles.

18.4 Overview

Gildea and Palmer (2002) show that semantic role labels can be predicted given syntactic features derived from the PTB with fairly high accuracy. Furthermore, they show that this method can be used in conjunction with a parser to produce parses annotated with semantic labels, and that the parser outperforms a chunker. The features they use in their experiments are:

- Head Word (HW.) The predicate's head word as well as the argument's head word is used.
- Phrase Type. This feature represents the type of phrase expressing the semantic role. In figure 18.3, phrase type for the argument *prices* is NP.
- Path. This feature captures the surface syntactic relation between the argument's constituent and the predicate. See figure 18.3 for an example.
- Position. This binary feature represents whether the argument occurs before or after the predicate in the sentence.
- Voice. This binary feature represents whether the predicate is syntactically realized in either passive or active voice.

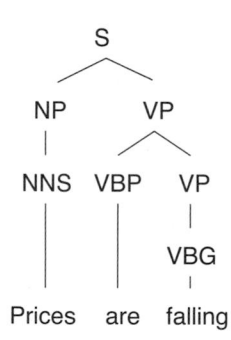

FIGURE 18.3 In the predicate argument relationship between the predicate *falling* and the argument *prices*, the *path* feature is VBG↑VP↑VP↑S↓NP.

Notice that most of the features solely represent surface syntax aspects of the input parse tree. This should not be taken to mean that deep syntax features are not important. For example, in their inclusion of voice, Gildea and Palmer (2002) note that this deep syntax feature plays an important role in connecting semantic role with surface grammatical function.

Aside from voice, we posit that other deep linguistic features may be useful to predict semantic role. Here, we explore the use of more general, deeper syntax features. We also experiment with semantic features derived from the PropBank.

Our methodology is as follows. The first stage entails generating features representing different levels of linguistic analysis. This is done by first automatically extracting several kinds of TAG from the PropBank. This may in itself generate useful features because TAG structures typically relate closely syntactic arguments with their corresponding predicate. Beyond this, our TAG extraction procedure produces a set of features that relate TAG structures on both the surface-syntax as well as the deep-syntax level. Finally, because a TAG is extracted from the PropBank, we have a set of semantic features derived indirectly from the PropBank through TAG. The second stage of our methodology entails using these features to predict semantic roles. We first experiment with prediction of semantic roles given gold-standard parses from the test corpus. We subsequently experiment with their prediction given raw text fed through a deterministic dependency parser.

18.5   Extraction of TAGs from the PropBank

Our experiments depend upon automatically extracting TAGs from the PropBank. In doing so, we follow the work of others in extracting grammars of various kinds from the PTB, whether it be TAG (Xia, 1999; Chen and Vijay-Shanker, 2000; Chiang, 2000), combinatory categorial grammar (Hockenmaier and Steedman, 2002), or constraint dependency grammar (Wang and Harper, 2002). We will discuss TAGs and an important principle guiding their formation, the extraction procedure from the PTB that is described in Chen et al. (2006) including extensions to extract a TAG from the PropBank, and finally the extraction of deeper linguistic features from the resulting TAG.

A *TAG* is defined to be a set of lexicalized elementary trees (Schabes et al., 1988). They may be composed by several well-defined operations to form parse trees. A lexicalized elementary tree where the lexical item is removed is called a *tree frame* or a *supertag*. The lexical item in the tree is called an *anchor*. Although the TAG formalism allows wide latitude in how elementary trees may be defined, various linguistic principles generally guide their formation. An important principle is that dependencies, including long-distance dependencies, are typically localized in the same elementary tree by appropriate grouping of syntactically or semantically related elements.

The extraction procedure fragments a parse tree from a treebank that is provided as input into elementary trees (see figure 18.4). These elementary trees can be composed by TAG operations to form the original parse tree. The extraction procedure determines the structure of each elementary tree by localizing dependencies through the use of heuristics. Salient heuristics include the use of a head percolation table (Magerman, 1995) and another table that distinguishes between complements and adjunct nodes in the tree. For our current work, we use the head percolation table to determine heads of phrases. Also, we treat a PropBank argument (ARG0 ... ARG5) as a complement and a PropBank adjunct (ARGM's) as an adjunct.

Ideally, the extraction procedure will localize all and only the PropBank complements of a given predicate in the same elementary tree. This is the case for the vast majority (91.4%) of complement tokens in the PropBank. There are various reasons why it is not true of the remainder, typically involving conflict between the extracted TAG's domain of locality and the domain over which a predicate assigns complements. For example, consider the cases of predicative nouns and adjectives. The small clauses surrounding them are the extent of the extracted TAG's domain of locality, whereas in the PropBank, the predicative noun or adjective and their syntactic complements are all semantic complements of the clause in which they

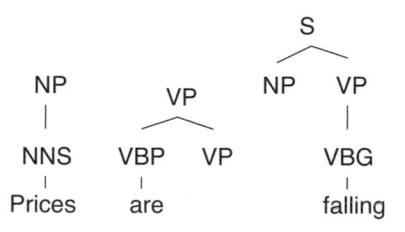

FIGURE 18.4 Parse tree associated with the sentence *Prices are falling* has been fragmented into three tree frames.

are embedded. Another example occurs in cases of subject-control PRO. Their argument labels are not localized by the extraction procedure because the surface subject of the main clause is labeled as the argument of the subordinate clause. Complements occurring in sentential adjuncts that corefer to complements of the main clause predicate are labeled as such in the PropBank, but will not be localized in the predicate's tree frame in the extracted TAG. Conjunction in the extracted TAG is treated as in XTAG (XTAG-Group, 2001). Consequently, instances of S conjunction lead the extraction procedure to localize complements properly with their predicates, but this may not be the case with VP conjunction or V conjunction.

Besides describing a procedure to extract elementary trees from a treebank, Chen et al. (2006) introduce other procedures to group the resulting elementary trees together into linguistically-related sets. In one approach, each tree frame is decomposed into a feature vector. Each element of this vector describes a single linguistically motivated characteristic of the tree.

The elements comprising a feature vector are listed in Table 18.1. Each elementary tree is decomposed into a feature vector in a relatively straightforward manner. For example, the POS feature is obtained from the preterminal node of the elementary tree. There are also features that specify the syntactic transformations that an elementary tree exhibits. Each such transformation is recognized by structural pattern matching the elementary tree against a pattern that identifies the transformation's existence. More details can be found in Chen (2001).

Given a set of elementary trees that compose a TAG, and also the feature vector corresponding to each tree, it is possible to annotate each node representing an argument in the tree with role information. These are syntactic roles including for example *subject* and *direct object*. Each argument node is labeled with two kinds of roles: a *surface* syntactic role and a *deep* syntactic role. The former is obtained through determining the position of the node with respect to the anchor of the tree using the usual positional rules for determining argument status in English. The latter is obtained from the former and from knowledge of the syntactic transformations that have been applied to the tree. For example, we determine the deep syntactic role of a *wh*-moved element by "undoing" the *wh*-movement by using the trace information in the PTB.

TABLE 18.1 List of each feature in a feature vector and some possible values.

Feature	Values
Part of speech	DT, NN, VB, RB, ...
Subcategorization	NP , NP_S , ∅, ...
MaxProj	S, NP, VP, ...
Modifyee	NP, VP, S, ...
Direction	LEFT, RIGHT
Co-anchors	{ of }, { by }, ∅, ...
Declarative	TRUE, FALSE
Empty Subject	TRUE, FALSE
Complementizer	TRUE, FALSE
Passive	TRUE, FALSE
By-Passive	TRUE, FALSE
Topicalized-X	TRUE, FALSE
Wh-movement-X-Y	TRUE, FALSE
Subject-Aux Inversion	TRUE, FALSE
Relative Clause	TRUE, FALSE

The PropBank contains all of the notation of the Penn Treebank as well as semantic notation. For our current work, we extract two kinds of TAG from the PropBank. One grammar, SEM-TAG, has elementary trees annotated with the aforementioned syntactic information as well as semantic information. Semantic information includes semantic role as well as semantic subcategorization information. The other grammar, SYNT-TAG, differs from SEM-TAG only by the absence of any semantic role information.

18.6   Corpora

Our extracted TAGs are derived from sections 02–21 of the PropBank. Furthermore, training data for our experiments are always derived from these sections. Section 23 is used for test data while section 00 is used as tuning data. In our experiments, we only consider those semantic roles that are semantic complements that are localized with their predicate in the same elementary tree. Thus, semantic adjuncts (ARGM's) are excluded, but the majority of semantic complements are included, over 91%.

18.7   Semantic Role Labeling

This section is devoted to evaluating different features obtained from a gold-standard corpus in the task of determining semantic role. We use the feature set mentioned in section 18.4 as well as features derived from TAGs mentioned in section 18.5. In this section, we detail the latter set of features. We then describe the results of using different feature sets. These experiments are performed using the C4.5 decision tree machine learning algorithm. The standard settings are used.

Furthermore, results are always given using unpruned decision trees because we find that these are the ones that performed the best on a development set.

These features are determined during the extraction of a TAG:

- Supertag Path. This is a path in a tree frame from its preterminal to a particular argument node in a tree frame. The supertag path of the subject of the rightmost tree frame in figure 18.4 is VBG↑VP↑S↓NP.
- Supertag. This can be the tree frame corresponding to either the predicate or the argument.
- Srole. This is the surface-syntactic role of an argument. Example of values include 0 (subject) and 1 (direct object).
- Ssubcat. This is the surface-syntactic subcategorization frame. For example, the ssubcat corresponding to a transitive tree frame would be NP0_NP1. PPs as arguments are always annotated with the preposition. For example, the ssubcat for the passive version of *hit* would be NP1_NP2(by).
- Drole. This is the deep-syntactic role of an argument. Example of values include 0 (subject) and 1 (direct object).
- Dsubcat. This is the deep-syntactic subcategorization frame. For example, the dsubcat corresponding to a transitive tree frame would be NP0_NP1. Generally, PPs as arguments are annotated with the preposition. For example, the dsubcat for *load* is NP0_NP1_NP2(into). The exception is when the argument is not realized as a PP when the predicate is realized in a nonsyntactically transformed way. For example, the dsubcat for the passive version of *hit* would be NP0_NP1.
- Semsubcat. This is the semantic subcategorization frame.

We first experiment with the set of features described in Gildea and Palmer (2002): Pred HW, Arg HW, Phrase Type, Position, Path, Voice. Call this feature set GP. The error rate is 6.86%.

We now experiment with our surface syntax features: Pred HW, Arg HW, Ssubcat, and Srole. (Feature set SURFACE.) The error rate is 4.83%, which is a sizeable reduction in error rate over GP. One reason for the improvement could be that this model is assigning semantic labels with knowledge of the other roles the predicate assigns, unlike previous models.

Our next experiment involves using deep syntax features: Pred HW, Arg HW, Dsubcat, and Drole. (Feature set DEEP.) The error rate in this case is 4.71%, better than both previous models. Its performance is better than SURFACE presumably because syntactic transformations are taken into account by deep syntactic features.

In our final experiment, we use supertag features: Pred HW, Arg HW, Pred Supertag, Arg Supertag, Drole. (Feature set SUPERTAG.) The error rate is 4.91%. It outperforms the model that uses surface-syntactically oriented features (GP), possibly because supertags provide both surface and deep syntactic information. We can postulate that SUPERTAG performs slightly worse than SURFACE or DEEP because sparse data afflicts supertag features more than subcategorization features.

TABLE 18.2 Error rates of models that label semantic roles on gold-standard parses. Each model is based on its own feature sets, with features coming from a syntactic extracted grammar.

Feature Set	SYNT-TAG
GP1	6.86
SURFACE	4.83
DEEP	4.71
SUPERTAG	4.91

18.8   Semantic Roles from Raw Text

In this section, we are concerned with the problem of finding semantic arguments and labeling them with their correct semantic role given raw text as input. In order to perform this task, we parse this raw text using a combination of supertagging and TAG parsing. We in particular compare the use of two different kinds of parsers for semantic parsing. The first is Lightweight Dependency Analyzer (LDA) which is a fast (quadratic-time), deterministic parser (Bangalore and Joshi, 1999). The second is a statistical TAG parser along the lines of Sarkar (2001); Schabes (1992); Resnik (1992). In addition to this dichotomy, we also investigate the impact of the use of either a syntactic grammar or semantic grammar on a semantic parser.

18.8.1   Supertagging

As a preprocessing step before parsing, we perform supertagging and n-best supertagging of the input sentences. In this section, we describe this preprocessing step, its motivation, and details of its implementation.

Supertagging (Bangalore and Joshi, 1999) is the task of assigning a single supertag to each word given raw text as input. For example, given the sentence *Prices are falling*, a supertagger might return the supertagged sentence in figure 18.4. Supertagging returns an *almost-parse* in the sense that it is performing much parsing disambiguation. The typical technique to perform supertagging is the trigram model, akin to models of the same name for part-of-speech tagging. This has the advantage of linear-time performance in the length of the input sentence, but it suffers in terms of accuracy.

n-best supertagging is a variant of supertagging in which a small subset of supertags is assigned to each word in the sentence. The idea is to sacrifice some ambiguity so that the accuracy may be higher. N-best supertagging accomplishes this by application of the usual trigram model of supertagging, followed by assigning N supertags to each word corresponding to the highest ranked backpointers of the nodes along the highest probability path through the Viterbi lattice. Chen et al. (1999) show that in this way a relatively small amount of ambiguity may be traded off for large increases in accuracy.

TABLE 18.3 Supertagging and n-best supertagging results.

n-best	SYNT-TAG		SEM-TAG	
	Pct Acc	Ambig (tags/wd)	Pct Acc	Ambig (tags/wd)
1	80.98	1.00	79.21	1.00
5	92.44	4.56	90.82	4.50
30	94.79	15.14	93.80	14.93
∞	97.80	148.14	97.15	182.43

Data sparseness is a significant issue when supertagging or n-best supertagging with an extracted grammar (Chen and Vijay-Shanker, 2000). For this reason, we smooth the emit probabilities $P(w|t)$ in the trigram model using distributional similarity following Chen et al. (2006). In particular, we use Jaccard's coefficient as the similarity metric with a similarity threshold of 0.04 and a radius of 25 because these were found to attain optimal results in supertagging experiments using the Penn Treebank (Chen et al., 2006).

Training data for supertagging is sections 02–21 of the PropBank. The results for supertagging and n-best supertagging are shown in table 18.3. A supertagging model based on SEM-TAG performs with 79.21% accuracy on section 23. The corresponding model for SYNT-TAG performs with 80.34% accuracy. Accuracy is measured for all words in the sentence, including punctuation. The SYNT-TAG model performs better than the SEM-TAG model, understandably, because SYNT-TAG is the simpler grammar. Compared to 1-best supertagging, 30-best supertagging achieves accuracies over 90%. In the latter case, the average number of tags per word increases to around 15, but this is much less ambiguity than the baseline approach of associating each word in the sentence with all of the supertags with which it is seen in the training corpus (150 to 180 tags per word).

18.8.2   LDA

LDA is an acronym for Lightweight Dependency Analyzer (Srinivas, 1997). Given as input a 1 best supertagged sequence of words, it outputs a partial dependency parse. It takes advantage of the fact that supertagging provides an almost-parse in order to dependency parse the sentence in a simple, deterministic fashion. Basic LDA is a two step procedure. The first step involves linking each word serving as a modifier with the word that it modifies. The second step involves linking each word serving as an argument with its predicate. Linking is restricted by the grammatical requirements stipulated in the supertags. The version of LDA that is used in this work differs from Srinivas (1997) in that there are other constraints on the linking process.[2] In particular, a link is not established if its existence would create crossing brackets or cycles in the dependency tree for the sentence.

TABLE 18.4 Accuracy of dependency parsing using LDA on supertagged input for different kinds of extracted grammar.

Grammar	Recall	Precision	F
SEM-TAG	74.12	80.19	77.03
SYNT-TAG	74.92	80.54	77.62

We perform LDA on two versions of section 23, one supertagged with SEM-TAG and the other with SYNT-TAG. The results are shown in Table 18.4. Evaluation is performed on dependencies excluding leaf-node punctuation. In accordance with the method that is described in Collins (1999), each dependency is evaluated according to both whether the correct head and dependent is related as well as whether the dependent receives the correct part of speech tag. The F-measure scores are in the 77% range, with LDA based on SYNT-TAG performing about 0.5% better than the one based on SEM-TAG. One obvious explanation for this result is that the accuracy of LDA correlates with the accuracy of its supertagged input.

These F-measure scores are relatively low compared to Collins (1999) which has a corresponding score of around 90%. This is perhaps to be expected because Collins (1999) is based on a full parser. Furthermore, the different parsers' outputs are in some sense incomparable because the parsing tasks are different. This is clear in the case of LDA based on SEM-TAG, since it performs the full semantic parsing task, whereas Collins (1999) is strictly a syntactic parser. It is also true in the case of LDA based on SYNT-TAG, because the form of the SYNT-TAG grammar is different from the one underlying Collins (1999). For example, a parser based on SYNT-TAG implicitly assigns null elements such as traces, whereas the highest accuracy parser in Collins (1999) does not. Another difference is that SYNT-TAG is a semantically headed grammar, whereas the grammar implicit in Collins (1999) is syntactically headed; for example, in the situation where the grammar of Collins (1999) would assign a dependency link between the modal verb and the subject, SYNT-TAG would assign a link between the main verb and the subject.[3]

18.8.3   Statistical TAG parsing

Our statistical TAG parser has a statistical model that is based on Sarkar (2001); Schabes (1992); Resnik (1992), and a parsing strategy modeled after Rogers (1994). The statistical model is generative. Basically, it models the probability of generating the TAG derivation tree, the sequence of TAG operations of substitution and adjoining that is necessary to construct the parse tree. In particular, if TOP is a substitution node representing the root of a derivation tree T, and α represents an initial tree, γ represents an initial tree or an auxiliary tree, $\langle \gamma, \eta \rangle$ represents the address of a particular node η in tree γ where a TAG operation occurs, then

TABLE 18.5 Accuracy of dependency parsing using a statistical TAG parser on supertagged input for different kinds of extracted grammar.

Input	Grammar	Recall	Precision	F
1-best	SEM-TAG	67.45	87.71	76.26
1-best	SYNT-TAG	68.22	87.32	76.59
30-best	SEM-TAG	77.93	78.29	78.11
30-best	SYNT-TAG	78.81	78.99	78.90

$$P(T) = P(\alpha_0|TOP) \prod_{(\gamma_j, \gamma_i) \in T} P(\gamma i | \langle \gamma_j, \eta \rangle) \tag{18.1}$$

Using the parsing strategy of Rogers (1994) has several advantages over those used by other statistical TAG parsers. For example, its running time complexity is $O(n^3)$ in length of the input sentence n, as opposed to $O(n^6)$, at least for languages such as English where the set of possible grammatical constructions by and large do not warrant the additional complexity. Also, it does not impose any restrictions on the form of the elementary trees in the grammar that is used for parsing, as for instance is the case with the variant of TAG called tree insertion grammar (Chiang, 2000; Schabes and Waters, 1996).

As with LDA, we perform statistical TAG parsing on two versions of section 23, one supertagged with SEM-TAG and the other with SYNT-TAG. Also following LDA, supertagging is performed as a preprocessing step before parsing. In this case, however, we experiment with feeding the parser 1-best supertag output as well as 30-best supertag output. The results are shown in table 18.5, with the same evaluation metric as before. We can see that the LDA parser approaches the accuracy of the full statistical TAG parser. Note also that when the 1-best supertagged output is used as input to the statistical parser, the accuracy is, perhaps counterintuitively, worse than LDA. From an error analysis, we see that this is primarily because this particular statistical TAG parser builds constituents strictly bottom-up, whereas LDA is more opportunistic. For example, let us consider the frequently occurring situation where the sequence of NP and VP is combined to form S. In this case, LDA will attach NP to the head of VP, even if the VP cannot be entirely constructed, unlike the statistical TAG parser. These results also show again that the overall accuracy of parsing using SEM-TAG is worse than SYNT-TAG.

18.8.4   Semantic roles from parser output

Parser output is a either a full or partial dependency parse annotated with TAG structures. We can use this output to predict semantic roles of arguments. The manner in which this is done depends on the kind of grammar that is used. Parser output using SEM-TAG is already annotated with semantic role information because it is encoded in the grammar itself. On the other hand, parser output using

TABLE 18.6 Evaluation of semantic argument recognition on SYNT-TAG corpus via LDA or statistical TAG parser.

Task: determine			LDA Recall	Precision	F
base +		arg	70.67	91.11	79.60
base +	bnd		54.34	70.06	61.21
base +	bnd +	arg	54.34	70.06	61.21

Task: determine			Statistical TAG Parser Recall	Precision	F
base +		arg	76.95	90.96	83.37
base +	bnd		64.96	76.78	70.37
basc +	bnd +	arg	64.96	76.78	70.37

SYNT-TAG contains strictly syntactic information. In this case, we use the highest performing model from section 18.7 in order to label arguments with semantic roles.

We have performed experiments on two different kinds of parsers. For LDA, we assume that the input to LDA is the 1-best supertagged version of the input sentence. For the statistical parser, we assume that 30-best supertagged output is used as parser input.

Evaluation of prediction of semantic roles takes the following form. Each argument labeled by a semantic role in the test corpus is treated as one test case. Certain aspects of this trial are always checked for correctness. These include checking that the semantic role and the dependency-link are correct. There are other aspects which may or may not be checked, depending on the type of evaluation. One aspect, "bnd," is whether or not the argument's bracketing as specified in the dependency tree is correct. Another aspect, "arg," is whether or not the headword of the argument is chosen to be correct.

Table 18.6 shows the results of first supertagging the input with SYNT-TAG and then using a model trained on the DEEP feature set to annotate the resulting syntactic structure with semantic roles. Use of the statistical TAG parser leads to performance increases of about 5 to 10 percent over use of LDA. When the boundaries of a semantic argument are correctly discovered, additionally finding the head word does not result in a decrease of performance. Note that if the head word of a semantic argument is more important than its boundary to an application that uses the output of semantic parsing, then we can see that this approach leads to promising results. We can also see that in this case, use of LDA leads to a model that approaches the accuracy of a model that uses a statistical parser, within 4%. Using a statistical parser always gives better performance, however. Its chief merit in particular seems to be the fact that it helps boundary detection.

TABLE 18.7 Evaluation of semantic argument recognition on SEM-TAG corpus via LDA or statistical TAG parser.

			LDA		
Task: determine			Recall	Precision	F
base +		arg	70.60	93.01	80.27
base +	bnd		54.21	71.42	61.64
base +	bnd +	arg	54.20	71.40	61.62

			Statistical TAG Parser		
Task: determine			Recall	Precision	F
base +		arg	76.88	93.15	84.23
base +	bnd		65.28	79.09	71.52
base +	bnd +	arg	65.28	79.09	71.52

Table 18.7 show the results when we use SEM-TAG in order to supertag the input and parse. We see that this approach leads to better results than when SYNT-TAG is used in a pipelined process. This is the exact opposite of the results obtained by Chen and Rambow (2003). This can be explained by the fact that in Chen and Rambow (2003), an incompletely annotated version of the PropBank is used, with the result that for example a parser trained on SEM-TAG would sometimes predict semantic arguments that were correct, but not yet annotated as such in the test corpus. The overall form of the results between the SEM-TAG and SYNT-TAG sets of experiments are the same, with identifying the semantic argument headword being easier than finding its boundary, and with statistical parsing being more effective than LDA.

18.9   Conclusions

We have presented various alternative approaches to predicting PropBank role labels using forms of linguistic information that are deeper than the PTB's surface-syntax labels. These features may either be directly derived from a TAG, such as Supertag path, or indirectly via aspects of supertags, such as deep syntactic features like Drole. These are found to produce substantial improvements in accuracy. We believe that such improvement is due to these features better capturing the syntactic information that is relevant for the task of semantic labeling.

We have also performed various experiments on semantic parsing. We show that predicting labels using a lightweight parser that generates deep syntactic features gives good results, especially in those situations where semantic dependency information is required more than semantic argument boundary information. For the latter case, we show that a statistical TAG parser boosts performance substantially. In a comparison between a pipelined syntactic parser and semantic labeler and a one-stage semantic parser, our experiments show that the one-stage parser is preferable.

There are many future directions for this work. It is doubtless that we can obtain an increase in accuracy by including morphological and lemma information as features in the models. We might also pursue the possibility of adding an additional post-processing step to label those semantic arguments that are not within an extracted TAG's domain of locality. More speculatively, instead of a post-processing step, another way to deal with those cases is to extract from the PropBank a grammar from a more powerful formalism, such as D-Tree substitution grammars (Rambow et al., 2001).

Notes

1. The relative ease of roleset disambiguation that is shown here parallels that which is found in the literature on word sense disambiguation, such as Kilgarriff (2004).

2. We thank Srinivas for the use of his LDA software.

3. In contrast with SYNT-TAG or SEM-TAG, the TAG that is used in the parser of Chiang (2000) is very much closer in form to the grammar of Collins (1999). It would not be straightforward, however, to repeat our experiments using Chiang (2000)'s TAG. Specifically, feature extraction would be made more difficult. For example, our subcat feature partly relies on information of a connection between a subject and its main verb rather than its modal verb.

References

Bangalore, S. and Joshi, A. K. (1999). Supertagging: An approach to almost parsing. *Computational Linguistics*, 25(2).

Carreras, X. and Márquez, L. (2004). Introduction to the conll-2004 shared task: Semantic role labeling. In *Proceedings of the Ninth Computational Natural Language Learning (CoNLL-2004)*, Boston, Massachusetts.

Carreras, X. and Márquez, L. (2005). Introduction to the conll-2005 shared task: Semantic role labeling. In *Proceedings of the Ninth Computational Natural Language Learning (CoNLL-2005)*, Ann Arbor, Michigan.

Chen, J. (2001). *Towards Efficient Statistical Parsing Using Lexicalized Grammatical Information*. PhD thesis, University of Delaware.

Chen, J., Bangalore, S., and Vijay-Shanker, K. (1999). New models for improving supertag disambiguation. In *Proceedings of the 9th Conference of the European Chapter of the Association for Computational Linguistics.*, Bergen, Norway.

Chen, J., Bangalore, S., and Vijay-Shanker, K. (2006). Automated extraction of tree-adjoining grammars from treebanks. *Natural Language Engineering*, 12(3).

Chen, J. and Rambow, O. (2003). Use of deep linguistic features for the recognition and labeling of semantic arguments. In *Proceedings of the 2003 Conference on Empirical Methods in Natural Language Processing*, Sapporo, Japan.

Chen, J. and Vijay-Shanker, K. (2000). Automated extraction of tags from the penn treebank. In *Proceedings of the Sixth International Workshop on Parsing Technologies*, pages 65–76.

Chiang, D. (2000). Statistical parsing with an automatically-extracted tree adjoining grammar. In *Proceedings of the the 38th Annual Meeting of the Association for Computational Linguistics*, Hong Kong, pages 456–463.

Collins, M. (1999). *Head-Driven Statistical Models for Natural Language Parsing*. PhD thesis, University of Pennsylvania.

Gildea, D. and Hockenmaier, J. (2003). Identifying semantic roles using combinatory categorial grammar. In *Proceedings of the 2003 Conference on Empirical Methods in Natural Language Processing*, Sapporo, Japan.

Gildea, D. and Palmer, M. (2002). The necessity of parsing for predicate argument recognition. In *Proceedings of the 40th Annual Meeting of the Association for Computational Linguistics*, Philadelphia, PA.

Hockenmaier, J. and Steedman, M. J. (2002). Acquiring compact lexicalized grammars from a cleaner treebank. In *Proceedings of the Third International Conference on Language Resources and Evaluation*, Las Palmas, Spain.

Kilgarriff, A. (2004). How dominant is the commonest sense of a word? In Sojka, P., Kopecek, I., and Pala, K., eds., *Text, Speech, Dialogue*, pages 103–112. Springer Verlag.

Magerman, D. M. (1995). Statistical decision-tree models for parsing. In *Proceedings of the 33th Annual Meeting of the Association for Computational Linguistics*.

Palmer, M., Gildea, D., and Kingsbury, P. (2005). The proposition bank: An annotated corpus of semantic roles. *Computational Linguistics*, 31(1).

Pradhan, S., Hacioglu, K., Ward, W., Martin, J. H., and Jurafsky, D. (2003). Semantic role parsing: Adding semantic structure to unstructured text. In *Proceedings of the Third International Conference on Data Mining (ICDM-2003)*, Melbourne, FL.

Rambow, O., Vijay-Shanker, K., and Weir, D. J. (2001). D-tree substitution grammars. *Computational Linguistics*, 27(1).

Resnik, P. (1992). Probabilistic tree-adjoining grammar as a framework for statistical natural language processing. In *Proceedings of the 15th International Conference on Computational Linguistics (COLING 92)*, Copenhagen, pages 418–424.

Rogers, J. (1994). Capturing cfls with tree adjoining grammars. In *Proceedings of the 32nd Annual Meeting of the Association for Computational Linguistics*, pages 155–162.

Sarkar, A. (2001). Applying co-training methods to statistical parsing. In *Proceedings of Second Annual Meeting of the North American Chapter of the Association for Computational Linguistics*, Pittsburgh.

Schabes, Y. (1992). Stochastic lexicalized tree-adjoining grammars. In *Proceedings of the 15th International Conference on Computational Linguistics (COLING 92)*, Copenhagen, pages 426–432.

Schabes, Y., Abeillé, A., and Joshi, A. K. (1988). Parsing strategies with 'lexicalized' grammars: Application to tree adjoining grammars. In *Proceedings of the 12th International Conference on Computational Linguistics*, Budapest.

Schabes, Y. and Waters, R. C. (1996). Stochastic lexicalized tree-insertion grammar. In Bunt, H. and Tomita, M., eds., *Recent Advances in Parsing Technology*, pages 281–294. Kluwer Academic.

Srinivas, B. (1997). Performance evaluation of supertagging for partial parsing. In *Proceedings of the Fifth International Workshop on Parsing Technologies*, pages 187–198.

Wang, W. and Harper, M. P. (2002). The superarv language model: Investigating the effectiveness of tightly integrating multiple knowledge sources. In *Proceedings of the Conference on Empirical Methods in Natural Language Processing (EMNLP)*, Philadelphia, pages 238–247.

Xia, F. (1999). Extracting tree adjoining grammars from bracketed corpora. In *Fifth Natural Language Processing Pacific Rim Symposium (NLPRS-99)*, Beijing.

XTAG-Group (2001). A Lexicalized Tree Adjoining Grammar for English. Technical report, University of Pennsylvania. Updated version available at http://www.cis.upenn.edu/~xtag.

Xue, N. and Palmer, M. (2004). Calibrating features for semantic role labeling. In *Proceedings of the 2004 Conference on Empirical Methods in Natural Language Processing*, Barcelona.

Applications of HMM-Based Supertagging

Karin Harbusch, Jens Bäcker, and Saša Hasan

19.1 Introduction

Applications providing natural language processing require robust and fast components in order to serve in situations where the utterance is either error-prone due to spontaneous speech production or caused by incorrect speech recognition results. Moreover, these systems have to work in real time to maintain the user's attention and acceptance in a human-computer dialogue. Statistical language modeling perfectly fits these two requirements (for a good overview see Jurafsky and Martin, 2000 and Manning and Schütze, 2000).

In the following, we elaborate on the statistical method of *Supertagging*, which provides the best lexicalized elementary tree, that is, its syntactic structure, for every word in a sentence (Bangalore, 1997). Our supertagger is based on a second-order Hidden Markov Model. The selected supertags, that is, elementary trees of a Tree-Adjoining Grammar (Joshi and Schabes, 1997), are composed by a shallow parser called Lightweight Dependency Analyzer (LDA; Bangalore, 1997). We have tailored the system to provide either only the very best hypothesis or its n-best hypotheses. We describe two applications that rely on the supertagger and LDA. For both our application domains, the supertagger is trained with a German corpus. These systems work in two rather different application domains. However, the task for the supertagger and the shallow parser remains the same, namely, to find the best hypothesis or the n-best hypotheses, respectively, for a given string and a trained supertag model.

First we describe the component KoHDaS–ST,[1] which serves as a parser in a user-initiative dialogue system in a call center. The user can freely speak to the system. KoHDaS analyzes the user's turn in order to extract the *task parameters*, that is, the information provided in the user's turn to perform the user-intended task by the system. KoHDaS solicits missing information from the user, in a manner similar to a system-initiative system. As for evaluating such component, we investigate in the following whether deploying a shallow parser based on Supertagging increases the performance of the system — with respect to both the classification and the extraction of the task parameters. We shall demonstrate that the accuracy increases when compared to a basic version of KoHDaS that only relies on recurrent plausibility networks.

In the second application domain, we address the problem of typing on ambiguous keyboards. Ambiguous keyboards host several letters, symbols, or numbers on one and the same button (such as telephone keyboards). Ambiguous keyboards are prevalent in watch-sized devices which lack space for a full keyboard, that is, unique keyboards with addressable keys. They are also common for typing Asian languages and on devices for speech- and motor-impaired users. In such devices, a full keyboard would result in too many buttons that are not manageable in reasonable time and these devices make use of so-called *ambiguous* or *reduced* or *cluster* keyboards (for one of the earliest systems, see Witten, 1982). Typing with ambiguous keyboards basically can be performed in two different manners. *Multitapping* as basic encoding method for short message sending (SMS) on cellular phones uniquely addresses a symbol by a predefined number of button hits in a row. Obviously, this method is cumbersome and time-consuming. So, hitting the button only once, although the code remains ambiguous, is more convenient. Based on frequencies of words, suggestion lists for the ambiguous codes can be presented to the user. (S)he selects the presented word out of the list.

In this chapter, we explore a sentence-wise disambiguation method based on Supertagging and shallow parsing (AkKo–ST^2) serving the primary goal of ordering these candidates in a way that the most appropriate words are placed on top of the suggestion list for minimal selection costs. Moreover, it allows us to postpone the attention to suggestion lists to a final editing step. We report on promising results compared to wordwise disambiguation approaches.

The chapter is organized as follows. In the next section, the methodological background of Hidden Markov Model-based Supertagging is presented. Furthermore, we outline the two variants of the system, namely a one and an n-best model, respectively. In this section, we also describe our training and test corpus imposed on both applications. In section 19.3, Lightweight Dependency parsing is described. After having elaborated on the formal descriptions, the next subsections describe two application areas for the system in turn. In section 19.4, a robust dialogue system is presented and evaluated. Subsequently, the second application, the sentencewise disambiguation for typing on ambiguous keyboards, is presented in section 19.5. Section 19.6, finally, summarizes our approach and the conclusions we reached.

19.2   Second-Order HMM-Based Supertagging

Both applications discussed in this chapter use second-order supertagging, that is, a *trigram model*. It is based on *Hidden Markov models (HMMs)*, enabling the use of the well-known algorithms on HMMs (see, e.g., Rabiner, 1989) to predict the most likely syntactic structure of a sentence.

Supertagging (Joshi and Bangalore, 1994; Bangalore and Joshi, 1999) is a disambiguation method that extends *Part-of–Speech Tagging* (*POS–Tagging*). In a *Lexicalized Tree-Adjoining Grammar*, every rule has at least one lexical anchor that cannot be the empty string (Schabes, 1990). As is the case for Part-of-Speech Tagging, the model is trained with a labeled corpus that provides the correct derivations for the sentences in the text. In the test phase, each word of each input sentence becomes associated with a lexicalized rule according to the model (*supertag*).

In the area of Supertagging, various approaches for the model have been proposed in the literature (Bangalore, 1997). On the basis of a training corpus of 1,000,000 English words, the supertagger provides an accuracy of 92.2%. *Head Trigram Supertagging* Bangalore (1997) is a similar method based on trigrams. However, the two previous supertags are not used to compute the current supertag; instead, the two previous *Head supertags* do so. A Head supertag is a previously computed supertag that influences the choice of the current supertag. This method works in two phases. In the first one, all Head supertags are determined. In the second phase, the Head supertags are used to compute the probabilities of all supertags. This method assigns in 91.2% of the cases the correct Head supertags using a training corpus of 1,000,000 words. Its overall supertagging accuracy is 87%.

Transformation-based Supertagging by Bangalore (1997); Bangalore and Joshi (1999) adapts the central idea of transformation-based POS-Tagging by Brill (1993, 1995). For this method, any word in the corpus is labeled with its most frequent tag. During tagging, these tags can be changed by a list of transformations. Such a transformation consists of a pattern, that activates the rule and a rewriting rule. In order to train this supertagger, a set of transformation patterns and a labeled reference corpus has to be provided. The training algorithm determines the best order of rule applications by minimizing the error rate of the tagger compared to the reference corpus. The supertagger based on this model has been trained with 200,000 words and reaches an accuracy of 90%.

19.2.1 Hidden Markov models for supertagging

Many variants of Supertagging use models similar to POS-Tagging (see the previous section for a brief description of the variants Trigram Supertagging, Head Supertagging, and Transformation-based Supertagging). Here, we discuss the details of a supertagger based on Hidden Markov Models (HMMs). Let us assume the notational conventions adapted from Rabiner and Juang (1986) and Charniak (1993) (see, Rabiner, 1989, for a good introduction).

A *Hidden Markov Model (HMM)* is a five-tuple $(\Omega_X, \Omega_O, A, B, \pi)$. Let $\lambda = \{A, B, \pi\}$ denote the parameters for a given HMM with fixed Ω_X and Ω_O. This means that a discrete-time, discrete-space dynamical system governed by a Markov chain emits a sequence of observable outputs: one output (observation) for each state in a trajectory of such states. From the observable sequence of outputs, the most likely dynamical system can be inferred. The result is a model for the underlying process. Alternatively, given a sequence of outputs, the most likely sequence of states can be inferred. The model can also be used to predict the next observation or, more generally, a continuation of the sequence of observations. Three basic problems can be formulated for HMMs:

1. Find $Pr(\sigma|\lambda)$, i.e. the probability of the observations given the model.
2. Find the most likely state trajectory given the model and observations.
3. Adjust $\lambda = \{A, B, \pi\}$ to maximize $Pr(\sigma|\lambda)$.

Efficient algorithms are known for all these questions (Rabiner, 1989). The *Forward-Backward algorithm* (Baum and Eagon, 1967) solves the first problem, problem 2 is solved by the *Viterbi algorithm* (Viterbi, 1967) and problem 3 can be solved by the *Baum-Welch algorithm* (Baum, 1972).

In this framework, the supertags are encoded as states and the words as symbols of the output alphabet of the HMM. Assuming a bigram model, the realization is easy and straightforward. Any supertag becomes an individual state and any terminal an individual output symbol. The resulting tagger can be trained with the Baum-Welch algorithm. The observation sequence is provided by the sentences of the training set (unsupervised learning). However, this method lags behind supervised learning methods (Merialdo, 1994). Supervised learning relies on an annotated corpus and using a trained model and the *Viterbi algorithm* (problem 2), the optimal sequence of states for a given observation sequence — in our case, the optimal sequence of supertags for a given test sentence.

The supertagger we report on in this chapter uses a trigram model (see Bäcker, 2001 for an evaluation of the HMM-based supertagger using bigrams). According to the trigram model, two previous states (that is, supertags) are encoded in the HMM in a well-known manner (El-Beze and Merialdo, 1999):

- The states of the HMM correspond to pairs of supertags (t_{i-1}, t_i).
- The transition probability $Pr[(t_{i-1}, t_i)|(t_{i-2}, t_{i-1})]$ is denoted by the trigram probability $Pr(t_i|t_{i-2}t_{i-1})$.
- The output symbols are provided by the words that are tagged with t_i and that are emitted in states $(\_, t_i)$.

At the beginning of a sentence, pseudo states $(\emptyset, t_j)$ with $\emptyset$ a pseudo category are assumed.

In general, the Baum-Welch algorithm (problem 3) can be applied to optimize the model parameters in order to maximize $Pr(\text{training set}|\lambda)$. Our results are gained on the basis of a labeled corpus. Hence, we do not use the Baum-Welch algorithm on our supertagger. On the basis of the labeled corpus, we directly estimate the model parameters according to the *Maximum Likelihood Estimation (MLE)* method. In order to overcome problems with *sparse data* — not all trigrams occur in the training set — *smoothing techniques* (for a good introduction see

Jurafsky and Martin, 2000 and Manning and Schütze, 2000; in Chen and Goodman (1996) the performance of various smoothing techniques is evaluated.) are applied in our system. Furthermore, the treatment of unknown words is described in the following.

In our system, we employ *Good-Turing discounting* (Good, 1953) and the *backoff method* (Katz, 1987). If the frequency of a trigram (bigram, resp.) is zero, the frequency of the bigram (unigram, resp.) is considered.

Unknown words are treated in our system in the following manner. The probability $Pr(w_k|t_j)$ is computed by the backoff method. In case w_k is an unknown word, we adapt the method by Weischedel et al. (1993), which deals with *features* of words. The prefixes and suffixes of words are considered to estimate the probabilities according to the following formula:

$$Pr(w_k|t_j) = \begin{cases} Pr_{MLE}(w_k|t_j) & \text{if } c(w_k, t_j) > 0, \\ Pr(unknown|t_j) * Pr(features|t_j) & \text{otherwise.} \end{cases} \tag{19.1}$$

The probability of the occurrence of an unknown word $Pr(unknown|t_j)$ for the currently considered supertag is estimated according to:

$$Pr(unknown|t_j) = \frac{N_1(t_j)}{c(t_j)}, \tag{19.2}$$

where $N_1(t_j)$ is the number of words that occur in the training set exactly once with the supertag t_j; $Pr(features|t_j)$ denotes the probability whether a word with the same prefix or suffix as w_k, respectively, occurs together with the supertag t_j.

Now we face the task of tagging itself. Formally speaking, this means the following. Let $t_1^N = t_1 t_2 \cdots t_N$ be a sequence of supertags for a sentence $w_1^N = w_1 w_2 \cdots w_N$. We are interested in the most probable tag sequence $\hat{t}_1^N$, which is defined by

$$\hat{t}_1^N = \text{argmax}_{t_1^N} Pr(t_1^N|w_1^N). \tag{19.3}$$

According to Bayes' law and additional assumptions that the words are independent of each other, the probability of a supertag sequence given a sentence, $Pr(t_1^N|w_1^N)$, can be rewritten as:

$$Pr(t_1^N|w_1^N) \approx \prod_{i=1}^{N} Pr(t_i|t_{i-2}t_{i-1})Pr(w_i|t_i), \tag{19.4}$$

where *maximum likelihood estimation* (MLE) is used for the probabilities by relative frequencies derived from an annotated training set of supertagged sentences. For unknown events, Good-Turing discounting in combination with Katz's backoff is applied as outlined earlier.

The tagging is performed by the Viterbi algorithm. For a given observation sequence $O = \{O_1, O_2, \ldots, O_N\}$, the most likely sequence of states $Q =$

$\{q_1, q_2, \ldots, q_N\}$ is computed in four steps (Initialization, Recursion, Termination, and Reconstruction (Path Backtracking); the time complexity of the Viterbi algorithm is $O(NT^2)$, where T is the size of the supertag set).

19.2.2   Implementation of the HMM-based supertagger

The overall system is implemented in Java. In this section we highlight some implementation details that reduce the space and time complexity of our system (see Cutting et al., 1992 for a discussion of efficiency matters for POS-Taggers).

Let us first bear in mind the complexity of an HMM model. The model parameters of a HMM consist of N states and M output symbols, form a transition probability matrix A, a $N \times N$ matrix; an observation probability matrix B, a $N \times M$ matrix and an N-dimensional vector π for the initial state distribution. All these parameters have to be computed, that is, the space complexity is $O(N^2 + MN)$.

The states of our HMM comprise pairs of supertags. Hence the number of states equals the square of the number of supertags T. Consequently, the space complexity is $O(T^4 + MT^2)$, and the run time of the Viterbi algorithm is $O(T^2 n)$. From this fact it directly follows that the model parameters cannot be represented by a two-dimensional array (for the 127 supertags in our system, the two-dimensional array of 64-bit digits for the transition probabilities requires 2 GB space). As a consequence, all model parameters are stored in an *associative* manner in our system.[3]

A reasonable space reduction results from only storing probabilities greater than zero.[4] With respect to the transition probabilities, the following holds. These probabilities are computed during the training phase, where they are not smoothed. Smoothing is performed during tagging. During that process the trigram, bigram, and unigram models are determined. Furthermore, the factors of the backoff method are computed. A smoothed probability is only computed on demand $(\text{getA}((t_{i-2}, t_{i-1})))$. Consequently, the overall space complexity depends on the actually deployed training set (unseen trigrams are not stored).

With respect to the run time, the following improvements can be performed to gain more efficiency in Supertagging. The Viterbi algorithm iterates over all words and all states by nesting loops for each word w_i in sentence {for each state m {for each state n {...}}}.

Shortcuts for states with an observation probability zero and unique POS can reduce the run time reasonably. The associative hash tables allow us to access all states of the currently considered word occurring in the training phase. These sets computed for the current word and its predecessor build the basis to collect the set of *relevant states* of the current word (backoff method for the observation probabilities). For these states, the iteration needs to be performed instead of the nested iteration over all states. More formally speaking:

$$\text{relevantStates}(i, j) = \{(t_k, t_l) \mid Pr(w_i|t_k) > 0 \wedge Pr(w_j|t_l) > 0\}$$

is supposed to be regarded in the two nested loops mentioned earlier. When $i < 0$ and $j < 0$, w_i and w_j, respectively, denote the pseudo words at the beginning of a sentence. Assuming only relevant states decreases the average run time reasonably. Our supertagger requires approximately 28 ms for the tagging of a sentence conducting only relevant states, whereas it takes over a one second to tag a sentence if all states are considered.

19.2.3   N-best supertagger

As described before, a dynamic programming technique (such as the Viterbi algorithm) finds the best supertag sequence of a sentence (equation 19.3) for a given HMM efficiently by storing the best local sequence probability and a backpointer to the predecessor state for each word position in the sentence. In order to find the n-best paths through the HMM trellis, we have to allow the backpointer table to store not only the best predecessor but also the n best predecessor states sorted by the corresponding logarithm of the probability. Since we deal with trigrams in equation 19.4, the states of the HMM have to be coded as supertag pairs; thus $Pr(t_i | t_{i-2} t_{i-1}) = Pr[(t_{i-1}, t_i) | (t_{i-2}, t_{i-1})]$. This leads to the following recurrence formula for state probabilities at position k in the sentence w_1^N, $1 \leq k \leq N$:

$$
\delta_k(\langle t_{i-1}, t_i \rangle) = \max_{\langle t_{i-2}, t_{i-1} \rangle} \left[\delta_{k-1}(\langle t_{i-2}, t_{i-1} \rangle) \cdot \\ Pr(\langle t_{i-1}, t_i \rangle | \langle t_{i-2}, t_{i-1} \rangle) \right] \cdot Pr(w_k | \langle t_{i-1}, t_i \rangle)
$$
(19.5)

The values in the δ-table are used to build an additional table that yields the n-best local hypothesis scores

$$
\phi_k(s_j, s_i) = \delta_{k-1}(s_i) Pr(s_j | s_i) Pr(w_k | s_j)
$$
(19.6)

for states $s_i = \langle t_{i-2}, t_{i-1} \rangle$ and $s_j = \langle t_{i-1}, t_i \rangle$. For each s_j, the number of predecessors s_i can be limited to n. The corresponding backpointers are stored in a table $\psi_k(s_j, m) = s_i$ where $m = 1$ denotes the best and $m = n$ the nth predecessing state.

Now, after this forward-trellis step, a backward-tree search is applied in order to find the n most promising supertag sequences, which are used to adjust the candidate lists and move likely matches to the top. The evaluation function $f(\langle t_{i-1}, t_i \rangle)$ that associates the current path cost with a state $\langle t_{i-1}, t_i \rangle$ can directly use the logarithm of the probabilities from the forward-trellis step as a heuristic $h(\langle t_{i-1}, t_i \rangle)$. This approach leads to *greedy search*. An important note is that the heuristic is optimal, since it actually returns the *exact* path costs to the goal. By also incorporating the backward partial path costs $g(\langle t_{i-1}, t_i \rangle)$ of the search process, i.e. $f = g + h$, we arrive at A^* *search*. The resulting system is able to generate the n-best supertag hypotheses for a given sentence. For a more detailed presentation of the system, see Hasan (2003).

19.2.4   Training and test corpora

Our German corpus comprises 250 labeled sentences (approx. 2,000 words), of which 225 are used for training and 25 for testing. The German training and test corpus has been constructed by hand for one of our application domains in the following manner. We looked at written German dialogues in news groups in the area of first level support for computer hardware. We developed an LTAG with 127 elementary trees covering the domain of the KoHDaS system (Bäcker, 2002) and automatically parsed these dialogues. The reviewed results of all parses constitute the tagged corpus. We trained our Supertagger using 250 tagged sentences. For the estimation of the HMM's model parameters we used Good-Turing discounting combined with Katz's backoff model to smooth the parameters resulting in better estimations of unseen trigrams. We use word features similar to Weischedel et al. (1993) (such as prefixes and suffixes of words) to estimate the observation probability of unknown words.

For a German test set of 30 sentences, 78.3% of the words were assigned the correct supertag. Due to the limited size of our corpus the results lag behind the ones for English. In the final section, we argue to extend the corpus considerably. However, special problems such as word order variation with German remain to be tackled in the future.

19.3 Lightweight Dependency Analysis (LDA)

A well-studied method to extract relevant information from potentially ill-formed (as is the case for spoken utterances) or not completely mastered (as is the case for automatically analysed spoken utterances) input is *chunk parsing* (also called *chunking*) (Abney, 1991; Appelt et al., 1993; Grishman, 1995; Hobbs et al., 1997). Cascaded finite-state automata analyze various phrase types expressed in terms of regular expressions. The main advantage of this approach is its robustness and the fast run time. The main limitation of such a chunking approach arises from the restricted formal power of finite-state automata. Cascades of several levels (FASTUS by Appelt et al. (1993) and Hobbs et al. (1997) has five levels) allow for the analysis of recursive structures to some extent. The basic level accepts smaller linguistic constructions, whereas in the next levels these elements become grouped into larger linguistic units. Accordingly, FASTUS can recognize "complex words" such as proper nouns consisting of several individual words. However, the coverage remains restricted to the static number of cascaded phases.

Statistical parsing is another robust and fast parsing method. Generalization rules can be extracted using a labeled corpus, *Treebank* (Marcus et al., 1993). These rules can be *grammar rules* (Charniak, 1997; Collins, 1996) or *decision trees* (Magerman, 1995). Each rule is associated with a probability, which is determined in the training phase with respect to the corpus. Parsing amounts to finding the most likely derivation according to these rules. The term statistical parsing subsumes a further variant where the rule set is also determined beforehand (Black et al., 1993). In the training phase, probabilities for these rules are computed according to the corpus resulting in a *Probabilistic Context-Free Grammar* (*PCFG*) (Booth, 1969).

Here, we focus on Lightweight Dependency Analysis (LDA; Bangalore, 1997) which composes derivations out of the supertags for individual words of the sentence. The LDA composes supertags using the two operations of Tree-Adjoining Grammar, namely, substitution and adjunction. So, after LDA, the supertags become interrelated in an appropriate and fast manner. Another favorably comparable method is presented in Nasr and Rambow (2004). In future work, we will run our systems with this variant and compare the parse accuracies.

In a supertag two node marks occur. On one hand, nodes marked for substitution have to be filled by the complements of the lexical anchor, whereas on the other, the foot nodes (i.e., nodes marked for adjunction) take words that are modified by the supertag. In the Supertagging terminology, one distinguishes a *derived* tree from a *derivation* tree. The derived tree is used for showing the phrase structure of the parsed sentence, and the derivation tree embodies the dependency links obtained from the LDA.

The algorithm of the lightweight dependency analyzer[5] is given in figure 19.1. It computes the dependency links for the n words of a given sentence in linear time. In order to achieve this, it first takes the modifier supertags, that is, the ones that are adjoined to a node, and computes the dependency links for them. Every node is associated with polarity values that reflect the directions of its arguments. For example, the tree β_1 takes an NP (complement) to the left and an S (modifier) to the right of the anchor *think*, which is noted with a plus or minus sign in front of the node, respectively. In this case, the node requirements of β_1 can be coded as "$-$NP• $+$S∗", where the bullet "•" symbolizes a complement relation and the asterisk "∗" a modifier relation. After having computed all dependencies for the modifier supertags of the sentence, the second step works on the remaining supertags (the substitution nodes) in order to obtain the links for their complements similar to the procedure in the first step. For the example sentence dealing with long distance extraction, the LDA result is summarized in table 19.1. The notation of "•" and "∗" was introduced in Bangalore (1997) and is also used by the supertagger that is freely available from the XTAG Research Group.

Step 1: For each modifier supertag s in the sentence
  ○ compute the dependencies for s
  ○ mark the words serving as complements as unavailable for step 2
Step 2: For the non-modifier supertags s in the sentence
  ○ compute the dependencies for s
Compute dependencies for s_i **of** w_i**:** For each external node d_{ij} in s_i do
  ○ connect word w_i to the nearest word w_k to the left or right of w_i depending on the direction of d_{ij}, such that label(d_{ij}) $\in$ internal_nodes(s_k) skipping over marked supertags, if any.

FIGURE 19.1 The two-pass LDA algorithm (from Bangalore, 2000).

The lightweight dependency analyzer presented in this section is an efficient means of determining the dependency links of the supertags that are annotated to the words of a sentence. For a sentence length of n, the LDA's runtime is linear;

TABLE 19.1 The summary of the LDA on the sentence *who does Bill think Harry likes.* The last column shows the final dependency links found by the procedure. The signs "+" and "−" indicate whether the dependencies are located to the right or left of the lexical anchor, whereas "•" and "∗" denote the type of the relation, namely complement or modifier, respectively.

Pos	Word	Supertag	Requirements	Step 1	Step 2	Dependencies
0	who	α_3	$\varnothing$	−	−	−
1	does	β_2	+S∗	3∗	−	3∗
2	Bill	α_5	$\varnothing$	−	−	−
3	think	β_1	−NP• +S∗	2• 5∗	−	2• 5∗
4	Harry	α_4	$\varnothing$	−	−	−
5	likes	α_2	−NP• −NP•	−	0• 4•	0• 4•

$O(n)$. It is a robust procedure and thus can be used to produce even partial linkages that span only a fraction of the sentence. If there are wrongly annotated supertags, an LTAG parser fails to parse the whole sentence. But the LDA is able to find "working islands" within the sentence without failing, thus resulting in a partial parse.

Now the basic method of our system is defined. In the following we describe two rather different application areas.

19.4 A Robust Analysis Component in the User-Initiative Dialogue System (KoHDaS)

Wizard-of-Oz experiments show that users of automatic dialogue systems would preferentially take the initiative in many dialogues instead of being asked a long list of tiny little questions by the system (Boje et al., 1999). Empirical evaluations demonstrate that adaptation to the user's dialogue preference leads to significantly higher user satisfaction and task success (Strachan et al., 1997; Litman et al., 1998). In contrast to these results, it can also be observed that in such *user-initiated dialogue systems* the user is sometimes left without a clear understanding of his/her options at a given point in the dialogue. This can cause frustration or even breakdown of communication. Consequently, an *adaptive system*, which reacts to the user's preferred mode, that is, it is able to ask explicit questions when the user does not take the initiative and to react to user-provided complex turns adequately as well at any particular state of the dialogue, serves as a user-friendly dialogue system.

19.4.1 The user-initiative help desk system (KoHDaS)

The strict dialogue structure with an explicit and inevitable initiative by the system (henceforth called *system-initiative* in contrast to *user-initiative*) entails that the user's answers to system's questions can be reliably recognized by some small subgrammar and sublexicon (e.g., a simple number or yes/no grammar and lexicon, respectively). Clarification dialogues caused by incorrectly analyzed words can be circumvented by this method. Hence it is essential for a user-initiative or adaptive (or also called *mixed-initiative*) system to remedy the shortcomings resulting from the less reliable analysis of the user's spoken turn with a general grammar and lexicon, respectively. Furthermore, the *task parameters*, that is, the information provided in the user's turn to perform the user-intended task by the system, have to be extracted without knowing exactly where in the user's turn or whether at all they have been uttered yet. In the case that not all task parameters are provided, even a user-initiative system has to ask questions – similar to a system-initiative system.

In the so-called KoHDaS-NN system, we have looked at a total of more than 400 spoken dialogues on hot lines and written dialogues in news groups in the area of first level support for computer hardware (in German and English). In spoken turns nearly almost and in written turns — by their nature — always, the user's problem is stated in one turn which can consist of several sentences (see example 1). In many of these cases, only a subset of all task parameters has to be asked in a consecutive manner after the initial turn by the user.

Example 1: Cannot get this printer to work with this computer.
I have follow all of the setup instructions
from the book and on the screen and
still nothing. Can you help.

In order to analyze such a user turn that outlines the whole problem, we supply the speech analysis component (Nuance, 2000) with a broad-coverage grammar and lexicon for the whole domain of computer hardware, see Laumann (2000) for a description of the context-free rules and a list of the words together with their part-of-speech information. From the word hypotheses graph that the speech analysis system provides, the best path is taken as input for the next steps in KoHDaS. Furthermore, a reduced vocabulary with 131 *word groups (w)* was defined, made up of general concepts in this domain (such as "cable", "capacity", "setup") with all in all containing 616 English and German words, which can be said more or less synonymously for a concept. Table 19.2 lists some of the defined general concepts.

TABLE 19.2 Word groups with their corresponding words.

word groups (w)	corresponding words
cable	cable, connection, ...
capacity	capacity, gig, GB, 8gig, ...
setup	setup, install, uninstall, ...
hard disk	hard disk, harddrive, disk, ...
monitor	monitor, screen, TFT, ...

Each word group is represented in the following processing by a significance vector $(c_1, c_2, c_3, c_4, c_5, c_6, c_7)$, with c_i corresponding to one of the seven problem classes. For each c_i a *significance vector* $v(w, c_i)$ is computed by equation 19.7.

$$v(w, c_i) = \frac{\text{occurrences of a word from } w \text{ within class } c_i}{\sum\limits_{j=1}^{n} \text{occurrence of words from } w \text{ within class } c_j} \tag{19.7}$$

Hence, a text is represented by a sequence of significance vectors. Although different words could be theoretically represented by the same significance vector, the probability is small that such a vector sequence describes different phrases.

The user's turn circumscribing the problem as a whole is handed to a hierarchy of recurrent plausibility networks (Wermter, 1995) that classify the problem accordingly. Such a neural net (NN), which basically compares to simple recurrent networks by Elman (1990), consists — beside one input and one output layer — of n (> 0) hidden layers each of which has recursive link(s) to its context layers. Our test system differentiated between seven classes forming a hierarchy according to figure 19.2 which we found optimal after a series of test with various topologies. The classes are outlined in table 19.3.

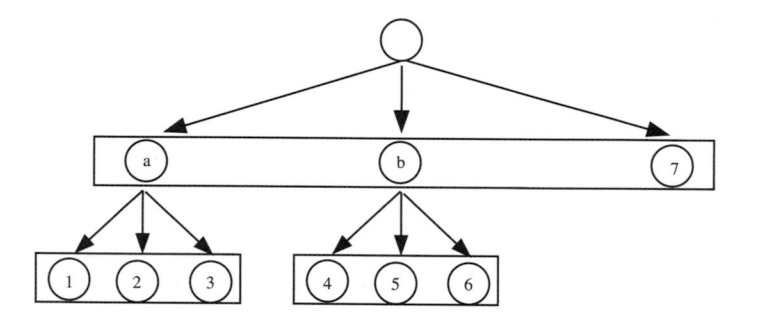

FIGURE 19.2 Hierarchy of our three different plausibility networks.

Before the system starts to extract the task parameters according to the classification in the current mode[6] the system asks the user for a confirmation of the proposed classification result. If the user doesn't agree (s)he can repeat or rephrase the turn. After a second mismatch between the user's actual problem and the system's guess, human assistance is provided. As the system allows for barging-in at any state of the dialogue, the user can always ask for human assistance by saying "operator". Then KoHDaS hands over the initiative to a human agent in the call center.

Assuming the confirmation is given by the user, in the next step, the system extracts even only implicitly mentioned task parameters of this problem class from the turn by a graph-matching technique. Remaining or unidentified task parameters

TABLE 19.3 Problem classes.

a	Problems with the hard disk	
1		Problem with two hard disks in the computer
2		Problem with wrongly identified hard disks
3		Another problem with hard disks
b	Problems with the monitor	
4		Problem with glimmering monitor
5		Problem with colour shifting
6		Another problem with the monitor
7	Another general problem	

required to solve the problem are asked by the system in an ordinary question answering manner. The results of the KoHDaS-NN where the classification and the extraction of the task parameters is performed only on the basis of simple words are promising. However the number of wrong classifications and questions for yet uttered task parameters has to be further decreased in order to provide a user-friendly dialogue with the customers. Hence we investigate in the following whether deploying a shallow parser based on supertagging increases the performance of the system — with respect to both the classification and the extraction of the task parameters.

19.4.2   Baseline of the system KoHDaS-NN

In order to have a baseline to compare the results of the suppertagging and the shallow parsing to, we first describe the version KoHDaS-NN, where the output of the recognition component is immediately handed to the classification. In KoHDaS-NN, the user's turn is classified according to *significance vectors* (see equation 19.7) where only 616 words are actually regarded and matched with a reduced vocabulary with 131 word groups c_i, that is, general concepts in our domain (such as *"hard disk"*, *"monitor"* and *"capacity"*) containing words, which can be considered to be synonymous (e.g., words in class *"hard disk"* are *"disk"* or *"harddrive"*). Generally, significance vectors account for the importance of the word in a specific problem class.

19.4.3   Supertagging and LDA in KoHDaS-ST

The supertagger in KoHDaS-ST relies on a *Hidden Markov model* and is trained with German input texts as outlined in section 19.2.1. Its results for a test sentence allow an LDA (see section 19.3) to discover dependencies between the supertags in the user's turn. The dependency structure accomplished by this method is used in classification and in information extraction in the following manner. In KoHDaS-ST, the significance vectors for classification are adjusted using the results of the structural information collected by the supertagger and the LDA. The adjusted significance vectors v^* are computed by:

$$v^*(w, c_i) = \begin{cases} \alpha^d \, v(w, c_i) & \text{if } v(w, c_i) > \frac{1}{n} \sum_{j=1}^n c_j, \\ (1 + \beta d) * 0.1 & \text{if } v(w, c_i) = 0 \text{ and } d > 0, \\ (1 + \beta d) \, v(w, c_i) & \text{otherwise} \end{cases}$$

where d represents the syntactic depth of the sentence in which the current word occurs and α and β are constant values. Tests have shown that suitable values for α and β are $\alpha = 0.8$ and $\beta = 0.6$.

19.4.4 Evaluation

The results of this approach compared to the pure neural net-based version of KoHDaS are outlined in table 19.4. The table shows that the Mean Squared Error (MSE) of three subnetworks of KoHDaS-NN is decreased in the top level net as well as in the local net for disk problems but increased in the local net for monitor problems. The reasons why the monitor problems behave in this unexpected manner are topics of future investigations.

TABLE 19.4 Mean Squared Error (MSE).

Net	MSE in Test	
	KoHDaS-NN	KoHDaS-ST
NN differentiating monitor and disk probs.	3.85	3.45
Local NN - disk probs.	10.33	9.65
Local NN - monitor probs.	4.72	4.91

In the graph-based information extraction step, each node of the graph corresponds to the information already extracted from the turn. Nodes can be associated with questions to be asked by the system. Edges are labeled with sets of word groups enabling a transition if an appropriate word occurs in the user's input. See figure 19.3 for a partial dialogue graph of KoHDaS-NN.

In KoHDaS-ST, the results of the dependency analysis together with features in the lexicon are used to create a kind of *semantic representation* of the user's turn (Bäcker, 2002). Edges in the new dialogue graphs are labeled with this representation (see figure 19.4) resulting in improved processing of the turn. For example, the turn *"Sometimes my computer drives me mad. My monitor started flickering 3 days ago".* would enable the transition from node 5 to 51, since *"sometimes"* is found in the input. In KoHDaS-ST this will not happen, because *"sometimes"* is not related to *"flickering."*

Comparing the results of German Supertagging (78.3%) to English (92.2%), two different reasons lead to less good results. First, our training set (1,973 words) is small compared to the English one (1,000,000 words). Accordingly, many unseen

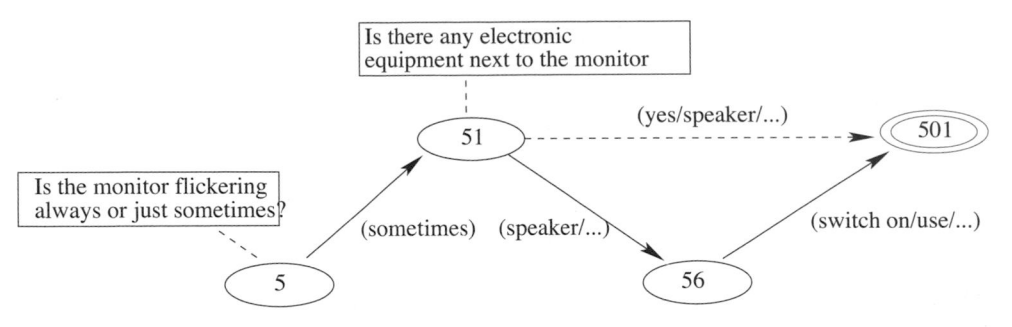

FIGURE 19.3 Part of a dialogue graph in the problem class of flickering monitors in KoHDaS.

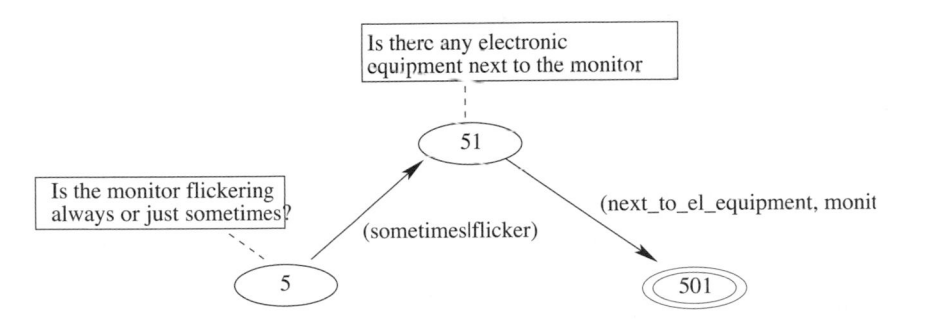

FIGURE 19.4 Part of a dialogue graph in the problem class of flickering monitors in KoHDaS-ST.

trigrams are imposed on the system. Second, German is a language with free word order. This fact amplifies the effects of sparse data (for example, Spanish Supertagging has an accuracy of about 80% Bangalore, 1998). In future work, the training set of KoHDaS-ST will be extended. Furthermore, unsupervised learning methods integrated with supervised methods (Montoya et al., 2002) will be deployed in our system. How far we can get with a free word order language like German is currently an open problem.

19.5 Sentencewise Disambiguation for Typing with an Ambiguous Keyboard

As a consequence of an observation by Witten (1982), namely that in a dictionary with 24,500 words only 8% are ambiguous if the respective button on a phone keyboard is pressed only once, predictive methods have emerged on the market. *Predictive* text entry devices (e.g., the product T9 by Tegic Communications for SMS typing; Kushler, 1998) have been developed that reduce the number of keystrokes needed for entering a word by proposing possible candidates matching the current input. Moreover, the possible candidates for *completion* all match the already entered prefix of the word. By selecting one of the available suggestions (irrespective of prediction or completion mode), the number of key presses decreases, but the overall time to enter the word is not necessarily reduced due to the cognitive load that emerges while scanning the suggested candidate list (see, Horstmann Koester and Levine, 1994).

Most frequently, *wordwise* systems are deployed for this problem. The easiest way to achieve appropriate suggestion lists is to sort the list according to word frequencies obtained from large corpora (see the proceedings of the EACL-workshop on language modeling for text entry methods edited by Harbusch et al., 2003 for an overview of recent *n*-gram systems). In Tanaka-Ishii et al. (2002), an adaptive language model utilizing prediction by partial match (PPM; Cleary and Witten, 1984) is proposed, which actually originates from the information theory domain and deals with the problem of improving the compression rates of arithmetic coding, and that lowers the entropy of a language model by maintaining a list of already seen contexts and its corresponding successors. In Matiasek et al. (2002), a system based on word *n*-grams with additional part-of-speech information is outlined. In Fazly and Hirst (2003), a system is outlined that also imposes part-of-speech information on prediction. Surprisingly, additional part-of-speech information hardly improves the prediction lists. Thus, other information sources have to be investigated.

The only approach that goes beyond a wordwise step-by-step disambiguation we are aware of is reported in Rau and Skiena (1996). Instead of permanently changing between two modes, a phase where a word is typed and a phase where it is disambiguated in a list of current suggestions, the user can solely concentrate on the process of text entry in a *sentencewise* approach. Here, a telephone keypad that distributes the 26 letters and the blank character (word delimiter) on 9 keys serves as and ambiguous keyboard (i.e., 3 letters are placed on one key at a time). The end of the sentence is marked unambiguously using the "#" key. Sentence disambiguation applies the Viterbi algorithm and involves word bigram probabilities and part-of-speech information extracted from the Brown Corpus. The results obtained by simulating the typing of various text samples with this framework look promising. For various domains, the percentage of correct words ranges from 92.86% to 97.67%. This is due to the relatively high number of keys and low number of ambiguous words, respectively.

19.5.1   The keyboard layout in AkKo

The distribution of the letters on the keys that is used in our system, AkKo, is language-specific and is obtained by applying a genetic algorithm that optimizes the candidate lists' length and overall selection costs for a given lexicon.[7] For German and English, the dictionaries are based on the CELEX lexical database Baayen et al. (1995). The current keyboard layout of the letter keys for the German language is depicted in figure 19.5. In contrast to the approach in Rau and Skiena (1996), the word delimiter (space) is coded unambiguously by entering the command mode.[8]

So for example, in order to enter *guten Morgen* (good morning), the user types the code sequence $\boxed{1}\boxed{2}\boxed{2}\boxed{3}\boxed{3}\boxed{\llcorner}\boxed{1}\boxed{2}\boxed{1}\boxed{1}\boxed{3}\boxed{3}$. For the first code, there exist 48 possible words (*guten, außen, wohin, . . .*), for the second, there are 30 entries (*wollen, morgen, Morgen, . . .*). This small example already allows for a total of 1,440 sentence hypotheses.

a g j l m	c f h k o s	b d e i
q r w z ä	t u v x y ü ß	n p ö -
Button 1	Button 2	Button 3

FIGURE 19.5 The layout of the letter keys for German.

19.5.2 Supertagging on suggestion lists

The starting point in AkKo-ST is an ambiguously coded word sequence typed with a reduced keyboard, as introduced in the beginning of this section. Every code generates a list of words and every word has several supertags associated with it. A supertagger is used to find the most likely supertag sequence for the sentence, and on the basis of this information, the candidate list becomes reordered such that the most likely words (which are the lexical anchors of the supertags) appear at the top. Due to the ambiguous coding, the number of supertags for a code (which corresponds to the supertags of all word expansions of a code) is so large that the best supertag sequence is not sufficient to improve the results significantly. Therefore, we use the n-best tree-trellis approach from section 19.2.3 in order to produce more than one hypothesis. At this point, the code sequence of each sentence is associated with a list of the n-best supertag sequences found by the supertagger.

Every word usually has several supertags, since the lexical items of an LTAG are almost always associated with several elementary structures that encode the various local dependencies of each word. And since every code expands to several matching words, the result is a set of supertag sets that form a trellis (cf. detailed view in figure 19.6). This trellis is the basis for the tree-trellis search that finds the n-best supertag hypotheses for a given sentence. Figure 19.6 also shows the different expansion steps for the sentence *ich habe ein kleines Problem* (I have a little problem).

After typing the words of a sentence with the ambiguous keyboard, the code sequence is expanded, and the candidate list is obtained according to the CELEX lexicon. After that, the possible supertags are looked up in the trained language model, that is, all supertags that occurred in the training corpus with its corresponding lexical anchor are primed for the n-best tree-trellis search. The hypotheses that are returned by the search are then used to reorder the candidate lists. The effect is that likely words of the trained language model will move to the top of the match lists and improve the overall accuracy of the system.

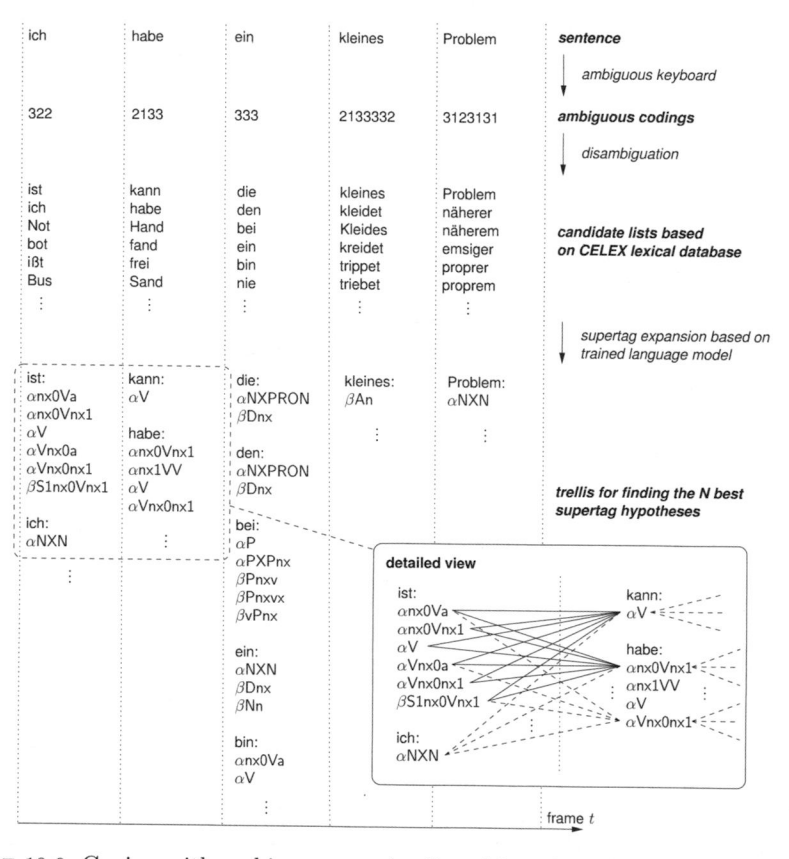

FIGURE 19.6 Coping with ambiguous words: disambiguation of coded words and the corresponding supertag expansion.

19.5.3 Filtering ungrammatical hypotheses by an LDA

In a second step, a *lightweight dependency analysis* (Bangalore, 2000) on the list of supertag hypotheses found by the n-best search is used as an additional knowledge source in order to determine likely chunks of the sentence. The dependencies coded in the elementary trees (supertags) can be used to derive a shallow parse of the sentence in linear time.[9] We use a *dependency coverage* criterion, which determines how many dependency slots of each supertag are filled to the left and right of its lexical anchor. The hypotheses that have a maximum number of covered elements are used to adjust the final candidate lists, that is, the supertag hypotheses that span the largest portion of the sentence and seem most "consistent" are moved to the top. This method is applied in order to discard hypotheses that have syntactic inconsistencies.

Figure 19.7 illustrates the rearrangements of the ambiguously typed sentence *ich habe ein kleines Problem* (I have a little problem). The three marked hypotheses all have a maximum coverage of 5; all supertags have their dependency slots filled, whereas the other hypotheses have coverages less than 5. One can see that local word probabilities would suggest *ist kann die kleines Problem* (is can the little problem). The information that is provided by the surviving hypotheses is used for additional final adjustments of the candidate lists to be presented to the user. We call this reordering process *match list reranking*, or shortly *reranking* (see figure 19.7 for an example).

19.5.4 Baseline

For an evaluation, we use as performance criteria the *accuracy* and the *average rank* of the correct word. Coping with unknown words in ambiguous typing is a more complicated problem. If the word is not in the dictionary, it has to be disambiguated letter by letter for all the keys of the code. Since the primary goal was not to simulate a specific keyboard but to evaluate whole sentences with the n-best Supertagging framework, the dictionary was patched by adding the unknown words with zero-frequency and thus contained all words of the corpus.

The baseline results are achieved with the simple unigram approach, where the frequencies of the words that are stored in the lexicon order the candidate list in descending order, with highest frequency first. As evaluation criteria, the *accuracy of rank r* and the *average match position* is chosen. More formally, let

$$f_r(w|c) = \begin{cases} 1 \text{ if } w \in \text{matches}(c) \wedge \text{rank}(w) = r \\ 0 \text{ else} \end{cases} \tag{19.8}$$

be a binary function that returns 1 if a disambiguated target word w correctly occurs on the rth position of the candidate list of its code c, which is given by matches(c). For a test corpus containing a total of N words, the accuracy of rank r for the given corpus can be computed as

$$\text{acc}(r) = \frac{\sum_w f_r(w|c)}{N}. \tag{19.9}$$

N–Best Hypotheses: Score:

1:	αNXN	αV	βDnx	βAn	αNXN	-240.06063154421645
2:	αNXN	αnx0Vnx1	βDnx	βAn	αNXN	-240.38368902077767
3:	αNXN	αV	αNXN	βAn	αNXN	-243.89617070437882
4:	αNXN	αnx0Vnx1	αNXN	βAn	αNXN	-244.12911205503033
5:	αNXN	αV	βvPnx	βAn	αNXN	-244.40697282629282
6:	αNXN	αVnx0nx1	βDnx	βAn	αNXN	-246.6986704928599
7:	αnx0Vnx1	αV	βDnx	βAn	αNXN	-246.922667216602
8:	αNXN	αnx0Vnx1	βvPnx	βAn	αNXN	-247.11626881520166
9:	αnx0Vnx1	αnx0Vnx1	βDnx	βAn	αNXN	-247.3293388332044
10:	αNXN	αV	αP	βAn	αNXN	-247.3614360472363
11:	αnx0Vnx1	αVnx0nx1	βDnx	βAn	αNXN	-247.6594103415739
12:	αNXN	αV	βPnxv	βAn	αNXN	-247.71859453097068
13:	αV	αVnx0nx1	βDnx	βAn	αNXN	-247.84025957497477
14:	αNXN	αnx0Vnx1	αV	βAn	αNXN	-247.8574589280952
15:	αNXN	αV	αNXPRON	βAn	αNXN	-248.16301458965847
16:	αNXN	αV	αV	βAn	αNXN	-248.19436643686464
17:	αnx0Va	αV	βDnx	βAn	αNXN	-248.53326733917402
18:	αVnx0a	αV	βDnx	βAn	αNXN	-248.6975767283041
19:	αV	αnx0Vnx1	βDnx	βAn	αNXN	-248.77906034631118
20:	αnx0Va	αnx0Vnx1	βDnx	βAn	αNXN	-248.93993895577637

LDA

maximum coverage

boosting

ist	kann	die	kleines	Problem
ich	habe	den	kleidet	näherer
Not	Hand	bei	Kleides	näherem
bot	fand	ein	kreidet	emsiger
ißt	frei	bin	trippet	proprer
Bus	Sand	nie	triebet	proprem
⋮	⋮	⋮	⋮	⋮

FIGURE 19.7 Example for rearranging word hypotheses according to the results of Supertagging and LDA.

For a *cumulative accuracy*, where the target words appear within the first r ranks of the candidate lists, the single accuracy values are summed:

$$\operatorname{cac}(r) = \sum_{i=1}^{r} \operatorname{acc}(i). \tag{19.10}$$

The second evaluation measure is the *average rank* of words of the test corpus. It is simply computed by

$$\bar{r} = \frac{\sum_w \operatorname{rank}(w)}{N}. \tag{19.11}$$

TABLE 19.5 The baseline results of ambiguously typing the test corpus.

Reference test set evaluation, $\bar{r} = 3.02$					
	$r = 1$	$r = 2$	$r = 3$	$r = 4$	$r = 5$
$\operatorname{acc}(r)$ [%]	50.26	28.04	5.29	7.41	1.59
$\operatorname{cac}(r)$ [%]	50.26	78.30	83.59	91.00	92.59

The results for the baseline are outlined in table 19.5. Apparently, the unigram approach places approximately 50% of the target words on the first position of the candidate lists; 92.6% of the words appear within the first five ranks. The rank expectation for the reference test set is 3; that is, the user has to scroll two times on average before selecting the desired word.

19.5.5 Evaluation of the n-best typing system AkKo-ST

As reported in Hasan and Harbusch (2004), on a 1.4GHz AMD Athlon, the evaluation of the reference test set needs approx. 10.58s for $n = 250$, that is, 423ms per sentence. The adjustments of the match lists can therefore be performed in real time for smaller values of n. The results show that the approach yields better rankings than the simple wordwise prediction method (baseline) and also outperforms a trigram language model. The overall results are shown in table 19.6. The first part (a) shows the values computed for the reference test set, namely the average for the full evaluation runs with hypothesis sizes ranging from 1 to 1,000. When comparing the values to those in table 19.5, a significant improvement for the reference test set is visible. The cumulative accuracy of rank 1 raises by approximately 12%, that is, 61.8% of the target words are now placed on top of the candidate lists. For the other ranks, the improvement is not as big as for rank 1, but there is still a significant increase. With the n-best approach, 95.6% are placed within the top five ranks, whereas the average rank drops down to 2.18. The overall best run of this evaluation session is given in (b.1). The maximum occurred for the hypothesis size $n = 592$; the 592 best supertag sequence hypotheses for the ambiguously coded sentences are used for adjusting the candidate lists. This result also shows that the biggest variation takes place for rank 1. The changes in cumulative accuracy for ranks ≥ 2 are very small for larger values of n. The graphs in figure 19.8 give an

TABLE 19.6 The improved results using the n-best supertagger/LDA system and additional experiments with trigrams and an upper bound.

Reference test set evaluation				(a)
Average for $n = 1, \ldots, 1000,\ \bar{r} = 2.18$				
	$r = 1$	$r = 2$	$r = 3$	$r = 4$	$r = 5$
acc(r) [%]	61.84	23.01	1.84	8.38	0.55
cac(r) [%]	61.84	84.85	86.69	95.07	95.62
Single best results				(b)
Overall best for $n = 592,\ \bar{r} = 2.11$				(b.1)
acc(r) [%]	66.67	18.52	1.59	8.47	0.53
cac(r) [%]	66.67	85.19	86.78	95.25	95.78
Best accuracy/time trade-off for $n = 250,\ \bar{r} = 2.16$				(b.2)
acc(r) [%]	61.90	22.75	2.12	8.47	0.53
cac(r) [%]	61.90	84.65	86.77	95.24	95.77
Trigram experiment				(c)
Average for $n = 1, \ldots, 1000,\ \bar{r} = 2.91$				
acc(r) [%]	60.01	19.64	4.09	6.59	2.26
cac(r) [%]	60.01	79.65	83.74	90.33	92.59
Upper bound experiment				(d)
Average for $n = 1, \ldots, 1000,\ \bar{r} = 2.11$				
acc(r) [%]	68.07	16.92	1.85	8.22	0.55
cac(r) [%]	68.07	84.99	86.84	95.07	95.62

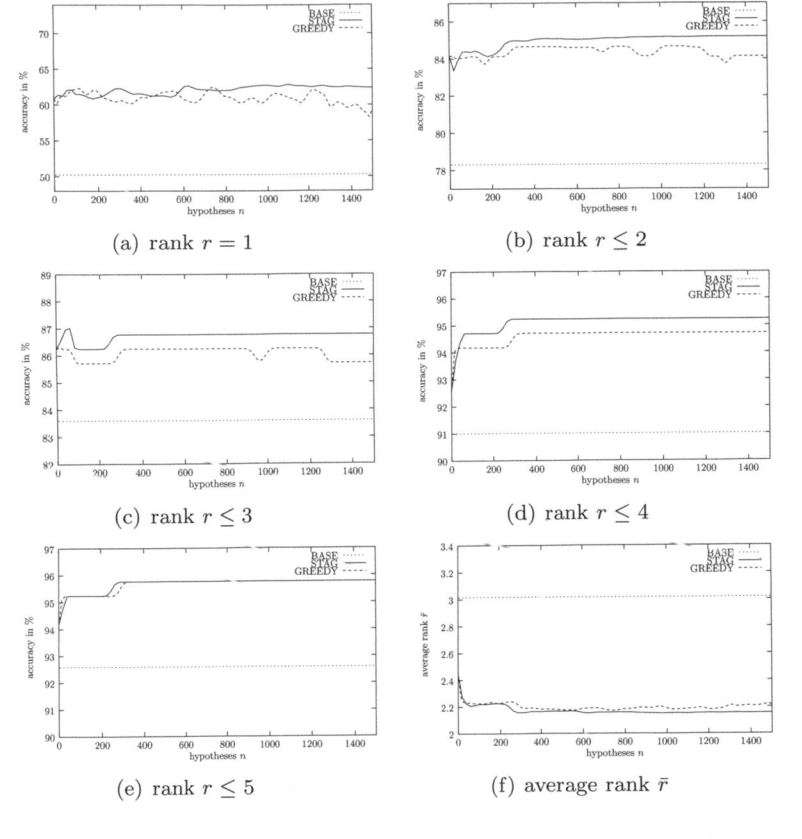

FIGURE 19.8 Backward search: Λ^* vs. Greedy, cumulative accuracy for ranks $r = 1, \ldots, 5$ and average match position $\bar{r}$. BASE refers to the unigram baseline, STAG/GREEDY is the Supertagging+LDA approach with Λ^* and Greedy search, respectively.

overview on the differences between the n-best approach and the baseline and also show the slightly better performance of Λ^* search when compared to greedy search.

As can be seen in all graphs, enhancing the search from 1-best (Viterbi) to n-best has the largest effect for values of $n < 250$. After approximately 250 hypotheses, the results do not improve significantly, at least for higher cumulative ranks. In general, a hypothesis size of $n = 250$ (see table 19.6b2) shows good results, since the value for cac(5) does not increase any more for $n \geq 250$ and the computation time is quite fast.

Another method of evaluating the n-best supertagger is the possibility to look at the target words of the sentences that are typed ambiguously and use only the hypotheses that match closest for adjusting the candidate lists (see the results in table 19.6). Clearly, this procedure is illegal for an objective evaluation since we are already looking at the desired result we want to achieve, but nevertheless it gives

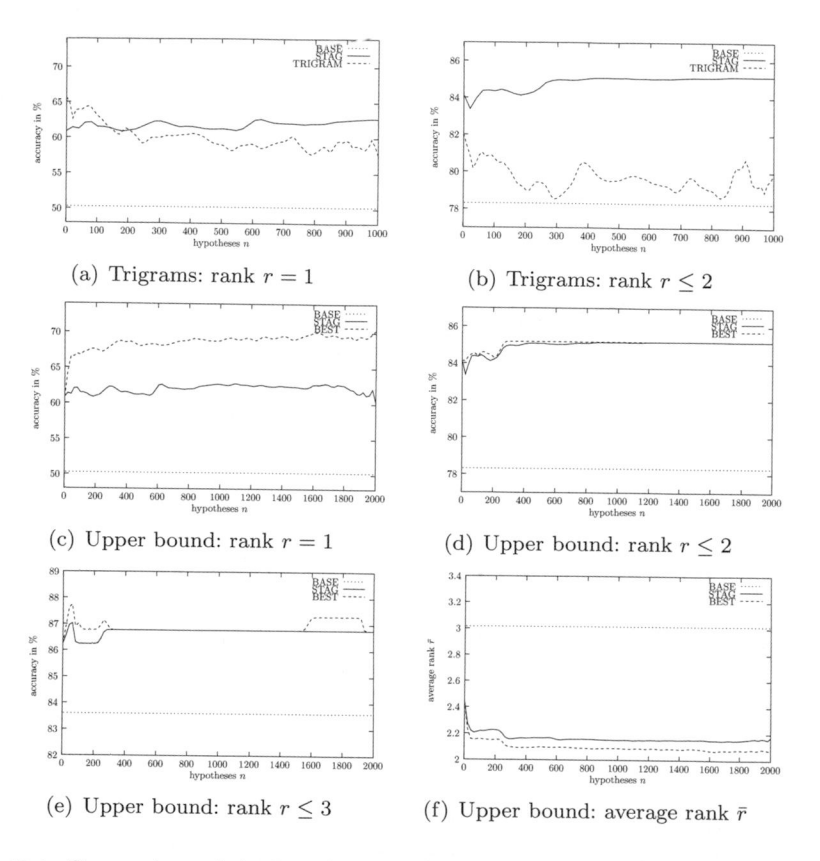

(a) Trigrams: rank $r = 1$ (b) Trigrams: rank $r \leq 2$

(c) Upper bound: rank $r = 1$ (d) Upper bound: rank $r \leq 2$

(e) Upper bound: rank $r \leq 3$ (f) Upper bound: average rank $\bar{r}$

FIGURE 19.9 Comparison of the baseline (unigram model, BASE), Supertagging+LDA (STAG), a trigram approach (TRIGRAM) (figures (a) and (b)) and an upper bound experiment (BEST) (figures (c)–(f)).

an upper bound of what accuracy the n-best supertagger can theoretically reach by just picking the most promising hypotheses. The detailed evaluation graphs are given in figure 19.9. As can be seen, the accuracy between the two approaches differs only for lower ranks (such as c), while for higher ranks (such as d and e), the graphs are nearly identical. This means that for the higher rank accuracy, the n-best supertagger already performs in an optimal way for the reference test set, and it actually cannot get any better with this kind of training material. It is assumed that with a larger training corpus and thus better language model, the rankings can be further improved.

An interesting constellation is revealed in figure 19.9 a, where the trigram approach outperforms Supertagging for lower hypothesis sizes considering rank 1, whereas the accuracy cannot compete for higher ranks (such as b). This is possibly due to the sparseness of data; the few learned estimations lead to disproportionately many misclassifications for a small hypothesis search space. This claim has to be verified on the basis of more data.

19.6 Conclusion

We propose to base Supertagging on Hidden Markov models in order to easily access efficient algorithms such as the Viterbi algorithm. A shallow parser combines the best supertags according to a language model estimated from our German corpus. In both application domains, we could improve the results compared to the baselines. However, comparing the results of German Supertagging (78.3%) to English (92.2%), two different reasons lead to less good results. First, our training set (1,973 words) is small compared to the English one (1,000,000 words). Accordingly, many unseen trigrams are imposed on the system. Second, German is a language with free word order (see, e.g., frequency studies on word order variation by Kempen and Harbusch (2004). This fact amplifies the effects of sparse data. So, in the future the training set for both our domains will be extended. Furthermore, unsupervised learning methods integrated with supervised methods (Montoya et al., 2002) will be deployed in our system. How far we can get with a free-word-order language such as German is currently an open problem.

Notes

1. The acronym KoHDaS stands for *Koblenzer Help Desk with automatic Speech recognition*. The extension ST represents *SuperTagging* in contrast to the baseline system with the extension NN for *Neural Network*. This project is partially funded by the ministry of work, social, family and health and the ministry of economy, traffic, agriculture, and viticulture in Rheinland-Pfalz, Germany.

2. The acronym AkKo stands for *Adaptive, kompakte Texteingabe zur freien Kommunikation*, an adaptive and compact text entry method to allow

communication for severely motor-impaired users. As for KoHDaS, the extension "ST" represents the Supertagging variant. The project is partially funded by the DFG — German Research Foundation — under grant HA2716/2–1.

3. The associative storing in Java is realized by the class HashMap, which provides a Hash table (see, for example, Flanagan, 2002).

4. It is important to notice here that because the real-digit arithmetics cannot differentiate between zero and very small values (as holds for the products of probabilities computed in the Viterbi algorithm) we deal with the logarithms of the probabilities in the hash table of the probabilities of supertags. This states a suitable method here, because not probabilities themselves but the arguments of such probabilities are maximized; the Viterbi algorithm computes the maximum sum of the logarithms of the probabilities instead of the maximum product of the probabilities.

5. Here, we only discuss the n-best variant.

6. It is also possible to suppress this confirmation dialogue completely in KoDHaS.

7. In AkKo, the distribution — e.g., an alphabetic one as for telephone keypads — and the number of keys can be tailored; even only a stop button for a circularly presented list is accessible (cf. *scanning*; see, e.g., Harbusch and Kühn, 2003) to the particular needs of a disabled user. Here we demonstrate a system with optimized letter distribution on four buttons.

8. In command mode, the mapping of the letter keys is changed to commands like *delete last key* or *space*. Thus, the command button functions as a meta key and allows for hierarchical menu structures, which are not further discussed here.

9. We decided for LDA because it considers more syntactic knowledge than simple chunking techniques, while still being very efficient in comparison to full TAG parsing.

References

Abney, S. (1991). Parsing by chunks. In Robert Berwick, Steven Abney, and Carol Tenny, editors, *Principle-based parsing: Computation and Psycholinguistics*, pages 257–278. Kluwer Academic.

Appelt, D.E., Hobbs, J.R., Bear, J., Israel, D., and Tyson, M. (1993). FASTUS: A finite-state processor for information extraction from real-world text. In *Proceedings of the 13th International Joint Conference on Artificial Intelligence (IJCAI–93)*, pages 1172–1178, Chambéry, France.

Baayen, H., Piepenbrock, R., and Gulikers, L. (1995). The CELEX lexical database (release 2). CD-ROM, Linguistic Data Consortium, University of Pennsylvania.

Bäcker, J. (2001). *Entwicklung eines supertaggers für das deutsche*. Studienarbeit, Universität Koblenz-Landau, Institut für Computerlinguistik, Koblenz, Germany.

Bäcker, J. (2002). *Kohdas–ST — Supertagging in dem automatischen Dialogsystem kohdas.* Diplomarbeit, Universität Koblenz-Landau, Institut für Computerlinguistik, Koblenz, Germany.

Bangalore, S. (2000). A lightweight dependency analyzer for partial parsing. *Computational Linguistics*, 6(2) 113–138.

Bangalore, S. and Joshi, A. K. (1999). Supertagging: An approach to almost parsing. *Computational Linguistics*, 25(2) 237–265, 1999.

Bangalore, S. (1997). *Complexity of Lexical Descriptions and its Relevance to Partial Parsing.* PhD thesis, University of Pennsylvania.

Bangalore S. (1998). Transplanting supertags from English to Spanish. In *Proceedings of Fourth International Workshop on Tree-Adjoining Grammars (TAG+4)*, pages 5–8, Philadelphia.

Baum, L. E. and Eagon, J. A. (1967). An inequality with applications to statistical estimation for probabilistic functions of markov processes and to a model for ecology. *Bulletin of American Mathematical Society*, 73:360–363.

Baum, L. E. (1972). An inequality and associated maximization technique in statistical estimation for probabilistic functions of markov processes. *Inequalities*, 3:1–8.

Black, E., Jelinek, F., Lafferty, J., Magerman, D. M., Mercer, R., and Roukos, S. (1993). Towards history-based grammars: Using richer models for probabilistic parsing. In *Proceedings of the 31st Conference of the Association of Computational Linguistics (ACL–93)*, pages 31–37, Columbus, Ohio.

Boje, J., Wiren, M., Rayner, M., Lewin, I., Carter, D., and Becker, R. (1999). Language-processing strategies and mixed-initiative dialogues. In J. Alexanderson, L. Ahrenberg, K. Jokinen, and Jönsson, editors, *Special Issue on Intelligent Dialogue Systems. ETAI (Electronic Transactions on Artificial Intelligence)*.

Booth, T.L. (1969). Probabilistic representation of formal languages. In *IEEE Conference Record of the 10th Annual Symposium on Switching and Automata Theory*, pages 74–81.

Brill, E. (1993). Automatic grammar induction and parsing free text: A transformation-based approach. In *Proceedings of the 31st Annual Meeting of the Association for Computational Linguistics (ACL–93)*, pages 259–265, Columbus, Ohio.

Brill, E. (1995). Transformation-based error-driven learning and natural language processing: A case study in part-of-speech tagging. *Computational Linguistics*, 21(4) 543–566.

Charniak, E. (1993). *Statistical Language Learning.* MIT Press.

Charniak, E. (1997). Statistical parsing with a context-free grammar and word statistics. In *Proceedings of the 14th National Conference on Artificial Intelligence (AAAI–97)*, pages 47–66, Menlo Park, CA.

Chen, S. F. and Goodman, J. (1996). An empirical study of smoothing techniques for language modeling. *Proceedings of the 34th Annual Meeting of the Association for Computational Linguistics (ACL–96)*, pages 310–318.

Cleary, J.G. and Witten, I. H. (1984). Data compression using adaptive coding and partial string matching. *IEEE Transactions on Communications*, 32(4) 396–402.

Collins, M. J. (1996). A new statistical parser based on bigram lexical dependencies. In *Proceedings of the 34th Annual Meeting of the Association for Computational Linguistics (ACL–96)*, pages 184–191, San Francisco.

Cutting, D., Kupiec, J., Pederson, J. O., and Sibun, P. (1992). A practical part-of-speech tagger. In *Proceedings of the Third Conference on Applied Natural Language Processing (ANLP)*, pages 133–140, Trento, Italy.

Elman, J. (1990). Finding structure in time. *Cognitive Science*, 14:179–211.

El-Beze, M. and Merialdo, B. (1999). *Hidden Markov Models*, Chapter 16, pages 263–284. Kluwer Academic.

Fazly, A. and Hirst, G. (2003). Testing the efficacy of part-of-speech information in word completion. In Harbusch et al. 2003, pages 9–16.

Flanagan, D. (2002). *Java in a Nutshell*. 4th ed., O'Reilly.

Good, I. J. (1953). The population frequencies of species and the estimation of population parameters. *Biometrika*, 40:237–264.

Grishman, R. (1995). The NYU system for MUC-6 or where's the syntax? In *Proceedings of the 6th Message Understanding Conference (MUC-6)*, pages 167–175, San Francisco.

Harbusch, K. and Kühn, M. (2003). An evaluation study of two-button scanning with ambiguous keyboards. In *Proceedings of the 7th European Conference for the Advancement of Assistive Technology (AAATE 2003)* Dublin.

Harbusch, K., Kühn, M., and Trost, H. eds. (2003). *Proceedings of the Workshop on Language Modeling for Text Entry Methods*, Budapest, Hungary.

Hasan, S. (2003). *N-Best Hidden Markov Model Supertagging for Typing with Ambiguous Keyboards*. Diplomarbeit, Universität Koblenz-Landau, Fachbereich Informatik, Koblenz, Germany.

Hasan, S. and Harbusch, K. (2004). M-best hidden Markov model supertagging to improve typing on an ambiguous keyboard. In *Proceedings of the 7th International Workshop on Tree Adjoining Grammar and Related Formalisms. (TAG+7)*, pages 56–63, Vancouver.

Hobbs, J. R., Appelt, D. E., Bear, J., Israel, D., Kameyama, M., Stickel, M., and Tyson, M. (1997). FASTUS: A cascaded finite-state transducer for extracting information from natural-language text. In Emmanuel Roche and Yves Schabes, editors, *Finite State Devices for Natural Language Processing*, pages 383–406. MIT Press.

Koester, H.H. and Levine, S.P. (1994). Modeling the speed of text entry with a word prediction interface. *IEEE Transactions on Rehabilitation Engineering*, 2(3) 177–187.

Joshi, A. K., and Schabes, Y. (1997). Tree Adjoining Grammars. In Grzegorz Rozenberg and Arto Salomaa, editors, *Handbook of Formal Languages*, volume 3, pages 69–214. Springer.

Joshi, A. K. and Bangalore, S. (1994). Disambiguation of super parts of speech (or supertags): Almost parsing. In *Proceedings of the 17th International Conference on Computational Linguistics (COLING–94)*, pages 154–160, Kyoto, Japan.

Jurafsky, D. and Martin, J. H. (2000). *Speech and Language Processing*. Prentice Hall.

Katz, S. M. (1987). Estimation of probabilities from sparse data for the language model component of a speech recognizer. *IEEE Transactions on Acoustics, Speech and Signal Processing*, 35(3):400–401.

Kempen, G. and Harbusch, K. (2004). Generating natural word orders in a semi–free word order language: Treebank–based linearization preferences for argument NPs in subordinate clauses of German. In *Proceedings of the Fifth International Conference on Intelligent Text Processing and Computational Linguistics (CICLING)*, pages 350–354, Seoul.

Kushler, C. (1998). AAC using a reduced keyboard. In *Proceedings of the Technology and Persons with Disabilities Conference 1998*.

Laumann, C. (2000). KoHDaS — Koblenzer Help Desk mittels automatischer Spracherkennung. Diploma Thesis at the Department of Computer Science, Universität Koblenz–Landau, Germany.

Litman, D., Pan, S., and Walker, M. (1998). Evaluating response strategies in a web-based spoken dialogue agent. In *Proceedings of the 36th Annual Meeting of the ACL and the 17th International Conference on Computational Linguistics (COLING-ACL-98)*, pages 780–786, Montreal.

Magerman, D. M. (1995). Statistical decision-tree models for parsing. In *Proceedings of the 33rd Annual Meeting of the Association for Computational Linguistics (ACL-95)*, pages 276–283, Cambridge, MA.

Manning, C. D. and Schütze, H. (2000). *Foundations of statistical language processing.* MIT Press.

Marcus, M. P., Santorini, B., and Marcinkiewicz, M. (1993). Building a large annotated corpus of English: The Penn treebank. *Computational Linguistics*, 19:313–330.

Matiasek, J., Baroni, M., and Trost, H. (2002). FASTY — A multilingual approach to text prediction. In K. Miesenberger, J. Klaus, and W. Zagler, editors, *Computers Helping People with Special Needs — Proceedings of the 8th International Conference ICCHP 2002, Linz, Austria*, volume 2398 of *Springer Lecture Notes in Computer Science*, pages 243–250, Berlin.

Merialdo, B. (1994). Tagging English text with a probabilistic model. *Computational Linguistics*, 20(2):155–172.

Montoya, A., Suárez, A. and Palomar, M. (2002). Combining supervised–unsupervised methods for word sense disambiguation. In Alexander Gelbukh, editor, *Proceedings of the 3rd International Conferences on Intelligent Text Processing and Computational Linguistics (CICLING)*, pages 156–164, Mexico City.

Nasr, A. and Rambow, O. (2004). Supertagging and Full Parsing. In *Proceedings of the 7th International Workshop on Tree Adjoining Grammar and Related Formalisms. (TAG+7)*, pages 56–63, Vancouver.

Nuance Communication. (2000). Nuance Speech Recognition System (Version 7.0), Application Developer's Guide.

Rabiner, L. R. and Juang, B.H. (1986). An introduction to hidden Markov models. *IEEE ASSP Magazine*, pages 4–15.

Rabiner, L. R. (1989). A tutorial on Hidden Markov Models and selected applications in speech recognition. *Proceedings of the IEEE*, 77(2) 257–286.

Rau, H. and Skiena, S. S. (1996). Dialing for documents: An experiment in information theory. *Journal of Visual Languages and Computing*, 7:79–95.

Schabes, Y. (1990). *Mathematical and Computational Aspects of Lexicalized Grammars.* PhD thesis, University of Pennsylvania.

Strachan, L., Anderson, J., Sneesby, M., and Evans, M. (1997). Pragmatic user modelling in a commercial software system. In *Proceedings of the 6th International Conference on User Modeling*, pages 189–200, Chia Laguna, Italy.

Tanaka-Ishii, K., Inutsuka, Y., and Takeichi, M. (2002). Entering text with a four-button device. In *Proceedings of the 19th International Conference on Computational Linguistics (COLING '02)*, pages 988–994, Taipei, Taiwan.

Viterbi, A. J. (1967). Error bounds for convolutional codes and an asymptotically optimum decoding algorithm. *IEEE Transactions on Information Theory*, IT-13:260–269.

Weischedel, R., Meteer, M., Schwartz, R., Ramshaw, L., and Palmucci, J. (1993). Coping with ambiguity and unknown words through probabilistic models. *Computational Linguistics*, 19(2) 359–382.

Wermter, S. (1995). *Hybrid Connectionist Natural Language Processing.* Chapman and Hall.

Witten, I. H. (1982). *Principles of Computer Speech.* Academic Press.

Author Index

Subject Index